CHILDCRAFT
THE HOW AND
WHY LIBRARY

SEE THE
WORLD

World Book, Inc.
a Scott Fetzer company
Chicago

Childcraft—The How and Why Library

CHILDCRAFT, CHILDCRAFT—THE HOW AND WHY LIBRARY, HOW AND WHY, WORLD BOOK and the GLOBE DEVICE are registered trademarks or trademarks of World Book, Inc.

World Book, Inc.
233 N. Michigan Avenue
Chicago, IL 60601

The Library of Congress has cataloged a previous edition of this title as follows.

Childcraft: the how and why library.
    v. cm.
    Summary: Presents illustrated articles, stories, and poems, grouped thematically in fifteen volumes.
    Includes bibliographical references and indexes.
    Contents: v. 1. Poems and rhymes -- v. 2. Once upon a time -- v. 3. Art around us -- v. 4. The world of animals -- v. 5 The world of plants -- v. 6. Our earth -- v. 7. The universe -- v. 8. How does it happen? -- v. 9. How things work -- v. 10. Shapes and numbers -- v. 11. About you -- v. 12. Who we are -- v. 13. See the world -- v. 14. Celebrate! -- v. 15. Guide and index.
    ISBN 0-7166-2203-3 (set)
    1. Children's encyclopedias and dictionaries.
    [1. Encyclopedias and dictionaries.]
    I. Title: Childcraft. II. World Book, Inc.
    AG6 .C48 2004
    031--dc21   2003008722

This edition:

ISBN-13: 978-0-7166-2219-2 (set)
ISBN-10: 0-7166-2219-X (set)
ISBN-13: 978-0-7166-2232-1 (Volume 13, See the World)
ISBN-10: 0-7166-2232-7 (Volume 13, See the World)

Printed in China
4 5 6 7 8 9 09 08 07 06

For information on other World Book publications, visit our Web site at **http://www.worldbook.com** or call **1-800 WORLDBK (967-5325)**. For information on sales to schools and libraries, call **1-800-975-3250 (United States)**, or **1-800-837-5365 (Canada)**.

Contents

Introduction

Let's go on a trip around the world today! Just open the pages of *See the World,* and your journey will begin.

You will start by exploring the seven huge land areas called continents. But were there always seven? Are they all alike? And do they stay the same? You'll enjoy discovering the answers in the pages that follow.

You will also find out the many ways that people travel from place to place—for example, in cars and buses on roads, in boats across water, and in airplanes

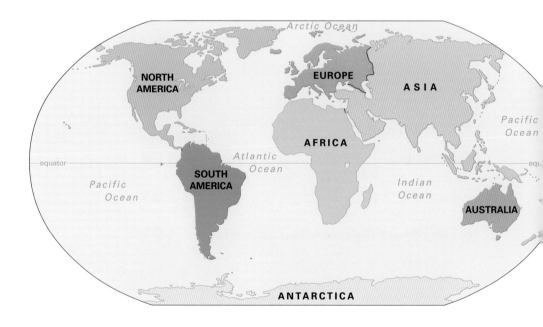

through the sky. But other ways of traveling are far less common. Some people travel on camels across the sand. Others use dogsleds to cover the distance on snow and ice.

There are lots of famous places to visit throughout the world, including castles, skyscrapers, towers, bridges, and monuments. Some of the world's most amazing structures were built long ago, such as the Great Pyramid of Giza in Egypt and the Great Wall of China.

If all this armchair travel has made you want to get out there and see the world in person, the book can help more. You will learn how maps help you find your way around, and then you can start planning your own trip!

There are many features in this book to help you find your way through it. The boxes marked **Know It All!** have fun-filled facts. You can amaze your friends with what you learn!

This book also has many activities that you can do at home. Look for the words **Try This!** over a colored ball. The activity that follows offers a hands-on

Know It All! boxes have fun-filled facts.

Each activity has a number. The higher the number, the more adult help you may need.

An activity that has this colorful border is a little more complex than one without the border.

way to learn more about the world. For example, you can make your own map or compass.

Each activity has a number in its colored ball. Activities with a 1 in a green ball are simplest to do. Those with a 2 inside a yellow ball may require a little adult help with tasks such as cutting or measuring. Activities with a 3 inside a red ball may need more adult help.

A Try This! activity that has a colorful border around its entire page is a little more complex or requires a few more materials. Take a moment to review the list of materials needed and to read through the step-by-step instructions before you begin.

As you read this book, you will see that some words are printed in bold type, **like this.** These are words that might be new to you. You can find the meanings and pronunciations of these words in the **Glossary** at the back of the book. Turn to the **Index** to look up page numbers of subjects that interest you the most.

If you enjoy learning about places around the world, find out more in other resources, such as those listed below. Check them out at a bookstore or at your library.

Alice Ramsey's Grand Adventure, by Don Brown, 1997. *This book describes the adventures of Alice as she takes a car trip from New York and San Francisco in 1909, becoming the first woman to drive across the United States.*

Amelia Hits the Road, by Marissa Moss, 1999. *Amelia writes about her family's road trip to California and some of the national parks they see on the way.*

Boats Afloat, by Shelley Rotner, 1998. *This book is filled with photos of all kinds of boats.*

Children Just Like Me: A Unique Celebration of Children Around the World, by Barnabas and Anabel Kindersley, 1995. *Beautiful photographs in this book show the clothing, housing, work, and play of children from all parts of the world.*

Houses, by Gallimard Jeunesse and Claude Delafosse, 1998. *In this book you will see the different kinds of houses in which people from around the world live.*

How to Make an Apple Pie and See the World, by Marjorie Priceman, 1996. *Take a trip around the world to gather the ingredients to make an apple pie.*

Illustrated Atlas by World Book, Inc., 2003. *Visit all the regions of the world. Meet the people and see what the land, animals, and plants are like around the world in this well-illustrated, oversized atlas.*

Market, by Ted Lewin, 2000. *Find out what people grow, catch, or make as you visit markets around the world.*

Roundabouts: Our Globe, Our World, by Kate Petty and Jakki Wood, 2000. *Harry finds out about maps, globes, the equator, continents, and much more as he takes a trip with his dog, Ralph, in a hot-air balloon.*

World Adventure, by World Book, Inc., 2000. *Imagine if you and three of your friends could take a trip around the world in a year. What would you see and do? Find out what these four characters did by reading their group journal, postcards, guidebook, newspaper clippings, snapshots, and more!*

Continents of the World

The earth has seven huge land areas called continents. Some are connected to each other. Others are completely surrounded by water. These chunks of land are so large that some may have snowy mountains on one part and steamy forests on another. They may have dozens of countries or just one. What are the names of these seven continents, and how is each one special? Which one is the largest? Which one has the most people? Read on to find out!

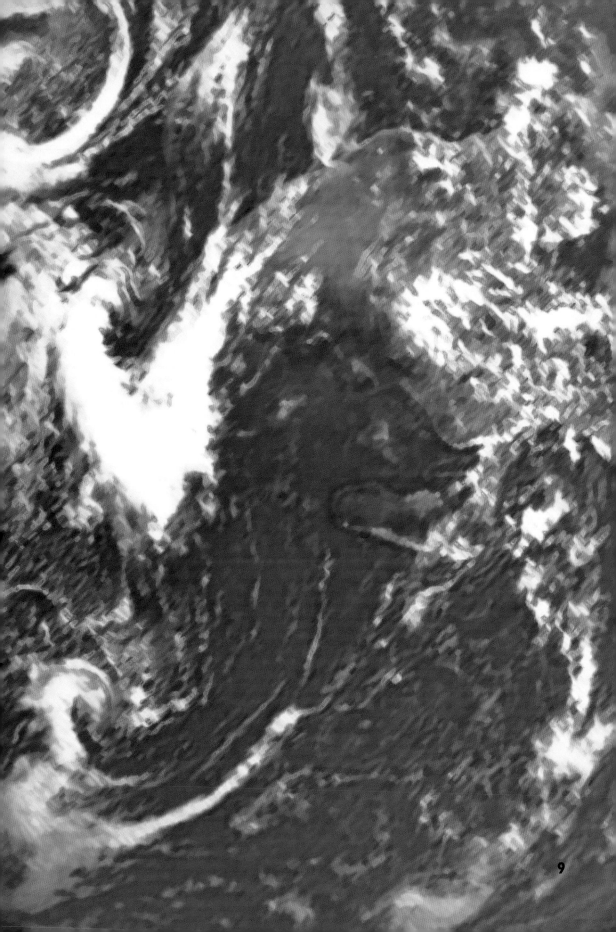

9

What Are the Seven Continents?

The seven **continents** are Africa, Antarctica, Asia, Australia, Europe, North America, and South America. Australia is an island, a piece of land totally surrounded by water. But it is such a huge island that it is also a continent. Other continents, such as Europe and North America, have islands that are considered a part of them. There are also thousands of smaller islands, such as a group of islands called the Pacific Islands, that are not counted as part of the continents. Europe and Asia are joined on one side, but they are thought of as two continents.

This map of the world shows where the seven continents are. You can tell a lot about the continents by studying the map. For example, if you look closely, you will see that each continent has a different shape. Use tracing paper to trace the shape of each continent.

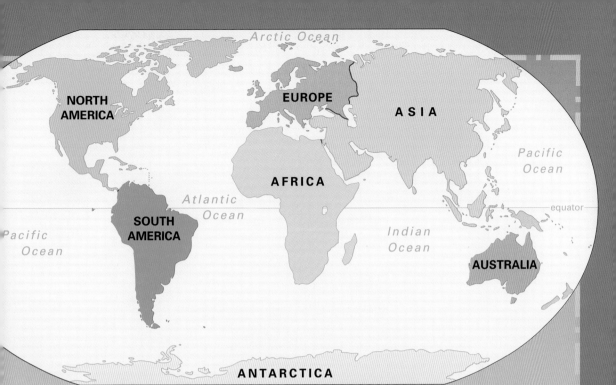

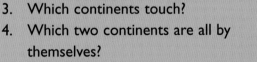 Now look at the map. Can you answer these questions?

See answers below.

1. Which continent is biggest?
2. Which continent is smallest?
3. Which continents touch?
4. Which two continents are all by themselves?
5. Which three continents cross the line called the equator?

Arctic Ocean

EUROPE

Russia

Turkey
Cyprus
Lebanon
Israel
Egypt
Jordan
Syria
Armenia
Georgia
Azerbaijan
Turkmenistan
Uzbekistan
Kyrgyzstan
Tajikistan
Kazakhstan

Iraq
Iran
Afghanistan
Kuwait
Bahrain
Qatar
United Arab
Emirates
Pakistan
Saudi
Arabia
Yemen
Oman

Mongolia
Beijing
Gobi

Huang He

China

Yangtze

Delhi
Nepal
Bhutan
Ganges
Bangladesh

India

Myanmar
Thailand
Laos
Cambodia
Vietnam

North
Korea
Tokyo
South
Korea
Japan

Taiwan

Philippines

Brunei

Malaysia

Singapore

Indonesia
East
Timor

Sri Lanka

AFRICA

Red Sea

Equator

Indian Ocean

Pacific
Ocean

Great Wall
of China

Mt. Everest

Taj Mahal

Asia

Asia is the largest continent by far. It has more land and more people than any other continent. It is so big that Australia and North America could fit inside it. Asia and Europe are joined along one side.

Asia has some of the world's highest mountains, largest deserts and **plains**, and thickest jungles. There are cold deserts in central and northern Asia, hot deserts in the southwest, and steamy tropics in the southeast. Many Asians live in crowded cities, such as Tokyo in Japan, Delhi in India, and Beijing in China. But there are also many places in Asia where very few people live.

There are 50 countries in Asia. Two of the world's largest countries, Russia and China, are in Asia. In fact, Russia is so big that it lies on two continents. Part of it is in Europe and part of it is in Asia.

Visitors to Asia often visit the Great Wall of China. It was built more than 1,000 years ago and stretches thousands of miles long across north-central China. Many mountain climbers are drawn to Asia's Mount Everest, the highest peak in the world.

Highest mountain:
Mount Everest,
29,028 feet
(8,848 meters)
Longest river:
Yangtze (yahng dzuh),
3,915 miles
(6,300 kilometers)
Largest desert:
Gobi (GOH bee),
500,000 square miles (1,300,000 square kilometers)

The Taj Mahal is a famous tomb in India. An Indian shah, or king, built it for his wife in the 1600's.

Africa

Africa is the second largest continent. Steamy tropical rain forests cover parts of western and central Africa. The Sahara Desert stretches across most of the northern part. The longest freshwater

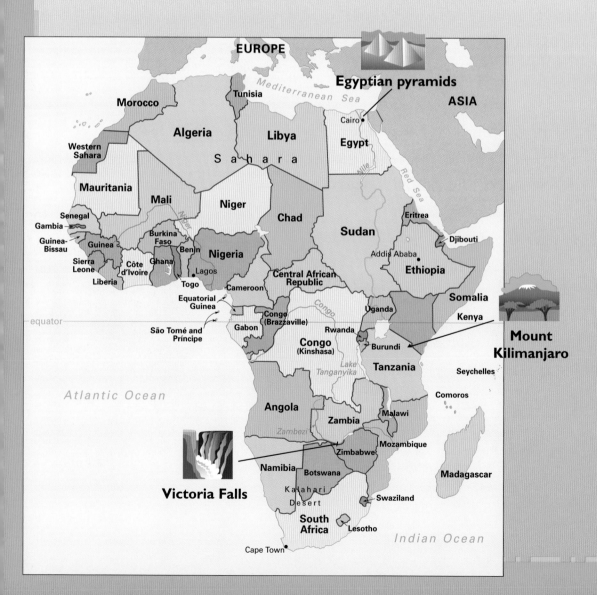

EUROPE

Mediterranean Sea

Egyptian pyramids

ASIA

Tunisia

Morocco

Cairo

Algeria

Libya

Egypt

Western
Sahara

S a h a r a

Mauritania

Mali

Niger

Nile

Red Sea

Senegal

Gambia

Guinea-
Bissau

Guinea

Burkina
Faso

Sierra
Leone

Côte
d'Ivoire

Ghana

Benin

Nigeria

Togo

Liberia

Lagos

Cameroon

Chad

Sudan

Eritrea

Djibouti

Addis Ababa

Ethiopia

Central African
Republic

Somalia

Equatorial
Guinea

Congo

Uganda

Kenya

equator

São Tomé and
Príncipe

Gabon

Congo
(Brazzaville)

Rwanda

Mount
Kilimanjaro

Congo
(Kinshasa)

Burundi

Lake
Tanganyika

Tanzania

Seychelles

Atlantic Ocean

Comoros

Angola

Zambia

Malawi

Mozambique

Zambezi

Zimbabwe

Victoria Falls

Namibia

Botswana

Madagascar

Kalahari
Desert

Swaziland

South
Africa

Lesotho

Indian Ocean

Cape Town

These school children visit the pyramids in Giza, Egypt, a popular spot for tourists.

lake in the world, Lake Tanganyika (TANG guhn YEE kuh), lies in eastern Africa.

A sea separates most of Africa and Asia, but in one place the two continents meet.

Africa has 53 countries. Its largest country is Sudan. The smallest is Seychelles (say SHEHL). Most Africans live in rural areas, but some live in cities such as Addis Ababa in Ethiopia, Cape Town in South Africa, and Lagos in Nigeria.

Many people travel to Africa to study its wild animals, visit such ancient sites as the pyramids of Egypt, or see such natural wonders as Victoria Falls and Kilimanjaro, a towering volcano that is no longer active.

Highest mountain: *Kilimanjaro*, 19,340 feet (5,895 meters)
Longest river: *Nile*, 4,145 miles (6,671 kilometers)
Largest desert: *Sahara*, 3 1/2 million square miles (9 million square kilometers)

15

North America

North America is the third largest continent. It has fewer people than Europe, Asia, or Africa. The northern part of the continent is near the North Pole. The southern part is connected to South America by a narrow strip of land. The north has icy plains. The south has sunny beaches.

Bikers enjoy the view at Acadia National Park, Maine.

North America includes magnificent mountain peaks, sandy deserts, flat grasslands, and thick forests.

North America has 23 countries. Canada is the biggest, but the United States has the most people. Major North American cities include Calgary, Montreal, and Toronto, in Canada; Chicago, Los Angeles, and New York, in the United States; Havana, in Cuba; and Mexico City, in Mexico.

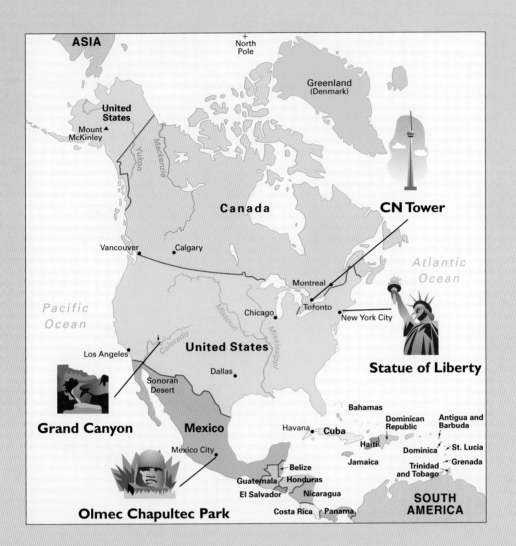

ASIA

+
North
Pole

Greenland
(Denmark)

United
States

Mount ▲
McKinley

Yukon

Mackenzie

Canada

CN Tower

Vancouver • Calgary •

Montreal •

Atlantic
Ocean

Pacific
Ocean

Missouri

Chicago •

Toronto •

New York City

Statue of Liberty

Colorado

United States

Los Angeles •

Mississippi

Dallas •

Sonoran
Desert

Bahamas

Grand Canyon

Mexico

Havana •

Dominican
Republic

Cuba

Antigua and
Barbuda

Haiti

Dominica

St. Lucia

Mexico City •

Jamaica

Grenada

Belize

Trinidad
and Tobago

Guatemala / Honduras

El Salvador

Nicaragua

SOUTH
AMERICA

Olmec Chapultec Park

Costa Rica • Panama

Highest mountain: *Mount McKinley,* 20,320 feet
(6,194 meters)
Longest river: *Missouri,* 2,540 miles (4,090 kilometers)
Largest desert: *Sonoran,* 70,000 square miles
(181,000 square kilometers)

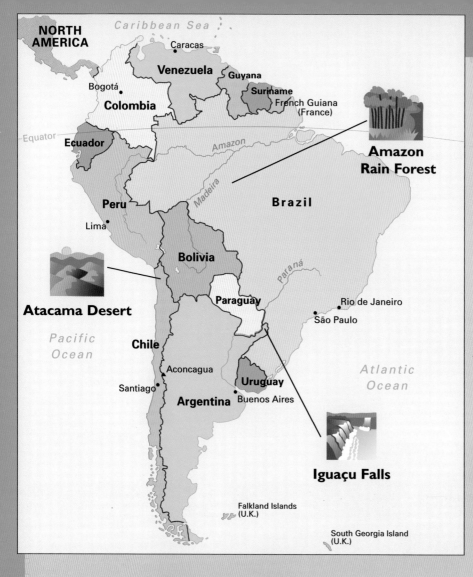

South Georgia Island
(U.K.)

South America

South America is the fourth largest continent. It has tropical rain forests, deserts, snowy peaks, volcanoes, and rolling grasslands. South America has fewer people than North America.

Most of South America lies south of the **equator**. At the north, the continent is joined to North America by a narrow strip of land. The southern part of the continent is close to Antarctica.

South America has 12 countries. The largest country in South America is Brazil. The smallest is Suriname. Most people in South America live in crowded cities.

People travel to South America to see such ancient ruins as Machu Picchu. The Amazon rain forest and Iguaçu Falls are also in South America.

The government of Brazil meets in these congress buildings in the country's capital city, Brasília.

Highest mountain: *Aconcagua* (AH kawng KAH gwah), 22,831 feet (6,959 meters)
Longest river: *Amazon*, 4,000 miles (6,437 kilometers)
Largest desert: *Atacama* (AT uh KAM uh), 51,000 square miles (132,000 square kilometers)

Antarctica

Antarctica is the fifth largest continent. Although Antarctica is larger than Australia, nobody lives there all the time. That is because Antarctica is the coldest and iciest place in the world. The South Pole is located in Antarctica.

The stormy waters of the Atlantic, Indian, and Pacific oceans surround Antarctica. Ships must steer around towering icebergs and break through huge ice fields to reach the continent. On Antarctica, most of the land is buried in ice. This ice can measure thousands of feet thick, about five times as tall as the world's

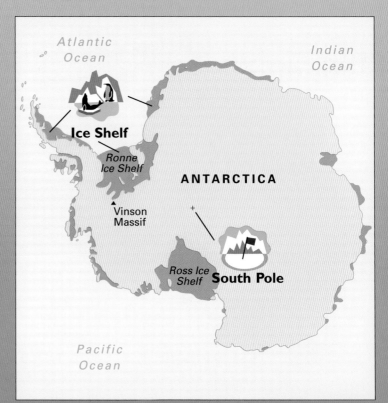

tallest building. But under the ice, Antarctica has mountains, lowlands, and valleys, just like the other continents do. One area near the South Pole is called a "polar desert" because so little snow falls there.

Scientists and travelers visit Antarctica for short periods. Scientists from many nations come to study the continent's animals and plants, ice, and rocks. Only a few small plants and insects can survive on Antarctica's dry land. But many animals, including fish, penguins, whales, and flying birds, live in the cold waters around Antarctica.

The cold **climate** of Antarctica is perfect for these penguins.

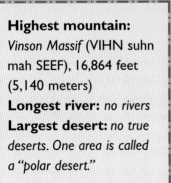

Highest mountain: *Vinson Massif* (VIHN suhn mah SEEF), 16,864 feet (5,140 meters)
Longest river: *no rivers*
Largest desert: *no true deserts. One area is called a "polar desert."*

Europe

Europe is almost the smallest of the seven continents. Only Australia is smaller. Europe is a region of mountain ranges, rugged coastlines, deep valleys, and plains. Thousands of islands, including Iceland, Corsica, Great Britain, and Ireland, are part of Europe.

All of Europe lies north of the equator. The parts that are farthest north are close

Iceland

Atlantic Ocean

Alps

Norway

Finland

Sweden

North Sea

Estonia

Latvia

Lithuania

Russia

Ireland

Denmark

United Kingdom

London

Netherlands

Belgium

Germany

Poland

Belarus

Moscow

Stonehenge

Paris

Luxembourg

France

Switzerland

Czech Republic

Slovakia

Austria

Slovenia

Hungary

Croatia

Ukraine

Moldova

Romania

Mount Elbrus

ASIA

Russia

Ural

Volga

Kazakhstan

Caspian Sea

Portugal

Spain

Corsica (France)

Italy

Rome

Vatican City

Bosnia-Herzegovina

Serbia

Montenegro

Albania

Macedonia

Bulgaria

Danube

Black Sea

Georgia

Azerbaijan

Turkey

Greece

ASIA

Rock of Gibraltar

AFRICA

Malta

Mediterranean Sea

Europe is known for the scenic beauty of its small towns, such as Stryn, Norway.

to the North Pole. Europe is joined to Asia on the east. It is separated from Africa by the Mediterranean Sea. A mountain range called the Alps cuts across the southern part of the continent.

There are 48 countries in Europe. The largest country, Russia, is also the largest country in the world. Part of Russia is in Europe, and part of it is in Asia. Vatican City is the smallest country in the world. It is so small it fits entirely within the city of Rome, Italy.

People from all over the world love to visit Europe for its museums and historic buildings. People also visit Stonehenge, an ancient monument in England.

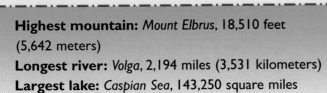

Highest mountain: *Mount Elbrus*, 18,510 feet (5,642 meters)
Longest river: *Volga*, 2,194 miles (3,531 kilometers)
Largest lake: *Caspian Sea*, 143,250 square miles (371,000 square kilometers)

Map labels: Darwin, Indian Ocean, Pacific Ocean, Great Sandy Desert, **Great Barrier Reef**, **Australia**, Uluru, Great Victoria Desert, Brisbane, Darling, Perth, Adelaide, Murray, Sydney, Canberra, **Sydney Opera House**, Melbourne, Mount Kosciuszko, Indian Ocean, Tasmania

Australia

Australia is the smallest continent. It is famous for its huge open areas of land, its bright sunshine, and its unusual animals. Australia is a dry land with few people. In fact, it has fewer people than any continent except Antarctica. Australia lies entirely south of the equator. For that reason, it is often called "The Land Down Under."

Australia is completely surrounded by water. It is often grouped with the island of New Zealand and other Pacific islands, which together are called Oceania (OH shee AN ee yuh). Australia is a country, and it is the only country that is also a continent. The island of Tasmania is part of Australia.

In Australia, most people live in cities near the coasts, such as Sydney and Melbourne. But some people live in the outback, a vast area of dry, flatland far from the cities. Here, in the center of the continent, is a very famous rock called Uluru (or Ayers Rock) that is several miles in diameter.

These children live in northern Western Australia.

People go to Australia to hear music at the beautiful Sydney Opera House. Divers visit the Great Barrier Reef, a chain of coral reefs. Other people go to Australia to see kangaroos and koalas.

Highest mountain: *Mount Kosciuszko*
(KAHZ ee UHS koh), 7,310 feet (2,228 meters)
Longest river: *Murray*, 1,609 miles (2,589 kilometers)
Largest desert: *Great Victoria*, 250,000 square miles (647,000 square kilometers)

25

Make Your Own Continent Map

Just as you can learn a lot about a place by looking at a map, you can learn a lot by making your own map. Choose a continent in this chapter that you would like to learn more about, and map it!

You Will Need:

books or encyclopedia
    articles about your
    favorite continent
a pencil
a large sheet of paper
crayons or markers

What To Do:

1. Read about the continent and answer the following questions: What is the tallest mountain? What is the longest river? What is the largest lake or desert? What animals live there? What are the biggest cities?

2. Look through encyclopedias and other books to find different maps of your continent. How do these maps show important information, such as the locations of mountains, rivers, and large cities?

3. Trace or copy the outline of the continent onto the large sheet of paper.

4. Now use a pencil to fill in the map outline. Choose symbols to show cities, rivers, mountains, deserts, and the animals that live in different places on the continent.

5. Color your map. Use green for land, blue for water, and brown for mountains.

6. Decorate the border of your map with pictures of the continent's people, animals, and any other features you want to show.

Now, laminate your map or put it in a plastic cover.

One World

The seven continents are far apart from one another, but they are all part of the earth. No matter how far apart the continents are, the people who live on them are connected because they have the same needs. In addition to needing food, clothing, and a place to live, they all need to learn, to communicate, and to plan for the future.

Years ago, people knew very little about the continents. The only way they could learn about them was by traveling on ships. Today, TV's and computers zip information around the world with the flick of a switch or the click of a mouse. People watching TV in Australia can see

In the 1400's, it took Christopher Columbus two months to sail from Spain to the Bahamas. Today, a jet plane could make the same trip in just a few hours.

Many people in the world like to watch television. These children from Saudi Arabia enjoy a show together.

a person rafting down the Amazon River in South America. A scientist in North America can send an instant message to a scientist in Antarctica by computer.

Yes, the continents are very far apart. But **transportation** and technology have brought the people who live on them much closer together.

Telephones allow people to communicate over long **distances.** Imagine what a person living in Christopher Columbus's time would have thought of that!

Say "Ahalan!" or "Ni hao" to the World

Around the world, people speak more than 6,000 languages. If you learn to say *hello* in just a few of these languages, you could say hello to millions of people! Here are some important words in other languages.

Hello

Arabic ahalan
Hebrew shalom
Japanese konnichiwa
Mandarin Chinese ni hao
Russian priven
Swahili jambo

Goodbye

Arabic ma'a el salaama
Hebrew shalom
Japanese sayonara
Mandarin Chinese zai jian
Russian do svidaniya

Please

Arabic min fadlak
Hebrew b'vakashah
Japanese douzo
Russian pazhaluysta
Swahili tafadhali

Thank you

Arabic   shokran
Hebrew   todah
Japanese   arigatoo
Mandarin Chinese   xie xie
Russian   spasibo
Swahili   asante

Yes

Arabic   na'am
Hebrew   kein
Japanese   hai
Mandarin Chinese   shi
Russian   da
Swahili   ndiyo

Friend

Arabic   sadik
Hebrew chaver, chavera
Japanese   tomodachi
Mandarin Chinese   peng you
Swahili   rafiki

School

Arabic   madrassa
Hebrew   beit sefer
Japanese   gakkou
Mandarin Chinese   xue xiao
Russian   shkola
Swahili   shule

Mystery Continents

Looking at a globe can help you learn important information about continents. It is also fun! Use a **globe** to play this guessing game with a friend.

You Will Need:

a globe
a long piece of string
   for measuring
   distance
a friend

What To Do:

1. Think of a continent you want to learn more about. Have your friend think of one too. Keep your continents a secret!

2. Take turns finding your continent on the globe. Don't let your friend see which continent you are looking for.

3. Study the continent you chose. Notice important information about it. The questions on the next page might help.

4. Take turns giving clues about the continent to your friend.

5. The first one who guesses the other person's continent wins.

You might want to choose a different continent each time you play this game. Then every time you play you will learn something new!

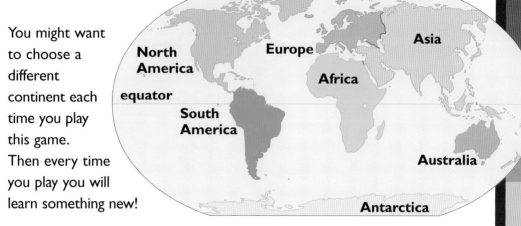

Questions to help you make up clues about your continent.

• Does the continent have a large mountain chain, river, or desert that you notice right away?

• Which ocean is the continent near?

• Which continent is farthest away from it? Use the string to find out.

• Is the continent close to—or far away from—the North Pole? The South Pole?

• Is the continent completely surrounded by water?

• Does the continent touch another continent?

• What other continents are close to it?

• Does the continent have lots of countries?

• Is the continent above or below the equator? Or does the equator cross through the continent? If it does, is most of the continent above or below the equator?

How Will You Get There?

To get around your neighborhood, you probably take a walk or ride your bike. But in parts of the world where houses stand on stilts and are surrounded by water, children paddle canoes from house to house.

To travel longer distances, people use other kinds of transportation. Buses and trains take many people from city to city, or even across one or more countries.

People can travel on rivers, canals, lakes, and oceans in boats of all shapes and sizes. There are many different kinds of airplanes, too. Some are big, some are small, and some are even fast enough to jet from one side of the world to the other in just hours!

What Is Wheel Power?

If walking is too slow, use wheels! A bicycle, skateboard, or pair of in-line skates can take you places you want to go. You can roll as far as the roads or paths—and your legs—will take you!

In China, there are not many cars. Most roads are unpaved, and few Chinese people can afford to buy a car. So most people get around on bicycles. There are so many cyclists that special traffic police are needed to direct them on their way.

Some people use their wheels—and their legs—to take other people where they want to go. Pedicabs are popular in India and other parts of Asia. Comfortable seats at the back can hold two people, while the cyclist pulls them along.

Using muscle power does not cost a lot of money, and it can be fun, too. Be sure you know the rules of the road, and always pay attention to traffic. Keep your bike and safety equipment in good working order so you are ready to roll anytime.

an owner of a cycle-rickshaw in India

Why Are There Roads?

This mountain pass in the South Tyrol, Austria, is a challenge to drivers.

The road zigzags farther and farther upward. You peer out of the car window and gulp as you look back. It's a very long way down!

You are traveling over a mountain pass in the South Tyrol (tuh ROHL), Austria. It is too steep to go straight up, so the roads to the top wind backward and forward like a slithering snake.

Today, there are roads across all the countries of the world. Some are little more than dirt trails, and others are six-lane or eight-lane highways that carry heavy traffic in each direction.

In Western Australia, roads are strong enough to support these powerful trucks.

This icy road winds through Keystone Canyon in Alaska.

Roads of some sort have existed for thousands of years. Often a road started as a rough trail—the easiest route from one place to another. Over the years, the feet of people and animals wore it down until it became a smooth, wide path. As towns grew, the paths became wider still. Some were covered with gravel, pebbles, or other materials to make them permanent roads.

In Uganda, a country in Africa, people take their banana crop to market along a dirt road.

Why Ride Cars and Motorcycles?

This African man lives in a traditional Nigerian village but uses a modern motorbike for transportation.

Before automobiles were invented, people walked, cycled, rode animals, or rode vehicles pulled by animals to work or to visit friends and family. So people usually lived near their work and family.

The invention of the car allowed people to live farther away from their work. Today, cars zoom over roads and highways to take

people to work. Cars also take people to the homes of friends and family. Many people drive to vacation spots such as theme parks, national parks, mountains, or seashores.

There are more than 450 million passenger cars in the world. While cars help people in many ways, they cause problems, too. These problems include accidents, pollution, and frustrating traffic jams. Many people try to help solve these problems by carpooling, or sharing rides with several people. Some cities set aside special highway lanes to be used only by carpooling passengers.

In some countries, motorcycles are a popular way to get to work. Most motorcycles are less expensive than cars and take up less space. Many police officers use motorcycles because they are small enough to move easily through traffic.

KNOW It All!

Some cars are able to give directions! Such cars use GPS (Global Positioning System) technology. GPS can track the location of a car using a satellite. A device installed in the car allows it to map out a route based upon the car's location.

How Do People Travel Across Snow and Ice?

Dogsleds are used to cross huge icy areas in Alaska.

In Canada, winters are long and cold. In some parts of the country, deep snow covers the ground for months at a time, and it is hard to go from place to place. Some of Canada's people have solved this problem by using sleds pulled by dogs.

The sleds are handy, but today, some people use snowmobiles to move heavy loads. A snowmobile is a kind of sled on skis, with a motor to push it through even the thickest snow. The driver uses handlebars to steer the snowmobile.

Another way of moving through frozen places is to put on skates. People travel on skates across ice in cold northern countries, such as Finland, Norway, Sweden, and Russia.

The Lapps use reindeer to pull their sleds.

The Lapps of northern Europe use both old and new ways to cross the snow-covered ground. Some use skis to travel with their herds of reindeer, while their belongings are strapped onto a sled pulled by reindeer. Others use snowmobiles, and some even use helicopters.

An Inuit woman in Canada uses a snowmobile to carry home the supplies brought by the airplane.

This man rides a reed boat on Lake Titicaca, in South America.

How Do People Travel Across Water?

Some of the first boats were made thousands of years ago by the ancient Egyptians. They built their boats out of a reed called **papyrus** (puh PY ruhs).

These people are riding a small Egyptian sailboat ferry across the water.

Today, the same kind of boat making still goes on. Some people cut tall reeds. They bend and weave them into fishing boats.

Other people build long, thin boats called canoes. They build or carve the boats from wood. Both kinds of boats are light enough to carry across the mud to the river's edge.

Today, many boats are complicated machines. They are built to go on long journeys in any kind of weather, and they often carry heavy loads.

Ferries are like taxis. They carry people and sometimes cars across a body of water.

Ocean liners are much bigger. They carry people across an ocean, sometimes traveling for many days.

The Queen Mary 2 pulling into port in Fort Lauderdale, Florida.

All Aboard!

You're at a place where there are lots of things to see, hear, smell, and taste. You can hear the cawing of hungry sea birds.

Harbors often create lovely scenes, such as this one in the Cyclades Islands of Greece.

You can see boats loading and unloading, tiny tugboats hauling enormous ships, and sailors getting ready for a cruise. Where are you? At a **harbor!**

Boats and ships begin and end their voyages at a harbor. A harbor is a protected body of water. Some harbors are partly surrounded by land. The land protects them from dangerous ocean waves and strong winds. Other harbors are built near narrow channels of water. On open coasts, huge walls are built to protect a harbor.

At a harbor, you might smell the salty air and motor fuel. At small harbors, people dock and refuel their boats. These harbors may have ramps that people use to unload the boats from their trailers. Other harbors are big enough to hold many large ships and barges.

Clang clang clang. The captains of boats and ships carefully move their vessels around the clanging colored buoys (BOO eez). The buoys warn them of dangerous places, such as shallow water and rocks.

If you are lucky, the harbor might even have a snack bar with delicious seafood to taste!

How Do People Travel on Sand?

All is quiet except for the tinkling of harness bells and the shifting of sand, as the great animals lift their feet. Everywhere you look there is sand—as far as the eye can see. There is no road to follow, not even a track, but a string of camels winds its way across the vast desert.

A Tuareg tribesman and his wife lead their caravan of camels across the Sahara in Africa.

A string of camels carrying goods is called a **caravan** (KAIR uh van). Camel caravans are still a common sight in the desert. But, small airplanes and sturdy all-terrain vehicles are now used in some desert places.

A camel caravan may make its way to Timbuktu in Mali, western Africa. Timbuktu is near the southern edge of the Sahara. Every year from December to May, great camel caravans gather there. People come from many places to trade goods.

The camel is the ideal animal to use for transportation in a desert, because its wide feet do not sink into the sand. Also,

camels can go for several days without water and use fat in their humps to keep them alive. If you think the desert seems like an ocean of sand, you can see why camels are often called "ships of the desert."

Why Do People Ride Buses?

The bus driver eyes the back of the school bus. "Stay in your seats," he says firmly and loudly enough to be heard over the roar of the engine and the noisy chatter of the children. Many people recognize school buses by their flashing lights. But buses come in all different sizes and colors, depending on how they are used. Not only do buses take children to and from school, but they also take people to and from work, stores, or parks. People often take buses on trips to other cities, across the country, or on group vacations. Tour buses take groups of people to see a city's important places.

Buses can carry up to 70 passengers, but they take up much less space than 70 cars. They cause less pollution because they use less fuel per person than cars do. They also cost less per person to operate.

Why Do People Ride Trains?

They can move people at speeds of more than 170 miles (275 kilometers) per hour. They carry goods weighing thousands of tons across a **continent**. Almost every country has them, and many children

In France, many people travel from the suburbs to jobs and cultural activities in the city.

collect toy models of them. What are they? Trains!

Every day, in many places throughout the world, trains carry thousands of people along railroad tracks. People who want to travel from one city to another use trains. Many people who live in one town and work in another take a train to work. Some trains make longer trips. They have beds for sleeping and serve meals in dining cars.

Subways are underground city trains that zoom people from place to place. Elevated trains, or els, crisscross a city on tracks that are built above the streets.

Every day, thousands of commuters board trains in the New York City subway system.

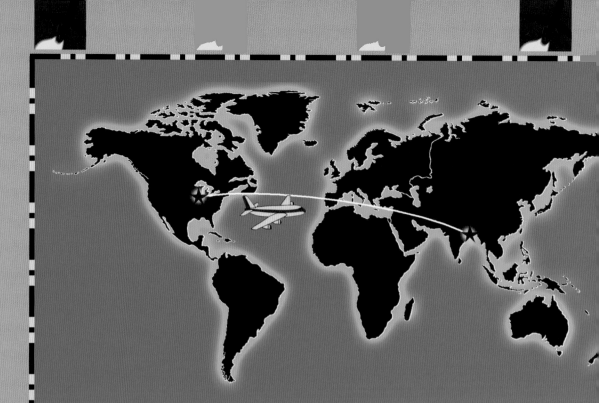

Why Do People Fly?

Airplanes and helicopters are two ways to get far in a hurry. They carry people and goods thousands of feet above the ground.

The first thing you might notice about an airplane is its wings. When an airplane starts moving, the special shape of its wings helps it rise in the air and fly. Under the airplane wings are its engines. The fastest planes have jet engines that help them travel halfway around the world—

from Chicago, Illinois, to Kolkata (Calcutta), India—in about 15 hours! Sometimes people can watch a movie, listen to music, or eat a meal or a snack while flying in the clouds.

Helicopters do not have the same type of wings that airplanes do. A helicopter is powered by whirling blades that lift it into the sky. Helicopters are not as fast as some airplanes, but they can change directions and land more easily. They can fly forward, upward, and sideways. They can also hover, or stay in one place in the air.

One of the world's largest passenger airplanes is the Airbus A380. The A380 can carry more than 550 passengers.

What Is an Airport?

The day has finally arrived! You are at the airport and about to board the plane that will take you on your dream vacation. There are many things you need to do  at the airport before takeoff.

At the check-in counter, an airline worker checks you in, tells you which seat is yours, and gives you a boarding pass. Your luggage is put onto a moving belt. It carries your suitcase through rubber flaps in the wall to large bins that are wheeled to the plane. The agent tells you which departure gate your plane will leave from.

At the airport, you and other travelers may also pass through a gate that has special machines. The machines make sure nobody is carrying anything dangerous.

At the departure gate, another airline worker takes your boarding pass. You are ready to board the plane.

You may have to walk through a tunnel or upstairs to get to the plane. When you enter the plane, a flight attendant helps you find your seat. You find a bin above your head in which to put your coats, small bags, or toys. Of course, you fasten your seatbelt!

Suddenly the plane's engines roar to life. The plane is moving! It moves slowly, at first, then faster and faster down a long paved path called a runway. Finally, you're up! Sit back and enjoy the ride.

TRY THIS! 1

It's a good idea to get to the airport an hour or more before the plane is supposed to take off. Bring a quiet toy or a book to help pass the time. You might also want to bring a journal to write down everything you see on your trip. Put stickers or tape on your luggage, especially if you check it instead of carrying it on the plane yourself. That will help you spot it after your flight.

Walk, Ride, or Fly?

Could you cycle to an island? Would you take a plane to school? The type of transportation you use depends on where you are going, how far away it is, and how fast you want to get there. Sometimes it even depends on the weather! The map on these pages shows a small town called Our Town. It has lots of places to visit. Take a look at all the different places on the map. Now turn the page and test your travel I.Q.!

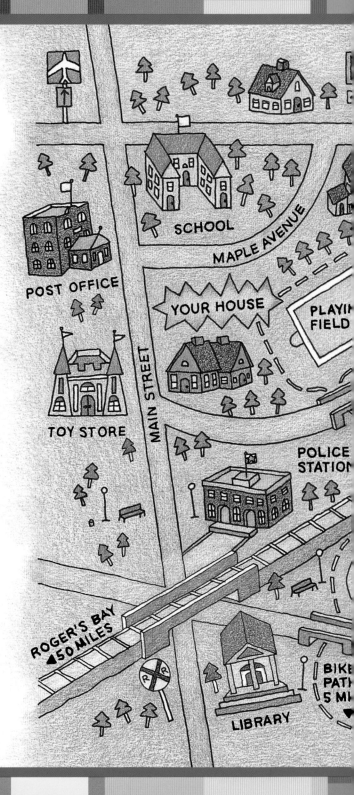

SCHOOL

MAPLE AVENUE

POST OFFICE

YOUR HOUSE

PLAYING FIELD

TOY STORE

MAIN STREET

POLICE STATION

ROGER'S BAY ◄ 50 MILES

BIKE PATH 5 MI

LIBRARY

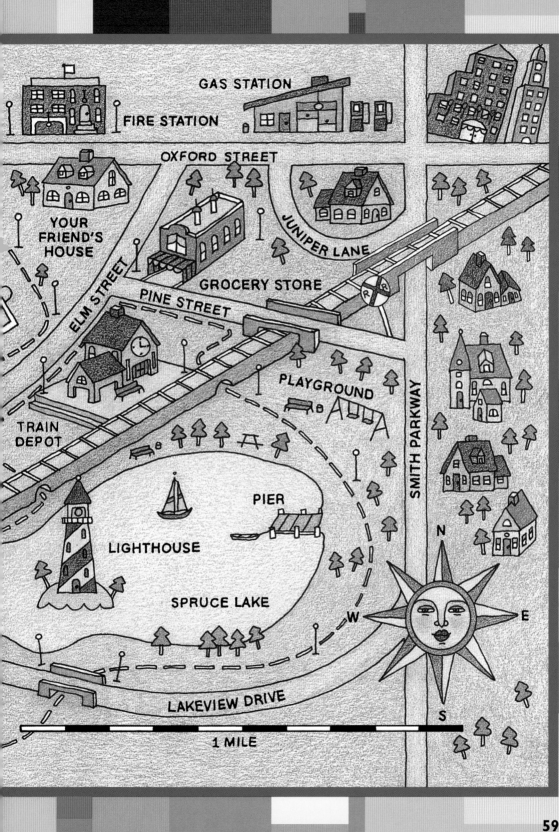

FIRE STATION

GAS STATION

OXFORD STREET

YOUR FRIEND'S HOUSE

JUNIPER LANE

ELM STREET

PINE STREET

GROCERY STORE

PLAYGROUND

SMITH PARKWAY

TRAIN DEPOT

PIER

LIGHTHOUSE

SPRUCE LAKE

N

W

E

S

LAKEVIEW DRIVE

1 MILE

Now that you have had a chance to study the map of Our Town, you can use it to find your way around. It will help you figure out the best way to get to different places.

1. You want to pick up your friend at the playground and then go to the playing field. But you're not allowed to cross busy streets. How can you get where you want to go?

2. What shortcut could you take if you were walking from the school to the grocery store?

3. How would get to the lighthouse from the pier? Which roads would you take to get closest to the pier if you were coming from the airport and you needed to buy gas?

4. How far away is Roger's Bay from this town? What is a good way to get there if you don't have a car?

5. If you wanted to get from the school to the toy store, how might you go there on a warm, sunny day? In the pouring rain, could you take a train?

6. Name the places you could visit if you rode your bike along the whole bike path. Could you go to the post office without leaving the bike path?

Where in the World?

Airplanes, trains, and ships can take you almost anywhere in the world. You can fly in a plane to a crowded city in Japan, sail on a boat down the Amazon River in South America, or ride on a train across country.

But did you know that you can feel as if you've been to these exciting places without even leaving your own house? Reading books and looking at pictures can make you feel as if you've been there!

The World in a Day

Kyle was bored and grumpy. All of his friends were away on vacation, and he had nothing to do. "Some school vacation," Kyle grumbled as he slumped into his chair and started eating his breakfast. He was about to start munching on his Crispy Crunchies when he spotted a stack of cards tied with a red ribbon.

When he untied the ribbon, Kyle saw that the cards were postcards. They were from far-off places: Japan, Kenya, and Brazil. Kyle was puzzled.

"Grandmother, what is this?" Kyle asked.

His grandmother came and stood beside him. "Hmm," she said. "It looks like you won't be bored today! Better go put on your gym shoes. You're in for an adventure. First stop, Kenya!"

Kyle followed his grandmother toward the living room. In the hallway, she stopped him and handed him the postcard from Kenya. It showed an elephant walking across a grassy plain in the sun. Kyle looked up and could not believe his eyes. Grandmother had turned the living room into an African **plain**. On the walls were pictures of lions, elephants, and zebras. On the table sat an African mask and a bowl carved out of wood.

Kyle was amazed. He never knew his grandmother had such wonderful things. "Jambo (JAHM boh)," his grandmother said. "That's Swahili for 'hello.'

"In Kenya, cassava (kuh SAH vuh) is an important food. It's a root vegetable like a potato. Here, try some." Kyle took a big bite. It tasted like sweet potatoes.

Then his grandmother handed Kyle a book called *African Safari*. It had pictures of people and wild animals. His grandmother touched his shoulder. "You can read that book when you return from your journey," she said.

"OK, time for our next adventure," she continued. "On to Tokyo!" Kyle clutched the book under his arm and followed his grandmother to his grandparents' room.

"Konnichiwa (koh nee chee wah)," she said, bowing. Then she handed him the postcard from Tokyo. The postcard showed two women hiding their faces behind beautiful paper fans.

Kyle looked into his grandparents' room. Paper fans covered the walls. The pillows from the chair were on the floor. On the bed was the most amazing kite

Kyle had ever seen. Kyle wanted to touch it. "Wait!" his grandmother said. "You must take your shoes off before you go inside. That is the custom in Japan." Kyle did as he was told.

Then his grandmother placed a tray with a teapot and tiny cups on the table. Kyle drank the tea. It didn't taste anything like the tea he was used to. It had no cream and no sugar!

After they finished their tea, his grandmother handed Kyle another book. This book was called *A Journey Through Japan*. The cover showed a kite festival

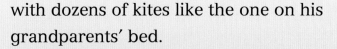

with dozens of kites like the one on his grandparents' bed.

As Kyle followed his grandmother out to the yard, he heard lively music. "Here, put this on," she said and handed Kyle a mask covered with bright feathers.

"We went to Rio de Janeiro for Carnival," she said. "It was one big party—four days of dancing, singing, and parades. In Brazil, a favorite food is black beans with rice. Here, try this. It's a little spicy." Kyle tried the beans. Were they hot!

Then his grandmother handed Kyle another book. This one was called *Discovering Brazil.*

"Well, sir, that's the end of our very quick trip. But you can do some more traveling on your own."

Kyle didn't care if it rained tomorrow—or the next day, either. If it did, he would just pick up one of his grandmother's books and take another trip!

Be an armchair traveler. Pick a faraway country. Look for books that will help you answer these questions:

• What language do the people speak?

• Do the children go to a school like yours? Say why it might be different.

• What are some of the names people give to children?

• What kinds of work can children do when they grow up?

• Can both women and men do these jobs?

The Clothes People Wear

No one knows exactly why—or when—people first wore clothes. But early people probably began to wear clothes for the same reasons that we wear clothes today. Clothes keep us warm and dry. Some people—nurses, police officers, priests, and many others— wear clothes that show who they are or what they do. And sometimes we wear clothes that make us look like part of a group or clothes that make us stand out in a crowd.

young Buddhist monks wearing orange robes

Think about your own clothes as you read the following pages about clothes worn by people around the world. How are they like the clothes you wear, and how are they different? What do you like about the different kinds of clothing? When you are finished looking at all of the clothing, choose a kind you would like to try. Then, draw a picture of yourself wearing it.

a Ndebele woman in South Africa

children in bright colors, ready to play

Clothes for Cold Climates

Brrrrrrrr, it's cold outside! You want to go out and play. What do you wear to keep warm? Perhaps you wear a heavy coat, hat, scarf, gloves or mittens, and warm boots.

Some people must wear warm clothes most of the time. People in northern Canada, Greenland, and other places that are far north live in **climates** that are cold most of the year. In these cold regions, people wear heavy clothes made of fur or wool.

An **Inuit** man wears clothes made from animal skins. A hooded jacket, or parka, protects the top part of an Inuit's body. Can you guess what he wears under his jacket? Another jacket! He also wears two pairs of pants to protect his legs. The heat from his body stays between the two layers of clothes, and this helps to keep him warm. Thick fur mittens protect his hands, and he wears sealskin boots on his feet.

An Inuit man of northern North America wears a furry parka and trousers.

Clothes for Hot Climates

You are midway through your soccer game, and the sun is beating down on you. Sweat drips off your forehead. To keep cool, you are wearing a T-shirt and shorts.

In warm places, people wear clothes made of a lightweight material, such as cotton or linen, to stay cool. Much of the clothing in warm regions is white or light-colored, because these colors reflect the sun's rays. Darker colors absorb heat from the sun, so they make a person feel hotter.

A man rides a long-legged camel across the Sahara. The sun burns bright and hot. This man is a Tuareg (TWAH rehg). He raises animals in the desert. A light blue robe

In India's hot climate, most people wear light, loose clothes.

covers him from shoulders to ankles. The loose folds of the robe shield him from the hot sun. They also let air flow around his body, helping to keep him cool. He has a long cloth wrapped around his head. Part of the cloth can be pulled over his mouth and nose to keep out blowing sand. Just as your lightweight clothes keep you cool in the hot sun, this man's clothing protects him from the weather.

This Tuareg man can pull the extra cloth of his headdress over his mouth and nose to keep out blowing sand.

Weave Your Own Friendship Bracelet

In many countries, people make rugs, baskets, and blankets. They make them by **weaving.** Weavers use a machine called a **loom** to cross threads over and under one another. The threads are made of cotton, silk, or even grass. Sometimes the threads are colored with dyes made from plants. You can make a simple hand loom out of straws and use it to weave a bracelet for your friend.

You Will Need:

2½ feet (1 meter) thin cotton twine
2 plastic drinking straws, each cut in half
different-colored yarn

What To Do:

1. Cut the twine into four equal pieces and thread each piece through a straw. Tie the four ends above the straws into a knot.

2. Knot the other end of each piece of twine.

3. Tie a piece of yarn to the twine just below the top knot.

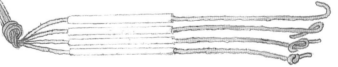

4. Weave the yarn under and over the straws from side to side. Use your fingers to push up each row of yarn onto the twine and slide the straws down. To change colors, tie a new piece of yarn to the end of the first one and weave in the loose ends.

5. Make your bracelet long enough to tie around your wrist. When your bracelet is the length you want, remove the straws. To fasten the last row, tie the end of the yarn to the piece of the twine. Then tie a knot with the two pieces of twine on the left. Repeat with the pair on the right. Finally, tie together the four twine pieces with another knot.

Now you are ready to give your bracelet to a friend!

The Work People Do

People have always had to work. Early people hunted animals and gathered plants. Some people fished. Later, they learned to farm. They made their own clothes, tools, and furniture. They swapped some of the things they made, grew, or caught for other things they needed. This is called **bartering.** Then people began to use money. Some people paid others to work for them. Workers used that money to buy what they needed.

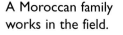
A Moroccan family works in the field.

A teacher leads her students on a field trip.

In some places in the world today, people still live as the early people did. They hunt, fish, or farm in small groups near their homes, and they make everything they need for everyday life.

In other places, people who farm or fish sell much of what they grow or catch. Some people make things for other people to buy. They are craftworkers and factory workers. Some people work as teachers, scientists, nurses, and doctors. They help other people.

Year after year, people learn, discover, and invent things. As they do this, they find different kinds of work to do.

Homes for All Places

Zulu people of South Africa build homes of reeds and straw.

Some of the very first houses were caves. They had walls and ceilings that kept out wind, rain, and prowling animals. They had floors where people could sit or sleep.

In time, people learned to build different kinds of homes. They needed homes that were right for the place where they lived. They used materials they found nearby.

In dry places, houses were made of mud or clay. Where there was plenty of wood, people built houses of logs or boards. On grassy plains, they built homes of dry grass.

People who lived near rivers made rafts or houseboats, or built their houses on stilts.

Steep roofs let snow easily slide off these colorful houses in Norway.

Today, people still build homes that are right for the place where they live. People who live in very hot places need houses that keep them cool. People in the frozen north need houses that keep the cold out.

On the banks of the Amazon River in Peru, houses are built on stilts to protect them from flooding.

In such large cities as Chicago, many people live in high-rise apartments.

Our homes—even apartment buildings—have much in common with those first caves. They protect us against the weather and give us a safe place to sit and sleep.

In Hong Kong, many people live in boats on the harbor.

What House Will You Build?

Here is your chance to design your own house. For each place listed below, decide which materials from the next page you would use to build your house. *See answers on page 83.*

stilt house

Where You Live

1. An area close to a swamp. Floods occur quite often.

2. A very rainy place.

3. A dry rural place with few trees.

4. A crowded big city with buildings that are homes for many people.

5. A place close to a river, lake, sea, or ocean.

mud house

Materials for a House

A. mud for making bricks

B. wooden poles on which to build your house

C. waterproof shingles for your roof

D. concrete bricks and steel beams

E. wood, fiberglass, or aluminum for making a house that floats

cottage

apartment building

houseboats

83

Famous Places

When you travel to places near and far, you can see with your own eyes the work of great architects and engineers. They are the people who have designed and built skyscrapers, churches and **temples,** castles, and bridges.

When you travel, you can see the wonders of nature, too. You can gaze at magnificent canyons, mountains that seem to reach the clouds, and rivers so wide you can't see the other side.

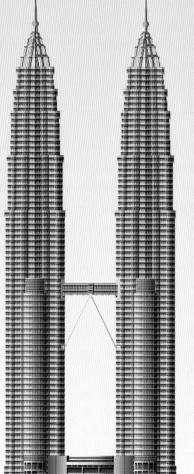

What Are Castles?

Some of the world's most amazing buildings were built for protection, not

The famous French author Michel de Montaigne lived his whole life in this castle.

beauty. Hundreds of years ago, people in different parts of the world had many rulers. The rulers often fought each other. Powerful rulers built castles to live in with their family, helpers, priests, soldiers—and farm animals!

Many of the castles were made of stone. Often they were built around an open courtyard. They had high walls that could be 30 feet (10 meters) thick to protect against enemies. Some castles had towers at each corner.

Sometimes the walls were surrounded with deep, wide ditches that were usually filled with water. These were called moats. To protect the castle, guards looked out from the towers and walked along the tops of the walls. They hid behind stone fences called battlements and shot arrows at attackers. When visitors came, the guards would lower a drawbridge so people could walk or ride across the moat. Then the visitors would have to pass a gatehouse.

Inside, there was a large great room where people met and ate meals. A huge fire in the fireplace took away the chill. So did tapestries, or hanging cloths, placed around the castle walls. People spread sweet-smelling plants on the floors and changed them every month.

The king slept in this bedroom in the Linderhof Palace in Bavaria, Germany.

The Tower of London has been a fort, a palace, and a prison. Today it is a museum.

Castles had a kitchen, a chapel in which to pray, and apartments for the family. They also had a barracks, or sleeping room, for soldiers. Many had dungeons in which to keep prisoners.

In many places around the world, ancient castles still stand. One is the Tower of London on the River Thames in London, England. This group of stone buildings has a wall and moat surrounding it. The Tower of London was first built as a castle in the 1000's. In later times, it was a palace and a prison. Today it is a museum.

The Loire (lwahr) Valley in France is famous for its castles, called chateaux (shah TOHZ) in French. One of the oldest French chateaux is in Angers (ahn ZHAY). Visitors can still see the remains of the 17 towers and the moat. This chateau was built in the early 1200's.

The Chateau D'Angers is one of many famous castles in France's Loire Valley.

In Syria, near the northern border of present-day Lebanon, is a castle called Krak des Chevaliers (KRAHK day shuh VAH lyay). This fortress was built during the 1100's.

In Syria stands the Krak des Chevaliers, a castle built during the 1100's.

The picture on these pages shows a typical castle. Find the following parts of the castle.

a. A moat surrounded the castle. It was filled with water to keep enemies out.

b. Strong towers helped soldiers defend the castle. People also lived in them.

c. Soldiers hid from enemies behind battlements.

d. The outdoor space inside the castle was the courtyard.

e. Meals were cooked in the kitchen.

f. The chapel was where people prayed.

g. The gatehouse was where soldiers raised and lowered the gate.

h. The dungeon was where prisoners were kept.

i. The great hall was the room that most people used during the day.

j. A drawbridge crossed the moat. It could be pulled up when an enemy was near.

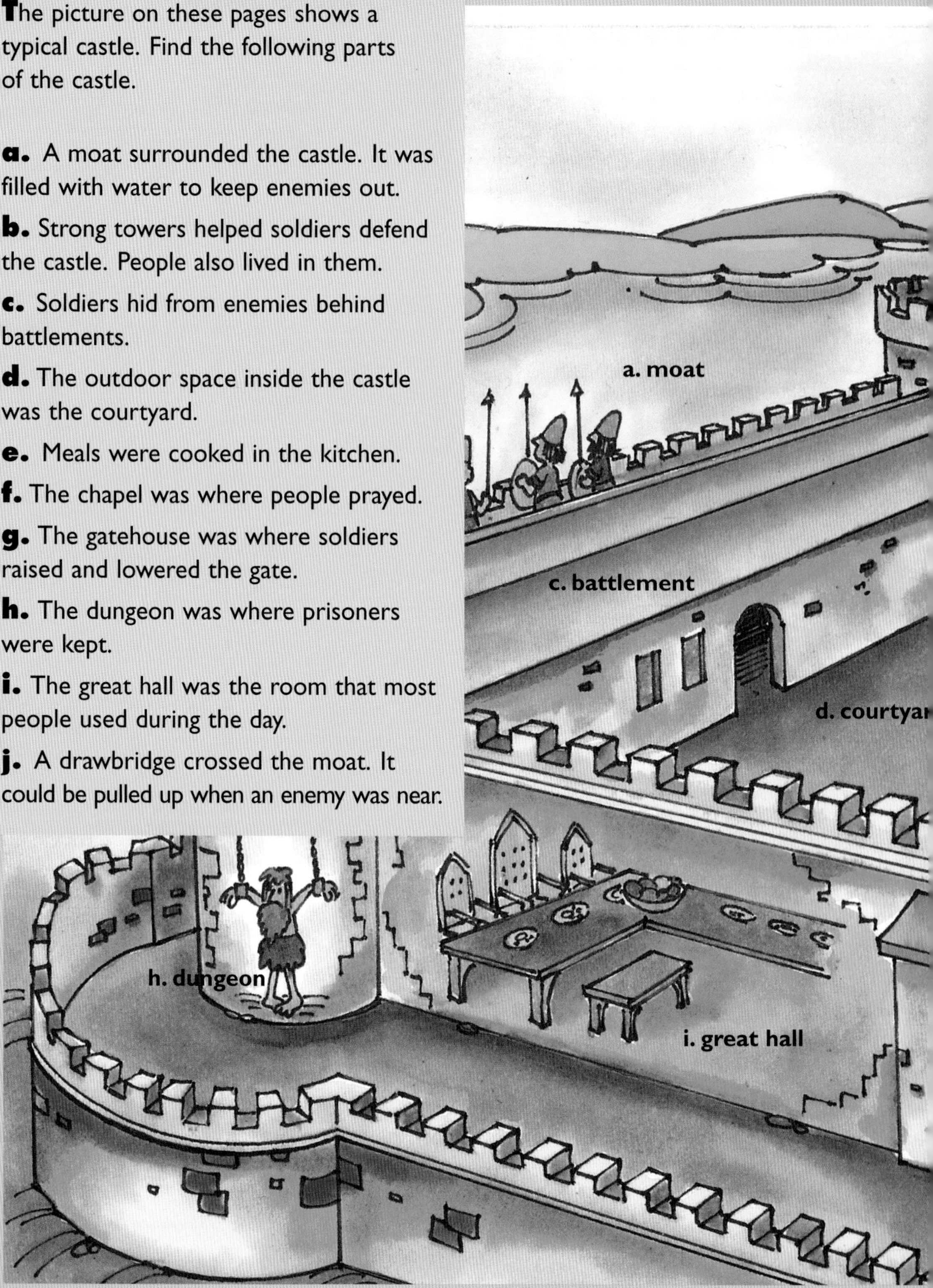

a. moat

c. battlement

d. courtyar

h. dungeon

i. great hall

b. tower

e. kitchen

f. chapel

g. gatehouse

j. drawbridge

Home Is Their Castle

A stone bridge over a moat leads to the imperial castle in Tokyo, Japan.

Many castles were designed as homes for rulers rather than as fortresses. Many of the world's most famous and fancy palaces were built hundreds of years ago.

The rulers of the United Kingdom live at Windsor Castle when they are not in nearby London. William the Conqueror built a castle in that place about 1070. Since then, many rulers have added to the castle, which now covers 9 acres (3.6 hectares). It has 15 majestic towers and a beautiful chapel.

Another famous castle lies on a hill in the city of Osaka, Japan. The elegant Osaka Castle was built during the 1500's. Visitors can still see three of the original towers as well as the castle's main gate.

A famous palace is in Versailles (ver SY), France. The Palace of Versailles is more than 1/4 mile (0.4 kilometer) long and has

The magnificent Hall of Mirrors thrills visitors to the palace of Versailles in France.

about 1,300 rooms. It was built by the French King Louis XIV in the 1600's.

To see a real fairy-tale castle, go to Neuschwanstein (noy SHVAHN shtyn) Castle in Germany. It has a walled courtyard, spires on its roof, and a blue arched ceiling decorated with stars. Built for King Ludwig II in the 1860's, the castle is now a popular place to visit.

This castle, Neuschwanstein, was the inspiration for the make-believe Fantasyland castles at Disney theme parks.

The government of Andorra, one of the world's smallest countries, meets in the House of the Valleys.

Where Do Leaders Work?

Many people work in tall skyscrapers, small office buildings, or tiny stores. And people who run governments often work in places that are works of art that look powerful or grand. The buildings in which they work might be gleaming white mansions, majestic palaces, or buildings tucked behind the walls of a fortress. Here are some famous government buildings around the world.

The White House, in Washington, D.C., is the home and the office of the United States president.

Both houses of the Indian parliament meet in the Parliament House in New Delhi.

The Kremlin, in Moscow, is an old fort. It contains many of Russia's government buildings.

The British government meets in the Houses of Parliament in London, England.

The Eiffel Tower, in Paris, France, was built for the 1889 World's Fair.

What Are Modern Wonders of the World?

People have built many incredible structures. Some soar to dizzying heights. Others cross huge lakes or rivers. Here are just a few modern wonders you can see around the world.

The Eiffel Tower is a huge iron tower in Paris. Built for a world's fair in 1889, the tower rises 984 feet (300 meters). You can take stairs or elevators to the top. The Eiffel Tower was the highest structure in the world for many years.

In Toronto, Canada, stands the CN Tower, one of the world's highest free-standing structures. The communications and observation tower stands 1,815 feet (553 meters) high. It was completed in 1976.

At night, the CN Tower and SkyDome brighten the Toronto sky.

The Akashi Kaikyo Bridge in
Japan took 10 years to build.

In 1998, the Akashi Kaikyo Bridge
opened in Japan. Its main suspension span,
the world's longest, stretches 6,527 feet
(1,990 meters) across the Akashi Strait.
The bridge took about 10 years to build.

The Channel Tunnel, or "Chunnel," carries traffic between the United Kingdom and France.

The Channel Tunnel is an undersea railway that connects the United Kingdom with France. It opened in 1994. Fast electric trains carry cars and buses, people and goods through the tunnel, under the English Channel. The journey can take less than 35 minutes.

The Suez Canal waterway joins the Mediterranean Sea and the Red Sea in Egypt. It is 118 miles (190 kilometers) long and 64 feet (19.5 meters) deep. When the canal opened in 1869, ships traveling between England and India no longer had to sail around Africa. This shortened the trip by 5,000 miles (8,000 kilometers)!

Another famous canal was built between North America and South America to link the Atlantic and Pacific oceans. When the Panama Canal was finished in 1914, it

The Suez Canal, in Egypt, is a shortcut for ships traveling between Europe and Asia.

A ship enters the locks of the Panama Canal, in Central America.

shortened the trip between New York City, New York, and San Francisco, California, by 9,000 miles (14,500 kilometers). Ships no longer had to sail around South America.

Wonders of Long Ago

Did you know that there are monuments, tombs, and huge walls that were built hundreds or even thousands of years ago? Sometimes only small parts, or ruins, of these places remain. But you can still visit them today.

Ancient peoples built Stonehenge, in England, more than 3,500 years ago.

In England, tourists and scientists alike are amazed by Stonehenge, a group of huge, rough-cut stones set in circles. Scientists believe that ancient people built Stonehenge as a gathering place. Much of the monument is gone, but scientists think that when it was first built, an earth wall about 320 feet (98 meters) across circled it. Thirty blocks of gray sandstone stood like guards 13 1/2 feet (4 meters) above the ground.

Another wonder from long ago is the Great Pyramid at Giza in Egypt. Pyramids were built by Egyptians about 4,500 years ago as tombs for their kings. The Great Pyramid contains more than 2 million stone blocks.

The pyramids of Egypt at Giza were one of the Seven Wonders of the Ancient World.

The Inca people built Machu Picchu in what is now Peru during the late 1400's.

In Peru, you can visit the ruins of Machu Picchu (MAH choo PEEK choo), which was once a walled city. It was built during the late 1400's by the Inca and was probably a home for the Inca royal family.

The longest structure ever built, the Great Wall of China, stretches nearly 4,000 miles (6,400 kilometers). The wall was built to protect the northern Chinese border against enemies. Most of the wall that stands today was built in the 1400's.

The Great Wall of China stretches for thousands of miles.

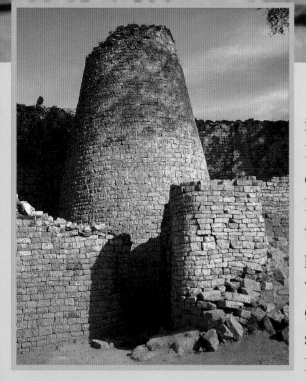

This tall stone tower is part of the remains of an ancient African city called Great Zimbabwe.

Another famous ruin is the Colosseum in Rome. The structure was completed in A.D. 80. From that time until 404, the Colosseum was a place where people could watch fights between gladiators who were slaves or paid fighters. Battles between men and wild animals and other events entertained Romans. The Colosseum was later abandoned. Many of its stones were used to build other structures.

The Colosseum was the largest outdoor theater in ancient Rome. It could seat

Ancient Greeks built the Parthenon to honor the goddess Athena. It stands on top of a hill called the Acropolis.

The Colosseum, in Rome, is one of the finest examples of Roman architecture.

about 50,000 people. It is made of brick and concrete and is surrounded by 80 entrances.

The Parthenon is a famous ruin perched on a hill in Athens, Greece. It was constructed between 447 and 432 B.C. The Parthenon was a temple built to honor the Greek goddess Athena.

The Parthenon is shaped like a rectangle. It stands about 60 feet (18 meters) high. When the Parthenon was built, it had many brightly colored statues and sculptured panels that showed stories from ancient Greece. Today, many of those statues are at museums in Athens and in London, England.

When maps are printed, the direction north is usually toward the top of the paper, and south is at the bottom. On these maps, east is at the right edge of the map, and west is at the left edge. But sometimes, north is not at the top of the map. How do you know if it is or isn't? Often a pointer on the map tells you which direction is north.

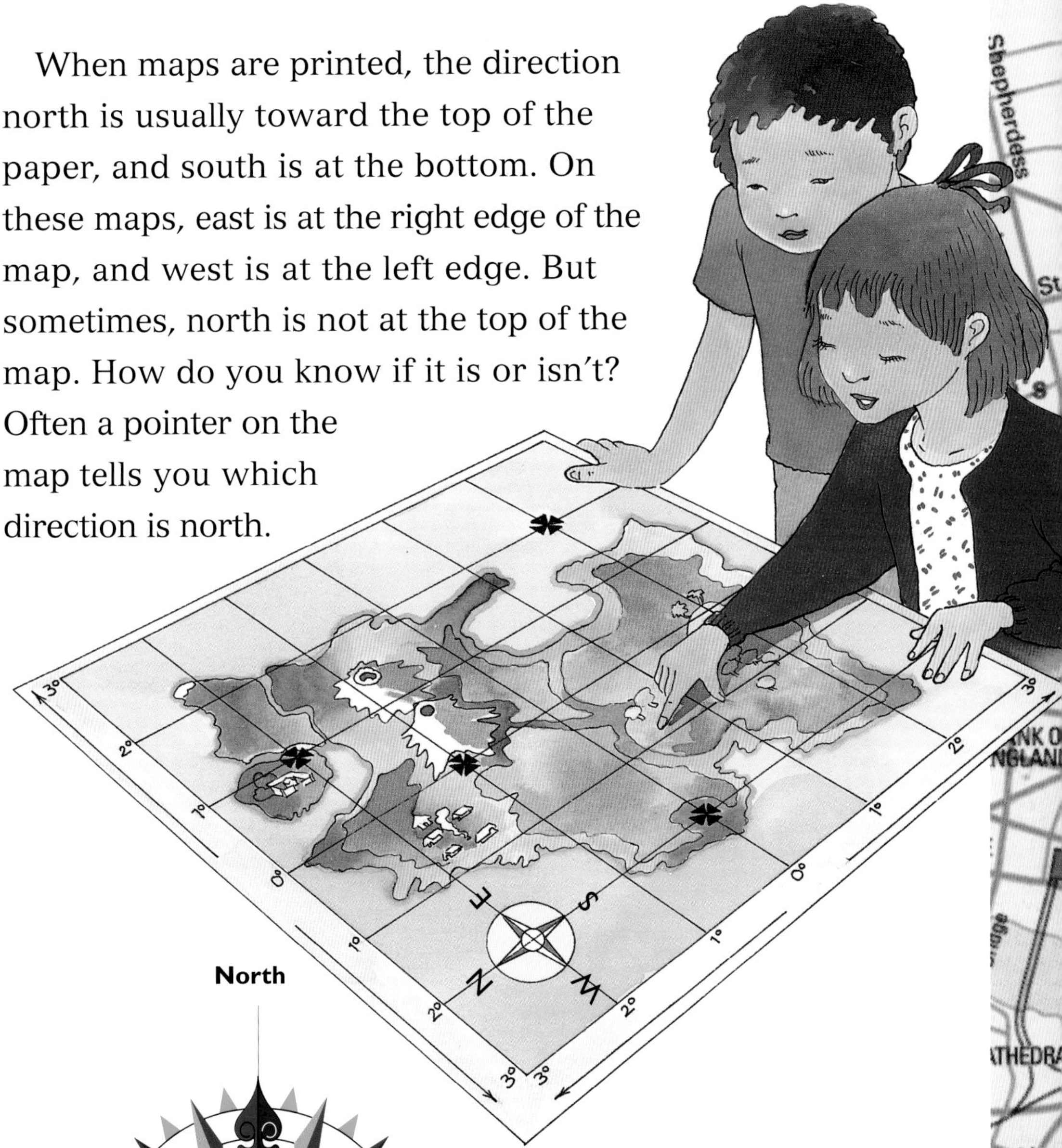

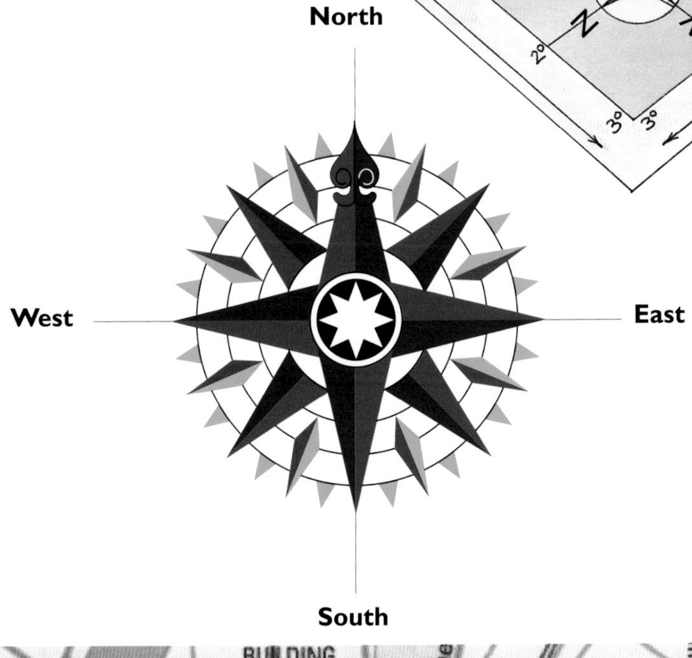

North

West

East

South

137

Understanding Map Symbols

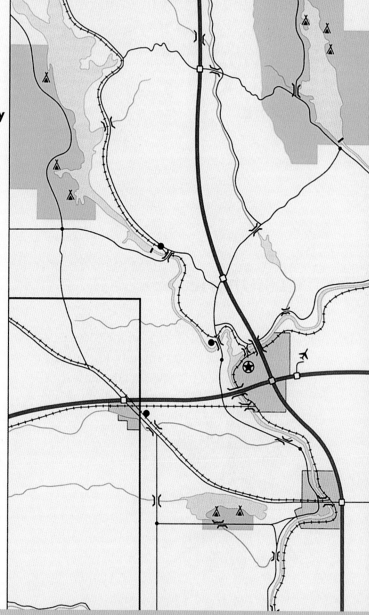

Legend:

- forest
- water
- county boundary
- highway
- other road
- railroad
- bridge
- dam
- capital
- large city
- medium city
- small town
- airport
- campsite

When you walk to the park, you might see trees, grass, flowers, and buildings. You won't see these things on a map, but the map will still help you find out where the park is. How does it do this? With symbols.

Map symbols stand for real things on the surface of the earth. The map legend shows what the symbols mean. The colors help, too. Highways are usually shown as red or black lines. The wider the line, the bigger the highway. Crossed black lines stand for railroad tracks, and a small black dot stands for a city. A star or dot inside a circle means a capital city. To find an airport, look for a tiny airplane on the map.

Water is shown in blue, so squiggly blue lines show rivers. Sometimes color is used to show the height of the land. Low land may be green. High mountains may be dark brown.

The next time you see a map, take a close look at it. You'll be surprised to find how much a small map can show.

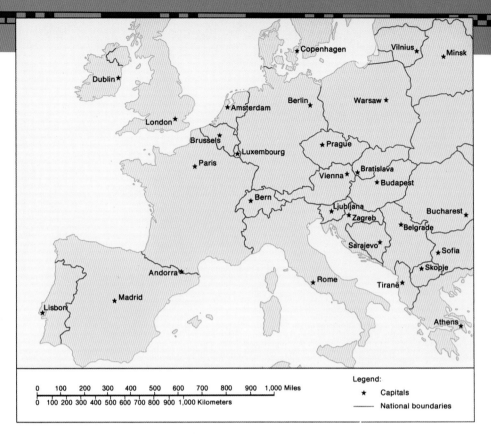

Legend:
★   Capitals
——   National boundaries

0   100   200   300   400   500   600   700   800   900   1,000 Miles
0   100 200 300 400 500 600 700 800 900 1,000 Kilometers

How Do You Measure Distance?

If you are using a map to get to your friend's house, you can figure out how far you have to travel. First, you have to learn something about distance. The word *distance* means the space between things.

A map has to show distance much smaller than it actually is. So, at the top or bottom of most maps, you will see what looks like a ruler. This is called the **map scale**. The scale shows what the distance on a map equals in real distance.

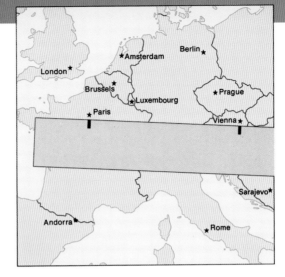

The scale shown on the previous page is a straight line on which distances are marked.

Each mark stands for a certain number of miles or kilometers. To find the real distance between two places, you first measure the distance between them on the map. To do this, line up the two places on the edge of a piece of paper. Make a mark for each place. Then, move the paper down to the scale. Line up one mark with the 0 on the scale. Then read the number that lines up with the other mark.

TRY THIS!

1

To measure distance on a winding road on a map, place a string along the route you want to take. Let the string curve along the curves of the road. Then straighten the string and measure its length on the map scale. The number you get will be the total distance.

Large Scale or Small Scale?

On a map, real land and real oceans are made small enough to fit on paper. The scale of a map is the difference between the map size and the real size. When a map is drawn to scale, everything is made smaller by the same amount.

A large-scale map shows a small area with lots of details. It is what you would see if you were looking down on an area from very close. The highways, streets, parks, and buildings would look large.

A small-scale map shows a large area with not many details. It is what you would see if you were looking down on an area from very far away. You might see main roads, large towns, and rivers or

This large-scale map shows some of Tokyo's important buildings.

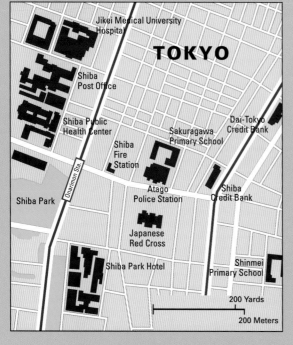

Jikei Medical University Hospital

TOKYO

Shiba Post Office

Shiba Public Health Center

Shiba Fire Station

Sakuragawa Primary School

Dai-Tokyo Credit Bank

Atago Police Station

Shiba Credit Bank

Shiba Park

Japanese Red Cross

Shiba Park Hotel

Shinmei Primary School

Onarimon Sta.

200 Yards

200 Meters

mountains. The roads and towns would look small.

The maps on these pages show the same place drawn in different scales. All the maps have useful information. Which map tells you how many towns are near the shore? Which map tells you the main roads in the area? Which map tells you how far it is from the school to the post office?

This small-scale map tells you that Tokyo lies in east-central Japan.

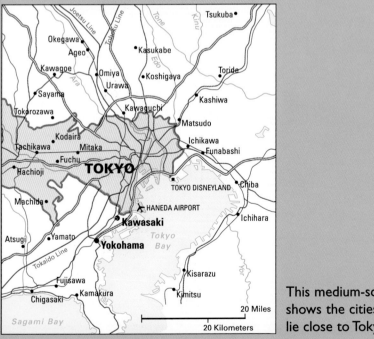

This medium-scale map shows the cities that lie close to Tokyo.

Draw a Map to Scale

You don't need rulers or tape measures to draw a map to scale. Make different maps of your own room—using just your feet!

You Will Need:

graph paper
crayons or markers
a ruler

What To Do:

1. Select two things in your room, such as your dresser and bed, or the door and the window.

2. Estimate, or guess, the distance between the two objects you have chosen.

3. Now use steps to measure the distance. Walk in a straight line, placing your feet from heel to toe. Count how many steps it takes to get from one object to the other. Write down that measurement.

8×16? ? steps

Bed Dresser

First map

4. Decide on a scale, such as the length of one square of graph paper equals one step. Draw a map of your room using the measurements (in steps) you just took. Use your scale to show the distance between the two things you chose. At the top or bottom of the map, mark the map scale.

5. Now draw more maps to different scales. For example, one step equals two squares.

6. Give each of your maps a title, such as "first map," "second map," and "third map."

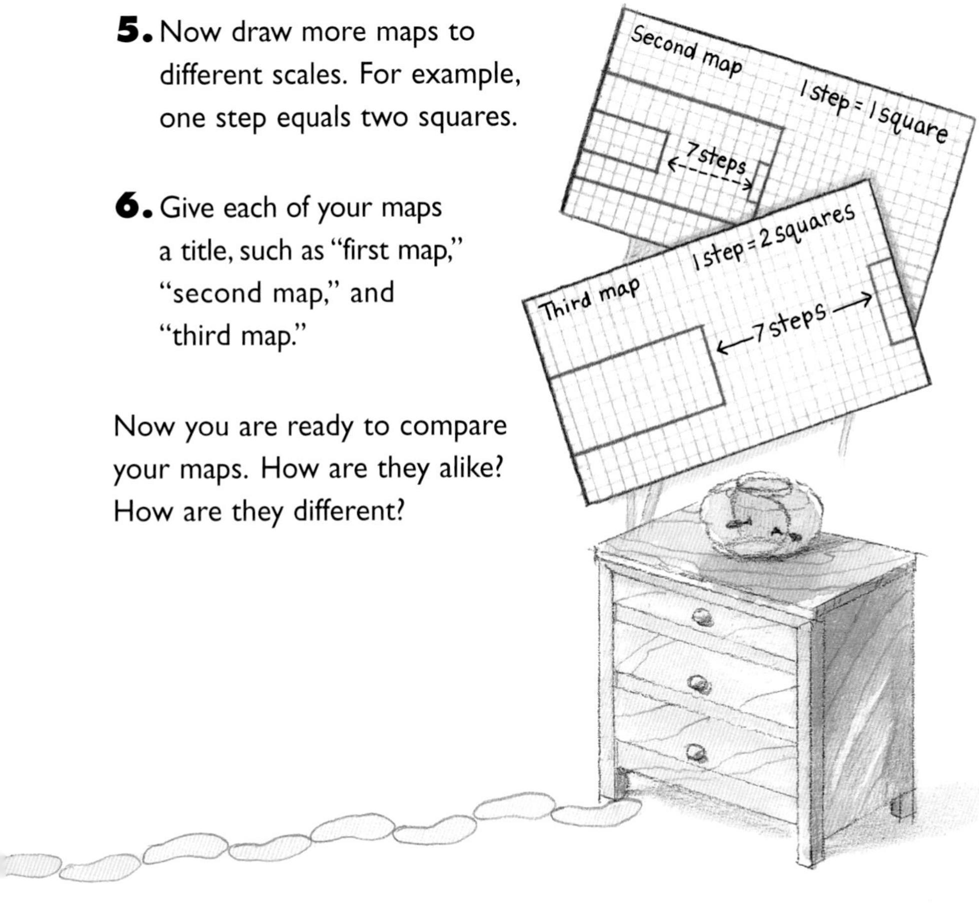

Now you are ready to compare your maps. How are they alike? How are they different?

Second map

1 step = 1 square

7 steps

1 step = 2 squares

Third map

7 steps

What Is a Compass?

If you are standing in your front yard, how do you know which way is east? If it's a sunny early morning, you can easily tell. The sun rises in the east, so you just have to face the direction of the rising sun. But what if it is cloudy outside?

Even on a cloudy day, a good way to tell direction is with a **compass.** A simple compass has a magnetized needle that's mounted so that it can turn freely. No matter which way you face or turn the compass, the needle will continue pointing north.

How does a compass tell which way is north? The needle of a compass is a magnet. It points north because it is pulled by a larger magnet—the earth. One end of the earth's magnet is near the North Pole, and the other end is near the South Pole. The north-seeking end of a magnetic needle always points toward the earth's north magnetic pole.

Underneath a compass's needle are the words *north, south, east,* and *west,* or the letters *N, S, E,* and *W.* When you turn the compass so that the needle points to the word *north* or the letter *N,* it is in the right position to show which way is east, west, or south.

Make a Compass

TRY THIS!
2

See for yourself how the north-seeking end of a magnetic needle always points toward the earth's north magnetic pole.

What To Do:

1. Ask an adult to help you rub one end of the needle along the magnet about 12 times. Rub in one direction only and lift the pin up each time. Then place the needle on the cork.

2. Gently place the cork in the bowl of water. At first, the needle and cork will swing around. Then the needle will point steadily in one direction. It points along the line between the earth's magnetic North and South poles. Ask an adult to tell you which end points north.

You Will Need:

a magnet
a straight pin or
   needle
a piece of cork about
   1 in. (2.5 cm) wide by
   1/4 in. (0.6 cm) thick
a bowl of water

To test your compass, walk to different places around your house or in your yard. Does your compass point to the north all the time?

What Does a Globe Show?

Do you like globes? Great! But don't throw away all your maps just yet. Globes are not very easy to carry when you are on a hike or traveling in a car. And they don't show close-up views of places, either.

The earth looks like a big, blue marble to astronauts in outer space. It's easy for them to see the round shape of the earth because they are so far away from it. If you want to see the whole earth at one time, you might look at a map. But mapmakers must squeeze and stretch parts of the world so that they can draw them on a flat map. That means a flat map does not show the true shape of the earth.

A **globe** is a round model of the earth. Globes show the size, shape, and location of land and oceans. Many globes show the boundaries of different

If you want to see the shape of the earth
and you don't have a spaceship, use a globe!

countries. Some globes show how the
mountains, hills, valleys, and oceans
would appear from the sky.

Do you know why most globes are
tilted on their stands? It is because the
earth really is tilted. It spins at a tilt as it
travels around the sun. With a globe, you
see part of the earth at one time. To see
places on the other side, you just turn
the globe.

What Is the Equator?

Maps and globes have all kinds of signs and symbols. Often they have certain lines, too. Nearly every map and globe of the world has one very important line. It's called the equator.

An imaginary line called the equator lies around the middle of the earth. The equator divides the earth into the Northern and Southern hemispheres, or halves. The word *hemisphere* means "half of a sphere or ball."

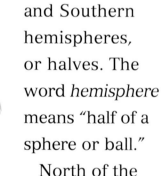

North of the equator is an imaginary line called the Tropic of Cancer. South of the equator is another line called the Tropic of Capricorn. Both lines are named for groups of stars. The areas between the equator and these

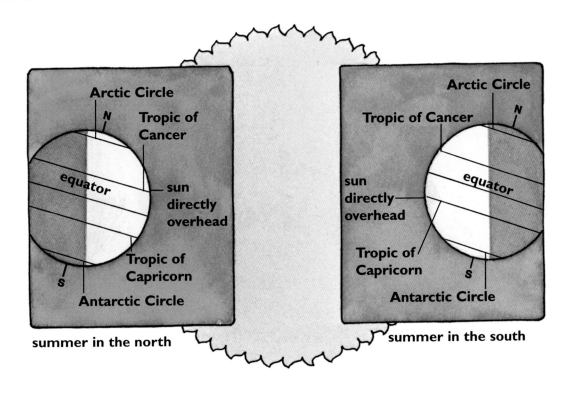

summer in the north

summer in the south

two lines are called the tropics. Once a year the sun is directly over the Tropic of Cancer. That marks the first day of summer in the Northern Hemisphere. Once a year, the sun is directly over the Tropic of Capricorn. That marks the first day of summer in the Southern Hemisphere.

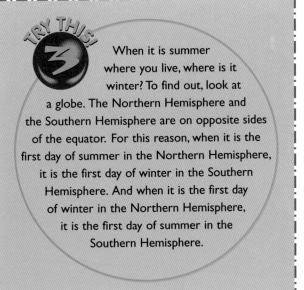

TRY THIS!

When it is summer where you live, where is it winter? To find out, look at a globe. The Northern Hemisphere and the Southern Hemisphere are on opposite sides of the equator. For this reason, when it is the first day of summer in the Northern Hemisphere, it is the first day of winter in the Southern Hemisphere. And when it is the first day of winter in the Northern Hemisphere, it is the first day of summer in the Southern Hemisphere.

What Are Longitude and Latitude?

Look at a globe or a map of the world. Have you ever wondered why they have so many lines? There are no lines on the earth, so why are there lines on globes and maps?

On a map, the prime meridian passes through Greenwich, England.

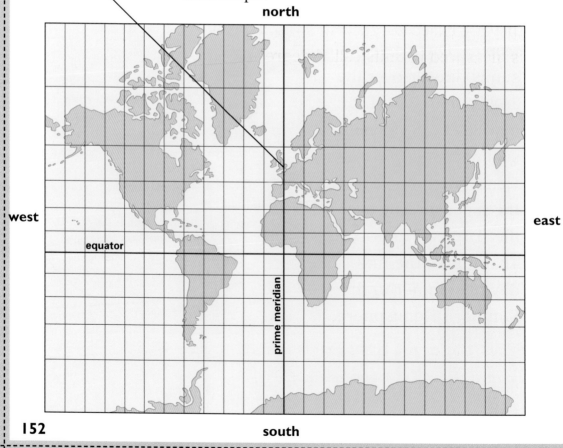

The lines help people find places. The lines are something like city streets. When two friends meet at a corner, they are meeting where two streets cross. On a globe or map, the east-west lines cross the north-south lines. Every place can be found on a map by looking near where two of the lines cross.

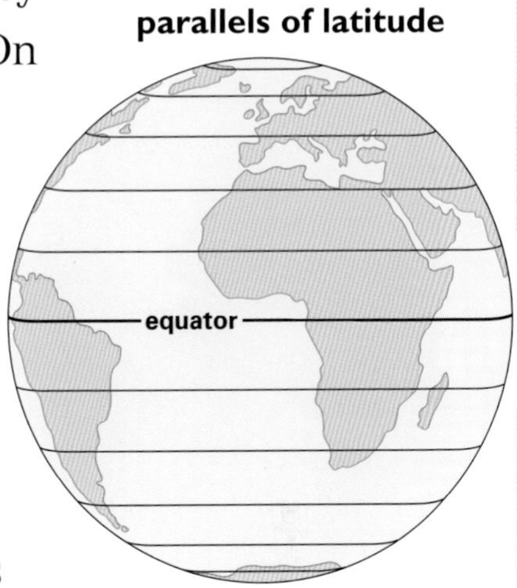

parallels of latitude

equator

The east-west lines measure how far north or how far south a place is from the equator. This measurement is called latitude. Because the lines are parallel—always the same distance apart—they are called parallels of latitude. Latitude is measured in units called degrees. The symbol ° after each number is a degree sign. Latitude is always given as so many degrees north or south of the equator. The equator is 0° latitude.

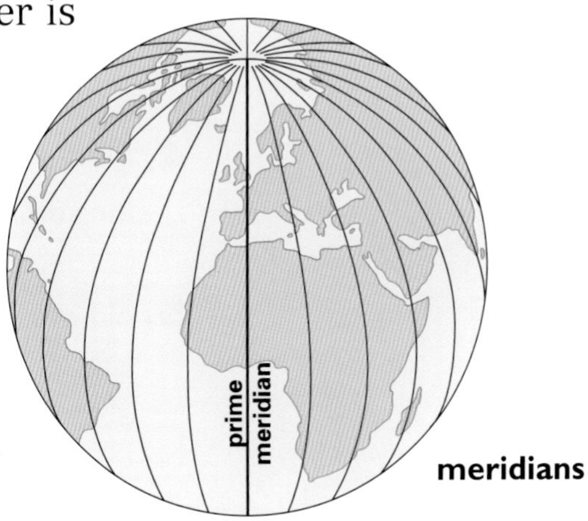

prime meridian

meridians

The north-south lines measure distance east and west, or longitude. These lines are called meridians. A line called the prime meridian is 0° longitude. All other meridians are measured as so many degrees east or west of this line.

TRY THIS! 2

Find the Buried Treasure

Have you ever wanted to hunt for buried treasure? You can do just that with this buried treasure map. Read a clue below. Then use the longitude and latitude to find the place of each hidden treasure on the map. Write the name of the place where you find each treasure on a piece of paper. *Check your answers against those on page 155.*

You Will Need:

paper
a pencil or pen

1. sunken treasure ship, latitude 2° north, longitude 2° east.

2. buried chest, latitude 2° south, longitude 0°.

3. ancient jars, latitude 0° north, longitude 2° east.

4. silver cups, latitude 1° north, longitude 2° west.

5. old musical instruments, latitude 2° south, longitude 2° east.

6. ancient carvings, latitude 0°, longitude 1° west.

7. another sunken treasure, latitude 1° north, longitude 1° east.

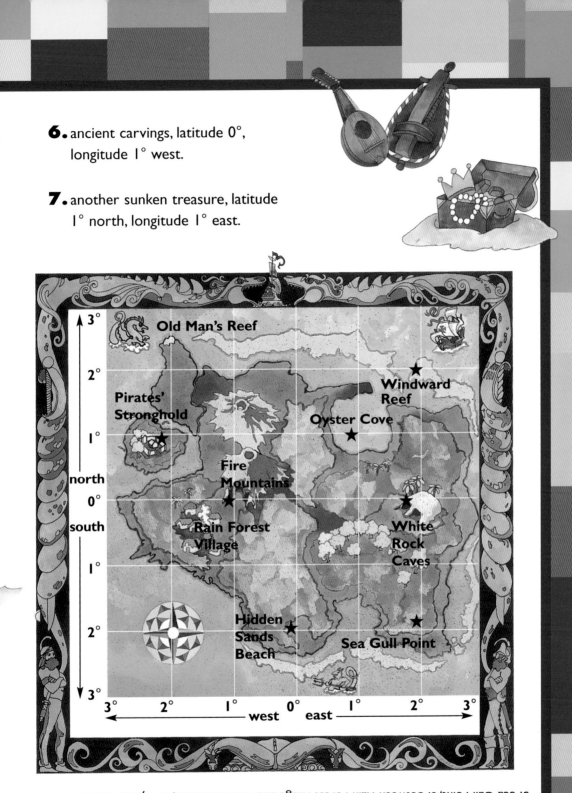

Answers: 1. Windward Reef; 2. Hidden Sands Beach; 3. White Rock Caves; 4. Pirates' Stronghold; 5. Sea Gull Point; 6. between Rain Forest Village and Fire Mountains; 7. Oyster Cove.

155

Maps of Long Ago

People have used maps for thousands of years. The earliest maps probably were simply scratches in the dirt. Early people made these scratches to show where to find water, food, or their caves. Later, people used nearby materials to make maps. Early Chinese people carved maps of their empire into bamboo or stone or painted them on rolls of silk. Certain people of the Pacific Islands mapped out their region with palm sticks and shells.

Long ago, in the Middle Ages, some people thought the earth was flat. They believed you could fall off the edge of the world if you sailed too far out to sea. Explorers such as Christopher Columbus and Ferdinand Magellan changed these ideas. They collected information about countries outside Europe for European mapmakers.

KNOW It All!

The earliest known map is a clay tablet found in Iraq. It was made more than 4,000 years ago. It shows settlements, waterways, and mountains.

156

a map more than 700 years old

When hot-air balloons were invented in the 1780's and airplanes in the 1900's, people finally got a bird's-eye view of the world. This helped them to make better maps.

Today, we use computers and photographs taken from airplanes and satellites to make maps of the world. We can even make maps for areas that nobody can get to.

Mapmakers

This surveyor in Hawaii uses a special instrument to measure the area where a building will go.

There are many different kinds of maps and many different jobs for people who help create them. Let's take a look at some of the people who help make maps.

A person called a **surveyor** (suhr VAY uhr) uses special instruments to measure distances, angles, and heights to figure out where a place is and how big it is. Surveyors measure and record the positions of things and the shape of the earth's surface.

Some people photograph the land from an airplane. The aerial photographs are used by people called **photogrammetrists** (FOH toh GRAM uh trihsts) to measure land areas, lakes,

This photograph of the Allard River in Quebec, Canada, was taken from the air and can be used to make a map.

Cartographers make many of
today's maps on computers.

and other features of the earth. The photographs show
wide areas of land and can give much more information
than a person could gather while on the ground.

Cartographers (kahr TAHG ruh fuhrz) use
information from surveyors and photogrammetrists to
make maps. Many cartographers use computers to
draw an actual map. They add symbols and colors to
help people understand all of the different kinds of
information on a map.

A **geographer** (jee AHG ruh fuhr) studies
how people and animals relate to the land. Some
geographers study the places where people live.
Others study the resources people use, such as water,
land, and oil. Still others study rivers, mountains, and
oceans. They put all of the information they find on
maps to show other people.

Taking a Trip

Before you take a trip, there is so much to do! It helps to be prepared, whether you are going on a weekend campout, a week-long visit to a relative's house, or a two-week vacation to another country. Even on the most carefully planned trips, there are changes and surprises. That is part of what makes travel interesting!

What's Your Favorite Place?

Uluru, Australia

Disney World, U.S.A.

Sahara Desert, Africa

Taj Mahal, India

Iguaçu Falls, Brazil

Statue of Liberty, U.S.A.

Buckingham Palace, United Kingdom

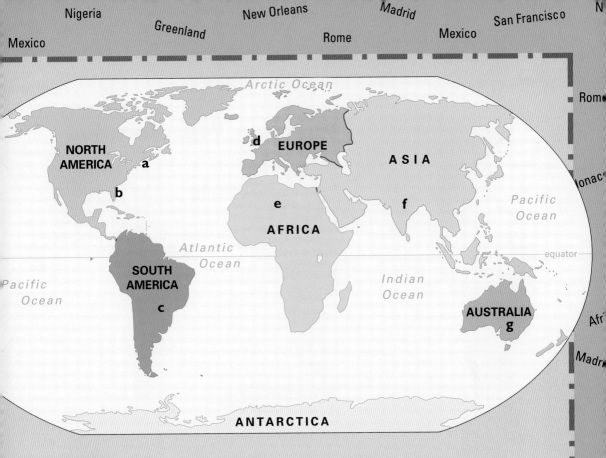

What is your dream vacation? Is it going on the thrilling rides of a theme park? Or would you rather visit Buckingham Palace, the home of a royal family? Would you like to see the Statue of Liberty or the Sahara Desert? Perhaps you want to see an amazing waterfall, or hike through the Australian outback. Or are there other exciting places you want to see?

Before you could visit any of these places, you'd have to know where they are in the world. Can you find these exciting places on the world map?

Answers: a. Statue of Liberty, United States; b. Disney World, United States; c. Iguaçu Falls, Brazil; d. Buckingham Palace, United Kingdom; e. Sahara Desert, Africa; f. Taj Mahal, India; g. Uluru (or Ayers Rock), Australia.

Planning Your Vacation

The more you know about where you are going, the more prepared you will be once you get there. Planning ahead helps you remember to pack the things you need. And it helps you avoid disappointments, too. How will you feel if you find out that the museum is closed on Monday—the day you're there?!

Making a to-do list can sometimes help you plan a trip. The travelers below are going on very different trips. Each one has to make a plan to prepare for the trip. Can you match each traveler with a to-do list?

Henry is planning a week-long trip to his grandmother's house.

Joe is taking a day trip to the beach.

Yoshi is taking a weekend trip to the city.

To-Do List 1

- Bring lots of snacks and cold drinks.
- Pack sunscreen and beach cover-up.
- Don't forget the towels!
- Find out if it's OK to use inflatable rafts or beach balls.

To-Do List 2

- Pack enough jeans, shirts, socks, and underwear.
- Bring favorite stuffed animal and book.
- Pack camera.
- Pack notebook for jotting down stories.

To-Do List 3

- Get a visitor's map.
- Bring money for **souvenirs** and entrance fees. Don't forget change for the bus!
- Check out must-see places to visit and find out when they are open.

Do you want to take a trip somewhere new? Get the facts about new places before you go:

- Head to your local library. Check out books about the history and the people in the area you plan to visit. Find stories set in that area, too.
- Ask permission to check the Internet to find the Web sites of tourist bureaus or chambers of commerce.
- Write to organizations to request maps and calendars of events.

Answers: Henry, list 2; Joe, list 1; Yoshi, list 3.

What Should You Pack?

What you pack for your trip depends on where you are going, how long you will be there, and what your interests are. You also need to think about what the weather will be like! Don't stuff your suitcase too full, though. It will be too heavy. You might want to bring along a backpack for day trips or the plane ride.

It's a warm summer day. Mia, Rob, and Jake have planned very different vacations, and they don't know what to pack! Mia is going camping, Rob is going sightseeing in the city, and Jake is going to the seashore. Take a look at the list and choose which things Mia, Rob, and Jake should put in their suitcase.

Some items will be needed by more than one person. Other items won't be needed at all.

See answers on page 167.

- beach towel
- snowshoes
- small radio with earphones
- visitor's map
- sandals
- camera and film
- hiking boots
- coins for the bus
- tent and sleeping bag
- bathing suit
- cup, plate, fork, and spoon
- bug spray
- flashlight
- sunscreen
- toothbrush and soap
- parka

Never a Dull Moment

Part of your vacation will be spent standing in line. You may have to stand in line to board a plane, get a table at a restaurant, or ride a roller coaster. Here's how you can keep busy while you wait:

- Play an alphabet game. With a friend or a brother or sister, take turns finding things that begin with A, then B, then C, and so on.

- Guess the mood of other people in line. What does their **body language** tell you? What do their facial expressions say? Are they tired? Bored? Excited?

- Make a count. How many people in line are wearing sunglasses? How many have backpacks? How many children are under the age of 6? How many people are over 70?

- Read, read, read. Read a brochure, guidebook, or map about the place you are visiting. If you're at a restaurant, read the menu. Then you'll know what you want to eat before you sit down. If you are at an amusement park, read the safety rules or study the park map to decide what you want to do next!

TRY THIS! 1

Did you pack your gorilla? Here's a fun game for two or more people to play on a long ride. Players take turns adding silly objects to their suitcases, trying to remember them all in the correct order. Older kids might want to list the contents of their suitcase in alphabetical order. For example, **Person 1:** "I'm going on a trip, and I'm going to pack my gorilla."

Person 2: "I'm going on a trip, and I'm going to pack my gorilla and a peanut butter sandwich."

Person 3: "I'm going on a trip, and I'm going to pack my gorilla, a peanut butter sandwich, and a snowman. . . ."

Keep this up until a player forgets an item. Then that player is out of the game. The winner is the last person remaining.

Are You a Savvy Traveler?

The word *savvy* (SAV ee) means "smart." Smart travelers are ready for new sights, new sounds, new tastes, and new experiences. They respect other people's languages, customs, and foods, even though they might seem strange at first. Savvy travelers expect surprises, and they know that each journey is a chance to learn something new.

Take this quiz to find out if you are a savvy traveler. You can pick more than one letter for each number. Then count the number of a's, b's, c's, and d's you score. *See what your score means on page 173.*

1. You are taking a stroll down a wooded path. You spot a flower you've never seen before. You:

    a. pick the flower so no one else will find it.

    b. ignore the flower. Woods are boring!

    c. look up the flower in your nature guide and make a sketch of it in your notebook.

    d. have a contest to see how many unusual flowers you can find.

2. It is late afternoon in a Spanish village. All the stores and restaurants are closed for **siesta.** You:

a. bang on the windows and tell everyone to wake up because you are hungry.

b. pout in your hotel room.

c. use the time to read about local customs.

d. have a picnic in the park with the snacks you packed in your backpack.

3. It is your only day to go to the beach. Suddenly, it starts to rain. You:

a. tell everyone that your trip is ruined and you want to go home.

b. sit in your room all day and watch it rain.

c. use the time to write postcards to your friends.

d. check out a museum you hadn't planned to visit.

4. You are in a restaurant and the waiter brings you an odd-looking dish you've never had before. You:

a. pinch your nose and yell "Gross!"

b. push the plate away from you when no one is looking.

c. ask the waiter to tell you the name of the dish and how to pronounce it.

d. try the dish even though you don't know whether you will like it.

5. Your parents tell you that you are going to an art museum instead of the amusement park. You:

a. plan to bring your in-line skates so you can play tag with your sister.

b. sigh loudly and dawdle behind your parents once you get there.

c. take the museum tour and learn about the paintings.

d. go on an art museum treasure hunt.

What Your Score Means:

Mostly A's:
Tourist, go home! You won't enjoy your trip, and you may keep other people from enjoying theirs.

Mostly B's:
B is for boring. You need to put more effort into your travels if you want to have fun!

Mostly C's:
Your willingness to learn about the places you visit makes you a savvy traveler.

Mostly D's:
You're savvy, too. Your adventurous spirit guarantees that you will have fun wherever you go.

Make the Memories Last and Last

While you are on vacation, you can do things that will help you remember your trip when you return home.

• Snap Away—Photographs are sometimes better than postcards. Photos are a record of things you have actually seen. Be sure your camera has plenty of film and batteries. You have to take lots of pictures to get a few great ones.

• Write a Note to Yourself—Mail yourself a postcard every day. You will have pictures that you couldn't take by yourself, and you'll have a daily record of your thoughts and adventures.

• Start a Collection—Keep menus, maps, and ticket stubs for your scrapbook. You might want to buy one or two souvenirs, such as a T-shirt or key chain with the name of the place you visited. But don't overdo it—you'll have to carry them all home!

• Share and Remember—Once you are home, it is fun

to show off your treasures. It also feels great to eat your favorite snacks and sleep in your own bed again. Traveling gives you a break from your everyday life, but it also makes you appreciate the things at home!

Start a postcard collection. Collect them when you travel, and save the ones that people send you. By studying postcards from different places, you can learn about their climate, culture, geography, places to visit, money, and even language.

TRY THIS!

1

Surprise!

My Grandpa went to Myrtle Beach
And sent us back a turtle each.
And then he went to Katmandu
And mailed a real live Cockatoo.
From Rio an iguana came,
A smelly goat arrived from Spain.
Now he's in India, you see—
My Grandpa always
    thinks of me.

Contents

Contents • ix

Illustrations follow page 254

Preface

This book was born by chance in 2002 while I was researching a biography of General Carlos de Alvear (1789–1852), one of the leaders of South American independence. I was at the National Archives in London looking for information about Alvear's three-year exile in Brazil in the dispatches of the British consul in Rio de Janeiro. Given England's strong interest in what was happening in the breakaway Spanish colonies the consul kept a close watch over Alvear, who had played a prominent role in the revolution in Buenos Aires. During my research I not only found plenty of information about Alvear, including some illegally intercepted correspondence, but also a "Secret and Confidential" dispatch sent to Lord Castlereagh, England's foreign secretary, at the end of 1817, reporting the occurrence of an extraordinary affair:

> Some weeks ago an American schooner landed four passengers either at or near Pernambuco. . . . They soon attracted the notice of the Governor and were arrested. Upon being examined they acknowledged that they had come from America and their object was to obtain employment in the rebel army. Two of these (one of whom appeared to be the chief) were then sent down here as prisoners and put in confinement on board the line of battleship *Rainha,* where they now remain. It was found difficult to draw from them more than has been just stated . . . except that the chief, who is a man beyond the middle age, was called Latapie, and that he had been a Lieutenant Colonel in the French Army under Buonaparte. . . . He made a confession of a very extraordinary nature, which will no doubt at-

tract the attention of His Majesty's government. He said that his object was to assist the rebels in establishing their independence and that he had flattered himself he should obtain the command of their troops. That he had entered into this project not from any view of hostility or ill will to the King of Portugal, but in the hope of establishing an independent post southward of the Line* from whence he might subsequently carry into effect with greater felicity his ulterior and real designs; these were nothing less than the liberation of general Buonaparte from St. Helena.[1]

Liberating Napoleon from St. Helena? I didn't have to be an expert in European history to realize the importance of discovering, and derailing, this plot. I had barely digested this information when I came across another dispatch dated a day later warning the chief of the British naval station in Buenos Aires that "General Brayer, now in the service of the government of Buenos Aires, is the leader to whom the subordinate agents look up and from whom they are to receive their orders when the preparations are ready. . . . Although General Brayer appears to be solely occupied by the military duties entrusted to him, it will be very necessary to keep a strict eye upon his motions as well as those of all other Frenchmen [in Buenos Aires]."[2]

A veteran of Napoleon's army, Brayer had arrived in Buenos Aires in early 1817 to join the patriots in the war of independence against Spain. He eventually became a friend and an ally of Alvear. Despite this connection and being intrigued by these dispatches, I could not see a direct link to my research.

But after I finished Alvear's book, an irrepressible curiosity brought me back to the National Archives. I wanted to know what had happened to Brayer and the plans to rescue Napoleon. I assumed that if these plans had originated in the United States, the dispatches of the British ambassador in Washington would provide some clues. As it turns out, I found details there of a much vaster conspiracy, which contemplated not only rescuing Napoleon but also creating a new Bonapartist empire in America. The instigator and financier of this grand plan was Joseph Bonaparte, Napoleon's older brother, who had fled to America after Waterloo. The dispatches of the British ambassador also suggested that certain well-known British subjects were involved: "Lord Cochrane and Sir Robert Wilson are both deeply engaged in it. . . . Lord Cochrane's intended voy-

---

*This could mean south of the Equator or south of Brazil's borders.

age to South America was connected with this design and . . . there was to be a general rendezvous of all the agents on the island of Fernando de Noronha, which is a small island off the coast of Pernambuco."[3]

Cochrane played an important role in the independence of the Spanish colonies. I knew that before embarking on the expedition to liberate Peru, he not only planned to rescue Napoleon but also offered him a throne in South America.[4] Since this was in mid-1820, it seemed that the plans to rescue Napoleon had not been abandoned.

I had no idea who Sir Robert Wilson was or another French general named Charles Lallemand, also mentioned in the dispatches as being part of the conspiracy. As I uncovered more clues, I could not resist the temptation to find out what had happened with these men who had risked their lives to rescue Napoleon. What motives drove former enemies to join forces in such a daring enterprise? Did they plan to take Napoleon to South America after setting him free? What happened to their plans? Did Napoleon know about and encourage them?

We may never have a complete answer to these questions. But a thorough investigation in public and private archives on both sides of the Atlantic unveiled an amazing story that has never been told. It will force us to reconsider many aspects of Napoleon's captivity at St. Helena and challenge the "official" version of the history of Latin American independence. It will also bring to life four of the most fascinating and least known characters of the Napoleonic era: Brayer, Cochrane, Wilson, and Lallemand. Theirs is the story of Napoleon's last campaign and of the efforts of the world's powers to ensure that it failed.

～

It is impossible to understand this story without understanding the role played by the Spanish colonies in Napoleon's fifteen-year struggle for global domination against England. At the beginning of the nineteenth century, the Spanish domains in America extended uninterruptedly for almost seven thousand miles from Cape Horn to San Francisco. It was one of the largest and wealthiest empires the world had ever known. Its political backbone was formed by four large viceroyalties: Mexico, Peru, New Granada (Colombia) and Buenos Aires and a number of smaller administrative entities. The viceroyalty of Mexico, or New Spain, which included modern Mexico, parts of Central America, and almost a third of the current territory of the United States, was the "crown jewel" of the Spanish empire, generating half of the revenues of the Spanish treasury. Mexico's mines produced more silver than the rest of the world combined and the ports of Vera Cruz and Acapulco were gateways to European and Asian markets, including the Philippines, another Spanish possession.[5] Next in importance was Peru, the fabulously rich Incan empire conquered by Pizarro. The enormous wealth of its American colonies made Spain, a barren country, one of the richest nations in the world and the envy of all of Europe. However, it was a fragile empire. The independence of the British colonies in North America and the French Revolution had shaken the empire's foundations. And when Napoleon came to power, the Spanish colonies became another front in his war with England.

A perennial enemy of Spain, England had always craved a piece of its colonial empire but had to content herself with plundering Spanish galleons. And France, which had lost Louisiana to Spain after the Seven Years War, had long coveted an American empire. French imperial yearnings survived the political upheaval of the Revolution. In 1793 the French Republic sent Edmond Genet to the United States to propose an alliance to wrest Canada from England, and Florida and Louisiana from Spain. George Washington refused to get entangled in this intrigue. Nevertheless, Genet began recruiting an army of adventurers to invade Louisiana. Fearing that the United States would be plunged into a war with Spain, Washington intervened.[6] At almost the same time, in Paris, Jacques Pierre Brissot proposed an expedition to liberate the Spanish colonies under the command of General Francisco de Miranda but the guillotine put an end to this plan.[7] The names of Brissot and Genet would remain forever linked to French intrigues in America.

A few years later, England considered seizing the Spanish colonies in South America to open their markets to British trade.[8] Meanwhile, Napoleon, having failed in his efforts to build an empire in Egypt, set out to create one in America. Shortly after becoming first consul, Napoleon signed a secret treaty with Spain and recovered Louisiana. He planned to use it as the base of a vast American empire that would also encompass French possessions in the Caribbean, particularly Haiti (then known as Santo Domingo). As a major exporter of coffee and sugar, the island was not only an important revenue source for France but also close to the Isthmus of Panama, a point of great strategic importance for launching further conquests in South America.[9] But Napoleon's carefully laid plans were unexpectedly derailed, first, by a slave rebellion in Haiti, and then by an epidemic of yellow fever that virtually annihilated the expeditionary force he sent from France to quash the rebellion.[10] Without an army to occupy and defend Louisiana, Napoleon sold it to the United States for $15 million. "I would have given it to them for nothing, for when war came I could not have protected it and the English would have taken it," he would say later.[11]

Despite these setbacks, Napoleon didn't abandon his American dream. However, as he was, at the time, allied to Spain, his only permissible targets were the Portuguese colonies. Napoleon knew the continent was ripe for change. In 1801 a group of Brazilian patriots in Pernambuco attempted to establish a republic independent of Portugal and sought his support.[12] But their efforts were quickly quashed. Two years later, Napoleon considered a plan to conquer Brazil using Buenos Aires as a base.[13] The resumption of war with England turned his attention to Europe, but in 1804 the Spanish colonies again caught his attention. Although Spain was neutral, her agreement to pay subsidies to France worried the British ministers, who suspected Napoleon would use them to finance an invasion of England. Prime Minister Pitt ordered the Royal Navy to intercept a Spanish convoy with a cargo of gold and silver from Peru estimated at 2 million pounds. The object was accomplished at the end of 1804, but at an enormous human cost, as during the battle that ensued one of the Spanish frigates blew up killing all on board, including several innocent passengers.[14] Irate at this unprovoked aggression, Spain declared war against England. Pitt was unapologetic: "Suppose we had suffered these two millions of treasure to go into Cadiz, and from thence, as of course it would, to the coffers of France."[15] With Spain firmly allied with France, the British government attempted to seize the Spanish colonies. A failed attempt to invade Buenos Aires in 1806 caught Napoleon's attention. Although lacking the silver mines of Mexico or the gold of Peru, Buenos Aires had a population of sixty thousand and was the gateway to the growing South American markets. If British exports reached these markets his continental blockade would be ineffective.*

In July 1807 a British expeditionary force ten thousand strong again attempted to take Buenos Aires. For a second time a local force led by a Frenchman named Jacques de Liniers, whom many suspected of being Napoleon's agent, repelled the invaders. It was the worst defeat of British arms during the Napoleonic Wars. This setback convinced Lord Castlereagh, England's secretary of war and the colonies, to follow a new policy toward the Spanish colonies. Castlereagh recognized that military expeditions would not lead to any "permanent national advantage" and that smuggling, although very lucrative for some merchants, would not produce any long-term benefits either. In his view, the

* Napoleon's "Berlin Decrees" sought to blockade England's trade.

Spanish colonies in South America were "a matter of British economic interest exclusively" and not a target for territorial expansion. To achieve her goals, England had to create and support an amicable local government supported "by a native force to be created under our countenance." Castlereagh's objective was to deprive Napoleon "of one of his chief resources and the opening to our manufactures the markets of that great continent." Although Castlereagh opposed "deliberate incitement" to revolution, he did not exclude the possibility that Napoleon might "so fasten himself upon Spain" that Britain would be forced "to work for the dismemberment of the Spanish Empire."[16]

Two failed British invasions of Buenos Aires and rumors of a third convinced Napoleon to act. If France didn't control the wealth of the Spanish colonies, England soon would.[17] In early 1808 Napoleon's army invaded Spain and Joseph Bonaparte was installed on the throne of Madrid. In a matter of months, England found herself unexpectedly allied with the dethroned Spanish Bourbons. Meanwhile, Napoleon evaluated a proposal from a Colombian envoy to extend Bonapartist rule to all of Spanish America. Two deputies from Buenos Aires went further and proposed invading Brazil to add its vast territory to a new American empire.[18] Years earlier Napoleon had received a similar proposal from the brother of Jacques de Liniers, who thanks to defeating the British invaders had been appointed viceroy of Buenos Aires.[19] While he pondered his options, Napoleon sent a special emissary to confer with Liniers.[20]

Initially, Napoleon hoped to keep the Spanish colonies under his control, but he quickly changed his mind, as the local authorities in Mexico and Peru remained loyal to the Bourbons and opposed Joseph's rule. Seeing that the treasures from the New World "contributed so decidedly to protract the war in Spain," he formed a plan "to excite a revolt in Spanish America."[21] In Napoleon's view, one of France's greatest glories was having helped the United States achieve their independence. He planned to do the same for the Spanish colonies. To accomplish this objective he sent several "special" agents to America to tell the patriots that Joseph would free them from the despotism of the Bourbons and to offer "troops and war materials to aid [them] in gaining their independence."[22]

At the end of 1809 when Napoleon seemed to have a firm grip on Spain and only a provisional government in Cadiz defied his rule, he publicly announced that he would support the independence of the Spanish colonies. "Whether the people of Mexico and Peru should wish to remain united with the motherland, or whether they should wish to elevate themselves to the height of a noble independence, France will never oppose their desires provided that these peoples do not form any relations with England."[23] This declaration had a strong impact in America. In early 1810, juntas in Caracas, Buenos Aires, and Santiago replaced the authorities appointed by Cadiz. A civil war pitting royalists against independents followed. The latter were split into two factions: one looked to France for support and the other sought England's backing. The execution of Liniers in early 1810 was a big blow for the French party. From then on, its members were more circumspect about disclosing their Bonapartist sympathies. By the end of the year, although Caracas had declared her independence and Buenos Aires and Santiago threatened to follow suit, the rebellion faltered in Mexico and Peru, which financed the armed resistance to the French occupation of Spain. Promoting the independence of these two colonies became a strategic objective for Napoleon, and to accomplish it he enlisted the support of the United States.[24]

In the summer of 1811, Napoleon instructed his ambassador in Washington to communicate to President Madison that he expected the cooperation of the United States not only in supplying military equipment and assistance to the rebels but also in providing naval protection to French vessels transporting weapons to South America.[25] Napoleon conveyed a similar message to the American ambassador in Paris, who took the opportunity to ask whether France would consent to the possession of Florida by the United States.[26] Napoleon replied that it would "entirely accord" with his policy and weeks later he announced that Spain still under Joseph's rule would sell Florida to the United States for $2 million.[27] Florida was the key to trade in the Gulf of Mexico, enormously important to British merchants, and had been coveted by the Americans since purchasing Louisiana. The transaction fit well with Napoleon's strategy of strengthening the United States to offset England's naval power in the Caribbean. Napoleon also ordered his minister of marine to send two frigates with weapons and ammunition to South America, where he envisioned a stronger naval presence.[28]

The invasion of Russia and the War of 1812 the following summer delayed the Florida transaction. Napoleon wanted to reach an agreement but his empire was crumbling.[29] At the end of 1812, as he dashed back to Paris to salvage his throne he told one his closest aides that he believed the independence of the Spanish colonies would be "the most important event of the century." He believed that if France moved quickly and established good relations with the insurgent republics it could keep them free from England's commercial influence. In Napoleon's view the main beneficiary of an independent Spanish America would be the United States.[30]

Madison was delighted with Napoleon's new policy, particularly as it related to Florida.[31] He was also interested in expanding U.S. influence in South America to counterbalance British commercial supremacy.[32] However, at the brink of war with England, Madison could not aid the rebels. But he offered his network of agents to transmit Napoleon's views to the rebels.[33] Meanwhile, the negotiations between France and the United States continued, and months later, Madison learned that Napoleon was prepared to sell not only Florida but also Texas.[34]

Don Luis de Onis, the Spanish ambassador in the United States was determined to derail Napoleon's plans. Cold, diligent, and wily, the forty-six-year-old diplomat was a zealous defender of the interests of the Spanish crown.[35] He had arrived in the United States in 1809, and for the next twelve years he fought relentlessly against the insurrection in Spanish America. Onis believed that Napoleon conspired with the United States "for the subversion of these rich and beautiful provinces" and sent agents to "inflame the minds of the people against the Spanish government and to promote the revolution."[36] In fact, since 1810 the Madison administration allowed several filibustering expeditions* against Mexico, in open violation of U.S. neutrality.[37] Onis' fears increased when at the end of 1811 a renegade Spaniard named Jose Alvarez de Toledo arrived in Philadelphia. Toledo, a member of a secret society that sought the independence of the Spanish colonies, had left Spain to join the Mexican revolution. Onis suspected that the U.S. government, Napoleon, or both secretly supported Toledo. In fact, Toledo met several times with Secretary of State James Monroe and obtained his unofficial support for an expedition against Mexico. Despite Onis' protests, Toledo moved to New Orleans and in early 1813 invaded Texas at the head of a small army. Partly thanks to Onis' early warnings, the Spanish authorities were able to defeat him.[38] But then a more dangerous threat appeared: General Jean Joseph Humbert, a hero of the French army. The intrepid general had arrived in the United States in mid-1812 charged by Napoleon with the mission of "establishing advantageous negotiations with the chiefs of the independent party in the Spanish colonies."[39]

---

* Filibusters were individuals who organized and launched unauthorized, and many times illegal, military expeditions into a foreign country to foment or support a revolution or for financial gain.

The following year Humbert moved to New Orleans and started organizing an army to invade Mexico.[40] He was well qualified for the enterprise. In 1798 he had led the invasion of Ireland and had participated in the expedition to Haiti. It was there that Humbert committed a faux pas by seducing Pauline Bonaparte. Napoleon was not pleased, and when Humbert returned to France he was discharged and ostracized. His banishment ended six years later when Napoleon recalled him to active service. The following year Humbert was allowed to retire, and in early 1812 Napoleon entrusted him with an important mission in America.[41] Onis knew that Napoleon had sent Humbert to lead the Mexican insurrection. By late 1813 Onis' agents in New Orleans confirmed that the French general was planning an invasion of Mexico with the legendary smuggler and privateer Jean Laffite, who, based on the island of Barataria, not far from New Orleans, commanded a squadron of fearsome corsairs. Even more worrying, as far as Onis was concerned, were the rumors that Colonel Aaron Burr would join Humbert's expedition.[42]

Burr was no stranger to intrigue. In 1806 President Jefferson had accused him of planning "to usurp the government of the United States, to sever the Western States from the Union; to establish an empire west of the Allegheny Mountains . . . and to invade and revolutionize Mexico."[43] In his defense, Burr claimed that he had only planned the latter. Following a short trial, he was acquitted. But his reputation was ruined, and Burr embarked on a voluntary European exile. He did not, however, abandon his ambitious plans, which in many ways resembled Genet's. In 1810 he went to Paris and submitted to Napoleon a plan to "liberate" all the Spanish colonies. Burr argued that it was the right time to "bring on a revolution in the Spanish colonies through French help and in favor of France" and that the independence of Spanish America had "to be the work of France and not of England." Unless Napoleon intervened, England would control commerce with the Spanish colonies. Burr predicted that once his plan was put into execution, the United States would declare war on England and seize all her possessions in North America. Napoleon had his own strategy for the Spanish colonies so, at least for a while, he discarded Burr's plans.[44] But Humbert later followed them closely.

With the tide of war in Europe turning in England's favor, Lord Castlereagh, who became foreign secretary in 1812, sought to take advantage of Napoleon's weakness to advance British interests in Spanish America. Although English public opinion was sympathetic to the cause of South American independence, Castlereagh openly supported the cause of the Spanish Bourbons, hoping to obtain as a reward the lucrative American markets. But just in case the South American patriots succeeded, he kept alive their hopes of obtaining England's support. It was the beginning of a devious foreign policy that for years played both sides to serve the interests of the British Empire.

Napoleon remained committed to the independence of the Spanish colonies. In early 1813 he agreed to help a group of Venezuelan rebels. "Every arrangement was made to give the necessary assistance to the Americans when the battle of Leipzig took place."[45] After Leipzig, Napoleon could no longer help the patriots in South America. His abdication in early 1814 left the insurrection without its main foreign sponsor. The Holy Alliance believed that the establishment of independent republics in the New World threatened the principle of legitimacy that underpinned Europe's ancien régime. And Ferdinand VII, restored to the throne of Madrid, hoped to quash the revolutionary spirit of his American subjects with a massive punitive expedition. Dethroned and exiled on a Mediterranean island, Napoleon did not forget his American dreams. On Elba at the end of 1814 he told a sympathetic English visitor that he had a "great project" for Mexico.[46]

Coincidentally, a few months earlier General Humbert had landed in Mexico at the head of a small army, but his invasion was derailed by the timely intervention of the Royal Navy.[47] Discouraged by this setback, Humbert returned to New Orleans. The War of 1812 had not yet ended* and together with Laffite and many other Frenchmen, Humbert joined General Jackson in defeating the British army at the battle of New Orleans. Although Jackson praised the French, their contribution to his famous victory was conveniently downplayed.[48]

By early 1815, Napoleon was aware of Humbert's failure. He must have thought that his own prospects in France were better than in Mexico, as in late February he escaped from Elba and in twenty days regained his throne. As the Hundred Days began to unfold, the fate of the Spanish colonies once again hung in the balance.

---

*A peace treaty was signed at Ghent at the end of 1814 but the news did not arrive in time to prevent a battle.

Acknowledgments

I owe a debt of gratitude to Professor Rafe Blaufarb, director of the Institute of Napoleon and the French Revolution at Florida State University, for his encouragement, support, and valuable comments. Thanks also to Felix Luna in Buenos Aires; Patrick Puigmal at the Universidad de Los Lagos; Armando Moreno Martín in Santiago; José Miguel Barros from the Chilean Academy of History; and Manuel Ortuño Martinez in Madrid. I also benefited from conversations with Inès Murat and Antonello Pietromarchi. The staff at the British Library and the National Archives where I did most of my research deserve special thanks. Many thanks also to the staff at the National Archives of Scotland in Edinburgh; the Manuscripts Department at Yale University Library; the Massachusetts Historical Society; the American Philosophical Society; the New York Public Library; the Archivo General de la Nación in Buenos Aires; the Archives Nationales and the Bibliothèque Thiers in Paris; the Archives Historiques de la Armée de Terre and the Archives du Ministère des Affaires Etrangères also in Paris; the Archivo Histórico Nacional de Madrid; and the Archivo General de Simancas.

Any errors are my sole responsibility.

The Emperor's Last Campaign

I
1815

I
After Waterloo

The thunder—clouds close o'er it, which when rent
The earth is covered thick with other clay,
Which her own clay shall cover, heaped and pent,
Rider and horse,—friend, foe,—in one red burial blent!
— Lord Byron, *Childe Harold's Pilgrimage,* Canto 3

As the sun set over the plains of Waterloo, Napoleon tried to make sense of what had happened. He couldn't believe he had been defeated. It seemed as if the outcome of the battle had been predestined. Hoping to save his throne, Napoleon raced back to Paris. When he arrived two days later, his political support had vanished. France was tired of war, and his enemies, led by his own minister of police, the devious Joseph Fouché, plotted his downfall. After a forty-eight-hour crisis, and under enormous pressure, Napoleon abdicated the throne in favor of his four-year-old son, Napoleon II, who lived in Vienna with his mother, the Empress Marie Louise.

Although his career in Europe was over, Napoleon was only forty-six and healthy. What was left for him to do? "Perhaps a new Empire might be forged in Mexico, Peru or Brazil," Churchill suggested when he analyzed Napoleon's options after Waterloo in his *History of the English-Speaking Peoples.* "The alternative was to throw himself upon the mercy of his most inveterate foe."[1] Framed in these terms it was an easy decision. After abdicating the throne, Napoleon told his closest aides that he would move to the United States.[2] Count Lavallette, chief of the post office, instead suggested seeking asylum in England.[3] But Carnot, the minister of justice, opposed this idea arguing that he had "excited too much hate there" and the British government would not welcome him. Carnot advised Napoleon to go to America, where "you will still make your enemies tremble; and if France falls again under the yoke of the Bourbons, your presence in a free country will sustain public opinion and restrain the designs of the new government." Napoleon had already made up his mind. His future was in America.[4] Eager to get rid of him, Fouché put two frigates at his disposal at Rochefort and promised to obtain passports from Wellington.[5]

Before leaving France forever, Napoleon decided to rest for a few days at Malmaison, Josephine's former palace on the outskirts of Paris. The sweet memories of Josephine, his lucky charm, helped him recover from the shock of his recent defeat. Napoleon called his brothers Joseph, Jerome, and Lucien to a closed-door family meeting to discuss his plans. No record of what transpired has survived but given that he had already decided to seek exile in America and knowing what happened next, it is not hard to imagine what he said. The political prospects of the Bonaparte family in Europe following Waterloo were not encouraging. Although the French people would oppose another Bourbon restoration, the Allied powers would never allow Napoleon to return to power. Maybe his son, Napoleon II, being an Austrian prince and thus related to the reigning dynasties of Europe, could one day recover the throne of France. For the rest of the family, America "was the only place where our children can succeed, for if the Bourbons come back on the throne they will stay longer than people think."[6] Joseph, Lucien, and Jerome agreed to accompany Napoleon to the United States.[7]

Napoleon's mind was already in the New World. He ordered his librarian to send to Malmaison any books related to America and to ship the rest of his vast library to the United States.[8] Days later he was seen reading Humboldt and Bonpland's *Voyages aux Régions Equinoxiales du Nouveau Continent.*[9] Napoleon thought it was a "particularly interesting book" for anybody who was thinking of living in America. It was another hint of what he had in mind, as the book focused only on the Spanish colonies. Aimé Bonpland, the longtime manager of Malmaison, was very close to Hortense, Napoleon's stepdaughter. Like many of his colleagues at the Institut de France, the fifty-two-year-old botanist was a staunch believer in the principles of the French Revolution and an ardent supporter of the independence of the Spanish colonies.[10] Napoleon called him to talk about the affairs in Spanish America and invited him to come to the United States.[11]

Not everybody believed that an American exile was a good idea. Pierre Fleury de Chaboulon, Napoleon's faithful secretary, advised against it. "The Americans love and admire you but you have a great influence over them and you would perhaps excite them to enterprises fatal to England," Fleury de Chaboulon said. The Allied powers would pressure President Madison to expel him from the United States. Napoleon dismissed these concerns. If the Americans didn't want

him, he said, "I will go to Mexico. I shall find patriots there and will put myself at their head." And if the Mexicans didn't want him, he would go to Caracas, and "if I do not find myself well received there, I will go to Buenos Aires!"
Napoleon exclaimed. His secretary politely observed that the South American
insurgents already had their leaders. "People bring about revolutions for themselves, not for others, and the chiefs of the independents would be disconcerted
by Your Majesty's presence."[12]

It was a valid point. Even though Napoleon had plenty of supporters in the
Spanish colonies, he also had many enemies. Simon Bolivar, the leader of the
Venezuelan insurrection, worried that if the deposed French emperor came to
America, the "hatred of the English" would follow him and the cause of inde-
pendence "would be damned forever."[13] Bolivar, who had good contacts at the
Foreign Office, believed that England was a better ally than Napoleon in the
struggle against Spain.[14] But even if Madison and Bolivar didn't welcome him,
Napoleon would certainly be well received in Louisiana, where the majority of
the white population was of French origin.

Napoleon dithered at Malmaison a few more days. He worried that without
a passport he risked being captured at sea by the Royal Navy. He was also concerned about his safety, since to reach the port of Rochefort he had to travel
across the Vendée, a royalist enclave. Napoleon's inner circle was divided about
what to do. Some argued that it was madness to leave without passports. Others, fearing Fouché had already sold Napoleon to the Allies, advised him to leave
at once. But Napoleon decided that without passports and as long as communications with Rochefort were not open, he would remain at Malmaison, and he
sent a messenger to communicate his decision to Fouché.[15]

In the early morning of June 29, 1815, the silence at Malmaison was broken by shouts of "Vive l'Empereur!" It was a regiment of the Young Guard led
by General Michel Sylvestre Brayer, who demanded to see the emperor.[16] Coming from anybody else such a demand would have been considered imperti-
nent, particularly at such an early hour. But since Napoleon had returned to the
throne of France, the Alsatian general had become one of his most trusted confidants. Brayer, forty-six years of age, was a tall and strongly built man. With
his stylish moustache and closely cropped black hair, he cut a handsome though
slightly haughty figure, and despite his many wounds and a slight limp—he had
almost lost his left leg at the Battle of Albuera—he still carried himself with a
proud military bearing. Brayer had started his military career in 1782 as a ca-
det and after the French Revolution he had risen rapidly through the ranks.

Commended for his bravery at Hohenlinden, promoted to colonel at Austerlitz, wounded at Friedland, he had participated in the Peninsular War as a general and had returned to France in 1813 to witness the fall of the empire. Despite Brayer's having fought in some of Napoleon's most celebrated battles, Napoleon had barely noticed him until March 1815, when after escaping from Elba he prepared to enter Lyon, the main obstacle in his march to Paris.[17]

At that time Brayer had been the commander of the 19th Military Division garrisoned at Lyon. On March 4, 1815, he had received an urgent message from Marshal Massena advising him that Napoleon had landed near Cannes and was marching toward Paris at the head of a thousand men. Since Lyon had the only telegraph station in the south of France, Massena had ordered Brayer to send an urgent warning to Paris. But Brayer deliberately waited until the following morning.[18] When King Louis XVIII learned the news, he called Marshal Soult, the minister of war, and asked for his advice. Soult was incredulous but as a precaution ordered Brayer to bring two cannons from Grenoble to defend Lyon.[19]

Napoleon had had good reason to escape from Elba. He suspected that the Count of Artois, brother of Louis XVIII, planned to assassinate him, and he had heard that the Allied powers intended to send him to St. Helena, a remote island in the middle of the South Atlantic.[20] On February 26, taking advantage of the absence of the British commissioner who guarded him, Napoleon left the island with a thousand men of his Imperial Guard. Three days later, he disembarked near Cannes and started one of the most famous second acts in history. The political situation in France favored his gambit. The Bourbons were perceived as the puppets of England; the economy was in a slump; and the aristocracy wanted to turn the clock back to 1789. The peasants feared that the king would restore their land to the aristocrats, from whom it had been confiscated by the Revolution, and in the army, resentment against the Bourbons ran high. They all longed for the return of their emperor, who according to a popular legend, would come back when violets bloomed at Malmaison. Violets, which under the Bourbon regime had become an underground symbol of Bonapartism, usually flowered in late February.[21]

The news of Napoleon's landing in France bewildered and surprised the Bourbon court. A royal decree calling Napoleon "a rebel and a traitor" declared him outside the protection of the laws. Louis XVIII asked Artois to stop Napoleon's advance at Lyon, which as France's second largest city was a political objective of great importance. Artois welcomed the opportunity to teach the Corsican upstart a lesson. For fifteen years his agents had tried unsuccessfully to kill Napoleon. With a bit of luck, in a matter of days he would be able to capture him and hang him like a highway robber. Marshal Etienne Macdonald was ordered to meet him at Lyon.

By the time Artois reached Lyon on March 8, Napoleon had already entered Grenoble, in part thanks to Colonel Charles de La Bedoyere, who disobeyed orders and joined him with his entire regiment.[22] The possession of Grenoble gave the returning emperor a huge moral and material boost; he was not only able to enlarge his army but also obtained much-needed horses, ammunition, and artillery. Napoleon expected to face much stronger resistance at Lyon. He knew that Artois would try at all costs to prevent him from crossing the Rhone and that he counted on ten thousand men to do so. Fortunately for Napoleon, Artois had no artillery, as Brayer had ignored Soult's orders and left it at Grenoble.[23] Napoleon spent that night twenty miles south of Lyon. He worried about the presence of Marshal Macdonald, as he was a talented military commander. What would Macdonald do? Before going to sleep, Napoleon received an urgent message from Brayer: support for his cause in Lyon was strong, Macdonald wanted to defend the city but had no artillery and only the presence of Artois prevented the troops from "exploding and coming out to meet him."[24] Napoleon told the messenger to go back and "assure Brayer of my friendship."[25] Then he tried to sleep for a few hours but a nagging doubt kept him awake: Was it a trap?

Meanwhile, when Macdonald arrived in Lyon on the evening of March 9, he found Artois completely distraught and ready to flee. Macdonald convinced Artois that the best way to deal with the situation was to review the troops the next day. But at four o'clock in the morning Brayer woke him up with bad news: The soldiers refused to be reviewed by Artois. Macdonald, who had thought he could count on Brayer's loyalty, soon realized that he was on Napoleon's side.[26] The old marshal went ahead with his plan, and hours later, under a cold rain, he reviewed the troops with Brayer at his side. Macdonald's impassioned harangue failed to stir the troops, so he called Artois, hoping his presence would inspire, if not enthusiasm, at least obedience. He got neither, so he convened a meeting of all officers and tried to convince them that it was necessary to stop Napoleon and protect the life of Artois. His forceful appeal was met with a long silence, which was interrupted by Brayer. "Marshal, don't be under any illusions. The prince is secure among us but if a tri-colored *cocarde* enters Lyon, nobody can answer for his security or his life. All the generals, officers, and soldiers of this garrison share the same feelings. Who do you want us to fight against? The one to whom we owe our glory, our position, our honor; the one who guarantees all our rights, all our interests, and the rights and interests of the French people?" "*Eh bien,*" said a disappointed Macdonald. "You cover yourselves with shame and dishonor, but since such is your resolution, what advice should I give to the princes?" Brayer replied, "They should leave as soon as possible." Shortly after, Artois and Macdonald left Lyon.[27]

It was Brayer who opened the city gates to welcome Napoleon. Any doubts the emperor had about his loyalty quickly disappeared. "It was not until I was near Lyon that I was convinced he had told me the truth," Napoleon recalled years later. "Brayer is a remarkable man. He deceived the Count of Artois up to the last moment, preserved his confidence, and gave him lots of advice." Lyon was the defining moment in Napoleon's return from Elba. The road to the throne of France was once again open. From then on, Brayer became part of his inner circle and one of his most trusted confidants. Napoleon never forgot his encouragement and support during those critical days. "It was especially during our trip from Lyon to Paris that I was able to appreciate all the force of his character," he remembered years later.[28] At reports that a large army threatened Napoleon's advance, Brayer kept his cool. "Go Forward. Have no fear," he said. "I know the soldiers and they are all for you." When a military plot in Napoleon's favor failed, many in Napoleon's entourage despaired but not Brayer. "I never saw a man stick so firmly to his own opinion," Napoleon would remember.[29] At the gates of Paris, Brayer even suggested attacking the city with a few hundred men to surprise the Bourbons "in their beds," but Napoleon thought it was better to let them escape.[30] After Napoleon recovered his throne he rewarded those who had helped him. First on the list were Brayer and La Bedoyere, who had "helped immensely along the way." Napoleon made Brayer a count, a peer of France, a chamberlain of the Imperial Palace* and a commander of the Imperial Guard.[31]

After Napoleon's defeat and abdication, Brayer again demonstrated his devotion. He hadn't participated in the Waterloo campaign, as Napoleon had put him in charge of a division of the Young Guard and ordered him to join the Army of the Loire, which after a swift campaign defeated the royalist rebels.[32] When Brayer learned of Waterloo, he immediately raced back to Paris with his two battalions of the Guard. When he arrived at Malmaison, Count Charles de Montholon announced his presence to the emperor. "What is the matter?" Napoleon asked brusquely. "Sire, it is General Brayer who returns from the

---

*With this title Napoleon rewarded those who had rendered him valuable services or members of the old aristocracy who supported his government.

Loire with some of his men," replied Montholon. What the hell did he want at this hour of the morning, asked Napoleon. "He wants to see you on behalf of his troops who demand that you put yourself at their head," replied Montholon. Napoleon agreed to see Brayer, who entered the room alone. Nobody witnessed their conversation, but minutes later Brayer and his troops marched to Paris hoping to see their emperor "again on the battlefield."

Brayer's visit and the news of a victory in the Vendée led Napoleon to consider taking command of the French army to attack the Prussians, which had dangerously detached themselves from the British army. He sent a messenger to communicate his idea to Fouché who, already in negotiations with Wellington to surrender Paris, replied with an ultimatum: If Napoleon didn't leave immediately for Rochefort he would be arrested. Napoleon realized that to avoid a civil war he had no alternative but to leave France. It was a decision he would later regret. "I should have mounted a horse when Brayer's division appeared in front of Malmaison, let them put me at head of the army, launched a quick offensive, beat the enemy and became a dictator with the support of the people of the suburbs of Paris. This 24-hour crisis would have saved France from a second [Bourbon] restoration. "I would have erased with a big victory the bad impression created at Waterloo and I could have always put my son on the throne if the Allies didn't accept me."[33] But Napoleon didn't dare. He had another private meeting with Joseph, who afterward left on his own, carrying a substantial amount of money.[34] As Napoleon watched his brother leave Malmaison, he told one of his companions: "I will settle in the United States. In a short time, my abode will gather the remains of the Empire. . . . My old veterans will find an asylum around me."[35]

2
Ah, la Perfide Albion!

To watch and mock thee shrinking, thou hast smiled
With a sedate and all-enduring eye;—
When Fortune fled her spoil'd and favourite child,
He stood unbowed beneath the ills upon him piled.
                    —Lord Byron, *Childe Harold's Pilgrimage,* Canto 3

General Sir Robert Wilson was at Brooks's explaining to a rapt audience how Boney would defeat Wellington when he heard the shouts on the street celebrating a British victory.[1] Wilson's career prospects in England suddenly dimmed. His absence in the recent campaign was notable, as he was a twenty-year veteran and the only British general who had faced Napoleon in at least half a dozen battles. Decorated by the sovereigns of Austria, Russia, and Prussia,[*] he had also been praised by Joachim Murat—Napoleon's brother-in-law and one of the greatest cavalry leaders of all time. "Wherever I am in all the great battles, I have seen General Wilson. He is certainly one of the most distinguished officers, and if it had not been for him, we should in various instances in Russia have got through much better. He has done us infinite harm," Murat once said.[2] According to a contemporary portrait, Wilson was a tall, handsome, distinguished-looking fellow with light brown hair, fashionably long sideburns, and a determined but friendly look in his eyes. To his admirers he was an "astonishing fellow," his detractors considered him "very slippery." Both recognized his courage and his charm. Some compared him to a character out of one of Sir Walter Scott's novels.[3] A polished courtier and an accomplished raconteur, Wilson could entertain any audience with an account of his adventures in Egypt, Russia, and Turkey. But his liberal views and penchant for self-promotion had not endeared him to the Tories. Wilson had particularly irritated Lord Castlereagh during missions to Russia and Italy. He had also annoyed the

---

[*] In 1801 George III granted Wilson a knighthood in recognition of a title awarded by the emperor of Austria.

prince regent by consorting with his estranged wife, the unruly Caroline. And if this were not enough, he had antagonized the Duke of Wellington.[4] Wilson and Wellington couldn't have been more different. In politics, the former was a Foxite Whig,* the latter an unreconstructed Tory. On the battlefield, Wilson, a light cavalry officer, almost always favored the offensive whereas Wellington favored defensive infantry tactics. And while Wilson "identified with the private soldier," the Iron Duke favored corporal punishment.[5]

Wilson's enmity with the most powerful men in England contributed to the poor treatment he received when he returned to London in the summer of 1814. Despite his experience and foreign decorations, the thirty-eight-year-old general was given an unattached commission and denied the order of Knight Commander of the Bath, the most coveted award in the British army. In the prime of his career, he was forced into retirement. Lacking an aristocratic pedigree also hurt him. Had Wilson been born in France, Napoleon would have already made him a marshal of the empire. There was a bitter irony in this because during most of his career Wilson had been one of Napoleon's harshest detractors.[6] But following the campaigns of 1812 and 1813, he had become disappointed with British foreign policy. Wilson thought that Castlereagh's obsession with dethroning Napoleon and his opposition to the independence of Poland and Italy were not in England's best interests. Conversations with Murat and Eugene de Beauharnais in Italy had given him a different perspective on Napoleon. After the first Bourbon restoration in France, Wilson completed his political transformation and became one of Napoleon's strongest supporters. "With all his faults, crimes and misrule, Buonaparte did more for the advantage of mankind than can ever be effected by the repeal of his acts and abolition of his establishments," Wilson wrote in the summer of 1814. In his view, Napoleon's empire and conquests were "lofty memorials" and his attempt to restore the independence of Poland and Italy were "magnificent traits of policy and intelligence which will secure him immortality."[7] Wilson believed that by dethroning Napoleon, Castlereagh had tipped the European balance of power in Russia's favor. Therefore, he cheered Napoleon's return to Paris and opposed the new war against him.[8]

Wilson was not alone. Ever since the start of his meteoric career, Napoleon had counted on the support of Englishmen who had followed his changing for-

* Founded in 1648, the Whig Party stood for limiting royal power in favor of Parliament. Under the leadership of Charles James Fox (1749–1806), the Whigs advocated parliamentary reform, opposed war against Revolutionary France, and supported Catholic emancipation.

tunes with a mixture of dread and admiration. For years it had been Charles James Fox who had led the pro-Bonaparte faction in the House of Commons. Fox was a charismatic liberal politician who briefly served as prime minister and whom the Tories often accused of being the "apologist of France" and the "agent of Bonaparte."[9] Following Fox's death in 1806, Samuel Whitbread, heir to England's largest brewing fortune, took up the Bonapartist mantle in the Commons, and Lord Grey and Lord Holland did so in the upper chamber. Outside of Parliament, Napoleon's supporters included Henry "Orator" Hunt, a fiery Radical activist who advocated parliamentary reform; the journalist William Cobbett, editor of the *Political Register;* and literati such as Lord Byron, William Godwin, and William Hazlitt.[10]

How could the enemies of tyranny in Europe's most liberal nation be such fervent supporters of England's most implacable enemy? In Cobbett's view, despite Napoleon's many faults, he was entitled to "the gratitude of mankind" for pulling "down the Pope, the monks in Spain and Italy, the Inquisition in those countries," for carrying "light and liberal principles to dark and enslaved regions," and for establishing "a code of wise and just laws."[11] Hazlitt argued that Napoleon had "conquered the grand conspiracy of kings against the abstract right of the human race to be free."[12] And Hunt admired Napoleon because he was more disposed "to tyrannize over mighty tyrants than he was to crush the weak and the unprotected." Constrained by a liberal constitution, Napoleon would have been "one of freedom's brightest ornaments, one of liberty's safest, staunchest guardians." It wasn't Napoleon but the European monarchs who had tried to dethrone him, financed by funds from the British treasury, who were the "greatest tyrants of the universe," Hunt said. Napoleon had subdued them and under his rule, "despotic as it might have been, and governed by the excellent code of laws that bears his name," the French people had enjoyed much greater freedom than anywhere else in the continent. "Had I been a Frenchman," Hunt wrote, "I should have adored him."[13]

During the Hundred Days, the English Bonapartists enthusiastically rallied to Napoleon's cause, as they considered that the French people had freely chosen him as their ruler. "I know thousands of Englishmen that rejoiced at the escape of Napoleon from Elba, and at his return to the French capital, but I know of no one except myself who had the courage to testify [to] his joy by any open demonstration," remembered Hunt.[14] This enthusiasm was soon replaced by anger and disappointment at the British government. Despite Napoleon's enormous popularity, his overtures for peace, and his promises of good behavior, the Allied powers declared Napoleon "an enemy and disturber of the tranquility of the world" deserving "public vengeance."[15]

In Parliament, Whitbread fiercely opposed the war; Cobbett attacked the government's decision in his *Political Register;* and Hunt asked why the already-overburdened English taxpayers had to finance a new war to "endeavor to force upon France a government which all the French nation detested and abhorred."[16] Godwin went further: "I do not even wish we should succeed."[17] Wilson took the news from Waterloo in stride; other English Bonapartists were dismayed. Hunt got sick; Hazlitt was "prostrated in mind and body"; and Whitbread, overtaken by depression and mounting debts, slashed his throat. Byron felt that "nothing was left but to follow Whitbread's example" but he did not have "the Roman in him to take his life."[18]

As the English Bonapartists digested the news of Waterloo, Napoleon traveled to Rochefort to board the ship that would take him to America. During the journey he received messages from Brayer and other generals asking him to make a stand and return to Paris at the head of the armies of the Loire and Pyrenees. Napoleon refused, as he was loath to trigger a civil war and had already made up his mind to go to the United States.[19] But when he reached Rochefort he had a nasty surprise. Although the frigates promised by Fouché were waiting for him, his passports had not arrived. To make matters worse, the winds were adverse and the Royal Navy blocked the estuary. A retired French admiral who lived in Rochefort advised Napoleon to embark on the *Bayadere,* a French corvette anchored at Royan under the command of Captain Baudin.[20]

A few hours later, an unexpected visitor arrived in Rochefort and curtly demanded to see the emperor. It was General Charles Francois Antoine Lallemand. Of medium height, muscular frame, with curly black hair and penetrating eyes of the same color, the forty-one-year-old general cut a fearsome figure. He was as well known for his impetuosity and bravery as for his arrogance and bad temper.[21] Lallemand exuded an intensity that did not endear him to strangers. He looked like a man not at peace with himself, as if he felt guilty for having survived so many cavalry charges when many of his comrades had died.[22] But Napoleon, who had known him for twenty years, thought he had the "sacred fire" and never forgot how days after he had escaped from Elba, "in a moment of the greatest danger," Lallemand had led "a movement of primary importance amongst the troops of his division."[23] Among Lallemand's accomplices were his younger brother Henri, also a general, and his friend Charles Lefebvre-Desnouettes, commander of the Chasseurs of the Royal Guard. Both will play a role in this story.

The conspiracy had quickly unraveled. Lefebvre-Desnouettes sought refuge with his friend General Antoine Rigaud commander of the Chalons garrison; the Lallemands were arrested by royalist troops while marching to Lyon to meet Napoleon. Both brothers were brought in chains to the village of Soissons, fifty miles north of Paris, to face a court-martial and certain death.[24] While they were in prison, a young boy suddenly appeared and introduced himself as Alexander Dumas. Lallemand asked him if he was the son of General Dumas, with whom he had served in Egypt. The boy assented and offered Lallemand "a pair of pistols and 50 Louis." The proud general thought for a moment and then said, "Thank you, little friend. The Emperor will be in Paris before our trial takes place." He then kissed Alexander's head and said, "You are a brave boy. Go and play and make sure they don't suspect that you came to see us."[25] It's a pity Dumas never wrote a novel about Lallemand, whose adventures rivaled those of Monte Cristo.

When Napoleon entered Paris, he freed Lallemand and rewarded him with a peerage, the title of count, and the rank of major general. At Waterloo, Lallemand was wounded while charging the enemy at the head of the Chasseurs à Cheval of the Imperial Guard. After Napoleon ordered a retreat and it seemed everything was lost, his commander, General Lefebvre-Desnouettes, proposed launching a suicidal charge against the advancing British army to follow Napoleon's dictum: better to die gloriously in battle than to live in defeat. But Lallemand brought his friend to his senses. The war wasn't over and the emperor would need his Guard in the next campaign.[26] Lallemand was one of the last generals to leave the battlefield, and when he returned to Paris, he was devastated to learn of Napoleon's abdication. While Fouché convinced Davout, the minister of war, that it was pointless to resist the Allied advance and the inevitable restoration of the Bourbons, Lallemand and other generals argued that Wellington and Blucher could be stopped. No other general was willing to take up their cause.[27]

Lallemand knew that only Napoleon could lead the army, and he set out for Rochefort at full gallop to convince him. Two days later, exhausted and still hurting from a wound in his arm, he walked into Napoleon's room. Without losing any time and in his usual blunt style he asked the emperor to put himself at the head of the army. Brayer still had his two battalions of the Young Guard;

Lamarque had the Army of the Loire; Grouchy's division was almost intact; and Clausel had ten thousand men at Bordeaux. It was still possible to save France. Lallemand's words "spurred" Napoleon's imagination, but after giving it some thought he rejected the idea. "Any such attempt would be civil war, to which I feel invincible repugnance," he said.[28] Joseph Bonaparte, who had come to Rochefort, suggested embarking on Baudin's ship or on the *Pike*, an American schooner anchored at Bordeaux. To Joseph's dismay, Napoleon refused, and remained two more days at Rochefort.[29] Worried that if more British warships appeared on the coast the emperor would never be able to escape, Lallemand again advised him to leave. "Sire, the English vessels are numerous." Napoleon cut him short. "Yes, undoubtedly they are numerous, so numerous in fact that I will not be able to avoid them. Maybe it would be better to deliver myself to the English." Lallemand pleaded with him: "You can't deliver yourself to England! Think of France, Sire. Think of the King of Rome!" But to avoid a civil war Napoleon had no option but to surrender to the British. Lallemand wouldn't give up. "Will Your Majesty allow me to go to find Captain Baudin? . . . I will find him and will arrange everything with him. In three days you will be at sea, defying your enemies and carrying your fortune to the New World, where so many opportunities await you! You will then be the hero of two worlds!"[30]

Napoleon was moved by Lallemand's devotion but remained undecided. He embarked on one of the French frigates and sailed toward the island of Aix, at the mouth of the Charente.* The following morning he received an ultimatum from the provisional government to leave French soil within twenty-four hours. By now Napoleon had almost decided that if he obtained certain guarantees he would surrender to England. On July 10, he sent Count Las Cases and General Savary to confer with Frederick Maitland, captain of the HMS *Bellerophon*, which blocked the estuary.† They were instructed to ask whether the passports promised by Fouché had arrived and if not, what attitude would Maitland take toward the emperor. The captain responded negatively to the first question and emphasized that without safe conducts he would stop, if necessary by force, any French ship attempting to leave Rochefort. He also said that he had no instructions regarding the possibility of receiving Napoleon on board his ship.

With the Bourbons back in power and the Army of the Loire disbanded, Na-

---

* It was at Aix, in 1809, that Lord Cochrane almost single-handedly destroyed the French fleet.

† The *Bellerophon* formed part of the squadron sent months earlier to support the royalist insurrection in the Vendée, which forced Napoleon to divert troops from the Waterloo campaign.

poleon's options were limited. Still undecided on the night of July 12, he agreed to send Lallemand to confer with Captain Baudin.[31] When Lallemand described the situation at Rochefort, Baudin said Napoleon should embark on the *Pike*, the American schooner. General Clausel and William Lee, the American consul at Bordeaux, had arranged everything for him to embark on that ship. Otherwise, Napoleon could leave on one of the French frigates anchored at Aix. "It is a matter of hours. He should leave immediately," Baudin said. "I will put myself between him and the English and will give him enough time to avoid the British cruisers." Lallemand galloped back to deliver this message. At Aix, Joseph was making a last-ditch effort to save his brother. "I will take your place and will appear to be ill in your room for two or three days," Joseph said. "No one will know anything of your departure until you are far away." Napoleon refused. He would never put his brother's life in danger to save his own and deemed it below his dignity to escape in disguise. Seeing all hope was lost, Joseph fled to Bordeaux where an American ship waited to take him to New York.[32]

Meanwhile, the British ministers debated what to do if Napoleon fell into their hands. Castlereagh, who had entered Paris with Wellington, asked John Wilson Croker, secretary of the Lords of the Admiralty, to convene an urgent meeting with Fouché and Talleyrand to discuss the situation. Croker, who thought Napoleon was better dead than alive, suggested attacking Rochefort under a white flag and executing him.[33] Ironically, at this time Napoleon entertained hopes that the British government would treat him hospitably and allow him to continue his journey to the United States. Lallemand argued that it was foolish to trust the British ministers and believed that the emperor could still avoid falling into their hands. Still unsure about what to do or perhaps simply playing for time, Napoleon sent Lallemand and Las Cases to the *Bellerophon* to ascertain if Maitland had received instructions. It was a strange meeting for Lallemand, who during the Egyptian campaign had briefly been Maitland's prisoner. The British captain, who remembered him well, found his manners unpleasant and his appearance "by no means prepossessing." Las Cases explained that Napoleon was so anxious "to stop the further effusion of blood that he would go to America in any way the English government would sanction." Maitland replied that he had been authorized to offer the emperor safe passage to England, where he would be under the protection of English laws. Las Cases emphasized that Napoleon's sole objective in going to England was "finding there all facilities to continue his journey to the United States." Maitland replied that he could not guarantee safe passage but insisted that Napoleon had nothing to fear, as England was a hospitable nation.[34]

After hearing this response, Napoleon consulted his inner circle. Everybody favored surrendering except Lallemand. The impetuous general had no doubt that Maitland was "a man of honor"* but didn't trust the British ministers and persisted in advocating his escape plan. Napoleon again refused. Maybe influenced by Voltaire's writings, he placed great faith in the English legal system. Disappointed, Lallemand asked for permission to leave. "Do you want to abandon me?" Napoleon asked. "No," replied Lallemand, "I think I can serve your interests better if I remain free. I can always go to England on the ship that was going to take you to America. Once there I can make your situation known to the public in case my worst fears about the British government prove to be true." Napoleon dismissed his concerns. "You would be useful to me," he said. "I would be sad to see you leave."[35] That was enough for Lallemand. He would remain with Napoleon.

On the morning of July 15, Napoleon sealed his fate. Confident that he would be treated as the former sovereign of France, he boarded the *Bellerophon.* "I board your ship to put myself under the protection of the laws of England," he told Maitland.[36] All the efforts to save him "from the humiliation of falling into the hands of the English are now to no purpose," complained the American consul at Bordeaux.[37] While on board the *Bellerophon,* Napoleon charmed and awed her crew. Maitland admitted privately that he had never met "a man more agreeable and engaging" and treated him with "every mark of respect." Whether he misled Napoleon has been a matter of debate. What is beyond dispute is that his popularity among officers and sailors of the Royal Navy remained a source of concern for the British and French governments until his death.[38]

Napoleon's surrender was a big blow for the English Bonapartists. "It makes my heart ache to think that such a man should have been so deceived and deluded as to the character of the English government," wrote Henry Hunt. A fierce debate followed in the London newspapers. The *Times* and the *Courier,* which expressed the views of the government, viciously attacked Napoleon and even suggested executing him. The opposition *Morning Chronicle* argued that the rules of hospitality should apply, and Cobbett warned that even if the ministers executed Napoleon, they would never be able "to efface the memory of his deeds."[39]

Napoleon's hopes of being treated hospitably by the British government quickly vanished. On reaching Torbay, he was not allowed to disembark and the *Bellerophon* was ordered to sail to Plymouth. During the voyage Lallemand

---

* Maitland was the nephew of Lord Lauderdale, a Whig peer who had served as envoy to France under Fox's ministry.

seemed "morose and abstracted," probably worried at the prospect of being delivered to the Bourbons, which meant certain death. But his loyalty never wavered. He rotated in the duty of aide-de-camp, taking turns to guard Napoleon's cabin.[40] Plymouth Bay, where the *Bellerophon* dropped anchor, soon became a major tourist attraction. Every day, boats and vessels of all types arrived "filled with curious spectators" from all over England "to snatch such a glimpse of him."[41] Napoleon walked along the deck of the *Bellerophon,* well aware of the impact he exerted on his audience, which applauded him when he retired to his cabin. "It is dangerous, I think, to the loyalty of the people to keep him here long; they all seem fascinated," observed an awed spectator.[42] The Tory ministers agreed. Something had to be done, quickly.

Among those who were not surprised at the way the British ministers treated Napoleon was Lord Thomas Cochrane, Tenth Earl of Dundonald. Born near Glasgow in an ancient but impoverished Scottish clan, Cochrane was a celebrity in England. His naval exploits during the Napoleonic wars were legendary. Turned radical politician, he had advocated reform in Parliament and campaigned against corruption in the navy with the same fearlessness and determination with which he had fought against the French. In the process he had riled the establishment. Cochrane had his comeuppance in early 1814 when the government accused him—falsely as it turned out—of spreading rumors of Napoleon's death to profit in the stock market. Tried and found guilty, he was expelled from Parliament, stripped of the Order of the Bath, discharged from the Royal Navy, condemned to the pillory, and thrown into a dungeon.[43] It is hard to imagine a greater insult to a man who so many times had put his life in danger to defend his country. "Such a man should not be made to suffer such degrading punishment," Napoleon said when told about Cochrane's fate.[44]

This act of injustice did not prevent Cochrane from being reelected as junior MP for Westminster. On March 6, 1815, as Napoleon marched to Paris and three months before completing his one-year sentence, Cochrane escaped from prison. The news caused almost as much sensation as the reports of Napoleon's escape from Elba, which reached London four days later. The marshal of the King's Bench Prison offered a hefty reward for information leading to the capture of the fugitive, who in leaflets distributed all around town was described as "about five feet eleven inches in height, thin and narrow-chested, with sandy hair and full eyes, red whiskers and eyebrows."[45] With the exception of the color of his hair and sideburns, the description was oddly inaccurate, as Cochrane was over six feet tall and broad shouldered. It also failed to mention his prominent roman nose, which gave his face the full force of his character.[46] Cochrane remained in hiding until March 21, the day after Napoleon entered Paris, when he defiantly appeared in the House of Commons. After a short struggle he was overpowered and, refusing to walk, was carried back to prison by the constables. He was confined in a cold, underground dungeon. It was a turning point in Cochrane's life. For years, the Tories had unfairly persecuted him. As England embarked on a new effort to dethrone Napoleon, there was no doubt about where Cochrane's sympathies lay. He believed his country had embarked on a "war of corruption" and confidently predicted that Boney would "beat them all."[47] Cochrane had to eat his words, but in early July, after completing his prison sentence, he took his seat in Parliament. Now he witnessed how the ministers treated Napoleon.

The British cabinet decided that the rules of hospitality would be sacrificed for reasons of state. Executing Napoleon, as advocated by the *Courier*, was not a realistic option. On the other hand, as no other man could "play the same part that he has done and is likely to play again if he should be allowed the opportunity," allowing him to go to the United States was too dangerous.[48] The Spanish government was particularly alarmed at this possibility as "the United States was the receptacle for all the disaffected and if Napoleon were to reach that point it was impossible to estimate the damage that he could cause us by leading the insurgents in the Americas."[49] Napoleon had to be exiled again, but this time to a place from which he could not escape. After consulting the Admiralty, Lord Liverpool, the prime minister, chose St. Helena as "the place in the world best calculated" to confine the fallen emperor. Considered impregnable, the forty-six-square-mile island was 5,000 miles away from Europe, 1,200 miles off the coast of Africa, and 1,800 miles from northeastern Brazil. And the dominance of the seas by the Royal Navy almost guaranteed that escape would be impossible. Lord Liverpool believed that "at such a distance and in such a place, all intrigue would be impossible, and being withdrawn so far from the European world, he would very soon be forgotten."[50] He could not have imagined how mistaken he was.

The government reached an agreement with the East India Company, which used the island as a watering station, to accommodate the prisoner and his entourage. Only vessels of the Royal Navy or the company would be allowed to enter the port. Lord Henry Bathurst, secretary for war and the colonies, was charged with the safety and custody of the prisoner. Bathurst appointed Lieutenant Colonel Hudson Lowe to be Napoleon's guardian. Since it would take

Lowe a few months to arrange his private affairs, Admiral Sir George Cockburn, recently appointed chief of the naval station at the Cape of Good Hope, would fulfill this role on an interim basis. Cockburn was ordered to get his ship, the HMS *Northumberland,* ready to depart for St. Helena.

When Napoleon learned that St. Helena would be his prison, he realized the grave mistake he had made. Privately, he said he would rather die than go to that dreadful island, but outwardly he maintained a calm composure. "Here indeed was adversity, and here was true greatness struggling against it," observed one of the officers on board the *Bellerophon.*[51] Being sent as a prisoner to St. Helena was a bitter irony for Napoleon, as ten years earlier he had tried to invade the island.[52] Now it would be his prison. In a letter to the prince regent, Napoleon appealed to history: "I hereby solemnly protest, in the face of God and man, against the violation of my most sacred rights, by the forcible disposal of my person and liberty. I came voluntarily on board the *Bellerophon.* I am not a prisoner; I am the guest of England."[53]

Napoleon's English followers were incensed at the government's decision. Several efforts to render it illegal were contemplated and rejected by the High Court.[54] But a clever lawyer convinced a London judge to subpoena Napoleon to testify as a witness in a trial. Conscious of the illegality of its proceedings and fearful that these efforts would succeed, the British government took immediate action.[55] A cabinet minister explained that "the foolish curiosity of the people and the refractory spirit of his suite rendered his longer stay in Plymouth Sound very inconvenient."[56]

Only a few officers were allowed to accompany Napoleon to St. Helena. Lallemand and Savary, deemed too dangerous, were excluded. Since Napoleon's doctor declined to go for health reasons, Barry O'Meara, surgeon of the *Bellerophon,* volunteered to take his post. His fluency in Italian made him amenable to Napoleon. The British government agreed, hoping to use him as a spy. Before Napoleon transferred to the *Northumberland* he received a visit from William Lyttelton, a Whig MP, who gave him the news of Whitbread's death. Lyttelton was struck by Lallemand, who had "a very dark, strong significant countenance and I think a rather noble one."[57] Napoleon felt guilty for having asked his general to surrender to the English. But Lallemand had no regrets. "Sire, I did my duty. I have no regrets for myself but for my country and Your Majesty, who has been treated more poorly than I have."[58] Lallemand never forgot the last minutes he spent with Napoleon and swore that one day he would set him free. The following morning, the *Northumberland* departed for St. Helena.

3
The Revenge of the Bourbons

Fit retribution! Gaul may champ the bit
And foam in fetters;—but is Earth more free?
Did nations combat to make *One* submit;
Or league to teach all kings true sovereignty?
—Lord Byron, *Childe Harold's Pilgrimage,* Canto 3

The relief of the British government at getting rid of its worst enemy was matched by the indignation of the Bonapartists. Cobbett argued that Napoleon had "committed no crime against our laws" and that banishment was "the severest of punishments allotted to well known and clearly defined crime." The "violation of national law in his person" only exalted "his unexampled worth."[1] According to Henry Hunt, Napoleon's confinement at St. Helena was a "disgraceful, damnable, imperishable blot on the escutcheon of England's character."[2] Sir Robert Wilson, who had once visited the island and found it "one of the most unhealthy and dank climates of the world," was also incensed.[3] Wilson thought England's fear of Napoleon proved "the most indisputable record of the majestic force of his character." Not even Hannibal had been "honored by a more flattering homage when Rome acknowledged that his life was incompatible with her summit." He prophesied that if Napoleon survived a few years, he would "see his triumph in the establishment of his dynasty."[4]

Henry Richard Fox, Third Lord Holland, scion of one of England's most powerful families and nephew of the legendary Charles James Fox, shared these views. The forty-three-year-old Whig politician had just returned to London after a long European sojourn. Holland thought Napoleon's banishment to St. Helena was a barbaric and illegal act of vengeance. Capel Lofft, an eminent jurist and devoted Bonapartist, advised him that the best strategy to obtain his release was to table a motion for an inquiry in Parliament and to oppose any bill of indemnity likely to be submitted by the ministers to justify their measures.[5]

As Lord Holland prepared to launch his parliamentary crusade, his wife started her own campaign on behalf of the exiled French emperor. Lady Holland's admiration for Napoleon, whom she had met in 1802, bordered on the fanatical and as her husband admitted, it was "more unqualified and more enthusiastic" than his own.[6] Although forty-four and mother to ten children, Lady Holland was an extremely attractive woman. Described by one of her many admirers as a "beautiful structure of flesh and blood," her flowing chestnut hair, seductive ruby lips, and intriguing personality were irresistible to the guests of Holland House.[7] To soften Lowe's attitude, Lady Holland invited him to several dinners attended by other celebrities who shared her sympathy for the fallen emperor.

Lowe had arrived in London in the fall of 1815 and was arranging his personal affairs—including getting married—before leaving for St. Helena. Despite a mediocre military career, he was awarded the order of Knight Commander of the Bath, a distinction which months earlier had been refused to Wilson and stripped from Cochrane, two men who had done a lot more than Lowe for the glory and honor of British arms. Despite being a snob and thrilled at the possibility of rubbing elbows with London's high society, Lowe did not succumb to Lady Holland's charms. But she was a most determined woman and never gave up in her efforts on behalf of Napoleon. For the next six years, her house became the headquarters of Bonapartism in England.[8] Contrary to Lord Liverpool's hopes, Napoleon did not sink into oblivion. His sins were quickly forgotten and as Cobbett predicted, he was "followed by the admiration and gratitude of every brave and every free man in every nation in the world."[9] As time passed and the harsh terms of his captivity became known, he became a symbol of the struggle against absolutism.

Although a regular guest at Holland House, Sir Robert Wilson never met Lowe. In early September he left for Paris to witness the second restoration of the Bourbons, which had started on a bloody note. His friends feared he would soon get into trouble. "I do know not what business you have at Paris," wrote Lord Hutchinson, his old mentor. "You are more than a suspected person and you will get yourself into some scrape or another."[10] When Wilson arrived, the "white terror" was being violently unleashed. Louis XVIII's first measure was to punish the "traitors" who had helped Napoleon in his last adventure. The instigators of this measure were the Count of Artois and his followers, known as Ultra-Royalists, or the Ultras. Fanatically attached to the monarchy, they detested the Bonapartists and viewed liberal ideas as a dangerous virus that had to be extirpated from society. The Ultras wanted to bring France back to the days before the French Revolution. The British government supported punishing Napoleon's supporters not only to sustain the Bourbons but also to maintain "a safe and lasting peace."[11]

The first victim of the Bourbon vengeance was the Bonaparte family, which was banned forever from France. Hortense sought refuge in Switzerland; her brother Eugene remained in Bavaria; Jerome fled to Wurttemberg; and Lucien escaped to Rome to join his mother and sister. Since Lucien and Joseph were considered particularly dangerous, the police made a special effort to track them down and put them under the strictest surveillance. Despite their efforts, they failed to discover Joseph's whereabouts for several months. The French police suspected that he was hiding in Switzerland, where he owned a large property.[12] Instead he walked as a free man in Manhattan.

The next victims of the white terror were those suspected of having plotted Napoleon's return. Fouché was put in charge of preparing the list of culprits, which originally included more than three hundred names but was later reduced to only thirty-one.[13] It was an odd list, not only because Fouché had omitted "none of his friends" but also because he was as guilty as any of them. On July 24, the king published an *ordonnance royale* accusing thirty-one men of high treason. There were two groups. The first included those accused of conspiring in favor of Napoleon before March 20. This group included Brayer, Clausel, Grouchy, Ney, La Bedoyere, Count Lavallette, Lefebvre-Desnouettes, and the brothers Lallemand, among others. In the second group were those who had aided Napoleon after he entered Paris. Among them were generals Fressinet and Rigaud and Count Regnault de St. Jean d'Angely, one of Napoleon's ablest ministers.[14] Those in the first group would stand trial for high treason and faced the death penalty. Those in the second group would be exiled.

The king's edict violated both the letter and the spirit of the Treaty of Paris signed by Wellington and the representatives of the Allied powers. Days before the edict was published, Marshal Davout convened a meeting in his office and alerted those generals who were included so that they could escape. Brayer's first reaction was to submit to the tribunal. One of his comrades argued that such a decision would be unwise as it meant a certain death. Brayer replied, "*Eh bien!* If the judges are political assassins, if my death could bring all civil discord to an end and contribute to the happiness of France, I would die without regret." Marshal Macdonald, forgiving Brayer for his conduct three months earlier, advised him to flee. Brayer realized that he would more useful to Napoleon alive than dead. Disguised as a gendarme he fled to Bavaria, where his wife's family was well connected.[15] Lefebvre-Desnouettes, Exelmans, Rigaud, and Henri Lallemand also escaped. La Bedoyere, Lavallette, and Ney were arrested. Other suspected Bonapartists were not as fortunate.[16]

Other high-profile Bonapartists who remained in Paris were placed under surveillance by the prefecture of police, which was led by a young protégé of Fouché named Elie Decazes. The Ultras, under the leadership of Count of Artois, had their own covert weapon to fight Bonapartism: a secret political-religious society known as la Congregation, which since 1789 had worked to restore the Bourbon monarchy. Now their mission was to ensure its survival.[17] It was pressure from Artois and la Congregation that led to the collapse of the cabinet formed by Talleyrand and Fouché—"vice supported by crime." By September a new cabinet was formed under the leadership of Armand du Plessis, Duke of Richelieu,* who was devoted to the Bourbons and a staunch enemy of Bonapartism. The clever and handsome Decazes survived the purge and replaced Fouché at the powerful Ministry of Police. Decazes was a peculiar choice for a cabinet post as he had served the Bonaparte family for years and was a high-ranking Freemason.[18] In the coming years he would become one of the most powerful men in France. Had he chosen to write his memoirs, he might have shed light on the many enigmas surrounding this story.

Within three months the army was purged of any suspected Bonapartists.[19] The revenge of the Bourbons led to the creation of an underground network called L'Association Fraternelle Européenne designed to help the victims of political persecution.[20] Its members, calling themselves the Friends of Freedom, could be found in government, the army, the police, and the diplomatic legations of foreign powers. Most of them were Freemasons and a good number were British subjects. Sir Robert Wilson was one of its most famous members. Together with Michael Bruce, Lord Kinnaird, John "Radical Jack" Lambton, and other Englishmen living in Paris at the time, Wilson made it his mission in life to help the persecuted Bonapartists. The association's members believed that Waterloo had dealt a fatal blow to the cause of freedom in Europe and that Castlereagh and Wellington had made a huge mistake by restoring Louis XVIII to the throne.[21] Wilson and his English friends were dismayed when, after a brief trial, La Bedoyere was found guilty and executed. Ney and Lavallette expected to meet the same fate.[22] Wilson was particularly irate at Wellington, who had signed the Treaty of Paris and now condoned a blatant violation

---

* One of Richelieu's ancestors was the sister of the famous Cardinal Richelieu.

of its articles. He kept Lord Grey and Lord Holland abreast of events in France through a regular correspondence. His well-known opposition to the Bourbons raised his profile and made him the subject of constant surveillance by the police and also a target of the *cabinet noir,* the unit within the post office that intercepted correspondence.[23] Aware of this surveillance, Wilson relied on the diplomatic pouch of the British embassy or trusted messengers for his correspondence. Among the latter was the botanist Aimé Bonpland, one of the last people Napoleon talked to about his plans at Malmaison. Wilson established a good and lasting relationship with Bonpland. Both shared the same ideals, an admiration for Bonaparte, and an interest in the New World. At the end of October, Bonpland left Paris carrying a letter from Wilson to Lord Holland. "The bearer of this letter is Mr. Bonpland, the companion of Humboldt and a scientist of the most sensible character," Wilson wrote. He explained that Bonpland was "one of the Empress Josephine's executors and is one of the most cherished friends of Prince Eugene." He recommended giving Bonpland "special notice and more especially as he is on his way to South America."[24]

As time passed and as the fury of the Bourbons claimed more victims, the Friends of Freedom became more resourceful. Marshal Grouchy hid for forty days in an attic and eventually managed to escape to the United States.[25] General Clausel escaped to New York with the help of William Lee, the American consul in Bordeaux, who had tried to arrange Napoleon's escape from Rochefort. The trial of Ney, the "bravest of the brave," attracted a lot of attention in England. Wilson zealously campaigned with Lord Holland and Lord Grey to secure Ney's pardon. In mid-November the British general learned "that the Court has resolved in executing Ney despite publication of the Treaty of Peace there being an article in it assuring a general amnesty."[26] With the passing days, Wilson's indignation grew. "My blood boils when I think that all this iniquity has executive force solely by the aid of our bayonets. It makes England as abhorrent to myself as to the sufferers," he wrote to Lord Grey a few days later.[27] As a last resort, Wilson asked his friend Sir Charles Stuart, the British ambassador, to delay the proceedings "until the crown lawyers in England will give their opinion." He feared that Ney would "be poisoned or stabbed in his dungeon" and offered to guard his cell. "What is passing at Paris annoys me more than I can well describe," Wilson said.[28]

When Ney was executed Wilson could barely contain his anger. He blamed the British cabinet for being an accomplice in the cold-blooded murder of an innocent man. "How can we expect freedom and justice at home when despotism and murder are the basis of our foreign policy?" he complained to Lord Grey.[29] Ney's execution also made a great impression in France. Even those liberals who had facilitated Napoleon's fall, like the Marquis de Lafayette, now regretted it. But the Friends of Freedom did not despair. Count Lavallette was still alive and maybe he could be saved. The death sentence pronounced against him was widely considered unfair and many expected the king to pardon him. Unfortunately, despite his protestations of innocence, Lavallette was not only known for his devotion to Napoleon but also for his closeness to Hortense and Eugene de Beauharnais, who were both under strong suspicion of having secretly conspired for their stepfather's return. The Ultras were not prepared to show any mercy.[30]

While lobbying in favor of Lavallette, Wilson continued his quixotic efforts to save England's honor by facilitating the escape of other proscribed Bonapartists. He counted on some "unofficial" help from the British ambassador. "I have an excellent friend in Stuart and indeed he is a most excellent man," he told Grey at the end of December. "In proof of his liberality he has just given me *entre nous* a passport for General Lamarque, who is in the proscribed list."[31] Wilson could hardly contain his joy when a day before his scheduled execution, Lavallette escaped from prison by walking out dressed in his wife's clothes. When the police found out they had been tricked, they started a massive manhunt. Poor Madame Lavallette remained in jail for six weeks. She never recovered from the traumatic experience. All of France was shocked. The Ultras accused Decazes of secretly allowing the escape. While everybody believed Lavallette had fled Paris, he had been hidden in an attic at the Ministry of Foreign Affairs, close to the office of the Duke of Richelieu.[32] The French prime minister never imagined that the most sought after fugitive in France slept only a few feet away from his office.

Although free, Lavallette was not out of danger. His friends knew that sooner or later the police would discover him.[33] On New Year's Eve, Michael Bruce received an anonymous note: "I place his life in your hands. You alone can save him," said its author.[34] It was a challenge that the young Englishman would not decline but one that he could not attempt on his own. The next day he confided the secret to Wilson who embraced the project with enthusiasm. As one of Wilson's comrades observed, few men were better suited to do it, as he had "a fertile imagination, ready courage, great assurance, and singular power of command over others."[35] It was just the beginning. The defiant British general would soon play an even more important role in Napoleon's last campaign.

4
America: Bonapartist Haven

How fortunate would it be for this country if Bonaparte on his arrival in America should select it as his residence. How many smiles would greet him—how many noble defenders of his tyranny and crimes, would give him welcome.

—*Dedham (Mass.) Gazette*, August 18, 1815

Joseph was lucky. As news of Napoleon's surrender spread, the Royal Navy relaxed its vigilance. At the end of August after thirty-four days of travel he arrived in New York, disguised as a merchant from Bordeaux. Anybody who had ever seen Napoleon in person or in a portrait could have easily believed that the former French emperor had landed in America. Joseph's physical resemblance to his younger brother was striking. He was slightly taller and less corpulent, and, although he didn't have his charisma, he had the gravitas of a former monarch. And unlike Napoleon, who was the ultimate political pragmatist, Joseph was a republican at heart and felt very much at ease in the United States. After resting in Manhattan for a few days, he decided that as a former king of Spain it would be appropriate for him to visit President James Madison. Joseph didn't know Madison personally, but he had met Secretary of State James Monroe during the negotiations for the sale of Louisiana and expected to be welcomed in Washington. But Madison had no interest in meeting him.[1] Monroe also thought it prudent to avoid him. When Joseph reached Baltimore he was told that the president and the entire cabinet were out of the capital. Realizing he was persona non grata, he returned to New York.[2]

Aside from this awkward official reaction, Joseph was warmly welcomed in America. Despite British propaganda, Napoleon was very popular, particularly after rumors spread that he would seek asylum in the United States. Most of the American press criticized the British government for exiling Napoleon to St. Helena, and sympathy for the deposed emperor increased even more when it was known that his guardian would be Admiral Cockburn, infamous in America for having burned Washington during the recent war.[3] Joseph's Masonic links also helped him. The Masonic brotherhood had played an important role in the American Revolution and remained very powerful. Its rosters included some of the country's most influential businessmen and politicians. Since 1804, Joseph had been the leader of the Grand Orient de France, which had played a central role in Napoleon's regime. Although it is not clear whether Napoleon was a Freemason—at St. Helena he said Freemasons were nothing but a bunch of "imbeciles" that got together to "perform ridiculous fooleries"—he had strong links with *la franc-maçonnerie* and strongly encouraged its development throughout his empire.[4] All of Napoleon's brothers were Freemasons and many high-ranking imperial functionaries and army officers occupied key roles in the French Masonic hierarchy.[5] Although there were no formal links between the lodges of France and the United States, there was sympathy toward the persecuted French "brothers."[6]

Don Luis de Onis, the Spanish ambassador in the United States, did not share this sympathy. When he had learned of Napoleon's return to Paris, he feared that he would again attempt to seize the Spanish colonies. Therefore he welcomed the news of Waterloo and Napoleon's exile to St. Helena. But by mid-August 1815, the Spanish diplomat learned that General Jean Humbert had again teamed up with Toledo and Laffite to invade Texas. Their plan was to join forces with the leader of the Mexican patriots, Jose Maria Morelos,* and launch a combined offensive against the royalists.[7] Onis at once warned the Spanish viceroy in Mexico, emphasizing that Humbert had "served under the orders of Bonaparte, has been in Louisiana for several years and participated in the Battle of New Orleans at the side of General Jackson. His military valor is beyond doubt and his engagement with the rebels will do us a lot of harm."[8] A few weeks later Onis learned that Joseph had arrived in New York.[9] It was the beginning of Onis' worst nightmare.

As soon as Joseph settled in New York, he focused on fulfilling his brother's instructions. It is true that Napoleon had not always treated him well, and had even humiliated him publicly, but blood ran thick in Corsican families. Joseph had already proved his devotion at Rochefort. He owed Napoleon everything and would spare no resources to obtain his freedom. With a vast fortune and the support of thousands of followers on both sides of the Atlantic, Joseph could contemplate almost any option. In fact, soon after he arrived in the United

---

*Jose Maria Morelos y Pavon (1765–1815) was a Mexican priest and leader of the Mexican independence movement after the death of Miguel Hidalgo in 1811.

States, rumors about secret plans to rescue Napoleon started to spread. According to one of these rumors, Joseph discussed these plans with Jean Laffite, who at this time was on a tour of the East Coast. According to a contemporary description, Laffite was "a well-formed, handsome man, about six feet two inches in height, strongly built, with large hazel eyes, black hair and [he] generally wore a thick moustache."[10] When it relates to Lafitte, separating myth from reality is often difficult. However, the possibility of his meeting Joseph is not so far-fetched. To rescue his brother, Joseph needed ships and daring seamen. Laffite could provide both. On the other hand, only a few weeks after Laffite supposedly met Joseph, his brother Pierre was in New Orleans agreeing to work as a spy for Onis. In the correspondence of the Spanish diplomat the two brothers became agent number 13. Did the Laffites sell themselves to Spain or were they double agents working for the independence cause "from inside"? Many historians believe Laffite was nothing more than a scoundrel devoted to his own interests, but the evidence is contradictory.[11] The services the Laffite brothers rendered to Spain were of limited value. By contrast, they were quite valuable to Humbert in all his attempts to invade Mexico. In fact, while Pierre was agreeing to work for Onis, the redoubtable French general was landing near Veracruz at the head of a small army accompanied by Dominique Youx, who was rumored to be a third Laffite brother. Humbert's plans failed because Morelos was captured and shot by the Spaniards. When faced with the prospect of encountering superior forces alone, Humbert returned to New Orleans.[12]

By the end of 1815 hundreds of Bonapartist émigrés had arrived in the United States and all paid their respects to Joseph.[13] The most prominent among them was Count Regnault de St. Jean d'Angely, Napoleon's former interior minister. The French consul in New York reported that there was no cause for alarm as Regnault rarely saw Joseph, who lived quietly in a house overlooking the Hudson.[14] In fact, Regnault saw Joseph regularly and became his political adviser. Another prominent émigré was General Clausel whom Joseph knew well as he had served with distinction in Spain. During the Hundred Days, Clausel had been among the first generals to join Napoleon and one of the last to abandon him. Clausel was also fluent in Spanish and was familiar with America; he had participated in the ill-fated expedition to Haiti and had lived for a short time in New Orleans.

Joseph arrived in the United States at a critical juncture.[15] For the first time since 1776, the country had a clear sense of purpose. Even though from a military standpoint the recent war with England had been disastrous, the defeat of the British army at New Orleans had instilled in the American people a strong sense of self-confidence. The rebellion of the Spanish colonies presented interesting opportunities. According to Onis, the American government "believed that the time had arrived when a considerable portion of Spanish America was about to fall into their power, and the rest, after being emancipated, to submit to their influence."[16] However, since England had signed a treaty of friendship with Spain, the United States could not openly support the rebels in Spanish America without risking a new war. Any enterprise against Mexico had to be disguised as the effort of filibusters. If they were defeated, the American government would distance itself from their efforts; if they succeeded it would take advantage of the situation.

The rebellion in the Spanish colonies also played to Joseph's advantage. He had learned in Spain that to succeed in establishing a new empire in America he could not appear as a conqueror but as a liberator. It was a challenging but not impossible objective. After all, Cortes and Pizarro had conquered the entire continent with fewer than five hundred men. Besides, Joseph was almost as powerful as if he still ruled a kingdom. And with no one else to turn to for help, the rebels would soon knock on his door.

But by the end of 1815 the insurrection against Spain had failed everywhere except in Buenos Aires. With the exception of Port-au-Prince in Haiti, no other major port south of New Orleans was free from the control of a European power. This made Buenos Aires an ideal base not only for any expedition to rescue Napoleon but also for any efforts to build a new empire in the Spanish colonies. Not surprisingly, the city soon became a haven for exiled Bonapartists. Since defeating two British invasions, Buenos Aires had gained a certain prominence. In early 1810, together with Caracas and Santiago, it had led the revolutionary movement. But the collapse of the Napoleonic empire and the restoration of Ferdinand VII in Spain had deepened the divisions among the patriots. According to Captain William Bowles, chief of the British naval station in Buenos Aires and the eyes and ears of the Foreign Office in South America, two opposing factions sought to control power. One party had as its objective "an accommodation with the mother country under the mediation of Great Britain" while the other, which included "all the North Americans and the greatest part of what may be called the anti-English faction," still aspired to "absolute independence."[17]

In Captain Bowles's opinion, only two men counted in Buenos Aires: Jose de San Martin and Carlos de Alvear. Born in South America, they had arrived from Spain in early 1812 after serving for many years in the army. Although they came from different social backgrounds—Alvear the scion of an aristocratic Castilian family and San Martin the fourth son of an undistinguished Spanish officer—they had initially seemed close friends. And although they had a certain physical resemblance—San Martin was slightly taller and had a darker complexion—and carried themselves "with a formality and dignity of deportment uncommon among the natives," their personalities and political objectives couldn't have been more different.[18] Only twenty-four, Alvear was, according to Bowles, "the director of the whole political machine," but his brashness and undisguised ambition had earned him powerful enemies. San Martin was twelve years older, and although as capable and self-confident, was more mature and had a personality as inscrutable as Alvear's was transparent. A severe, calculating man, San Martin was circumspect in his views and austere in his tastes. His long career in the Spanish army had been unremarkable, more because of lack of social standing than lack of ability. To break into Buenos Aires' society San Martin had depended entirely on Alvear, whose mother belonged to one of the city's oldest families. But their friendship, if it had ever truly existed, had been replaced by a rivalry that for the next years would shape the revolution in South America and complicate Napoleon's plans.

Bowles thought England had an ally in San Martin, who was "extremely friendly to the English" and entertained "a sincere dislike of the French" but he didn't trust Alvear, even though he apparently no longer favored "a connection between this country and France" and had recently expressed views favorable to England.[19] Alvear had strong personal reasons to dislike the British and many believed he concealed them "due to the delicate political situation of the revolutionary government."[20] He was also the leader of the Caballeros Racionales, a Masonic secret society that was founded in Spain in 1809 to establish independent republics in Spanish America and had ties to Napoleonic France.[21] While living in Cadiz, Alvear had arranged the escape of an imprisoned French officer and given him a letter addressed to Napoleon asking him to support the cause of independence.[22] San Martin had joined this secret society in early 1811, after spending a year attached to the British army in Portugal.[23] His motives for joining the Caballeros Racionales remain unclear. But during his Portuguese stint San Martin made contacts with British officers and acquired a lifelong admiration for England. It is not at all improbable that the British government, worried by Napoleon's influence over the South American rebels, decided to infiltrate them with someone more sympathetic to its interests. Be that as it may, in the fall of 1811, Alvear and San Martin left Cadiz for London with a small group of followers. Their final destination was Buenos Aires.

London had long been a gathering place for exiled revolutionaries. Colonel Aaron Burr, who was also there at the time, met several times with a certain Mariano Castilla, another a native of Buenos Aires. Burr advised Castilla that only the United States could help the rebels in South America.[24] Castilla also met with Alvear and San Martin, and he may have introduced them to Burr, although no records of such a meeting exist. Castilla, unbeknownst to the others, moonlighted as an informer to the British government. After Alvear and San Martin left for Buenos Aires, Castilla warned the Foreign Office that Napoleon had secretly financed their trip and that "the negotiation was opened by the *aide-de-camp* of Marshal Victor some time since a prisoner in Cadiz, but who was liberated and sent to France."[25] The suspicions about Alvear's French connections followed him to America. When he arrived in Buenos Aires, British agents reported that one of his companions had brought a special message from Napoleon offering arms and support to the patriot cause.[26] Months later, when Alvear led a coup d'état, the chief of the British naval station reported that the new government was "unfavorably disposed" toward England and tried "by every underhand means to create in the minds of the people distrust of the British government and suspicions of their views towards these Americas."[27]

British agents in South America watched the growing influence of the United States with concern. By the end of 1812 American agents were not only encouraging independence but also trying to persuade the patriots that the United States "has taken the most lively interest in their concerns and to make them believe that they may expect the most active assistance from it." Joel Roberts Poinsett, the American consul in Chile, was "particularly diligent and active in propagating doctrines and opinions prejudicial to the British government and its subjects."[28] The second war between England and the United States had just started and South America was one of its front lines.

In early 1813 the rebel government in Buenos Aires called a national assembly to draft a constitution and declare independence from Spain. Under Alvear's leadership it abolished noble titles, freed the children of slaves, and eliminated the Inquisition. These reforms, inspired by the French Revolution, raised a few eyebrows among many locals, who were attached to old customs and viewed Alvear and his faction as dangerous Jacobins. The commander of the British naval station shared this view. He described Alvear as an "adventurer" and the members of the assembly as "men without respectability or connection, but turbulent, ambitious, democratic demagogues, who in revolutionary times like these, have everything to gain and little to lose but their heads."[29] However, by the end of 1813, when news of Napoleon's defeat at Leipzig reached Buenos Aires, enthusiasm for the cause of independence had started to wane and the gulf between Alvear and San Martin deepened. After almost two years in Buenos Aires, San Martin had lost hope in the cause of independence. The return of Ferdinand VII to Madrid seemed imminent, and the patriots did not have the resources to resist a renewed effort by Spain to subdue them. San Martin believed the conflict had to end through England's mediation, and when he was appointed commander of the patriot troops stationed on the border with Peru, a thousand miles away, he suspected Alvear was trying to get rid of him. Before leaving Buenos Aires he had a secret meeting with Captain Bowles in which he disclosed that the government had recently made overtures to France through an American agent. San Martin warned Bowles about the danger posed by the United States and recommended the interception of "any agents or supplies that might be sent from that country." He also promised that if "any anti-English revolution should take place here," he would "return from Peru and oppose it." He proved to be a man of his word.[30]

With San Martin out of the way, Alvear strengthened his hold on power.[31] But Napoleon's empire was in decline and by early 1814 the Peninsular War had ended, freeing the Spanish army to quash the insurrection in South America. Five thousand troops loyal to Ferdinand VII were garrisoned in Montevideo, a day's travel from Buenos Aires. This fortress had enormous strategic importance for any punitive Spanish expedition. For two years, the patriot armies had blockaded Montevideo without success as the Spanish navy continued to provision the besieged garrison. With the help of two American businessmen living in Buenos Aires, Alvear set out to build a squadron to neutralize Spanish naval superiority and force the surrender of Montevideo. The creation of a patriot fleet "under the direction of citizens of the United States" and manned mostly by American officers and sailors put Captain Bowles on alert.[32] England was at war with the United States and a powerful American warship, the USS *Essex* under the command of Commodore David Porter, had wreaked havoc on British commercial interests in the Pacific.[33] Porter used a Chilean port as a base and received protection from the revolutionary government led by Jose Miguel Carrera. Carrera was under the influence of Joel Roberts Poinsett who, according to Bowles, was not only an agent of the United States but also of Napoleon.[34]

Bowles pressured the Buenos Aires government to scrap its new fleet at once as it "might commit acts of hostility or piracy upon the subjects of His Majesty."[35] San Martín also thought the idea of a fleet was absurd. He believed a punitive expedition would soon arrive from Spain and that it was better to negotiate with the Spaniards before it was too late. But Alvear stood firm and the squadron set sail. Claiming to be deadly ill, San Martín resigned his command and moved closer to Buenos Aires. His unease at the course of events was not unwarranted. Weeks earlier, the rebel government had requested the military and diplomatic support of the United States.[36] Soon after, the patriot fleet won its first victories.

But by early June, news that Ferdinand VII had returned to Madrid reached Buenos Aires. The supporters of negotiations with Spain thought it was time to suspend hostilities. Alvear instead forced the surrender of Montevideo, capturing more than five thousand Spanish troops and two hundred pieces of artillery. It was the biggest military victory for the cause of South American independence since 1810.[37] Weeks later, news of Napoleon's abdication arrived. Now the patriots in Buenos Aires had no one to turn to for help. England was allied with Spain, and the United States was still at war and could offer only moral support. This isolation, coupled with the prospect of a punitive expedition from Spain, deepened the divisions among the patriots. Many, including San Martín, favored England's mediation. A crisis ensued and Alvear took over the government. British agents reported that the army and public opinion had "taken alarm at the tone of moderation" adopted by the former government and noted the bellicose stance of the new authorities, who acted "with more than their usual energy in raising and drilling troops."[38] San Martín, who had just been appointed governor of Mendoza, decided it was time to act. Months earlier he had promised Captain Bowles that he would not allow an anti-English faction to take power in Buenos Aires, and the only country at war with England was the United States.

San Martín had already started to take measures to fulfill his promise. At the end of 1814, after being defeated by the Spaniards, Jose Miguel Carrera arrived in Mendoza at the head a contingent of Chilean patriots. Taller than average, of slender but athletic frame, Carrera was a striking looking man. A high forehead, pale white skin that contrasted with his jet black hair, an aquiline nose, and lively black eyes completed the portrait of an aristocratic Spaniard born in the Americas. Carrera's attractive appearance was matched by a magnetic personality that quickly earned him the sympathy of strangers.[39] But his charm didn't work with San Martín, who considered Carrera a puppet of the United

States. After a few days he arrested Carrera, sent him to Buenos Aires under escort, and asked for his immediate deportation.

Carrera had been born in Santiago in 1785 in one of the city's oldest and most respectable families. A string of frivolous duels and scandalous affairs in his youth had led his embarrassed father to send him to Spain, where he joined the army. It was an experience that changed Carrera forever. For two years he participated in some of the bloodiest battles of the Peninsular War. Imbued with revolutionary ideals, in mid-1811 he returned to Chile "with no profit but a wish to join in the struggle for independence and no desire but to imitate Napoleon."[40] A few months later, Carrera led a coup d'état and placed himself at the head of the revolutionary government. Less than a year later he had declared independence from Spain and become Chile's first president. An internal power struggle led to his downfall in late 1813. Captured by the Spaniards, he managed to escape and return to Santiago where he wrested control of the army from Bernardo O'Higgins, the leader of an opposing faction. The battle lines were drawn. Carrera allied himself to the United States while O'Higgins, the son of an Irishman, sought England's support. Events favored the latter. In early 1814, one of the bloodiest naval battles of the War of 1812 took place in Chilean waters, a British squadron defeated Commodore Porter, thus ending American influence in Chile. A new offensive by the royalists forced Carrera and O'Higgins to forget their differences, but a crushing defeat deepened their enmity and forced them to seek exile in Mendoza, across the Andes.[41] It was there that San Martin met them. It was easy for him to pick sides. O'Higgins would be his man.

Fortunately for Carrera, by the time he arrived in Buenos Aires, Alvear, whom he had befriended while they served in the Spanish army, was supreme director. Alvear not only revoked Carrera's deportation but also supported his plans for an expedition to liberate Chile. This irked San Martin and increased his fears that a pro-American party had taken over in Buenos Aires. To oust Alvear he sought the assistance of his father-in-law, the leader of the Cabildo,* which represented the interests of the city's conservative elite, and a group of disgruntled army officers. He achieved his objective in April 1815. Alvear was forced to resign and seek exile in Rio de Janeiro. Captain Bowles explained to his government that Alvear had "the means of bringing the war in this country

---

*The Cabildo was a remnant of the Spanish colonial administration. In essence it controlled a city's government.

to a satisfactory termination, . . . [but] the apprehension to which his popularity amongst the troops had given rise" had led the Cabildo to oust him.[42]

Alvear's downfall didn't end the war with Spain. Despite England's efforts at mediation, the negotiations with Madrid stalled due to the intransigence of Ferdinand VII. Buenos Aires had no choice but to continue fighting. But the patriots now counted on a powerful ally. During the War of 1812, hundreds of American vessels, most of them financed by merchants in Baltimore and New York, had been commissioned as privateers. Privateers were not pirates but warships legally authorized by a belligerent government during a time of war to seek out and capture enemy vessels, known as prizes. They made money by receiving a percentage of the proceeds from the sale of captured prizes.[43] When the war ended, these privateers were unemployed. They made up a powerful mercenary navy that only needed a friendly government, at war, to survive. They soon found one in South America. In May 1815 the rebel government of Buenos Aires issued its first privateering patent to the *True Blooded Yankee*, an American privateer that had wreaked havoc on British trade during the recent war. Its captain was a certain George Sonntag, an enigmatic character who had served in the Russian military and was known as "the Cossack."[44] The *True Blooded Yankee* had left France in mid-1814 on her fifth cruise. By early December the privateer had arrived at the Brazilian port of Bahia with her crew in mutiny. The Portuguese authorities detained the ship and the American consul was forced to intervene. To his surprise, the consul learned that Sonntag's privateering patent had been issued by none other than Joel Roberts Poinsett on behalf of the rebel government of Chile.[45] The British consul in Bahia assured the Foreign Office that the career of the American corsair was "near its final close."[46] It proved to be an optimistic prediction; under the flag of Buenos Aires, the *True Blooded Yankee* would again trouble British authorities. Other American seamen followed in Sonntag's footsteps, and by the end of 1815, privateering was a thriving business in Buenos Aires.

The local newspapers reported that Napoleon had been taken to St. Helena, which with favorable winds was less than a month away. Maybe a daring privateer would try to rescue him.

5
Prometheus Chained

What was thy pity's recompense?
A silent suffering, and intense;
The rock, the vulture, and the chain,
All that the proud can feel of pain.

—Lord Byron, "Prometheus"

Napoleon's voyage to St. Helena took longer than usual. To approach the island at this time of the year it was generally necessary to sail along the Brazilian coast to Bahia and then tack to the east to take advantage of the strong southeasterly winds that prevailed in the South Atlantic. Admiral Cockburn instead sailed close to Africa despite the deadly calms that made this route so unappealing. He made this decision after being warned of the presence of a dangerous American privateer in Brazil that might attempt to snatch his prisoner.[1] It was the *True Blooded Yankee*.

By mid-October, after the *Northumberland* had sailed for two months, St. Helena appeared on the horizon. As its profile became clearer, the crew's excitement was replaced by an uneasy foreboding. Perhaps no island presented a more menacing and unfriendly appearance. Its coast looked like a massive wall of black rock. It was hard to imagine how such a place could be inhabited, for it seemed that in its creation humans "had been intentionally excluded."[2] Only after the ship rounded a tall rocky promontory were the first signs of human life apparent. With its neat little church, white houses built in a typical English style, and narrow streets lined with coconut trees, Jamestown, the tiny capital of St. Helena, presented a slightly more inviting prospect. The town was situated in a narrow ravine, flanked by steep, stony ridges that towered above it. To the left was Rupert's Hill, to the right, Ladder Hill, up whose almost vertical side led a zigzag road that led to Plantation House, the residence of the governor of St. Helena. As the ship approached the harbor, Napoleon's mood worsened. "I should have remained in Egypt. By now, I should be the Emperor of all the

East," he said.[3] Landing failed to cheer him up. Cockburn noted days later that Napoleon "appeared less resigned to his fate and has expressed himself more dissatisfied with the lot decreed him than he did before." Nevertheless, the admiral felt "quite confident" of being able to ensure "the safe custody of the general."[4]

Cockburn's confidence was the result of a misleading first impression. Although it seemed impregnable, St. Helena had been invaded several times during its long history. In 1673 the Dutch landed at the end of Lemon's Valley, on the western side of the island. Repulsed, they launched a second attack, this time landing at Bennet's Point, climbing up Swanley Valley, and then marching eastward to capture Jamestown. The following year a British expedition led by Sir Robert Munden succeeded in retaking the island. This time the invading forces landed at Prosperous Bay, only a mile away from Longwood Valley, site of Napoleon's future residence.[5] Colonel Wilks, the acting governor of St. Helena, warned Cockburn that he "must receive these impressions with considerable reservation if we are to contemplate an enemy well guided and perfectly informed." Wilks pointed out that "a stranger, or indeed any persons inspecting, for example, the post named Hold Fast Tom overlooking Prosperous Bay, would pronounce that particular spot to be an inaccessible precipice and all access from the bay within his view be nearly impracticable. Yet this is the very spot at which the party under Lieutenant Kedgwin ascended from Prosperous Bay when Sir R. Munden recovered the island from the Dutch. The bay is a favorite fishing place daily frequented from abroad, and of such landing places, all presenting a much easier access, there are fourteen."[6]

Heeding this warning, Cockburn set out to find a suitable residence for the imperial prisoner and his large entourage. Wilks suggested Longwood House, which was located on the Longwood Plateau, on the eastern side of the island. Originally built as a farmhouse, it served as a summer residence for the deputy governor of the island and was only used from July through November, when the heat in Jamestown was unbearable. During the rest of the year, the violent changes in temperature, the constant humidity, and the incessant wind made it inhospitable. But isolated and approachable only by a narrow road, it was an ideal place to keep the prisoner under strict surveillance.

In mid-December, after Longwood had been refurbished to accommodate him, Napoleon moved in with all his entourage, which included Count Henri Bertrand; his wife, Fanny, and their three children; Count Emmanuel de Las Cases and his son Count Charles Tristan de Montholon with his wife, Albine, and their young boy; and General Gaspard de Gourgaud. With the exception of

Count Bertrand, who at his wife's insistence moved to a separate house at Hutt's Gate, a mile away, everybody lived at Longwood.

Napoleon's companions made an odd group. Although only forty-two, Bertrand was an old veteran of the Grande Armée. Ever since the expedition to Egypt he had been part of the inner circle. In 1813 Napoleon had appointed him grand marshal of the palace, the highest-ranking position at the Imperial Court. After the first abdication, Bertrand had accompanied him to Elba. Trained as an engineer, he was dull and unimaginative but totally devoted to the emperor. His Irish wife, Fanny, was "a beautiful woman" according to Napoleon, who greatly enjoyed her conversation, and maybe something else. Although Bertrand would maintain a preeminent position in Napoleon's court in exile, Fanny's decision to live at Hutt's Gate left a vacuum that was quickly filled by Las Cases.

At fifty-two, Las Cases was the oldest of the group. A member of the aristocracy, he had left France shortly after the Revolution and had returned in 1802, after the Peace of Amiens. He then joined the Imperial Court, rose rapidly through the ranks and eventually became a member of the influential Council of State and served Napoleon loyally. After the first Bourbon abdication he sought exile in England. During the Hundred Days, Napoleon had reappointed him chamberlain of the Imperial Palace, and after learning of the disaster at Waterloo he had immediately gone to the Elysée Palace to support the emperor. Since becoming England's prisoner, Napoleon had increasingly relied on Las Cases, who was the only one of the "chosen four" who spoke English fluently. Due to Las Cases's penchant for intrigue, Napoleon called him "a little Talleyrand."[7]

Equally adept at intrigue was thirty-eight-year-old Count Montholon, also a member of the old nobility. Although he had participated in many of Napoleon's campaigns, Montholon's military career had not been particularly distinguished. In 1812 he had obtained the much-coveted appointment of chamberlain of the Imperial House but had been forced to resign after marrying a pretty divorcée named Albine Vassal without Napoleon's approval. Nevertheless, Montholon remained loyal to Napoleon until his first abdication. He then sought the favor of the Bourbons, who promoted him to general. Accused of misusing public funds, at the end of 1814 he avoided a court-martial thanks to the intervention of the Count of Artois. Napoleon did not reappoint him to any government post during the Hundred Days, but after Waterloo, Montholon showed up at the Elysée wearing the chamberlain's uniform and professing his devotion. Napoleon, who had known him for decades, did not question his presence or motives and allowed Montholon to follow him to Rochefort. Montholon was a vain and devious character, but Napoleon liked him and appointed him Longwood's manager.[8] His wife, Albine, eventually became Napoleon's mistress. He found she possessed "more firmness and *caractère* than most of her sex."[9]

At thirty-two, Gourgaud was the youngest member of the group and the only bachelor. A graduate of the Ecole Polytechnique and an artillery officer, he had fought in the Austrian, German, and Polish campaigns and later became Napoleon's chief aide-de-camp. Napoleon had rewarded him for his bravery and loyalty with a promotion and the title of baron. However, during the Elban exile Gourgaud had served under the Bourbons. When Napoleon returned to Paris in March 1815 he had refused to see Gourgaud and had only agreed to reappoint him as chief aide-de-camp after listening to his hysterical and tearful pleas. Gourgaud had been with Napoleon at Waterloo and, except briefly, had not deserted him since.* He was so stubborn and temperamental that Napoleon chided him for having the character of a "Corsican." At Longwood he served as Napoleon's equerry.

Two British subjects completed Napoleon's entourage: Barry O'Meara, who had become Napoleon's personal physician and had his own room at Longwood, and William Balcombe, in whose house Napoleon had spent his first two months on the island. Little is known of O'Meara's personal background, except that he was Irish. His name would have been familiar to Napoleon, as Daniel O'Meara, maybe a relative, had served in the Grande Armée as colonel of the Legion Irlandaise. As to Balcombe, he became Longwood's purveyor. Napoleon had become very fond of him and particularly of his teenage daughter, Betsy. Both were regular guests at Longwood. According to rumors Balcombe was the illegitimate son of England's prince regent.

With this motley set of companions and assisted by numerous staff supervised by Cipriani Franceschi, a mysterious Corsican who served as maître d'hôtel and moonlighted as a spy, Napoleon started a new life as England's prisoner. The strictest etiquette was followed, and Bertrand, Montholon and Gourgaud always wore their uniforms in Napoleon's presence. But the bickering started almost at once. Usually Bertrand and Gourgaud sided together against Las Cases and Montholon. If not, it was Madame Montholon against Madame Bertrand

---

*When he boarded the *Bellerophon,* Napoleon sent Gourgaud to England on another ship with a letter to the prince regent.

or Gourgaud. Napoleon had no patience for these petty quarrels and reminded everybody that they were still "on the battlefield."[10]

Longwood was not exactly an ideal place to encourage an amicable and cheerful atmosphere. Napoleon considered it "the worst place on the entire island." The house was uncomfortable and filled with vermin. The weather was dreadful: unbearable humidity, a constant wind that got on everybody's nerves, rain, fog, and except during the summer, a sky covered by hazy clouds. The surrounding landscape was equally uninspiring. To the north, the horizon opened up to the South Atlantic; the rest of the view included dull plains, huge rocks, deep ravines, and far away, the greenish slopes of Diana's Peak, St. Helena's tallest mountain.

To prevent an escape attempt, Colonel Wilks recommended that the prisoner be seen by an officer "within as short periods as courtesy and humanity shall admit" and that his staff should exclude "blacks and all natives of the Island, who are the best guides, and perhaps also persons who have been long resident and possess local information." Napoleon's movements were limited to a perimeter marked by the road leading to Alarm House, a house called Miss Mason's, and to sentry posts on the plains of Longwood and Deadwood.[11] If he wanted to visit any other part of the island, he had to be escorted by an English officer. Nobody could enter or leave Longwood's enclosure after sunset. All communications had to be screened by the governor or Lord Bathurst. Guns were used to send special messages. During Napoleon's captivity, a cannon was fired to announce dawn and sunset and also to announce the arrival of any ship at Jamestown.[12] A nearby telegraph station, which was linked with the island's efficient telegraph system, provided additional security. And as if this was not enough, Admiral Cockburn sent a detachment of marines to Ascension, an island seven hundred miles northwest of St. Helena that had been regularly used by American privateers during the recent war, to remove the facilities "which the said island might afford to persons desirous of effecting the escape of Napoleon Bonaparte."[13] Napoleon was furious at these restrictions and the presence of sentries outside his house. "You can be certain they have instructions to kill me," he told Gourgaud. "Oh! I know the English!"[14]

Despite these precautions, apparently at the end of the year the first plan of escape reached Longwood. Only Las Cases knew the secret and every day he scouted the horizon in search of "the vessel that was to end our exile." His hopes were fulfilled at the end of December. It was a clear day and from Longwood's veranda, Las Cases saw three ships, two of them hoisting an English flag. He immediately alerted Napoleon who, after a breakfast, asked him and Gourgaud to join him on a riding expedition. The regulations limiting Napoleon's movements were still loosely enforced, and no British officer came along. According to Las Cases, they rode to the end of the Longwood plateau and went down a very steep valley with deep ravines covered with sand and pebbles and strewn with brambles. It seems their destination was Prosperous Bay, one of the few points of the island that was easily accessible from the sea.

The uneven terrain forced Napoleon and his companions to dismount. Gourgaud took the horses through another road. Napoleon and Las Cases continued on foot and laboriously walked down the ravines. Napoleon quickly got tired and complained about his lack of exercise. After a while, more frustrated and exhausted, he exclaimed: "Only a Frenchman could come up with this idea!" Completely breathless, they managed to reach the bottom of the ravine. The trail ahead crossed over a narrow stream. Napoleon led the way but the surface cracked and both men started to sink "as if on broken ice." In a few seconds they were up to their knees in mud. "We were in danger of disappearing," remembered Las Cases, who extricated himself with difficulty and then helped Napoleon, who struggled to get out. It was a sobering experience. "My dear Las Cases, what a nasty adventure!" Napoleon said. "Can you imagine the reaction in Europe if we had died here? The hypocrites would have surely said that we were gobbled up for all our crimes!" Minutes later Gourgaud arrived with the horses and Napoleon returned to Longwood. Somebody noted that among the ships sighted earlier "was an American schooner."[15] Was it the *True Blooded Yankee* or a corsair sent by Jean Laffite?

This episode left a big impression on Napoleon, who imagined the reaction that the news of his death or injury while trying to escape would cause in Europe. It would be an indignity worse than being imprisoned at St. Helena. Even though he was a prisoner, he was still an emperor. He would never attempt to escape as a common criminal and risk death or capture or "attempt anything where concealment or disguise or bodily exertion were required." If he left St. Helena, he would do it "with his hat on his head and his sword at his side" as befitted his status.[16] Either the British government would set him free or his followers would have to rescue him by invading the island.

Napoleon considered both alternatives. In his view a political solution was possible "if the Jacobins become masters of Europe" or if Princess Charlotte succeeded George III as queen of England, bypassing her father, the prince regent.[17] As to an invasion of St. Helena, it wasn't such a far-fetched idea. Invading

St. Helena was a daunting enterprise but Napoleon had faced worse odds in his career. Although distance and the difficulties of landing weakened the odds of success, unlike Malta, Gibraltar, and Capri, St. Helena did not have a fortress. All that was needed was surprise and overwhelming force, as previous invasions had proved. Napoleon was quite familiar with the logistical and tactical challenges involved, as in 1804 he had planned on taking St. Helena from British hands. The objective was to use the island as a base to launch raids against East Indiamen returning from Asia. The expedition had included a squadron of four frigates and two brigs escorting two transport vessels carrying sixteen hundred men and failed due to the timidity and incompetence of its commander.[18] A year later the British used St. Helena as a base to launch an invasion of Buenos Aires.

The successful invasion of Capri in 1804 offered another precedent. With its steep, rocky cliffs and inaccessible coastline, the island resembled St. Helena. And Sir Hudson Lowe had been in charge of Capri's defense when French troops led by General Lamarque had successfully invaded the island in 1808. Lowe had twenty-three hundred men to defend the island, roughly the same number soon to be stationed at St. Helena. Lamarque only had eighteen hundred men, but counted on the element of surprise. He launched a diversionary attack on Capri while the bulk of his army attacked the opposite side of the island. Against all odds Lamarque had succeeded. It was a humiliation Lowe never forgot.[19]

Napoleon only had to update his plans of 1804. The invaders would need fast sailing ships and good sailors. It would be easy for Joseph to find them in America. Money was not an obstacle. The invaders could even use steamboats similar to those designed by the American inventor Robert Fulton. Napoleon believed steam power was a revolutionary technology that "could change the face of the world."[20] Joseph shared this view and while in the United States invested in several steamboat companies. Any rescue expedition would also need a good naval commander. Although there were many able and loyal French officers, it would be easier for an American or British officer to fool the Royal Navy cruisers guarding St. Helena. With the end of the war, there would be plenty of candidates. Perhaps Joseph could convince Lord Cochrane, who had been treated so shabbily by the British government, or maybe Commodore Stephen Decatur, the American naval hero. Joseph also had to pick a good general to lead the attack. Bertrand Clausel would be an excellent candidate. Napoleon thought Clausel was the ablest general in France and superior to any of his marshals when it came to planning and executing complex military operations.[21] "I see nobody capable of doing anything big," Napoleon said. His stepson Eugene had "a good head, judgment, and good qualities, but not that genius, that resolute character that distinguishes great men. Soult is incapable of being anything more than an army commander. There is only one who could succeed me: Clausel! He is young. He has resources and strength."[22] In late December, when Napoleon learned that Clausel had escaped to the United States, he was ecstatic.

The day after his perilous expedition to Prosperous Bay, Napoleon had a private conversation with Captain Charles Piontkowski, who had just arrived from England with secret messages.[23] The loyal Pole had escorted Napoleon from Malmaison to England but initially had not been allowed to follow him to St. Helena. Napoleon greeted him with kindness and asked for news of Joseph and "all the members of his family." The captain reported the efforts of Lord Holland to obtain Napoleon's release. According to Piontkowski, Napoleon was still "under the impression that the English government had only momentarily yielded to the necessity of making so evil a return for the noble trust that the Emperor had extended to them in his voluntary surrender."[24] Napoleon decided to wait before making a decision about his escape. The situation in France might deteriorate so fast under the Bourbons that maybe England would agree to restore Napoleon II and let him go to America.

2
1816

6
Wilson Enters the Scene

There is a turbulent sect which wants to stir the revolutionary ferment everywhere.

—Richelieu to Osmond, January 1816

During the first days of January, Sir Robert Wilson made final arrangements for the escape of Lavallette, who remained in hiding. Wilson made "quite a military expedition of the business" and, not surprisingly, reserved for himself the riskiest role: carrying the fugitive out of Paris. He planned to disguise Lavallette as an English officer and take him to Bavaria using false passports: one in the name of General Lewis Wallis, who happened to be Wilson's brother-in-law, the other for a fictitious colonel named Lesnock. Wilson obtained the passports from his friend Sir Charles Stuart, the British ambassador, who didn't ask any questions.[1] He also enlisted the help of Colonel Hely-Hutchinson* of the Horse Guards and a man named Ellister, both officers of the British army, "independent men, of liberal opinions, who might be disposed to play off a good trick on the government of the Bourbons."[2] Hutchinson was in charge of finding the best road out of Paris and following the carriage carrying Wilson and Lavallette with two extra horses that could be used to escape if they were discovered. Ellister guarded the fugitive's hiding place and on the day of the escape would leave Paris by a different route in Wilson's carriage.

The police were suspicious. A day before the planned departure, a gendarme came to the house where Lavallette was hiding and asked to see Colonel Lesnock. Sensing a trap, Ellister introduced himself as Lesnock. The agent, who was hoping to see Lavallette, was disconcerted and left.[3] The following morning, Wilson went ahead with the plan. "In five minutes, I had seated Lavallette

*He was the nephew of Lord Hutchinson, Second Earl of Donoughmore, under whom Wilson had served in Egypt.

and we were on our way to the gate of Clichy," he recalled later. "We met an English officer who appeared surprised at seeing a general officer whom he did not know, but my servant avoided all questions; I passed the barrier at a moderate pace; the gendarmes looked earnestly at us, but the presenting of arms gave Lavallette the opportunity of covering his face in returning the salute." Eventually, they made it to the border. Lavallette continued alone to Munich, where he hid under the protection of Eugene de Beauharnais. Wilson returned to Paris.

"I have just returned from a journey of about 350 miles and the first half was certainly the most interesting I ever made," Wilson wrote to Lord Grey three days later. He then provided a detailed account of his adventure.[4] To avoid having his letter intercepted, he sent it with a servant to the British embassy. But the police bribed the servant and got hold of it. The police also intercepted a letter to his brother with compromising language.[5] A day later Wilson was arrested. A police report described him as "1.89m,* chestnut hair and eyebrows, broad forehead, gray eyes, long nose, average mouth, round chin and oval face."[6] Bruce and Hely-Hutchinson were arrested soon after and Lord Kinnaird, who had also been involved, was deported from Paris. Defiant, Wilson complained that the main evidence against him had been obtained "by unfair means and yet on a letter so obtained we were arrested and extorted confessions."[7]

The Duke of Richelieu complained to the British ambassador that Wilson and his accomplices had taken "an active part in culpable maneuvers directed against the government" and been "accused of having favored the escape of Lavallette."[8] Richelieu was convinced it was part of a sinister conspiracy to dethrone the Bourbons organized by a "turbulent sect which wants to stir the revolutionary ferment everywhere it can find the means to do so. Under the pretext of bringing freedom to nations, it attacks the legitimate governments, and is essentially an enemy of law and order. The home base of this sect is in England and among its members are many members of the opposition."[9] Pozzo di Borgo, the Corsican-born Russian ambassador in Paris, reported that "the English revolutionaries" in Paris were becoming every day more dangerous and tried "to incite confusion in France, to coordinate with all the disaffected in this country, to irritate them against the Bourbons, to attack the conduct of the Duke of Wellington and particularly to make him unpopular in his own army." Their objective was to put Napoleon II or the Duke of Orleans on the throne and Wilson was "the man chosen to lead this work of confusion; his boldness and

---

* Six foot three.

energy were sure means of success, but his thoughtlessness and carelessness exposed him at every moment to be discovered and compromised."[10]

To the dismay of the Bourbons, Wilson became an instant hero. Even the devious Fouché, ostracized in Dresden, made "a pompous eulogium" of Wilson.[11] The English Radicals were also ecstatic. They felt that Wilson's feat atoned for the disgraceful passivity of the British ministers at the violation of the Treaty of Paris by the Bourbons. Henry Hunt thought that with their deed Wilson and his accomplices had "secured to themselves immortal honor."[12] The Ultras were enraged and demanded the death penalty for the three Englishmen. Richelieu expected them to spend at least two years in prison.[13] The British government, embarrassed and angered by the affair, soon realized that a harsh sentence would not only have a negative political impact at home but could also have serious repercussions in the army, where Wilson was very popular.

The ensuing trial was highly publicized and increased Wilson's popularity. Among the mostly female fans that attended it was Wilson's older sister, Fanny Wallis, who according to one of her French friends admired Napoleon "with an excess of enthusiasm." Fanny fearlessly flaunted her Bonapartism in the courthouse, wearing at all times "a tricolored scarf and a gold chain with a medal of Napoleon's head attached to it."[14] Her passion for the fallen French emperor was the result of a chance encounter in Paris in 1802, shortly after the Treaty of Amiens. One day while attending a public parade at the Tuileries she tried to get a close view of Napoleon and was hit by a guard so hard that she fell unconscious. Hours later she woke up inside the palace surrounded by the doctors and ladies of the court. Then she received a visit that changed her life forever. It was Napoleon in person who had come to check on her condition and to express his displeasure at the tragic accident. He assured Fanny that the soldier who had hit her would be punished. Fanny was so overwhelmed that she begged Napoleon to pardon the culprit as he had given her the opportunity to meet "the greatest man that the world had known." When she left Paris a few months later she had become a lifelong Bonapartist and for many years resented her brother for falsely accusing Napoleon of poisoning wounded soldiers in Egypt. Fanny felt that by rescuing Lavallette, Wilson had "nobly retrieved his character and obliterated all recollection of his former error."[15] Until she died in mysterious circumstances three years later, she rendered valuable services to the Bonapartist cause.

The prosecutor accused Wilson of being part of a conspiracy to overthrow the Bourbons.[16] In a heavily accented French that the female public found irresistible, Wilson denied all charges and attacked the Bourbon regime and the policies of his own government. When the prosecutor asked him why he had interfered with the internal affairs of France, he replied that the trial and sentencing of Lavallette was "not foreign to any Englishman" as it had violated "a ratified convention signed by an English general and ratified by an English government." He argued that the execution of La Bedoyere and Ney was an outrage to the "honor and good faith of the English nation."[17] Therefore, his involvement in Lavallette's escape was based on principles of "liberty and humanity." When Wilson finished his speech there were "great acclamations, which incensed the Judge, who shouted for the gendarmerie."[18] To the dismay of Richelieu and the Ultras, the three Englishmen were sentenced to just three months in prison. Having faced the possibility of the death penalty, Wilson was relieved. "Our battle has been fought and if we have not succeeded in redeeming our persons, we certainly have not left our honor in the hands of the Philistines," he explained to Lord Grey.[19] To Bonapartists everywhere, the renegade British general became a much-needed hero; to the supporters of absolutism, a feared enemy.

Richelieu worried that Lavallette's escape might shake the stability of the French monarchy. He saw Napoleon's long hand behind it and feared that his escape from St. Helena, which was reportedly being organized in America, could plunge France into a civil war.[20] Richelieu had valid reasons to be concerned. Across the border, some of Napoleon's most devoted supporters plotted the fall of the Bourbons. By early 1816 many high profile émigrés banned by the *ordonnance royale* had made Brussels their home.[21] Among them were General Brayer and his wife, Philippine, a "colorful creature given to coarse and picturesque language" who, despite being Bavarian, was a fanatical Bonapartist.[22] Brayer established contact with Joseph and started organizing the passage of a large number of discharged French officers to the United States and South America. The émigrés in Brussels frequently gathered at the house of "la merveilleuse" Fortunée Hamelin, a close friend of the late empress Josephine who at the end of 1815 had been forced into exile for her Bonapartist sympathies. Fortunée was in close contact with Eugene de Beauharnais.[23] According to French spies, the Bonapartist émigrés secretly gathered at the house of "the old priestess of their fallen idol" to revive "their old dreams and their wild hopes, which cannot be based on any fact." In the middle of March, as the first anniversary of Napoleon's return to Paris approached, the spies reported a troubling increase in conspiratorial activity. A meeting between Madame Hamelin and Colonel* Paul Latapie particularly caught their attention.[24]

Latapie had attracted the wrath of the Bourbons for having ordered the interception of the carriages of the Duke of Berri as he escaped from Paris on March 19, 1815. Born in 1789 in a noble family of Cahors, he had been orphaned during the Reign of Terror. At sixteen he joined Napoleon's army and received his baptism of fire at Austerlitz. He had then participated in the campaigns of Prussia, Poland, Spain, and Russia, where he had earned the order of the Legion of Honor. Put on half-pay during the first Bourbon restoration, during the Hundred Days he had rallied to Napoleon's cause and had been rewarded with an appointment in the Ministry of War. After the second restoration, Latapie was discharged, transferred to Lille, and put under strict police surveillance.[25] When he found out he would stand trial for treason he decided to escape. Using official stationery—which he must have kept from his stint at the Ministry of War—he falsified an order transferring him to Paris, where he planned to obtain the means to escape to America. The police quickly found out his whereabouts and tried to ensnare him in a "honey trap." But when the gendarmes showed up to arrest him, Latapie jumped out of the window. Disguised as a British officer, the following day he escaped to Brussels, where he joined Les Chevaliers de l'Epingle Noire, a secret society that plotted to dethrone the Bourbons.[26]

According to the *Morning Chronicle,* Austria would support Napoleon II; England, the Duke of Orleans; and Russia, the Prince of Orange.[27] The Duke of Richelieu believed that the first and the second alternatives were possible but that the third was absurd. Nevertheless, given that Orange was the brother-in-law of Tsar Alexander, he thought it merited some attention.[28] Although the Belgian prince was deemed sympathetic to the Bonapartist émigrés, installing him on the throne may have been simply a deception to distract the Bourbons.[29] French spies in Brussels, sure that the true objective of the exiled Bonapartists was to bring Napoleon's son to the throne, reported that Brayer's wife confidently stated that a "foreigner could never be the ruler of France; only Napoleon II would unite the country."[30] This had been Napoleon's objective when he abdicated.

Fearful of the political impact of these intrigues, Richelieu pressured the Belgian authorities to expel the most dangerous Bonapartist émigrés.[31] Brayer es-

---

* It is unclear whether his rank was colonel or major.

caped to Antwerp and months later sailed to the United States. Latapie and others fled to Aix-la-Chapelle, over the Prussian border. But the French ambassador in Brussels, the Marquis of La Tour du Pin, was determined to prevent Latapie from escaping. Even though he had served Napoleon for many years, La Tour du Pin had developed the zeal of the recently converted.* As soon as Latapie reached Aix-la-Chapelle he was arrested and put in secret confinement.

The Bourbon regime faced dangerous menaces from other quarters. The Duke of Richelieu had also been informed that the Austrian police had intercepted a letter addressed to Count Charles-Antoine Morand, a Bonapartist general exiled in Krakow, containing "an obscure allusion to St. Helena, Ascension and Philadelphia and a reference to future communications in cipher which General Morand is to receive from General Gilly explaining several circumstances of material importance regarding the present situation of Bonaparte."[32] These and other reports convinced Richelieu of the urgency of sending a new ambassador to the United States to uncover and derail Joseph's plans.

Richelieu also worried about England. When Parliament reopened in January 1816, Lord Holland launched the first of his crusades on Napoleon's behalf, attacking the legal foundation of his detention by questioning the treaties England had signed with the Allied powers to restore the Bourbon dynasty. Holland described England's postwar foreign policy as "a general and perpetual guarantee of all European governments against the governed." He felt that England, which prided itself on being a liberal nation, had become the supporter of despotism on the continent. Sending Napoleon to a barren island was an "unjustifiable and ungenerous" treatment that he would have never received had "he descended from a line of princes."[33] With this speech Lord Holland laid the ground for a more serious attack. But many in the House of Lords considered the Whig leader "too violent" and "a friend of Buonaparte" and did not support his motion.[34]

The Tory ministers, realizing that Napoleon's supporters in England could become a dangerous nuisance, launched a counteroffensive. It was necessary to dissuade any adventurous British subjects from emulating Wilson. After all, if he had saved Lavallette "why couldn't others attempt to do the same with his master?"[35] In April the government submitted new legislation to Parliament that imposed the death penalty on "any subject of, or owing allegiance to His

* La Tour du Pin's wife was the sister of Fanny Bertrand, who had accompanied her husband to St. Helena.

Majesty, his heir or successors" found guilty of rescuing or attempting to rescue Napoleon.[36] Lord Holland opposed the new law, arguing that Napoleon's detention was illegal and that his exile at St. Helena showed "neither magnanimity nor sound policy." But the law was passed without much opposition. Lord Holland issued a written protest: "To consign to distant exile and imprisonment a foreign and captive chief who after the abdication of his authority relying on British generosity had surrendered himself to us in preference to his other enemies is unworthy of the magnanimity of a great country."[37] The only other signatory of this document was Frederick Augustus, the Duke of Sussex, younger brother of the prince regent, the black sheep of the English royal family.[38] Sussex, known for his liberal ideas and was the leader of England's Freemasons. The new law incensed Napoleon's supporters in England. Hunt considered it "arbitrary, cruel, unjust and most cowardly" and predicted it would forever remain "a hateful and foul blot upon the statute book of England."[39] It was obvious that in the near term, Parliament would not release Napoleon or soften the terms of his captivity. The stakes had been raised.

In addition to lobbying on behalf of Napoleon, Lord Holland actively supported another cause dear to his heart: freeing the Spanish colonies from the yoke of Ferdinand VII. Although this cause was increasingly popular in England, the alliance with Spain had put the cabinet in a difficult position. According to American ambassador John Quincy Adams, Castlereagh's position was "decided against the South Americans, but by a political obliquity not without example, it is not so equivocally in favor of the mother country." And since the South Americans "may ultimately prove *de facto* independent," the British ministers held "ready to take advantage of the proper moment to acknowledge them, if it should occur."[40] This policy was at odds with England's liberal values and commercial interests, and Lord Holland was determined to correct it. In recent months he had taken under his wing a twenty-five-year-old Spaniard named Xavier Mina whose ambition was to liberate Mexico.[41] Mina also got financial support from Lord John Russell. A protégé of Lord Holland who would become prime minister during the Victorian era, Russell was the third son of the Duke of Bedford, head of one of "the proudest and the richest families in England." Considered "the boldest democrat possible," the young aristocrat was well known for his Bonapartist sympathies and had been one of the few Englishmen who had met Napoleon at Elba.[42]

During the Peninsular War, Mina had acquired fame leading a band of guerrillas. In 1811 he had been captured and spent almost three years in a French prison. When he returned to Spain after Napoleon's first abdication, Mina realized that Ferdinand VII was a much more despotic ruler than Joseph had ever been. Persecuted for his liberal views, he escaped to France in October 1814. What happened next is a matter of historical debate. At St. Helena, Napoleon assured O'Meara that during the Hundred Days Mina had asked him for help to dethrone Ferdinand VII.[43] He also told Las Cases that "some of the Spaniards who had been the most relentless against my invasion, who had acquired the greatest fame in the resistance, called immediately upon me: they had fought me, they said, as their tyrant; they were coming to implore me to be their liberator." Napoleon took these proposals so seriously that he put Joseph in charge of organizing an insurrection in Spain. It is unclear whether Mina ever got entangled in these intrigues, but after he arrived in London in the summer of 1815 he renewed his Bonapartist ties.[44] Spanish and British agents watching Mina's preparations at Liverpool reported that most of his officers were "French and Italians who were in the service of Bonaparte and Spaniards who were in that of Joseph Bonaparte in Spain" and that his objectives were hostile to the interests Ferdinand VII.[45] The Spanish ambassador asked Castlereagh to stop the expedition immediately. Castlereagh replied that since Mina had committed no crimes on English soil there were no grounds for his arrest. For a Spaniard accustomed to absolutism, respect for the law by a high-ranking government official did not ring genuine. Spanish suspicions of England's connivance with the South American rebels would never disappear.

At the end of April, as Mina sailed to New York, France was shocked by a new plot against the Bourbons. A mob stormed the city of Grenoble and proclaimed Napoleon II as the new ruler of France. Their leader claimed to be an agent of Marie Louise, Napoleon's estranged wife.[46] Wilson, who was still serving a three-month sentence, was linked to this conspiracy. The British general was amused. "In yesterday's *Journal des Débats,* I see myself figured as one of the Brissot, Robespierre and Buonarotti* conspirators," he wrote to Lord Grey.[47] The authorities acted swiftly and all suspected plotters were executed.[48] But within days, the Paris police uncovered two other Bonapartist plots.[49] At the same time, rumors intensified that several expeditions to rescue Napoleon had left from America. Richelieu had no doubt that everything was part of a conspiracy to overthrow the Bourbons.[50]

---

* Filippo Michele Buonarotti (1761–1837) was one of the leaders of the French Carbonari.

Still in prison, Wilson waited for his release and planned his next move. Convinced that England under the Tories was on the road to despotism, he set his sights on the New World. "America seems to be the only country where an individual obnoxious to any of the European governments can avoid the reciprocal actions of their engines of tyranny."[51]

7
Dreaming of New Empires

Oh, dull Saint Helen! Why thy gaoler nigh—
Hear! Hear Prometheus from his rock appeal
To earth, air, ocean, all that felt or feel
His power and glory, all who yet shall hear.
                    —Lord Byron, *The Age of Bronze,* Canto 5

"A year ago I was at Elba," Napoleon said. Napoleon started the year in a gloomy mood. The incessant rains contributed to a depressing atmosphere at Longwood. Days later an unexpected visit shook Napoleon's gloom. An English sailor sneaked past the sentries to pay him his respects and wish him happiness. If we are to believe Las Cases, the poor man had brought flowers and was so overwhelmed with emotion that he had tears in his eyes. Napoleon was touched and told Las Cases: "What is the power of imagination! What it cannot do to men! Here are some people who did not know me, who had never seen me, they had just heard of me; and what do they not feel, what would they not do for me! And the same oddity can be found in all countries, in all ages, in both sexes! This is fanaticism! Yes, imagination rules the world!"[1] He would need this kind of devotion to succeed in his next campaign.

Napoleon's mood improved a few days later when he learned that Joseph was safe in the United States. "If I were in his place, I would build a great empire in all of Spanish America," he told Montholon.[2] He then turned to Gourgaud and said that Joseph had all the money he needed and, unaware of the tragic fate of his brother-in-law, added: "Murat will probably join him."[3] Napoleon believed Ferdinand VII was a "fool and coward" who by his "bigoted misconduct" would inevitably lose all of Spain's colonies.[4] In his opinion, with an army of five thousand men led by his best generals and the help and support of the patriot leaders, all of South America could be quickly brought under Joseph's control. The Spaniards would not be able to stop him. And in contrast to that bloody war in Spain where the people had fought against him, in America they would rally to his support and see him as a liberator from Spanish despotism. Napoleon thought the colonial system was over for everybody, even England. "You grow tired of waiting for orders from five thousand miles away, tired of obeying a government which seems foreign to you because it is remote, and because of necessity it subordinates you to its own local interest, which it cannot sacrifice to yours," he once said.[5]

To conquer the Spanish colonies Joseph only had to follow the plan proposed by Aaron Burr in 1810, which required seizing the Spanish port of Pensacola in West Florida, the only natural harbor in the Gulf of Mexico that could berth large ships carrying troops and supplies from Europe. Florida would then serve as the launching pad to attack Veracruz, the gateway to Mexico, and eventually the rest of South America.* As Burr had pointed out, the invaders would be welcomed by the locals, as it would not be a conquest "but only the taking of them away from the Spanish domination."[6] The next step after occupying Florida was to cut the communications between Mexico and Peru by taking the fortress of Portobello on the Isthmus of Panama. Once in control of Portobello, Napoleon's generals could sail down the Pacific coast, and following the footsteps of Francisco Pizarro, conquer Peru, the former Incan empire. Alternatively or in parallel, Peru's conquest could be attempted from Chile. Then Joseph could sell Florida to the United States for $2 million, as Napoleon had proposed to Madison in 1811.† It wasn't such a crazy idea. Madison was still president; the United States still coveted the Floridas; and a deal with Joseph could avoid a war with Spain. Joseph in turn could use the proceeds to finance the creation of a new empire in the Spanish colonies. And if Madison didn't agree, Joseph could offer Florida to England in exchange for Napoleon's freedom.

But who could lead such an ambitious enterprise? Joseph had already shown himself to be a poor military commander. He would need the help of Lucien, who was more decisive, and a general with energy, ambition, and determination. Joseph had plenty to choose from, as Clausel, Brayer, and Lefebvre-Desnouettes had all arrived or were on their way to the United States.[7] Lallemand, who had given so many proofs of his loyalty, could not be discarded. Napoleon thought he had the "sacred fire." Where was he now? Piontkowski told him he had been sent to Malta as a prisoner.

---

*This was the same spot from which Hernan Cortes had started his conquest of Mexico in 1519.

†The transaction had never been closed due to the disastrous campaign in Russia and the end of Bonapartist rule in Spain.

Napoleon didn't expect to remain at St. Helena much longer. He believed the turmoil in France would work in his favor. And neither he nor his supporters in England had given up hope of obtaining his release by a parliamentary measure. If nothing else worked, he would have to resort to force. His reconnaissance of the island continued. During his morning rides he explored Longwood's surroundings. Countess Bertrand noted that Napoleon's "quickness of observation never so much excited my astonishment as during these rides and promenades."[8] One morning in early January, he decided to visit Sandy Bay, one of the few spots in the island where invading troops could easily disembark.[9] Captain Poppleton, the British orderly officer stationed at Longwood, unexpectedly showed up to accompany him on the ride and Napoleon abandoned the idea. Days later Cockburn visited Longwood. During dinner the admiral mentioned that another infantry regiment would soon arrive to reinforce the island's garrison. Napoleon laughed. "Don't you have enough troops here? A frigate would be much more valuable than a regiment." He told Cockburn that only ships could assure the safety of the island, as an attack made with superior forces would always succeed if distance prevented immediate reinforcements.[10]

Two days later, Napoleon went on another reconnaissance ride with Count Bertrand. Poppleton followed them at a close distance. Annoyed at his presence Napoleon ordered Bertrand to ask the captain not to follow them so closely. Slightly embarrassed, Poppleton agreed to ride far behind. He soon wished he hadn't. After riding over a hill that temporarily kept them out of Poppleton's sight, Napoleon ordered his companions to escape at full gallop. Unable to find them, the captain returned to Longwood and sent a frantic message to Cockburn: "General Bonaparte has escaped!"[11] To Poppleton's relief, Napoleon was back at Longwood at sunset. But Poppleton had learned his lesson. A few days later when Napoleon decided to go on another riding expedition, Poppleton insisted on riding alongside him. Napoleon considered this demand such an affront that he never again rode outside the limits.[12] As far as his plans were concerned, it didn't matter anymore.

From then on Napoleon spent most of his days dictating his memoirs to Las Cases. The name of Lewis Goldsmith, the editor of the *Anti-Gallican,* a London weekly, came up during their conversations. Goldsmith had moved to Paris after the French Revolution and returned to London in 1809. Then, with the support of the British government he had founded the *Anti-Gallican* and become one of Napoleon's harshest critics. Napoleon told Las Cases that Goldsmith now insulted "the idol that he had for a long time praised."[13] Interestingly, during a conversation with Cockburn, Napoleon said that while he was planning his invasion of England, Goldsmith had provided him with valuable intelligence and had been well compensated for it.[14] Given Goldsmith's strange conduct during Napoleon's captivity, these comments seem odd. But Goldsmith was a master of the art of double and triple dealing.[15] On whose payroll was he now? In the next months the *Anti-Gallican* would be connected to St. Helena in a bizarre way.

Napoleon's boring routine was occasionally broken by news from Europe, usually with a three-month delay. The tragic deaths of Murat and Ney saddened him, but the report of Lavallette's escape, which reached him in late March, lifted his spirits. "We shivered with joy on our rock," remembered Las Cases. He and others were puzzled at the involvement of Sir Robert Wilson and wondered whether he was the same man who had falsely accused the emperor of killing his own soldiers in Egypt. "And why not?" asked Napoleon. "How little do you know about people and their passions! How do you know he is not one of these burning, passionate spirits, who at that time only wrote what he believed to be true? Besides, then we were enemies, we fought each other, today that we are beaten, he knows better. Maybe he was deceived, misled or dissatisfied, and maybe he now wishes to help us as much as he then sought to harm us."[16]

To confirm his views about Wilson, Napoleon asked William Warden, the surgeon of the *Northumberland,* if he "knew anything of his military character and the tendency of his writings." Warden said he didn't know. Napoleon insisted and asked him "from what motive this officer has acted in the escape of Lavallette, the decided and avowed friend of the man whom he has so wantonly calumniated?" Warden replied that undoubtedly "they were such as did honor to his heart," maybe "an adventurous and romantic spirit might have governed him." Napoleon was pleased with this answer, which agreed with his opinion, and added: "I believe every word you have said, at the same time you may be assured that money would not have been wanting to save Lavallette. I desire you also to give your particular attention to my opinion, which is a decided one. That this act of Sir Robert Wilson for the preservation of Lavallette, is the commencement of his recantation of what he has written against me." Napoleon could have been reading the future. For as Las Cases noted years later, "Nobody showed a deeper indignation about Napoleon's treatment or gave stronger evidence of his burning desire to see them stopped [than Wilson]."[17]

Napoleon expected a change in his situation. He learned from Piontkowski that Lord Holland would raise the issue of his detention in Parliament. His hopes may have been encouraged from other quarters. One day in early March, he went for an early outing with Las Cases. During the ride, he dismounted from his horse five or six times and scanned the horizon with his field glasses. He could see several ships in the distance, one flying a tricolor flag. When they returned to Longwood, he talked privately with Las Cases "about serious subjects, which I cannot trust to lay on paper."[18] Was it about the ships that kept hovering around St. Helena?

Cockburn suspected that a rescue plan was afoot and sent a detachment of marines to Ascension with orders to occupy the island and resist "any sudden attempt of any persons of any station whatsoever to dispossess you" and prevent "any nation desirous of effecting the escape of Napoleon Buonaparte from possessing themselves of that island, thereby to procure shelter for the shipping they might employ on such errand and otherwise to afford them facilities for such undertaking." Cockburn's orders emphasized that "if general Bonaparte or any of the French persons who accompanied him hither, and in the event of him, or any of them being discovered in any such vessels or boat, to take forcibly if necessary him, or them as the case may be, on board His Majesty's ship for the purpose of them being conveyed back to St. Helena unless they produce a certificate from under my hand."[19] When the marines disembarked at Ascension they found a message on the beach saying "May the Emperor Napoleon live forever!"[20]

Napoleon followed the news from Europe with interest. The French Bourbons had unleashed the "white terror" with fury, and popular unrest was on the rise throughout the continent. Even England was in the midst of political turmoil. "Ah! How unfortunate that I wasn't able to reach America!" Napoleon exclaimed with frustration. "Even from another continent I could have protected France against reaction! Fear of my return would have bridled this senseless violence; my name alone would have had the power to contain all excess!" Deep down he was convinced that the ideas of the French Revolution would eventually succeed and that not only would he remain the leading light of the rights of free people but even after his death his name would be "the war cry of their efforts and the currency of their hopes." Napoleon predicted that a revolutionary fervor would soon spread throughout the continent. Men would no longer be divided by their nationality but by their opinions. It would all boil down to legitimacy versus democracy. He had no doubt about the ultimate outcome of this struggle. It would be only a matter of time before the principles of the French Revolution succeeded.[21]

The arrival of Sir Hudson Lowe at St. Helena in mid-April opened a new battlefront for Napoleon. Their relationship started on the wrong footing. Napoleon took an immediate dislike to his new guardian. Lowe hadn't even led a British regiment in his entire career. His haughty attitude made matters worse. Lady Holland's efforts in London to predispose him in favor of his prisoner had been in vain. Although Bathurst had advised him to adapt his instructions as much as possible to local circumstances, Lowe enforced them in the strictest possible manner.[22] Even before arriving at St. Helena, Lowe was obsessed with the possibility of Napoleon's escape. He had no doubt that many British subjects would gladly help him. He had been warned in London that an officer serving in the island's garrison had Jacobin ideas and also that the strong winds prevalent at St. Helena "would very quickly carry a small boat (obtained and easily launched with connivance) over to the Spanish settlement now so much disturbed of South America."[23] Lowe took this warning seriously. If Napoleon escaped, it would be the end of his career.

Napoleon realized that his new guardian would make his life impossible and only a few days after his arrival, the atmosphere at Longwood changed dramatically. The bad weather exacerbated Napoleon's displeasure. "In this damned island there is neither sun nor moon to be seen for the greatest part of the year. Constant rain and fog. It is worse than Capri. Have you ever been at Capri?" he asked O'Meara.[24] Napoleon was well aware of Lowe's pathetic performance defending Capri. If Lamarque had defeated Lowe, there was no reason why Clausel or Lallemand could not do it. Cipriani, Napoleon's maître d'hôtel and spy, also didn't miss the connection. The wily Corsican, more experienced in the art of spying and intrigue than in managing staff, had been in Capri at the time of Lamarque's invasion. "It was to Cipriani that the taking of Capri was owing," remembered Montholon, "and we always felt inclined to laugh when we saw Sir Hudson Lowe and Cipriani in each other's presence at St. Helena."[25]

Suspicious that Lowe would try to plant a spy at Longwood and that O'Meara was the obvious candidate, Napoleon decided to preempt the situation. "Are you my private surgeon or surgeon *d'un galère* and are you expected to report my conversations?" Napoleon asked his doctor. Taken slightly aback, O'Meara replied that he would never agree to be Lowe's spy. The other person who might have spied on Napoleon was Alexander Baxter, a physician who had served under Lowe for many years and was more malleable and reliable than O'Meara. But Napoleon always refused to see Baxter. "What a *coglione* to think that a man in my situation would take a surgeon selected and sent to him by his jailer? Being sent by him, I could have no sure idea that he hasn't come for the purpose of poisoning me," he told O'Meara.[26]

Napoleon was convinced that Lowe would to try to kill him. Once when he fell ill, Lowe suggested he would send one of his officers to check on him. But Napoleon was determined to defend his privacy. "Any person who endeavors to force his way into my apartment shall be a corpse the moment he enters it," he said. "Then I should be of course dispatched."[27] O'Meara tried to dissuade him from these ideas and argued that the British government would never attempt to assassinate him. Napoleon did not agree and next time he saw Lowe he said: "If Lord Castlereagh has given you orders to poison us and kill us please do it as soon as possible. I have governed and know that there are men for all missions: there are men of honor for honorable missions and others for dishonorable missions." Lowe calmly replied that he hadn't come to Longwood to receive lessons. "It isn't for the want of needing them," Napoleon retorted. Barely containing his rage, Lowe turned around and left. Later that evening, Napoleon assured Las Cases that he would be assassinated at St. Helena.[28]

Shortly after this heated exchange, Las Cases proposed a new escape plan. The organizer was a captain of an East Indiaman, and according to Montholon the plan had a good chance of success.[29] The captain came to Longwood to communicate his proposal to Napoleon, with Las Cases translating. Napoleon listened carefully and then asked the captain what kind of reward he expected. "Nothing!" was his emphatic reply. Not satisfied, Napoleon asked what motivated him to make a proposal that could expose him to death. The captain said that he wasn't doing it gratuitously. "Can you imagine having my name linked to yours?" he said. Napoleon smiled, thanked the captain and told him he would give him an answer the next day. But after three hours of deliberation, and despite Las Cases's insistence, he discarded the plan.[30] Weeks later, in early June, another escape plan came to Napoleon's attention. We ignore its details, but its timing was perfect as an eclipse of the moon was expected.[31] Napoleon again refused to consider it. He thought any bodily exertion or the use of disguise was beneath his imperial dignity. If this new plan came from Europe, it could have only arrived on board the HMS *Mosquito*.[32] It wouldn't be the last time this vessel would be implicated in the confusing affairs of St. Helena.

Napoleon never abandoned hope of leaving St. Helena. And when he learned that Joseph had purchased large tracts of land near Canada and that a large number of French émigrés had gathered around him, he said: "America was our asylum in every respect. It is an immense continent where you can enjoy a very special kind of freedom. If you are sad, you can get on your carriage and travel a thousand miles enjoying the pleasures of a simple traveler. In America you are everybody's equal; you can get lost at your will in the crowd without difficulty, with your customs, your language, your religion, etc." Napoleon believed that a Bonapartist enclave in America would soon attract the most talented people in the world, who "would provide a sound refutation to the system that currently rules Europe." He told Las Cases that if he had reached America, he would have founded the core of "a new homeland," as he had planned at Elba. In this new empire Las Cases could have ruled over the provinces of Orinoco, Napoleon joked.* "I would have loved to realize this dream," he said more seriously. "It would have brought me new glory."[33]

It was not too late. He recognized that his presence in America "would be of an immense interest to our poor France, it would stop the royal reaction. I would be the nightmare of the King." On the other hand it would be better for his son if he remained at St. Helena. "My martyrdom will return him the crown of France."[34] Napoleon had still not abandoned hope that the British government would set him free. He told Montholon that if Lord Holland didn't succeed in Parliament, a revolution would do it.[35]

By the beginning of the Southern Hemisphere winter, all evidence in Lowe's hands confirmed the existence of plots to rescue his prisoner. Worried that certain locals were involved, Lowe published edicts all over Jamestown announcing that Parliament had passed a resolution "adjudging capital punishment" to anybody found guilty of assisting in Napoleon's escape.[36] Among the evidence that troubled Lowe was a letter addressed to Count Bertrand that had been intercepted. The letter, which had no date but was postmarked in London, provided Bertrand with detailed instructions for effecting Napoleon's escape:

> I told you before the boat that will drift to the back of the island will be in the shape of an old cask but so constructed that by pulling at both ends to be seaworthy and both boat and sail which will be found inside will be painted to correspond with the color of the sea and when the Emperor and one more, which will be requisite to transform the boat as I said above, is all ready, he must bear away right before the wind, for the ship, after

---

*Napoleon's comment was a pun on the similarity of Las Cases's name with that of Fray Bartolome de las Casas, a Spanish priest who denounced the treatment of the American natives by the conquistadors and attempted to create an experimental colonial enclave in Venezuela, in the province of Orinoco.

drifting the boat to the island, will maneuver so as to get right to leeward and display a light of one of the portholes, for to show it at the masthead would endanger it to be seen by the enemy.

"It will depend on circumstances what port in the United States His Majesty will land at, but he may depend upon the most cordial and fraternal reception," added the mysterious correspondent. The Americans adored Napoleon "as a deity" and "to remedy his loss of France they will seize on all South America." Then Spain and Portugal would be invaded, and once this was accomplished, the French Bourbons would fall. "There is not the least doubt but the exalted hero will have greater fleets & army than ever." The strange letter was signed "L. Meu."[37]

Lowe was still trying to figure out what to make of this letter when another note from the same correspondent was intercepted. This one was addressed directly to Napoleon and advised him to "exert yourself to the utmost to get away before the new regulations take place or else your situation will be most critical. I told Bertrand all about the methods and sent him everything for your use. Be circumspect and everything will go well. God grant you speedy release is the sincere wish of your never failing friend." The whole thing was bizarre.[38] Why would anybody send details of such plans through the post office? Also, it is hard to imagine that Napoleon would agree to climb down a cliff using a rope. Was this the plan he had discarded a few days earlier? Was it a joke? Was Napoleon trying to torment his guardian? Whatever it was, it intensified Lowe's paranoia.

It was at this time, mid-June, that representatives of Austria, France, and Russia arrived on St. Helena. Baron Barthelemi von Sturmer, recently married to a young and beautiful French woman who was strongly attached to Napoleon and was suspected of being a secret messenger, represented the Austrian emperor.[39] Sturmer had also brought along a botanist named Philip Welle, who had been sent by the Austrian emperor to gather some native plants from St. Helena for his garden at Schönbrunn.* The Bourbon representative was Claude Marie Henri, Marquis de Montchenu, a bumbling old French aristocrat of firm royalist opinions. "The greatest blockhead on earth" according to Napoleon, who knew him well. "When you have seen Montchenu, you have seen all the old nobility of France before the Revolution . . . ignorant, vain and arrogant. They

---

* Welle had been sent to St. Helena at the suggestion of Alexander von Humboldt, a close friend of Aimé Bonpland, the coauthor of the *Voyages aux Régions Equinoxiales*.

have learned nothing and forgotten nothing."[40] Captain de Gors, who was probably a spy of Artois, accompanied the old marquis as secretary. Count Alexander Balmain de Ramsay, thirty-seven and the youngest of the three commissioners, represented the tsar of Russia. A man of liberal views, some thought he was not the right man for the job.[41] In his first dispatch Balmain reported that Napoleon was "in good health and promises to live a long time. As yet nobody has been able to discover whether he is resigned to his fate or whether he entertains hopes. It is said that he bases any hope of leaving the island on the English opposition." The Russian diplomat reported that St. Helena was the "saddest, the most isolated, the most unapproachable, the easiest to defend, the hardest to attack, the most unsociable, the poorest, the dearest and especially the most appropriate for the use to which it is now put."[42]

On the same ship came a gift for Napoleon from John Cam Hobhouse, a well-known English Radical of strong Bonapartist sympathies. It was a volume of letters he had written to Lord Byron from Paris during the Hundred Days. The book cover was stamped with the words "Imperatori Napoleone" in gold letters.[43] Lowe glanced at the book and decided to take it away, although nothing in Bathurst's instructions authorized him to do so. Although Napoleon didn't care much about the book he was annoyed at Lowe's high-handedness.

The first anniversary of Waterloo brought Napoleon painful memories. "Incomprehensible day," said he in a tone of sorrow. "Concurrence of unheard of fatalities! . . . Was there treachery, or only misfortune? Alas! Poor France!" He then covered his eyes with his hands as if seeing the battlefield and added. "In that extraordinary campaign, thrice, in less than a week's space, I saw the certain triumph of France, and the determination of her fate slipped through my fingers."[44] Despite Lowe's constant harassment and the realization that, without a cabinet change, England would never set him free, Napoleon did not lose hope.[45] He had just learned that Lord Holland and the Duke of Sussex had supported a motion on his behalf in the House of Lords.[46] It was an encouraging sign. Napoleon now talked about joining Joseph in America, surrounded by "a little France."[47]

8
A Bonapartist Court in Philadelphia

Joseph loves me sincerely and would do anything for me.
—Napoleon to O'Meara, St. Helena, 1816

"What I like most about this country is the freedom that one can enjoy," Joseph wrote to his wife in January 1816.[1] After almost six months in the United States, he had comfortably settled in as head of the Bonaparte clan in exile. In the early spring he moved to Philadelphia, where he established his residence. Around this time, the Bonapartist community gained another celebrity: Marshal Emmanuel de Grouchy. Grouchy, fifty-five, was the highest-ranking officer of the Grande Armée to seek exile in America. Although a member of the old nobility, he had supported the French Revolution. In 1796, after leading an ill-fated invasion of Ireland, Grouchy had joined Napoleon in Italy and tied his fortune to him. A gifted cavalry commander, in the Russian campaign he had performed extraordinary feats of bravery. During the Hundred Days he had quickly rallied to Napoleon's cause, quashing royalist resistance in the south and arresting Louis XVIII's nephew.[2] Napoleon had rewarded him with a marshal's baton and, during the Waterloo campaign, put him in charge of a large division. But on that fateful June 18, Grouchy was miles away from the battlefield, pursuing the remnants of the Prussian army. Ever since, he has been blamed for the defeat of the French army.

Despite the shadow cast by Waterloo, Grouchy enjoyed a reputation as one of Napoleon's legendary marshals, and his arrival caused great excitement and was amply reported by the press. After meeting Joseph, Grouchy contacted Stephen Girard, a native of Bordeaux who had become one of the wealthiest men in the United States. Girard had built his enormous fortune trading overseas, and his considerable fleet regularly touched on the ports of Europe, South America, and Asia. Huge profits had allowed him to establish a powerful bank in Philadelphia. During the recent war with England, Girard had almost single-handedly saved the U.S. Treasury from bankruptcy. As a result he had access to the top ranks of the Madison administration. But Girard had not forgotten his roots. He was a strong believer in the French Revolution and belonged to a Masonic lodge established by his compatriots in Philadelphia. Grouchy introduced Girard to Joseph and the two of them soon became friends. Over the years the banker would render Joseph valuable services.[3]

Two other veterans of Napoleon's Imperial Guard, generals Charles Lefebvre-Desnouettes and Henri Lallemand, also arrived in Philadelphia at this time. In Washington, Philadelphia, and Baltimore, Grouchy, Clausel, Lallemand, and Lefebvre-Desnouettes were "treated with great sympathy."[4] At every event they attended, Napoleon was the topic of conversation. When asked what made him a great man, Grouchy replied: "The great art of Bonaparte was the firmness and determination that accompanied all that he undertook. . . . There was a certain attraction in his manners, something which interested . . . [the French] people [who] were charmed to find in the chief of government a brilliant soldier, an excellent mathematician, a man of science, that he inspired respect."[5] The popularity of the former French emperor was at an all-time high in the United States. Napoleon had "never showed himself more fully as a hero than he now does," wrote an influential journalist in Baltimore.[6]

In addition to rubbing elbows with the East Coast establishment, Napoleon's former generals also established contact with exiled South American rebel leaders. Luis de Onis, the alert Spanish ambassador, soon learned about these contacts. Months earlier, he had complained without success to the U.S. State Department about an expedition to invade Mexico being organized in New Orleans by the rebel leader Alvarez de Toledo and General Humbert, whom he had long suspected of being Napoleon's agent.[7] The French ambassador, who had now conveniently switched his allegiance to the Bourbons, warned Onis that Grouchy planned to join Toledo's expedition and that Clausel was on his way to New Orleans to meet Mexican rebel leaders.[8] Onis also learned that Joseph was "trying to buy an immense property near the border with Canada and that he intends to set up an establishment there for his family and all the French who support the cause of the Bonapartes" and was organizing his brother's rescue. "Someone named Kalender or Carpenter, who captained one of the most terrible corsairs of this country, has proposed to go to St. Helena at his own expense to bring Napoleon Bonaparte back here. He only asks for 100,000 *duros** in escrow to be paid if he succeeds in rescuing that illustrious prisoner. I do not know whether Joseph accepted the offer but it is very likely that he will do so if it is true that his fortune is 10 million *duros,* even without counting the diamonds that his wife is bringing from Europe."⁹

Onis was right about Joseph's fortune and about his links with the Yankee privateers and the South American rebels. He quickly realized that the Bonapartist émigrés were as dangerous to the Spanish Bourbons as to their French relatives. Where else could Napoleon go but America? With the passing weeks, Onis' fears about the complicity of the United States with the Bonapartists in intrigues against Spanish interests intensified. In early March, Onis sent an urgent warning to Madrid: "Every day more French revolutionaries or Bonapartists arrive and they are all received with particular attention. I have informed Your Excellency that General Clausel was going to New Orleans to take up the cause of the insurgents. I have similar suspicions about Marshal Grouchy. He remains in Washington receiving the highest proofs of consideration from this government. His presence in the most disagreeable point in the globe cannot be for pleasure. He must be negotiating something extremely important with the [U.S.] government."

Onis believed Napoleon's hand was behind these intrigues. He observed that escaping from St. Helena was not impossible, "particularly if one of the powers considered it useful to its objectives to renew the scenes of horror and violence in Europe or to start them in this continent."¹⁰

Joseph was preparing to launch his campaign but needed guidance from Napoleon. The problem was communicating with him. It was more a question of timing than delivery, as Napoleon had effectively managed to circumvent Lord Bathurst's restrictions.¹¹ But it could take between three and six months for a message to reach St. Helena. As Joseph and Napoleon soon found out, during that time the world could change radically thus rendering any instructions irrelevant. Although Joseph had not yet received any messages from Napoleon, they had talked about the American project at Malmaison. Joseph would never attempt such an ambitious undertaking without his brother's blessing. In the meantime he started organizing his staff under the leadership of Grouchy, who as if wanting to atone for his absence at Waterloo, undertook his role with

---

* A *duro* was equivalent to a dollar or a peso.

great zeal. Bertrand Clausel, who had served as Grouchy's chief of staff during the first Italian campaign, was second in command.[12] Lefebvre-Desnouettes and Henri Lallemand completed Joseph's cadre of military advisers, which was expected to expand with the arrival of Brayer, Fressinet, Vandamme, and the elder Lallemand. In addition to this first-rate military talent, Joseph counted on the advice of some of the best and the brightest of Napoleon's court such as Count Regnault de St. Jean d'Angely, former conseiller d'etat; Count Pierre Real, former prefect of police; and several exiled luminaries from the Institut de France such as Jean-Augustin Penieres, Nicholas Quinette, and Joseph Lakanal. It would have been hard to find a better group of people to assist Joseph in his projects.

Onis was now on full alert and his agents throughout the East Coast kept him informed of the movements of the émigrés. At the end of May, he learned that the *Orb,* a fast-sailing schooner, was about to depart to Buenos Aires from Baltimore carrying on board a certain Fournier, "the same who brought Bonaparte back from Elba" and "a large number of French officers." The ship was partly owned by an American businessman named David Curtis DeForest, one of the largest outfitters of privateers sailing under the rebel flag of Buenos Aires.[13] Onis learned that "some cannons have been hidden in the cargo and are to be armed after sailing." He also worried about two other vessels that were ready to depart from Baltimore. "Maybe they will join the *Orb* and proceed to Buenos Aires and from there attempt a *coup de main* on St. Helena to rescue Bonaparte. General Lallemand, younger brother of the man who was Bonaparte's great favorite, is rumored to be in one of these schooners. Other versions indicate that Marshal Grouchy and generals Clausel and Lefebvre Desnouettes, who recently went from Philadelphia to Baltimore, will also embark on the expedition."[14]

Despite Onis' protests, the *Orb* eventually left port but no French general was on board.[15] It is unlikely that she was part of an expedition to rescue Napoleon but she could have been on a scouting mission and she could very well have been the Buenos Aires privateer spotted hovering around St. Helena months later. Onis was on to something. Almost at the same time, British agents independently confirmed that Grouchy, Clausel, Lallemand, and Lefebvre-Desnouettes were planning to "put themselves in some manner in connection with the insurgents in Mexico and South America."[16]

Pedro Gual, a leader of the Venezuelan insurrection, was one of the links between both groups. Gual had arrived in Baltimore months earlier and was organizing an expedition to liberate Mexico. His name must have been familiar to

Joseph, as at the end of 1812, Gual had met the French ambassador in Washington and requested Napoleon's military aid for the rebels in Venezuela.[17] While one of his fellow revolutionaries embarked to Paris to make his case directly to Napoleon, the following year Gual returned to Cartagena, the last stronghold of rebel resistance in Venezuela, and brought along with him a valuable French ally: Commodore Louis Aury.

The details of Aury's life before arriving in America are almost as sketchy as those of Jean Laffite, with whom he was many times associated. It is very likely that he was one of the many agents Napoleon sent to America to advance his plans. Born in Paris shortly after the French Revolution, Aury had at some point served as a lieutenant in the French navy under the orders of Jerome Bonaparte.[18] Around 1808, he had become a corsair, using the Gulf of Mexico as his base. As he explained to his worried parents, corsairs were "the only French ships, war or merchant, in this country," and they waged war "as loyally as the ships of his Imperial Majesty."[19] In fact, with the French navy neutralized after Trafalgar, Napoleon relied heavily on corsairs or privateers to pursue war against England and many times entrusted them with delicate missions.[20] In 1813 Aury joined the navy of Cartagena, and for the next two years, Aury and his fleet wreaked havoc on Spanish commerce in the Caribbean.[21] However, by mid-1815 the South American republic finally succumbed to superior Spanish forces. Gual barely escaped the scaffold, thanks to Aury, who took him to New Orleans.

The South American rebels had strong allies in the United States. Among them was an enterprising young man named John Stuart Skinner, who was Baltimore's postmaster general. Skinner's job was much more important than his title suggests. Even in democratic America, the post office served as a key piece of the government's intelligence network. Skinner, who was only twenty-eight at the time, not only was well connected to the highest ranks of the Madison administration but also was one of the leading members of the Improved Order of Red Men, a patriotic society whose objective was to defend the principles of the American Revolution.[22] Skinner believed that there was no better way to defend these principles than to support the cause of independence in the Spanish colonies. He admired Napoleon as much as he hated England, an "accursed nightmare" that in his view tried "to extinguish the first sparks of liberty as they arise in all parts of the world."[23] Skinner also had close ties to a group of Baltimore merchants actively involved in outfitting privateers now sailing under the flag of the insurgents of Buenos Aires.[24]

As time passed, the connection that Onis had uncovered between the Bonapartist émigrés, the South American rebels, and the American privateers became increasingly clear. In early June the British consul in Rhode Island reported:

A combination of moneyed men at Baltimore and Charleston, and I believe at other places, which have purchased several of the largest class of fast sailing privateer vessels used during the late war and have fitted them out, manned with more men that are apparently necessary, old privateers and other desperadoes, and under different pretences, some clearing out for one place and some for another; but they are ultimately to meet at some appointed rendezvous to the southward in South America, perhaps the River La Plata.* Extreme secrecy is observed; yet, there is a strong suspicion that the real object of this combined expedition (as they are called) in those parts, perhaps to go round Cape Horn and fall on some of the points of Chile. It is also whispered that there may be an attempt to release general Bonaparte included in this plan and land him among the patriots. Several Frenchmen and probably Mr. Joseph Bonaparte are concerned.[25]

It was the first time Chile had been mentioned as being in the sights of the Bonapartists. But Chile was simply a step to Peru, the other "crown jewel" of the Spanish empire. This explains why Joseph took a sudden interest in an obscure Chilean revolutionary named Jose Miguel Carrera.

Carrera had arrived in the United States in early 1816, after a year's residence in Buenos Aires. His plans to liberate Chile had been frustrated by the fall of his friend Carlos de Alvear. Months later, San Martin had accused Carrera of being the leader of a secret Masonic society that promoted a mutiny among Chilean troops under his command and tried to get him arrested.[26] To avoid prison, at the end of 1815, Carrera embarked for the United States, where he expected to obtain support for his plans. To liberate Chile, and eventually Peru, Carrera needed ships, crews, weapons, and ammunition. He had no money but counted on the assistance of two well-connected friends: Commodore David Porter, a hero of the War of 1812, and Joel Roberts Poinsett, former American consul in Santiago.

---

*The River Plate.

As soon as he landed in the United States, Carrera visited Porter in Washington, where he had just been appointed to the Navy Board of Commissioners. The commodore had not forgotten the warm welcome and support he had received from Carrera's government in early 1813, when he had arrived in Valparaiso in command of the USS *Essex*. Porter introduced Carrera to Madison and Secretary of State James Monroe, who expressed words of encouragement but offered no tangible support for the Chilean's cause. Porter also introduced Carrera to John Stuart Skinner. The two men struck up an immediate friendship. Skinner thought Carrera embodied the ideal South American patriot and offered his valuable connections. Over the next several weeks, the Chilean saw a large number of potential sponsors for his expedition in Baltimore, Philadelphia, and New York. He faced a daunting challenge as the cost of a typical privateer, usually a fast sailing schooner, could reach fifty thousand dollars and required a crew of between eighty and a hundred men.[27] Carrera needed at least four vessels, which was well beyond his financial means. Without a financial sponsor, his expedition to Chile would go nowhere. He hoped Poinsett would help him.

Although Poinsett's name will forever be associated with a popular Christmas flower, his activities in Chile between 1811 and 1814 had nothing to do with botany. Born in Charleston in 1779 to a family of French Huguenot émigrés, he had spent most of his adult life in Europe. A Francophile and a believer in the ideals of the French Revolution, by the time he arrived in Paris in the summer of 1808, he was already a member of the Masonic brotherhood.[28] This allowed him to be introduced to many high-ranking members of the empire and the Grande Armée, including a promising general named Bertrand Clausel, who had served in the armies of Italy and Dalmatia and was on his way to acquire fame in Spain.[29] Poinsett returned to the United States in early 1810 and a few months later Madison appointed him as special agent to South America. Besides promoting trade, his secret instructions were to communicate to the patriots that if they decided to pursue their independence from Spain, it would "coincide with the sentiments and policy of the United States."[30]

After a brief residence in Buenos Aires, Poinsett settled in Santiago and befriended Carrera, who had just taken over the revolutionary government.[31] Their instant rapport was helped by a closeness in age and shared republican ideals. More importantly, Carrera viewed Poinsett's arrival as a semiofficial recognition of his government by the United States. Poinsett soon became one of Carrera's closest advisers and encouraged him to declare independence from

Spain. Poinsett's influence was so strong that he wrote the first draft of the constitution for the new republic and the fourth of July was chosen to celebrate the creation of the new national flag. Irritated at these developments, at the end of 1812 the viceroy of Peru sent an army to quash the Chilean rebels. Carrera prepared his army to defend Chile. Riding alongside him was the American consul. Carrera called Poinsett *el mejor chileno*—the best Chilean—and appointed him a general in his army.[32] British agents in Buenos Aires noted with concern the growing influence of the United States and recommended establishing a stronger naval presence in Chile to support the party opposed to the Carreras and "to counteract the very unfavorable impressions which Mr. Poinsett, the American agent or consul, or whatever else he is, is doing his utmost at this moment to make against the English." All evidence suggested that Poinsett worked "as much in the interests of France as America."[33] Fortunately for England, with Carrera's fall from power and the destruction of the *Essex,* American influence in Chile ended.

Poinsett probably introduced Carrera to Aaron Burr, the controversial former vice president and perennial intriguer. Their first meeting took place in New York in early February. Carrera was very impressed with Burr and thought he was a talented man. "Some call him traitor, others too ambitious," he wrote in his diary. "The truth is that everybody respects him for his courage, although he is generally hated."[34] While in New York, Carrera also met with Captain David Jewett, a former U.S. naval officer who had become a Buenos Aires privateer. Jewett was trying to buy the *True Blooded Yankee* and planned to use the ship in some "crazy projects" for South America in association with Burr.

It was at this time that Carrera started paying attention to the growing numbers of Bonapartist émigrés. Through the newspapers, he learned about Grouchy's arrival and of "an unsuccessful attempt to liberate Napoleon from St. Helena." He also heard rumors that Joseph had offered "a million dollars for his brother's rescue."[35] These rumors must have excited his imagination, as he desperately needed money to finance his expedition. In the coming months Carrera continued to look for a financial sponsor throughout the East Coast; he even met with John Jacob Astor. In April he met again with Burr, who still dreamed of building an empire in the Spanish colonies. But this time Carrera was much less enthusiastic, particularly after he heard that Jewett had invited Burr to go to Chile. It may have been Burr, Jewett, or maybe Poinsett, who convinced Carrera of the advantages of joining the Lodge of St. John in New York, one of the most influential Masonic lodges in the country. Although undetected by Onís' spies, he caught the attention of a Bourbon agent who watched the Masonic proceedings.[36]

At the beginning of the summer, Carrera started to gravitate toward Joseph's orbit. Poinsett helped, as his French connections were strong. In early June, Carrera met a Spaniard called Novoa, who was a member of Joseph's inner circle. After inquiring about his expedition to Chile, Novoa promised assistance and told Carrera that Joseph wanted to meet him. "Friendship with Bonaparte," wrote a hopeful Carrera in his diary.[37] Even for a self-assured man such as him the idea of meeting face to face with Joseph Bonaparte, former king of Spain and Naples, and brother of the great Napoleon, could not fail to generate certain excitement.

What could Joseph want to talk to him about?

9
Napoleon Loses His Patience

Plunged in a dungeon he had still been great;
How low, how little was this middle state,
Between a prison and a palace, where
How few could feel for what he had to bear!

—Lord Byron, *The Age of Bronze,* Canto 5

Napoleon's patience was severely tested in mid-July, when Sir Hudson Lowe visited Longwood to discuss plans for a new residence. Napoleon took advantage of his presence to give vent to all his grievances. He reproached Lowe for intercepting a letter from Countess Bertrand to Montchenu, the French commissioner. Lowe denied having done so, but Napoleon knew he was lying and got furious. Besides, he didn't want a new residence. Construction would take six years and he didn't expect to remain that long at St. Helena. There would soon be a change of government in England or France and he would be released. Napoleon then complained about the many annoyances he suffered and claimed that Cockburn had never enforced regulations so strictly. Slightly embarrassed and unsure about what to do, Lowe turned around and left. "He is a galley-slave driver—a *sbirro!*" angrily exclaimed Napoleon.[1]

After this unpleasant incident, Napoleon seriously began to reassess his situation. He detested Longwood and his guardian with equal intensity. "Why choose this vile island? I thought there was nothing I could hate so much and now I do, her Governor," he said.[2] But a political solution seemed unlikely in the short term. With O'Meara, who had become a close confidant, Napoleon spoke about escaping and said that "if he was inclined to try it, which he was not, there were ninety-five chances in one hundred against his effecting it." As long as he lived there was a chance he could escape and the only sure way to stop him was murder. "Then all uneasiness on the part of the European powers and Lord Castlereagh would cease," Napoleon said. O'Meara was worried enough about this conversation that he warned Countess Bertrand that any escape attempt would lead to "inevitable death by hunger, thirst, or being drowned, even allowing they could get a boat victualed, etc, and escape the cruisers, which I thought impossible." Fanny replied that perhaps Napoleon could slip away and board an American vessel sailing near the island. O'Meara asked her "how he was to know of an American vessel being near" as no American vessels "would be let in or allowed to stay near the island; that an attempt of the kind could only be supposed to be made by people under sentence of death to whom the slender chance was open and who could only die at best."[3] Surely the countess knew more than she was willing to share.

O'Meara was also unaware of preparations under way in the United States. Besides, there was a difference between escape and rescue. Napoleon had discarded the former but seriously considered the latter. His hopes were high and he assured Gourgaud that "sooner or later" they would leave the island.[4] The United States was the country "most convenient for a Frenchmen," Napoleon told Bertrand. Particularly now that so many of his followers lived there. "It seems that Joseph is going to build an establishment over there; there are already three hundred French families. There are already more Frenchmen in America than in any [other foreign] country." Regnault, Grouchy, and Lefebvre-Desnouettes had already settled in the United States. "Where else in the world can one encounter such company?"[5]

It was at this time, mid-July, that Lowe received a dispatch from Lord Bathurst warning him about an attempt to rescue Napoleon from Brazil:

We have information that the crew of the notorious privateer, called the *True Blooded Yankee* are at Bahia. They are buccaneers of the most enterprising and desperate character. Men of all countries though the great proportion are Americans. The captain is named Sonntag, probably a German. There are some Italians, and they live at the house of an Italian who keeps the *café* at St. Salvador and this man's wife it is stated resides at St. Helena. All these adventurers are full of schemes as well as wishes to effect the release of Buonaparte; and they seem to be much favored by the American consul at Bahia. The Italian tavern keeper has lately endeavored to get a passage to St. Helena under the pretext of visiting his wife. The [American] consul is shipping presents of oranges for Bonaparte. One of the principal officers of the privateer lives in the consuls' house. In the meantime the crew are kept together and appear to have no employment but in their design to assist Napoleon.

Bathurst suspected that some of Napoleon's money supported these adventurers, who "talked of fitting out a schooner or two and it was believed they meant to send one to Tristan da Cunha and keep one cruising at a certain distance from St. Helena as a point to which Napoleon might steer if he could be apprized of their intentions and could contrive to push off in a boat."[6] This plan was very similar to the one described by Fanny Bertrand.

Sonntag, the captain mentioned in the dispatch, had obtained the first privateering license from the government of Buenos Aires in mid-1815. Although at this time he was in Brazil, he had lost control of the *True Blooded Yankee* to David Jewett, a former American naval officer and a friend of Joel Roberts Poinsett and Jose Miguel Carrera. Jewett had also obtained a privateering patent from Buenos Aires and after taking a share of the ship had taken her to Rhode Island.[7] Once there, he got entangled in a fight with the other owners over the fate of the *True Blooded Yankee*. But in years to come the fearsome privateer would continue to haunt Napoleon's guardians. Although the scheme seemed far-fetched, Bathurst thought it deserved attention, as there "could not be fitter instruments" for its execution than "these desperate adventurers who are good seamen withal and responsible to no government [for] their actions." Among other things Bathurst recommended using "the strictest vigilance with regard to vessels," particularly American schooners, sailing between St. Helena and Brazil, and to "send away the Italian's wife (if there be such a person at St. Helena) and any other woman or man through whom a clandestine communication is likely to be kept up with the coasts of South America." He also ordered Lowe to occupy Tristan da Cunha, an island twelve hundred miles to the south of St. Helena that could be used as a base of operations. "If the Americans should have anticipated you in the occupation of Tristan da Cunha, you will feel how doubly necessary the strictest vigilance will become."[8]

In no time Lowe found the wife of the Italian tavern keeper and sent her to Brazil. He also advised the British consul in Rio de Janeiro to be especially vigilant of any American adventurers as he had "been made acquainted of some designs that had been formed by a set of desperadoes who were formerly the crew of an American privateer to use some efforts for the liberation of Bonaparte."[9] Bathurst's warning prompted Lowe to assess the state of the island's defenses against a possible invasion. His conclusion was disheartening:

The general idea that has been presented of this island is, that it is as *impregnable* a post as Gibraltar, Malta or any other regularly fortified place, but how this term can be applied to an island of *twenty-eight miles* circumference, within which there is no regular *fortress or fort whatever* and only sea batteries I am really at a loss to understand except if it is founded on the idea of the inaccessibility of the coast and of the difficulty which may be opposed to boats approaching those parts which are accessible. I have recently visited in minute detail every one of those points. I have been struck as every other person has been with the extreme difficulty of landing at any part of them and I consider the island to be altogether as strong a post as nature alone ever formed, considering its extent, but there are still various parts where, by particularly waiting for a lull of fine weather, and bringing a powerful fire from ships of war and gun boats, or rather men of war's boats armed as such, it would not be impossible for a very active and enterprising enemy to force a landing if there was not a sufficient number of troops at hand to oppose him.

During his inspection, Lowe found no less than twenty-three points where an invading force could land. In his view the best landing spots were James Valley, Rupert's Valley, Lemon Valley, Sandy Bay, and Prosperous Bay. He wasn't concerned about the first four being taken if he had enough troops to defend them but worried about Prosperous Bay, which was dangerously close to Longwood. Lowe thought it was an ideal landing spot for an invasion as it had "no line of defenses, its strength principally consists in the difficulty of ascent from it. It is however by no means impracticable." Lowe warned that an attack on St. Helena would be "made in a very sudden manner, and by a very powerful armament, such as might possibly sail from some of the ports of France in the event of any new revolutionary movement in that country."[10]

With great zeal and energy, Lowe set out to reinforce the island's defenses. He must have surely remembered his experience at Capri. After a few weeks he assured Bathurst that he had taken every step to prevent the escape of his prisoner and warned that it was only "by an additional number of small cruising vessels" that the risk could be completely eliminated. To prevent someone "coming in close to the shore during the nighttime, sending in a boat, and disappearing before the morning," he considered it essential to place "a small corvette well to windward."[11] According to an English captain who visited the island months later, Lowe's "vigilant arrangements by sea and on land" made it almost impossible for Napoleon "to attempt an escape without being detected." There was not "a seemingly accessible point but that a battery was established there." There were 500 officers and 2,300 soldiers plus 500 cannons stationed at Deadwood, Ladder Hill, and Jamestown. Lowe also put sentries at Sandy Bay, High Peak, Lemon Valley, Egg Island, and Tag Lake. The telegraph system kept him informed of everything that went on in the island. In addition, three frigates and two men-of-war, each carrying twenty guns, and six brigs "constantly patrolled the island's coast and surroundings."[12]

Even as paranoid as he was, Lowe couldn't have imagined that soon after he assured Bathurst that he had taken all necessary precautions, an English captain would propose to take Napoleon to the United States in exchange for a million dollars. Montholon refused to provide any details about this plan to avoid compromising "the political existence of men to which I owe recognition." Both Montholon and Gourgaud thought the plan had a good chance of success but Napoleon refused to consider it.[13] He had decided he would only leave the island with "his hat on his head and his sword on his side."

To prevent Napoleon from having cash to bribe the natives to help him escape, Lowe decided to reduce Longwood's budget by one-third. On August 16, the day after Napoleon's birthday, he showed up at Longwood to deliver the bad news, and as Napoleon refused to see him, he met Bertrand. After a short but heated discussion both men swore never to speak to each other again. When Napoleon found out about Lowe's designs, he told O'Meara that the objective of the British ministers was to force him to rely on his own money and thus find out where he kept his fortune. Two days later, Lowe returned to Longwood to complain about Bertrand's conduct. This time Napoleon lost his temper and told Lowe he was not an Englishman but a *sbirro siciliano*. Lowe, livid, turned around and left. Napoleon refused to ever see him again.[14]

Count Balmain noted "there was too much incompatibility between the two men." The Russian commissioner was surprised at "the enormous ascendancy which this man, surrounded by guards, by rocks, by precipices still keeps over men's minds. Everything at St. Helena reflects his superiority." He also noted that O'Meara was a "clever and discreet man" whom he suspected of being "the secret agent of Sir Hudson Lowe at Longwood."[15] In truth, the Irish doctor was taking the brunt of Lowe's ire. "If he continues his abuse, I shall make him feel his situation," Lowe told O'Meara after his last spat with Napoleon. "He is a prisoner of war and I have a right to treat him according to his conduct." To justify himself, Lowe claimed to be following orders from London and said that Napoleon had already caused the death of millions and might do the same again if he escaped.[16]

The budget reduction took place at the end of September and, according to O'Meara, caused "great distress" at Longwood, as the "number of mouths to be fed was forty-five, independent of the Chinese."[17] Incensed, Napoleon asked Montholon to draft a letter detailing the vexations, insults, and humiliations he suffered at Lowe's hands. Napoleon wanted this document, known as Montholon's "Remonstrance," to be published in London so that the British people could learn how he was being treated. He also launched measures to neutralize Lowe's new restrictions. He ordered Cipriani Franceschi, his enigmatic maître d'hôtel, to sell some of the imperial silver he had brought from France to buy provisions. It was a symbolic protest that caused quite a stir in Jamestown and that months later would cause a political storm in Europe.

Lowe suspected a sinister plan was afoot. Bathurst had just warned him about another rescue attempt and ordered him to take even stricter precautions, including an immediate reduction of Napoleon's attendants at Longwood: "The conduct of General Bonaparte and his followers, the information which I have from time to time directed to be forwarded to you, and many concurring circumstances cannot fail of impressing you with an expectation of some attempt being made to effect his escape and it is to be apprehended that he may be much assisted in such an undertaking by the number and character of the persons who are about him. You will therefore remove from General Bonaparte's [presence] at least four of the persons who went out with him. You will understand that I include Piontkowski among this number."[18]

At this time Napoleon thought Lowe had sinister designs directed toward him. Recurring colics had revived his fears about poisoning. Gourgaud and Montholon suspected the wine served at Longwood contained lead and asked O'Meara to analyze it.[19]

Napoleon's patience had run out.

The Last Campaign Begins

After ravaging Europe the Bonaparte family plans to spread the germs of its iniquities in this hemisphere.
> —Luis de Onis to the Court of Madrid, November 1816

Baron Jean Guillaume Hyde de Neuville, the new French ambassador, arrived in the United States in the early summer of 1816. The forty-year-old diplomat was fanatically devoted to the Bourbons and considered one the "most violent *ultra* royalists" in the Chamber of Deputies.[1] In his youth he had participated in several attempts to assassinate Napoleon. Captured, he had been forced to seek asylum in America. He returned to France in 1814 and was sent to Tuscany, supposedly to watch Napoleon's movements at Elba but probably with more sinister objectives. As it turned out, it would be in the United States where Hyde de Neuville rendered his most valuable services to the Bourbons. His instructions were to keep a strict watch over Joseph and use any means to derail his plans.

Hyde de Neuville's arrival was marred by an unpleasant incident. During a celebration of Independence Day in Baltimore attended by Lefebvre-Desnouettes and other Bonapartist émigrés, John Stuart Skinner, the city's postmaster general, made a public toast to "the generals of France in exile, the glory of their native land—not to be dishonored by the proscriptions of an imbecile tyrant."[2] Enraged at the disrespectful manner in which Skinner referred to Louis XVIII, Hyde de Neuville sent a protest to the State Department demanding his dismissal. Secretary of State James Monroe replied that he could take no measures against Skinner because he had not violated any laws.[3] Hyde de Neuville also demanded the recall of William Lee, the American consul at Bordeaux, who had helped many Bonapartists escape from France. Since Lee was visiting the United States and had decided to stay, Monroe avoided another embarrassing incident.[4] It was not a coincidence that Lee and Skinner caught the attention of Hyde de Neuville; both had strong links to the Bonapartists and the Madison administration.

These distractions prevented Hyde de Neuville from detecting the contacts between Joseph and Jose Miguel Carrera. The Chilean rebel leader was screened by several of Joseph's underlings: first, a Spaniard named Novoa, then Colonel Antoine Bellina-Skupieski, a thirty-seven-year-old Polish aristocrat. Skupieski was a strange man. Many suspected he was an impostor, but he had followed Napoleon to Elba and while there had served as equerry to Madame Mere.* It had been Magdalena, his attractive Spanish wife, who had opened for him the doors to Joseph's inner circle. She had been one of Napoleon's lovers at Elba. Thanks to her influence Skupieski had been promoted to colonel during the Hundred Days. After Waterloo, husband and wife followed Napoleon to Malmaison and then to Rochefort. When Skupieski arrived in the United States at the end of 1815, it was again thanks to Magdalena that he was allowed into Joseph's inner circle.[5]

A few days after the interview with Skupieski, Carrera met Colonel Rafael Gravier del Valle, a Spaniard who had served in Joseph's army. Finally, in early July, he met with Joseph in Manhattan. It was an odd moment for Carrera. Six years earlier he had fought against Joseph's rule in Spain and now he was discussing a possible alliance! Their conversation lasted more than three hours. Initially, Joseph tried to convince Carrera of the futility of revolution. Then he complained about the way Napoleon had treated him. Sensing he was being tested, Carrera remained circumspect. When his turn came to talk, he reviewed events in South America, emphasizing the prominent role he had played as first president of Chile. He then explained his plans. Joseph offered to help him. "Many proposals, evidence of friendship, etc." Carrera wrote in his diary.[6]

At this time, Joseph and his generals were analyzing several options to advance Napoleon's plans. One was Carrera, another, the Spaniard Xavier Mina who had just arrived from London with Lord Holland's backing. After a quick visit to Washington, Mina visited Baltimore and discussed his plans with the Venezuelan Pedro Gual, who was also planning an expedition to Mexico and counted on Joseph's support. Whether Mina met with Joseph is a subject of debate but there is little doubt that he received his backing.[7] When Mina left Philadelphia he was accompanied by two of Joseph's men, the Spaniard Novoa and Arago, a former quartermaster in Napoleon's army.[8]

* Napoleon's mother.

Since the newspapers reported Mina's plans to join the Mexican insurgents, Onis put him under surveillance. Hyde de Neuville believed that a greater danger lay in store. His agents had alerted him to the imminent departure of an expedition from Baltimore: "The opinion of the consul general is that this expedition is for St. Helena and that it is only to divert attention that a rumor has spread stating that its purpose is to join the rebel Bolivar."

Undeterred by reports that "a certain Bolina"—none other than Skupieski—wanted to kill him Hyde de Neuville promised Richelieu that he would "make every effort to find out the truth."[9] Onis already knew the truth. The Bonapartist émigrés, the South American insurgents, and the American privateers were working together to destroy the Spanish empire. Sir Charles Bagot, the newly appointed British ambassador to the United States, dismissed the rumored plans to rescue Napoleon as chimerical but had no doubt that Joseph and his generals were "deeply engaged in some design now carrying on in this country for the assistance of the revolutionists in the Spanish settlements," probably with American encouragement: "The great interest taken here by all parties in the success of the insurrection of the Spanish settlements leaves little doubt that any attempt to assist it would meet with every encouragement from hence which could be afforded with safety to the existing relations between the court of Spain and this country, while the military reputation and desperate fortunes of the French officers who have sought refuge here, naturally point them out as the fittest and readiest instruments by which assistance might be indirectly afforded."[10]

Hyde de Neuville was convinced that an expedition to rescue Napoleon was under way. His spies in Baltimore discovered another suspicious ship that was about to depart under the orders of Captain Thomas Taylor, a Buenos Aires privateer who was a friend of Carrera. Among the passengers were Colonel Jacques Roul, a former French naval officer named Fournier, and other French émigrés. Hyde de Neuville believed their objective was St. Helena:

> If an expedition against St. Helena were possible, that of Taylor would be more dangerous than any other. This man is of an extreme boldness and a very big admirer of the prisoner of St. Helena, as the pirates of his sort are. . . . It is necessary to ascertain well whether St. Helena can be taken by force or by surprise. He will figure this out. Such an attempt will be made ten or twenty times if necessary by the people of this continent. The Spanish insurgents are not sparing anything to get him [Napoleon]

as their leader. What they want from him is his reputation and we cannot deny that if he appears in South America we will again see him armed with formidable power.[11]

We will never know Taylor's real objective, as customs officials arrested him for violating neutrality laws, probably at the instigation of Onís. Fournier was also arrested for larceny and accused his compatriot Roul of setting him up.[12] This confusing episode was a warning sign that the French colonel was a troublemaker. Carrera had met Roul in New York a few months earlier and had been impressed with his stories about Napoleon's march from Elba to Paris and the battle of Waterloo. Roul told Carrera that he wanted to join the patriots in South America to take revenge against Spain. Convinced that "the services of these disciples of the great Napoleon" would be of immense value for the cause of independence, the Chilean had helped Roul obtain a commission in the army of Buenos Aires.[13] Roul finally set sail on Taylor's ship and arrived in Buenos Aires in late October. He will soon resurface in this story.

While in New York, Carrera also met Xavier Mina. He found him inexperienced and conceited, and he feared that Mina would get all of Joseph's support. Given Mexico's importance, the expedition to Chile was of secondary importance. Nevertheless, Joseph and his generals, maybe influenced by Poinsett, were impressed with Carrera and wanted to combine both expeditions. At the end of July, Carrera went to Philadelphia and again met Colonel Gravier, who brought "all sorts of proposals" from Joseph and updated him on Mina's plans.[14] Then Carrera met Mina, who suggested combining their expeditions. Carrera was not convinced, so Poinsett proposed a meeting with Grouchy and Clausel to discuss the issue. The following evening, they had dinner at Poinsett's house in Philadelphia. Carrera argued against combining the expeditions and persuaded Grouchy and Clausel. Mina would go to Mexico and Carrera would use Chile as a base to launch the Peruvian campaign.[15] Grouchy promised to help Carrera and gave him letters of recommendation for several French merchants in Baltimore. He also agreed to seek funds from Stephen Girard. As Grouchy was on his way to Wilmington to visit Pierre Dupont de Nemours,* he invited Carrera to come along in his carriage. During the trip, they went over the details of the plan. Grouchy told Carrera that he wanted his two sons, both veteran officers, to join the patriot army.[16]

---

* Dupont was a Frenchman who had become the largest manufacturer of gunpowder in the United States.

Thanks to Grouchy's recommendation, Carrera succeeded in negotiating the purchase of a ship in Baltimore. On his way back to Philadelphia he stopped at Wilmington to update Grouchy, who told him that Girard would finance his expedition and Dupont would provide him twelve thousand pounds of powder. When he reached Philadelphia, Carrera saw Colonel Gravier who assured him that he would get everything he needed. "Bonaparte protects you," Gravier said.[17] It was a turning point for Carrera. Suddenly dozens of French émigrés volunteered to join his expedition. Among them was Colonel Jean Joseph Dauxion-Lavaysse, a thirty-nine-year-old veteran of Napoleon's army. "Before I contacted you for two months I had investigated you and your character," Lavaysse said in a flattering letter. "I promise not to defect until your country has recovered its independence."[18] Despite suspicions that Lavaysse was a spy of the Bourbons, Carrera took him on board. It was a decision he would later regret.

Meanwhile, Mina went to New York to visit General Winfield Scott, whom he had befriended at Holland House in London months earlier. The American general was a strong supporter of the independence of the Spanish colonies even if it meant war with Spain, a view not shared by his government.[19] French agents reported that Scott was helping Mina recruit "the most disreputable French, Irish, Spanish and American types of men willing to sail to join the insurgents in Latin America" and to liberate "the usurper."[20] Scott never imagined that thirty years later he would be the one conquering Mexico.

Onis informed his government that Joseph was financing the expeditions against Mexico and Buenos Aires. He identified Novoa as Joseph's agent in his dealings with the insurgents. Onis' agents were now on Carrera's tracks and reported that he had unlimited credit with Baring Brothers, where Joseph was rumored to keep part of his fortune.[21] Onis also suspected that an American banker named David Parish was acting as Joseph's courier. Parish, who had just left for France, was a partner of Hope and Company, an Amsterdam-based bank that had been involved in many dealings with Napoleon.[22] Coincidentally, a few weeks earlier, Hyde de Neuville's spies had linked Parish to the plans to rescue Napoleon.[23] The banker's exact role is unclear, but we know for certain that he served as a courier for Grouchy.[24]

In Philadelphia, Grouchy and Clausel arranged the final details of the campaign. They had been so impressed with Carrera that they were now trying to convince Mina to join him. It was at this time, mid-August 1816, that Jose Alvarez de Toledo entered the scene. Together with Carlos de Alvear, former supreme director in Buenos Aires, Toledo had belonged to the secret society of the Caballeros Racionales, which since 1809 had plotted the insurrection of the Spanish colonies.* Toledo had already organized several expeditions to invade Mexico with General Humbert, so his name was well known to Joseph. It was certainly well known to Onis, who had long suspected him of being an agent of Napoleon or the United States.[25] Toledo wasted no time in offering Joseph the throne of Mexico.[26]

Joseph now had a third option besides Carrera and Mina. This one seemed the best. Toledo's reputation as a rebel leader was very strong, and unlike Mina, he had been born in the Spanish colonies. If Toledo delivered Mexico, the rest of the colonies would soon fall under Bonapartist rule. Joseph was so excited that he sent a secret message to Napoleon. Unaware of Toledo's proposal, Carrera met frequently with Grouchy, and thanks to his support he was able to acquire two more ships in Baltimore. Only one thing was missing from his expedition, "the presence of the marshal himself."[27] From Joseph's mansion in Bordentown, Grouchy replied: "I had suspected that General Mina would not agree to join his resources to those you could deliver in Chile. I deplore this circumstance more for his interests and those of my fellow compatriots who will accompany him in the expedition. . . . I hope you will succeed with your own efforts. . . . I will not go to Baltimore until Mina departs, since I do not want the spies of the Bourbons to accuse of me of taking part in matters that I ignore. I would prefer not [to] go there unless Mr. Smith† does not deliver on his promises given the influence that my opinion about the success of your expedition could exert over him and to support you as much as I can."[28]

Carrera's hopes that Grouchy would join him were not unrealistic. Even though the marshal publicly expressed his wish to return to France, he not only asked Carrera to take his sons to South America as officers but also prepared a long memorandum for the government of Buenos Aires in which he proposed to take the command of the patriot army in the war against Spain. South America "would be the new theater of glory" for Napoleon's officers exiled in the United States. "Their support for the cause will be one of the surest means to attract a great number of men who had served under their orders," he wrote. Grouchy promised that once he and his officers liberated the colonies from Ferdinand's tyranny they would resign and leave the country. His only condition: a deposit

* Another member of this secret society was Servando de Mier, Mina's political adviser.
†Junius Smith, a Baltimore merchant.

of 120,000 *duros* in escrow to compensate him if his properties were confiscated in France.[29]

Seeking an approving nod from the Madison administration Carrera went to Washington accompanied by Pedro Gual, who had joined Mina's expedition.[30] Unable to meet Commodore Porter they visited William Thornton, head of the U.S. Patent Office. Thornton was one of the most enthusiastic supporters of the cause of independence of the Spanish colonies in the United States.[31] At fifty-six, he had lost none of the revolutionary enthusiasm of his youth and felt a responsibility to spread the ideas of Thomas Paine around the world. More importantly, he was a close friend of Madison and Jefferson. As a result, Gual and Carrera interpreted his enthusiastic support as an indirect endorsement of the administration.[32] Next day, when they returned to Baltimore, they were surprised to learn that Toledo's intrigues with Joseph had cost Mina "half his expedition."[33] Gual was not too disappointed and quickly changed his allegiance. Toledo's prospects now looked much brighter than Mina's. Gual switched sides and days later, he returned to Washington with Toledo. Since Monroe avoided them, they met with one of his aides. During the conversation Toledo made no reference to his offer to Joseph but openly discussed his plans to invade Mexico and explained that "the want of a convenient port on the Gulf of Mexico might perhaps induce them to take possession of Pensacola, but if they did so it would be with no view ultimately to keep it, as it ought to belong to the United States." Toledo emphasized that he would make every effort to avoid violating U.S. neutrality laws and "seemed anxious to know how such an act on their part would be viewed by this [the U.S.] government." Monroe's aide advised Toledo against taking Pensacola, as it could trigger a reaction from England.[34] Toledo's plan was essentially the same that Aaron Burr had proposed to Napoleon in 1810. In fact, Toledo even invited Burr to join the expedition.[35] Aware of Toledo's intentions, Monroe started planning his own moves in Florida.

Meanwhile, while in New York, Carrera learned that Joseph had promised Toledo that he would finance an army of twelve thousand men to invade Mexico under Clausel's orders.[36] Nobody suspected that Toledo had sold out to the Spaniards. At the end of 1815 the young revolutionary had lost faith in the cause of independence and had approached Onis' agents in New Orleans to seek Spain's pardon. During a brief visit to Manhattan in August 1816, Toledo met secretly with Onis to negotiate his change of allegiance. The Spanish ambassador offered him a pardon if he helped disrupt the schemes of Mina, Carrera, and Joseph. Toledo agreed. Onis thought Toledo's defection was worth more to the cause of Spain than "the destruction of a couple of armies."[37]

Unaware of this but determined to go ahead with his own plans, Carrera refused Toledo's overtures to join the Mexican expedition. His plan was to lead a small squadron to South America. "It is a grand plan that is not constrained by our little Chile," he explained to his brother. "If we succeed, I will be the happiest man on earth for being one of those who has most actively contributed to the emancipation of the Americas."[38] This "grand plan," agreed to with Grouchy and Clausel, consisted of the liberation of Chile and Peru. After a brief stop in Montevideo to embark more troops, Carrera intended to sail with his squadron around Cape Horn and take the fortress of Valdivia, in southern Chile. Once this was accomplished, he intended to raise an army of four thousand men to liberate Chile or, if he received the reinforcements promised by Grouchy, to proceed directly to Guayaquil and attempt to take Quito. In essence, Carrera would complete half of Joseph's master plan for South America. The other half would be accomplished by an expedition that would leave from Pensacola, sail across the Caribbean, cross over to the Pacific at the Isthmus of Panama, and march south to Guayaquil. Together the two forces could attack Lima, the capital of the viceroyalty of Peru.[39]

The stars seemed to be aligned in Carrera's favor. Porter assured him that the administration supported him and would soon recognize the independence of the Spanish colonies. His endorsement proved to be as unsanctioned as Thornton's. Encouraged by both men, Carrera attempted to buy the *True Blooded Yankee*.[40] The legendary privateer had been unable to sail due to a dispute between her owners, and strange rumors swirled around her. In early September the British government was warned that a plan to rescue Napoleon was under way involving the *True Blooded Yankee*. Reportedly, the privateer and a French warship called *Eurydice* were about to leave the United States with instructions for Commodore Stephen Decatur, who was in the Mediterranean with an American squadron. The *True Blooded Yankee* and Decatur's squadron would rendezvous at the island of Cape Verde, off the coast of Africa, and from there would launch an attack on St. Helena.[41] But the *Eurydice* had just brought Hyde de Neuville to the United States and Decatur was in Washington serving on the Navy Board of Commissioners. However, the report helped build the legend of the *True Blooded Yankee*.

Rumors about Joseph's designs for Mexico were now rife. Baltimore's *Niles'*

Weekly Register reported "that the unambitious character of Joseph, ex-king of Spain and the Indies, has been powerfully worked upon, by a numerous body of generals, who regained their fame under Bonaparte, and who having fled to America for refuge, are uneasy at the state of inaction to which they have been reduced. The persons, we are told, have urged Joseph to resume his pretensions as King of the Indies, and have offered to unite their means with those of the insurgents of Mexico to drive the Spaniards from the colonies and to establish a mighty empire on the shores of the Pacific. We are further informed that nothing has prevented the immediate engagement in this enterprise but the refusal on the part of the government of the United States to undertake any ostensible cooperation."[42] Another Baltimore newspaper wondered "why would not a South American diadem become him [Joseph] as well as a Spanish one? . . . The deuce is in it, if the mines of Mexico will not furnish diamonds enough to make a crown as brilliant as Ferdinand's."[43] Onis reached the same conclusion. One of his spies reported that Toledo had convinced Joseph that all the Americas would welcome him if he agreed to accept a liberal constitution. Onis was unsure whether this was an intrigue by Toledo "to take Joseph's money or whether they are seriously trying to get him to spend it all with the crazy design of becoming King of Mexico." But he had no doubt that Joseph was "the principal actor" and had contributed the most "to the arming of the expedition of Mina and others that are being prepared here."[44]

Joseph was certainly backing Carrera, as Clausel reiterated during a private meeting in New York at the end of September.[45] But Carrera was running out of funds and again began to suspect that Joseph's attention—and money—had shifted to Toledo.[46] Carrera's doubts disappeared after a meeting with Edmond Genet. Not surprisingly, Genet, who in 1794 had attempted to create a French enclave in the Spanish colonies, was also involved in Joseph's plans. He assured Carrera that he would get everything for his expedition. Grouchy, who was visiting Manhattan, reassured the Chilean the following morning.[47]

Meanwhile, despite Onis' protests to Monroe, Mina departed from Baltimore with 250 men, including many Napoleonic veterans and a spy sent by Onis with orders to kill Mina at the first opportunity.[48] The schooner *Ocean* was also ready to depart for Buenos Aires with Colonel Skupieski and a dozen veterans of Napoleon's Imperial Guard on board. Carrera had introduced the Polish officer to Martin Thompson, a recruiting agent from Buenos Aires, and then had introduced Thompson to Ruggles Hubbard, the owner of the schooner who paid for their transportation. Hubbard was the grand sheriff of the City of New York, a former state senator, and a supporter of South American independence.[49]

It is difficult to ascertain the exact nature of Hubbard's relationship with the Bonapartist émigrés but for many years he had been linked to Aaron Burr.[50] Both belonged to the Tammany Society, or Columbian Order, a patriotic society created a few years after the American Revolution to safeguard its principles.[51] During the war with England, some members of the society had founded the Society of Red Men, which had chapters in New York, Philadelphia, and Baltimore and counted John Stuart Skinner among its members.

After a violent incident involving Skupieski and another Pole, who accused him of being an impostor, in mid-October the *Ocean* put to sea.[52] Onis reported Skupieski's departure and noted that the Polish officer had been close to both Napoleon and Joseph. He also reported his connection to the "dangerous" Carrera. According to Onis, Joseph not only wanted to be the king of Mexico but also believed he could rule all the Americas "fomenting the war against our sovereign." In his view it was "a clear demonstration that the American rebels are no less shrewd in taking advantage of his weakness and silliness to get money from him."[53]

With Mina gone, Toledo again invited Carrera to join his expedition. Carrera declined, as he now felt confident that his expedition would succeed. In the following weeks he secured more ships and weapons and recruited soldiers and crews. By mid-October everything seemed ready. Carrera invited Clausel to join him: "I have received the memorandum from our Marshal [Grouchy] and some separate conditions related to his own person. I assume you would want to do the same. If that is the case, please send them over to me as soon as possible. I will deliver them loyally and secretly."[54]

Unsure whether to go to Mexico or South America, Clausel replied vaguely and inquired about the progress of the expedition. Carrera said that he planned to leave on the *Clifton,* a ship he had acquired with Grouchy's help, and that the rest of his squadron would depart soon after. He thanked Clausel for all his help and expressed confidence he would "beat the Spaniards."[55]

Onis noted that the French generals were very active. Although Clausel remained in Philadelphia, Lallemand and Lefebvre-Desnouettes had left for New Orleans, and Grouchy was reportedly headed to Charleston. Onis suspected they were all waiting for Joseph's orders.[56] In fact, they were busy setting up the French Agricultural and Manufacturing Society. Charles Lallemand, whose whereabouts were unknown, was appointed president, and William Lee, the former American consul at Bordeaux, vice president. Lee informed President Madison that the purpose of the society was "making a settlement in the Western country" and that several of its members had been dispatched to the Ohio and Mississippi rivers to search for a tract of land in a climate "which will produce, among other things, the vine and olive."[57]

Carrera embarked at the end of October. Some influential friends intervened to ensure that customs officials didn't stop him. Neither Grouchy nor Clausel accompanied him but another French general came along. It was Michel Brayer, whom Carrera had met in Baltimore. Brayer had arrived in the United States sometime in the fall of 1816, weeks after a French court had sentenced him to death.[58] Despite his high profile, neither Onis nor Hyde de Neuville detected Brayer's presence in Baltimore or his departure to Buenos Aires.[59] In addition to Brayer—who traveled as a private individual—Carrera's expedition included almost thirty veterans of the Grande Armée and three former officers of the U.S. army.[60]

With Carrera and Brayer bound for South America, Joseph and his generals turned their attention to Mexico. With help from William Lee, they lobbied Henry Clay, the influential speaker of the house, to obtain a land grant from Congress for the French Agricultural and Manufacturing Society somewhere on the frontier with Mexico, along the Ohio and Mississippi rivers, where Napoleon had said he would settle after abdicating the throne. Onis believed that the Vine and Olive colony was simply a screen to hide the "perverse designs" of the Bonaparte family, who "after ravaging Europe" planned "to spread the germs of its iniquities in this hemisphere." He was convinced that these plans were secretly encouraged "by certain powers interested in weakening Spain and promoting the independence of Spanish America."[61]

At the beginning of December, when it appeared that Joseph's plans would be crowned with success, the first signs of trouble appeared. Before leaving the United States, Carrera had intercepted a package of correspondence for Onis, containing a letter from Toledo confirming his betrayal. From his ship, Carrera warned Clausel, who was planning the expedition to Mexico with Toledo. "I would hang him if I could. I am sure he informed that barbarous ambassador of all my plans," Carrera said.[62] When confronted, Toledo said that he had only tried to get money from Onis. John Stuart Skinner wrote to Carrera that Toledo was "wandering in disguise, a wretched victim of his own treachery and indecision." Skinner, who remained the link for all the expeditions to South America, also confirmed that the rest of his squadron would soon set sail. "The *Savage* will follow in 12 days and Mr. D* has told me that the *Regent* would not be far behind you." Skinner believed Congress would "not interdict those enterprises of our citizens which are calculated to aid in your struggles against the damning embraces of the mother country." After sending his best wishes to Brayer, Skinner warned Carrera "not [to] be surprised if you see General Clausel in the *Savage*."[63]

Toledo's defection forced Clausel to reconsider his plans. Joseph had been left without a leader to "liberate" Florida and Mexico. Even worse, Toledo had revealed to Onis that Clausel and the other French generals had "joined the imbecile Joseph Bonaparte, . . . and disposing of Spanish America in the delirium of their exalted arrogance, have offered the crown of Mexico to this fatuous one and that of Peru to his brother Lucien."[64] Although these plans faced huge challenges, Onis thought they were real. He had just learned that Lucien had recently proposed to exchange his properties in Rome for land in the United States to an Italian residing in Philadelphia.[65] As usual, Onis was right.

---

* Probably Henry Didier, a merchant and an outfitter of privateers in Baltimore.

II
United in a Common Cause

Parliament or Mexico are the only two fields which afford any interest.
—Sir Robert Wilson, July 1816

At the end of July 1816, after serving a three-month prison sentence, Sir Robert Wilson was deported to England. He was in great spirits, but his wife, Jemima, had not recovered from a nervous breakdown she had suffered as a result of his trial and imprisonment.[1] She felt increasingly uneasy about her husband's quixotic adventures. Wilson's friends and the British public welcomed him as a hero. Lord Grey invited him to his country manor, where he received many visitors, including General Charles de Flahaut, the most prominent Bonapartist exiled in England and a permanent guest at Holland House. But the Tory ministers were not pleased and the Duke of York publicly criticized his conduct in France.[2]

In France, Brayer, the Lallemands, Lefebvre-Desnouettes, and Rigaud were condemned to death in absentia.[3] The fact that so many high-profile Bonapartists had escaped to the United States worried the Duke of Richelieu, who was sure they would attempt to rescue Napoleon. If they succeeded "it would be an endless source of troubles for our unhappy country, no matter where he [Napoleon] decides to go."[4] He also worried about American public opinion, even though the American ambassador in Paris assured him that sympathy for Bonaparte was caused by "hatred of Great Britain."[5] John Quincy Adams, American ambassador in London, lamented that "all the victims and final vanquishers of the French Revolution abhor us as aiders and abettors of the French during their career of triumph." He wondered how long "it will be possible for us to preserve peace with all Europe."[6]

The British government remained unconcerned about the possibility of Napoleon's escape. At the end of August, the Austrian ambassador in London warned Prince Metternich, the Austrian chancellor, that "the government here does not seem to admit more the probability of an attack against St. Helena or its likelihood of success if they however have the audacity to attempt it." Nevertheless, Lowe had been ordered "to double surveillance toward Bonaparte and to prevent especially that he has no communication with the inhabitants of the island."[7] Admiral Cockburn, who had just returned from St. Helena, confirmed that Napoleon had received "some propositions (mad and wild to be sure) from America on this subject" and that Napoleon's liberation would surely be attempted from America, but he remained convinced that he could not escape if "common vigilance" was used.[8] Cockburn's warnings were confirmed by a report "containing intelligence of an expedition stated to have lately sailed from Baltimore, the real object of which is represented to be to afford the means of General Bonaparte's escape from St. Helena." A certain Fournier, "a former naval officer of Bonaparte that followed him to Elba," was the leader of this expedition. Once at St. Helena, during daylight the rescuers would remain outside the range of the British cruisers and at night they would approach the island "on various points, and will send a rowboat from every vessel with a man disguised as an English soldier. They will carry Bonaparte secret messages informing him of the rescue project and the different points in the island to which the rowboats will go at night to pick him up." According to the report "considerable funds in gold and diamond have been put at the disposal to corrupt those that will be able to be necessary for him. They seem to be sure of obtaining the cooperation of certain individuals that have taken up residence or are employed at St. Helena."[9]

At this time the Tory cabinet was more concerned with domestic issues. The economy was in recession, and the discharge of thousands of soldiers after decades of continuous wars had contributed to an increase in unemployment. The ministers feared that food shortages in the fall and winter could lead to widespread social unrest.[10] To reduce the risk of a popular uprising, they encouraged the creation of an Association for the Relief of the Manufacturing and Laboring Poor, which at the end of August convened its first meeting. The Duke of York, the archbishop of Canterbury, and other high-ranking dignitaries were invited to attend. The organizers made the mistake of inviting Lord Thomas Cochrane, who in the middle of the proceedings launched a violent tirade against Tory policies, blaming the economic crisis on excessive public spending that fed a growing public debt, which in turn imposed an enormous tax burden on the British people. Cochrane also criticized the life sinecures paid to members of the

House of Lords and the Church of England, which made the efforts of the association look hypocritical.[11] Cochrane's speech greatly irritated the government. The Tory press predictably condemned him. "Many of the poorer classes of this country are crying aloud for relief and Lord Cochrane and the philanthropic patriots of 1816 instead of bread would give them a stone." With the parliamentary reforms proposed by Cochrane, England could "expect all the horrors, confiscation, plunder and massacre of the French Revolution."[12] William Cobbett defended his friend, who in his view had "performed ten million times more services to this Kingdom than he ever performed during the whole of the former part of his life. His conduct at the London Tavern meeting merits the thanks of every man in this Kingdom who does not live upon the taxes. It was an instance of the wonderful effect which a single man is able to produce upon a critical occasion if he has but the courage to avail himself of the opportunity."[13] When Napoleon heard about this episode at St. Helena he said, "If I were at the head of affairs in England I would devise some means of paying off the national debt. I would appropriate to that purpose the whole of the church livings. . . . I would appropriate to a similar purpose all sinecures."[14] Cochrane would have completely agreed with this view.

Weeks later Cochrane was brought to trial for escaping from prison. Since he believed that his detention had been illegal he refused to defend himself. The jury found him guilty but recommended "mercy because we think his subsequent punishment fully adequate to the offence." Cochrane defiantly replied: "I want justice, not mercy."[15] Instead he was slapped with a fine of one hundred pounds. Cochrane's hatred of the Tories reached new heights. Having suffered similar vexations at their hands, Wilson sympathized with his plight. During the summer of 1814 he had followed Cochrane's trial for fraud with great interest. Puzzled by the accusation and guilty verdict, he had asked the opinion of Samuel Whitbread, the Whig leader, who told him he was convinced that Cochrane "was totally and entirely innocent."[16] Although Wilson and Cochrane hadn't seen each other much in recent years, their mutual hatred of the Tories now brought them together.

Wilson believed that as long as his government pursued misguided policies it was his right and duty to correct them. Although he had considered running for Parliament, he was more inclined to join the cause of Mexican independence. "I am still unsettled in my plans," he wrote to Lord Grey in early August. "I should like to hear your opinion on the subject of my going abroad again or re-establishing myself in England. I have no desire to please the Government but [to do] what would be most approved by the Public." In truth, Wilson had already made up his mind, but he feared that England would intervene in the war between Spain and her colonies and complicate his plans.[17] Determined to go ahead, he prepared a memorandum "on the expediency and policy of fitting out an expedition on the present period to aid in the emancipation of the Kingdom of Mexico or New Spain." The new government would be established "on the most liberal principles of civil religious and commercial policy."[18] The Spanish ambassador in London got wind of these plans. He informed Madrid that an unnamed British general was organizing an expedition to Mexico and that its departure had been put on hold "until a packet from New York arrived with the results of the negotiations between the rebel Congress of Mexico and Joseph Bonaparte."[19]

Wilson coordinated his plans with the Bonapartist émigrés on both sides of the Atlantic. Among his contacts in London was General Frederic Guillaume de Vaudoncourt, who for the next five years would play an active role in advancing Napoleon's cause. In the middle of the summer Vaudoncourt left for Brussels with letters from Wilson to his sister Fanny Wallis, whose open and irreverent displays of Bonapartism had led to her deportation from Paris.[20] In Brussels, Fanny had joined other Bonapartist émigrés and opened a valuable channel of communication with her brother. Wilson's involvement in these intrigues prompted Lord Grey to warn him that "the general feeling in this country is decidedly hostile to everything connected with the French Revolution or Buonaparte and that everything which might proceed from a motive favorable to either would be severely judged."[21] True to form, Wilson ignored this warning.

Meanwhile, the Friends of Freedom were as active as ever. The *Anti-Gallican* reported that "there are at this moment organizing in every state of Europe, except Russia and Spain, political associations, denominated the *European Fraternal Association,* in which no Frenchman is admitted but regicides or those who have been condemned to death *par contumace.* I cannot say anything at present on the subject of these societies, but their effect will soon be felt."[22] Lewis Goldsmith, editor of the *Anti-Gallican,* who had been or would be on the payroll of Napoleon, Louis XVIII, Ferdinand VII, and Bathurst, was probably tipped off by the French ambassador in London or by a spy of Decazes, France's interior minister.[23]

Richelieu's conviction that a vast Bonapartist conspiracy was afoot was reinforced by a report from Hyde de Neuville suggesting that Joseph, Grouchy, and Clausel were on their way to Mexico. Richelieu asked his ambassador in London to alert the British government: "Given the presumption that an expedition could be launched to release Buonaparte no precaution would be too costly to prevent it. This rock in the middle of the Atlantic is a point on which we always have to keep our sights fixed. It would be nice to say that he has lost all support in France. I would like to believe this, but I will never be foolish enough to test this assumption and I wouldn't want for anything in this world to learn that he is free."[24]

Richelieu's warning coincided with the publication of a report in the *Anti-Gallican* about three expeditions that had "sailed from South America and from the United States for the purpose of carrying off Buonaparte from St. Helena."[25] Goldsmith was obviously well informed. In fact, he was so well informed that in late October, he reported the latest movements of General Charles Lallemand. We saw him last with Napoleon on board the *Bellerophon*. The British government had deemed him too dangerous to go to St. Helena and had instead confined him at Malta with Savary and other members of Napoleon's retinue. Lallemand left Malta in April 1816; a few weeks later he resurfaced in Smyrna, an important port on the coast of Turkey, where he hid under the protection of an English merchant.[26] In Smyrna he met Count Paul Lascaris-Vintimille, a fellow Bonapartist and a knight of Malta who had served as Napoleon's spy in the Middle East for many years.[27] The impetuous Lallemand soon got into trouble. The French consul in Smyrna invited Lallemand to dinner at his house with other Frenchmen. The subject of Napoleon came up. Lallemand referred to him as the "emperor," whereas a naval officer of royalist sympathies called him "Buonaparte." A sensible man under most circumstances, Lallemand could get "a little bit violent" with anybody who insulted Napoleon.[28] The discussion heated up and the consul stepped in to prevent a duel. Shortly after this incident, Lallemand left for Istanbul, where he gathered other stranded veterans of the Imperial Guard and organized their departure for the United States.[29]

The French and Austrian ambassadors at the Ottoman court requested his deportation, and at the end of the summer Lallemand left Istanbul.[30] A rumor reached London by late October that he was on his way to the United States. The *Anti-Gallican* reported that the French general had left the Ottoman capital "with an officer of the name of Vintimelle [*sic*], who formerly served in Buonaparte's army. . . . He has embarked on board an American ship for Salem."[31] The report was partially true, as Lallemand had not yet embarked for America. According to another version he went to Teheran to offer his services to Ali-Shah, the despotic ruler of Persia, who apparently turned him down because he only wanted British officers in his army.[32] But this explanation doesn't hold water as one of Lallemand's French comrades joined the Persian army at this time and served for more than a year.[33] In any case, Lallemand reached Cairo. Lallemand's movements in Turkey, Persia, and Egypt remain unclear, but it seems that from the moment he left Malta he was determined to join Joseph in the United States.[34] In early November the *Anti-Gallican* reported that the French Agricultural and Manufacturing Society had invited Savary and Lallemand "to fix their residence in the United States. A vessel fitted out solely for that purpose has sailed for the Levant in order to take them on board as well as others of the proscribed French who took refuge in Turkey."[35]

By this time rumors about Napoleon's escape were rife in London. According to one, "Buonaparte had escaped from St. Helena" and according to another "he had not escaped, but that a correspondence between him and the Court of Vienna, carried on by the intervention of the Austrian commissioner at St. Helena with a view to his escape had been detected."[36] Weeks later the *Anti-Gallican* confirmed that "a scheme for the abduction of Buonaparte from St. Helena" had already "assumed shape and consistency." A vessel had recently arrived from Jamestown but nobody had been allowed to disembark. "The mystery which hangs over this business is further increased by the strict silence which is observed; all I could learn is that Buonaparte is neither dead nor sick, nor has he escaped," said Goldsmith, "but I have been informed that a discovery has been made of a project to carry him off, and that too by vessels fitted out in North America."[37] It was around this time that the *Anti-Gallican* carried a strange ad on its back page. It was a collection of numbers, without apparent meaning. The secretary of the Austrian legation in London noticed it and thought it looked like a ciphered message so he sent it to Vienna to be decoded.

The British government remained unconcerned about these rumors and focused its attention on halting the unrest spreading throughout England, particularly in industrial cities such as Manchester. The Radicals inside and outside of Parliament, such as Cochrane, Cobbett, and Hunt, exploited the situation to advance the cause of parliamentary reform. Although England was still the most liberal nation in Europe, its political system was far from democratic by today's standards. According to Lord Russell, a future prime minister, before 1832, parliamentary representation was "a mockery and a scandal."[38] The roughly two hundred members of the House of Lords held their seats by hereditary right, and although the members of the House of Commons were elected, strict property ownership requirements limited the electorate to no more than 5 percent of adult males. No Roman Catholic could hold high civil office or be admitted to Parliament. The Irish were also excluded. In essence, the landed aristocracy, the "oligarchy" as the reformers called it, controlled Parliament.[39] The Whigs and Radicals wanted to reform this system but internal divisions undermined their cause.* Wilson, traditionally a Whig, moved closer to the Radicals, particularly to Cochrane and Major Cartwright, the "father" of the reformist movement.[40]

It was a fringe Radical faction, the Spenceans, led by Arthur Thistlewood, who in mid-November organized a public demonstration against the government at the London Spa Fields. Many other Radical leaders were invited to address the crowd, but fearing that the organizer's intentions were not peaceful and disagreeing with the basic tenets of the Spenceans, they declined the invitation. Only Hunt accepted, as long as it was a peaceful demonstration in favor of parliamentary reform. Hunt was no ordinary rabble-rouser and had no working-class credentials. In fact, he was a well-educated and wealthy Wiltshire farmer who had entered Radical politics after a short stint in prison. In the coming years he would become a leading figure in the reform movement and a thorn in the side of the Tory government.

Hunt's presence attracted large crowds waving tricolor flags and cockades.† The government watched the gathering with apprehension as it had been warned by one of its spies that the organizers planned to start a popular uprising to depose the British monarchy. But the highlight of the demonstration was an electrifying speech by Hunt blaming the government's policies, particularly the high level of taxation, for the economic distress, and demanding universal suffrage, secret ballots, and annual general elections. When the meeting was adjourned, it was agreed that Hunt would ask Radical politician Sir Francis Burdett to present a petition with these three points to the prince regent at the opening of Parliament. A second meeting was convened for early December to hear Burdett's response.[41] With the exception of Cobbett most of the press vilified Hunt and Thistlewood for threatening England's "social peace."

Burdett declined to accept the demonstrators' petition. Hunt realized that no one but Cochrane would dare submit the petition to the prince regent or Parliament and invited him to attend the December meeting. However, the government made sure the rebellious MP could cause no trouble. Cochrane received a

---

* Most Whigs opposed universal suffrage as proposed by Henry Hunt and favored some form of property restriction.

† It is estimated that ten thousand people attended the Spa Fields demonstrations.

summons to appear at Westminster Hall to pay "a fine of £100 to the Crown."[42] Boiling with indignation, he refused. He would never agree to pay a fine imposed for escaping from what he considered an illegal detention. On November 21, he was arrested and confined once again in a cold dungeon.

Cochrane's arrest almost coincided with the publication of another ciphered ad in the *Anti-Gallican*. (To avoid raising suspicions, pro-Bonapartist messages would be placed in anti-Bonapartist publications.) The secretary of the Austrian legation in London, convinced that it was a secret message, sent a copy to Vienna to be deciphered. Who was trying to communicate with Napoleon? The main suspects were the members of the Bonaparte family, particularly Eugene and Hortense de Beauharnais and Lucien Bonaparte, who lived in Rome and was reportedly in active correspondence with Joseph.[43]

The Bonapartists had not given up their hopes of bringing Napoleon II back to the French throne. Austria's endorsement was needed, and the man in charge of assessing whether Metternich would agree was General Vaudoncourt, Wilson's friend and a diehard Bonapartist.[44] By the end of October, Vaudoncourt was in Brussels, where he stayed at the house of Wilson's sister. Weeks later he left for Munich to confer with Eugene de Beauharnais, under whose orders he had served for many years. By the end of 1816 Vaudoncourt had arrived in Vienna and requested an audience with Metternich. The Austrian chancellor knew something was afoot involving the young Napoleon. He had just learned that the American consul in Trieste had conveyed secret communications from Marshal Grouchy to Marie Louise, who had thrown them into the fire without even opening them.[45] And the Austrian police had confirmed that the *Anti-Gallican* was being used to carry out a clandestine communication with Napoleon. According to the Austrian code-breakers the hidden message published in November said the following: "The noise made by the sale of your silver has made a big sensation here. It is a mistake on your part. You can't be short of money because Joseph has promised to pay for your needs. We have received satisfactory letters from Vienna. B is always there. In two months we will try again."[46]

Did B stand for Beauharnais? Metternich suspected that Vaudoncourt's mission was connected with this message. Through his secretary, he told the general that he appreciated "the affection and loyalty for the son of the legitimate sovereign of his country but the actual political situation in Europe prevents Austria from supporting the views described."[47] Vaudoncourt returned to Munich to convey Metternich's response to Eugene. If the emperor of Austria would not support the claims of his own grandson to the throne of France, the only hopes of the Bonaparte dynasty rested in America. Metternich warned his ambassador in London that the secret message published in the *Anti-Gallican* seemed to give hope to the prisoner at St. Helena that he would soon be rescued. He had recently been informed that among the means considered to rescue Napoleon were air balloons, and that "the expedition of air vessels seems to be related to the one that Grouchy is preparing." Fortunately, this plan appeared "more than impossible."[48] Air balloons? These Bonapartists were quite ingenious.

Meanwhile, in England, concerns about clandestine communications between Napoleon and his followers in Europe were overshadowed by more domestic turmoil. In early December the second Spa Fields meeting took place. The government had been tipped off that the demonstrators were "going to liberate Lord Cochrane and the prisoners in the bench prison and then proceed to enter Carlton House to see the Prince Regent."[49] Another spy revealed that Thistlewood's plan was to seize the Tower of London and establish a Committee of Public Safety, which was to include Hunt, Burdett, and Cochrane among its members. Once in power, they planned to send a ship to St. Helena to bring Napoleon back to England.[50] Based on this intelligence, the government sent the army to disperse the crowds and "a company of infantry" to guard Cochrane.[51] Some confusing riots took place. Wilson, who attended the meeting incognito, believed that the violence was orchestrated by the government to gain support for "large military establishments and perhaps for the abolition of the right to assemble."[52] Thistlewood and three of his associates were arrested and accused of high treason. The ministerial papers portrayed him as England's Robespierre and accused Hunt, Cobbett, and Cochrane of being his accomplices in a conspiracy to overthrow the monarchy. Cobbett angrily denied the charges and accused the government of trying to divert public opinion from the country's economic crisis.[53]

Five days after the Spa Field riots, Cochrane was released from jail thanks to a "penny levy" organized by Hunt.[54] "I will now be able to get my Westminster friends to look into the cruel injustice that has been done to me," Cochrane wrote to a friend. "I have no doubt of beating all my enemies most completely and of exposing such a scene of villainy as scarcely ever before was carried on."[55] Having dealt with the Radicals, the British ministers turned their attention to Napoleon, who seemed to exert a dangerous influence over British politics and public opinion. William Warden, former surgeon of the HMS *Northumberland,* had just arrived from St. Helena and published a pamphlet about Napoleon's life in captivity that had caused a great sensation. Even American ambassador John Quincy Adams, never a fan of the captive emperor, admitted after reading Warden's pamphlet that Napoleon endured "his confinement at St. Helena with dignity and composure, if not philosophical tranquility." Adams noted that Castlereagh seemed anxious "to keep up the sentiment of fear and hatred against the ex Emperor in this nation."[56] Wilson launched a campaign to counteract Castlereagh's efforts. He had been energized after Warden told him of Napoleon's joy on hearing the news of Lavallette's escape.[57] As part of his efforts, Wilson frequently contributed articles to the *Morning Chronicle,* which was edited by his friend James Perry. Wilson found an active collaborator in Colonel Francis Maceroni, Murat's former aide-de-camp. They had met during Wilson's mission to Italy in the summer of 1814 and had probably seen each other in a French prison in early 1816.[58] In the coming years Maceroni would become Wilson's right-hand man.

The twenty-seven-year-old Maceroni had already built an impressive résumé as an intriguer. Born in England of an Italian father and an English mother, he was fluent in English, French, and Italian. He had served Murat as aide-de-camp during the last years of his reign and acted as his special envoy to Paris and London during the Hundred Days. After Napoleon abdicated the throne, Fouché had chosen Maceroni to deliver to the Duke of Wellington his proposal to surrender Paris.[59] Metternich then entrusted him with the mission of negotiating the surrender of Murat, who had sought refugee in Corsica. But Murat instead embarked on his ill-fated attempt to recover the throne of Naples. Many suspected Maceroni had secretly encouraged him, so as a result, when Maceroni returned to France at the end of 1815, he was thrown in jail.[60] After arriving in London in the summer of 1816, Maceroni became a regular contributor to the *Morning Chronicle* and started to write an account of Murat's last days, in which he sharply criticized Castlereagh. Wilson considered it a work of "great importance."[61]

Wilson's efforts to neutralize Castlereagh's policies were not limited to writing articles. As long as England remained neutral, he was determined to join the cause of Mexican independence. He told Lord Grey that the patriots in Mexico had "gained quite an advantage and [you should] not be surprised if you hear of an expedition to that quarter; £200,000 to equip and arm four thousand men are promised. The command has been offered to your humble servant."[62] Grey again felt compelled to try to dissuade his protégé from embarking on a dangerous adventure. "I hope you will weigh all the considerations belonging to it, particularly the danger to which any foreign leader would be exposed in the event either of good or bad fortune, from the jealousies, the disappointment, the envy and the traits of a barbarous and murderous people. You have an example before you in the fate of Liniers.*"[63] As usual, Wilson ignored Grey's warnings. It was at this time that he established contact with Cochrane, who had just been released from prison. "I have had no peace for these three years past," Cochrane wrote to a friend upon his release, "and those who have attempted my destruction shall have none for the next."[64] What sweeter revenge than liberating Napoleon and putting him on the throne of South America? It would be quite easy to send a message to the illustrious prisoner. "My son—the sailor—sails for St. Helena next week on the *Conqueror*," Wilson wrote to Grey. "I presume you have no commissions to execute in that part of the world as yet, but I hope and believe before three months that you will."[65]

---

* Liniers had led the defense of Buenos Aires against two British invasions but was later accused of treason and executed by the patriots.

Lowe's Nightmare Begins

Vain his complaint,—my lord presents his bill,
His food and wine were doled out duly still;
Vain was his sickness, never was a clime
So free from homicide—to doubt's a crime.

—Lord Byron, *The Age of Bronze,* Canto 3

Even if Lowe had heard of aerostats, not even in his worst nightmare could he have imagined that they could be used to liberate his prisoner. However, warnings about more conventional means kept piling up on his desk. The latest involved an American privateer who was reportedly "equipping a fast sailing vessel in the Hudson River for the express purpose of facilitating the escape of general Bonaparte."[1] Sightings of a suspicious ship sailing close to St. Helena confirmed Lowe's worst fears. When sighted, the ship had "hauled down the English colors and hoisted a blue, white and blue flag with a pendant of the same colors." These were the colors of the rebel government of Buenos Aires. Asked where she came from, "she answered from Buenos Aires and was bound to Gibraltar."[2] Was it one of the privateers that had left Baltimore months earlier under suspicion it would "attempt a coup on St. Helena to rescue Bonaparte"?[3]

This report increased Lowe's fears that some scheme was in progress to liberate Napoleon. He was under a lot of pressure as he had just received a dispatch from Bathurst expressing displeasure at the unauthorized communications that continued to take place between Longwood and Europe and stressing the need to stop them at once, particularly those directed to England, as they had a strong political impact. "There can be no doubt of attempts being made to appeal to the compassion of the nation," wrote Bathurst. "Materials for this object will be furnished by the representations of the foolish and ill disposed who come from St. Helena and by the clandestine communications sent over by Bonaparte's followers. It will be impossible to counteract this evil, but one must try to limit its extent. You had better impose some restrictions on the visits of those who are on their return to England."[4]

Eager to fulfill his instructions, on October 1, Lowe visited Longwood. Napoleon refused to see him, taking advantage of one of the few privileges he still enjoyed. Since Lowe refused to talk to Bertrand, he sent Colonel Thomas Reade to inform the grand marshal that all of Napoleon's attendants would be required to sign a declaration stating their intention to remain at St. Helena and abide by all the restrictions. Those who did not sign the declaration would be sent to Cape Town and later transferred to Europe. Those who chose to remain in the island and were found to violate any rules would be deported at their own cost. Napoleon was furious and advised everybody to refuse to sign the declaration, which referred to him as "General Bonaparte." He also saw sinister objectives behind the decision. "Their design is to send everybody away who might be inclined to make my life less disagreeable," Napoleon told O'Meara. They would get rid of everyone and sooner or later "they would kill him."[5] He believed Lowe's conduct dishonored England. Surely Parliament did not know what was happening and would not condone such behavior.

Napoleon used the forced staff reduction as an opportunity to send four messengers to Europe. Natale Santini was a loyal Corsican and former sergeant of hussars who served as Napoleon's tailor and barber. He was "a most determined character and brave as a lion" and months earlier had threatened to kill Sir Hudson Lowe.[6] Maybe this convinced Napoleon that it would be better to get him off the island. Theodore Archambault was a footman and Pierre Rousseau a domestic in charge of the silver. The fourth messenger was Captain Charles Piontkowski, whose exit from St. Helena had already been ordered by Lord Bathurst. Piontkowski was deemed too dangerous, and in any escape attempt he would be particularly useful. Lowe expected the four men to be "quarantined" at the Cape for six months and then taken to Malta. They would not reach the continent for a year.

As he did in all his campaigns, Napoleon gave each messenger separate instructions to minimize the risk of interception. Archambault and Rousseau would sail to America with letters for Joseph. Rousseau also carried a detailed map of St. Helena sewn inside his jacket. Santini would go to London and publish the "Remonstrance." "You will find in England brave people who don't share the hatred of their government towards me. They will help you fulfill your mission. After you finish go see my family and tell them everything about what is going on here. Go to Munich to see Eugene."[7] Santini was also instructed to deliver a message to Marie Louise, Napoleon's estranged wife. Piontkowski would help Santini as needed and deliver messages for Lucien, Madame Mere, and Marie Louise. Piontkowski was reminded to keep "prudent and discreet silence" and to "lose no time in compassing my object, nor jeopardize its attainment by any unauthorized publication whatever."[8] The loyal Pole memorized Montholon's "Remonstrance" in case Santini's copy was intercepted. On October 19, after being thoroughly searched, the four men left St. Helena.

To reduce the risk of escape, Lowe imposed stricter limits on Napoleon's movements. Within these new limits Napoleon was ordered "not to stir off the high road, nor to speak to any person he met, nor to enter any house unless in the presence of a British officer who had directions to interfere whenever he thought proper." With these measures Lowe hoped to stop clandestine communications with England aimed at "disseminating libelous and incendiary statements to mislead the public mind as to the mode in which the Allied Powers (and England in particular) have treated him." However, he still believed that the risk of Napoleon's escaping was unacceptably high:

> There is still a considerable period of the day (from the time the sentries are withdrawn in the morning until sunset) in which it is by no means difficult for general Bonaparte to effect his escape from the boundaries assigned as his limits[;] . . . the road to the Alarm House contains a circuit of about eight miles. It is impossible so effectually to watch all their extent by sentries as to prevent his passing unperceived through some part of the line, particularly in rainy and foggy weather. The principal security therefore during the day rests in his being seen or its being ascertained by some other nearly certain means that he is in the house in the morning and at the close of the day.[9]

As a result of Lowe's restrictions, Napoleon was forced to limit his movements to a very small area. If he moved off these limits "only for a few minutes any of the numerous sentinels posted on it would be fully justified in shooting him for an attempt to escape." Napoleon was enraged at these new measures and to avoid the possibility of being stopped, insulted, or detained by the sentinels, as regularly happened to all members of his suite who ventured out of Longwood, he confined himself to his rooms.[10] Lowe soon realized the mistake he had made. Unless he forced Napoleon's door he would never be able to ascertain whether he was actually at Longwood. It became critical for him to have someone close to Napoleon to act as a spy. Lowe tried to recruit O'Meara for the job. Meanwhile the warnings from London piled up on his desk. All evidence confirmed that Napoleon was secretly communicating with his supporters in Europe. Bathurst demanded stronger measures, including searching the private papers of Napoleon's companions. He advised Lowe to keep the strictest surveillance over the prisoner, particularly at night. Bathurst also warned Lowe that "if evasion be the object of General Buonaparte, . . . no part of the twenty-four hours is better calculated for its successful execution than that between dark and morning and it is therefore least of all possible during that period to abandon the precautions which have at other times been considered important."[11]

Lowe could scarcely keep up with the barrage of communications arriving from Bathurst's office. In another dispatch he was told that Napoleon had already "gained over a person at St. Helena" and advised him to remain alert. Who could that person be? Lowe suspected it was William Balcombe, the purveyor of Longwood, who had unrestricted access to Napoleon's residence. By early November, Lowe received yet another report "containing intelligence of an expedition stated to have lately sailed from Baltimore the real object of which is represented to be to furnish the means of General Buonaparte's escape from St. Helena."[12] Lowe could hardly sleep. He woke up in the middle of the night and rode to Longwood to make sure his prisoner had not escaped.[13]

Around this time, Napoleon was offered a plan of escape. According to Montholon, he "listened without interest." Was he already thinking of his own plan? One thing is clear, Napoleon was fed up with Lowe and St. Helena. "It requires great resolution and strength of mind to support such an existence in this horrible abode," he told O'Meara. It seemed as if Lowe's only objective was to irritate him. "He wants to shorten my life by daily irritations." Napoleon couldn't even talk freely with anybody he met during his rides. "It is a piece of tyranny unheard of except in the instance of the man with the iron mask." To make matters worse, Longwood was the worst part of the island. There was "either a furious wind with fog . . . or a sun which scorches my brains." Napoleon couldn't believe Parliament could possibly know what was happening at St. Helena.[14]

Napoleon was up to something. Las Cases, who had become his most trusted adviser and spokesperson, believed that the tsar would intervene in his favor.[15] The wily count started having mysterious interviews with Balmain, the Russian commissioner, who reported back to St. Petersburg that the prisoner was "quite impatient" to talk to him.[16] Lowe noticed these accidental encounters.

He thought Las Cases was dangerous and had long suspected Balmain of being one of the channels through which Napoleon communicated with his supporters in Europe and determined to get rid of him. Lowe also suspected the Austrian commissioner's pretty, young French wife who was devoted to Napoleon. In late November, Lowe was warned that a servant of Las Cases's had carried a message from his master to Baroness Sturmer. Las Cases had no choice but to fire the servant.

To entrap Las Cases, Lowe enlisted the help of the dismissed servant, who one night surreptitiously returned to Longwood and told his former employer that he had been hired to go to England and offered to take some letters with him. Las Cases took the bait and gave him two letters to be sewn inside a vest. One was addressed to Lady Clavering, a French woman who lived in London, and the other to Lucien Bonaparte. Both letters were promptly delivered to Lowe. One paragraph in the letter to Lucien caught Lowe's attention:

> You will ask me maybe if it is possible to escape from our rock? The military men and the sailors think it is almost impossible; but they also agree that the rigorous measures and the harassments of every kind that we have to endure do not alter the probabilities. Having answered that escape is almost impossible, it remains to ask what does the Emperor want? At first we have to consider the insuperable difficulties of attempting an escape, then, where to go? Wouldn't the ocean become a second prison? Aren't all of Europe, Africa, India, and almost all of the Americas closed to him? The Emperor is and remains today positively in the same frame of mind, the same position, and has the same wishes he had at the island of Aix. At that time he wanted to go to America and retire on the shores of the Mississippi or the Ohio or to take asylum in England.[17]

Although the letter did not seem to have any details of an escape plan, Lowe thought it was not "entirely free from incitement to have it attempted."[18] The letter left no doubt about Napoleon's wishes, which were already known to his supporters in the United States. Representatives of the recently created French Agricultural and Manufacturing Society, with Charles Lallemand as its president, were scouting for land near the Ohio and Mississippi rivers, in the wild and unexplored frontier between the United States and the viceroyalty of Mexico.

Las Cases was arrested, all his communications with Longwood interdicted, and his personal papers with the details of his conversations with Napoleon confiscated.[19] Lowe informed Bathurst that the count had recorded all the details of Napoleon's life. "His acts, his conversations, including Count Montholon's letter,—even his gestures are noted. The whole kept with the minuteness of Boswell's *Life of Johnson* with the force of Bonaparte's own language and the embellishment of Las Cases' own . . . [with] the great object of presenting to posterity in the person of General Buonaparte a model of excellence and virtue."[20]

Napoleon viewed the arrest of Las Cases as another outrage against his dignity.[21] He was particularly annoyed because the fruit of nine months of dictation, with information about the death of the Duke of Enghien and other sensitive matters that he did not wish to disclose to the British government, had fallen into Lowe's hands.[22] But Napoleon's mood improved in early December, when he received news from the United States.[23] Joseph asked for instructions. He expected his family to join him in America soon and would get the diamonds of the crown of Spain, which he had hidden in his property in Switzerland.[24] Napoleon was pleased with the conduct of his older brother. In a conversation with O'Meara he described Joseph as "a most excellent character. . . . His virtues and talents are those of a private character and for such, nature intended him: he is too good to be a great man. He has no ambition. He is very like me in person, but handsomer. He is extremely well informed." O'Meara noted that on all occasions Joseph's name came up, Napoleon spoke of him in terms of "warm affection."[25]

Joseph would receive Napoleon's instructions much sooner than expected. On December 18, the *Orontes,* carrying Piontkowski, Santini, Rousseau, and Archambault dropped anchor at Jamestown on their way back to England. Lowe was puzzled and irritated at their appearance; he had hoped they would remain in Cape Town for several months. Napoleon was obviously quite pleased, as it meant that his messengers would reach their destination sooner. Lowe would not make the same mistake with Las Cases. He had no doubt that if left free to roam Europe, the scheming count would launch a very effective campaign in favor of his master. "This governor is a man totally unfit to fill the situation he holds," Napoleon told O'Meara. "Does he think that Europe is a mine of gunpowder and Las Cases the spark to blow it up?"[26]

With Las Cases out of Longwood, Lowe stepped up his efforts to recruit O'Meara as his spy. Two months earlier he had supported a petition by the Irish surgeon for a salary increase, "having had experience of Dr. O'Meara's zeal and useful information to me in several instances."[27] O'Meara seemed compliant and sent Lowe a detailed memorandum on Napoleon's health and what transpired at Longwood. Although the report didn't contain much valuable information, in it O'Meara claimed to have tried to convince Napoleon that Lowe was not trying to kill him.[28] But O'Meara refused to be Lowe's spy, maybe because he had already negotiated a better deal. Napoleon had made sure long ago that the doctor was firmly on his side.

As the year ended Napoleon became more melancholic. "What a fool I was to give myself up to you," he told O'Meara. "I had a mistaken notion of your national character; I had formed a romantic idea of the English. There entered into it also a portion of pride. I disdained to give myself up to any of those sovereigns whose countries I had conquered, and whose capitals I had entered in triumph and I determined to confide in you, who I had never vanquished. Doctor, I am well punished for the good opinion I had of you and for the confidence which I reposed in you."[29] Napoleon had learned from his mistake. According to Balmain he often said, "If I were in the power of the Emperor Alexander I should be better off. That Prince is noble and generous."[30] Was he trying to soften the tsar? Determined to leave St. Helena, Napoleon was playing all his cards.

3
1817

13

Hope Rises at Longwood

There sunk the greatest, nor the worst of men,
Whose spirit antithetically mixt
One moment of the mightiest, and again
On little objects with like firmness fixt.
　　　　　　　—Lord Byron, *Childe Harold's Pilgrimage,* Canto 3

Napoleon started 1817 in a better mood, convinced his situation would improve. "Perhaps I shall be dead, which will be much better," he told O'Meara laughing, "Worse than this cannot be."[1] Sir Hudson Lowe started the year badly. Not only was he completely estranged from Napoleon but also was at open war with Baron Sturmer, the Austrian commissioner. The cause was Welle, the Austrian botanist. Like many other botanists in this story, Welle had other interests besides studying plants. In fact, he had brought from Vienna a letter for Napoleon's valet from his mother, who was Napoleon II's nanny. Inside the envelope was a lock of the young boy's hair.[2] When Lowe learned that the letter had been delivered without his permission, he accused Sturmer of complicity and demanded Welle's immediate recall.[3]

The "Welle affair" proved once again how the world communicated with Napoleon in defiance of Lowe's regulations. Napoleon was well aware of the preparations being made in the United States. At the end of January, he received a message from Joseph saying that a group of Spanish rebels had offered him the crown of Mexico. Joseph's message improved the mood at Longwood. Napoleon was "gayer than ever."[4] According to Montholon, months later the rebels offered the throne to the emperor himself "and had foreseen all the obstacles resulting from the emperor's captivity and forgotten nothing to ensure the success of their design."[5]

In his message Joseph asked Napoleon for instructions on how to respond to the offers made to him "by several representatives of states belonging to Spanish America and also regarding those men in France that are raising their hopes."[6]

Napoleon thought Joseph would refuse these offers. "Although possessing the mind, talents, and all the qualities necessary to make a nation happy," he told Montholon. "He loves his liberty and the enjoyments of social life too much to have any wish to launch into the storms of royalty for a second time." Joseph was not the right man to lead the conquest or liberation of the Spanish colonies; he had a good head but did not like to work, Napoleon said. Besides, he knew nothing about the military profession.[7] "Surely he has a big fortune, maybe 20 million francs,"* he added. "But he is wrong to mix himself up in a revolution. To succeed it is necessary to be much more wicked than he is, to have better brains and not to be afraid to chop some heads. His personality is too mellow. On the other hand he has a lot of ambition and believes [in] his own capabilities and resources. A crown is a big temptation and he can count on the French officers who are with him in America. Maybe it is better for England to separate the colonies from Spain. However, a Frenchman ruling there seems too much." Napoleon's wishes were clear. "If I am told that he has succeeded, I would reply that I am very happy," he said. "I have been told he will tempt his fortune, which concerns me." Napoleon then unfolded his maps of South America on the billiard table and after careful study, he turned to Montholon and Gourgaud and said: "We would be so happy in Buenos Aires!"[8] He would have certainly been welcome in Buenos Aires, where in the past eighteen months, scores of his supporters had settled, including General Michel Brayer and the botanist Aimé Bonpland. Not surprisingly, Brayer's name came up in the conversations at Longwood. Napoleon recalled how much he had helped him after escaping from Elba. He had never seen such a determined man.[9]

Napoleon wanted Joseph to take the crown of Mexico; he told Bertrand that doing so would not only be useful to himself but also "to those unfortunate people by saving them from the calamities of a long civil war." Napoleon also thought the objective was within reach, as he estimated Joseph could count on at least fifteen thousand Frenchmen. "If he has only a third, even only two thousand, and among them officers of artillery, logistics and cavalry, it would still be enough," he told Bertrand. "The officers make the troops; with them, he can aid the Mexicans, who by themselves would be worth nothing."[10] Who could lead this campaign? Maybe Clausel, or even better Lallemand, who was reportedly on his way to the United States. Their names, as well as Brayer's, kept coming up in the conversations at Longwood. Clausel was one of Napoleon's best

* Five francs were roughly equivalent to one dollar.

generals but he had a warm spot for Lallemand. "He has the sacred fire," he told O'Meara, "*beaucoup de décision,* is capable of making combinations, and there are few men more qualified to lead a hazardous enterprise."[11]

Napoleon had a vested interest in Joseph's success. He believed a Bonapartist empire in the Spanish colonies would be "very advantageous to England, because she would acquire all the commerce of Spanish America," as trading with Bourbon Spain or France could be out of the question. And Joseph "would avail himself of these new means to obtain from the English ministers some change in my position."[12] Napoleon's speculations about the attitude England would take toward Joseph's rule in Spanish America were not far-fetched. "Your nation," Napoleon told O'Meara, "is chiefly guided by interest in all its actions."[13] Trade with the Spanish colonies was crucial to the British economy, particularly in the current recession. As long as Spain ruled the colonies, British merchants would never be able to obtain any significant commercial advantages. Napoleon reasoned that it would be much better for England to have a Bonaparte ruling the Spanish colonies than Ferdinand VII. A "nation of shopkeepers" would not oppose a scheme that offered greater commercial prospects. In recent months Napoleon had articulated his ideas on this subject in several conversation with O'Meara.

Napoleon thought the situation in England was unsustainable and would lead to popular unrest and perhaps a revolution. He blamed this state of affairs entirely on the "imbecility" of Lord Castlereagh. "If your ministers had paid attention to the interests of the country instead of intriguing they would have rendered you the most happy and the most flourishing nation in the world," he told O'Meara.

> At the conclusion of the war they should have said to the Spanish and Portuguese governments: "We have saved your country, we alone supported you and prevented you from falling a prey to France. We have made many campaigns and shed our best blood in your cause. We have expended many millions of money and consequently the country is overburdened with debt on your account, which we must pay. You have the means of repaying us. Our situation requires that we should liquidate our debts. We demand therefore, that we shall be the only nation allowed to trade with South America for twenty years and that our ships shall have the same privilege as Spanish vessels. In this way we will reimburse ourselves without distressing you."

Napoleon thought neither Spain nor Portugal could have refused and England's economy would be in a strong position. But as a consequence of Castlereagh's misguided policies, France could soon dominate trade with Brazil. "You have in your own colonies more cotton and sugar than you want, and consequently will not take the production of the Brazils in exchange for your merchandise. . . . [France] will exchange their manufactured goods, silks, furniture, wines, etc., against colonial produce and soon have the whole trade of the Brazils. In like manner they will have the preference in trading with the Spanish colonies partly on account of the religion and also because the Spaniards, like other nations, are jealous of a people all-powerful at sea, and will constantly assist to lessen that power; which is most effectually to be done by lessening your commerce."[14]

Having Joseph as king of Mexico "would be of great advantage to England, as you would have all the commerce of Spanish America," Napoleon assured O'Meara. In his view Joseph "would not, and indeed could not, trade with either France or Spain for evident reasons and South America cannot do without importing immense quantities of European goods. By having me in your hands, you could always make advantageous terms with Joseph, who loves me sincerely and would do anything for me."[15] Days later he told his doctor that Castlereagh and Liverpool "would have done better to have left me upon the throne. I would have given the English great commercial advantages which the Bourbons dare not offer."[16]

In conversations with O'Meara, Napoleon insisted that England's economy desperately needed free trade with the Spanish colonies and saw "no feasible measure to remedy the distress of your manufacturers except endeavoring by all means in your power to promote the separation of the Spanish South American colonies from the mother country. By means of this, you would have an opportunity of opening a most extensive and lucrative commerce with the South American, which would be productive of great advantages to you." Otherwise the Americans would gain the upper hand. But if England acted "as I have said, they [the colonies] could trade with no other nation than you."[17] Days later, Napoleon insisted: "As long as the Spaniards and Portuguese retain their colonies in South America, so long will they be against England. The world is too enlightened to allow you to usurp the whole of the trade and manufactures."[18]

Napoleon knew O'Meara would report back these opinions to his contacts at the Admiralty. In fact, O'Meara's reports were read by all the cabinet ministers. At this time, the British government certainly thought O'Meara was rendering valuable services. A few months later Lord Bathurst recommended an increase in his salary, as it was inadequate "for the delicate and disagreeable duty imposed upon him" and could make him "desirous of abandoning it." Bathurst emphasized that he attached "much much [*sic*] importance to retaining about the person of General Bonaparte's a person so familiarized with his habits and constitution as Dr. O'Meara must necessarily be."[19] Just in case O'Meara didn't transmit his views about the Spanish colonies, Napoleon made them clear during a conversation with Admiral Sir Pulteney Malcolm, chief of the St. Helena naval station. He said that England should favor the separation of the Spanish colonies from the mother country. "That no matter how kind, or how well England treated Spain, or how ill France behaved to her, that as long as Spain retained her colonies, she would be jealous of England, from the fear that her commerce would be destroyed by our navy."[20] Napoleon's views on the subject were also reproduced in the *Letters from the Cape of Good Hope,* a pamphlet published in London in 1817, which he apparently authored. One of the letters said that the emancipation of Spanish colonies "would be of the greatest advantage to England because as long as the principal policy of Spain is directed towards the preservation and administration of her American colonies, she will consider the power which rules the seas her natural enemy, and will adhere to France to counterbalance the maritime preponderance of England; but America once set free, the policy of Spain becomes purely continental and consequently in rivalry with France, as the only power in contact with and in opposition to her continental interests."[21]

Was Napoleon trying to send a message to the British cabinet? In his mind any personal animosity toward him could not enter into the equation. Napoleon thought "a distinction must be made between the actions of a sovereign, who acts as a collective person, and those of a private individual, who has only his own feelings to consider. Politics allows the one to do what would be inexcusable in the other."[22] He obviously underestimated how much the Tories hated him. Besides, Castlereagh had its own plan for the Spanish colonies and the Bonaparte family had no role in it. The British foreign secretary was playing both sides in the conflict to ensure England achieved commercial supremacy in South America.

The American dream was part of the daily conversation at Longwood. In early March, Napoleon received another message from Joseph. "Ah! If I had been able to govern France for forty years, I would have created the most amazing Empire the world has ever known," exclaimed Napoleon during dinner. "Who knows?" said Countess Montholon, "perhaps Your Majesty will some day build a vast Empire in America."[23]

At the end of March several East Indiamen arrived in Jamestown and many of their passengers were allowed to visit Longwood. The captain of one of these vessels offered to take Napoleon "wherever he wished." He explained that he had been inspired to do so by his strong indignation at the conduct pursued by the British government—and above all, that of Sir Hudson Lowe—an indignation, he added, "which was shared by all classes in England, with the exception of a few private friends of the ministers." Napoleon listened with attention to this new offer of escape, but after thanking the captain he refused. Was this the same plan that one of the British officers garrisoned in St. Helena presented to him? The unnamed officer claimed to be in agreement with one of the captains of one of the ships anchored in the harbor. His plan required Napoleon to escape from Longwood and reach Sandy Bay, where a boat would to take him to a ship anchored nearby. Montholon did not know whether Napoleon refused these proposals because he had abandoned all ideas of escape or "whether he doubted the sincerity of the offers that were made to him or their probability of success."[24]

Lowe probably never found out about this plan but was alarmed by a report that an unidentified boat had approached the island without permission. "We have not been able to find out to what ship she belongs," reported Colonel Reade.[25] Then, after learning that four English sailors had entered Longwood without being noticed by the sentries, Lowe increased his precautions. He could hardly sleep, and he visited the compound twice a week to ascertain the presence of his prisoner.[26]

Napoleon also suffered from insomnia. According to Countess Bertrand, he woke up during the night and "can never go off to sleep again, but turns over in his mind all his mistakes and compares his present position to the past."[27] If he had gone to America it would have been different. "He would have had plenty of books to read and Frenchmen with whom he could associate, but here, he has nothing."[28] Napoleon was anxious. Had his messengers reached London?

14
Napoleon's Message Delivered

Save the Emperor Napoleon my master who is dying under the tortures of
St. Helena!

—Natale Santini to Sir Robert Wilson, February 1817

The Bourbon court started 1817 in a state of full alert. A conspiracy had recently been discovered at Bordeaux "to restore the Buonapartean dynasty and
declare the Archduchess Marie Louise as Regent during her son's minority." According to the London papers a "considerable number of persons" had been arrested.[1] In Vienna the police were "making active researches to discover the
principal agents of the late plan to rescue the young Napoleon" and had arrested many individuals suspected "of being concerned in this affair."[2] A second
ciphered message appeared in London's *Anti-Gallican*. Metternich suspected it
was from Lavallette, who was hiding in Bavaria under the protection of Eugene
de Beauharnais. Metternich thought "it would be very helpful to pass the *Anti-
Gallican* to St. Helena" to provoke Napoleon's response through a London newspaper.[3]

The activities and movements of the Bonaparte family, particularly Lucien,
also caused alarm in Paris and Vienna. At the end of 1816, Lucien had asked
for a passport for himself and his son to go to the United States. In February,
Richelieu met with the representatives of the four Allied powers in Paris to review this request. The interception of Las Cases's letter and the information provided by Madrid about Joseph's plans for the Spanish colonies called for immediate action. One Bonaparte in America was already one too many.

While elsewhere in Europe everybody was speculating when the Bourbons
would fall, Richelieu was more concerned about a cabinet change in England.
Political and social unrest were on the rise. Taking advantage of the situation,
the Whigs and the Radicals criticized the government's domestic and foreign

policies, particularly England's attitude toward the war in the Spanish colonies and Napoleon's treatment at St. Helena. Richelieu warned the Marquis of Osmond, his ambassador in London, that a cabinet change "would produce a shock that would be harmful to us and good for the man on the rock. Couldn't he obtain a bit more freedom in the name of philanthropy and maybe the means to escape and trouble the world again? We need to have our sights constantly fixed on St. Helena, because this little black spot on the horizon can still cause a storm."[4] Napoleon also believed that if Lord Holland was chosen as prime minister or if Charlotte was crowned queen he would be released.[5] But Charlotte could only become queen if the prince regent abdicated or died.

A strange incident at the beginning of 1817 suggested that the latter scenario was not so improbable. Since the Spa Field meetings the Radical politician Henry Hunt had gathered dozens of petitions around the country in favor of parliamentary reform. At the end of January, Hunt organized a big demonstration in Hyde Park to decide who would present these petitions to the prince regent at the opening of Parliament. Since Burdett had declined, Hunt proposed to ask Lord Thomas Cochrane and led a crowd of demonstrators to his house. "Refuse their request if you please," the Radical leader told the surprised Lord. "But if you do, I am sure that you will regret is as long as you live." At the sight of the demonstrators and at the insistence of his friend William Cobbett, Cochrane accepted. The demonstrators carried him all the way to the doors of Parliament.[6]

Hours later, as the prince regent returned to Carlton House, a window of his carriage was broken. Whether it was a pistol shot, as the government claimed, a potato or a stone we will never know, but the ministers quickly promoted the incident as an attempt on the life of the prince regent and the English monarchy. The Tories feared that Thomas Paine's dire predictions were turning into a reality and that the virus of the French Revolution was infecting England. The Tory press, particularly the *Courier*—the "greatest liar of the whole" according to Lord Byron—accused Cochrane, Cobbett, and Hunt of being "the panders of the tyranny of Buonaparte, of the usurpations, oppressions of France, and [they] cannot pass themselves off as friends of freedom."[7] Naturally, the Radicals were blamed for the attack on the prince regent. The strategy worked and when Cochrane presented Hunt's petitions in the House of Commons nobody supported him. Cochrane's attempt to bring parliamentary reform to England was dead on arrival.

The government, claiming that the alleged attempt on the prince regent was part of a conspiracy "centrally controlled and organized with demonic skill by cold-blooded revolutionaries," took drastic measures to save England from a dangerous revolution.[8] In the following weeks the home secretary presented a "mountain of documents" to Parliament's Secret Committees showing that the recent meetings at Spa Fields were part of a vast plan conceived by Arthur Thistlewood and others to depose the monarchy. The conspirators had "the fullest confidence of success."[9] The objective of the second meeting at Spa Fields had been "to establish a new government, attack the prisons and provoke a rebellion among the troops." The government alleged that among the first measures planned by the conspirators if they succeeded was to send a fast sailing vessel to St. Helena "to fetch Bonaparte and bring him to England."[10]

Although the evidence was of dubious value, the Secret Committees approved taking measures to prevent a dangerous revolution. Thistlewood and his accomplices were tried for high treason.* The next victim was the habeas corpus act, which since 1679 had protected English citizens from arbitrary imprisonment. To support overturning this law, the home secretary asserted that "a traitorous conspiracy" had been discovered "for the purpose of overthrowing the established government," the result of "a malignant spirit which had brought such disgrace upon the domestic character of the people . . . which had long prevailed in the country, but especially since the commencement of the French Revolution." Lord Cochrane replied that instead "of bringing in these bills, he thought the best way of quieting the people would be to abolish all sinecure places, to reduce the military establishments and to give them a fair representation in parliament."[11] As usual, his views were ignored, and on March 3 a majority in both houses agreed to suspend the habeas corpus for three months. The suspension was later extended until the end of 1818.[12]

The turmoil in England had a great impact across the Channel. Richelieu was particularly concerned about the increasing popularity of the Radical Party and the activism of Cochrane, Hunt, Hobhouse, and Burdett—"seditious agitators" who would stop at nothing for parliamentary reform—and by Cobbett's incendiary articles in the *Political Register.* The French minister also noted with concern that Sir Robert Wilson, had embraced the Radical cause. Wilson felt the Whigs had lost their enthusiasm for reform, which he thought was "absolutely necessary for the salvation of this country."[13] Reform also meant the end of the Tory ministry and the release of Napoleon. Wilson was still determined

---

*Thistlewood and his collaborators were later acquitted for lack of evidence.

to join the patriots in Mexico but it seems the arrival of Napoleon's messengers in mid-February changed his plans. "General, I just arrived from St. Helena. Please save the Emperor Napoleon my master who is dying under the tortures of St. Helena! Save him or soon it will be too late!" Santini said upon meeting him.[14] It was a plea Wilson could not ignore.

Santini gave Wilson and Lord Holland copies of Montholon's "Remonstrance."[15] Piontkowski also provided them additional details about Napoleon's captivity.[16] With this material, the general began drafting a scathing attack of Sir Hudson Lowe to be published under Santini's name.[17] He found an eager and able assistant in Francis Maceroni, who was already a relatively well-known author in England; he had just published an account of the last days of Joachim Murat that was highly critical of the British government.[18] Wilson considered Maceroni's book "a publication of great importance" and enthusiastically recommended it to Lord Grey.[19]

Meanwhile, the Austrian police had just deciphered the third ad published in the *Anti-Gallican.* The message added another twist to the intrigue. In a book published a year earlier, William Warden had said that Napoleon considered Lewis Goldsmith a double-dealer and a spy. This had prompted the latter to refute this accusation, reaffirming his anti-Bonapartist credentials and arguing that "the principles which I put into a state of activity were chiefly instrumental in conducting Buonaparte to his present abode."[20] This in turn had raised suspicions that Goldsmith had "a wish to be reconciled with Buonaparte." The ciphered message specifically referred to Goldsmith's letter, and its content, although vague, suggested that an attempt to rescue Napoleon was imminent.

The *Anti-Gallican* has just arrived here; it is annoying that the editor sent you a letter, it raised attention; it will hurt us if I cannot communicate with you through the newspaper because I am afraid that the others will not want to insert announcements in cipher; so it is not necessary to answer him. Harel* left for America; funds were sent to your brother Joseph; Lucien has become greedy; Hortense is always well disposed. The army will be increased by 500.000 men. Russia raises its army. Pozzo di

* It is probably Charles-Jean Harel (1790–1846), Prefect of Landes during the Hundred Days. Included in the *ordonnance royale* of July 24, Harel sought exile in Brussels after Waterloo and became the lover of Mademoiselle George, an actress who had at one point also shared Napoleon's affections. It is unclear whether Harel ever went to America. He returned to France in 1820.

Borgo sounded Davout. Carnot has turned completely Russian. If the English government makes you any propositions, say nothing to Sturmer. Although Metternich promised to be useful to you, it is not necessary to confide in him. In any case, follow the advice given to you: do not sleep at night.[21]

Metternich was now almost certain that Lavallette was the author of the message and he advised Prince Esterhazy, his ambassador in London, to communicate the contents of the message to the British government.[22] Esterhazy reported back that the prince regent suspected Goldsmith, "known for his venality, to be in concert in this correspondence."[23] Lord Bathurst agreed to send a copy of the deciphered message to Sir Hudson Lowe. Richelieu also suspected Lavallette's involvement and thought Wilson might have had a hand in it as well. It was certainly a possibility, as the two men remained in close contact.

At this point, Wilson was considering all options to alleviate Napoleon's captivity, including a rescue plan. Piontkowski and Santini confirmed his worst suspicions about the high-handed manner in which Lowe treated his prisoner and convinced him of the need to do something about it. Even Sir George Cockburn "put implicit merit in Santini's relation" and told Wilson that Napoleon's complaints were "founded in truth and justice." Cockburn was even considering the possibility of returning to St. Helena.[24] Wilson had enlisted a new ally in his quest to liberate Napoleon: Lord Cochrane. Against Lord Holland's advice, who insisted on sticking to the law, both wanted to take matters in their own hands.

In mid-March, Wilson had Montholon's "Remonstrance" published in the *Morning Chronicle.* He also helped Santini draft a pamphlet describing in great detail the "petty and mean" vexations to which "the worthy Governor Lowe subjected his illustrious prisoner." Piontkowski asked Lord Holland to intervene and stop its publication, as Santini's head had been "turned" by Wilson, who had "charged himself with this affair."[25] Maybe Santini had instructions that Piontkowski ignored or maybe the Pole changed his mind. A few days later he wrote to Gourgaud: "General Wilson has written a brochure that will appear in French and English in Santini's name."[26]

The publication of Santini's pamphlet—titled *An Appeal to the English Nation*—caused a great sensation. The *Courier* disclosed that the pamphlet had been "ushered into the world under very extraordinary patronage and protection; no less than that of an English General."[27] Wilson was quite pleased with his work. "Santini's *Appeal* is in great request and the public feeling is better than expected," he exultantly informed Grey.[28] To the dismay of the Tories, the British public devoured "every scrap of news from St. Helena."[29] Santini's pamphlet became an instant best seller and quickly went through several editions.[30]

Wilson had fired the first salvo; the next was fired by Lord Holland, who introduced a motion in the House of Lords to investigate Napoleon's situation at St. Helena. In the debate that followed, Lord Bathurst denounced all the accusations against the government as hogwash. He also disclosed that Napoleon's supporters were trying to communicate with him through ciphered messages inserted in several London newspapers. By doing so Bathurst lost a chance to find out who was the author of these messages. None were ever published again. Wilson desperately tried to enlist the support of the Whig lords for Holland's motion. "I hope you will not yet determine that the selection of Santini is untrue," he wrote to Grey. "Notwithstanding Bathurst's garbled extracts without dates I am certain of the fact of the allegations are correct and Santini is now employed in authenticating them."[31] Wilson even arranged a private meeting between Grey and Santini, which was duly reported to Metternich by Austrian spies.[32] Despite all these efforts, Lord Holland's motion was defeated. The *Courier* thanked him "for affording so official and decisive an opportunity of putting down the charges brought against us."[33]

Lord Holland's defeat in Parliament confirmed that as long as the Tories remained in power, Napoleon would remain in prison. For Wilson and Cochrane it was time for action. Rumors that they were preparing to depart for South America soon filtered to the press. The *Globe* reported that they planned to join the patriots in the war against Spain. The *Anti-Gallican* echoed this rumor: "Lord Cochrane has announced by public advertisement his intention of joining the insurgents in South America. His Lordship wants to raise £10,000 upon security. It is reported that Sir Robert Wilson likewise intends to proceed to South America. I hope this is not true." A week later Goldsmith reported that Cochrane had "raised the £10,000 and bought a fine vessel, nearly as large as a frigate, which he proposes to man with the best sailors he can procure for his voyage to South America."[34]

Wilson's association with Cochrane in a South American adventure raised a few eyebrows in Whig circles. Cochrane's reputation had not yet recovered from his involvement in the 1814 stock scandal. Even though he was an aristocrat, his virulent brand of reform and his antiestablishment attitudes were too extreme for most Whigs, who still held a good opinion of Wilson. Lord Hutchinson immediately wrote to his former aide. "Surely you are not about to rush into some mad scheme and with such an adventurer as that unfortunate man Lord Cochrane." Lord Grey also expressed his concerns to Wilson. "You will think, I know, the South America project wild and injudicious," Wilson replied. "There is however a fatality which seems to make such combinations as will render the attempt inevitable." As to Cochrane's company, in his view South America presented "sufficient field for more than one Quixote."[35]

At about this time, Charles Lallemand—who had arrived in England incognito—and the two messengers from St. Helena left for the United States. What Lallemand did during his brief stay in England remains a mystery. The British government never detected his presence. If Wilson had anything to discuss with Lallemand he could have done it face to face. Under the banner of South American independence they would rescue Napoleon and put him on the throne of a new empire.

While in England Lallemand, Wilson, and Cochrane prepared for their South American adventure, in France the political struggle between the Ultras and the liberals intensified. Santini's pamphlet was followed by the publication of an anonymous tract *A Manuscript Transmitted from St. Helena by an Unknown Channel*, which was attributed to Napoleon himself. Written in the first person, the manuscript was a politically charged manifesto in which the former emperor presented himself as a champion of liberalism and blamed his enemies for the wars that had afflicted Europe for fifteen years.[36] Copies of the *Manuscript* were smuggled into France, where the document had great impact. The Bonapartists felt as if Napoleon spoke directly to them.[37] Richelieu believed that the *Manuscript* and the sudden interest of the public in the former emperor threatened the political stability of France.[38] Napoleon agreed. "The author says that there will be a revolution in Europe. That is not at all improbable," he said after reading it.[39] A play titled *Germanicus* provided a forum for the Bonapartists. At its heavily attended opening in Paris, the public booed the actor playing Tiberius, who represented the Bourbons, and cheered Germanicus, who represented Napoleon. The Ultras were troubled by these demonstrations.[40] The *Courier* noted that "this disturbance is the more deserving of attention, as from a variety of circumstances, it is evident the Revolutionary Party are bestirring themselves, particularly at this moment, for some purpose or another, at the very moment the seditious in England expected to effect a revolution in Spa Fields!"[41]

Fearing a new conspiracy was afoot, the French police kept a close surveillance over any suspected Bonapartists. The beautiful Laure Regnault de St. Jean d'Angely, whose husband was exiled with Joseph in the United States, was at the top of their list. She had recently returned from Brussels, and her house was a meeting point for many disgruntled Bonapartists.[42] One of her assiduous visitors was a young man named Charles Robert, a former captain of the Grande Armée and subprefect of Nievre during the Hundred Days. At the end of March the countess wrote to her husband asking him to hasten his return to France. "A revolution is inevitable. It will be terrible," she said. "If we had been able to judge beforehand the effect of *Germanicus,* maybe we would have been freed from these obnoxious wretches." Laure was fanatically attached to Napoleon and had at times been rumored to be his lover. Now that Napoleon was in the clutches of "our cruelest enemies," she felt France's honor was attached to his liberation. "All my force, all my courage give in to this thought," she told her husband. "Believe me we shall soon reach a big crisis. Come quickly so you can judge for yourself."[43] Thanks to the efficient intervention of the *cabinet noir,* Regnault never received this letter; his wife was arrested and confined at the infamous Conciergerie.[44]

Countess Regnault's letter confirmed the Ultras' worst suspicions—that a conspiracy to bring Napoleon back to France was afoot. One of her protégés, Captain Robert, escaped to Buenos Aires with a group of fellow Bonapartists. The arming of expeditions in England and the United States and the immigration of Napoleon's veterans to South America troubled Richelieu, who again pressed Castlereagh for a quick solution to the conflict between Spain and her colonies. The French minister suspected that Castlereagh's reluctance to openly support Spain was shortsighted, and he sought to strengthen England's commercial interests in South America. Richelieu was convinced that it was in the best interest of Europe's dynasties to stop the anarchy in the New World, which provided a fertile ground for the plans of the Bonapartist émigrés. Months earlier Hyde de Neuville had suggested establishing two monarchies in South America under Bourbon princes. With the support of the Portuguese monarchy in Brazil, they could arrest the spread of revolutionary ideas in the Spanish colonies and reduce the influence of England and the United States.[45] This ambitious scheme slowly started to take shape in Richelieu's mind.

The king of Spain had rejected Castlereagh's offers of mediation, which precluded the use of force, and had turned to the tsar of Russia, who promised ships and troops in exchange for the island of Minorca. Castlereagh soon learned of these secret negotiations and warned Russia to stay away from the Spanish colonies.[46] Castlereagh still had a card up his sleeve. He had just received a letter from General Jose de San Martin, commander in chief of the patriot army of Buenos Aires, requesting England's mediation in the war against Spain and proposing the establishment of a European monarchy in South America. Castlereagh liked this idea, as years earlier he had seriously considered it to achieve the same objective: reducing Napoleon's influence in the Spanish colonies.[47] The British foreign secretary launched again his mediating efforts and proposed five conditions to the court of Madrid: the abolition of the slave trade, an amnesty for all insurgents, legal equality for the Spanish Americans, free trade for all the colonies with "a fair preference" for Spain, and no use of force. Ferdinand VII scoffed at these conditions and started preparing a massive punitive expedition to quash the rebels.[48] John Quincy Adams, the American ambassador in London, observed that while Castlereagh negotiated with Spain, "Lord Cochrane and perhaps Sir Robert Wilson are following upon the track of Sir Gregor MacGregor and are going to offer the insurgents a mediation of their own."[49]

As the spring arrived, England's political situation grew increasingly tense. Convinced that the suspension of habeas corpus was not enough to defeat the threats against the monarchy, the cabinet proposed more repressive measures, including restricting freedom of the press. Cobbett's *Political Register* particularly troubled the ministers, who instructed the Lords Justices to arrest people selling seditious literature. While the *Times* and the *Morning Chronicle* severely criticized these measures, the *Courier* shamelessly sided with the government. Cobbett, afraid he would be arrested, embarked for New York at the end of March, almost at the same time as Lallemand, Rousseau, and Archambault. Santini left for Brussels, a stopover on his way to Munich to meet Eugene de Beauharnais.

The *Courier* celebrated Cobbett's departure. "Cobbett to North America and Lord Cochrane to South America! What wonders may not be expected!"[50] John Quincy Adams was amazed by the enormous influence that Napoleon still exerted over England's political affairs. "It is remarkable though perhaps according to the ordinary workings of human nature and human passions, that the enemies of this man grow more inveterate against him and his partisans more enthusiastic in his favor, as the term of his captivity lengthens and as the prospect of its being perpetual acquires probability," wrote Adams. "Chained to his rock, he is at this moment more dreaded and detested, and at the same time more admired and beloved than when he was at the summit of his power." Adams thought that by forcing Cobbett into exile, the Tories had succeeded

in breaking up "the main pillar of parliamentary reform." They had also succeeded "in silencing the itinerant orator of the same cause, Hunt." As to Lord
Cochrane, he also appeared "to have found it expedient to seek another field for
his active energy and is going upon some project not fully disclosed to South
America."[51]

Wilson was extremely disappointed at the state of affairs in England. He believed that, if permanent, the measures taken by the government would provoke
a massive "transfer of intellect, spirit of enterprise" to the New World.[52] Cochrane, who viewed the Tories as despotic tyrants, shared Wilson's disappointment. He had decided to go to South America and break all ties with England.
"My opinion of the government here is such that I have nothing to expect from
them—no, not even my just right. But then there are other countries, and I have
in my head enough to make me useful in any part of the world."[53]

15
Brayer Arrives in Buenos Aires

The occupation of Chile has entirely defeated the plans of the Carreras.
—Robert Staples to Foreign Office, May 1817

In early February 1817, almost two months after leaving Baltimore, the *Clifton* finally dropped anchor in the outer roads of Buenos Aires. From the ship's deck, General Michel Brayer observed the outline of the city with curiosity. From what he could see, Buenos Aires didn't look at all like a European city. It didn't look like New York, Philadelphia, or Baltimore either. Its most noticeable feature, the one that always struck foreign visitors, was its dull flatness, which was broken here and there by the spiking white church towers. There were no other buildings of any architectural importance and most of the houses, also painted in white, had only one story. There wasn't even a proper harbor, and to reach land the arriving passengers had to transfer to boats, or if the tide was low, to horse-driven carriages with huge wheels that slowly negotiated the muddy riverbed.

It was hot summer day and as Brayer disembarked he couldn't shake off a strange foreboding. Some unexpected obstacles had complicated the plan agreed upon with Grouchy and Clausel in Philadelphia. First, the city of Montevideo, across the river from Buenos Aires, had fallen into the hands of the Portuguese and therefore could no longer serve as a base of operations for an expedition to St. Helena.* Second and more important, Carrera's erstwhile enemy, General San Martin, had crossed the Andes at the head of an army to liberate Chile. Car-

---

* At the end of 1816, the Portuguese invaded the territory that now comprises Uruguay and that then formed part of the Spanish viceroyalty of the River Plate, of which Buenos Aires was the capital.

rera had arrived too late and it was unclear how useful he could be to Brayer's plans.

The political situation in Buenos Aires had changed dramatically during Carrera's twelve-month absence. The old rivalries between monarchists and republicans were still very much alive. Although a national congress had declared independence from Spain in mid-1816, the secret objective of the faction now in power was to establish a monarchy in South America under the protection of the Holy Alliance. The main sponsor of this scheme was San Martin, who had engineered the fall of Alvear in 1815 and the recent appointment of Juan Martin de Pueyrredon as supreme director. San Martin was frustrated by the anarchy created by the revolution and was convinced that his compatriots were incapable of establishing an independent nation under a republican form of government.[1] He also feared that the European powers would never accept the creation of new republics in South America. But San Martin and Pueyrredon had to move cautiously as the republican sentiment was still strong, particularly in the army. Commodore William Bowles, chief of the British Naval Station in South America and a close friend of San Martin, explained to his government that the recent declaration of independence had not been sincere and was "easily explained by the necessity of giving way to those whose violence and revolutionary enthusiasm rendered it dangerous either to oppose or entrust with the real secret."[2]

Another noticeable change that had taken place in Buenos Aires had been the arrival of large numbers of Bonapartist émigrés, not only French but also Spanish *josefinos,* Poles, Italians, and Germans, most of whom had served in the foreign regiments of the Grande Armée. Among them was Colonel Skupieski, who had followed Napoleon to Elba and been part of Joseph's circle in the United States.[3] The Polish baron had introduced himself to the local authorities as one of Napoleon's top cavalry officers and was given a commission as "colonel general" of the revolutionary army. Skupieski had left for Chile a few days before Brayer's arrival in the company of a dozen veterans of the Imperial Guard.

The recently arrived émigrés also included civilians who had been employed in the imperial household or who had strong links to the Bonaparte family. Such was the case of Aimé Bonpland, the famous botanist and a friend of Wilson. Bonpland had left London months earlier in the company of his young wife, Adeline. Officially, he had come to Buenos Aires to study the plants of South America but like other botanists in this story scientific pursuits were not his only concern. Bonpland, a man of firm political convictions, had long supported the independence of the Spanish colonies. He was not only close to Eugene and Hortense de Beauharnais but also had been one of the last people who had talked to Napoleon about his American plans at Malmaison.[4]

The simultaneous arrival of Carrera and a large number of French émigrés caught the attention of Commodore Bowles, who remembered well how in 1813 and 1814, the Chilean leader had intrigued with the French and the Americans and shown an "inimical disposition towards Great Britain."[5] Carrera's presence in Buenos Aires did not bode well for British interests, particularly as reports of an approaching war between Spain and the United States had given "great hopes to the warlike and revolutionary party here, and their agents in North America are sending a considerable number of French and other foreign officers to take service in the troops of this country," wrote Bowles in a report to the Admiralty. Just in case, he requested immediate reinforcements.[6]

In early March news that San Martin had defeated the Spaniards in Chile reached Buenos Aires. The British consul noted that the victory had "entirely defeated the plans of the Carreras," who favored an alliance with the United States.[7] Not surprisingly, the government's attitude toward Carrera grew increasingly hostile. Supreme Director Pueyrredon assured San Martin that Carrera and his brothers would not go to Chile, "no matter how hard they try."[8] Carrera realized that unless he left Buenos Aires, his freedom, and possibly his life, would be in danger, so he embarked on the *Clifton* and left orders for the rest of his squadron to meet him at Valparaiso. But before he could embark, the government arrested him. Colonel Jean Joseph Dauxion-Lavaysse, one of the French veterans Carrera had recruited in New York, had betrayed him. In a letter he sent to John Stuart Skinner, Lavaysse tried to discredit Carrera and accused him of being "the purest of impostors."[9]

Lavaysse's motives for joining and then betraying Carrera are unclear. He had joined the French army as a young man and had participated in the campaigns in Egypt and Haiti. After the Haitian debacle he had chosen to remain in the Caribbean. When he returned to France in 1812, he gained some notoriety with the publication of an account of his travels in Venezuela and the Orinoco.[10] Lavaysse rejoined the French army and briefly served under Eugene of Beauharnais in Italy. But during the first Bourbon restoration, he had "vociferously" criticized Napoleon and served as a special agent of the government to Haiti.[11] He had not taken any prominent role during the Hundred Days. In June 1815 he was found guilty of bigamy in a Paris court and condemned to twenty years forced labor.[12] He avoided the sentence by escaping to the United

States, where he joined the growing community of Bonapartist émigrés. One of Joseph's underlings first introduced him to Carrera in New York. Against the advice of Skinner and Clausel, who suspected Lavaysse of being a spy of the Bourbons, Carrera had agreed to bring him on board.[13] As a reward for his services, Lavaysse was given the rank of colonel in the army of Buenos Aires. If Lavaysse's objective had been to disrupt the plans of the Bonapartists in South America, he accomplished a lot by betraying Carrera.

Pueyrredon took advantage of San Martín's victory to crack down on the opposition and deport any troubling dissenters. Among those forced into exile was a man who will play an important role in this story: Jacques Roul, another veteran of Napoleon's army. Roul had arrived from the United States in late 1816 with Carrera's recommendation, but his career in South America had been short and undistinguished. Pueyrredon, who was a Francophile, had initially welcomed him into the patriot army and had even recommended him to San Martín. "He has served in the cavalry and has general knowledge of the army," Pueyrredon wrote. "See what you can do with him and make him useful."[14] But Roul never joined the army. Weeks later Pueyrredon told San Martín that Roul had "shown some new developments for the artillery that could be extremely valuable. . . . He will also show you other interesting innovations."[15] What sort of innovations Roul could have developed is a mystery, as he had never served in the artillery and in recent years he had served as a forestry inspector. By the end of 1816 Roul still had not joined San Martín's army. It seems Pueyrredon suspected something as he advised San Martín that it would be impossible to give Roul the rank of colonel or the command of the cavalry. Besides, he said, it was not a good idea "to trust a stranger so much."[16] Shortly after Brayer's arrival, the government deported Roul for "insults directed to the Supreme Authority of the State."[17] Before leaving Buenos Aires, Roul met Brayer, who gave him a secret message for William Lee, the vice president of the French Agricultural and Manufacturing Society recently founded in Philadelphia. Brayer told Roul that he felt confident he would be able to raise troops in Buenos Aires for an expedition to rescue Napoleon from St. Helena.[18]

The government crackdown coincided with San Martín's sudden return from Santiago, which was puzzling, since from a military point of view, the liberation of Chile was far from complete. Nobody knew that San Martín had returned to Buenos Aires to meet with Commodore Bowles and decide what to do next. The British naval officer had befriended San Martín during his first stint in Buenos Aires in 1813 and had already identified him as sympathetic to England. Their friendship and correspondence had recommenced after Bowles returned to South America in mid-1816. Shortly after his victory, San Martin had asked for an interview. Bowles reported to London that the rebel general had "some plan to confide to me in which the intervention of His Majesty's government may be necessary and which he will not venture to commit to paper."[19] Basically San Martin wanted Castlereagh to support his plans to establish a monarchy in South America. But Bowles had not expected San Martin to come back from Chile so soon and had left for Brazil. Therefore San Martin was forced to communicate his views to the unofficial British consul in Buenos Aires, Robert Ponsonby Staples.

San Martin told Staples that he wanted the British government to inform him privately what course of action "might meet its approbation." He explained that his secret plan was to install monarchies in Argentina and Chile with European princes under the protection of Great Britain. Staples reported to the Foreign Office that San Martin "earnestly requested some person might be authorized to point out to him by consulting with whom he might give that turn to the affairs of Chile necessary to accomplish the end proposed." At the conclusion of this meeting, San Martin told Staples: "Should any one be authorized to treat with me on the affairs I have mentioned, let it be in the most private manner and be assured of my conviction that whatever advantages this country has to offer, its prosperity depends on conceding them to England." He clarified that he not only spoke about Chile, but also Peru, "in the event of Lima being added to the number of those territories now free of Spain." The general asked Staples to make his views known to the British government "in the most expeditious and private manner."[20] San Martin also sent an emissary to London to purchase ships "which may be armed and employed against the Spaniards in the South Seas" and to engage "officers for the naval service of Chile." The emissary also had to "open some communication with His Majesty's Government" and was authorized to "enter into any political negotiations which circumstances may allow of."[21]

Before returning to Chile, San Martin met with Carrera. At San Martin's recommendation, the government rejected Carrera's offer of a squadron to liberate Peru and Grouchy's proposal to take command of the patriot army. San Martin also met with Brayer. Not totally familiar with the internal politics of the revolution in Buenos Aires, the French general probably thought he could work around San Martin. He must have received a favorable report from one of his former subordinates, Lieutenant Colonel Ambrose Cramer, who had joined the patriot and had distinguished himself in the recent campaign.[22]

Brayer introduced himself as a professional soldier without any political ambitions or attachment to Napoleon and agreed to serve under San Martin's orders. Why would a general of the legendary Imperial Guard agree to become a subordinate of an obscure Spaniard who had only achieved the rank of lieutenant colonel in the mediocre Spanish army? Brayer's decision was evidence of his commitment to the cause of his master, who at this time, was praising his determination at St. Helena. Fortunately for Brayer, during the voyage from the United States, he had kept to himself and had taken Clausel's warnings about Lavaysse more seriously than Carrera. His low profile probably saved him from suspicion and after meeting him, San Martin assured O'Higgins, that he would "like him immensely." Neither Brayer nor San Martin ever imagined each other's real plans. By late April, Brayer was on his way to Chile, accompanied by several French and North American officers recruited by Carrera with San Martin's "best recommendations."[23]

San Martin was informed of the plans agreed by Carrera in the United States and did not approve them. He was informed by Pueyrredon of Grouchy's proposal to lead the army and probably learned more details from Colonel Lavaysse, who accused Colonel Skupieski of being Joseph's agent.[24] Even though San Martin had never met Skupieski he asked O'Higgins to "get the Baron Bellina the hell out of the army before the mountain passes close."[25] Skupieski's antics in Chile had infuriated O'Higgins and other officers, but such behavior did not deserve a discharge without a court-martial, particularly given his rank. To confuse things further, at this time a pamphlet authored by Colonel Roul circulated around Buenos Aires accusing Pueyrredon of conspiring with the courts of Madrid and Rio de Janeiro to put Buenos Aires again under Spanish rule. The pamphlet accused Skupieski of being part of this conspiracy and of being a spy sent by Onis to disrupt Carrera's expedition.[26] The expulsion of Roul and Skupieski from the patriot army was received with relief by Commodore Bowles, who reported to London that the French émigrés had met "with very little success or encouragement" from the government and that a few had been dismissed "on account of excessive insolence and misconduct." Bowles noted that Brayer was the only one "who appeared likely to get forward and he was now serving in Chile with San Martin."[27]

The trip to Santiago proved as enlightening for Brayer as his arrival in Buenos

Aires. The French general had probably never seen a landscape like the barren pampas. The endless plains had scarcely any trees; roaming cattle and horses were the only visible inhabitants. Although unseen, the ferocious Indian tribes were always present in the mind of the traveler. After almost three weeks, Brayer and his companions reached the city of Mendoza, in the foothills of the Andes. They missed an early snowfall and in another week they reached Santiago, a sleepy town on the western side of the Andes. Once in Chile, Brayer quickly proved his mettle. Shortly after his arrival, he participated in several successful combats against the Spaniards.[28] Many French veterans who had recently joined the revolutionary army were delighted by his presence. Some of the locals were also impressed. "He had the most martial and arrogant bearing I have ever seen," said a Chilean who met him; "his mere presence imposed respect."[29] However, most of the native officers were resentful. Brayer's enforcement of strict discipline and his attachment to European style drilling made him unpopular.[30] San Martin soon removed him from direct troop command and put him in charge of an officer training school.

While Brayer tried to settle in to his new job in Santiago, Carrera escaped from prison and fled to Montevideo. Since early 1817 the city had been occupied by Portuguese troops led by General Lecor, a veteran of the Peninsular War. Lecor had been one of the officers who in 1808 had helped Sir Robert Wilson organize the Loyal Lusitanian Legion. Lecor also happened to be a Freemason and welcomed his Chilean "brother" with open arms. From Montevideo, Carrera wrote to Skinner, Grouchy, and Clausel to explain why the expedition had unraveled and why Pueyrredon had rejected Grouchy's proposals.[31] Despite this setback, Carrera's political career was far from finished. He still counted on numerous supporters on both sides of the Andes. His strongest allies were his two brothers, Juan Jose and Luis, who were in Buenos Aires waiting for his instructions, and Manuel Rodriguez, his childhood friend, who was very popular in the army and had gained San Martin's confidence. Carrera also counted on the support of a large number of French veterans who kept arriving in Buenos Aires to join the patriot army. Among the new arrivals were Charles Robert, Frederic Brandsen, Benjamin Viel, and Alexis Bruix, all of them fanatical Bonapartists. Robert was a former captain and had been close to Countess Regnault; Brandsen had been aide-de-camp of Eugene de Behaurnais; Viel was a veteran of the campaigns in Prussia, Poland, Spain, France, and Waterloo; and Bruix, the son of Admiral Bruix, one of Napoleon's most devoted supporters, was a veteran of the Russian campaign and Waterloo. They had all been discharged from the army and had managed to leave France in the early spring. The French authorities, suspecting the ship that carried them was part of an expedition to rescue Napoleon from St. Helena, had unsuccessfully tried to delay her departure.[32] Desperate for experienced officers, the government incorporated these veterans into the army and dispatched them to Chile. Robert remained in Buenos Aires to liaise with other arriving émigrés and with Carrera, who from Montevideo was planning his comeback. The Frenchman lodged at the house of Carrera's sister Xaviera, a beautiful and strong-willed woman who was determined to see her family regain political prominence in Chile. Her house soon became the gathering place for those who were disaffected with the government.

From Montevideo Carrera wrote to his brothers who remained in Buenos Aires. "Tell me who can we count as our friends in Santiago? How are the officers of the expedition behaving? How is General Brayer? Where is [Manuel] Rodriguez? What troops does San Martin have and how are they employed?"[33] Shortly after receiving this letter, the two brothers left for Chile incognito. Once in Santiago, they planned to depose San Martin and O'Higgins.

16
The Guard Regroups

As to South America, I continue to believe that only one man, Buonaparte,
can effect a big revolution there.

—Hyde de Neuville, January 1817

At the start of 1817, Hyde de Neuville knew that Joseph, Grouchy, and Clausel
were plotting something, but he did not know exactly what. He was particularly
puzzled by Grouchy's conduct. While some of his informers spoke of "his desire not to do anything that could displease the King," others held a completely
opposite view. Hyde de Neuville also had doubts about Lefebvre-Desnouettes,
who was allegedly ready to "throw [in] his lot with the Spanish rebels." In a
ciphered dispatch Hyde de Neuville warned Richelieu that although Joseph
dreamed of being "the King of the Indies" only Napoleon could lead a revolution in South America. He also mentioned in his dispatch that some émigrés
had "joined Mr. Lee, who is at the head of a French colonial establishment that
will be formed on the banks of [the] Ohio and the Mississippi."[1] The Vine and
Olive colony had been set up as a screen to disguise the Bonapartist plans for
Mexico, but things had gotten a bit complicated. Toledo's defection and the unfriendly attitude of the Madison administration had forced a change of plans.
Any attack on Spanish territory launched from U.S. soil would violate the neutrality of the United States and trigger a war with Spain, and possibly England.
The Madison administration had submitted to Congress a new neutrality law
that if approved, would seriously undermine Joseph's plans.

This may explain why the Vine and Olive colony was now seeking land just
a few miles away from Pensacola. As Colonel Burr had explained in his 1810
memorandum to Napoleon, "without the Floridas, no success could be attained,
either in Mexico or in Texas."[2] Pensacola had the best natural harbor in the Gulf
of Mexico and was an ideal launch pad for an invasion of Mexico. Burr had also

noted that the settlements of Mobile and Tombigbee in Alabama were the best points from which to attack Pensacola. If the patriots of Mexico or other parts of South America seized Florida, declared their independence from Spain, and then asked the French generals to help them, then U.S. neutrality would not be compromised. Once in "friendly hands," Florida could be used to launch expeditions to Mexico and the rest of South America. Eventually, the territory could be sold to the United States, as Napoleon had envisioned in 1811.

Joseph and his generals needed someone to liberate Florida. The candidate had to combine military experience, local connections, and a strong reputation as a freedom fighter. One possibility was to approach Xavier Mina, whose plans had been rejected in favor of Toledo's only a few months earlier. Mina had left Baltimore in September and after a brief stop in Haiti had established his base in Galveston, an island off the coast of Texas that was conveniently occupied by the French corsair Louis Aury.[3] In mid-February, Mina was invited to discuss the attack of Pensacola in New Orleans, where Charles Lefebvre-Desnouettes and Henri Lallemand had just arrived. But when Mina heard that the ultimate objective of the scheme was to sell Florida to the United States, he refused to participate.[4] To liberate the colonies from the despotic rule of Ferdinand VII was one thing. To cede Spanish territory to the U.S. was another.

Joseph then decided to approach Gregor MacGregor, who had just arrived in New York. MacGregor seemed like a good candidate for the Florida project. A tall, well-built man with thick brown hair, long sideburns, and bushy eyebrows, MacGregor had the right *physique du rôle*. Vain and self important, he styled himself the Rob Roy of South America and pretended he was descended from the legendary Scottish hero, but his military and revolutionary credentials seemed solid. For a brief period he had served in the British and Portuguese armies in the Peninsula, and in early 1811, he had joined the cause of independence in Caracas as aide-de-camp of General Miranda. In 1815, following the defeat of the Venezuelan patriots, MacGregor had escaped to Haiti; the following year he had joined Bolivar on an ill-fated expedition to liberate Venezuela. During this campaign, he had skillfully led the retreat of his troops in the face of superior Spanish forces. This earned him not only the rank of brigadier general in the patriot army but also the praise of Bolivar.[5] It wouldn't have been difficult for MacGregor to establish contact with Joseph. He not only knew Pedro Gual, who had served as Miranda's secretary and had been involved in Toledo's expedition, but also the Colombian botanist Francisco Zea, who had been part of Joseph's inner circle in Madrid.

Shortly after arriving in New York, MacGregor was approached by Count Regnault, Napoleon's former minister, who sounded out "his willingness to connect himself with the views of Joseph Bonaparte." MacGregor agreed and Regnault disclosed "the outlines of several different projects which were in contemplation and which had been discussed by the principal French officers in the United States." The count assured MacGregor that Joseph "possessed funds to a very large amount" nearing 3 million dollars "exclusively of what they could command for a such a purpose through the means of their European connection and many of the leading men" in the United States. Regnault also talked to MacGregor about another secret project that was under consideration: "It was conceived that with the funds which he [Regnault] had mentioned, and with the privateers which several of the principal merchants in this country were willing to furnish, it would be perfectly practicable to fit a squadron of ships to be manned with all the desperadoes now engaged as pirates under the revolutionary flags of South America which would be sufficiently strong to effect the rescue of Buonaparte and that having obtained possession of his person it was proposed to carry him to the *Rio de la Plata** and from thence to place him at the head of the revolution in Chile where he might establish an Empire."[6]

The rescue of Bonaparte must have seemed like a bold enterprise to Mac-Gregor. The *New York Evening Post* had just published a letter from the Marquis of Montchenu, the French commissioner at St. Helena, detailing the multiple precautions taken to prevent such a rescue from happening. The British garrison had "about 2,500 men with 500 odd pieces of artillery and about a score of mortars" and the governor was "made acquainted hourly with whatever passes by means of telegraphs erected throughout the isle, so that in a minute he knows whatever is passing." In addition, there were "at least two frigates at anchor while two brigs are sailing night and day round the island." Montchenu's letter, probably published at the instigation of Hyde de Neuville, concluded with a veiled warning. Napoleon's escape was "physically impossible." All roads to Longwood were guarded; "the rocks are nearly impracticable, and there is not a point where ten men without arms, and with stones only . . . could not stop a thousand men well armed."[7] A Baltimore newspaper speculated that "an army of 10,000 men and a fleet of 20 sail of the line would not be sufficient to release the captive."[8]

Regnault enlisted MacGregor for "the attempt which it was proposed to

---

* Buenos Aires.

make upon the Viceroyalty of Mexico" and for an invasion of Florida. The plan initially contemplated the occupation of Amelia Island, a deep-water harbor on Eastern Florida. Once MacGregor took possession of this point and declared independence from Spain, he would call for the assistance of Clausel, who would be waiting in Mobile, pretending to set up the Vine and Olive colony. If invited by the patriots in Florida, Clausel could take Pensacola without violating American neutrality. Attacked from both sides, the Spaniards would quickly surrender. As the spring arrived, hundreds of former veterans of Napoleon's legendary Imperial Guard began arriving in New York, Baltimore, and Philadelphia to join this campaign. Joseph hoped that the American government would support this plan, as it would be able to take possession of Florida at a lower price than Napoleon had offered in 1811.

In mid-March, MacGregor told a Venezuelan friend that he would soon "leave here with a big squadron taking weapons, ammunitions and uniforms, etc. . . . I am planning to take with me Gual, Roscio and many other friends."[9] To lend an appearance of legality to the expedition, it was necessary to give MacGregor an authorization to occupy Florida on behalf of the independent republics of Spanish America. A document dated March 1817 in Philadelphia, drafted by Gual, and signed by him and by representatives from Buenos Aires, Colombia, and Mexico instructed MacGregor to "adopt such measures as in your judgment may most effectually tend to procure" the liberation of Florida.[10] The ultimate objective of the expedition was to use Florida as a base to send expeditions to liberate Mexico and South America and then to sell it to the United States.[11]

The principal obstacle facing this plan was the U.S. government. Despite the opposition of Henry Clay, Congress had just approved a new neutrality law that provided harsh penalties for any U.S. citizen engaged in armed enterprises against nations not at war with the United States. As a result, not only the profitable business of privateering under the flag of Buenos Aires but also any filibustering expedition against Florida or Mexico launched from U.S. territory was rendered illegal.[12] Despite this setback, Joseph's plans received a big boost in late March, when thanks to Clay's active support, Congress granted the Vine and Olive colony one hundred thousand acres of public land near Mobile.[13] On March 20, a significant day for all Bonapartists, Clay informed one of the members of the French Agricultural and Manufacturing Society "of the success of the request that was made in favor of the French immigrants who desire to establish a colony on the Tombigbee [River]."[14] Although Tombigbee was far from the Ohio and Mississippi rivers, the original objective of the society, it was relatively close to Mobile and to Pensacola. The grant, worth almost half a million dollars, was not only an excuse to gather a large number of Frenchmen in the area but also a potential source of funds to purchase supplies and ammunition.

The Spanish ambassador Luis de Onis had no doubts about the real designs of the Vine and Olive colony. The traitor Toledo, who was now safely ensconced in Europe, had revealed its true objectives. At the head of this enterprise were Clausel, Lallemand, and Lefebvre-Desnouettes, and "with good reason I believe that they will try to establish a military port in our frontiers instead of a colony of farmers." Toledo believed that the U.S. government, "if not an active part in these plans, is at a minimum guilty of a cover-up."[15] Onis realized that to protect Mexico, sooner or later Florida would have to be sacrificed.[16]

Not everybody in Washington supported the plans of the French émigrés. An anonymous article in an influential newspaper criticized Joseph's plans. "Suppose brother Napoleon could be liberated from his cage, put himself at the head of the South American patriots and bluster as loudly as he once did about the rights of the people." The article speculated how Napoleon could accomplish his goals. "The best plan that I can devise is to throw out to the world, ideas of emigration—I may inform Congress for example, that the poor and oppressed emigrants from Europe wish to preserve their own customs that have been handed down from their ancestors—we will say for example that we wish to purchase a tract of territory for the sake of planting vines—Congress will be flattered by an application of this kind and will undoubtedly lend their patronage to the proposal."[17]

In late April, the newspapers reported that General Charles Lallemand had arrived in Boston. After leaving Egypt, Lallemand had traveled to England and then to the United States. To avoid detection by British customs, "the general was passed in a boat to and from several ships" and boarded a ship bound for Boston.[18] At almost the same time Lallemand arrived in Philadelphia, Napoleon was praising him at St. Helena. Lallemand's energy and enthusiasm gave a strong morale boost to the émigrés. Joseph was also relieved. After the passage of the new neutrality law, his position had become very delicate. If directly implicated in any enterprise against Spain he risked being deported or prosecuted. It was a risk he could not take, but Lallemand would. Although he wasn't as brilliant as Clausel or as senior as Grouchy, Napoleon liked him. The general immediately joined the Florida campaign and started recruiting veterans of the Grande Armée who were arriving from Europe daily. Lallemand's arrival coincided with that of Rousseau and Archambault, who had brought messages from Napoleon, a detailed map of St. Helena, and a plan of attack.

Ironically, at this time Hyde de Neuville had almost dismissed the possibility that such a plan was seriously being considered. Curiously, it was Sir Charles Bagot, the phlegmatic English ambassador always wary of Hyde de Neuville's conspiracy theories, who first confirmed its existence. In mid-April the British ambassador received a visit from Gregor MacGregor. Bagot knew of MacGregor's reputation, his links to Miranda and Bolivar, and his involvement in the Venezuelan insurrection. But he couldn't have suspected what he was about to hear. MacGregor explained that the real purpose of his visit was to make "a communication which he thought interesting to the British government." MacGregor then gave Bagot a long-winded account of the state of the revolution in South America to ascertain "the real feelings of the British government upon the subject." Bagot replied that England followed a policy of strict neutrality and that she was firmly allied with Spain. After hearing this response, MacGregor disclosed the real purpose of his visit. He told Bagot about his meeting with Count Regnault in New York. He explained that the Bonapartists' main objective was Mexico and that "all the French officers in the United States were ready to join in the undertaking and that the settlement recently made by French Refugees upon the Tombigbee River in the Mississippi Territory was connected with this project." Bagot was shocked, despite having been warned about this project months earlier by Onis. After listening to MacGregor, Bagot had no doubt that "the views of Joseph Bonaparte are seriously directed towards Mexico."

But there was more. MacGregor disclosed details of other plans the Bonapartists were considering. One was to rescue Napoleon. Another "was directed against Spain itself and was founded in an idea that by abandoning all pretensions to the crown and professing only to have in view the establishment of the government of the Cortes,* Joseph Bonaparte might so connect himself with the party of the Cortes as ultimately to effect the expulsion of Ferdinand VII and not improbably, his own restoration." And a third plan "was to endeavor to obtain possession of the Grand Duchess of Parma and her son† as the surest means of turning to the advantage of Buonaparte's family any resolution which might take place in France." MacGregor said that he had a meeting scheduled

*The Spanish Parliament.
† The Archduchess Marie Louise and Napoleon II.

with Joseph in Philadelphia to discuss these plans. He assured Bagot that his own views on South America were beneficial to England. In fact, he was "apprehensive that the interference of any of Buonaparte's family would so indispose the British government to the general cause of the Revolution that he hesitated to accept the proposals which Joseph Buonaparte would make to him, and this was the point upon which he pretended to be desirous of consulting me."

Bagot assured MacGregor "that any political cause would be made worse, and I trusted weaker, in proportion as it was connected with the family of Buonaparte." The next morning, MacGregor returned and told Bagot that Spain would soon settle its differences with the United States, which would obtain possession of Florida. MacGregor told Bagot that Monroe had secretly ordered American troops to move into the Spanish territory. The Scot was anxious "to learn the real sentiments of the British government respecting the independence of the Spanish provinces as he had no doubt that he could now take possession of the Floridas* in the name of the patriots and that he was furnished with a commission as captain general granted to him by the five revolted vice royalties of South America by which he was authorized to do so." And although he was aware that the Floridas would "in all probability ultimately fall into the hands of the United States, it might still be an object to Great Britain to delay this event as long as possible."[19]

Was MacGregor a traitor, a charlatan, or a messenger sent by Joseph to ascertain England's views? Interestingly, almost at the same time this meeting took place in Washington, Napoleon was telling O'Meara and Admiral Malcolm that Joseph's rule in the Spanish colonies would be favorable to British commercial interests. But if Napoleon and Joseph entertained any hopes that England would not oppose their enterprise, they were quickly disappointed.

Bagot was very suspicious and tried to ascertain with whom MacGregor had met while in Washington. MacGregor claimed he had met with the secretary of the navy to discuss "private matters" and said that his plans were not only well known to the American government but also "that they would not be averse to seeing him take possession of any parts of the Spanish dominions." Maybe he was referring to Commodore David Porter a member of the Navy Board of Commissioners and a friend of John Stuart Skinner, with whom MacGregor had spent several weeks in Baltimore planning the invasion of Florida.[20] MacGregor did not tell Bagot that while in Washington he had met several times with

*They were called Floridas because under Spanish rule they were divided into two separate provinces, East Florida and West Florida.

William Thornton, the head of the Patent Office, and had sounded him out on the idea of selling Florida to the United States for $1.5 million. Thornton had assured MacGregor that the United States would view an expedition against Florida with sympathy.

The British ambassador was skeptical. He knew MacGregor's influence with the South American revolutionaries was "nearly lost" and he seemed to have misrepresented the intentions of the American government or the status of its negotiations with Spain. Bagot believed rescuing Napoleon from St. Helena was the craziest idea he had heard since arriving in the United States, a point he made clear in his dispatch to Castlereagh: "The report of his conversation with Regnault may I think be relied upon—and so far as it relates to Joseph Bonaparte's views upon Mexico is important. The rest is but a history of the *reveries* with which the excited officers of France may naturally be supposed to beguile their time."[21]

News of MacGregor's meeting with Bagot soon reached Onis and Hyde de Neuville and confirmed their suspicions that England had secret designs on the Spanish colonies. Rumors about an expedition to Florida were already rife on the East Coast, and the Spanish ambassador feared that the British were secretly financing it. Onis repeatedly warned Madrid, but England was still Spain's most powerful ally in Europe. Aware of these suspicions, Bagot debriefed Onis about his meeting with MacGregor and assured him that England would not take any action against Spanish interests. In fact, it was the United States government who "had agreed to help MacGregor take the Floridas to later cede them in exchange for money." Bagot also warned Onis that the Americans would use MacGregor to take Pensacola.[22] The problem was whom to believe. Hyde de Neuville, who had long suspected a British intrigue, believed that the Americans were waiting for an opportunity to seize not only Florida but also Cuba, which was the key to all the Caribbean trade.[23] If the objective of MacGregor, or of Joseph, had been to fuel mistrust among the ambassadors of France, England, and Spain, that had certainly been achieved.

Although still suspicions of England, Onis started worrying again about U.S. support for Joseph's plans. The expedition to Florida posed a serious threat to Spain, and if the Americans were secretly helping MacGregor, it would be necessary to dissuade them. Maybe it was better to cede them Florida to placate their appetite. In the grand scheme of things it was a small price to pay. Onis felt something had to be done soon as he saw other dangerous threats in the horizon. According to newspaper accounts, Cochrane had "raised £10,000 and bought a fine vessel, nearly as large as a frigate, which he proposes to man with the best sailors he can procure for his voyage to South America," and Lucien had "demanded from the Pope a passport for the United States of America."[24] It was unlikely that Lucien would be allowed to leave Italy. But Cochrane was another story; according to newspaper reports, the British ministers were "glad to get rid of him."[25]

Hyde de Neuville concluded that France had to take a proactive approach to resolve the question of the Spanish colonies and avoid consequences fatal to the Bourbon regime. Instead of trying to fight against independence, France should favor the establishment of monarchical governments in the colonies. "Spain in my opinion, by appearing to make a big sacrifice, would actually protect its future interests if it decided to establish two independent monarchies in the South, whose thrones would be occupied by a Bourbon prince, who could only add to the political force of the family," he explained to Richelieu. An additional advantage of this scheme would be to stop the insurrection in the Spanish and Portuguese possessions and leave the Bonapartists without a cause to advance their intrigues.[26]

The news of a revolution in Brazil, confirmed Hyde de Neuville's fears. In March an independent republic had been established in Recife, the capital of Pernambuco, a province in northern Brazil.[27] The uprising had been planned since late 1816 by Brazil's leading Freemasons, the same group of men who fifteen years earlier had led a similar revolution and sought Napoleon's protection. Though the revolution had taken place ahead of schedule, it had been coordinated with a similar uprising in Portugal, also led by Freemasons of a republican persuasion.[28] Once in power, the rebels immediately sent an expedition to take control of the island of Fernando de Noronha. Only a hundred miles off the coast of Pernambuco, the island was the closest point to St. Helena on the American continent. With favorable winds, it would take a rescue expedition slightly over two weeks to reach the island. Hyde de Neuville viewed the revolution in Pernambuco as a serious threat, not only to the Portuguese, but also to all European dynasties.[29] But he initially made no connection between these events and the restless activity of the Bonapartist émigrés in the East Coast. At that time he was convinced that Grouchy and Clausel were ready to petition for a royal pardon.[30]

However, Hyde de Neuville's concerns intensified after the arrival in Boston of Antonio Gonçalves da Cruz, an emissary sent by the rebellious Republic of Pernambuco to obtain American support. At some point during his stay in the United States, Da Cruz discussed the situation with Joseph or some members of his entourage. By early June the Pernambucan envoy arrived in Washington and met Secretary of State Richard Rush, who confirmed the appointment of an American consul in Pernambuco.[31] Ray will play a role in this story.

Joseph had ways of knowing what had happened in Brazil. The Masonic connection was the most obvious one. Also, since 1815, a large number of Bonapartist émigrés had settled in Brazil. Among them were General Dirk van Hogendorp, a Dutchman who had been Napoleon's aide-de-camp; Joachim Le Breton, a former member of the prestigious Institut de France and a staunch republican; and a veteran of the Grande Armée of Danish origin called Flemming Holdt who lived in Pernambuco. The arrival of the former two caught the attention of the British consul in Rio de Janeiro, who alerted the authorities at St. Helena that attempts could be made "by some of them or at any rate by their means, to open a secret correspondence with General Buonaparte." Since Le Breton had been "one of Buonaparte's secret police" the consul advised checking "all correspondence from hence."[32] The events in Pernambuco forced Joseph to put on hold the Florida scheme and to support the Pernambucan rebels with money, weapons, and men. Fernando de Noronha was of strategic importance and had to be secured.

At the end of May, Marshal Grouchy's two sons and his nephew, twenty-two-year-old Louis Gustave Le Dulcet Pontecoulant, all former officers of the Grande Armée, arrived in Philadelphia. Together with Grouchy and "the ex-generals Lallemand, Lefebvre-Desnouettes, the ex-Colonel Latapie," they gathered at Joseph's house. According to the French consul, Lallemand intended to meet his younger brother "in the West" and Latapie was reportedly recruiting men for an expedition.[33]

There was a flurry of activity at Point Breeze. The events in Pernambuco had accelerated the timing of the expedition to rescue Napoleon. To aid the Brazilian rebels and secure the island of Fernando de Noronha, Joseph chose the intrepid Latapie. Thirty other veterans of the Grande Armée accompanied him. This advance guard would be reinforced later with men and ships from the United States and troops sent by Brayer from Buenos Aires. Cochrane was also expected to join them with a small squadron. Once in control of Fernando de Noronha they would launch the expedition to St. Helena. In mid-June, Latapie and his companions left New York on board the schooner *Paragon*. According to the *New York Evening Post,* the rebels still controlled Pernambuco.[34]

Hyde de Neuville's anxiety about Bonapartist intrigues reached a fever pitch. He reported that Archambault and Rousseau had arrived from St. Helena and "had several conferences with the zealous partisans of Bonaparte," who since then had raised "their hopes." Hyde de Neuville remained "persuaded that nothing is being done at present in the ports of America aimed at the removal of the prisoner." With respect to St. Helena he didn't fear force but cunning, and help from the locals, he told Richelieu. To discover what was going on he sent agents all over the East Coast and planned to visit New York to meet certain émigrés "who are very tired of being exiled."[35]

Latapie's expedition was prepared and launched in complete secrecy. However, Hyde de Neuville reported that since the arrival of the two emissaries from St. Helena "ridiculous rumors continue to circulate. They almost announce the escape of Napoleon. What seems likely is that these two individuals have a mission related to this object and they have been sent to coordinate with Joseph and his chiefs."[36] Hyde de Neuville couldn't help but link the presence of Napoleon's messengers in the United States and recent events in Europe—the *Germanicus* affair in Paris, the arrest of Countess Regnault, and the arrival of Santini in Brussels with "letters from Napoleon to his wife."[37] Even more troubling was the recent departure of Count Regnault for Europe. According to Bagot, Regnault had left "on board a vessel by Joseph Bonaparte's orders and immediately sent at his expense to Antwerp."[38] Napoleon's former minister had reportedly gone mad after learning of the arrest of his wife. Hyde de Neuville believed Regnault's madness was faked and that Joseph had sent him to prepare a revolution to install Napoleon II on the throne of France.[39] As time passed Hyde de Neuville's fears grew: "At the moment many shady characters are preparing to leave for Europe by the way of Liverpool. One of them, Mr. Galabert, an enterprising man and full of spirit, formerly chief of staff of Marshal Soult, and who really prepares to embark, has dared to say publicly that two months after his arrival, he would either succeed or be shot. An exiled officer has told me that they are recruiting men for a secret expedition."[40]

Days after the departure of Latapie, another contingent of Napoleonic veterans arrived in Philadelphia and were immediately recruited by Lallemand for an expedition against Florida "in accordance with a very secret agreement with the government of the United States."[41] It was at this time, the end of June, that MacGregor's troops led by Colonel Thornton Posey, a former U.S. Army officer and the son of the governor of Indiana, took possession of Amelia Island. Days later MacGregor issued a proclamation "in the name of the Independent Governments of South America" and promised to lead his men "to the continent of South America to gather fresh laurels in freedom's cause."[42] The Monroe administration knew about this plan. Thornton had discussed the plan with Rush, interim secretary of state, who although he had refused to give it an "official sanction," had led him to believe "he would not personally be sorry to see such an outcome." In fact, Thornton had assured the organizers of the Amelia Island expedition that he would intercede with the government on their behalf.[43]

Onis immediately complained to the State Department, emphasizing that MacGregor was "engaged in enterprises to invade or disturb the tranquility of His Catholic Majesty's possessions in that part of the world. . . . His subsequent proceedings and hostile preparations in the bosom of this union against the possessions of the Spanish monarchy are notorious and announced with a scandalous publicity."[44] What about U.S. neutrality? Onis' agents also reported that two expeditions bound for Buenos Aires were being outfitted in Baltimore and New York and were carrying a group of exiled French officers. Although the details were sketchy, Onis learned that Clausel was the leader of the expedition being prepared in New York and that he had recently discussed its details with Joseph.[45]

As Joseph looked out at the gardens of Point Breeze, his mansion in New Jersey, he was pleased. He was turning the property into a beautiful French chateau.[46] Over time, Point Breeze would become one of the most palatial mansions in the United States, rivaling the splendor of any French chateaux. But there were more important reasons for Joseph's contentment. Despite seemingly insurmountable obstacles, he was close to accomplishing Napoleon's dream. A few days earlier he had sent a ship to Italy to bring Lucien, and maybe the king of Rome, to the United States. Perhaps in a few months he would be able to embrace his two brothers and his nephew.

17
All Ready for Action

The affairs of South America are daily assuming a more important character.
—*Courier*, London, July 1817

By the early spring of 1817 Wilson was almost ready to depart for South America. "You have not condescended to state to me your reasons for adopting in such haste this line of conduct or what prospects and future advantages have been held forth to you in order to induce you to make such a sacrifice. The war in South America does not appear to me to be a war of soldiers but of plunderers and *banditti* affording no hope of glory or any opportunity of showing those military talents which you possess," wrote Lord Hutchinson, under whom Wilson had served in Egypt and Prussia.[1] Lord Cochrane was also ready and eager to depart. "His lordship has made up his mind to go to South America," his secretary wrote. "Numbers of gentlemen of great respectability are desirous of accompanying him . . . but Lord Cochrane discourages all."[2] Cochrane knew that aiding in the escape of Napoleon would mean a complete break with England. In the last four months Cochrane had presented four petitions for reform in Parliament and all four had been rejected.[3] He had lost all hope for parliamentary reform under Tory rule. Like Thomas Paine before him, Cochrane no longer attached much value to his British citizenship. He and Wilson shared the utopian dream that in South America it would be possible to create a new political system, free of the despotism that oppressed Europe.

These hopes were encouraged by news that General San Martin had defeated the Spaniards in Chile. Although it was an ominous signal for Spain, there was a silver lining for England; the patriot victory had reportedly caused great "demand for British goods at Buenos Aires."[4] The news excited "the lively interest and generous sympathy of the British public." The Spaniards, who during the

Peninsular War had been praised as heroes, were now stigmatized "as cowards in every battle, and dastards in every flight."[5] Press reports suggested that the demise of the Spanish empire in America was near. According to one newspaper, "the arrival of Joseph Bonaparte at Mexico" was imminent. The *Courier* reported that he would be soon joined in the United States by Generals Rigaud and Fressinet.[6] The Bonapartists seemed to be as active as ever. Captain Joseph Jeannet, a veteran of the Grande Armée exiled in London, departed for Philadelphia with messages for Joseph and Lallemand. Jeannet had recently returned from Brussels, where he had met Wilson's sister. Wilson and Cochrane were waiting for a signal to depart.

The Duke of Richelieu didn't know whether to worry more about what was happening in America or Europe. Whatever the designs of the Bonapartists, he was determined to stop them. First, he had to neutralize Lucien, the most dangerous of Napoleon's brothers, who was getting ready to depart for the United States.[7] Richelieu convened an urgent meeting of the representatives of the Allied powers in Paris to decide what to do. Under pressure from the French and Spanish ambassadors, the Vatican States refused to issue Lucien his passports and agreed to restrict his movements.[8] Richelieu informed Hyde de Neuville of this decision but nevertheless warned him that Joseph's presence in the United States "should increase your caution."[9] Second, it was necessary to eliminate the dynastic hopes of Napoleon II. This goal was accomplished by a treaty between Austria and France by which at the death of his mother the duchy of Parma would pass to the infanta Maria Luisa, sister of Ferdinand VII of Spain and queen of Etruria. Richelieu was quite pleased to see that Vienna showed no interest in defending the dynastic interests of the young Napoleon. Third, it was necessary to stop Napoleon's messengers before they reached their destination. After a stopover in Brussels where he had been "received by many of his late master's friends," Santini had gone to Munich to meet with Eugene de Beauharnais, who gave him money to continue his voyage to Italy to deliver a message to Marie Louise.[10] Austrian and French spies were on his tracks. Meanwhile, Rousseau and Archambault had sailed to the United States. Only Piontkowski remained in London.

The intrigues of the Bonapartists in America suddenly became less important when the Paris police discovered that some members of the Royal Guard planned to murder the Bourbon princes. The discovery caused "considerable alarm" in Paris, as its successful execution would have extinguished the branch of the Bourbons.[11] In London the *Times* reported that new plots had been detected "for favoring the escape of Buonaparte" and that the police had discovered "a correspondence carried on between the adherents of Buonaparte in different quarters, through the medium of certain agents, who had arrived with a mission from North America." It was additional proof of the "unwearied spirit with which the adherents of the late tyranny pursue their machinations."[12]

It was at this time that reports of a revolution in Brazil reached London. It was a threatening development for the supporters of monarchism. "It is a vast event!" announced the *Courier*. "A fearful one too, we may add, for who now after the experience of the French Revolution can contemplate a new one without fear?"[13] The details of this new revolution were sketchy even in Brazil, but as usual, British agents were well informed. They had intercepted a letter containing "exceedingly important details" of the Pernambucan plot. Its author was Carlos de Alvear, former supreme director of Buenos Aires, who was exiled in Rio de Janeiro and, due to his revolutionary and Masonic credentials, had strong links with the conspirators. When the British chargé d'affaires in Rio de Janeiro read Alvear's letter he fired off an urgent and confidential dispatch to Castlereagh. As he explained, the plot at Pernambuco had been forced into "premature execution" and its ramifications extended "all along the coast as well as through the interior" of Brazil. The country's leading Freemasons were behind the revolution in Pernambuco. The brothers in Pernambuco had planned the revolution with their brethren in other parts of Brazil and Portugal. Their plans had gone awry when the authorities had arrested some of the conspirators and precipitated the uprising. A leading "brother" of Bahia who lived in Rio de Janeiro, "a man of many talents and great fortune," had told Alvear that the events in Pernambuco had surprised the revolutionaries in Bahia, who had not dared to move due to the forceful measures taken by the authorities. The conspirators in Pernambuco not only "had anticipated the revolution but had not acted in accordance to what had been agreed" with the "brothers" in Lisbon, which was to force the king to call the courts and swear a liberal constitution. According to Alvear, the Brazilian Freemasons had tried to fool their Portuguese brethren with the idea of a constitutional monarchy, when their real objective had always been to create an independent republic in Brazil. The British consul in Rio believed that if the ramifications were as extensive as Alvear's letter suggested, it would "require the exertion of great prudence and skillful energy to prevent a general revolution through the whole of Brazil."[14]

The news of a revolution in Pernambuco coincided with the discovery of a dangerous conspiracy in Portugal. The plotters were army officers and high-ranking Freemasons. Their objective was to establish a constitutional monarchy in Portugal and Brazil. The leader of the Lisbon conspiracy was General Gomes Freire de Andrade, a popular army officer and grand master of the Gran Oriente Lusitano.[15] And there was a troubling Bonapartist link. Like many Portuguese liberals, Freire had loyally served in the Grande Armée for six years and had even participated in the invasion of Russia.[16] Following Napoleon's abdication, Freire had been pardoned and restored to the Portuguese army. At the end of May, Freire and other suspected conspirators were arrested. One of Freire's accomplices was Baron Eben, a Prussian officer who had served with Wilson in the Loyal Lusitanian Legion. Eben was also linked to the Duke of Sussex, brother of the prince regent and grand master of the Grand Lodge of London. Among his papers the Portuguese authorities found some Masonic tracts and letters addressed to Sussex.[17] The connection, however indirect, of a member of the British royal family with the Lisbon conspiracy created an embarrassing situation for Whitehall that was carefully managed. Freire was hanged and Eben was expelled from Portugal.[18]

The revolutions in Brazil and Portugal were followed by the discovery of a military rebellion in Spain led by generals Luis Lacy and Francisco Milans del Bosch. Both were heroes of the Peninsular War and Freemasons. Their objective was to implant a constitutional monarchy in Spain. Lacy was arrested and promptly executed; Milans managed to escape to Montevideo.[19] Almost at the same time, in early June, the French authorities discovered that some former officers of the Grande Armée in Lyon were plotting to proclaim Napoleon II as the new ruler of France. The police suspected that Eugene de Beauharnais, Marshal Grouchy, and Lazare Carnot were behind this plot. The authorities executed twenty-eight suspected conspirators.[20]

The simultaneous uprisings in the Old and the New World put all the European courts on high alert. They were also the signal Cochrane and Wilson had been waiting for. By the early summer Cochrane had sold his country house at Holly Hill and arranged all his personal and financial affairs.[21] Wilson was also ready, but the sudden decline in the health of his wife complicated his plans. The prospect of taking care of thirteen children without the help of her husband was probably too much for the poor woman. But Wilson still hoped to join Cochrane in this South American adventure.

Eager to aid Napoleon's cause, Wilson helped Captain Piontkowski fulfill his instructions. Having received funds from Napoleon's mother, by mid-July the Polish officer was ready to depart for Italy to deliver "verbal messages for every friend and relative of Bonaparte."[22] Piontkowski's sudden departure may have been prompted by Santini's arrest at the end of June near the Italian border, before he was able to deliver Napoleon's message to Marie Louise. Count Neipperg, Marie Louise's faithful guardian, had been forewarned by Metternich and asked the Austrian police to prevent either Santini or Piontkowski from ever reaching Parma.[23] Was Napoleon's message to Marie Louise to allow Napoleon II to join Joseph in America?

In mid-July, when Cochrane was ready to depart for South America, bad news arrived from Brazil. "Pernambuco is actually restored to legitimate authority," reported the *Courier.* There were also troubles in the United States. Although MacGregor had sailed to Florida and Lallemand had arrived safely in Boston, the newspapers reported that Count Regnault had gone mad. Other reports suggested that Brayer "whose departure for South America was announced, still resides at New York, and intends to take no part in the insurrectionary war. The name of this general has been confounded with that of a Sr. Roul, calling himself a French general who, after having gone to Buenos Aires, suddenly returned pursued by an order for arrest, by the insurgent Government, and who brings news not much calculated, as it appears, to induce European officers to take any part in that cause."[24] Roul would do a lot more damage than this rumor suggested.

The collapse of the Pernambucan revolution forced Wilson and Cochrane to change their plans. Cochrane left for France, ostensibly in consideration of his wife, who was supposedly not well, but most probably with other designs in mind. He arrived in Paris on August 15, Napoleon's birthday.[25] Richelieu was puzzled and worried by Cochrane's presence in the French capital, but there was not much he could do except to ask the police to keep him under strict surveillance. A servant at the hotel told Cochrane that he had been "instructed to collect all the bits of paper he threw into the fireplace, and even those he used at the close stool."[26]

Richelieu needed any piece of information he could get. He feared that revolutionary virus in the New World was now spreading to Europe. It was necessary for the peace and tranquility, if not for the survival, of the European monarchies to "find some means to calm these vast and interesting countries." First, he explained to Hyde de Neuville, it was imperative to prevent a war between Spain and the United States over their border disputes in Louisiana and Florida, as it "would decide the issues in a very unfavorable manner."[27] Second, it was necessary to stop the growth of republican and liberal ideas in the New World.

If the Spanish colonies became independent, and it seemed they would, they had to be governed by a monarchy supported by the Holy Alliance.

Richelieu knew that there was support for this idea in Buenos Aires. Juan Martin de Pueyrredon, the supreme director, had just sent him a message suggesting that he would welcome a rapprochement with France. Pueyrredon's overtures were part of a strategy designed by General San Martin, the all-powerful chief of the patriot armies, to establish monarchies in all the Spanish colonies with the sponsorship of the Holy Alliance. There were only two dynasties San Martin didn't like, the Spanish Bourbons and the Bonapartes.

The Argentine general was so convinced of the advantages of his project that he had sent an emissary to London to open a direct channel of communications with Foreign Office. San Martin had also entrusted his agent with the mission of buying ships and recruiting experienced naval officers in England to help in the naval war against Spain. Cochrane seemed the ideal candidate for the job but had already left for Paris. However, Wilson and other supporters of South American independence, unaware of San Martin's real designs, welcomed his envoy with open arms. With the end of the war in Europe, public opinion eagerly looked for new heroes in South America. The legend of San Martin was born. The Abbé de Pradt felt compelled to compare his battle dispatches to "the bulletins of Bonaparte's Grande Armée."[28]

18
Keeping the World Awake

Behold the scales in which his Fortune hangs,
A Surgeon's statement, and an Earl's harangues!
A bust delayed, a book refused, can shake
The sleep of Him who kept the world awake.
—Lord Byron, *The Age of Bronze*, Canto 3

Napoleon was anxious for news from Europe but the flow of newspapers to Longwood suddenly stopped. Bathurst had informed Lowe about the ads published in the *Anti-Gallican* and explained that the Austrian government wanted "to discover if possible the person by whom this letter has been written, and as they are now masters of the cipher, they consider it very desirable that no means should be taken to prevent the *Anti-Gallican* from reaching General Bonaparte in the hope that some evidence may hereafter be obtained of the person in Vienna who proposes to carry on such correspondence and of its objects. You will therefore permit *The Anti-Gallican* newspaper to reach General Bonaparte in the usual manner."[1] But then Bathurst changed his mind and recommended that Napoleon not be allowed to read the *Anti-Gallican* because in one of the letters "the advice given to General Bonaparte was not to go to bed in the night." Bathurst suspected the *Morning Chronicle* and the *Times* also carried secret messages for Napoleon.[2]

To circumvent Lowe's restrictions, O'Meara brought Napoleon any newspapers he could get at Jamestown. Napoleon believed that the political troubles in France would help his cause. He warned his doctor that the "revolutionary spirit which exists now against the actual government of France may find its way to England, and if so, there is no knowing how it may terminate."[3] At the end of May, Napoleon learned that his messengers had safely reached London and that they had published Montholon's "Remonstrance." The surgeon of an East Indiaman brought a letter from Piontkowski to Gourgaud saying that they had fulfilled their mission in London and that Rousseau and Archambault were on their way to America.[4]

This news somewhat compensated for Napoleon's disappointment at the defeat of Lord Holland's motion in the House of Lords. A pessimistic Gourgaud thought it was "obvious that we are to stay at St. Helena."[5] Napoleon disagreed. "Whatever they say will have a good effect in Europe." He believed Santini had done "marvelously well."[6] However, it seems he wanted the British government to think otherwise as O'Meara told Lowe that Napoleon considered Santini's *Appeal* "a foolish production exaggerated, full of *coglionere* and some lies" and that he regarded Maceroni, its supposed author, as "*un intrigante*—a mongrel Englishman, who, born in England, had an Italian name, is employed by Murat in Naples, afterwards by Fouché and Metternich."[7]

However, Napoleon could not disguise his anger at Bathurst. "That noble lord is a beast, an ignoramus who doesn't know what he is talking about. He will soon see how I am going to torment him."[8] Napoleon was so indignant at Bathurst's speech in the House of Lords that he immediately began writing a rejoinder. In it he argued that his confinement was contrary to the laws of nations and that there was no instance in the history of England or France "in which prisoners of war were sent away to be in a state of detention in another hemisphere, and on an isolated rock in the midst of the seas." The minister of a civilized European country could not impose restrictions on such a prisoner "according to the measure of his alarm, his caprice, or his passion." It was "magistrates of the administrative or judiciary order, who determine upon them, and protect his responsibility," Napoleon argued. Otherwise, "there would be no dungeons safe enough in the eyes of the man responsible for the detention. For, after all, prisoners shut up in towers, fettered and manacled, have found means to escape. In whatever situation living men are placed, they have always certain chance, more or less numerous, of regaining their liberty." There was only one way to "enclose a man without any chance of freeing himself, without even one chance in a thousand, you find only one: a coffin!" The restrictions imposed on him were not only illegal but also unnecessary. "If there were not any land guards at St. Helena, the brigs alone which cruise round the island might suffice to render all egress impossible, or, in other words, to give ninety-nine chances to the keeper and scarcely one to the prisoners."[9] Page after page Napoleon dissected Bathurst's speech to refute his arguments. Months later the document was smuggled to London and published as *Observations to Lord Bathurst's Speech.*

Recent messages from Joseph, Piontkowski, and Santini had encouraged

Napoleon's hopes that he would soon leave St. Helena. Even if his plans failed, he was convinced that the turmoil in Europe would work in his favor. Informed about the recent demonstrations in London, he assured Gourgaud that "the rioters in England were speaking of no one but him, that they had a tricolor, and that they were crying out for the Emperor to lead them in defense of the rights of people. They might seize several vessels and come and rescue us, after which, they would go to France and expel the Bourbons."[10] William Balcombe, who visited Longwood a few days later with gifts from Lady Holland, instead thought that the Spa Fields riots had injured the emperor's image.[11] Napoleon brushed off these concerns. "If Lord Holland were to enter the Ministry, I would perhaps be recalled to England," he told Gourgaud. "Our greatest hopes lie in the death of the Prince Regent. In this event, little Princess Charlotte would ascend to the throne. She would recall me."[12]

In a conversation with O'Meara, Napoleon insisted that the only remedy to relieve the misery that existed in England was to provide

a vent for your manufactures and by a reduction of expenditure. . . . This would contribute essentially to calm the public agitation. Had the ministers come forward like men at the opening of the session of Parliament and thrown up their sinecures, this with the example set by the Prince Regent, would have quieted all tumults and complaints. . . . An exclusive commercial treaty for twenty years with the Brazils and Spanish South America might still be demanded with success. Or assist the colonies in rendering themselves independent and you would have all their commerce. . . . All your miseries I maintain to be owing to the imbecility and ignorance of Lord Castlereagh and his inattention to the real prosperity of his own country.[13]

His words would have been music to the ears of the English Radicals.

News of the uproar caused in Paris by the staging of the *Germanicus* play greatly amused Napoleon, and a few days later he was seen reading it in his study. Napoleon predicted that within three years Louis XVIII would die and that the Duke of Orleans or Napoleon II would succeed him. "I have still a great many years to live. My career is not finished," he told Gourgaud.[14] The improved atmosphere at Longwood was almost shattered when Napoleon learned that Lowe had threatened to break a marble bust of his young son brought by a sailor of an East Indiaman because he was convinced that there was a hidden message inside. Napoleon was enraged and ready to take advantage of the situation for his own purposes. Fearful of the repercussions in Europe, Lowe relented and the bust made its way to Longwood.

Napoleon was quite moved at seeing an image of his son, whom he hadn't seen in almost five years, and placed the bust on the top of the chimney in his drawing room. "Barbarous and atrocious must be the man who would break such an image as that," he said. "This man [Lowe] appears to have no other goal but to kill me morally and physically with blow of pins," he told O'Meara. "A torturer would kill me out of only one blow. His conduct is tortuous and surrounded by mystery. Only the crime goes in darkness."[15]

Maybe it was because Napoleon hoped for his imminent release that he started to worry about an assassination attempt. "A man must be worse than a blockhead who does not perceive that I was sent here to be killed either by the natural effects of ill treatment combined with the badness of the climate or by the probability of my being induced to commit suicide," he told O'Meara.[16] To his companions Napoleon voiced more sinister suspicions. Once at dinner after tasting the wine he said: "This rogue Reade is quite capable of trying to poison me. He has the key to the wine cellar and he can change the corks." Having just finished Hume's *History of England*, Napoleon had lost any illusion that the British ministers would not try to assassinate him. "The English are ferocious people. What crimes we read of in their history!" Gourgaud thought the danger of poisoning was real and noted in his journal that the emperor would be well advised "not to be the only one drinking wine at Longwood." Napoleon felt safe for the time being "because Balcombe is responsible for our food supplies" and O'Meara and Poppleton were "decent fellows . . . above that sort of thing." But what if they were both removed from Longwood? "If Reade displaces Poppleton, I shall protest," Napoleon said. Maybe as a precaution, for several days O'Meara and Poppleton ate the same food as Napoleon did.[17]

Wilson was a regular topic of conversation at Longwood. Napoleon knew he was the real author of Santini's appeal, although for a while he pretended not to know.[18] "Guess who wrote Santini's memoirs?" he asked Gourgaud. "Las Cases," replied Gourgaud. "*Eh non!* It was Wilson."[19] Lord Cochrane was also mentioned. Napoleon learned that he had left or was about to leave for South America.[20]

In late June, Admiral Robert Plampin arrived aboard the HMS *Conqueror* to replace Malcolm. Napoleon had awaited the arrival of this ship for two months. It was no coincidence that Wilson's oldest son was a midshipman on the *Conqueror* and brought messages from London. On July 2 Admiral Plampin came to Longwood to introduce himself. Aware of the presence of the young Wilson, Napoleon told Plampin that he would take great pleasure in meeting the son of someone who had "saved the life of one of his best friends."[21] Suspicious, Plampin refused to authorize the visit. But the young man managed to meet Countess Bertrand, who on many occasions was the recipient of secret communications for the emperor, particularly from British subjects, as she spoke fluent English. After the meeting, the countess confidently reported that the emperor would "soon be on the throne again." Many people in England shared this view.[22]

Days later, an East Indiaman coming from China brought some gifts and a letter for Napoleon from Thomas Elphinstone, head of the East India Company in Canton. On the eve of Waterloo, the emperor had sent his own doctor to treat Elphinstone's younger brother, who had been left for dead on the battlefield. This gesture had not been forgotten. "The present consisted of a magnificent ivory chess set larger than the usual size, two large and beautiful openwork baskets, and an exquisite ivory basket filled with mother-of-pearl tokens."[23] Although the gifts were sent through proper channels, Lowe complained to Bathurst about Elphinstone's conduct, which he feared would encourage sympathy for Napoleon among naval officers returning to England. Lowe was irritated because the chess pieces had an *N* engraved with a crown.[24] After procrastinating for several weeks, he reluctantly agreed to send the chess set to Longwood. When Napoleon found out about the reason for the delay, he was furious.

It was a few weeks after receiving Elphinstone's gift that Napoleon told Montholon and Gourgaud that he had been offered a new plan of escape. The plan was well thought out and involved the assistance of some locals. Napoleon explained how he would leave Longwood without being noticed by the sentries, go to the shore, and then embark on a ship that was waiting for him. Montholon would stay behind to guard his room and fool Lowe who, used to not seeing his prisoner for several days, would not suspect anything. "We could send one of our ladies, or even both, to pay a visit to Plantation House on that day. Lady Lowe would make beautiful conversation about me while we left this cursed country."[25] Napoleon got carried away by the idea. He asked Gourgaud if Poppleton would be on their side. "If so," he added, "it is in the hope of receiving a bribe. Bah! The English are like that. With money one could buy them all over." After dinner, Napoleon continued to talk about escaping. He pulled out a map of the island and described the route he would take. "Through the town and in broad daylight would be best" he said. "On the coast, with our shot-guns we could easily rout an outpost of ten men—yes, even of twenty. Ah, if only the Governor knew what we were talking about!" Napoleon laughed. It would be complete madness to attempt to escape but the thought amused him. "I've added fifteen years to my life," he said.[26] How was this plan communicated to Napoleon? A hundred years later, at an exhibit in Prague, it was discovered that a set of chessmen used by Napoleon at Longwood contained a hidden escape plan.[27] Was it the same?

Days later, Cipriani, Napoleon's mysterious maître d'hôtel, came back from Jamestown with a letter for Napoleon from Lewis Goldsmith, the editor of the *Anti-Gallican*. Montholon noted that Goldsmith had been "the most active agent of the oligarchy, but after a long time he had mysteriously turned in favor of the Emperor." Coincidentally, Goldsmith was related to Lewis Solomon, a Jewish merchant in Jamestown whom Cipriani used to transmit clandestine messages back to Europe.[28] According to Montholon, Goldsmith's letter provided details of everything that was happening in France and assured Napoleon that the Bourbons would not be able to support themselves on the throne after the departure of the Allied armies at the end of 1818. Austria would support Napoleon II; England would support the Duke of Orleans; and Russia, maybe the Prince of Orange.[29]

Maybe it was Goldsmith's letter that convinced Napoleon of the need to send another emissary to Europe to ascertain what kind of support he could get from Russia and Austria. He hinted to Gourgaud that he had chosen him for this delicate mission. Gourgaud wasn't happy. He thought Montholon intrigued to get rid of him and feared that his reputation would be ruined forever if he left. But Gourgaud knew he had no choice. He was absolutely devoted to Napoleon. "If Your Majesty requires it, I will go," he said reluctantly.[30] To avoid having Gourgaud quarantined at the Cape like Las Cases, Napoleon would have to prepare his exit very carefully.

19
A Traitor in Their Midst

This revelation gives all the details of a plan formed by Buonaparte for his own rescue.

—Hyde de Neuville to Richelieu, July 26, 1817

If it ever existed, Joseph's complacency was shattered in mid-July, when he received reports suggesting the Pernambucan uprising had faltered.[1] As the days passed, he learned that the rebellion had been crushed and that the Portuguese authorities were in control. Troubles were also brewing in other quarters. The Monroe administration reacted negatively to the Florida incursion. From Amelia Island, MacGregor asked John Stuart Skinner to intercede with the administration as "you promised me at Baltimore." Skinner sent a letter to John Quincy Adams, the new secretary of state, explaining that MacGregor's objective had been to take Amelia Island, "thence to wrest the Floridas from Spain and encourage the existing disposition of the people in that section to confederate with the United States—leaving it to the will and policy of this Government and to political circumstances as they might arise, to indicate the most favorable time for their admission into the Union." In the meantime, Florida would be used as a base to further "South American independence." This scheme, Skinner explained, had two advantages. First, it would give the rebels "access to the resources and profit of the enterprising spirit of this country, without necessarily involving a positive violation of any of our strictly neutral or pacific obligations" and second, it would spare the administration "the embarrassment resulting from the uncontrollable propensity of our citizens" to join the rebels. More importantly, Skinner assured Adams that despite "strongly indicative circumstances," MacGregor was not a British agent. Besides, it was so clear that Florida belonged to the United States "that all apprehension of an attempt to hold them by any other power must be rebutted by the gross and manifest folly of such an undertaking."[2]

Adams was not receptive to these arguments. The son of former president John Adams, he was a man of "reserved, cold, austere and forbidding manners" and a "gloomy misanthropist," who compensated for his lack of social skills with a keen intellect and a great ability for intrigue.[3] He had accepted Monroe's offer to lead the State Department even though their views "upon subjects of great public interest have at particular periods of our public life been much at variance."[4] Henry Clay, who had openly aspired to that position, was clearly disappointed. During the country's short political history, the secretary of state had been the successor of the president. Clay had expected a reward for his loyalty to the Madison administration. For Monroe it was a political compromise.* After fifteen years of dominance by the Virginian junto, he needed to expand his support base. Clay, a Virginian, represented the western states, whereas Adams was from Massachusetts and led the "moderate wing of Federalism."[5]

Although they would become allies, in 1817 Adams and Clay had very different views on how to conduct U.S. foreign policy. An Anglophile, Adams believed that "no country or people that I have ever visited presents more solid, more numerous or more noble topics for panegyric than England."[6] Clay instead had been one of the strongest supporters of the war against England. Adams detested Napoleon. He had been in Paris in March 1815 and had described Napoleon as a "highway robber" and his escape from Elba as "the last struggle of desperation on his part."[7] Clay considered Napoleon the "master spirit of the age."[8] When he heard of Napoleon's escape from Elba, he exclaimed: "Wonderful age! Wonderful man! Wonderful nation!"[9] Regarding the Spanish colonies, Adams feared that support or recognition of their independence could plunge the United States into a war with Spain, and possibly England.[10] He was not only committed to a policy of strict neutrality but was also convinced that the United States should act in concert with England with respect to the Spanish colonies, where he saw dim prospects for the development of republican institutions.[11] In contrast, Clay was an enthusiastic supporter of the independence of the Spanish colonies and favored relaxing U.S. neutrality laws to allow filibustering and privateering.[12]

Other considerations entered Adams's mind. Spain was already dangling Florida to settle pending border disputes in Texas. Any deal with the Spaniards

---

* Ironically, Clay served as secretary of state during the presidency of John Quincy Adams (1825–1829).

would require neutralizing the plans of the French émigrés and delaying recognition of Buenos Aires' independence, as Spain desperately needed to narrow the fronts in the war against the rebels. Besides, Adams thought MacGregor was a brigand and he had a poor opinion of Skinner.[13]

Hyde de Neuville was not worried about MacGregor, as he had not yet linked him to Joseph's plans. However, he was sure that something awful was about to happen. He was puzzled by the frenzied activity of the émigrés. What to make of General Vandamme's arrival? And Regnault's departure for Europe? And what about Colonel Galabert, former chief of staff of Marshal Soult, who was ready to leave for France and boasted that in less than three months he would succeed or be dead? Hyde de Neuville also worried about the imminent departure of the *Morgiana*, a Buenos Aires privateer that he suspected was bound for St. Helena.[14] Hyde de Neuville's attention now focused on Europe. His spies had heard that a plot to topple the Bourbons would "explode in France" in November.[15] He warned Sir Charles Bagot that the émigrés were "secretly forming a mad and criminal project and talk about returning to France" via England.[16] Bagot listened with his usual coolness. He was not worried about a Bonapartist conspiracy in France as he had just discovered that Joseph had sent a ship to Italy to bring Lucien and Napoleon II to the United States.[17]

As summer approached, Hyde de Neuville grew more frantic and prodded his spies for information. At the end of July, his efforts finally paid off. The French consul in New York had been contacted by a man who introduced himself as General Jacques Roul, of the patriot army of Buenos Aires. Roul promised to disclose "all the details of a plan formed by Buonaparte for his own rescue." As Hyde de Neuville reported: "The plan was brought by the Messrs. Rousseau and Archambault and it seems it must be executed, not only by ships fitted in the United States but also by the other means supplied in Europe. Everything is prepared for St. Helena. Wilson and Cochrane are the main engines of this enterprise. Here, the main émigrés act under Joseph's orders. The officer who revealed everything also offered to provide irrefutable proofs. He claims to be one of the main agents behind the plan."

Roul, who had recently arrived from Buenos Aires, also disclosed that there was a plan for "the removal of the son of Bonaparte that must be attempted by a certain Colonel Poli." An agent had just left for Italy "carrying messages for Marie Louise and Lucien," the latter of whom was expected in America with the young Napoleon. "I repeat that November seems to be a watchword which everybody keeps repeating," warned Hyde de Neuville. Despite his anxiety, he had doubts. Was Roul a double agent? If so, his confession could hide a more dangerous project. If the objective was not St. Helena, "this army of determined and fearless desperadoes will disembark with weapons and ammunitions in one of our provinces and attempt one of these daring and unexpected coups which always bring trouble and provoke confusion. . . . Let us watch more than ever the movement of our enemies; they stir in a threatening way in both worlds."[18]

In early August, Hyde de Neuville prepared a detailed report for Richelieu. According to Roul, Grouchy and Clausel transmitted Joseph's orders to the rest of the French officers. The rescue expedition would be disguised as a privateering enterprise under the flag of Buenos Aires. The forces already gathered in the United States, the troops to be recruited by Brayer in Buenos Aires, and the group that had departed for Pernambuco under the orders of Colonel Latapie would meet with Cochrane at Fernando de Noronha and then sail to St. Helena. Cochrane and Wilson had discussed the plan in London with a certain Colonel Jeannet. Once at St. Helena part of the squadron would engage the British cruisers, while three simultaneous attacks were launched: one on Jamestown, another on Sandy Bay, and a third on Prosperous Bay. The first would be a diversion to draw the British garrison to the capital; the second would take a fort in the middle of the island; and the third would be directed at Longwood to liberate Napoleon. Roul said that he had discussed this plan with Brayer before leaving Buenos Aires and that Joseph had assigned Roul the duty of liaising with Grouchy and Lallemand. He also claimed to have participated in a meeting a few days earlier at Joseph's house to discuss the plan. According to Roul, a light schooner fitted by Stephen Girard was ready to depart for St. Helena to observe the position of the British cruisers and would later join the rescue expedition at Fernando de Noronha. Once freed, Napoleon would be brought to America and then "attempt a new march to Paris."[19]

Roul had never been popular among the émigrés and only thanks to Carrera had he been able to obtain a commission in the army of Buenos Aires. Although he was a veteran of some of Napoleon's most celebrated campaigns, it seems he tried to appropriate the celebrity of Nicholas Raoul, a member of the "immortal battalion" who accompanied Napoleon to Paris in March 1815.[20] Expelled from Buenos Aires, penniless and with few friends, Roul could only resort to treason. Thanks to a brief encounter with Brayer he had been able to enter Joseph's circle and learn enough details about his plans to sell them to Hyde de Neuville.[21]

Hyde de Neuville was stunned by Roul's revelations and warned Richelieu that any rescue expeditions "would find in all the ports of the United States, fearless auxiliaries, weapons and money" and that there was nothing that he could do to stop them. "I would be much less worried if my alarm had no other foundation than the revelations of Colonel, or General, Roul," he wrote. Hyde de Neuville also noted that "a very large number of French officers embark secretly, that St. Helena and November do not cease to be mentioned as their objective; that the two people arrived from St. Helena are awaiting orders for an imminent departure; that the leaders are at this moment gathered in Philadelphia at Joseph's house and that many former officers are assembled in New York and Baltimore, and that, finally, people who had no money some months ago, are now spending sums that would represent fortunes for them in taverns and other public places." He believed the arrival of Vandamme "undoubtedly strengthens any hopes that they may have which cannot exist without some foundation." As time passed, Hyde de Neuville's suspicions grew: "Then St. Helena is only a pretext and Regnault de Saint Jean d'Angely in his madness has only told the truth, which they have tried to dismiss as the dreams of a madman. Regnault, in one of his few lucid moments, as in delirium, mentioned an uprising, a movement being prepared in France and of an expedition sailing from the United States for the coast of Normandy with weapons, and ammunitions, which could serve as the signal for a new March 20."

"Almost all our enemies seem confident and what is secretly said in New York and Philadelphia, is also revealed and confided in New Orleans," Hyde de Neuville warned Richelieu. In his view St. Helena was "a diversionary point or simply an imaginary objective masking another project used to seduce and rally those for whom Napoleon's name will always be a dreadful talisman." Besides, the way to St. Helena could be indirect: "If the project of the Cochranes, the Wilsons, the Cobbetts, in short all the dissidents and refugees of both worlds, is currently the rescue of Bonaparte, I don't believe it can be effected with the means presented to us by Roul."

Wilson's involvement troubled Hyde de Neuville. The man who had saved Lavallette knew that "where force is lacking, guile and address can succeed." So either he was strongly mistaken or "this enterprise to St. Helena does not involve a plan of attack," wrote Hyde de Neuville. "Bonaparte can be saved by deception." The conspirators surely counted on other means to achieve their objective. "Here I can again be mistaken," he wrote, "but if I were Napoleon's man I would know well not [to] take part in such a plan and would not allow myself to be engaged in an impossible enterprise in which I could only see insurmountable difficulties." On the other hand, there were always people "who put their glory above anything and there is no point in us doubting their determination. Therefore, if such expeditions—which are certainly being prepared, but which after all may not be executed—have St. Helena as their objective, I remain persuaded that they are less likely to use force."[22]

Determined to uncover the truth, Hyde de Neuville met several times with Roul, but the more he listened to him the more suspicious he became. Even to a conspiracy theorist like Hyde de Neuville, Roul's confession seemed too far-fetched. And some of the leads he had provided turned out to be false. The French consul in Philadelphia, who wasn't on very good terms with Hyde de Neuville and maybe was on Joseph's payroll, dismissed Roul's story as the fabrications of a charlatan. In a report he sent directly to Richelieu, he said Grouchy and his sons were hunting, Vandamme lived quietly in Philadelphia, and the supposedly dangerous Galabert worked in a tavern. Nothing suggested that they were involved in a plan to rescue Napoleon.[23] Eventually Hyde de Neuville also concluded that Roul's confession was a sham. "Nothing more ridiculous than the pretensions of this man," who had tried to deceive him with "miserable boastings" and make him believe that all the preparations "which are undertaken under my eyes are only directed to South America!"[24] Despite his doubts, Hyde de Neuville communicated the results of his investigations to Luis de Onis, with whom he had an excellent personal relationship and with whom he shared the same obsession: disrupting the plans of the Bonapartist émigrés and ensuring the survival of the Bourbon dynasty in their respective countries. To his dismay and surprise, Onis told him that his agents had discovered that an expedition was actually being prepared to rescue Napoleon and put him at the head of the insurgents in Brazil or in Buenos Aires.[25]

Through other sources, British agents also confirmed the existence of an expedition to rescue Napoleon. A man named Joshua Wilder approached Gilbert Robertson, the British consul in Philadelphia, and offered to disclose details of a plan hatched by an American captain named Jesse Hawkins. Wilder claimed that Hawkins was building a specially designed fast sailing vessel made of "cedar and birch plank" and had chartered two other fast sailing vessels that were supposed to sail to China but instead were bound to St. Helena. The captain had also told him that General Henri Lallemand promised him "money to get the materials for this boat and to charter the vessels and hire the men to go with them." They planned to approach the windward side of the island at night and then lower a few boats and row to shore. The rescuers had hired a man who was well acquainted with the island and happened to know William Balcombe.

Hawkins had already sent one of his men to the Far East on an East Indiaman via England with messages for Napoleon. Joseph had promised a big reward and had already paid out money "to get this thing done." Clausel and Lallemand were also involved in the rescue plan, which was targeted for January or February and involved taking Napoleon "to South America [to] join the patriots." Wilder stated that Joseph had spent as much as a thousand dollars in silver and tableware to be used by Napoleon en route to Buenos Aires. He assured Robertson that he had seen several letters on the subject that suggested the execution "of the business immediately."[26] Robertson alerted Sir Charles Bagot even thought he was inclined "to believe the plan altogether impossible."[27] Bagot suspected that Wilder was after easy money even though he had just received a letter from an Englishman living in Kentucky confirming that Bonapartist agents were actively recruiting men in the western states for an expedition to St. Helena. The informer warned him that unless their efforts were derailed, they would "certainly end in the rescue of Napoleon."[28]

Despite all their spies and informers, Onis, Hyde de Neuville, and Bagot failed to notice the departure to Europe of Joseph's secretary, Louis Mailliard, on a secret and delicate mission: to recover the diamonds of the crown of Spain, which were hidden in the garden of Joseph's chateau in Switzerland.[29] An American passport obtained by Stephen Girard facilitated Mailliard's departure. It is unclear whether Joseph planned to encrust these diamonds in the crown of Mexico or use them to pay for his brother's rescue.

Somehow Joseph learned that his plans had been discovered. If the French consul in Philadelphia was not on his payroll, he had other ways to find out. In mid-August, Hyde de Neuville reported an attempted burglary at his house. Wilder was also discovered and the incriminating letters from Hawkins suddenly disappeared. Desperate for money, Wilder submitted a sworn statement to the British consul confirming the existence of a plan to rescue Napoleon and implicated another American captain as "one of the precious gang employed in this adventure" and a Frenchman named Fournier, "who was in jail for not paying his debts." Bagot agreed to spend £100 to buy more evidence.[30]

By the end of August, Joseph and his generals were trying to salvage the Florida scheme by getting rid of MacGregor, but the Monroe administration was increasingly hostile to their plans. Although the *Morgiana* under the command of Captain Taylor managed to leave New York, another privateer carrying weapons and reinforcements for Amelia Island was detained by customs for violating U.S. neutrality laws.[31] Taylor, whom Hyde de Neuville had described as a man of "extreme boldness and a very big admirer of the prisoner of St. Helena" was partners with Ruggles Hubbard, who had just resigned from the office of high sheriff of New York, and weeks later the newspapers reported he had embarked on a ship "that he himself had fitted out to join MacGregor."[32]

Hubbard was a longtime associate of Aaron Burr. He was also connected to John Stuart Skinner and was not new to the business of organizing filibustering expeditions.[33] In fact, a year earlier Hubbard had arranged the transportation of several French officers to Buenos Aires with Martin Thompson, one of the representatives of the insurgent South American republics who had authorized MacGregor's occupation of Florida.[34] Another moving piece of the Florida puzzle was the French corsair Louis Aury who was sailing with his squadron toward Amelia Island. Aury was a close associate of the Venezuelan lawyer Pedro Gual, the legal mind behind the Florida enterprise. Aury's Bonapartist sympathies and connections were strong and his right-hand man had once served as Napoleon's spy in England.[35]

Lallemand was determined to go ahead with the invasion of Mexico and had already gathered a large number of French veterans in Philadelphia.[36] Days later, Clausel and Lefebvre-Desnouettes left New York without difficulty after declaring that their objective was to settle the Tombigbee lands donated by Congress. But the two generals and almost forty veterans who accompanied them had no intention of cultivating vines and olives. Neither did Colonel Galabert, who planned to join them later at the head of more troops. Their real objective was to use Florida as a base to invade Mexico.[37] They didn't fool Onis who promptly alerted Madrid.[38]

Hyde de Neuville was still unsure about the true objective of the Bonapartists. Was it France or St. Helena? According to one source, it was the latter. November was again mentioned and Grouchy, Lallemand, Clausel, Lefebvre-Desnouettes, and Galabert were again implicated, as well as another French colonel named Pierre Douarche.[39] A veteran of the Peninsular War, Douarche had embraced Napoleon's cause during the Hundred Days and fought bravely at the battle of Waterloo. He had just arrived in the United States to join the emperor's last campaign and would become one of Lallemand's key lieutenants.

Then Hyde de Neuville made a shocking discovery. One of his spies intercepted correspondence implicating Joseph in a vast conspiracy to take over Mexico and the Spanish territories west of the Mississippi to create a Napoleonic confederation. The plan had been put together by Joseph Lakanal, a former member of the Institut de France and a banished regicide.* Hyde de Neu-ville noted that this plan was "practically the same [as] Colonel Burr's[;] it is the insurrection of the West and has as its objective to make Joseph the king of Mexico." Fearing it was too late to derail the plan, he vented his frustration in a lengthy dispatch to Richelieu:

> I can try to disrupt the Napoleonic intrigues in the New World, but those related to St. Helena can only be stopped in Europe. . . . The latest reports from St. Helena say Napoleon is behaving well but that he refuses to see anybody. Is he trying to figure out the way to escape without anybody immediately knowing about it? Maybe a fishing boat has been offered to him. With a good naval officer, nothing would prevent him from meet-ing a friendly vessel coming from America at prearranged latitude. I am not a seaman, but I have consulted this matter with good sailors and if the surveillance at St. Helena is not extraordinary, I say and I repeat, we have everything to fear. What are we going to do if this prodigious man arrives [in] an already conquered Mexico?[40]

Hyde de Neuville approached Onis and proposed disrupting the plans of the Bonapartists jointly because if those plans succeeded "neither Spain nor France could remain calm." The ever-suspicious Onis rejected the idea, arguing that it was a waste of money. In truth, he worried about the possibility of a French intrigue. Onis had no doubt that a project of "great importance" was afoot. According to his spies, Joseph had recently visited Manhattan and attended a long meeting with the émigrés, after which an urgent message had been sent to Paris. Onis warned Madrid that there were plans to rescue Napoleon and ini-tiate an uprising in France, "which could very well be linked to an insurrec-tion in Mexico." He recommended that all the European sovereigns protest to the United States in the strongest manner "for all these plans made in its soil to upset tranquility of neutral countries."[41] He also warned the Spanish authorities in Mexico and Cuba that "an expedition of 900 men, led by Napoleon's most famous generals, is preparing to invade the Kingdom of Mexico. . . . Joseph Bonaparte is supporting and aiding the expedition on the expectation that he will be proclaimed King."[42]

---

* Regicides were members of the Convention nationale who had voted in favor of Louis XVI's execution.

Hyde de Neuville then met with Bagot. To enlist England's support, he gave him copies of Lakanal's letters and assured him that the Bonapartist émigrés were recruiting men in the western states "with the secret objective of proclaiming Joseph as King of Mexico." It was another link in "the revolutionary chain" organized by the Bonapartists in America "to excite again troubles by anarchy and usurpation." Hyde de Neuville excitedly argued that the most urgent measures were needed on both sides of the Atlantic "to derail the plots of a family that has been disastrous for the world."[43] Although exasperated by his French colleague, Bagot realized this conspiracy was more substantial than he had imagined.

Hyde de Neuville also shared the information with Secretary of State Adams and demanded the intervention of the U.S. government to stop "a project for invading Mexico from the United States and declaring Joseph Bonaparte King of Spain and the Indies."[44] Adams replied that his attention would be "peculiarly directed to every object of information disclosing designs illegal in their character, or tending to disturb the public tranquility by menacing the peace of friendly nations." However, since the incriminating letters "found" by Hyde de Neuville had never reached Joseph, his involvement in a conspiracy could not be proved. Besides, under the laws of the United States, criminal intent per se was not a punishable offence, least of all when the intended crime was to be perpetrated by foreigners abroad. Adams said he would ask William Lee, former consul at Bordeaux and recently appointed auditor of the War Department, to conduct an investigation, as he was well connected to the Bonapartist émigrés.[45]

On September 26, Adams had another long meeting with Hyde de Neuville whose views "changed so much in the course of our conference from what they had been by his letter of last evening, as it made it necessary for me to consult with Mr. Rush and to write to the President."[46] The following day, Lee presented the results of his investigations regarding the projects of the French émigrés. Lee had obtained most of the information from Colonel Galabert, who had escaped from France with his help. Lee told Adams that the Lallemands were at the head of the expedition to Mexico and that they had already recruited eighty officers and one thousand men. They had also obtained the support of the Mexican patriots. According to Lee, merchants in Charleston, Philadelphia, Boston, and New York had provided money and ships for the expedition. Lallemand intended to establish a camp near Texas' Red River with a group of officers and about four hundred men that would serve as a base for future military operations. Lee also confirmed that Lallemand's expedition was connected to the Vine and Olive colony. The land granted by Congress in Tombigbee had been given as security to obtain sixty thousand dollars for the expedition from merchants in Philadelphia. According to Lee, "all the French officers of distinction except the Lallemands disapprove of this project." In fact, Vandamme had censured them "in so pointed a manner" that a serious quarrel ensued. Lee absolved Joseph from any responsibility, claiming that he had "pointedly refused all aid and assistance to this and the like schemes; that he has been solicited in every way and all means used to induce him to patronize these adventurers without success."

Lee claimed to have told Lallemand that his plans would not only bring opprobrium to all the French émigrés in the United States but also ruin "his reputation in violating our laws." Taken aback, Lallemand had promised not to proceed with his plans unless Congress amended the neutrality laws. The French general had been led to believe by "some influential" congressmen that some measures would be taken to favor the cause of the Spanish colonies. Everything he had done so far "was only under the expectation that this government would early in the winter give an opening to all those who wished well to the revolution in Spanish America." Lallemand also said that he "had determined not to engage in anything of this sort if disagreeable to [the] administration" and that he hoped the Monroe administration "wished him well" in his efforts to promote the independence of the Spanish colonies.[47] The "influential members" of Congress that supported Lallemand's plans included Henry Clay, the powerful Speaker of the House. Adams was shocked that Clay did not believe "in these levies of men in the Western States by French emigrants, and that he was determined at the next session of Congress to propose the acknowledgment of the South American insurgents."[48] Clay also sympathized with Napoleon and criticized England for surrendering him to the Allies and "her concurrence in his exile to St. Helena."[49]

The complaints of Onis and Hyde de Neuville put the Monroe administration in a difficult position. The president, who knew more about the Bonapartists' plans than he was willing to admit, was unsure about what to do. He continued to believe the publication of the Lakanal papers would be imprudent. He warned Adams that there was "a feeling in this country favorable to revolutionary men in France proceeding from the interest which was taken in the success of the [French] Revolution, which although the cause has long ceased, still has influence with many. It is well not to excite this feeling."[50] Adams in turn argued that Lee's report presented "the subject under an aspect altogether different from either of those in which it is exhibited by Mr. [Hyde] de Neuville. It is neither to conquer Mexico, nor to proclaim a King of Spain and the Indies; but whatever the purpose may be, it is evidently not warranted by, nor compatible with our laws." Adams warned Monroe that it would be necessary to stop "as soon as possible" the projects "in agitation among some of the emigrants from Europe."[51] Unfortunately, Adams didn't provide more details. If it wasn't Mexico, what else in Lallemand's plans was incompatible with the law? Rescuing Napoleon would violate American neutrality if it involved attacking British troops.

To get more information Adams contacted Peter Paul De Grand, a Frenchman in Boston who was an old family friend and was well connected with the Bonapartist émigrés. A business associate of Stephen Girard, he also knew Joseph, who during a recent visit to Boston had stayed at his house.[52] De Grand sent Adams a copy of a letter describing "certain projects" of the French émigrés that appears to have been written by Lallemand. The letter, of which only the first page has survived, stated that MacGregor was "devoted to the interests of England" and had been in contact with British agents while in Philadelphia, whereas Lallemand's plan contemplated the temporary occupation of Florida and the invasion of Mexico.[53] Lallemand was obviously trying to distance himself from MacGregor but could not stop movements planned months earlier. Another contingent of French veterans had recently left from New York bound for Florida and by the end of September, Aury and Hubbard had replaced MacGregor and annexed Amelia Island to the independent republic of Mexico.[54]

Adams completely disapproved of the Bonapartists' projects and warned De Grand "to have no concern with them." He also asked for more information about "the real and entire projects, for I have reason to believe that what you disclosed to me was but a small part of them."[55] Adams warned Monroe that the projects of the French émigrés, which he described as assisting the Mexican rebels "for consolidating their struggle for independence into a regular and legitimate form of government," required "the interposition of this government to prevent their further progress or execution."[56]

Alerted by his agents, Hyde de Neuville ordered a French warship anchored in New York to intercept Lallemand if he left for New Orleans or Mobile. He suspected that Joseph's sudden trip to Niagara Falls was to place himself "nearer to the Mississippi, which he can reach without observation and in a much shorter time than he could do from Philadelphia."[57] Bagot informed Castlereagh that the Confédération Napoléonienne appeared "to remove all doubt as to the real designs of Joseph Bonaparte against the Spanish provinces in South America," which were perhaps "upon the point of being carried into execution." He thought that the Monroe administration was "a good deal embarrassed." Although he didn't think they would resort to "vigorous measures," Bagot believed "they must be sensible that if they do not interfere, they will give such cause of complaints to Spain, at least as in the present state of their negotiations with that country they will hardly like to do."[58] A few days later he sent Castlereagh more details of the conspiracy. It had been planned by "a dangerous political society in this country composed of almost all the French officers in the United States and of several Americans." Bagot noted it was a "curious circumstance" that "the whole design was nearly being betrayed some months ago by Regnault," who had apparently gone mad. His dispatch added other shocking revelations:

> Two persons of the names of Rousseau and Archambault (the latter a servant of some inferior description) left the island of St. Helena with M. Santini. He [Hyde de Neuville] says that they parted with M. Santini in Brussels and arrived at Philadelphia. That Rousseau passed about a fortnight with Joseph Bonaparte and that he then went to Long Island, where he has resided ever since in the house of Cobbett, who as your Lordship probably knows settled there after his flight from England. M. [Hyde] de Neuville assured me that he knows that Cobbett is a principal agent in the plan which is in agitation for effecting the escape of Buonaparte from St. Helena and that he is the channel of communication for such of the English who are privy to the design. He says that Lord Cochrane and Sir Robert Wilson are both deeply engaged in it and that a correspondence is carried on upon the subject with some persons in France through the means of a female relation (he thinks a sister) of Sir Robert Wilson who resides at Brussels.

Bagot reported that Cochrane's "intended voyage to South America was connected with this design and that there was to be a general rendezvous of all the agents on the island of Fernando de Noronha, which is a small island off the coast of Pernambuco."[59] Where was Colonel Latapie now?

20

The Bourbons Strike Back

It is rather mortifying to see this country become the jailors and spies for the
Bourbon government; for to that condition Lord Castlereagh has brought it.
—Lady Holland to Mrs. Creevey, September 1817

By early September, Richelieu was so troubled by the dispatches from Hyde de
Neuville, that he asked his minister of marine to send a squadron to patrol the
eastern seaboard of the United States and intercept any expeditions bound for
St. Helena. To his dismay, he learned that it was impossible to do so.[1] He then
asked his ambassador in London to impress upon the British cabinet the need for
even stricter vigilance: "I know well that it seems impossible to free Napoleon
without the assistance of the British government, but I am surprised at the pres-
tige that this man has built around him and the influence that we see him exert
over anybody who approaches him; a plot could be hatched in St. Helena to facilitate his escape. I admit that this thought crosses my mind quite frequently
and disturbs me quite a bit. I would like you to direct the attention of the British government to this important issue."[2]

To raise the awareness of the British cabinet, Richelieu passed the details of
Roul's confession to Sir Charles Stuart, the English ambassador, who in a dispatch to Castlereagh expressed serious doubts about the whole scheme. "The
manifest absurdities and incoherencies in the whole statement would have rendered me unwilling to transmit such a communication to your Lordship had it
been received from a less respectable quarter."[3] Castlereagh passed the information to Bathurst who in turn passed it to Lowe, noting that he did not "attach
any importance to the information further than as tending to show the feeling
towards General Buonaparte which may naturally be supposed to animate those
of his adherents who have taken refuge in America."[4]

As he mulled over the plans of the Bonapartists, Richelieu also started to have doubts. Many details of Roul's confession seemed absurd. The participation of Fouché and Talleyrand in the conspiracy seemed unlikely. Equally implausible was the suggestion that an unnamed member of the cabinet was also involved. Who could it be? Decazes? On the other hand, Richelieu wasn't surprised at the involvement of Wilson and Cochrane, which confirmed his view that the biggest threat to the Bourbons was not in Philadelphia, but in London, where Wilson's campaign in favor of the prisoner of St. Helena continued unabated.

Wilson had in fact just received a message from Napoleon. "You will be astonished to find how well he knows what is going on here," Wilson wrote to Grey in mid-September. "He is in high health . . . [and] as fit to make a campaign as he ever was."[5] Days earlier, Wilson had published a pamphlet arguing that Russia, not France, had become England's most powerful enemy. He also presented his own version of the Napoleonic wars, interspersing it with favorable comments about Napoleon, who "on a rock in the centre of the ocean" was contemplating adversity "with the equanimity of a philosopher."[6] An anonymous appraisal in the *Quarterly Review,* probably written by John Wilson Croker, accused Wilson of being "the eulogist of Buonaparte and the apologist of those very actions which his own pen was the first to point out to general horror and execration!" According to the *Courier,* Wilson's pamphlet was "full of gratuitous assumptions, of false reasonings, of vain pretensions, of bold fictions and malignant misrepresentations."[7] Wilson was unfazed. "The *Courier* has been very vulgar but does not attack the matter of the book," he explained.[8]

The British ministers did not take Roul's confession very seriously but the Marquis of Osmond, French ambassador in London, did. During a hastily arranged meeting with Castlereagh he pointed out that the Portuguese held more than two thousand prisoners on the island of Fernando de Noronha and that given arms and hopes these men could be used to attack St. Helena.[9] How many troops did the English have at St. Helena? Noting Castlereagh's apathy, the marquis sent an urgent warning to his colleague in Rio de Janeiro:

> In the vast and complex plan of the Bonapartists, there is a preliminary expedition to the island of Fernando de Noronha. If it is true that it has over 2.000 prisoners, guarded by a small garrison, the plotters will find useful allies that could render their enterprise quite formidable. Whatever their objectives are, we must not lose sight of them. Your attention should be particularly fixed on Colonel Latapie in Pernambuco and Gen-

eral Brayer in Buenos Aires. These two officers, with any other men they can gather, are destined to join the forces departing from America and England at Fernando de Noronha.[10]

Weeks later, as reports began to confirm some of Roul's more far-fetched allegations, Richelieu changed his mind. Roul had claimed that Joseph had sent a certain Astolphi "in the American brig *General Jackson* to Leghorn with two packages, one for Marie Louise and the other for Lucien."[11] A report from Italy had just confirmed the arrival of this ship. Richelieu immediately asked the Vatican to increase its vigilance over Lucien.[12] Roul had also disclosed that Piontkowski carried letters from Napoleon to Cambaceres, Fouché, Carnot, and other leading exiled Bonapartists and that Santini had "other letters for the same people and besides three decorations of the legion of Honor, the iron crown and the *Réunion* with plaques and two locks of hair for the archduchess Marie Louise and her son." Santini had been arrested while trying to enter Italy.[13] Roul had said that Piontkowski was Napoleon's messenger. In late September the Polish officer sailed to Italy on board an American vessel and with a British passport. Richelieu had no doubt that Piontkowski carried messages for the Bonaparte family.[14] Roul had said that an Italian named Poli, who was a former colonel of the Grande Armée, would carry off Napoleon's son and hand him over to Lucien, who would take him to the United States.[15] Colonel Bernard Poli, a Corsican who was fanatically devoted to Napoleon and who had helped Murat in his last adventure, arrived in Leghorn in July 1817 for a secret interview with the Archduchess Marie Louise. A meeting between the two took place. The police were alerted and chased Colonel Poli all over Italy.[16]

As Richelieu put all the pieces together, he realized that Hyde de Neuville had been wrong in dismissing Roul's confession so quickly, and he was thrown into a state of great anxiety. He asked Osmond to tell the British ministers to change Napoleon's guards frequently, "as this devil of a man exerts an amazing seduction over all those who surround him."[17] He also warned the Austrian ambassador in Paris about Piontkowski's movements. These warnings paid off, and in late October on the night the Polish captain disembarked in Genoa, "he was seized by three gendarmes, his papers and effects taken possession of by the Police and now [he is] in confinement."[18] After a thorough interrogation, the Austrian police concluded that Piontkowski carried secret messages from Napoleon to his family. The unfortunate Pole was eventually transferred to Austria under a false name and remained a prisoner for several years.[19] The news of Piontkowski's arrest brought some relief to Richelieu. At least two of Napoleon's messengers had been stopped. Lucien would not be allowed to join Joseph, and Napoleon II was safely guarded in Vienna. Unfortunately, other more dangerous Bonapartist conspirators were at large. Brayer was in South America, Lallemand in the United States, and according to all reports, Wilson and Cochrane would join them.

Wilson had not yet abandoned the idea of joining the American campaign. In mid-October he wrote Lord Grey: "Destiny has unhappily not willed that I should participate in this great enterprise. I could not leave Lady W. unless there was a great amelioration."[20] But two weeks later he suggested that things had changed, "I have the command in chief offered of Chile with *carte blanche* on all other matters."[21] Cochrane, who was back from a summer vacation in Paris, was negotiating the command of the Chilean navy. Their plans were conveniently camouflaged behind the banner of South American independence, a popular cause in England. The papers announced the victories of San Martin in Chile and Bolivar in Venezuela. The men appeared as new heroes to the British public. Wilson organized a dinner to celebrate these victories, as it would "be a great encouragement to the patriots at the same time it might awe ministers in any hostile policy to that cause for the sake of legitimacy."[22]

Wilson was right. The British cabinet was finding itself in an increasingly difficult position vis-à-vis Spain. Castlereagh had asked Sir Henry Wellesley, his ambassador in Madrid, to inform the Spanish court that if South America continued "in its present state of anarchy and confusion [such a situation] would ultimately be productive of the greatest evils to all Europe." But Ferdinand VII stubbornly refused a British mediation and maintained a belligerent stance.[23] Castlereagh had at least managed to neutralize an alliance between Spain and Russia, and he launched new conciliatory overtures to Madrid. Wellesley informed the Spanish prime minister Jose Pizarro that Sir Charles Bagot had been instructed to act in concert with Onis and Hyde de Neuville "for the purpose of defeating the projects of the conspirators." Wellesley believed Pizarro would use the discovery of the Confédération Napoléonienne as an excuse to drag the Allied powers into a military expedition against the rebels in the colonies by "pointing out the danger to which Europe itself is exposed from the project of the expatriated French and from the possibility of their establishing themselves in some part of Spanish America, and drawing from thence an argument that the tranquilization of America being an object of equal interest to all the European powers they ought to adopt the most decisive measure with a view to effecting it."[24] Despite Castlereagh's efforts, Ferdinand VII did not relent. However, Castlereagh had an ace up his sleeve. He had just received a letter from General San Martin asking for his mediation and supporting the establishment of a monarchical scheme in the Spanish colonies. It was a timely proposal. On the other side of the Channel, Richelieu was working on a similar antidote to the Bonapartist schemes.

Cochrane and Wilson were also counting on San Martin to advance their plans, unaware of the divisions among the patriots that had led to the downfall and exile of Alvear and Carrera and of San Martin's real objectives. Although Wilson had some suspicions in this regard, he believed the South American patriots were firmly "resolved on [a] republican establishment and complete independence."[25] He continued negotiations with San Martin's envoy to lead the patriot army, and at the end of October he told Grey that he would make his acceptance subject to an improvement in his wife's health. But it seems Wilson saw other obstacles as well, as days later he informed Grey that there was "another consideration of a political nature as to the form of government to be established in that country."[26]

When weeks later Jemima's health improved, Wilson told Grey that if he did not go to Chile, "I should be tempted to join the *Mobile* establishment with a plough and a sword. It must be difficult to play the part of Cincinnatus with the golden harvest of Mexico in view."[27] Clearly he had no intention of planting vines. Grey again warned his protégé in the strongest language not to embark on this new adventure.[28] Lord Hutchinson also felt compelled to dissuade him from joining the cause of the South American independence. "Before you go to Chile," he wrote in early November, "it becomes my duty to make this my most solemn protest, which I accordingly do."[29] Wilson's involvement in a new campaign didn't go undetected by Spanish agents, who in early November reported that Wilson would lead an expedition that was ready to sail to South America.[30] But Wilson had not yet made up his mind.

The other two possible destinations were Mexico and Portobello, a Spanish fortress at the Isthmus of Panama, which could be used for a campaign to Lima. For both, the support and participation of local rebel leaders was essential. Fortunately, candidates were not in short supply; Ferdinand VII's reactionary absolutism had driven many Spanish liberals into exile in London. Among them was a Basque-born general named Mariano Renovales. A short and stocky man with thick eyebrows and jet dark hair, even in his dark blue uniform with its shiny medals, Renovales looked a bit ridiculous next to the comely Wilson and Cochrane. However, his revolutionary credentials were as good, if not better, than those of Mina, who had just been executed by Spanish authorities in Mexico. Renovales had grown up in Buenos Aires. His bravery during the Peninsular War had earned him the rank of brigadier general in the Spanish army. But after the return of Ferdinand VII, Renovales had participated in a failed conspiracy to overthrow him. In early 1815 he escaped to Bordeaux, where he met Clausel.[31] He seemed an ideal candidate to join the Mexican expedition.

As for Napoleon, any hopes that he would be released by a political decision of the British cabinet were dashed in early November with the tragic and sudden death of Princess Charlotte after giving birth to a stillborn baby. "The hopes of the country are dashed to the earth," the *Courier* lamented. Napoleon's hopes were also crushed and when he learned of her death he told O'Meara that he had hoped "that she would have caused a more liberal policy to be adopted toward himself."[32]

This meant Napoleon's freedom could only be obtained by force. Even though the *Courier* argued that it was a "perfectly childish" idea due to all the precautions taken by Lowe, Wilson and Cochrane counted on a powerful weapon to rescue Napoleon.[33] With his own money plus a loan, Cochrane had started building a 350-ton steam-powered frigate. The ship looked like a cross between a traditional sailing ship and a steamboat. One innovation in its design was the location of its paddle wheels, which were placed in the hold on both sides and enclosed in a watertight casing that was open to the sea at the underside through openings in the ship's bottom.[34] Cochrane had always been fond of this type of innovation. Although steam navigation was widely used in the United States, the Royal Navy resisted its adoption and viewed it as a threat to its naval preeminence.

Wilson's hopes of accompanying Cochrane had not entirely vanished. By early December, Lord Grey again warned him about the dangers of "your South American schemes," which he hoped he would abandon.[35] But there was no need to worry. Although his wife's health had improved, Wilson's negotiations with San Martin had stalled. The Argentine general would not relinquish command of the army. "I shall not go because I cannot obtain powers sufficient to my object," Wilson said. The next day he told Grey that "the naval expedition in favor of the Chileans is going on"—the steam vessel would be ready in three months—and that Cochrane would be in command. "Keep this to yourself," he asked Grey.[36]

Latapie Lands in Brazil

I had a mission of the highest importance, whose objective, if it had succeeded, was to rescue the Emperor from St. Helena.

—Paul Latapie, Court d'Assise, Paris Testimony, 1836

On the morning of August 25, 1817, a group of armed men disembarked on the
white sandy beaches of Paraiba, in northeastern Brazil. They asked the surprised
locals who greeted them what kind of government existed in the province. Mistakenly understanding the response to be "republican" they declared themselves
to be North Americans who had come to aid the rebels of Pernambuco.[1] The
men and the vessel that carried them were part of a squadron led by the *Paragon,*
which had departed from New York in mid-June carrying a group of Napoleon's
veterans led by Colonel Paul Latapie. A few days later the *Paragon* anchored in
Formosa Bay, in the neighboring province of Rio Grande do Norte, and Latapie
disembarked with three comrades: Louis Gustave de Pontecoulant, Pierre Raulet, and another officer of German origin named Hartong.

Latapie's companions were as determined and experienced as he was. Despite
his aristocratic origins—he was the nephew of Marshal Grouchy—Pontecoulant
was a fanatical Bonapartist. He had graduated from the prestigious Ecole militaire de St. Cyr in 1812, just in time to accompany Napoleon to Russia. Captured after the combat at Paroutina, he had been released a year later. He had
fought at the battle of Waterloo, and after the defeat he organized a group of
militias to resist the invasion of the Allied armies.[2] Captain Pierre Raulet was a
battle-hardened veteran of the Peninsular War and was "as familiar with Spanish prisons as even Gil Blas had been." During the Hundred Days he had rallied
to Napoleon's cause and had been wounded at Waterloo.[3] About Hartong we
know only that he was a native of Coblentz and that he had served in Napoleon's

army as a cavalry captain. They had all heeded Joseph's clarion call and arrived in the United States in early 1817.

But as Napoleon had once said, "Space we can recover, lost time never." By the time Latapie and his men left New York, the revolution in Pernambuco had already been quashed and most of its leaders had been arrested and executed.[4] Alerted by the earlier incident in Paraiba, the Portuguese authorities in Rio Grande do Norte lost no time in arresting the men. Latapie, Raulet, and Hartong declared that their objective was to set up a trading house in Rio de Janeiro, whereas Pontecoulant said he intended to stay in Pernambuco to do "botanical observations." The authorities were suspicious but the only thing they found out was that one of the four men arrested was a former officer of the Grande Armée who had been wounded at the battle of Busaco. This was Latapie.[5]

The appearance of four former officers of Napoleon's army in northern Brazil in the aftermath of a bloody revolution, was an issue well beyond the jurisdiction of a provincial governor. The foreigners had not committed any crime and their passports were in order, and the governor decided to pass the problem on to his colleague in Pernambuco, who having already dealt with the rebels would be in a better position to ascertain whether they presented any threat.[6] By mid-September, Latapie and his three companions had arrived at the provincial capital of Recife. Finding nothing wrong with their papers, the governor of Pernambuco set them free but kept them under surveillance.

While in Recife, Latapie and his companions lodged at the house of Joseph Ray, the recently appointed American consul. Not much is known about Ray except that he was from Philadelphia and sympathetic to the French émigrés. The Portuguese authorities also suspected him of trying to "advance the interest of the patriots."[7] In the coming months Ray would become a valuable ally for Latapie and his companions. It is likely that he knew about their plans, as his secretary was a Dane called Georges Flemming Holdt, another veteran of the Grande Armée who had arrived from the United States in early 1816.[8]

The *Paragon* had been forced to sail back to New York, so Latapie and his companions were stranded. Latapie realized that the original plan had to be revised, if not totally abandoned. With the defeat of the revolution in Pernambuco it would be impossible to use the island of Fernando de Noronha to launch an expedition to St. Helena. Latapie left for Rio de Janeiro with Hartong while Raulet and Pontecoulant remained in Recife. In the Brazilian capital lived two prominent Bonapartists who could help: General van Hogendorp, a Dutchman who was Napoleon's former aide-de-camp, and Joachim Le Breton, a former member of the Institut de France who had been forced into exile after the Bourbon restoration.

Latapie did not yet know how bad things had turned. Even if he had succeeded in Pernambuco, Brayer would not have been able to send him any troops. In fact, Brayer's position in the patriot army, and possibly his life, was in serious danger. In mid-August the Chilean government had arrested an agent of Jose Miguel Carrera who, under interrogation, had disclosed the existence of a vast conspiracy to depose San Martin and O'Higgins. Brayer would take command of the army and a friend of Carrera named Manuel Rodriguez would lead the new government. Once this was accomplished, Carrera would return to the United States to arm an expedition to liberate Peru and would return with Marshal Grouchy and other French officers, all supported by Joseph.[9] San Martin took active measures to derail Carrera's conspiracy. Juan Jose and Luis Carrera, who were on their way to Chile, were arrested before crossing the Andes. "Thirty or forty people of the Carreras party" were imprisoned in Santiago, including two American officers.[10] Several Frenchmen were expelled from the patriot army, including Lieutenant Colonel Ambrose Cramer, who had served with Brayer in France, and Captain François Drouet.[11] The authorities in Mendoza were ordered to prevent any foreigner, "particularly of French origin," from crossing the Andes.[12] Although Brayer was not free of suspicion, San Martin took no direct measures against him. Instead he sent him far away from Santiago to join the army besieging the fortress of Talcahuano under the command of General O'Higgins. In early September, Brayer left Santiago accompanied by a small number of French veterans who had survived the recent purges. As a friend and ally of San Martin, O'Higgins was informed of all the details of the recent plot, including Brayer's alleged role in it.[13]

The authorities in Santiago and Buenos Aires had received very accurate information about Carrera's plans. The traitor was probably Colonel Skupieski. Following his discharge from the patriot army in early 1817, the disgraced Polish baron had returned to Buenos Aires. Denied back pay, completely destitute, and unable to buy a passage for his wife from New York, Skupieski appears to have followed Lavaysse's example. Two months later his financial situation changed dramatically, when he received a large plot of land in Mendoza by direct orders of Buenos Aires' supreme director.[14]

From Montevideo, Carrera wrote to John Stuart Skinner about the arrest of his two brothers in Mendoza and the difficulties that he had encountered in trying to overthrow the "despots" in Buenos Aires. He also expressed his disappointment with Napoleon's veterans. "General Brayer will maybe repay me like Lavaysse . . . although I don't dare decide about him until I receive further notices. I can't see in these French gentlemen any qualities that would make them useful to our cause. . . . Lavaysse was a traitor. . . . Roul was a madman; Bellina [Skupieski] a rascal, he is miserable and abandoned in Buenos Aires."[15] Skinner replied that "no event has materially injured the cause of South America in this country [so much] as the treatment which you have experienced, it has disgusted the most unenthusiastic and struck the most sanguine with despair."[16]

Unsure about what kind of support he could obtain in the United States, Carrera contacted his old friend Carlos de Alvear, who was exiled in Rio de Janeiro and whose political prospects seemed strong. "You are the only genius of the Provinces of the Plate," he wrote to Alvear in early October. "Without your efforts we shall not be able to fight the perils that threaten this country."[17] Alvear assured Carrera that he would soon join him in Montevideo.[18]

At about this time Latapie arrived in Rio de Janeiro. Already warned by the authorities in Pernambuco, the police decided to interrogate him. Sensing that he was involved in something important, the prefect of police informed the minister of interior, who decided to invite Latapie for dinner at his house. Somehow the minister convinced Latapie to open up after giving him his word of honor that his confession would remain a secret and that he would be able to return to the United States. Days later the entire foreign diplomatic corps in Rio de Janeiro knew about Latapie's secret plans. The French chargé d'affaires had forced the Portuguese minister's hand, as he had just received a letter from his colleague in London warning him about the expedition to rescue Napoleon and the role played by Latapie. The Spanish ambassador reported that Latapie had told the Portuguese minister that "he owed his existence to Napoleon and that he did not care about his life if he did not devote himself to free him [Napoleon] from his captivity." He had arrived in Pernambuco "to put himself at the head of the insurgents and coordinate from there an expedition to the island of St. Helena." They had chosen Pernambuco because it was the closest point to the island and because of the insurrection. The attack would be carried out with small steamships that were expected to arrive from the United States.[19] The British consul in turn informed Castlereagh that Latapie's objective was to assist the rebels in establishing their independence and that he had flattered himself he should obtain the command of their troops. That he had entered into this project not from any view of hostility or ill will to the King of Portugal, but in the hope of establishing an independent post southward of the Line* from whence he might subsequently carry into effect with greater felicity his ulterior and real designs. These were nothing less than the liberation of General Buonaparte from St. Helena, which he said all the Frenchmen who had served under him that were gone to America are determined to attempt. That being chiefly indebted to him for all they possess they will never cease to regard him as their sovereign and that not only he, Latapie, but many thousand others are ready to sacrifice the last drop of their blood for his sake.

The British diplomat also noted that Latapie planned to use steamboats, a notion that was "entirely new and is worth attention, particularly when a landing is to be made at St. Helena."[20]

Following these disclosures, Latapie and Hartong were confined in a Portuguese warship. Latapie claimed it was the French consul who "did not ignore my departure from Philadelphia for Brazil, put the biggest zeal to obtain my extradition from King John VI and he succeeded."[21] Richelieu would later praise his chargé d'affaires for his zeal and initiative on this occasion. At the end of November, Latapie and Hartong were sent to Portugal "to be confined there for some time; probably until the wishes of the French government can be known respecting him."[22] A few weeks later, the Portuguese minister who had extracted Latapie's confession died of a stroke.

The British chargé d'affaires in Rio de Janeiro sent an urgent warning to Sir Hudson Lowe about the rescue expedition. Given the importance of the matter, the HMS *Blossom* was detached from the South American naval station and departed immediately for St. Helena. He also sent a message to Captain Sharpe, who commanded a British warship in Buenos Aires, asking him to keep strict surveillance over General Brayer, who was "the leader to whom the subordinated agents look up and from whom they are to receive orders when the preparations are ready." Sharpe was also asked to report "the preparation of any steamboats."[23]

Sharpe got the warning in early December and promised to keep "a strict

---

*This could mean south of the Equator or south of Brazil's borders.

look out on the motions of the Frenchmen and tell you all about them." He also reported that although there were no steamboats in Buenos Aires, three months earlier, "a young man formerly a midshipman of the *Orpheus* arrived here bringing with him the plan of a submarine boat invented in England and for which a patent has been obtained. This boat is of iron capable of containing six persons who are able to remain under water several hours and at the same time to pull the boat with considerable velocity; this machine was offered to this government but I fancy they refused to have anything to do with it as the sum demanded was very large."[24] Given the importance of the matter and the presence of Brayer in Chile, Sharpe decided to inform his boss, Commodore William Bowles, who was sailing in the Pacific. San Martin, who was a close friend of Bowles, would surely be interested in learning of Brayer's plans.

Bowles had just arrived in Chile and expected to meet San Martin soon. In a dispatch he sent to London around this time, he noted that there were fears in Chile of a new offensive by the royalists who had fortified their position in Talcahuano, which was "considered impracticable in front, and very difficult to be attacked in any other way while they have a naval superiority." Bowles also warned about the threat presented by the Carreras, who during the last war had openly supported the United States. In a ciphered passage of his dispatch he added that San Martin, "extremely desirous of pacification, is now all powerful here and much wishes our mediation. He has lately proposed to Pueyrredon to solicit it, and if the latter refuses, Chile will negotiate separately."[25] San Martin was very keen on bringing the war with Spain to a quick end. In early December he wrote a letter to James Duff, Earl of Fife, asking him to intercede with the prince regent to pressure Spain. Duff had served as a general in Wellington's army and was one of the many British officers San Martin had befriended during the Peninsular War. Maybe it was Duff who had "recruited" him to the British cause. In his letter San Martin explained that "democratic ideas" had lost support among the "leading men in this state." It was time for England to intervene: "How exalted in the eyes of the world has appeared the conduct of the Prince Regent of England! By giving liberty to Europe, he has arrested the torrents of blood that [Europe] was shedding. Shall not the unfortunate Americans be blessed with one of his compassionate looks I am certain that if the picture of horror exhibited by these delicious countries, could be held by Him, his tender heart would melt and I am equally certain that the gratitude of the Americans would soon display itself in favor of His Royal Highness' subjects."[26]

Brayer, Wilson, and Cochrane would have cringed had they known that

San Martin did not believe in "democratic ideas" and considered the prince regent the liberator of Europe. But San Martin was always very careful about disclosing his views. He never fooled Carrera who, stranded in Montevideo, now
pinned his hopes on his friend Alvear, whose political support in Buenos Aires
was on the rise.[27] If Alvear regained power, Carrera would be able to return to
Chile and launch an expedition to Peru with Brayer's help.

But Brayer was facing his own set of problems. "Brayer is here," O'Higgins
informed San Martin in early October. "As a foreigner, his presence has not been
agreeable to most of the officers."[28] Fully aware of Brayer's alleged role in the
recent conspiracy, in early December he ordered the French general to lead the
attack of Talcahuano following a plan approved months earlier by San Martin.
On the morning of December 6, Major George Beauchef, a veteran of Napoleon's Imperial Guard, led the main assault column in a surprise attack. After
an initial success Beauchef was wounded; his men lost heart and an early victory turned into a crushing defeat. In his report of the action O'Higgins praised
Brayer who "since joining the campaign and particularly in this fierce action"
had shown "clear proof of activity and military abilities."[29] Brayer knew that he
would nonetheless be blamed for the defeat. But this was the least of his problems. The throne of Peru suddenly seemed a lot more distant. Napoleon would
be disappointed. Days later, O'Higgins and his army abandoned Talcahuano
and marched north to meet San Martin.

22

The Shadow of Aaron Burr

Projects are in agitation among some of the emigrants from Europe to which it will be necessary for the government to put a stop as soon as possible.

—Adams to Monroe, September 27, 1817

The discovery of the Confédération Napoléonienne and the reports of Lallemand's plans for Mexico put Adams and the entire diplomatic corps in Washington on alert. With the passing weeks, Adams realized that all the European powers had a strong interest in suppressing any enterprises connected with Napoleon in the American continent. Otherwise the United States could be pushed into a costly war with Spain, and possibly also with England.[1] While an ambassador in London, Adams had feared this scenario. As he explained to Monroe, although the establishment of a Bonapartist regime in Mexico was a Spanish and not a French concern, "the consideration that the agents are French, the association said to be Napoleonic, and that the acquisition of power by these emigrants, with Joseph Bonaparte at their head, might prove in its immediate consequences of great importance to France, will, I think, justify the notice of the representations of the Minister of France." Independent of these considerations, Adams thought "the movement and projects complained of are of deep interest to the United States."[2] Hyde de Neuville had hit a sensitive nerve in Washington. The Confédération Napoléonienne seemed inspired by Aaron Burr.

Monroe remained undecided about what to do and asked for more information. Adams again contacted his Boston friend Peter Paul De Grand, who was quick to clarify that he had "no concern with the projects in question" and promised to communicate "any information really interesting to you."[3] De Grand must also have communicated Adams's views to Lallemand, who was engaged in damage control. In a letter to William Lee he denied his plans were contrary to American interests. "What can you reproach us for?" he asked

Lee. "Certain conversations in which particular wishes were expressed in concert with certain members of the American government?" Such conversations proved nothing, Lallemand said. He had no intention of violating the laws of the United States. His objective was simply to create a refuge for his compatriots banished from France.[4] If Florida was not available as a base to invade Mexico, Lallemand would have to consider an alternative. Unfortunately, the second phase of the Amelia Island occupation—MacGregor's replacement—was under way and there was no way for Joseph or Lallemand to stop it.

Oblivious of the political storm gathering in Washington, Aury and Hubbard had taken control of Amelia Island.[5] Their first measure was to annex all of Florida to the "Free Republic of Mexico." Aury issued a proclamation stating that he had come "to plant the tree of liberty, to foster free institutions, and to wage war against the tyrant of Spain, the oppressor of America, and the enemy of the rights of man."[6] Unfortunately, the invaders soon split into opposing factions: the Americans sided with Hubbard and the French with Aury. Hubbard's death from yellow fever allowed Aury to consolidate his power. In early November, Aury called for presidential elections.[7] By taking this step he tried to give legitimacy to the occupation, and more importantly, circumvent the restrictions imposed by U.S. neutrality laws. But the Monroe administration had its own plans for Florida and they did not include Aury. Among other things, the fact that Aury's men included a regiment of Haitian blacks and mulattoes had not sat well with the slaveholding states.

Back in Washington, Hyde de Neuville met Adams and demanded that the U.S. government publish the Lakanal papers. Adams refused because of legal concerns. As he explained to Monroe, there was nothing in the papers that proved Joseph was an "accessory to any part of the project, and it seems hardly equitable that he should be made responsible before the public for any schemes by which madmen or desperadoes use his name without his knowledge or consent."[8] Hyde de Neuville had confirmed through several sources that the Bonapartist émigrés planned to invade Mexico and that Lakanal's proposal was one of several under consideration. Although he believed that Adams would take measures to stop these projects, he feared that certain members of the administration secretly supported them.[9]

Although Hyde de Neuville kept him well informed, Onis had taken his own measures to find out what was going on. In early October he made a startling discovery. A Frenchman named Arsene Lacarriere Latour, an associate of Jean Laffite who had just arrived in Philadelphia, lodged at the same inn with

Colonel Galabert, Lallemand's right-hand man. A graduate of Paris's Ecole de Beaux-Arts, Latour had served as an engineer in Napoleon's army and later as his spy in New Orleans. He also knew Lallemand well; they had met during the ill-fated expedition to Haiti.[10] Latour had just returned from a mysterious visit to La Havana commissioned by Laffite. He told Onis that he knew Galabert and promised to help. Was Latour a double agent sent to dupe Onis? It is impossible to tell. He is one of the most unfathomable characters in this story.[11]

Latour told Onis what he already knew: that the Bonapartist émigrés had a vast plan to take the Spanish possessions in America and to launch a revolution in France. Galabert was very close to the Lallemands and played a key role in these plans. A member of the French aristocracy, the young colonel had left France after the Revolution and had traveled to China, the Philippines, Chile, and Mexico, where he settled for a few years and where he almost married a rich heiress. Years later Galabert had returned to France to join the Napoleonic empire and in 1808, he had submitted a memorandum to Joseph, then king of Spain, asking to be sent as a special agent to Mexico.[12]

Onis learned that Galabert was the nephew of the Count of Cabarrus, Spain's former finance minister and an old acquaintance, and invited him for dinner at his house. Galabert admitted that even though he hated the French Bourbons, he was very fond of Spain. Slightly surprised at this statement, Onis asked why was he not stopping the projects against Mexico and Florida. Galabert replied that he had dissuaded hundreds of French officers from joining MacGregor's expedition. Onis then asked about Joseph's projects for Mexico. Galabert explained that they were entirely feasible. He boasted that with only fifteen hundred men led by veteran French officers he could conquer all of Mexico. Galabert also said that "none of the émigrés actually likes Joseph Bonaparte, they only want to take money from him." Onis offered to compensate the Frenchman properly if he put together a plan to disrupt the expeditions against the Spanish possessions. Galabert smiled and said that for the time being there was nothing he could do, as a final decision about these expeditions had not yet been made.

Onis also learned that the innkeeper at the lodgings where Galabert and many of the French generals were staying had earlier requested his assistance in reclaiming some unpaid loans in Mexico. He had initially ignored the request but realized that he could now offer to help in exchange for information about the French émigrés. The innkeeper's scruples quickly disappeared and he told Onis everything he knew. Galabert had great influence over all the French generals, particularly the Lallemands, whose recent fight with Vandamme had actually delayed the invasion of Mexico. It was unclear whether they still planned to attack Florida or whether they would go to Buenos Aires. Joseph was very tight with his money, and as a result Lallemand was using the Tombigbee land grant to finance his enterprise. It was not a bad idea. At this time John Stuart Skinner advised Jose Miguel Carrera, that the Tombigbee lands had "already raised in value to $10 per acre."[13]

Onis was convinced that Lallemand would go ahead with his plan and that his first objective was Pensacola. He suspected that the Monroe administration supported these plans.[14] His suspicions were not unfounded. Certain members of the administration had unofficially encouraged Lallemand. However, this encouragement had not come from John Quincy Adams, who realized some intrigue was going on behind his back and was determined to stop it. Prodded by Adams, at the end of October, Monroe convened an urgent cabinet meeting to discuss the following questions:

Has the Executive [the] power to acknowledge the independence of new states whose independence has not been acknowledged by the parent country and between which parties a war actually exists on that account? Will the sending or receiving [of] a minister to a new state under such circumstances be considered an acknowledgment of its independence? Is such acknowledgement a justifiable cause of war to the parent country? Is it a just cause of complaint to any other power?* Is it expedient for the United States at this time to acknowledge the independence of Buenos Aires or any other part of the Spanish dominions in America now in state of revolt? What ought to be the future conduct of the United States towards Spain, considering, the evasions practiced by her government in procrastinating negotiations, amounting to a refusal to make reparation for injuries? Is it expedient to break up the establishments at Amelia Island and Galveston, it being evident that they were made for smuggling, if not for piratical purposes, and already perverted to very mischievous purposes to the United States? Is it expedient to publish the communication of the French minister of a projected movement of the French emigrants for the establishment of Joseph Bonaparte in Mexico and of the correspondence with him?[15]

* One wonders what would have happened to the United States if France had entertained any doubts about these questions in 1776.

After this meeting Monroe decided to take measures against the occupation of Amelia Island and Galveston, now occupied by Jean Laffite.[16] Several adventurers who had been recruited to reinforce Amelia Island were arrested in Philadelphia. According to Hyde de Neuville, among them was one identified "as one of the chiefs of the plot that had St. Helena as its objective."[17]

It was at this time that Galabert visited Onis in Washington. He had either agreed to the traitorous scheme proposed by the Spanish ambassador or was engaging in a dangerous double game on behalf of Lallemand. Galabert submitted to Onis a plan to disrupt, or at least delay, an attack on Mexico by the French émigrés and also defend the interests of Spain against an expansionist United States. In exchange for his services Galabert asked for six thousand dollars and land in Texas. Onis claimed to have no funds at his disposal and proposed that they meet again after he consulted with the Spanish authorities in Cuba.[18]

The hostile attitude of the Monroe administration had deepened the rift among the French émigrés in Philadelphia. "I know without doubt that divisions and discouragement exists among those loyal to Joseph," Hyde de Neuville informed Richelieu. "These gentlemen now reproach and threaten each other." In his opinion "discord had never been deeper."[19] The émigrés were divided into two camps: Grouchy and Vandamme believed that without American support the Mexican plan was impracticable, while Lallemand still believed success was possible and was determined to proceed. Lallemand's old friend General Antoine Rigaud, who had just arrived in Philadelphia, supported him. It appears that Clausel and Lefebvre-Desnouettes, who were in Mobile, also backed Lallemand. As for Joseph, he would follow his brother's instructions but would not involve himself directly in order to avoid problems with the Monroe administration.

If there were any hard feelings between the exiled generals, the wedding between Henri Lallemand and the niece of Stephen Girard provided an excellent opportunity for reconciliation. The reception held in Philadelphia in early November was presided over by Joseph and was attended by the most prominent Bonapartists in America, with the exception of Lakanal, who had been ostracized.[20] Once the wedding celebrations were over, Charles Lallemand went to Washington to explain his intentions to the American government. Monroe refused to see him, but he obtained an interview with John Quincy Adams. Lallemand assured Adams that the French émigrés harbored no designs contrary to the laws of the United States. He admitted having been invited to participate in MacGregor's expedition to Amelia Island and of having "warm sympathies" for the revolution in South America but claimed to have no intention of taking part in either one. He told Adams that if the U.S. government entertained any suspicions about him he would seek refuge elsewhere, as he wanted to preserve his independence. As to plans to liberate Napoleon from St. Helena, Lallemand denied their existence. Besides, he said, he wasn't such a strong supporter of the fallen emperor.

Lallemand was obviously lying. As of three days before the meeting with Adams, his name was still mentioned as the best candidate to lead an expedition to Florida.[21] Adams in turn lied when he told Lallemand that he "was in no way an object of uneasiness to this government." It was simply that the Allied powers "had received from various quarters information of a project for levying monies in the United States for an expedition to join the Mexican insurgents; that Joseph Bonaparte was to be placed at the head of this movement and that his name had been implicated in it." Since this project "was contrary to the laws of the United States which the government was bound to see executed, its existence had given them uneasiness, particularly as its tendency was to force them to take a decisive part against the exiles from France who had sought, and were enjoying an asylum in this country; that the government had now reason to believe this project was abandoned." Lallemand fiercely defended Joseph, arguing that it was unfair to hold him responsible for letters addressed to him, particularly as it was evident that he had refused to receive them. As to Lakanal, he "had never seen him, knew nothing, whether he had written the letters, whether they were forgeries or what they were."[22] That was another lie.

The meeting with Adams convinced Lallemand that the Florida scheme had to be abandoned, although an enterprise against Mexico was still feasible. Under no circumstances should Joseph be implicated. Adams in turn was quite satisfied with the conversation and felt that Lallemand had given him "the strongest and most satisfactory assurances that he will engage in no project of military adventure forbidden by the laws of this country. I am very happy to learn that schemes of that character which had been entertained are abandoned," he wrote to De Grand. "Lallemand's brother has got into better quarters than he would find in Mexico or Peru."[23]

By late November, American troops were ready to take over Amelia Island. To justify his actions, Monroe argued that the island's occupation by privateers "have done us great injury in smuggling of every kind and particularly in introducing Africans as slaves into the United States."[24] As Adams explained, MacGregor had occupied Amelia Island "pretending authority from Venezuela" and had been "succeeded by persons disgracing and forfeiting by such acts the character of citizens of the United States* and pretending authority from some pretended Government of Florida; and they are now by the last accounts received, sharing the fruits of their depredations, and at the same time contesting the command of the place with a Frenchman having under him a body of blacks from St. Domingo and pretending authority from a Government of Mexico." Since "the revenue, the morals and the peace of the country are so seriously menaced and compromised by this state of things" the president had to break up "this nest of foreign adventurers with pretended South American commissions."[25] It was a distortion of the truth, but served as a good excuse to invade Spanish territory.

In his first annual speech to Congress, Monroe announced that the United States would "suppress" the piratical establishments in Amelia Island and Galveston, which "if ever sanctioned by any authority whatever," had abused "their trust and forfeited all claim to consideration."[26] Three days later, Adams assured a much-relieved Hyde de Neuville that "whatever absurd projects may have been in the contemplation of one or more individuals, nothing is to be dreaded from them to the peace of the United States and the due observance of the laws."[27] But by invading Spanish territory, Monroe was setting the stage for a serious diplomatic crisis. Onis' reaction was predictable. In a strongly worded protest he emphasized that MacGregor had formed and armed his expedition at Charleston and Savannah and that it was composed "of citizens of this Republic, in violation of the laws of the United States, the law of Nations, and the existing treaty between Spain and the said states." As for Galveston, he warned that it "has not been, nor could ever be within the limits of Louisiana, because at no time, did it make part of it. It has constantly belonged to the dominions of the Crown of Spain. . . and as such, ought to be maintained and respected."[28] Onis was convinced that Amelia Island was the first step in a vast plan to extend the American border all the way to the Pacific and to take possession of Florida, Cuba, and parts of Mexico. Onis also feared that Monroe would eventually yield to pressure from Henry Clay and recognize the independence of Buenos Aires. Clay had taken up the mantle of the insurgents and was leading the ef-

---

*This was a harsh statement; Hubbard was a former state senator and sheriff for New York, and Jared Irwin was a former U.S. Army officer and the son of the governor of Indiana.

forts in Congress to recognize their independence, and he opposed negotiations concerning the limits of Louisiana and Florida. Onis feared American public opinion supported a war with Spain.[29]

Monroe's measures upset not only Spain but also the South American patriots. From Philadelphia, Nicholas Biddle warned Monroe that the South Americans "misapprehend the steps taken in relation to Amelia Island which they consider as indication not merely of an unfavorable change in the sentiment of the government, but in fact decisive against them and their cause." Biddle confirmed that Amelia Island had been occupied only to have "a rallying point for persons disposed to join them from Europe and that no other place united the double advantages of a supply of resources and a vicinity to the United States."[30]

Undeterred by Monroe's speech, Lallemand went ahead with his plan. Instead of Florida, he would use Texas as a base of operations and simply put into execution the plan that Toledo, Humbert, and Mina had failed to carry out. If he couldn't invade Mexico, he would direct his expedition to Colombia or Venezuela. During the last weeks of November, Lallemand worked intensely, recruiting men and gathering weapons and provisions. To raise money for his enterprise he used the Tombigbee land. During the first two weeks of December, the Vine and Olive land market "reached its all-time peak with forty-nine confirmed and eleven probable sales."[31]

On December 17, Lallemand's first contingent of troops left Philadelphia on board the *Huntress* under the command of General Rigaud. Among the veterans who accompanied Rigaud were Colonel Pierre Douarche, Colonel François Jeannet, and Major Jean Schultz of the Polish Lancers. As with many other Poles, Schultz' devotion to Napoleon had never wavered. He had accompanied him to Elba and then back to Paris. He had fought at Waterloo, attended Napoleon at Malmaison and Rochefort, and followed him to the *Bellerophon*. Imprisoned at Malta, he had later joined Lallemand in Istanbul and then left for the United States with several other veterans of the Grande Armée.[32] Officially, they were colonists bound for Mobile, and they disguised their real purpose by bringing on board agricultural equipment and vine and olive plants. At night, the ship was loaded with guns and ammunition. Rigaud had instructions to proceed to Galveston, which was conveniently occupied by Jean Laffite.[33]

The French consul in Philadelphia had no doubts about the real purpose of this enterprise. He reported that the French officers who accompanied Rigaud "took with them saddles, bridles, sabers and pistols."[34] His British counterpart warned Sir Charles Bagot that the *Huntress* carried 140 men, "all followers of Bonaparte and chiefly officers. . . . [And] four or five vessels are now preparing for the same destination at New York, some in Charleston, Savannah and Baltimore." Their objective was to rescue Napoleon. When the consul argued with his informer that it would be "foolish" to attack St. Helena when a British squadron permanently patrolled the island, the informer confidently stated that Louis Aury "had twenty vessels at least on the point of leaving Amelia Island and that it was not impossible [that] his intention [was] to aid the escape by a previous understanding to carry the persons intended for the object to Buenos Aires, whenever they might meet with a force adequate to the enterprise for he knew there was no lack of money to carry any project of that important nature into execution." Evidently, "a project is on foot to attempt the rescue of Bonaparte from St. Helena."[35] Days after the *Huntress* set sail, a servant of Colonel Jeannet was killed after he was found to be a spy.

Aware of Rigaud's departure, Onis realized that it was essential to reach an agreement with the United States and he requested a meeting with Adams. Adams did not give in on any point. Onis realized that unless Spain was prepared to back up its claims with military force, it would lose not only Amelia Island but the rest of Florida, Galveston, and maybe Mexico. He was convinced that the Americans would use the attacks of the Seminoles, an aggressive Indian tribe, as an excuse to invade Florida.[36] To stop the Americans, he resorted to intrigue, hoping that Galabert could bring the French émigrés over to the cause of Spain. For his part, Lallemand realized that his enterprise was in danger due to the hostility of the Monroe administration and he decided to raise the stakes. He secretly met with the Spanish consul in Philadelphia and told him that if the king of Spain was prepared to "hire" the French émigrés, they would set up an establishment in Texas to stop American expansionism. He also said he could not postpone his expedition for too long or the Americans would force him to attack Florida.[37]

The French consul in Philadelphia got wind of the negotiations between Lallemand and Onis' agent. The French general had reportedly said that he was in "a position to execute either one of our two projects. . . . We will serve for or against Spain." The French consul also reported that Spain planned to offer land in Texas to the émigrés as a way to defend Mexico against the expansion of the United States.[38]

Lallemand was playing a dangerous game. He knew that a war between Spain and the United States would help his objectives. In late December he and his brother Henri left for New York, where a ship fitted out by Stephen Girard was waiting to take them to New Orleans with a another contingent of troops. Hyde de Neuville's agents detected Lallemand's presence in New York and reported that "the general rendezvous is in Mobile and could equally serve Spain or the United States or maybe the latter against Spain." Onis was reportedly waiting for a response from Madrid. Lallemand was also waiting for orders and would "let Spain know immediately after his propositions are accepted and after giving all the guarantees that will be demanded from him. He demanded letters to put himself in contact with the Viceroy of Mexico to the Minister of Spain." According to these sources, Lallemand had rejected the offers made by British agents, whereas Galabert kept negotiating with Onis. "Grouchy and Vandamme ignore everything," added the French consul.[39]

By late December, Americans troops had taken Amelia Island and ordered Aury to evacuate it as soon as practicable. Puzzled by the demand but eager to avoid a conflict, the French corsair agreed. The following morning he sent a letter of protest to Monroe and sent an emissary to Washington to explain his actions.[40]

In Washington the political tension increased. "Clay came out with great violence against the course pursued by the Executive upon South American affairs, and especially in relation to Amelia Island," Adams wrote in his diary. The secretary of state had just met with a special envoy from Buenos Aires who told him that his government had sent emissaries to London, Vienna, and Madrid to gather support for a monarchical scheme and had even submitted a proposal to the king of Spain to crown one of his brothers as its sovereign as long as it remained independent.[41] These disclosures confirmed Adams's poor opinion of the South American revolutionaries. What kind of independence could they claim if they were begging to crown a European prince? The relationship between the United States and the European powers, particularly England, could not be jeopardized by the recognition of the "independence" of Buenos Aires.

The next day, Monroe convened a cabinet meeting to discuss whether American troops should retain possession of Amelia Island "or abandon it to be occupied again by the Spanish authorities from Florida." Monroe was inclined to the latter course but postponed a decision.[42] Fearing a congressional inquiry, Adams asked one of his agents in Florida to obtain more information about Aury's role and his links to MacGregor. He was particularly interested in knowing whether the Scotsman had "any real authority after he came to the United States." He suspected it was "rather of European than of South American origin." He also wanted confirmation that the British were secretly involved in the enterprise. "It can scarcely be supposed that in September last he [MacGregor] should have projected an expedition from New Providence to be carried [out] next April or May, and chiefly with British materials, if the British government, either at home or in the colony, should be very intent upon obstructing or defeating him," Adams wrote.[43] Alerted that Lallemand had already left for New Orleans, Adams wondered whether he was involved with Aury and MacGregor. Only five months into his job as secretary of state he was facing a diplomatic crisis that could plunge the country into war.

23
Napoleon Changes Strategy

Behold the grand result in your lone isle,
And, as thy nature urges, weep or smile.
Sigh to behold the eagle's lofty rage
Reduced to nibble at his narrow cage.

—Lord Byron, *The Age of Bronze,* Canto 3

Napoleon's boring routine at Longwood was broken in July with the visit of Lord Amherst, who was returning to England after a mission in China. Napoleon took the opportunity to air all his complaints. He said Lowe had stopped at nothing except violating his privacy. He would have preferred "to be shot on board the *Bellerophon* in the rage of the moment . . . [than] to be exiled to such a rock as this."[1] Amherst was unfazed. Napoleon's next visitor was Captain Basil Hall of the Royal Navy. A regular guest at Holland House, Hall was probably more sympathetic to Napoleon's complaints. Napoleon launched a charm offensive that overwhelmed the British captain. Napoleon told Hall that he remembered his father from the Academy of Brienne, where he had studied as a teenager. "Your father was the first Englishman I ever saw," he said. The effect was predictable. Hall was not the first and would not be the last British naval officer to fall under Napoleon's spell. The British captain found Napoleon "much broader and more square, larger indeed in every way, than any representation I had met with. His corpulence, at this time universally reported to be excessive, was by no means remarkable. His flesh looked, on the contrary, firm and muscular. . . . His skin was more like marble than ordinary flesh. . . . His health and spirits, judging from appearances, were excellent."[2]

The cheerfulness that Napoleon showed during Hall's visit faded a few days later when he learned that the revolution in Pernambuco had failed. "I hear there has been an insurrection and that the Prime Minister wanted to make himself king," Napoleon told Montholon. He suspected the recent news from Brazil had prompted Lowe to increase his vigilance.[3] The failure of the Pernambucan rebellion would delay any rescue attempt. But Napoleon kept dreaming about freedom. Days later he told Montholon and Gourgaud that he would be happy if he could establish a colony on a deserted island with two thousand men. It would be a model state. He would create everything from scratch without the need to fight with "false ideas." If he had gone to America, he would have done that "instead of amusing himself with palaces and gardens like Joseph." For a few hours Napoleon entertained himself with these thoughts and dictated a list of the things he would need to carry out this project.[4] Brayer's name came up in Napoleon's conversation. He regretted not having followed his suggestions at Malmaison.[5] If he had then taken the command of the army, he could have defeated his enemies, installed his son on the throne, and then left France to pursue his dream. "If we had gone to America we would have established a kingdom!" Napoleon said. "You would all require me as a chief," he added. "Bah! This is just a dream."[6]

Napoleon again set his hopes on a political solution. O'Meara observed that the present "disturbed state" of British politics would conspire against his being permitted to be transferred to England. "Bah," Napoleon replied, "your ministers are not silly enough to believe that I would lose my character so far as to put myself at the head of a *canaille,* even if the latter were willing to place a foreigner at their head, which is very unlikely. . . . I have too great a regard for the reputation I shall leave to posterity to act the adventurer. No, no, it is hatred and the fear they have of the information I could give. They are afraid I should say it was not true in reply to the histories of many political events which they have explained in their own way."[7] If the solution didn't come from England, then it would have to come from Russia or Austria. Lowe, suspicious as ever, prohibited the Russian commissioner from entering Longwood but his "accidental" meetings with Gourgaud continued to take place. Cipriani also carried messages for Balmain. Napoleon still hoped to recover his power and anxiously waited for news from Europe.[8] He believed that if Lord Holland became England's prime minister, he would agree to restore him to the throne of France.[9]

Napoleon again started to fear an attempt on his life. Montholon complained to O'Meara that the cooking pots were in such a state that exposed them daily "to the risk of being poisoned." Napoleon had been sick, and Montholon, who had experienced "diverse pains and commotions in his intestinal region," told O'Meara that "if it was not desirable to have them poisoned," the governor would have to fix the problem immediately. After inspecting the pots O'Meara found them "in a very dangerous position in consequence of all the tinning having been worn away from the inside" and warned Lowe to have them repaired to avoid any malicious accusations.[10] Napoleon wasn't afraid of the cooking pots. There were many ways of killing a man. He believed Bathurst's plan was "to impose restrictions of such a nature, that I, without degrading my character and rendering myself an object of contempt in the eyes of the world, must imprison myself; thereby in the course of time to bring on disease, which in a frame impaired by confinement and the blood being decomposed must prove mortal, and that I may thus expire in protracted agonies, which may have the appearance of a natural death. That is the plan, and is a manner of assassinating just as certain, but more cruel and criminal than the sword or the pistol."[11]

Napoleon's hopes of leaving St. Helena were dealt yet another blow at the end of October when he received a secret message from England. Montholon, who left no details about its content, observed that Napoleon's "gloominess was extreme."[12] It was necessary to start negotiations with Russia and Austria to end his captivity. Napoleon still remembered Alexander's "brotherly friendship" at Tilsit and Erfurt and hoped that Francis II would not forget their ties of kinship.[13] "Gorgoto," as Napoleon affectionately called Gourgaud, would be in charge of this delicate mission. However, it would be necessary to plan his exit carefully. Having grown up in a family of comedians, Gourgaud was well prepared to play the part. To soften the Austrian and Russian sovereigns, Napoleon asked O'Meara, who was now totally devoted to him, to diagnose him with hepatitis and suggest that unless he was moved to a healthier climate he would die in six months.[14]

Lowe still worried about the possibility of a rescue attempt, particularly after reading a dispatch from Bathurst warning him that "the turbulent and seditious in this, as well as in every other country, look to the escape of General Bonaparte as that which would at once give life and activity to the revolutionary spirit, which has been so long [a] formidable enemy to the best interests of Europe."[15] The sighting of an American schooner near St. Helena increased Lowe's anxiety. The British cruiser gave chase but failed to capture her.[16] Other troubling reports suggested something was afoot. A local farmer, father of an attractive young girl whom Napoleon had visited frequently, was heard talking while he was drunk about an invasion of St. Helena, which could be accomplished with "only" two thousand men. To avoid being detected, the invaders could approach the island at night, disembark at Stone Top Bay and "reach Hutt's Gate or Diana's Peak by *point du jour.*" The farmer claimed he was "the man who would assist Buonaparte in making his escape from the island, that it would make his fortune."[17] Lowe also found out that before leaving St. Helena, Piont-kowski had said that Napoleon "would not remain eighteen months on the is-land."[18] If Piontkowski was telling the truth, Napoleon's departure was near. Lowe reported to Bathurst that there had been unauthorized contacts between Longwood and the island's natives, one of whom had mentioned "the fortunes that might be made by those who assist him" in an escape attempt.[19]

Desperate to find out what was going on, Lowe again pressured O'Meara to be his spy. But Napoleon had stolen a march on him. "The doctor has only been good to me since I gave him money," he told Gourgaud.[20] Whether out of per-sonal conviction or financial reward, O'Meara resisted Lowe's overtures. "You may tell him that I conceive his object to be to deprive me of all medical aid and by that to arrive sooner at the end which he proposes," Napoleon told O'Meara. "I do not esteem life so much as to allow my physician to be made a spy. Tell him that I said his views are directed to lessen the confidence I had in you and to make you a spy or to make me suspect that you are one. In fact, had it not been for the confidence which I have in you, from the character Captain Mait-land gave of you, and from my own observation, the measures of this governor would long ago have induced me to tell you that I had no longer any occasion for your services"[21]

Napoleon's spirits were raised at the end of the year when he learned through the newspapers that English public opinion was strongly opposed to his impris-onment at St. Helena and that a change of cabinet was likely. Maybe he also knew of some of the plans that were afoot to obtain his release. Lord Coch-rane's name crept up in Napoleon's conversation. Napoleon greatly admired his talents as a naval commander and remembered well his role in the attack of the French fleet at Aix in 1809. He assured O'Meara that Cochrane could not only have destroyed all the ships but also "might and would have taken them out had your Admiral supported him as he ought to have done."[22] Could he get him out of St. Helena?

Lowe was so obsessed by the possibility of Napoleon's escape that he could barely sleep at night. He received a dispatch from London describing the plot discovered in Philadelphia by the French ambassador.[23] And Colonel Reade warned him that "in America bets run high on the possibility of taking Bona-parte off St. Helena."[24] Another report from British agents indicated that an American captain was planning to approach St. Helena and "then watch [for] a good opportunity and have the vessel early in the day and repair towards the island so as to be as near at night as they could be with their boat undiscovered from the island, and as soon as it was dark, immediately row to the island. As soon as the boat left, the vessels are to fall into the windward of the island on the other side of the island and there wait till the return of the boat, keeping a proper distance so as not to be discovered while waiting for the boat."[25] Could this be the American schooner that had been chased off by British cruisers days earlier?

By reading the European newspapers Napoleon could foresee a breakup in the Holy Alliance and the withdrawal of Russian troops from France. The contacts with Balmain intensified. Napoleon let it be known that the Russian commissioner would be "welcome with open arms."[26] But Lowe, always suspicious of Balmain, would not allow him to enter Longwood. A few weeks later, Napoleon's mood improved even further. "Great News!" he told Gourgaud. "I hear there is to be a change of Ministry in England. We shall see Wellesley, Holland and Grenville in power. The little princess will punish the Ministers for ill-treating her mother."[27] The "little princess" was Charlotte, the daughter of the prince regent, whom many believed would succeed George III. Napoleon couldn't have known that she had just died after giving birth to a stillborn baby.

Napoleon continued to plan Gourgaud's departure from St. Helena.[28] In recent months Gourgaud had even managed to fool Lowe, who was "perfectly satisfied with his behavior."[29] As an accomplished puppet master, Napoleon used Gourgaud's ongoing quarrel with Montholon and his wife as the perfect alibi for his departure. He also made sure Balmain sent reports of his health to the tsar: "Bonaparte's liver is seriously affected and his health is visibly deteriorating. The devouring air of the tropics, his excessive leisure, are altering his blood and his temperament. At night he does not sleep. In the daytime, he is torpid. His complexion is livid, his eyes sunken. His condition excites pity."[30]

4
1818

Between Florida and Texas

The possession of the Floridas, by treaty or force, will probably be among the interesting events of the new year.

—Niles' Weekly Register, January 1818

The news from Amelia Island reached Washington in the first week of January and the diplomatic crisis triggered by the discovery of the Confédération Napoléonienne took another dangerous turn. In the coming months it would give way to one of the most bizarre and least understood chapters in the history of U.S. foreign policy. And at its center was Charles Lallemand, who single-handedly attempted to advance the plans of his master against Spain, France, England, and the United States. Monroe convened an urgent cabinet meeting to discuss the situation. Afraid of war with Spain, he drafted a message to Congress announcing the withdrawal of American troops from Amelia Island. A discussion ensued in which only Adams and the secretary of war voted in favor keeping possession of the island. Monroe remained undecided.[1] Shortly after the meeting, Adams received a visit from Luis de Onis who vehemently protested against the "violent occupation of the dominions of Spain" by American troops "at the time of a profound peace." Well acquainted with the temperament of the Spanish ambassador, Adams listened silently. Then he proposed that the United States purchase Florida for $2 million, an offer that Onis flatly rejected.[2]

Meanwhile, Henry Clay rallied congressional opposition to the American occupation of Amelia Island and Adams's policy toward the Spanish colonies. Public opinion seemed to be on his side.[3] The *National Intelligencer* published an anonymous article that argued that Aury had been under the protection of U.S. neutrality laws and that his occupation of Amelia Island had weakened Spanish influence near the American borders. A passage censored by the paper's editors stated that Aury was not a pirate but "a hedge against the secret occupation of Florida by England." The author of the article was William Thornton, the head of the Patent Office, who was no stranger to the intrigues behind Amelia Island.[4] Under pressure from the administration, the next day the newspaper published an editorial claiming that the American occupation of Amelia Island was legal and that Aury's followers were "negroes, violators of the revenue laws, and adventurers."[5] The fact that most of these unsavory characters had fought alongside General Jackson at New Orleans was not mentioned. Aury's black regiment was a source of concern for the slaveholding states that shared borders with Florida.[6]

Stung by criticism, Monroe convened a second cabinet meeting. Adams again argued in favor of continued occupation of Amelia but still no decision was made.[7] Monroe's indecision ended a few days later when he received a message from his ambassador in Madrid suggesting that Ferdinand VII wanted to reach a settlement over the Louisiana borders and that Onis had received instructions to cede Florida for the best possible terms. Based on this information, Adams called Onis who, to Adams's surprise, said he had no new instructions and again demanded the immediate evacuation of American troops from Spanish territory. Adams replied that the United States had been forced to occupy the island in defense of its laws and commerce and that its actions had benefited Spain.[8] Then Adams met with Hyde de Neuville who was greatly alarmed and warned him that the French settlers in the Tombigbee colony "were engaged in a project against the Floridas." Adams said he knew nothing about such a project.[9]

On January 13 Monroe sent a message to Congress explaining that "the suppression" of the "piratical establishments" at Amelia Island, and at Galveston, which would soon follow, had prevented "the consummation of a project fraught with much injury to the United States."[10] The president, however, did not provide any evidence to support this serious accusation. Adams again called Onis and warned him that if they did not come "to an early conclusion of the Florida negotiation, Spain would not have the possession of Florida to give us."[11] But this bravado was not backed up with substance. In fact, when days later Monroe heard that a Spanish squadron had left Cuba to retake Amelia, he grew "alarmed at the idea of a war with Spain backed by the Allied powers" and seemed to regret not having "ordered our troops to withdraw." Adams's only consolation was that an envoy sent from Buenos Aires confirmed that "the adventurers who had taken possession Amelia Island" had no authority from his government and that the United States "were fully justified in breaking them up." This bolstered the administration's argument that the South American patriots had not been involved.[12]

To shore up congressional support, Adams prepared a dossier on Amelia Island that suggested that MacGregor was a British spy. Among the evidence supporting this claim was an anonymous letter stating that the Scottish adventurer operated in agreement "with the British Admiral on the Jamaica station."[13] Another anonymous letter stated that before returning to England, MacGregor had "issued instructions for making a settlement at Tampa Bay, stating that he expected to be there the last of April or first of May 1818" and that he had appointed an English officer named Robert Ambrister* to recruit troops.[14] It is unclear whether Adams believed these charges, but anti-English sentiment was strong and he needed the full support of Congress to fend off Clay's attacks.

At this time, Lallemand's first contingent of troops was landing at Galveston, where Jean Laffite welcomed them. Although Laffite had promised his Spanish employers that he would derail Lallemand's expedition, he gave General Rigaud a friendly reception. Maybe he realized that opposing 150 experienced French officers led by a battle-hardened general was an enterprise beyond his abilities. More likely, he was expecting their arrival and was part of their plan. With Laffite it is impossible to know. A master at double-dealing, he always sided with whoever offered him more money. Despite Laffite's warm welcome, during the five weeks they remained in Galveston, Rigaud and his men suffered "hunger, thirst (for there is no drinking water), rains and tropical downpours, wet clothes, vermin, and the stings of myriad mosquitoes."[15] Lallemand had just arrived in New Orleans and it would be another month before he could join them. Before leaving New York, the general had sent a message to Aury saying that he would assemble all his forces in Galveston. From there he planned to proceed to Tampico, not far from where Mina had started his ill-fated invasion a year earlier. Lallemand asked Aury to join him "with the greatest number of people" possible, and to bring the *Calypso,* a ship that Onis suspected of belonging to Joseph. If this plan failed, Lallemand would divert his expedition to Venezuela.[16]

With the help of Pierre Laffite, Lallemand and his brother started buying arms, ammunition, and provisions. Henri wrote to "uncle" Stephen Girard to report their progress: "We are constantly advancing toward our goal, albeit pru-

---

*Ambrister was later captured and executed by General Jackson.

dently and slowly."[17] In reality, the two brothers encountered more difficulties than they had expected. By mid-February, Henri had already drawn four thousand dollars against Girard's credit. "Living is horribly dear in this place and nothing can be done except for its weight in gold," he explained to the banker. "My brother is to leave presently for the new settlement where our first convoy has arrived. As soon as it is definitely known where the settlement is to be established, it appears we shall have a great many people."[18] Lallemand "has come several nights to the house, and you may believe that our interviews were solely concerning his project," Pierre Laffite wrote to his brother. Lallemand planned to set up his camp on the Trinity River, "and to this effect he has begun to transport the necessary supplies." As to his intentions, they were "to seize the province of Texas and that as soon as he has got enough men he will extend his frontiers farther; that is to say, his designs are the same as Mina's." His ultimate goal, however, was the conquest of Mexico, "as soon as he has got nine or ten thousand men, a number he counts on getting within a short time if only money is not lacking . . . it cannot be doubted that if they get money they will succeed in their intent." The Spanish authorities would have to deal with men "much different from those that Mina brought with him," Pierre added. "I suspect that the operations of this army will give us news that will astonish the Spaniards." Pierre also confirmed that Lallemand had "some arrangement with the Americans." In a postscript, he added that the general planned a massive strike and would "neglect nothing, always assuming that resources of money do not fail him." The Lallemands would be joined by General Humbert, a veteran of previous Mexican invasion, and General Clausel, who would "bring a good party with him, and since he is familiar with the project and will work for it." Pierre believed that with the aid of a general as talented as Clausel, "their operations cannot fail to have a good result."[19]

In Washington, Lallemand's intrigue took another unexpected twist. William Lee saw Colonel Jacques Galabert, who had fallen out of favor with Lallemand, entering Onis' house in Washington. When confronted by Lee, Galabert admitted that Onis had paid for his trip but refused to give any more details, except that he had asked for a passport to go to Mexico. Galabert also said that Joseph had advised him not to join Lallemand's "wild and extravagant" projects and had offered "him the means of settling himself in Pennsylvania."[20] Suspecting that Galabert was intriguing with the Spanish ambassador, Lee reported the news to Adams. Adams also smelled an intrigue. Was Spain planning to use the French émigrés against the United States? Adams asked Lee for more information.

A few days later Lee disclosed that the Lallemands were seriously engaged in an expedition to conquer Spanish America and had always counted on Aury's assistance. The two brothers had recruited more than three hundred men, and Lee estimated that they would soon have five times that number. Lallemand would concentrate his forces on a Caribbean island and then sail toward the Isthmus of Panama. His objective was to conquer the Spanish viceroyalty of Peru and use Lima as a base of operations for further conquests. To accomplish this objective he would cross the isthmus, travel by sea to Guayaquil, march south to Quito, and then take Lima, following the route taken by the conquistadors. Lee told Adams that the French generals were also considering an expedition to liberate Mexico with the help of the Count of Galvez.[21] This last detail particularly troubled Adams.*

In a letter to Adams, Peter Paul De Grand confirmed that Lallemand's plan was the same that Grouchy and Clausel had considered in 1816. In fact, it was the plan that they had agreed to with Toledo and Carrera. According to De Grand, at that time the Mexican patriots had approached Clausel and asked him "to take the lead of their armed forces" and offered ten thousand men near New Orleans and $2 million that had been borrowed in London. "They were to enter Mexico well organized. . . The whole plan was ready but Clausel and Grouchy kept it at bay, without decision for a while and finally said they must be assured in case of failure that their property in France would be mortgaged to them! Of course the plan dropped to the ground. Something like a sequel to it is now managed by the friends in question, but details are unknown to me."[22] Adams replied to De Grand that if Lallemand's objective was Peru, there was "nothing in the project disclosed in it which my duties enjoin upon me to oppose. . . . But the view of the subject presented by your communication is in some particulars new and important." Mexico was another matter. Adams asked De Grand for more information on "how far, or in what manner the Germans† are connected with a certain Count de Galvez."

---

* He must have been referring to the son of Bernardo de Galvez (1746–1786), governor of Louisiana. Galvez had played an active role in support of the American rebels during the War for Independence. He later became viceroy of Mexico.

† The "Germans," a literal translation of *les allemands,* was Adams's code word to describe the Lallemands.

I am not without suspicion that the disclosures made to you were only of "colorings." You have seen in the newspapers the proceedings of this government and the message of the president concerning the Amelia Island. You have observed that Commodore Aury talks very loudly about the rising Republic of the Floridas being at war with Spain and entering into all the rights of his enemies. But do you know that Aury is all the time acting in concert with the Germans and by consequence with the Spaniards here? There is so much double and treble treachery in the speculations of these auxiliaries to the South American revolutions that the principal difficulty is to discover on which side the chief acting personages are.

Adams realized that Lallemand was connected to MacGregor, who was in England preparing a new expedition against Florida. He complained to De Grand that during their meeting Lallemand had "solemnly protested to me that he had refused to have any concern with MacGregor, and never would have any; but Aury has certainly been connected with MacGregor, and Aury, if we are rightly informed, is connected with the present designs of the Germans. You say that the invitation to the Germans by the Spaniard here was obtained by a *coup de maitre*,* and afterward that it was his own personal act, which may be disapproved by his master." Adams was puzzled by the contacts between Onis and the French generals. What was Galabert's role? Was it all an elaborate intrigue to confuse Adams, Onis, and Hyde de Neuville? Adams asked De Grand for more information.[23]

De Grand replied that he did not know how the Lallemands were connected with Galvez, but "they had calculated on his cooperation." Apparently, the mysterious count, probably a code name for a leader of the Mexican patriots, had more than fifteen hundred men at his disposal in Texas. With respect to a British connection, De Grand assured Adams that Lallemand "would be one of the last men in the world to help Spain or England against the United States or to enter into any plans unfriendly to the United States." In fact, he said, Lallemand looked "to the United States as the great power that will check England." De Grand also confirmed that Aury was cooperating with Lallemand, but as far as he knew, MacGregor would be "altogether excluded, it being well understood by the Germans that he is in the British interests . . . anything that is English is

---

*A masterstroke.

to the Germans an enemy." De Grand didn't know anything about MacGregor's new expedition to Florida but had "no doubt that it is in no shape connected with the Germans." Regarding Onis' involvement, the offer "was first made by the Spaniard to the German at the close of October or the beginning of November." De Grand suggested giving money to the Lallemands to get more information and strongly defended their integrity: "I may be mistaken but I am very clear in the opinion that the plan as disclosed to me is the real plan and not mere coloring. I have no better opinion than you have of the generality of the chief personages engaged in aiding South America. But the Germans form a striking exception to their double and treble treachery. With the sentiments I know him to possess, I do not see how he can possibly act against the United States or in real concert with England or with old Spain."[24]

John Stuart Skinner, who hated the British probably as much as Lallemand, had assured Adams months earlier that MacGregor was not a British agent. In February 1818 he reiterated his opinion that the Scottish adventurer was "not a tool of England" and that his original plan had been to use Florida as a base to help the patriots in South America and then "to encourage and accelerate its annexation to the U.S." In a letter to a general close to the Monroe administration, Skinner also warned that British influence, "which has the malignity of the Devil and the ubiquity of God," was behind the persecution of his friend Jose Miguel Carrera in South America.[25] Despite all these assurances, Adams still believed, or wanted others to believe, that there was a connection between MacGregor, the British government, and Aury, from which it followed that the Lallemands were working, wittingly or unwittingly, for the "perfidious" Albion. In the coming months Adams persisted with this thesis, probably because he knew it would be easier to get congressional support for his policies.

At the same time Adams was raising the specter of British intrigue, he was also making overtures to Castlereagh to adopt a common policy regarding the Spanish colonies. By co-opting the British he mitigated the risk that the Holy Alliance would support Spain in a war with the United States. After a meeting at the White House in early February, the British ambassador reported that Adams and Monroe "have taken great pains to assure me that there is nothing which they so much desire as that the two countries should act in unison upon the whole of the great question of South America." Bagot believed that they were sincere, as "they would certainly gain from such union considerable strength to their own administration in resisting the great endeavors which are to be made at Congress by the Western States to force them into an absolute and unqualified acknowledgment of the independents of all the South American provinces."[26]

Adding a new twist to an already complicated plot, Adams discovered that before leaving for Amelia Island, MacGregor had met several times with William Thornton and had told him that it was the intention of the South American patriots to take Florida and later sell it to the United States for $1.5 million. Even more troubling was that Thornton had communicated this idea to Richard Rush, Adams's predecessor, who had tacitly approved it. Adams called Thornton into his office and asked him to provide in writing "the substance of his conversations with MacGregor and with Mr. Rush."[27] Adams was puzzled. Rush had been interim secretary of state while he was in London and couldn't have failed to inform the president of his conversation with Thornton. How much did the president know? Monroe now feigned complete ignorance and said that he disapproved of the whole scheme. During a second meeting, Adams told Thornton that the president was upset at his involvement with MacGregor. An embarrassed Thornton "equivocated a little about his having advised MacGregor to go to Mr. Bagot, but ultimately did not deny the fact. He said he was afterwards sorry for it, and had distrusted MacGregor when he found he was gone to an English island."[28] A few days later Thornton told Adams that he had never advised MacGregor to talk to Bagot about the Florida scheme, but "as a Scotsman, because his family estates had lately been restored to him, and he had a great distrust of MacGregor, as soon as he heard he had talked with Bagot about the Florida project."[29] On the other hand, a very reliable source told Adams that Lallemand operated independently of Onis.[30] At this point, Adams wasn't sure whom to trust. One thing was certain: Monroe knew more about Lallemand's plans than he was willing to admit. Any evidence of contacts between MacGregor, Thornton, and Rush would have to be excluded from the Amelia Island dossier being prepared for Congress.

Meanwhile, Onis made progress in his efforts to derail Joseph's plans. Colonel Rafael Gravier, who had just returned from Amelia Island, offered to disclose "the secrets of all the intrigues" of the French émigrés in exchange for a royal pardon. Gravier had been one of the Spanish officers who had formed part of Joseph's inner circle in Philadelphia and had served as a liaison with Jose Miguel Carrera, the Chilean rebel leader. During a meeting at Onis' country house in New Jersey, Gravier confirmed that MacGregor's expedition to Amelia Island was to be combined with another one that had Pensacola as its objective. Once Florida was taken, the plan was to use it as a base for other expeditions to liberate South America. Clausel had refused to be the leader so Gravier was offered its command, which he had declined because, he said, it was against the interests of Spain. Gravier assured Onis that he had tried to stop these plans from being executed but that MacGregor had gone ahead and his initial success had increased the hopes of his supporters. When Lallemand arrived from Europe he had been offered the command of the Florida operation but he had judged that the means available were not sufficient to accomplish the objective. The French general had nevertheless started to recruit men and had put Galabert in charge of the Pensacola project. Gravier claimed to have derailed Galabert's efforts and to have forced Lallemand to eventually abandon the expedition. Aury's arrival had given it new life until the Monroe administration intervened.[31]

To support his assertions, Gravier gave Onis a copy of a correspondence he had exchanged with Lallemand regarding the invasion of Florida. "The enterprise is beautiful and maybe not so difficult," Lallemand said in a letter dated July 1817. Occupying Florida would offer "enormous advantages" to his plans, but given the strong interests of the United States in annexing it, he had decided to stay away from the project. In case Gravier went ahead Lallemand recommended that the operation be designed as "a liberation campaign," and he detailed the measures that would need to be taken in conjunction with the Seminole Indians and the Spanish governor. The French general also emphasized that Pensacola was the key point for any military operation against Florida. In his response to Lallemand, Gravier said that as a Spaniard he could not accept "a commission which would conspire against the interests of Spain."[32] But Gravier had done nothing to stop the expedition against Amelia Island. In fact, in September 1817 he had joined a group of veterans of Napoleon's army to reinforce its occupation. And Gravier had just introduced Aury's envoy to the ineffable Dr. Thornton.[33]

Despite Gravier's assurances to Onis that the Bonapartist projects had been foiled, troubling reports of new intrigues surfaced in the press. One asserted that the French émigrés had "formed a plan to rescue Bonaparte from his prison," which would "undoubtedly succeed . . . [as] all the Spanish American provinces had proposed to Joseph Bonaparte through agents sent to him at his residence near Philadelphia that they would recognize him as King of Spain and assist with men and money."[34] The intrigue surrounding Lallemand became so impenetrable that Adams considered giving him money through De Grand to learn more about his objectives: "We must know distinctly, clearly, and minutely the whole plan—what has been done with the Spaniard [Onis], and what he has done, what his project has been, and how far the Germans have embarked in it, before we can authorize the advance of a dollar. . . . If they are to go to Texas, if will be ostensibly for annoyance to us. With that aspect, we must know very specially that other purposes are intended, what they are, and the ways and means of execution. . . . To be candid with you, we have reason to distrust semi-confidences. If assistance or even forbearance is expected from us we must know the whole."[35]

A few days later, Nicholas Biddle informed Adams that the Lallemands had asked Onis for twelve thousand dollars to "buy" their expedition. Onis had refused and "instead of buying off the party, he bought only the secret of their destination. This has, I presume, been conveyed long since to the local authorities in South America, so that the scheme will probably end in the ruin of these people." Biddle also confirmed that Lallemand had raised funds almost entirely by selling to French merchants in Philadelphia the land granted by Congress in Alabama. "This fact is very decisive as to their not going to cultivate vines and it is equally certain that they are destined against some of the possessions of Spain in South America," concluded Biddle.[36]

Hyde de Neuville suspected as much. He knew that Lallemand was in New Orleans and Rigaud at Galveston, and he was convinced that they not only had Mexico in their sights but also liberating Napoleon. The French consul in New Orleans also reported that "the expedition is really directed to St. Helena."[37] This led Hyde de Neuville to request a meeting with Adams, in which he expressed France's deep concern about the projects of the Lallemands. When Adams suggested contacting Onis for more information, the French ambassador assured him that Onis had protested "upon his honor that he knows nothing of them or their project." Adams smiled and told Hyde de Neuville that he could "rely upon it that Onis did know something of them."[38]

Onis clearly knew more than he was willing to tell his French colleague. In a ciphered report he sent to Madrid he explained that before leaving New York, Lallemand had sent him a message proposing an expedition against the United States. According to Onis, Lallemand had asked for land in Texas to establish a French colony and a passport for his emissary to go to Vera Cruz to negotiate with the Spanish viceroy. Onis admitted that he had been ready to agree to this proposal but a recent report from the Spanish consul in New Orleans suggested he had been fooled. The plans of the Lallemands were to conquer Mexico for

Joseph and to establish a Bonapartist empire in America. Their timetable was unknown but they seemed to have unlimited credit and to count on Aury's naval support. Onís explained that Lallemand intended to set up his base on the Trinity River, not far from Galveston. He was unsure about Galabert's recent visit. Was Lallemand planning to oppose the United States if Spain agreed to his proposal or would he go ahead and invade Mexico? To complicate matters further, Onís had heard rumors that the French Bourbons secretly supported Lallemand's expedition with the objective of recovering Louisiana. A similar rumor had reached Hyde de Neuville regarding Spain. Onís concluded that the Lallemands were trying "to sow the seeds of discord between the two embassies." He had no doubt that their objective was to establish "a branch of the Bonapartes in the Americas" and he suspected that the United States covertly supported their efforts.[39]

Onís feared Henry Clay, who led the opposition to the administration's policies regarding Amelia Island and the Spanish colonies. Clay had just proposed to amend the 1817 neutrality law. In his opinion "instead of an act to enforce neutrality, it ought to be entitled, an act for the benefit of His Majesty the King of Spain." Clay's proposed amendment stated that "neither the persons nor the property sailing under the flag of any colony, district, or people admitted in the ports of the United States" should be restricted provided that they claimed to be independent "at the time their engagement was granted" even if the United States had not recognized their independence.[40] If approved by Congress, this amendment would legitimize Lallemand's expedition and privateering under the flag of Buenos Aires. Clay also welcomed Aury's envoy and launched a congressional inquiry into the measures taken by the administration with respect to Amelia Island. He attacked Monroe's policies toward the Spanish colonies and proposed the immediate recognition of Buenos Aires. In his view the United States had the "deepest interest" in the independence of South America. "There is no question in the foreign policy of this country which has ever arisen, or which I can conceive as ever occurring, in the decision of which we have had or can have so much at stake," Clay said. "This interest concerns our politics, our commerce and our navigation."[41] Ready for Clay's offensive, Adams sent Congress a dossier that "proved" that MacGregor "had been funded by the British government." In private Adams explained to the British ambassador that this accusation was "totally without foundation."[42] To pressure Onís, Monroe assured Congress that "the project of seizing the Floridas was formed and executed at a time when it was understood that Spain had resolved to cede them to the United States and to prevent such cession from taking into effect."[43]

Onis worried that Clay would force the administration to recognize the independence of Buenos Aires. Madrid had warned him that "the recognition of the insurgents by the United States would be a terrible blow to us" and instructed him to do everything "humanly possible to avoid this outcome by muffling them with negotiations."[44] Maybe the Americans would agree to delay recognition in exchange for Florida. It wasn't such a far-fetched idea. Adams was not ready to give in to Clay's pressures and still hoped to act in concert with Castlereagh on this matter. Castlereagh in turn still hoped to cut his own deal with Madrid and did not respond to Adams's overtures. He knew Bolivar and San Martin were on England's side. There was no need to get the Americans involved.

As spring arrived, news from South America suggested the demise of the Spanish empire and the resurgence of Napoleonic power. The *National Intelligencer* reported that the patriot troops under General Michel Brayer, who was described as "a man of experience and a good soldier from the school of Napoleon," would soon defeat the Spaniards in Chile.[45] The reports from New Orleans were equally sanguine about Lallemand's prospects in Mexico. In fact, Napoleon's redoubtable general was already on his way to Galveston. "My brother left yesterday for the French settlement which we are beginning near Louisiana, in a beautiful, fertile and extensive country," Henri wrote to Girard on February 20. "I shall not go there until I know that he has arrived. Our first efforts have been successful and we shall follow them up with constancy and prudence. Our settlers from Philadelphia have arrived on the ground and have already planted corn." What he meant is unclear, as no one was farming and Girard knew it. "As soon as this settlement begins to be talked about (for the present we are still keeping it a secret) detractors and slanderers of the kind that is always base and disposed to do evil, will hasten to spread abroad all kinds of calumnies; but we care little for that. . . . Our enterprise is absolutely honorable." The younger Lallemand hoped "we shall be permitted to remain there unmolested and are firmly resolved to maintain and preserve peace and our liberties."[46] At the end of the month he wrote again to Girard. "I am expecting to hear from him every day and as soon as I receive news I shall leave this city." Henri, who drew on Girard's credit for his purchases, complained that New Orleans had become "exorbitantly expensive."[47]

The French consul in New Orleans informed Richelieu that Lallemand's objective was to conquer Mexico for Joseph. The project had been conceived in 1816 but was later discarded as impracticable, until Mina's initial success at the head of a small band of adventurers "had reanimated the hopes of Joseph and his friends." Lallemand had a better chance, as he had the support of the Mexican patriots for the establishment of an independent monarchy under the Bonaparte dynasty.[48] "The expedition must be composed only of Frenchmen led by the generals exiled in the United States. The number of recruits is between five or six thousand. Funds are abundant and easily available to the leaders. . . . They recently acquired two cannons and more artillery and guns are on the way. Clausel is expected from Mobile any day," reported the consul.[49]

On a date full of Bonapartist symbolism—the third anniversary of Napoleon's return to Paris—Lallemand landed at Galveston, where his old comrades welcomed him warmly. In addition to Rigaud, there was General Humbert, with whom he had served in Haiti; Captain Schultz, the loyal Pole who had followed Napoleon after the first and second abdication; Colonel Douarche, a veteran of the Peninsular War; Colonel Sarrazin, a veteran cavalry officer; Colonel Jeannet, who had served in Napoleon's Guard of Honor during the Hundred Days; and many others. At night they sang patriotic songs and drank to the glory of the emperor and the success of their enterprise. With his usual energy, Lallemand reestablished order and obedience and announced the beginning of the campaign. Days later, Lallemand set out for the shores of the Trinity River, where he planned to set up his camp, with all his men on boats provided by Jean Laffite. While crossing Galveston Bay the small fleet was hit by a violent squall. "The darkness of the night made our situation still more critical; several of the boats leaked badly, and were for a long time on the point of being swallowed up," remembered one of the French officers.[50] Five men drowned and many boats returned to Galveston.

The omens were not good, but Lallemand brushed aside this setback and moved forward. He put half his men under his command and the other half under Rigaud's and marched north in separate columns along the shores of the Trinity. The land journey was as disastrous as the bay crossing. After a six-day march under the scorching Texas sun, Lallemand and his men, half famished and worn out, arrived at the point chosen for their base. Additional supplies and provisions arrived a few days later. Lallemand divided his men into three cohorts: infantry, cavalry, artillerymen. The encampment, baptized Champ d'Asile (Field of Asylum), was built using the latest military engineering concepts. Discipline was strict and the men performed daily military drills. Everybody knew what the objective was. "The idea of colonizing Texas was a thousand miles away from our thinking," remembered one of Lallemand's officers. "We dreamed about the Mexican insurrection and the rescue of Napoleon."[51]

25
The London Connection

It is in the best interest of all kings and people that the affaires of Spanish America are quickly settled.

—Hyde de Neuville, July 1818

The negotiations between Wilson, Cochrane, and San Martin's envoy concluded with mixed results. Although Cochrane accepted the top command of the Chilean navy, Wilson had almost decided not to join the expedition as San Martin had refused to yield the post of commander in chief. For a man of Wilson's rank and reputation nothing less was acceptable. Even though he temporarily discarded Chile, Wilson contemplated joining Lallemand and Renovales in Mexico. "Pray see the map of America and see where Galveston is and the *Rio Grande del Norte* to which line the Americans . . . insist on advancing their frontier," Wilson wrote to Grey. "See how it bears on the line of communication between old and New Mexico, the distance from the [silver] mines, the Pacific [Ocean] and the Isthmus of Darien."[1] Wilson was also in contact with MacGregor, who had returned to England and was preparing a new expedition. The ineffable Scotsman had added a "Sir" to his name and went around London claiming to descend from Rob Roy. "Tomorrow I shall see MacGregor," wrote Wilson in mid-February. "He is *incognito* but he is, I presume, nevertheless under surveillance. He proposes to return to the charge." As to his own plans, Wilson admitted having received several letters from Europe that held "flattering & persuasive language to ears you will say prone to believe the tale."[2] Wilson may have been referring to his regular correspondence with Count Las Cases, exiled in Hamburg.[3]

The Duke of San Carlos, the new Spanish ambassador in London, watched Wilson and Cochrane closely. He had been appointed to his post to secure England's support in the war against the rebels in South America and in any conflict with the United States. San Carlos had just learned that two expeditions to aid the rebels were being organized in London. One was bound for Chile and Peru under the command of Lord Cochrane and Sir Robert Wilson. The second, bound for Mexico, was led by an exiled Spanish general named Mariano Renovales and a so-called admiral William Brown, an Irishman who had briefly led the navy of Buenos Aires.[4] Brown and Renovales had already commissioned several ships and were actively recruiting discharged Spanish, French, and English officers. San Carlos asked Castlereagh to stop them.[5]

Castlereagh did not tell San Carlos that weeks earlier Renovales had sent the Foreign Office a lengthy memorandum disclosing his plans to join the cause of the rebels in the Spanish colonies. "The Americas are lost for Spain," Renovales said in his memo. England had to help the independence of the Mexican patriots to balance the influence of the United States in North America.[6] Although Castlereagh didn't give much weight to San Carlos's warnings, he ordered customs officials to inspect any vessels departing for South America and to ascertain if Cochrane or Wilson had enlisted with the insurgents.[7]

The Marquis of Osmond, the French ambassador, was also aware of these expeditions and feared that Castlereagh would do nothing to stop them. In a letter to Richelieu he lamented that the "thirst for territorial expansion" was the disease of "this ill-advised cabinet."[8] Osmond wondered how it could be possible that the British government "doesn't have the means nor the will to prevent an attack of St. Helena?" He couldn't believe that if the U.S. Congress had passed a law prohibiting the arming of expeditions in favor of the insurgents, the British Parliament couldn't do the same. If Castlereagh was trying to maintain flexibility to gain commercial advantages in the Spanish colonies, it would be "a terrible miscalculation, and one that would have dangerous consequences for us," Richelieu replied. He urged Osmond to keep his eyes "wide open" and to use "any means at your disposal to foil any intrigues whose consequences could be disastrous to us. Our attention should be constantly focused on the island of St. Helena."[9]

Richelieu saw a link between the expeditions being armed in England and the "ridiculous plot conceived last summer by certain French émigrés in the United States with the objective of putting Napoleon Bonaparte on the throne of Mexico." He explained to his ambassador in Russia that the scheme had "as its auxiliaries certain men known for their devotion to the usurper, such as generals Clausel, Lefebvre-Desnouettes, Lallemand and others." Fortunately, the Monroe administration "had been alerted and has taken measures whose results are not yet known to us, but will easily destroy the hopes of the agitators" as one of the objectives of the plan "was to promote the revolt of the Western States and their secession from the Union."[10] The phantom of Aaron Burr was the best insurance against the success of the French émigrés in the United States. But Richelieu continued to receive reports from America regarding a "plan to release" Napoleon from captivity. "I want to keep proof in our files of our constant preoccupation with the island of St. Helena," he wrote to Osmond. "We can't let our guard down and have somebody one day reproach us for negligence." Given the involvement of Wilson and Cochrane, he could not understand "the indifference of the English cabinet."[11]

The possibility of Napoleon's escape obsessed Richelieu. "I ignore as you do, on what foundation the Buonapartists base their hopes," he wrote to Osmond weeks later, "but the fact alone that they have hope should put us on our guard and increase our vigilance. There is no doubt that the agitators and the disaffected of all countries have their sights on St. Helena, not certainly for love of the man confined there, but because they look to his appearance on the world scene as a means to disturb and destroy the present state of things." It was necessary to ensure that Napoleon could not escape and only the British government could give such assurance. What did Richelieu have in mind? There was only one way to ensure Napoleon never escaped: murder him. Richelieu instructed Osmond "to remind the English ministers of the importance of the duty entrusted to them, of which they are responsible to all of Europe."[12]

Although Castlereagh did not find any evidence that could incriminate Wilson and Cochrane, he tried to show San Carlos that he was taking measures to stop the expeditions against the Spanish colonies by providing him information about the activities of a certain Captain George Woodbine "of His Majesty's late corps of Colonial Marines and commissary for the Indian Tribes." Woodbine, who was in Jamaica, had been commissioned by MacGregor to purchase "arms and ammunition for assisting the insurgents against the Spanish government." MacGregor's plan was "to drive the Spaniards out of both the Floridas" at the head of a small army of Indians and runaway slaves. Castlereagh informed San Carlos that Bathurst had ordered the British authorities in Jamaica to "use every legal means for preventing the exportation of arms and ammunition to Florida for the purposes contemplated by Mr. Woodbine."[13] At this time, Adams was telling Congress that Woodbine was Bathurst's secret agent and that MacGregor's new expedition to Florida had England's support.

Castlereagh's show of goodwill pleased San Carlos, but not enough to prevent him from taking his own measures to stop Renovales and Cochrane.[14] Through his well-funded spy network he was able to confirm that their expeditions had links with the Bonapartists in Europe and the United States. He also confirmed that Cochrane was seriously considering a plan "to rescue Napoleon from St. Helena and take him to America, where they would link with the projects already known of the French émigrés in the United States." San Carlos again demanded urgent measures from the British government to derail their efforts.[15] In a conversation with Osmond, Castlereagh explained that English law prevented him from stopping the expeditions as there was no proof that they were directed against the Spanish colonies. On hearing this, the French ambassador replied that the interests of the British monarchy could not be subordinated to those of a few London merchants. Osmond was worried because he had just learned that General Brayer was in Buenos Aires and had allied himself with an influential leader of the insurgents.[16] Under mounting pressure from San Carlos and Osmond, Castlereagh decided to intervene. Customs officials assured him that they would take "immediate measures" to ascertain the accuracy of the intelligence provided by San Carlos and "to adopt forthwith all legal proceedings to prohibit the clandestine exportation of arms to South America."[17] But days later Osmond reported that Renovales had recruited several French veterans and that his expedition was going ahead.[18]

The fates of Napoleon and the Spanish colonies seemed inextricably linked. According to Osmond, the Bonapartists had joined the cause of independence to facilitate Napoleon's escape. Fortunately, their plans faced serious obstacles. A recently arrived report from Rio de Janeiro confirmed the arrest and deportation of Colonel Latapie. Osmond observed that at least in this instance, British agents had been cooperative.[19] Richelieu agreed that Latapie's arrest was good news, but Brayer, who was much more dangerous, was still at large. It was necessary to neutralize him and stop the anarchy that was spreading throughout the New World, which benefited Bonapartist designs in Europe.

In recent months Richelieu had been mulling over the idea of placing a Bourbon prince in Buenos Aires to stop the "republican emulation of the United States" and derail the plans of the Bonaparte family. This scheme could also provide commercial advantages to France and curb England's trade dominance in the region. Encouraged by recent overtures from Buenos Aires, Richelieu thought it necessary to first convince Spain and, if possible, also obtain the support of England and the United States. The French minister remained obsessed by the possibility of Napoleon's escape. "Unfortunately," he admitted to Osmond, "as it was the case in 1815 we are not in a position to prevent by ourselves an event that would have such fatal consequences. We cannot do anything but awaken the attention of those who guard him."[20]

An attempt to kill the Duke of Wellington during a visit to Paris heightened Richelieu's fears.[21] The French police confirmed that the plot had been hatched in Brussels and that Lord Kinnaird was somehow implicated in it. Kinnaird, who was a friend of Byron, Wilson, and Lord Holland, already had a bad reputation in Bourbon circles. Since 1816, he had lived in Brussels with his lover Fortunée Hamelin. Under threat of arrest, Kinnaird agreed to disclose what he knew about the plot. According to Richelieu, Nicolas Brice, former officer of Napoleon's Imperial Guard was the mastermind of the plot.[22] Brice was not new to conspiracy. He had participated in the 1815 uprising at La Fère with Lallemand and belonged to Les Chevaliers de l'Epingle Niore, a secret society created to restore the Bonapartist dynasty to the French throne. According to the *Courier,* General Philibert Fressinet was reportedly also implicated in the affair, as well as "several Belgian officers formerly companions in arms of the refugee French officers."[23] The only man who stood trial for this alleged assassination attempt was a former *grognard* named Cantillon, who had been employed by Brice in Brussels.[24] Fressinet would later resurface in Buenos Aires.

Even though Latapie's arrest in Brazil made Richelieu "a bit less anxious about St. Helena" he still worried about Napoleon's guardians. "I would like to know if the garrison and the squadron are regularly relieved," he wrote Osmond. "This [*is*] of the utmost importance because the influence of this man is such, that if the same troops remain attached [to] his guard for too long, he is going to find supporters among them."[25] Soon, however, news of Lallemand's progress in New Orleans again threw the French prime minister into a frenzy. *La Minerve Française,* the newspaper edited by Benjamin Constant, had started a public subscription to finance the establishment of a French colony in Texas, which had been baptized the Champ d'Asile.[26] "You will see the movements of our refugees and adventurers in the United States," Richelieu wrote to Osmond. "They want to go St. Helena and if the deliverance of the prisoner is not the first operation they will attempt, it is at least the main objective of all their efforts. It will be necessary that you pass these reports to Lord Castlereagh. I hope the precautions taken at St. Helena will guard us against any serious worries. Still, I can't stop thinking about this rock and of the evils that could be unleashed from it due to negligence or treason."[27]

The *Courier* made fun of reports from the United States that a fleet was under construction to rescue Napoleon. The men behind this project seemed to be the same who had "devised a plan for carrying off the great man in a balloon."[28] Lewis Goldsmith was also skeptical about these reports but claimed to "know some curious things relating to certain projects of the Buonapartists which are not on the *tapis* [carpet], but which I cannot, with propriety communicate to my readers at present."[29] Days later Goldsmith insisted that "immense preparations" were under way in American ports "for the delivery of Napoleon from St. Helena."[30]

In London the public debate about Napoleon's treatment intensified. Doctor Warden, former surgeon of the *Northumberland,* advised Lord Holland that he wanted to publish Napoleon's *Observations on Lord Bathurst's Speech.* Wilson supported the idea, as he thought the piece made a strong case against Lowe and Bathurst.[31] Lord Holland disagreed. He thought the document was too extreme and advised against its publication, particularly as it was clear evidence of clandestine communications with Napoleon. Probably encouraged by Wilson, Warden published the *Observations,* which had a great impact on public opinion. Whereas the *Examiner* criticized the government for its "petty and vindictive treatment of this fallen conqueror," the *Courier* blamed Napoleon's lack of exercise for his illness, as he had "not passed the threshold of his house these four months."[32]

Meanwhile, Cochrane's revolutionary steamship, the *Rising Star,* was about to be launched on the Thames. Wilson checked out the vessel at the shipyard and was impressed. "She is not only to effect a Peruvian revolution but a total one in naval affairs," he told Grey. Cochrane claimed that "with a few such vessels he could destroy all the navies in Europe." The ship carried four guns on deck and her two steam engines delivered 45 horsepower each. The paddling wheels were in the center of the hull and therefore protected from gunshot. Wilson observed that the ship had "a variety of other improvements all of which do honor to the genius of Cochrane."[33]

The Duke of San Carlos confirmed that MacGregor was part of the plan. Wilson had Maceroni appointed as MacGregor's chief of staff. In the new version of the plan Lallemand and Renovales would jointly invade Mexico; Cochrane and Brown would go to Chile, take over the patriot fleet and attack Spanish vessels sailing in the Pacific and provide naval support for an expedition to Peru; MacGregor and Maceroni would take the fortress of Portobello, at the Isthmus of Panama, cross over to the Pacific and send reinforcements to Mexico or Peru, as needed. Portobello was a point of enormous strategic importance, as it guarded the narrowest strip of land in Central America. Wilson met regularly with Cochrane and Maceroni to discuss the details of the upcoming campaign. At the end of March, he invited John Cam Hobhouse for dinner at his house. Hobhouse had just returned to England after a tour of Italy with Lord Byron. In addition to Cochrane and Maceroni, Hobhouse also found Michael Bruce, who had helped Lavallette escape. Wilson had known Hobhouse for years, and together with Byron, Bruce, Burdett, and Kinnaird they founded a political society called the Rota Club that advocated parliamentary reform.[34] Over dinner, Maceroni warned everybody that the Count Beaumont de Brivazac was "a paid spy of Decazes" who had contrived to get him arrested for "certain debts." He said that Lewis Goldsmith was also a spy and kept Wilson and Cochrane under surveillance. Hobhouse thought Maceroni was sharp but looked like a "rogue," whereas Cochrane looked like "a mild, very gentlemanly and agreeable man." As to MacGregor, he considered him a "stupid fellow."[35] But Wilson believed MacGregor was "a useful personage" who could render some services "before the rope suspends his functions as a freebooter."[36]

Having failed to obtain the command of the Chilean army, Wilson now considered a parliamentary career. If Cochrane left for South America, somebody would have to take up the torch of reform in the Commons. The borough of Southwark once again offered him a seat, and Hunt and the Westminster Committee supported his candidacy. Much relieved, Lord Hutchinson congratulated him for his decision to accept the candidacy.[37] The *Courier* lambasted the new candidate noting that his qualifications were "about as good as those of Lord Cochrane."[38]

The Duke of San Carlos again asked Castlereagh to stop the expeditions being organized by Cochrane, Renovales, and MacGregor.[39] The information quickly reached the press. The *British Monitor* reported that Renovales was fitting out an expedition in the Thames "destined perhaps [for] Spain, if not it is certain that it is intended for South America. Lord Castlereagh perhaps wishes for an Alien Act."[40] San Carlos was not going to wait until the British government took measures. Instead, he started his own campaign. Money was always a persuasive argument. First, he tried to bribe Cochrane, whom he considered the most dangerous, due to his talents as a naval commander.[41] The rebel admiral was not for sale, but he played the game for a few weeks to distract the Spanish ambassador. San Carlos then approached Renovales, who was more receptive.

The Marquis of Osmond was as determined as San Carlos to derail the expeditions against the Spanish colonies. The preparations of Wilson and Cochrane in London, Brayer in South America, and Lallemand in New Orleans presaged trouble. The European courts shared these concerns but neither the English nor the Americans moved aggressively enough to stop them. In recent months Osmond had established contact with Colonel Hilaire Le Moyne, a veteran of Napoleon's army who had been forced into exile in England due to problems with creditors. Le Moyne not only had a good relationship with the Bonapartist émigrés but had also been approached by Renovales to join his expedition.[42] Osmond offered him an opportunity to clear his name and shore up his finances by becoming his spy. Le Moyne agreed and started passing valuable intelligence to the French ambassador. Among other things, Le Moyne revealed that the Duke of Sussex supported Renovales's expedition.[43] This information was particularly disturbing, as the duke was the brother of the prince regent and was known for his "democratic" views. Osmond asked for more information. Le Moyne met again with Renovales, who this time refrained from implicating Sussex, but said that a monarchical system in South America would offer great advantages. Since most of the population was Roman Catholic, a French prince would be the most appropriate. Renovales also said that France could create a "beautiful kingdom in Buenos Aires" and that Supreme Director Pueyrredon would support such a project. It is unclear whether Le Moyne invented this story to get himself appointed to a mission in Buenos Aires. Was he a double agent? Unclear, but his report excited Osmond's imagination. "A kingdom in Buenos Aires certainly gives a lot to think about! Our commercial surpluses could be advantageously placed there," he wrote to Richelieu. The French ambassador recommended sending Le Moyne to Buenos Aires as soon as possible, as he not only was well informed about the expeditions being organized in England but also knew Brayer. At a minimum he would be able to obtain trade advantages for France.[44]

Richelieu agreed but advised Osmond to convince San Carlos that this plan was also advantageous to Spain.[45] Richelieu's decision was probably influenced by a memorandum he had just received from Marshal Serurier, who he had served for many years as Napoleon's ambassador in the United States and was very familiar with the plans of the Bonapartists. Serurier argued that all the world's agitators and revolutionaries were looking for a point of support and a base in South America. Buenos Aires was the ideal place. If they succeeded, the political impact in Europe, particularly in France, could be enormous. He therefore recommended the establishment of new monarchies led by Bourbon princes in the Spanish colonies.[46] At the end of May, Le Moyne embarked for Buenos Aires.

26

In His Majesty's Service

San Martin has always shown a marked predilection towards England.
—Commodore William Bowles, February 1818

Commodore Bowles was quite surprised when he read the urgent message from Buenos Aires. A plot to rescue Napoleon had been discovered in Brazil and General Brayer, who was serving in the Chilean army, played a leading role in it.[1] The warning about Brayer was timely, as Bowles was about to have an important meeting with General San Martin, commander in chief of the patriot army.

Unbeknownst to Bowles, since Latapie's arrest, the Portuguese authorities had uncovered more information about the rescue expedition. At the end of 1817, they arrested Captain Pierre Raulet and Flemming Holdt, the Danish secretary of Joseph Ray, the American consul in Recife.[2] Flemming Holdt declared that after Napoleon's abdication he had left the French army to join the American navy and at the end of 1815 he had embarked for Pernambuco. He confessed that in Recife he had liaised directly with Raulet and Latapie, both of whom were under the protection of Pernambuco's Freemasons. Latapie had told him that there were ten thousand Frenchman in the United States ready to rescue Napoleon from St. Helena and that over a million dollars had been raised for that purpose. Two men on the island "knew the secret and had offered to facilitate the landing of the troops." When news of the revolution in Pernambuco had reached the United States, Joseph decided "to support the revolutionary government to accomplish more easily the task of delivering the Emperor." Raulet in turn confessed that Latapie had recruited him for the rescue expedition in the United States. He claimed that Commodore Decatur, the best officer in the American navy, was aware of their plans and thought their chances of success were two out of three.[3] Was the legendary hero of Tripoli involved?

We shall never know, as he was killed in a duel in 1820. But twenty years later, Joseph Lakanal claimed that Decatur had proposed leading an expedition to rescue Napoleon but that Joseph had refused by "pusillanimity or avarice."[4] Decatur was a man of action and he loathed his bureaucratic responsibilities at the Navy Board.[5] In any case, Portuguese authorities deemed Raulet too dangerous and kept him in jail without trial for several weeks. The French consul in Rio de Janeiro made no effort to obtain his release but Ray tried to make his confinement more bearable by passing him money, food, and messages through corrupt prison guards.[6] Just when Raulet lost hope of ever leaving prison alive the Portuguese government deported him to Europe. It would not be Raulet's last adventure in South America.

The warning from Brazil confirmed Bowles's worst fears. Ever since retaking command of the British squadron stationed in Buenos Aires in 1816, he had watched with concern the endless arrival of Frenchmen, most of them veterans of Napoleon's army. He now understood why they had come to South America in such large numbers. During his first mission in Buenos Aires in 1813, Bowles had become a good friend of San Martin and they had kept up a regular correspondence. Although he took care to preserve an appearance of neutrality, Bowles was partial to the cause of the rebels and believed England's best interest would be served if the Spanish colonies became independent under the leadership of someone like San Martin, who had "always shown a marked predilection towards the English." During their conversations, which took place over several days, Bowles brought up the plans to rescue Napoleon. San Martin must have been shocked. He realized that Brayer was a much more dangerous enemy than he had ever suspected. San Martin must have promised to deal with Napoleon's general, as in his dispatch to London, Bowles explained that there was no reason to worry. "[A lack] of officers has lately obliged him [San Martin] to employ in his army a number of French and Americans who accompanied General Brayer to this country last year, but various opportunities have been taken to warn him of their intrigues, and having lately detected a conspiracy against his life in which many of them were concerned, he is now removing and separating them as fast as possible and they possess no influence whatever here at present."

Then the conversation moved on to political issues. Now that the capture of Lima seemed likely, Bowles wanted to ensure that British interests were well protected. When San Martin described his grand plan for Peru and the rest of Spanish America, it was Bowles's turn to be surprised. In his dispatch to London he transcribed verbatim San Martin's proposal. Bowles explained that San Martin had "from the very beginning of the revolution seen and lamented the want of talent and integrity which has hitherto opposed an insurmountable obstacle to the adoption of a regular system here, and although perhaps one of the most determined supporters of the cause of independence it has always been under the conviction that foreign interference would finally be necessary to establish a settled government in this country." The Argentine general was not only "decidedly in favor of a monarchical government, as the only one suited to the state of society in this country" but also proposed a scheme that, if known, would have outraged many of his compatriots.

> He threw out the idea of dividing South America amongst the principal European powers forming such a number of kingdoms as might provide for a prince of each royal house and by that means satisfy all parties and prevent those rivalries and jealousies which might otherwise produce opposition and difficulties. Spain might have Mexico. The other powers the different viceroyalties according to their existing divisions and to reconcile the court of Madrid to a sacrifice which appears so enormous he suggested the practicability of pecuniary and commercial indemnifications from the colonies thus relinquished. . . . The moderate and amicable interference of some friendly power can alone terminate the present convulsions and prevent new and more serious ones; and those who at this moment hold the principal authority here consider themselves so strong, and so completely in possession of the general confidence, as to engage for the adoption of any practicable plan which takes independence for its basis and excludes the Spanish branch of the house of Bourbons.

The "friendly power" was obviously England, and San Martin was prepared to offer special commercial advantages if a British prince accepted the throne of Chile. Such a pretender would be accepted "without any conditions except the establishment of a constitutional monarchy." There was more. San Martin, once again, requested "some communication from His Majesty's Government which might guide his conduct if the events of war place the whole of Peru in his possession; that he may be enable to take proper steps at once, and not find himself the receptivity of retracing mistaken ones."[7] This message was also conveyed to Castlereagh through the British Consul in Rio de Janeiro who confirmed San Martin's "extreme desire to be guided, if possible, by the [advice] of the British cabinet."[8] San Martin's plan for the Spanish colonies was completely at odds with the one that Brayer, Cochrane, Wilson, and Lallemand had in mind.

After his meeting with Bowles, San Martin headed south to join O'Higgins, who had abandoned the siege of Talcahuano and was returning to Santiago with Brayer and the rest of his army. San Martin was determined to deal with the French general at the earliest opportunity. In early March, four days after his rendezvous with O'Higgins, he removed Brayer from any direct troop command and appointed him chief of staff. By now Brayer knew what had happened at Pernambuco but he was not aware that the plans to rescue Napoleon had been discovered, and he did not imagine that his involvement had been disclosed to San Martin. Nonetheless, it didn't take him long to realize that his days in the patriot army were numbered.[9]

As Brayer mulled over his options, a Spanish force sent from Lima landed in Chile and marched toward Santiago. For several days the Spanish and patriot armies watched each other's movements, waiting for the right moment to attack. Then San Martin made the worst mistake of his military career. He camped in a position that left one of his flanks completely vulnerable. The Spaniards launched a surprise attack in the middle of the night and most of San Martin's troops fled in utter disorder.[10] It seemed that the end of Chile's independence was near. Brayer took advantage of the chaos and galloped back to Santiago to regain control of the situation. He counted on the assistance of Carrera's supporters, particularly the charismatic Manuel Rodriguez, who months earlier had been expelled from the army for conspiring against San Martin and O'Higgins.[11]

When Brayer reached Santiago, he helped Rodriguez stage a coup d'état.[12] Once in power, Rodriguez took drastic measures "to resist the advance of the Spaniards."[13] With Rodriguez in charge of the government and Brayer the only man capable of leading the army, it seemed as if San Martin's luck had ended. However, the coup was short lived. Two days later, learning from Napoleon's mistake after Waterloo, San Martin appeared in Santiago at the head of a division that had escaped unscathed from the battlefield. This show of force allowed him to regain control of the political situation.[14] San Martin could see Carrera's shadow everywhere and his links to Rodriguez and Brayer were now evident, and much more dangerous than he had ever imagined. He had to take drastic measures to end their plots. O'Higgins had long advised him that "an exemplary and quick punishment" was "the only remedy" to deal with his enemies. "That the three iniquitous Carrera disappear from amongst us. Judge them and execute them, as they deserve it more than America's worst enemies."[15] But what about Brayer?

27
A Mystery to Be Unraveled

We thought ourselves safe from all reverses of Fortune, from all the blows of Fate.

—Hartmann and Millard, Le Champ d'Asile, 1819

In late March, Joseph received a letter from Las Cases saying Napoleon's health was deteriorating and he would die if he remained at St. Helena.[1] He must have felt discouraged. So far his efforts to rescue his brother had failed. At least he had recovered the diamonds of the crown of Spain.[2] What could he do now? Joseph was anxious to free Napoleon but not desperate enough to support the scheme proposed by a Belgian aristocrat named Jean Hippolyte Colins, a former officer of the Imperial Guard. After being discharged from the army in July 1815, Colins had become obsessed with aerostats, which had been invented by Jacques Montgolfier at the end of the eighteenth century. Napoleon had considered using them for military purposes but eventually abandoned the idea. The main problem with hot air balloons was that they were very difficult to control while flying. Colins had developed a mechanism to resolve this problem, and he believed he could rescue Napoleon with a balloon. Austrian spies learned of his plan and reported it to Metternich, who never took it seriously. But Colins was quite serious, and in the spring of 1818 he left for the United States to meet Joseph. But Joseph told Colins that he had received strict orders from his brother not to make any attempts "of this kind." Instead, he persuaded the frustrated inventor to join Lallemand's expedition to Mexico.[3]

At this time, Lallemand faced formidable obstacles. Monroe and Adams had succeeded in misleading Congress, which rejected Clay's proposed amendment to the 1817 Neutrality Law and instead approved a stricter law that would make anybody who helped Lallemand liable to criminal prosecution. Public opinion was also turning against the French general. At the end of April, the *National*

Intelligencer reported that "an extraordinary assemblage of French gentlemen with a large quantity of warlike stores" had landed in Galveston. Two days later, the newspaper reported that the Frenchmen had "formed a plan, some time since, for taking possession of the Province of Texas" with funding from "the most wealthy to defray the incidental expenses. Mr. Girard is said to have subscribed 50,000 dollars; and Joseph Bonaparte, Marshal Grouchy and company are also believed to have contributed largely."[4] Since the *Intelligencer* was considered to be the mouthpiece of the Monroe administration, the report was particularly damaging and contributed to a negative reaction in public opinion. "They are upon the territories of the United States and cannot remain there for any purpose unfriendly to them," Adams complained to his friend De Grand. Besides, "the greater part of the funds with which the party sailed from Philadelphia were raised by the proceeds of the sales of the Tombigbee lands which Congress had generously granted to distressed French emigrants for the cultivation of the vine."[5]

De Grand surely informed Joseph of Adams's opinion. Sensing that his plans were in danger, Henri Lallemand wrote a letter to the *National Intelligencer* claiming his brother and the other Frenchmen that followed him were simply colonists who had no other objective in Texas, "but the choice of productive lands."[6] He explained to Girard that he thought it better "not to maintain silence in this case because of the incorrect reference to yourself, as well as to that of the Count of Survilliers and Marshal Grouchy, as my silence might have been misinterpreted." His brother had reached the Trinity River and built his camp "after many hardships caused by the bad conditions of the roads and bad weather." Henri told Girard that he planned to return to Philadelphia to see his wife, but most likely the reason was to confer with Joseph and decide on what course of action to take.[7]

Despite all these obstacles, the information arriving from New Orleans suggested that an invasion of Mexico was imminent. Onis explained in a lengthy dispatch to Madrid, that Lallemand was "one of Bonaparte's ablest officer and he will be accompanied by Clausel, Vandamme, Lefebvre-Desnouettes and other lesser known names but with similar military talents." He was in communication with Mexican rebels, knew the weakest points along the border, and "did not lack [for] funds or resources to achieve their enterprise." Onis also reported that Galabert had fallen out with Lallemand and offered to attract the entire expedition to the service of Spain. Although it was "impossible to penetrate the feelings of these people," Onis agreed to give Galabert a passport to go to Mexico to provide the viceroy with detailed information about the planned invasion.[8] Galabert had prepared a lengthy memorandum for Onis that revealed details of Lallemand's plans and described the means to defend Mexico.[9] Joseph, who was aware of the spat between Galabert and Lallemand, and maybe of Galabert's contacts with Onis, thought it would be better to take the disgruntled colonel away from the scene and asked his friend Girard to find him a position in Asia, "where it appears he is anxious to return. You will oblige me if you can procure passage for him on board one of your vessels."[10] But Galabert instead fled to Cuba with Onis' recommendation and continued to advise the Spanish crown on how best to protect its colonies in America.[11]

The rumors in Washington suggested that Lallemand and Rigaud were already in Galveston and that they would soon gather an army of four thousand men. According to a French newspaper, their intention was to land at Tampico "to appropriate and occupy a country which may become the asylum of discontented Europeans."[12] Even California seemed to be in their sights. Hyde de Neuville now believed the Lallemands were playing a dangerous game with Spain and the United States and would take the side of whoever supported them.[13] Onis had a different view. He informed Madrid that Lallemand had already raised an army of two thousand men in Galveston and would soon receive reinforcements from New York. Girard had given him credit in New Orleans, and as Onis pointed out, he was known "to be very miserly and stingy and also a very good speculator, nobody doubts that the credit has been provided by Joseph Bonaparte."[14] In a ciphered report sent a few days later Onis reported that he and many well-informed people believed that Napoleon had planned this enterprise "with the expectation that by faking a serious illness he could soften public opinion in England and [if] allowed to retire in America he would then take possession of those points conquered by his followers."[15]

Hyde de Neuville visited Adams and "expressed much anxiety and alarm at the Frenchmen landed at Galveston under the two Lallemands, and was much afraid there were Bonapartes concerned in the affair." Adams referred him to Onis for more information. Hyde de Neuville admitted that Onis "had tampered with Galabert—had given him money, and perhaps a letter to the Viceroy of Mexico; but he employed him only as a spy" and he was not intriguing with Lallemand. He also warned Adams that there was a great force coming from Europe to join Lallemand and urged him to settle any disputes with Spain as soon as possible. Sir Charles Bagot also expressed his alarm to Adams "at the Lallemand expedition to Galveston" and emphasized that "if there was a Bonaparte concerned in it, his government would of course consider it as deserving high attention." Adams was very circumspect and responded with "a great deal of caution," claiming to have no information beyond what was already publicly known. However, he added that he "had reason to think that the parties were largely provided with military equipment and that their expedition's expenses were supplied from sources which I was probably far from having any suspicion." Adams also took the opportunity to chide Bagot about MacGregor's expedition, "the numbers of people coming out from England to join it," including Lord Cochrane, and "the popular disposition in England favoring the cause of the South Americans."[16]

Adams's accusations were absurd. Having lived in London for two years, he knew perfectly well that Cochrane would never serve the Tories. Bagot reported to Castlereagh that the French émigrés had sold part of the land granted by Congress in the Tombigbee and used the proceeds to buy large quantities of "warlike stores of various kinds" and that no less than 250 Frenchmen led by Lallemand and Rigaud had set up a camp in Texas. "With what objects, by whose encouragement or by whose means they have done so, are points which by no means [are] equally evident," Bagot informed Castlereagh, but it seemed they were connected with the plans uncovered by Hyde de Neuville the previous fall. A much broader intrigue was also possible:

> It has been reported that it [Lallemand's expedition] has been undertaken with the knowledge and with the concurrence of the American government. It has, on the other hand been reported that it has been undertaken with the consent and by the means of the Spanish government, and it has also been reported that France, pursuing by every means her object of acquiring colonies, has, with the consent of Spain undertaken to interpose herself between the Mexican provinces and the United States, and that she has chosen as the instrument of her design the French officers now resident in this country, who have been given to understand that such services will be received as the atonement for their former offences.[17]

Onis realized that Lallemand was trying to confuse everybody. He had told some people that his expedition was under the auspices of France, others that he was supported by the United States, and still others that he had Spain's backing. Meanwhile in his public statements he claimed to have no hostile intentions toward either Spain or the United States. Onis noted that Lallemand had unlimited credit in New Orleans, which was provided by Girard, who was a miser and too good a businessman to finance an enterprise with no prospects of profitability, and Joseph knew he would be as unpopular in Mexico as he had been in Spain and therefore he would not have given Lallemand any money either. "All these well-known facts and the others which have reached me through very good sources lead me to believe that the plan in question has grand and secret designs." In fact, Onis was convinced that the plan "had been forged on the island of St. Helena by Napoleon himself, who ordered his brother Joseph to contribute to its execution. Only by a special order of Napoleon would a man of Joseph's weak character agree to provide funds for such an expedition." Napoleon's objective was to distract Spain, France, and the United States, so that Lallemand "could assemble all his partisans in a single point from where they would be ready to receive him if he was released by the British government, or if not, to launch an attempt to rescue him."[18] Onis had also learned that besides crowning Joseph as king of Mexico, Lallemand planned to seize Mexico's silver mines to obtain funds to "get Napoleon out of St. Helena, through bribes or intrigue." The plan was being coordinated with a campaign by Napoleon's followers in England to soften public opinion and lobby Parliament to allow him to retire to America. Its execution had been delayed by the negotiations between Spain and the United States regarding the limits of Florida and Texas.[19]

Hyde de Neuville agreed with Onis but believed that given the precautions recently taken in Europe and the measures taken at St. Helena "we may safely discard the probability of invasion and an attack by force to rescue the prisoner." He told Onis that "if such project actually exists, [it] would merely be a fantastic enterprise which would [serve] only to throw a gang of shady and unfortunate characters into the abyss."[20] However, Hyde de Neuville was troubled by persistent rumors that Cochrane was in the Caribbean at the head of a small squadron. "We cannot lose sight of the prisoner at St. Helena," he wrote to Richelieu. He did not reject the possibility that the expeditions being armed in London were encouraged by the British cabinet.[21]

Onis sent Adams a strong letter of protest in which he accused the United States of complicity with Lallemand, or at a minimum, of incompetence in enforcing its own neutrality laws, as the French general was currently in Galveston receiving "a considerable number of recruits and large supplies of military stores from the ports of New Orleans, Charleston, Savannah and others." Lallemand was executing the plan discovered by Hyde de Neuville the previous fall, and it was certain "that Joseph Bonaparte was at the head of it with the rash project of being crowned King of Mexico." The administration had taken no measures to stop them. "Seeing that this expedition daily takes a greater consistence and that the recruiting and supplies clandestinely sent from this Republic are not put a stop to, I can no longer refrain from again calling your attention, and, through you, that of the President, to the enormous abuse of the hospitality offered by this Republic, on the part of Joseph Bonaparte and his adherents with a view to disturb the tranquility of Europe," he wrote. Onis demanded a firm stance by the U.S. government to ensure "that Joseph Bonaparte, the generals Lallemand, and other Frenchmen now residing in this country, be compelled to keep themselves within the bounds prescribed by the hospitality and generosity with which they have been received and prevented from continuing to organize expeditions for the purpose of invading the territory of His Catholic Majesty and the peace enjoyed by his subjects."[22]

Two weeks later Onis returned to Adams's office and again asked for information about Lallemand's expedition. Adams smiled and told him that Onis knew more about it than he did. He then suggested that the United States would send troops to break up the establishment on the Trinity River, which according to Adams was on American territory. At hearing this, Onis reacted violently. The Trinity River was on Spanish territory, he replied. Besides, the viceroy of Mexico was at the head of an army of eighty thousand men and ready to quash Lallemand. Adams "laughed heartily" at Onis' exaggerations.[23] If indeed he laughed, he must have tried to hide his own anxiety. After only twelve months in the State Department he was facing a major crisis that could plunge the country into war. Adams advised his ambassador in London that he had made little progress in his negotiations with Spain and reiterated his interest in acting "in good understanding and harmony with Great Britain" in relation to "South American affairs."[24]

Bagot shared Onis' suspicions about the complicity of the Monroe administration with Lallemand. He knew that the ship that had taken Rigaud and his men to Galveston had violated U.S. neutrality laws, as it carried weapons and ammunition on board. He had an informer among the ship's crew who had just returned to Philadelphia and reported that Rigaud had landed at Galveston with more than a hundred men and "expected to be joined by various others who had been collected in the United States for the object and would when collected, amount to ten thousand men." Lallemand's first objective was to attack Vera Cruz, "to plunder that city, by which they would obtain sufficient booty to execute their grand scheme, which was the release of Bonaparte." The lack of reinforcements, in large part due to measures taken by the U.S. government, had forced a change of plans. The majority of the troops were "well aware of the real intention; that their songs, etc, were all the popular airs of the times of Bonaparte's successful days and that they hosted the tricolor flag in honor of him." The arrival of Lallemand from New Orleans had lifted everybody's spirits. However, the general seemed "disconcerted at the non-appearance of the expected force," and was trying to "find out the causes of the failure." His plans "appeared now frustrated unless they can rally them again by the force of money," Bagot's informer reported.[25]

The unexpected reappearance of Henri Lallemand in Philadelphia confirmed that the plans had changed. Henri had come back to confer with Joseph and Girard. To the latter he explained that the situation at the Champ d'Asile was very difficult and that although his brother would "be able to endure all privations and fatigues in order to succeed . . . he may be in need of provisions." To preempt any reproach, he added they had "calculated very accurately what was necessary but that everything was infinitely more expensive at New Orleans than in the previous year." Henri also said that Monroe's message to Congress had hurt the expedition and had kept several people from furnishing provisions. "It is not for me to decide whether the President has done well or ill. That is a matter of state which I do not permit myself to criticize," wrote Lallemand. "What is certain however is that this message has injured us. Who could have foreseen this?" Lallemand assured Girard that they had been careful to avoid "displeasing the American government" or "putting it in a position of being forced to declare against us." They had also done everything "to put ourselves in a safe position with the Spanish government, to give it no excuse to complain to the Americans that we had made an armed invasion of its territory from American soil." In everything "depending on foresight, on human wisdom, we have succeeded; we have endured disappointment only in what depended on heaven and on others for what we could not foresee."[26] French agents in Philadelphia reported that the younger Lallemand was still recruiting men for his brother's expedition while another former French officer was recruiting men for Aury, who reportedly planned to attack Haiti.[27]

Meanwhile, in Texas, the situation was coming to a head. It was an extremely hot and humid summer and constant rains flooded the Champ d'Asile. As the conditions in the camp became unbearable, morale started to wane. The news soon reached New Orleans. At the end of May, the French consul reported that "this fake army has vanished, the capital which was provided to finance the conquest of Mexico doesn't seem to be enough to ensure the subsistence of a hundred men." Nevertheless, a thousand "vague and contradictory rumors" circulated among the adventurers; "some spoke as if they plan something on St. Helena, others on Mexico." However, it seemed certain that Lallemand would "resist any attack by the Spaniards."[28]

Lallemand had become entangled in his own web of intrigue. Onis suspected that the French general was following Napoleon's orders and had been encouraged by the Americans. Bagot shared these suspicions but did not dismiss the possibility that the Spaniards, or even the French, were using Lallemand for their own purposes, whereas Adams suspected that Onis was behind him. Despite his paranoia, Hyde de Neuville had the clearest perspective, particularly after his last meeting with Onis. First, Spain was not supporting Lallemand. Second, Spain alone could not win the war against the insurgents in South America. Unless the rebellion was quickly brought under control, the anarchy in the Spanish colonies would only benefit the Bonapartists. Hyde de Neuville also realized that even though the French émigrés had found support for their projects among certain influential people in America, Adams was not among them. Hyde de Neuville believed the United States and France were natural allies. In his view the first step to resolve the situation was to help Spain reach an amicable peace with the United States, and the second was to establish two monarchies in South America, under Bourbon princes, which would not only serve Spain, but all of Europe, as it was "in the best interest of all kings and people that the affairs of America are quickly settled." Although always wary of England, Hyde de Neuville continued to think the most dangerous enemies of Bourbon France were the Bonapartist émigrés in America.[29]

Hyde de Neuville requested a meeting with Adams to discuss the tense situation in Florida, which he feared could trigger a war between the United States and Spain. Adams stated clearly that the territory could only belong to the United States. The French ambassador then talked to Onis, who expressed fears that "the adventurers under the influence of the United States will try to take Cartagena and Portobello," two strategically important points for any attempt to conquer the Spanish colonies. A natural harbor on the northern coast of the Isthmus of Darien, sixty miles north of Panama, Portobello was the hinge of the Spanish empire. If the insurgents took this fortress they would break communications between Mexico and Peru and have easy access to the Pacific.

With the arrival of summer, the Champ d'Asile became not only an embarrassment to the Monroe administration but also a potentially dangerous source of friction with Europe. Although Adams avoided giving any definite answers to Bagot, Onis, and Hyde de Neuville, he took measures to neutralize Lallemand's expedition. Besides a stricter enforcement of U.S. neutrality laws, the government appointed George Graham, the former secretary of war who had issued the orders that authorized Jackson to invade Florida and a personal friend of the president, to investigate the Champ d'Asile. Adams explained to Graham that Lallemand's plans were "of a wild and extravagant character" and that he contemplated "the invasion of Mexico for purposes of cooperation with the revolutionary party." Graham was instructed to proceed immediately to Galveston and "endeavor to ascertain the precise and real object of the expedition; the numbers of the persons already there; the sources from which they have derived the means of defraying the expenses of their undertaking; and those from which they expect future aid and support." In particular, Graham had "to ascertain whether any part of their funds are supplied by Joseph Bonaparte, or by Mr. Onis, or by both; and whether they have had intercourse with the Viceroy of Mexico."[30] Unknown to Adams, Graham had received a parallel set of instructions from the president. His mission belongs to the secret history of the Monroe administration, which as Adams would later admit, was a "continued series of intrigues."[31]

Days after Graham's departure, Washington was shocked by the news that General Jackson had taken Pensacola from the Spaniards. Jackson's incursion into Florida had been prompted by the alleged depredations of the Seminole tribes, which the Spanish authorities in Florida had supposedly encouraged. Jackson, who had been fighting the Seminoles for years, was convinced that the best way to terminate the Indian problem was to occupy Florida. At the end of 1817, Monroe had put him in command of a punitive expedition and warned him that he might "have other services to perform, depending on the conduct of the *banditti* at Amelia Island and Galveston."[32] Jackson had interpreted Monroe's letter as a presidential authorization to invade Florida. In late January he had marched through Georgia and two months later he crossed the border into Spanish territory. In early April, Jackson took the fort of St. Mark's and then marched west, took Pensacola and virtually annihilated the Spanish presence in Western Florida.[33] In the process he brought the two countries closer to war. Most Americans were thrilled by Jackson's exploits, which included the execution of two British citizens accused of conspiring with the Seminoles. Curiously, it was the usually bellicose Henry Clay who was shocked and outraged. He accused Jackson of engaging "in open warfare against a foreign government without constitutional authorization."[34] Monroe convened an urgent cabinet meeting to deal with the new crisis. Everybody opposed Jackson's actions except Adams, who argued they had been justified by the misconduct of Spanish authorities in Florida.[35] The *National Intelligencer* strongly defended the administration.[36]

Onis protested vehemently against the latest American military incursion into Spanish territory. However, he knew Spain could not afford a war with the United States while facing Lallemand in Texas and an insurgency in South America. Bagot requested a meeting with Adams to protest Jackson's execution of two British subjects in Florida. Adams claimed not to have accurate information about what had happened and took the opportunity to bring up the issue of the Spanish colonies. He told Bagot that it was the "earnest wish" of the United States to "proceed *pari passu* and if possible in the closest concert" with England with respect to the South American question and that "the time was fast approaching when the American Government could no longer avoid" recognizing the independence of the colonies. Adams knew that this message would get to Castlereagh in time for the discussions to be held at Aix-la-Chapelle by the sovereigns of the Allied powers.

Hyde de Neuville feared that the events in Florida could trigger a war, a scenario that could only help the Bonapartists. He expressed his concerns to Adams, who told him that Monroe was "much embarrassed about what course to pursue in this transaction."[37] Sensing an opportunity, Hyde de Neuville offered to act as a mediator. Adams and Onis accepted his proposal. Despite Jackson's actions, the French ambassador was optimistic, as he knew the Americans didn't want war with Spain either.[38] If he brokered an amicable resolution between both countries he would derail the intrigues of the Bonapartists in America.

It is unclear if and how Jackson's incursion into Florida related to the designs of the Bonapartist émigrés. On one hand, it preempted them, so it is possible that Monroe secretly encouraged them as MacGregor had suggested to Bagot a year earlier. On the other hand, Jackson put the United States at the brink of war with England and Spain. Adams argued that Jackson had taken Pensacola "not in a spirit of hostility to Spain, but as a necessary measure of self-defense." Interestingly, the Anglophile secretary of state also supported the execution of the two Englishmen, as the evidence produced at their trial proved "beyond all question" that they were connected with MacGregor.[39]

At the Champ d'Asile, Lallemand was unaware of the upshot of all the intrigues he had helped unleash and still entertained hopes of invading Mexico and fulfilling his last promise to Napoleon. He spoke little of his plans but held out hope "of great fortune."[40] "Perhaps we can help the illustrious prisoner," he said to a close subordinate. "Remember those plans which were laughed at by Clausel and Lefebvre-Desnouettes, as well as by Doctor Thornton, the chief of the Patent Office at Washington, that old independent who was always entertaining us with a fury for waging war and a mania for making constitutions for all the insurgents on earth? Well, that project which the ex-king himself [Joseph] regarded as chimerical we have just put into execution," wrote one of his officers.[41]

Meanwhile in New Orleans, Pierre Laffite, the master of double-dealing, assured Spanish agents that Lallemand would not be able to start operations in 1818 and proposed a plan to neutralize him by sending Spanish troops to blockade the mouth of the Trinity River.[42] Whom were the Laffites working for now?

Gourgaud Leaves St. Helena

Vain was his sickness, never was a clime
So free from homicide—to doubt's a crime;
And the stiff surgeon, who maintain'd his cause,
Hath lost his place, and gain'd the world's applause.

—Lord Byron, *The Age of Bronze,* Canto 3

The unexpected arrival of the HMS *Blossom* from Rio de Janeiro and a vessel from England in the first days of January caused great excitement at Jamestown. According to one rumor, some daring American corsairs were planning to attack the island.[1] According to another, Joseph had conquered Mexico and had sent Clausel at the head of a large army to attempt a coup de main on St. Helena.[2] Napoleon anxiously waited for news. He still did not know what had happened to Santini and Piontkowski. He also hoped his generals had delivered a crown to Joseph and that maybe he would get a message from Marie Louise.[3] Napoleon sent O'Meara to Jamestown to find out the latest news. But to his disappointment the doctor came back empty-handed and simply reported old rumors.[4]

Lowe was also anxious. The dispatches from Rio de Janeiro put him on alert. Latapie had confessed that "a large number of his comrades would gladly lay down their lives in the execution of this project" and that "they thought and dreamed of nothing else, and since they owed their all to the prisoner of St. Helena, they would surmount all obstacles to rescue him."[5] Lowe's worst fears had been confirmed. And days later a letter from a British captain in Buenos Aires reported that a young man had arrived from England with plans to build a boat "capable of navigating under the water" for several hours.[6] Could it be used to rescue the prisoner? After getting these reports, Lowe "doubled and even tripled the sentinels at Longwood." He worked incessantly on the fortifications, placed new telegraph posts and batteries at various points of the island. British cruisers were "more vigilant than ever," especially after four American ships passed near St. Helena and asked about Napoleon's health.[7] "The Bonapartist plots at Pernambuco have greatly excited the Governor," reported Balmain. "I see him always on horseback, surrounded by engineers and galloping in all directions. One cannot blame him for his extreme vigilance but he is pushing it quite too far."[8]

With the passing days, Napoleon realized how bad the situation was. Although he could not have known of Latapie's arrest and his deportation from Brazil before the arrival of the *Blossom,* he must have suspected that something had gone wrong with the rescue plan. The revolution in Pernambuco had been quashed in June 1817 and news of it had already reached St. Helena. General Hogendorp, Le Breton, or any other of Napoleon's many supporters in Rio de Janeiro could have informed him. Details of Latapie's misadventure soon trickled down to Longwood. It was Balcombe who told Napoleon that a group of French officers who had planned to rescue him "with a submarine" had been captured in Pernambuco.[9] Balmain told Gourgaud that Brayer and Latapie had been arrested when planning to rescue the emperor in a steamboat.[10] Napoleon sent a message to the Russian commissioner saying that it was simply an invention of the British ministry to justify Lowe's restrictions.[11]

Napoleon was "angry and in a very bad humor."[12] In a conversation with Bertrand he complained about Joseph and Lucien. Joseph loved women and pleasure too much and in Spain he had been "the worst possible head of government. He didn't do anything and didn't let anybody [else] do anything either." And Lucien was an "unprincipled" man.[13] Was Napoleon upset at his brothers for not being able to get him off St. Helena? Napoleon's spirits were dealt a further blow when he learned that Princess Charlotte had died in childbirth. For a long time, he had entertained hopes that the "little princess" would become queen and set him free. Napoleon thought her death "had a strange appearance." Napoleon couldn't help but see a sinister hand behind it.[14]

Faced with a string of bad news that dashed any hopes of a quick end to his captivity, Napoleon changed strategy. It was time for Gourgaud to leave, a decision he had planned for many months. Many historians assert that Napoleon was just fed up with his jealous and temperamental young aide, which is probably true.[15] But Montholon asserted that Gourgaud left St. Helena "with the consent of the Emperor and charged with an important mission."[16] The most likely explanation is that seeing little hope in a military expedition or a political decision in England, Napoleon decided to approach the emperors of Russia and

Austria. They would soon meet at Aix-la-Chapelle to discuss the situation in France. It would be an excellent opportunity to present his case. The problem was how to get Gourgaud off St. Helena without raising suspicions.

Many factors influenced Napoleon's decision to choose Gourgaud, who accepted his mission with reluctance and some resentment. No one at Longwood was better prepared for the mission. Bertrand was not an option as he had been condemned to death and was considered too attached to his master. Montholon had never met the tsar or the emperor of Austria. Gourgaud had met both and also knew Marie Louise. Napoleon thought Gourgaud would be well received in England. "Lord Bathurst loves you," he said, "You delighted him with your correspondence." In the letters he regularly sent to his mother, Gourgaud had never complained about St. Helena or the conduct of the governor.[17] From Lowe's perspective, his behavior had been beyond reproach. In contrast with Montholon and Bertrand he had never used insolent language or provoked silly disputes.

Balmain had encouraged Napoleon's hopes that the tsar would be receptive to his plea and there is no doubt he knew about Gourgaud's mission. In the last months Gourgaud had met several times with Balmain, who had passed important messages to Longwood that awoke the "dreams of a return to Europe and of royal hospitality in Russia."[18] A few days later Bertrand wrote in his diary: "The Emperor is suffering much. In this situation, he believes that a statement of the Emperor Alexander would be something that would honor him in the eyes of thinking people." Balmain told Bertrand that the public did not know what was happening at St. Helena and promised information about Santini and Piontkowski.[19] Lowe grew increasingly suspicious of the "casual" contacts between Balmain and Napoleon's companions. Balmain said that nothing of any substance was discussed and assured him that he would report back anything that passed between him and Longwood.[20]

Gourgaud also talked to the French and Austrian commissioners. When Montchenu asked him about escaping, Gourgaud replied that the emperor had had many occasions to escape to America but had chosen to remain on the island. "He can leave whenever he wants," he said. As to Latapie's attempt, Napoleon considered it the project "of a gang of adventurers." Gourgaud assured the marquis that Napoleon would never have agreed to "put himself in their hands."[21] Sturmer also thoroughly interrogated Gourgaud. Among other things, he asked what Napoleon's reaction had been to the death of Charlotte. "It was one misfortune more in his position," Gourgaud replied. "Everybody knows that the Princess of Wales has for him an almost fanatical admiration. He hoped that when her daughter mounted the throne, she would take advantage of the influence she has over her to have him taken to England." Gourgaud told Sturmer that Napoleon believed that he would not stay for long at St. Helena, as "the party of the opposition [in England] will succeed in removing him." In fact, he had not "renounced forever the hope of recovering the throne." When asked about Latapie, Gourgaud gave the same answer he gave Montchenu and insisted that Napoleon had been offered ten opportunities to escape and had refused them all. "What cannot be done when one has millions at [one's] disposal!" he told Sturmer. "He can escape alone and go to America whenever he desires." Napoleon hadn't escaped because he secretly enjoyed "the importance attached to his detention, the interest taken in it by all the powers of Europe, the care with which his smallest remarks are reported, etc." Besides, he felt he could no longer live as a private person and preferred "being a prisoner here to living free in the United States."[22] This was nonsense. Given the suspicious conduct of Sturmer before, during, and after his mission at St. Helena, his report of this conversation has to be interpreted with care. What is clear is that Napoleon was sending a message to the sovereigns of Russia and Austria: he was behaving responsibly and could leave St. Helena whenever he wanted to.

Sturmer's response was encouraging, even more so than Balmain's. Napoleon thought his father-in-law would take a greater interest in his situation. After all, the Austrian emperor had to think about the future of his daughter and grandson.[23] Napoleon had no time to waste. Gourgaud had to go straight to England without raising any suspicions. A duel with Montholon due to a quarrel between Gourgaud and his wife provided the perfect excuse. Supposedly, the challenge was accepted but Napoleon prevented it. Was this part of the charade? On February 10, Napoleon told Gourgaud to ask Lowe for permission to leave the island on grounds of "ill health" and dictated him instructions and a response to certain questions asked by Balmain.[24] Three days later, Gourgaud left Longwood. It would be another twenty years before he returned.

For the next month, Gourgaud carried on the deception beautifully. Lowe did not make a connection between his sudden fall from grace and recent events in Europe and America. He even believed the Frenchman when he said that Napoleon had treated him "like a dog."[25] In dispatches to Bathurst he praised Gourgaud for his behavior and for never violating the regulations. Gourgaud was doing his job so well that through a note written by Montholon, Napoleon advised him not to "overdo" it:

Be constantly on your guard and hasten your departure without showing any desire to do so. Your position is very delicate. Don't forget that Sturmer is completely devoted to Metternich. Avoid talking about the King of Rome, and on every occasion try to introduce in the conversation the affection of the Emperor for the Empress. Don't trust O'Meara. His Majesty fears that he still maintains a certain connection with Sir Hudson Lowe. Try to find out whether Cipriani is playing a double game. Ask Madame Sturmer whatever you think appropriate. As to Balmain, he is on our side as much as is necessary. Complain about the £500 and write to Bertrand about it. Don't fear anything from this side; he ignores the nature of your mission.[26]

Montholon's warning raises many doubts. Particularly puzzling are the comments about O'Meara and about Cipriani, who died only a few days later after suffering "awful intestinal pains." The evidence suggests that Cipriani was deeply attached to Napoleon and had served his cause faithfully for many years. Many on the island, including Balcombe, were convinced he had been poisoned. Did Cipriani know something? If he did, he would have told nobody but his master. He never had a chance to do so. During the night of February 25, Napoleon asked O'Meara if his visit would be good for Cipriani and the doctor advised against it saying that it "would hasten his death."[27] His grave site has never been found.

Lowe remained vigilant. In March he received another report with details of the Confédération Napoléonienne and the rescue expedition being prepared by Joseph and Lallemand. As on previous occasions, Bathurst did not think the report should "excite much alarm" but Lowe became increasingly paranoid.[28] He decided to tighten the regulations, as any breaches or evasions could only help Napoleon's "liberation from this island, through schemes and designs, which are as yet only in embryo."[29]

Despite Lowe's measures, Longwood's clandestine network continued to operate smoothly. In mid-March, William Balcombe left St. Helena carrying secret messages from Napoleon for his brothers, a commission for which he was amply remunerated.[30] In a letter addressed to Joseph, Bertrand said that the emperor had been "attacked by hepatitis, a deadly disease in this unhealthy climate." If left at St. Helena, "he will certainly die," wrote Bertrand.[31] Gourgaud embarked on the same ship with Balcombe. So far he had fulfilled the first part of his mission admirably well. "Gourgaud left this morning for England and was not first sent to the Cape of Good Hope, which is a mark of great favor," wrote Balmain in mid-March. "It is said at St. Helena that he has a secret mission from Bonaparte, that his troublemaking at Longwood was pure comedy, a clever way of taking in the English. I am not of that opinion."[32] Days later, the Russian commissioner told Montholon that Gourgaud had deceived everybody and would cause a great impact in London.[33]

Soon after Gourgaud's departure, Lowe again turned his attention to O'Meara, whom he had long suspected of facilitating clandestine communications. He and Balcombe were the only two people who had constant uninterrupted access to Napoleon and were not technically subject to Lowe's regulations. A few weeks after Gourgaud's departure, Lowe ordered O'Meara to stay inside Longwood's limits, in effect subjecting him to tighter restrictions than those applicable to Napoleon. O'Meara resigned, arguing that under such conditions he could not fulfill his role as Napoleon's personal physician. Napoleon sent a strongly worded protest to Plantation House.

Lowe suspected that Napoleon's illness was simply another intrigue. He told Balmain that O'Meara had committed "unpardonable mistakes" by keeping Longwood "in touch with everything that was happening in the town, in the country, on board vessels." Lowe claimed that the doctor had secretly given a gift from Napoleon to an Englishman. "What treachery!" he said indignantly. Balmain argued that maybe it was not part of a plot or scheme of escape but just "a little caprice." Lowe disagreed. He thought to use "such little tricks as these to corrupt and seduce Englishmen" was an abomination but admitted that the doctor had not violated the regulations. Balmain advised Lowe to retract his decision.[34] "If Dr. O'Meara is guilty, accuse him and try him publicly, so that in St. Helena, Longwood, and Europe they may know what he has done and why you have punished him," Balmain said. "But if he is innocent and should be reproached only for peccadilloes, forget about the affair and set him at liberty. Remember that if Bonaparte dies without having seen a doctor, as he seems determined on doing, the English will be accused of having poisoned him, and it will be easy for the Bonapartists to produce false witnesses in France and other places against you. And millions of men will henceforth look upon you as his assassin."[35] This last thought may have convinced Lowe, who allowed O'Meara to return to Longwood and resume his functions.[36] He would deal with the doctor later.

Days later Lowe issued a proclamation "interdicting" any communication between the residents of St. Helena and the "foreign persons under detention in the island." These measures did not have much effect. The Jamestown merchant Lewis Solomon continued to communicate with Bertrand and reported rumors that Lowe would be recalled and that Napoleon would be taken to a more temperate climate. On hearing this rumor, Napoleon said that if public opinion in England was as strong in his favor as it seemed, Parliament would have to release him and maybe even recall him to Europe. Bertrand assured Solomon that he would be well rewarded if he provided any more information.[37]

With the passing weeks, Lowe continued to receive disquieting news from London. The dispatches from Bathurst confirmed that Napoleon continued to communicate with the rest of the world. A packet of letters from Longwood had been delivered to a person in London by someone recently arrived from Brazil. It appeared that the person was an Englishman or an American living in Bahia who had been twice to St. Helena by way of the Cape and had met with somebody, maybe even Napoleon, at Longwood. Bathurst assured Lowe that there was "no doubt that measures have been in contemplation to proceed with a party of French and other adventurers from Pernambuco to St. Helena for the rescue of general Buonaparte."[38]

Lowe's opportunity to get rid of O'Meara arrived in mid-July when he received a dispatch from Bathurst ordering his dismissal. At the end of the month, O'Meara was removed from Longwood and sent back to England.[39] O'Meara's role as Napoleon's doctor raises many questions. It is clear that during the first months of captivity he spied for the governor and that at a certain point he was won over by Napoleon through a combination of money and personal charm. When he left St. Helena, he carried a message from Napoleon to Joseph asking him to publish a secret correspondence between Napoleon and the emperors of Austria and Russia. Although O'Meara would be a valuable messenger, his departure from St. Helena could have serious consequences for Napoleon, who a year earlier had discarded the possibility of any attempt to poison him as long as Balcombe, Poppleton, and the Irish doctor were at Longwood. They were all gone. "The crime will be committed much faster," Napoleon told O'Meara during their last meeting. "I have lived too long for them."[40]

Shortly after O'Meara's departure, Sturmer also left St. Helena after being recalled. He also took a letter from Napoleon for the emperor of Austria.[41] Napoleon probably expected this correspondence to have an impact on the proceedings at Aix-la-Chapelle. Coincidentally, Balmain told Lowe that he needed to recover his health in more favorable weather and departed for Rio de Janeiro. Before leaving the island, he reported to St. Petersburg that Napoleon had passed him a message through Montholon saying that he still "hoped for the magnanimity" of Alexander and "that he adjured him by the memory of old friendship to release him from this frightful exile and to give him another, less unhealthy; which being the arbiter of Europe he could easily do."[42]

It had been a very active six months at St. Helena. Gourgaud, Balcombe, O'Meara, Sturmer, and Balmain had left, all carrying messages from Napoleon. A new chapter of the St. Helena saga was about to begin.

29
Get Rid of Brayer!

I am exceedingly well pleased to be able to communicate another circumstance to your Lordship which appears quite certain, namely the total disgrace of general Brayer.
— Chamberlain to Lord Castlereagh, Rio de Janeiro, May 20, 1818

Early reports of San Martin's defeat at Cancha Rayada reached Brazil in late April. It was the opportunity that Carlos de Alvear had been waiting for. As a leader of the opposition in Buenos Aires, Alvear was a key ally of Jose Miguel Carrera, who since early 1817 had entreated him to join his efforts to overthrow the San Martin-Pueyrredon-O'Higgins faction that ruled on both sides of the Andes. At the end of April, Alvear embarked on *La Celeste,* a French schooner bound for the River Plate. It was the same ship that a year earlier had taken many Bonapartist émigrés to Buenos Aires.[1]

Count Casa Florez, Spanish ambassador in Rio de Janeiro, became extremely concerned when he learned of Alvear's planned departure. Since Alvear was almost destitute, the count figured an enemy of Spain must have paid for his passage. For months, Casa Florez had tried to convince the exiled revolutionary leader to rejoin the cause of the king of Spain, particularly now that the news from Chile presaged the demise of the independence cause. Alvear had consistently refused these entreaties. To stop him from leaving Brazil, Casa Florez requested the help of the French consul, Colonel Maler, who months earlier had convinced the Portuguese authorities to arrest Latapie. It is unclear why Maler agreed to help Casa Florez as Alvear was not French and was not traveling to a French possession, and his passport had been issued by the Portuguese. In his reports to Richelieu he explained that Alvear was "immoral" and had pernicious ideas. Obviously, he was a potential ally of the Bonapartists.[2]

Maler ordered the captain of the French ship to remain anchored while he and Casa Florez interceded with the authorities to withdraw Alvear's passport.

The Portuguese government considered this a violation of its sovereignty and a diplomatic crisis ensued. The Portuguese foreign minister told Casa Florez that there was no reason to detain Alvear as there was no evidence linking him to any conspiracy. Latapie's case had been different, he said, as "he had arrived in accord with the rebels of Pernambuco to lead them in the insurrection and had a secret commission from Joseph Bonaparte to examine the viability of the project of freeing Napoleon."[3] On May 9, *La Celeste* finally put out to sea. The British consul in Rio de Janeiro noted that Alvear's departure "was not merely allowed, but forwarded" by the Portuguese authorities who erroneously considered him "devoted to the cause of Brazil." He wondered about "the secret of the precise object for which he has been so earnestly pressed to repair to the [River] Plate and so effectually enabled him to overcome the obstacles placed in the way of his sailing."[4]

Three weeks later, as Alvear disembarked in Montevideo, a new contingent of Napoleon's veterans led by General Philibert Fressinet arrived in Buenos Aires. It is not unlikely they were in the same ship. Fressinet was a hot-headed, temperamental man, who together with Lallemand in the aftermath of Waterloo had unsuccessfully tried to rally the French army to fight the Allied advance to Paris.[5] At his initiative, at the end of June, thirty generals signed a petition to the National Assembly swearing to defend the national honor to the last man. Davout disavowed the document and at a meeting at his office, he had to prevent Fressinet from having a fistfight with a royalist agent sent to negotiate the return of Louis XVIII. Fressinet's vehement opposition to the Bourbons would cost him dearly, but he remained devoted to the Bonapartist cause until his death. Forced into exile in Belgium, in the past two years his name had been linked to several Bonapartist conspiracies, including an attempt to kill Wellington.[6]

With Fressinet were Colonel Georges Jung and Major Jean Bulewski, two other hard-core Bonapartists.[7] Jung had led the Corps Francs de la Moselle that had slowed the advance of the Prussian army in the Lorraine region after the battle of Waterloo.[8] Bulewski was a Polish aristocrat who had served as aide-de-camp to the Duke of Bassano, Napoleon's foreign minister, and during the Hundred Days had served in the Polish Lancers.[9] Some of the recently arrived French émigrés lodged at an inn run by the wife of Captain Taylor, the American privateer, others at the house of Xaviera Carrera, Jose Miguel's sister. Fressinet and his comrades immediately established contact with the growing Bonapartist community in Buenos Aires, particularly with Captain Robert. A veteran of the Grande Armée, Robert had been close to Countess Regnault, and after her arrest in the spring of 1817 he had been forced to leave France. After arriving in Buenos Aires, Robert had launched a newspaper with another Bonapartist émigré named Jean Lagresse, who was related to none other than Elie Decazes, France's interior minister.[10] Robert and Lagresse were in regular contact with Carrera who, together with Alvear, plotted the downfall of the government in Buenos Aires.

Their hopes that a change in government would take place as a consequence of San Martin's recent defeat in Chile were quickly dashed. Instead of taking full advantage of their victory, the Spaniards instead waited for reinforcements. This allowed San Martin to regroup his forces and achieve a decisive victory at the battle of Maipu, which strengthened his grip on power on both sides of the Andes. Having regained the upper hand militarily and politically, the Argentine general cracked down on his enemies. When it came to politics, "neither calumny nor murder was out of bounds" for San Martin.[11] Like Machiavelli, he thought the end justified the means. Carrera and his foreign and local allies were too dangerous and could derail his grand plans. O'Higgins had already advised him to kill them all.[12]

The first victims were Juan Jose and Luis Carrera, who were executed after a sham trial.[13] Next on the list was Manuel Rodriguez, who was placed under arrest. The charges against him were of having "an intention to overthrow the government of O'Higgins," but as there was no trial, no evidence was ever presented. Instead, Rodriguez was deported, and when he was on his way into exile, one of his guards murdered him. The assassin later confessed that he had received orders "from several persons high in authority to dispatch Rodriguez in the manner described."[14] Rodriguez would become such an enduring legend in Chile that in the 1970s a Marxist guerrilla group fighting Pinochet's regime took his name.

San Martin and O'Higgins tried to distance themselves from the cold-blooded murders of Rodriguez and the Carrera brothers. According to the American consul in Buenos Aires nothing could "save their reputations from an indelible stain in the page of future history."[15] But historians have conveniently cleared them of any responsibility.[16] Not surprisingly, Commodore Bowles didn't think San Martin was to blame for anything, not because he was innocent but because the Carreras were "men with the most turbulent ambition" and such "decided enemies to the English that their downfall may be considered as peculiarly fortunate for us." Bowles reminded his government that during "our late war with America they permitted English vessels to be condemned and sold at Valparaiso . . . [and] were entirely directed by an agent from the United States named Poinsett, who resided at their headquarters and accompanied them in all their military operations."[17]

San Martin then turned his attention to Brayer. As he was a decorated general of Napoleon's Grande Armée and a former *pair* of France, murdering him was not an option. A subtler solution was necessary. Many capable French officers were still serving in the patriot army and San Martin needed them to accomplish his objective of reaching Lima. To avoid their suspicions or resistance he had to completely discredit Brayer. Days before the battle of Maipu, Brayer asked for the command of a division. San Martin refused and after a bitter verbal exchange, the French general left for Santiago.[18] This gave San Martin the perfect opportunity to ruin the obnoxious Frenchman. Soon a rumor spread around the camp that San Martin had summarily dismissed Brayer after telling him that he had "less honor than the lowliest drummer in the army."[19] News of Brayer's disgrace traveled fast. By late May the British consul in Rio de Janeiro, who had issued the warnings about Brayer's participation in a plot to rescue Napoleon, gleefully reported to Castlereagh the news of Brayer's "total disgrace." As a result, the diplomat added, the government of Buenos Aires had declared "that no more Frenchmen shall be received into his [*sic*] service as they have all turned out ill."[20]

After rendering such valuable services to his majesty's government, San Martin turned his attention to his monarchical projects. In a letter to Castlereagh he confidently stated that his recent victory had "decided the fate of South America"* and that he ardently wished "the termination of a war which while it utterly prevents this portion of America from prospering subverts the interests of the Spanish government by insensibly aggravating the mutual animosity of two belligerents." It was England that, having "acquired the immortal glory of having dispensed peace to the old world," could now gain "fresh laurels by extending the same benefit to the new."[21] Before leaving for Buenos Aires, San Martin assured Bowles that "the events of the late campaign far from exciting ideas of conquest or personal ambition have only proved to him more clearly the necessity of speedily pacifying South America." San Martin not only requested England's mediation but also "expressed the greatest anxiety to prevent if possible any revolution in Lima, which might occasion bloodshed and

---

* San Martin's assertion proved too optimistic; it would take the Chileans more than five years to expel the Spaniards from their territory. .

calamity."[22] By early May, San Martin was in Buenos Aires to plan with Pueyr-redon the establishment of a monarchy in South America. Despite being more powerful than ever, they worried about the presence of Carrera and Alvear in Montevideo, as both had many supporters in the army. And the links between Carrera and the Bonapartists were now evident.

Carrera and Alvear now had to adjust their plans. The Chilean had just received a discouraging letter from John Stuart Skinner, suggesting that now that he had "no power and no prospects" it would be very difficult to obtain support for his plans in the United States.[23] But Carrera had not lost all hopes. His Bonapartist allies in Buenos Aires plotted the downfall of the government at the houses of his sister Xaviera and of the botanist Aimé Bonpland. Their ranks grew every day. Among the latest arrivals was Marc-Antoine Mercher, one of the loyal officers who had escorted Napoleon from Malmaison to Rochefort and then to the *Bellerophon*. The British government had prevented him from going to St. Helena and instead had sent him to Malta with Lallemand. Mercher had followed Lallemand to Turkey but instead of going to the United States he had gone to Tehran and joined the Persian army. Obviously the Middle East was not the theater for the emperor's last campaign, and after less than a year, Mercher joined his former comrades in Buenos Aires. Led by General Fressinet, the Bonapartists prepared their next coup. They hoped that under Alvear and Carrera, it would be easier to set up a Bonapartist enclave in South America.

Napoleon Bonaparte on board the HMS
Bellerophon in Plymouth Bay, by Sir Charles
Eastlake, 1815.

Portrait of Joseph Bonaparte when
he was king of Sicily and Naples
(1806–1808).

Lord Thomas Cochrane (1775–1860).

Sir Robert T. Wilson (1777–1840), by Henry
William Pickersgill.

Michel Brayer (1769–1840).

Charles Lallemand (1774–1839).

Jose Miguel Carrera (1785–1821).

Jose de San Martin (1778–1850).

Robert Stewart, Lord Castlereagh (1769–1822).

Emmanuel, Marquis de Grouchy (1766–1847).

30
Farewell to England

His character has been much mistaken or there are few things that would
gratify him more than to become the liberator of Napoleon.
—*Courier,* London, September 18, 1818

In early May the *Courier* reported Gourgaud's arrival in London as a consequence of a quarrel with Montholon. The newspaper dismissed as "most ridiculous" certain rumors "that a secret correspondence had been detected at
St. Helena."[1] Interestingly, two days earlier Bathurst had warned Lowe that
"a clandestine correspondence to a considerable extent is carried on by the inhabitants of Longwood; and as there is little or no communication between
Buonaparte and any individual in the island, this evasion of your regulations
must be effected by the opportunities which Generals Bertrand and Montholon
and the servants of the establishment of Longwood enjoy of having frequent
intercourse not only with those who visit Longwood but with the other inhabitants of the island."[2]

Gourgaud's revelations proved what Bathurst already knew: Napoleon communicated clandestinely with his family and supporters "without the knowledge
or intervention of the government." Most of the couriers were Englishmen who
visited St. Helena and had "free access to the attendants or servants of Bonaparte
and were willing, many without any reward and others for a very small payment,
to convey to Europe any letter or packet entrusted to their charge." The captains and passengers of the East Indiamen were also "peculiarly open to the seduction of general Bonaparte's talents, so much so indeed that the inhabitants
of Longwood have regarded it as a matter of small difficulty to procure passage
on board one of these ships for General Bonaparte if escape should at any time
be his object." This communication network had been used for sending and
receiving letters, pamphlets, money, and "other articles of which the party in

Longwood might from time to time be in want." Gourgaud also talked about the plans of escape and said "that there was no difficulty in eluding at any time the vigilance of the sentries posted around the house and ground and in short that escape from the island appeared to him in no degree impracticable." Several escape plans had been proposed, but Napoleon "was so fully impressed with the opinion that he should be permitted to leave St. Helena either upon a change of ministry in England or by the unwillingness of the English to bear the expense of detaining him that he would not at present run the hazard to which an attempt at escape might expose him." Bathurst concluded that Napoleon looked to the time of evacuation of the Allied armies from France as the "most favorable for his return."[3] Gourgaud also said that Napoleon was in good health and that O'Meara's reports were misleading. This information led Bathurst, who until recently had supported keeping O'Meara as Napoleon's personal physician, to have him removed from St. Helena.[4] Many historians claim that by making this statement Gourgaud betrayed his master. On the other hand, if Napoleon wanted to sway public opinion in his favor due to his health, nothing could be better than to have the British government deprive him of his doctor.

After meeting with Bathurst's underlings, Gourgaud had a four-hour session with the Marquis of Osmond during which, after describing Napoleon's life at St. Helena, he asked for authorization to return to France. Osmond replied that if he wanted a pardon, he should at all costs avoid the company of Sir Robert Wilson, Lord Holland, and Lord Grey.[5] When he heard about Gourgaud's confession, Richelieu was skeptical. He couldn't determine whether his departure from St. Helena had been the result "of a disagreement with his master, a quarrel with the Montholons, or a means to send a messenger to Europe." Richelieu still believed that the Bonapartists were planning to invade Mexico, St. Helena, or both.[6] He asked Osmond to find out how Napoleon communicated with Europe, how he received money, and what kind of communications he had with Eugene de Beauharnais.[7] After reflecting on the matter for a few days, Richelieu asked Osmond to interrogate Gourgaud again to ascertain if Napoleon could really escape. "We cannot have a moment of tranquility and all our thoughts and efforts must be directed to the means of preventing the incalculable damage that could result from his escape from St. Helena," he told Osmond.[8] Maybe Richelieu had been listening to Madame Krudener, a famous seer who had recently announced that God had told her that Napoleon "had already quitted St. Helena or will soon leave it." This time, she said, he would "disturb the world with his private intrigues."[9]

Osmond had another interview with Gourgaud, who expressed no doubts about the success of an escape plan. When Osmond pointed out the many obstacles that had to be surmounted, Gourgaud replied: "Mr. Ambassador, nothing would be easier than that." Osmond was shocked. "Maybe in theory," he said. "No, in reality," insisted Gourgaud, "and in many different ways. Suppose for example that Napoleon hid in one of the barrels that come to Longwood filled with provisions every day and then are taken back to Jamestown without ever being inspected. Do you believe it would be impossible to find a captain of a ship who for a reward of a million would agree to put the barrel on board and sail away to America? I could indicate many other ways if my position did not require my silence." Besides, added Gourgaud, by now "a *coup* has been made or failed."[10]

Gourgaud had played the charade perfectly. Napoleon would never prefer to be a prisoner at St. Helena than "to be free in the United States" and would have never agreed to escape hidden in a barrel. He had refused to consider much less hazardous and more dignified escape plans. Years later, Gourgaud revealed that the British government "never knew about our true means of communication and even less of our plans of escape." His disclosures to Osmond and Bathurst, as well as those made to Sturmer and Lowe at St. Helena, seem to have been part of his efforts to disguise his secret mission. To negotiate from a position of strength, Napoleon had to show that he could leave St. Helena whenever he wanted. By not doing so, he was acting responsibly and therefore expected reciprocity from the Allied powers. If he didn't get it, he could always resort to force.

The problem was that the most serious plan to rescue Napoleon was discovered at this time. Renovales had revealed to the Duke of San Carlos, the Spanish ambassador in London, that Cochrane, Wilson, and MacGregor were "in negotiations with the agents of the insurgents to join their cause."[11] San Carlos worried that Buenos Aires had become "the rallying point for all the adventurers that are seeking the evasion of Napoleon from St. Helena."[12] He warned Castlereagh, who remained unconcerned. With San Martin in power in Buenos Aires and Santiago, England had nothing to worry about. San Carlos asked Castlereagh to pass a foreign enlistment act to prevent any British subjects from enlisting in the armies of the South American insurgents. The end of the Napoleonic wars had left large numbers of unemployed British army and navy officers who were seeking new ways to gain fame, fortune, and glory. South America seemed the right place to get them.[13] Castlereagh did nothing, and hundreds of officers on half-pay joined the armies of Simon Bolivar, who was very friendly to England.

Richelieu shared San Carlos's concerns and also worried about the possibility of a war between Spain and the United States, which he thought would benefit the Bonapartists. His solution was for Spain to cede Florida to the Americans and in exchange the Americans would not oppose his monarchical project for Buenos Aires. As for Gourgaud, after reading the details of his conversation with Osmond, Richelieu no longer thought he was a fanatical Bonapartist. Maybe he was too much of a raconteur and this had inspired him to disclose so many details about the possibility of Napoleon's escape. If Gourgaud's testimony was true and escape was so easy, why hadn't Napoleon attempted it yet? Was he trying "to prolong his stay to excite interest" about his plight in Europe? Richelieu did not give any credence to rumors of an attack of the island. But he was "afraid of an escape, not necessarily aided by the English government, but in which a man shrewder than all of us will dupe it."[14] Gourgaud had said a coup had already taken place or was imminent. Richelieu was convinced that Napoleon's illness was faked and that it was part of an intrigue.[15] He insisted that Lowe should take every precaution at St. Helena, including checking any "empty barrels" leaving Longwood.[16]

In London, Napoleon was news every day. In mid-June a newspaper reported that a sailor of an East Indiaman had met Napoleon without obeying Lowe's regulations, demonstrating "the possibility of Bonaparte's escape on board of any English vessel, the captain of which might be inclined for a bribe, or otherwise, to convey him to Europe or America." Apparently, several such occurrences had recently taken place at St. Helena, inducing Lowe "to declare to the government, that if vessels are allowed to come to that island as at present, he cannot answer for the security of his prisoner."[17]

Meanwhile, Gourgaud continued his rounds of meetings. Among the people he met was Lewis Goldsmith, editor of the *British Monitor* (formerly the *Anti-Gallican*).[18] He also had an interview with Prince Lieven, the Russian ambassador, who completely believed the "official" story behind his departure from Longwood.[19] Lieven shared the information with Osmond, who every day grew more skeptical about Gourgaud's sincerity. At the end of May, Osmond warned Richelieu that the terms in which Gourgaud "expressed himself toward Count Lieven are not consistent with those of the submission that he showed me. It seems as if his plan is to join Eugene if we make it difficult for him to return to France." In fact, Gourgaud had already sent a secret message to Eugene.[20] Also, unknown to Osmond and against his advice, Gourgaud had secretly met with Wilson and also with Colonel Latapie, the leader of the failed expedition to Pernambuco, who was now in London after having escaped his captors. Latapie told Gourgaud that Lallemand had raised an army of two thousand men and that Joseph "would be well received in Mexico."[21]

Richelieu was greatly alarmed at "the intended expedition of Lallemand."[22] He was also concerned about Wilson's election to Parliament, as he was "an ardent enemy of the order existing today in France."[23] He asked Osmond to watch his movements. But Osmond's spies failed to observe the contacts between Wilson, Gourgaud, and William Balcombe. It was the latter who told Wilson that Napoleon "was very ill, with swelled legs and that his eyes were much sunk," and that Lowe's treatment of him was "infamous."[24] Something had to be done, quickly.

In early June, Lord Cochrane made a speech in Parliament in favor of parliamentary reform. In his speech, a "mighty pathetic oration" according to the *Courier,* he thanked his Westminster constituents who had "rescued him from a desperate and wicked conspiracy which has nearly involved me in total ruin." Cochrane also warned the Tory ministers to abandon their reactionary policies before they plunged the country into revolution.[25] In the past eighteen months real and imaginary fears of conspiracies had allowed the government to pass the most repressive legislation seen in the country since the time of the Stuarts. Cochrane, who felt that under the Tories the threats to civil liberties were dire, was making his farewell speech to the House of Commons. He didn't plan to return.[26] A few days after this speech, Cochrane attended a secret meeting with MacGregor, Brown, Renovales, and representatives of the South American rebels. It was agreed that Renovales would sail to New Orleans to join the expedition against Mexico, and Brown would go to Buenos Aires. MacGregor would follow soon after with a small squadron and a thousand men and would join Renovales. Cochrane would sail to Chile at the end of July with many British officers and two ships, "a beautiful one with 35 cannons and propelled by steam." Cochrane would attack Acapulco to distract the Spaniards while Lallemand attacked from the north and Renovales landed at Vera Cruz.[27]

Although Cochrane tried to disguise his intentions by naming his steamship the *North Star* and claiming he was bound for the North Pole, many suspected he had different plans. "His Lordship has a little tendency to stratagem. . . . His present vessel will never approach the North Sea, for she has not been doubled. Why there is so much in her ornaments relative to the North

Pole, we have not heard, nor what is her real destination. She is pierced for ten guns and has eight mounted," reported the *Naval Register*.[28] Richelieu believed the Bonapartists had financed the construction of Cochrane's ship.[29] What if he was connected with the French generals exiled in America? According to reports from the United States, Lallemand was already in Mexico, and his assertions that he intended "to cultivate the soil and remain in peace are now altogether discredited."[30] Coincidentally, the Bonaparte family had just requested permission to send a priest to St. Helena to attend to Napoleon's spiritual needs. Osmond thought it was just an excuse to send an emissary well informed of "plots in Europe and America." If it was true that Joseph had given Lallemand $2 million, as had been reported, it would be necessary to redouble the vigilance at St. Helena. "Fortunately, I believe this is what has been prescribed to Sir Hudson Lowe," he informed Richelieu.[31]

San Carlos had exceeded his instructions when negotiating with Renovales, but he believed the means justified the end. The protests he had sent to Castlereagh had achieved nothing, and everything made him fear new disasters for Spain "condoned and supported by England's public opinion." Renovales had agreed to get paid only if the expedition against Mexico was actually derailed. As part of the agreement, the renegade Spaniard not only promised to publish a manifest denouncing the insurgents and their foreign supporters, but also endeavored to persuade the French émigrés to abandon any projects against the Spanish crown. In early July, San Carlos confidently reported the results of his negotiations to the court of Madrid, including a detailed description of the plan to liberate Mexico. Renovales had been given command of an army of three thousand men that would leave shortly for New Orleans. MacGregor would follow him weeks later with another thousand men. While Lallemand attacked from the north, Renovales and MacGregor would join forces somewhere in the Caribbean and then strike at the port of Vera Cruz. Wilson and Cochrane would focus their efforts on the Pacific coast of South America. Together they expected to liberate all the Spanish colonies, from Mexico to Peru. The information provided by Renovales was confirmed by another of San Carlos's spies, a French renegade who had infiltrated the conspirators and had heard MacGregor boast that he would "soon lead an expedition which will disembark in Cartagena" with Maceroni as his chief of staff and that he would meet Cochrane at "the Isthmus of Darien in the Pacific Ocean."

In a dispatch to Madrid, San Carlos explained that by separating one of the chiefs "that would lead the land forces, at the same time whoever manned the ships would be left without objective, protection or resources" and by intercepting the "ships and weapons that they carry" the expedition to Mexico would be completely derailed. MacGregor would be stranded and "far away from it where its facilitators remain, without means to replace the loss of Renovales, will not be able to continue or attempt anything that would not lead him to complete ruin and our victory." Meanwhile, Cochrane and Brown, still confident in their two colleagues, would go ahead with the plan, "unaware that their attacks are expected everywhere."[32] It would be a miracle if they succeeded.

In late July, unaware that Renovales had betrayed him, Cochrane left London, traveled to the coast, and surreptitiously boarded a fishing boat that took him to Boulogne with his wife. His sudden departure caused much anxiety on both sides of the Channel. Richelieu had no doubt about Cochrane's objectives and tried to convince London and Madrid of the advantages of establishing independent monarchies in the Spanish colonies to neutralize the designs of the Bonapartists. Time was of the essence, as Richelieu feared "strong attacks in Parliament regarding the treatment of Buonaparte."[33] If the British government surrendered to these pressures and Napoleon was released, a political earthquake would take place on both sides of the Atlantic. Richelieu asked Osmond to sound Castlereagh out about his monarchical scheme. The reply was encouraging. The foreign secretary "was aware of the dangers that the establishment of a republic in the New World would entail for Europe" and thought that the idea "of a Spanish Prince in Buenos Aires could soften the bitterness of a sacrifice difficult to obtain from Spain." Osmond reported that Castlereagh was well disposed "to support the step which you have already made with Madrid."[34]

Napoleon's least movement at St. Helena was carefully watched. To the chagrin of the Tory ministry, O'Meara's articles in the *Morning Chronicle* regarding Napoleon's declining health and imminent death had produced "some effect on the public mind."[35] But the ministers were more worried about O'Meara's unpublished accusations. On his return from St. Helena, the doctor had confided to several people that his removal from Longwood "was the precursor of Bonaparte's death either by poison or from want of proper medical advice." O'Meara had said that if he "had attended to all that the Governor wished, Bonaparte would not have been alive at this moment and I should now be in great favor. . . . Poor fellow, he has been taking calomel* these last six weeks for

---

*O'Meara mentioned calomel as the favored treatment to deal with Napoleon's liver sickness as early as mid-1818.

the liver complaint, and when I left him, he said there was no doubt my removal was a prelude to assassination."[36] O'Meara told Wilson that Lowe had "wished him to connive at the death of Napoleon" and that all the foreign commissioners at St. Helena were convinced "such was his object." Not surprisingly, Wilson encouraged the doctor to disclose everything that was happening at Longwood. O'Meara replied that although he had had "various offers to leave the country" he was determined to stay and "do his duty." He also gave Wilson an important message from Napoleon. First, the tsar had "shown much feeling" and written Balmain a letter in his own hand asking him "to pass every respect" to the exiled emperor. Second, Napoleon's political hopes in Europe rested on the accession of his son to the throne of France.[37] Somehow, these hopes were also known in Paris and Vienna. Through his ambassador in London, Metternich learned that "Goldsmith, Beaumont [de Brivazac] and all the agents who arrived in London indoctrinated by Count Decazes" were spreading the rumor that Napoleon had 50 million francs in Vienna for the coronation of his son.[38]

After meeting with O'Meara, Wilson met again with Gourgaud, who was ready to publish an account of the battle of Waterloo that Wilson considered "comprehensive, impartial and . . . very useful." He did not believe the French general was a turncoat; he believed his conduct had been "very noble" and would "conciliate the good will of all who were prejudiced against him by vague or vicious reports." Gourgaud was "a very intelligent man, full of fire" and, Wilson had no doubt, "a complete fire-eater in the field of battle."[39] Gourgaud would be valuable in the campaign that was about to begin. According to the *Courier,* Joseph had sent "16,000 invitations individually to Frenchmen residing in France to join him in America."[40] On August 15—Napoleon's birthday—Lord Cochrane boarded the *Rose,* a ship owned by his friend Edward Ellice, and put out to sea, supposedly bound for South America. One of his companions was Henry Cobbett, a nephew of William Cobbett and a Royal Navy veteran.* On the day of Cochrane's departure, the *Journal des Débats* published a lengthy report on the affairs of South America, confirming that his arrival in Chile or Buenos Aires "was expected very soon."[41]

In London, San Carlos learned through one of his spies that Cochrane had a close relationship with "the leaders of the Bonapartist party" and that he was contemplating Napoleon's liberation. According to the informer:

---

*While serving under Cochrane, Henry Cobbett became close friends with Frederick Marryat, who, although he did not accompany Cochrane to South America, was later posted to St. Helena and brought news of Napoleon's death back to England.

If we are to believe what General Gourgaud has said, and it is almost the only thing that he said, nothing would be easier to Buonaparte than escaping if he wanted, the opinion of many people is always that General Gourgaud talks about a facility of escaping that doesn't exist in order to create some anxiety about the security of the prison of St. Helena and maybe to influence by this the decision to transfer Napoleon to another point. I share this opinion because what Santini, Warden and Piontkowski told me does not at all agree with the opinion that M. Gourgaud deliberately wants to convey. The rescue of Napoleon is not easy by subterfuge or by surprise and it is impossible by *vive force*. If that is the objective of Lord Cochrane, he will do it as an accessory to the grand enterprise. He could try on his way, particularly if he touches St. Helena under the British colors, in case he fails he would go to Chile where two expeditions await his reinforcement, one directed to the Isthmus of Darien, and the other for the Philippines, this last one is unknown in London at present. I learned from the major general of MacGregor's expedition [Maceroni] that part of his men would cross the Isthmus of Panama and embark on the ships coming from Chile for the expedition to the Philippines.

San Carlos also learned that Cochrane's steamboat could not sail due to problems with its engine. Cochrane apparently hoped that these problems would be fixed soon, as he had told MacGregor that he would meet him at the Isthmus of Panama with the *Rising Star*.[42] Richelieu was relieved when he learned the steamboat had not followed Cochrane to South America.[43] The *Rising Star* would remain docked on the Thames for almost three years even though she was ready to sail.[44]

In Frankfurt, Las Cases met with William Balcombe, who brought letters from Longwood. Bertrand assured him that Balcombe was trustworthy and could be used as a messenger. His message was clear: Napoleon was suffering from hepatitis, "a fatal disease in this unhealthy climate." If he remained in St. Helena, he would die soon.[45] Las Cases wrote to Joseph that communications with St. Helena were open. Undoubtedly something was afoot. "What one's imagination and the heart can suggest as being feasible has been, is, or will be attempted. Unfortunately up to now most efforts have been fruitless," Las Cases wrote. "Your Majesty's wisdom perfectly judged the consequences that could result from following certain risky speculations. . . . The Emperor often thought that the numerous Frenchmen in your neighborhood would not fail to

employ their known talents to fight alone or jointly the calumnies of our enemies against the great cause that triumphed here for so long."[46]

Among the Frenchmen still in Joseph's neighborhood were Pierre Real, Napoleon's former chief of police, the Lallemands, Lefebvre-Desnouettes and
Clausel, who hadn't abandoned hopes of setting the emperor free and continued
to fight for his cause. They also counted on Wilson. Despite the upcoming parliamentary elections, he was still thinking of joining the campaign. Richelieu
had no doubt that Wilson and Lallemand were planning to liberate Napoleon
and take him to America. Castlereagh would let the situation in the Spanish
colonies deteriorate for England's benefit but the political stability of Europe
required immediate measures. "I don't need more proof of the dangers that we
face [from] the community of interest that has been established among the revolutionaries everywhere and the insurgents in the Americas," Richelieu wrote to
his ambassador in Madrid. Ferdinand VII would never recover his colonies, particularly Buenos Aires, so it would be better if he reached an agreement with his
rebellious subjects and gave them a monarchy under a Bourbon prince. In this
way, Richelieu argued, Spain would neutralize "the most powerful and best organized" enemy she had ever faced: the Bonaparte family.[47]

By the fall of 1818, and probably for the first time, the British government
expressed concern about plans to rescue Napoleon. In early September the *Courier* reported that Lallemand was ready to invade Mexico at the head of five
thousand men and speculated whether this "force may be ultimately employed
in an attempt (fruitless we are sure it would be) to release Buonaparte."[48] A few
days later, the newspaper made an even more shocking revelation: Cochrane
planned to use his steamboat to rescue Napoleon. The well-informed article
noted that most of the British cruisers guarding St. Helena were anchored off
Jamestown, on the leeward side of the island, but the best landing places were
on the windward side, which was guarded by only two cutters. This was where
"seafaring men" thought Napoleon's escape had a better chance of success:

> The most practical chance they think would be for a strong cutter or two
> well appointed with oars to approach the windward side, beat off the cut-
> ters, take and row away with Buonaparte, their prize, to a large ship at
> some distance, perhaps out of sight of the island, which might convey
> him to his destination. A steamboat can approach the island on every
> side, its mechanical movement supplying the place of oars, and after tak-
> ing away Buonaparte, being large and heavily armed, it might beat off

any cutters. It might then work up to a large vessel to windward to deliver its prize, or it might itself convey away Buonaparte wholly. The power of going against the wind and tide would in those seas be a great protection against the King's ships and moving as it does without sails it would not easily be discovered at sea. Experienced nautical men, who have had an opportunity of inspecting the steam vessel of Lord Cochrane, have been struck with its remarkable adaptation for navigating upon such a coast as the windward side of St. Helena.

One ship alone—even one powered by steam—would not be enough to subdue the British garrison guarding St. Helena. To succeed, the rescuers would need overwhelming land forces. The *Courier* suggested it was "something more than mere speculation" that Cochrane and Lallemand were acting in unison:

> With respect to warlike means, the recent union of the Buonapartists in the province of Texas on the Trinity River may probably supply resources, long since contemplated, and which could not have been so available had these exiles remained contented with the grants of land made to them by Congress in the Alabama territory. As a naval officer, Lord Cochrane never showed himself deficient in enterprise, and to his natural ardor is now added the excitement of desperate fortunes. His character has been much mistaken or there are few things that would gratify him more than to become the liberator of Napoleon. The bare attempt, indeed, would seal his future destiny. If he succeeded, his fate would be linked with that of Buonaparte. If he failed, he might still become an insurgent admiral. He has nothing to lose in England; everything to gain out of it. Just such a man—one so completely with the world before him would be required for the hazardous and daring enterprise. But it is said he is going to Chile. Be it so. It will not be much out of his way to call at St. Helena.[49]

The *Globe* gave credence to the report and noted that Cochrane had "given repeated proofs of an enterprising spirit and of determined valor, and it is not impossible that his ideas of humanity might induce him to employ these high qualities in an attempt to restore to freedom one whom he might consider as unworthily treated."[50]

Lallemand Charges Again

It was certainly a fine conception, that of conquering Texas with the remains of the Imperial Army.

—Honoré de Balzac, *Les Celibataires*

By midsummer American public opinion had turned against the projects of the French émigrés, particularly as rumors spread that they had sold the land given to them by Congress in Alabama to finance them. A "splendid foolery" was how the *Weekly Register* described the land grant. According to the influential Baltimore newspaper the Lallemands had "seized upon a part of the province of Texas, which is claimed by the United States as a part of Louisiana, as purchased of France and as ceded to France by Spain."[1]

Hyde de Neuville was particularly pleased by this change in public opinion and informed Richelieu that the newspapers criticized "the Lallemands for their ungratefulness towards the United States for having sold the property in Alabama." On the other hand, they absolved Joseph of any blame.[2] Secretary of State John Quincy Adams was also pleased by the reaction of the media. He warned his friend Peter Paul De Grand that although Lallemand's intentions were "still very ambiguously and imperfectly disclosed, we now see enough of them to perceive that they are incompatible with the laws and the rights of the United States. They will know that the spot upon which they have made their lodgment belongs to the United States and the purpose to which general Lallemand has turned the grant of Congress on the Tombigbee has given such disgust to the people of this country that there is a general sentiment of indignation against him. I hope you have carefully avoided any speculation of property upon this project." Adams also said that the rumors that Spain had ceded Florida to the United States were "without foundation."[3] In truth, the negotiations with Onís had already started and Adams not only asked for Florida but to extend Louisiana's western border to the Sabine River in Texas.

Despite all the obstacles it faced, the project to rescue Napoleon "existed in the head and in the hearts of some individuals," reported the French consul in Philadelphia. He pointed out that Joseph and a daring American privateer were much more dangerous than any band of hot-headed Bonapartists. "The former can provide the money, and the latter the boldness needed for such an enterprise. One has to wonder that if the former has not tried whether it is because he considers success as impossible?"[4]

By rendering Lallemand's enterprise illegal, Congress had dealt him a serious blow. Sensing a mounting opposition to his plans in Washington, in early July he justified his actions in a letter to Girard: "Who could dispute our right to establish the settlement that we have begun? The Spanish government? Has it not, I repeat, abandoned its claim to this country by forcing Spanish subjects to evacuate it?" As to the Americans, they claimed ownership of this land "because it has formed part of a vast territory which has been ceded to the United States by the French government," more specifically by Napoleon. "The United States government, while claiming this territory, does not occupy it. This government has principles too sound and equitable to wish that under these circumstances a company of men worn out by adversity, be deprived of the right of coming to this country, breathing the air that enlivens it and seeking the peace which it offers. . . . If an attempt to oppress us is made, we are resolved to resist. We will maintain peace as long as we are not disturbed, but if we are attacked we will defend ourselves. . . . If the Spanish Government attacks us or attempts to remove us from this country, we shall be forced to call to its attention the fact that the land does not belong to it, that it was discovered by Frenchmen, that Frenchmen were the first to take possession of it."[5]

Lallemand had a chance to back up his boast much earlier than expected. In mid-July the Spanish governor of San Antonio, who had been forewarned by Onís, marched to the Champ d'Asile at the head of a substantial army. The governor issued an ultimatum to Lallemand, ordering the immediate evacuation of Spanish territory. Despite his numerical inferiority—he could muster 150 men at most—Lallemand was prepared to defend his camp to the last man. However, instead of attacking, the Spaniards blockaded the Champ d'Asile. Lallemand soon realized that he was in an impossible position. Lack of supplies made a defensive strategy unadvisable. On the other hand, attacking the Spaniards would be suicidal. Lallemand concluded that a strategic retreat was his best option. Once Henri sent him additional reinforcements, he would teach the Spaniards a lesson. In mid-July he embarked his men on a few boats and rowed down to Galveston.

But Galveston proved as inhospitable as the dry plains of Texas. If the Laffites had any intention of destroying Lallemand, as they had promised Onis, this would have been the perfect opportunity to do so. Faced with unusually hot weather, the situation of the French émigrés became desperate. Dysentery, fever, and other diseases wreaked havoc among the troops and hurt morale. Lallemand's "strength and courage seemed to increase in proportion as our resources diminished and imbued every one with a confidence and hopes which he could not himself have," wrote one of the suffering veterans.[6] As the weeks passed and no provisions or reinforcements arrived, Lallemand convened a council of his senior officers where it was decided that he should return to New Orleans to obtain the means necessary to continue the campaign. During his absence, Rigaud would be in command of the troops.

It was at this time, the end of August, that George Graham, Monroe's envoy, arrived in Galveston. Graham was quite surprised to see Lallemand, who in turn was quite embarrassed to be seen in the company of Jean Laffite. But the French general soon recovered his haughtiness and told Graham that he was determined to fight the Spaniards and showed him a declaration of war that he intended to publish that same day. Lallemand explained that he had made a treaty with the rebel Congress of Mexico and that he planned to "direct his operations against the Spaniards in the four internal provinces." The Champ d'Asile had been simply a depot and base to attack San Antonio, the capital of Texas. Lallemand assured Graham that although he had only a few men at Galveston, "there were a number of Frenchmen in different parts of the country who were ready to join whenever their active services were required." British and American merchants would supply everything they needed in exchange for special trading privileges granted by the new government, "which were to be allowed to none others except to the merchants of the nation which should first acknowledge the independence of Mexico." Lallemand asserted that he had no connection with Laffite's privateering activities.

Graham realized that in the current circumstances a declaration of war by Lallemand could have some very unfavorable consequences for the United States and persuaded him to postpone the decision. Although he could not condone the occupation of Galveston, he told Lallemand he would recommend such measure to Monroe and that "if any of his followers chose to remain for the purpose of cultivating the soil, I did not presume that the government would remove them." He also gave the French general a letter of introduction to General Ripley of the U.S. army who was based in New Orleans.[7] Graham wasn't simply giving Lallemand a tacit encouragement. He also promised him and Laffite "the greatest advantages, both political and pecuniary, offering them all sorts of assistance in order that they should extend their occupancy not only on the Trinity region but also as far as the Rio Grande, but on condition that after occupying these regions they should put them at the disposal of the United States in order that the country thus occupied might be made an integral part of the Union." Lallemand agreed to everything and sent an aide-de-camp back to Philadelphia "to arrange these matters."[8] He then embarked for New Orleans.

By mid-September the French consul in New Orleans reported that Lallemand had arrived but "nothing still transpired of the motive for this unexpected journey." The French émigrés were up to something. "Clausel had just left in all haste to Mobile on his way to New York, whereas the young Grouchy embarked here for Nantes. I have been assured that Lefebvre-Desnouettes had also left for Tombigbee." Lallemand's projects were "not totally knocked down." Aury and Cochrane, "with the ground and sea forces they have under their command, are, we are told, to join their efforts to those of the ex-generals Lallemand and jointly attempt a simultaneous attack on several points of the coast of Mexico." Everything augured "an imminent action in one theater or another (either Mexico or St. Helena) with the forces which they are now working to gather."[9]

Days later, French agents in New Orleans confirmed that Lallemand had adopted the title of captain general of the internal provinces of Mexico and was coordinating a new campaign with General Renovales, who had just arrived from London. The Bonapartists did not appear "to have abandoned their project" but on the contrary, "they take charge of its execution with more activity than ever." And it seemed that the government of the United States was "not foreign to their plan."[10] Renovales was determined to fulfill the agreement he had reached with the Duke of San Carlos in London to derail the plans of Cochrane, MacGregor, and Lallemand. "With my separation not only everything is destroyed but also whoever is left will not be in a position to gather his forces or to meditate another enterprise without this one having been consumed on its own without any success," he had assured San Carlos.[11] Renovales disclosed everything he knew to the Spanish consul in New Orleans: MacGregor would soon leave England with three ships carrying eight hundred men, muskets, and ammunition; Cochrane would embark "on his frigate *North Pole,* which is not for the northern Pole, but to Chile," Wilson would remain in London for a few months recruiting men and would eventually follow Cochrane to Chile, and Brown would go to the Pacific on another frigate.[12] Renovales explained how he could derail the plans of Lallemand:

> I am in direct communication with the troops of general Lallemand in Galveston. I am being approached by his top officers who offered their services to me and with my guarantee will leave Lallemand, who is here and will remain for five weeks. General Rigaud, with whom I am in agreement, has remained in command, and he believes that I will participate in the conquest of Mexico, they are waiting for me to show up with some forces. In consequence and in fulfillment of my duties, I must tell you that if you want to take advantage of this opportunity and avoid the results of Amelia and Pensacola, or worse, it is in my power to make them all prisoners, including the pirates and their ships.[13]

Meanwhile at Galveston, Lallemand's expedition faced even greater troubles. All the men had "the greatest respect for General Rigaud," but the departure of their leader had hurt morale.[14] As if this was not bad enough, a violent three-day hurricane hit the Texas coast and pummeled Galveston. "The sea burst its confines and inundated the island, rushing into camp and dwellings, submerging everything." Most of Laffite's ships sank and Rigaud's camp was wiped out. It seemed as if nature had taken sides against the Bonapartists. Galveston "was a picture of nature's destruction when her laws seemed to have gone awry."[15] Exhausted and without provisions, Rigaud tried to lift his men's spirits: "Well my friends, victory which remained faithful to our flag triumphed over all difficulties and the enemy armies disappeared like thin mist before our invincible phalanxes. Success will crown our efforts." But as the days passed, the situation worsened and the brave general was forced to order a full evacuation to New Orleans. Rigaud marched by land with some of his troops while others embarked with General Humbert on a vessel provided by Laffite.[16]

In early October, the French consul in New Orleans reported that at Galveston everything was "in confusion." "A hurricane had destroyed the vessels and establishments of the adventurers. Since the departure of their leader there is no more discipline and a lot of discouragement and discontent." One man named Durand had a fight with Lallemand and was "getting ready to leave him and go to Buenos Aires."[17] Weeks later, Spanish troops completely destroyed the

Champ d'Asile. To make matters worse, in New Orleans, Renovales succeeded in bribing many members of Lallemand's expedition and convinced them to desist from further attempts to invade Mexico.[18] But Renovales's treachery also went awry. On October 20, a manifesto he had addressed to Ferdinand VII disavowing the cause of independence and asking for a royal pardon was published by a newspaper in New Orleans.

Back in Washington, Graham reported the results of his mission to Adams, who was dismayed to learn that while at Galveston he "had a sort of negotiation" with Lallemand and Lafitte, which "did not exactly tally with my ideas of right, and they were altogether unauthorized." The secretary of state was particularly mortified because Graham had advised Lafitte to obtain a privateering patent from Buenos Aires and had given him a letter for David DeForest "to assist him in obtaining one, and that Laffite took his advice, and immediately dispatched a man to New York for that purpose." The involvement of DeForest, one of the most active outfitters of privateers and the newly appointed consul of Buenos Aires in the United States, added a new dimension to the intrigue. How this successful entrepreneur and follower of Thomas Paine's ideas got involved with Lallemand and Laffite is unclear. But DeForest had links to the Bonapartists and, as we shall see, to an attempt to rescue Napoleon from St. Helena.

Adams disapproved of Graham's negotiations with Lallemand and Laffite because he believed, wrongly as it turned out, that they complicated his own negotiations with Onis. The Spanish ambassador in turn doubted Adams's good faith as he suspected that an American naval squadron was sailing toward the Gulf of Mexico to aid Lallemand. Onis believed that Galveston would be a replay of Amelia Island, and he sent Colonel Galabert to Cuba to "help us to derail all the expeditions of the Frenchmen."[19] With news from New Orleans delayed by almost a month, Onis did not know that Lallemand was in serious trouble. To make matters worse, the divisions among the French émigrés had deepened. Henri Lallemand apparently disapproved of the conduct of his brother toward Galabert. Grouchy was furious at Gourgaud for publishing an account of the battle of Waterloo in which Grouchy was blamed for Napoleon's defeat. The marshal claimed never to have heard a word of reproach from Napoleon. Gourgaud had written a distorted version of the battle relying on "imaginary movements," "alleged orders," and "artificially woven calumnies."[20] Was it a way to punish Grouchy for not supporting Lallemand?

By the end of the year Onis was convinced that it was no longer Joseph whom Spain had to fear but the United States, which he suspected of secretly supporting a new expedition to Mexico. He reached this conclusion after he learned about the proposals Graham had made to Lallemand and Laffite at Galveston, which he learned about through Pierre Laffite.[21] Under the new plan, the Laffites, Aury, and Lallemand were to join forces to defend Galveston and occupy several points along the Texas coast from Galveston to the Rio Grande. American troops would then evict the illegal settlers and take possession of these points, as they had done at Amelia Island. It is hard to know whether this plan was real or whether it was invented by Pierre Laffite to take money from Onis or by Monroe to soften Onis' stance in the negotiations. What is certain is that Graham's proposals to Lallemand and Laffite threatened the territorial integrity of the Spanish empire.

Adams had another lever with which to pressure Onis. At this time the administration was facing a new offensive by Clay to recognize the independence of Buenos Aires. Adams believed that Clay's intention was to "push the Executive, if possible, into a quarrel with Spain" as a means of bringing the United States "into the Spanish colonial conflict on the side of the revolutionaries." Adams found an unexpected ally in Joel Roberts Poinsett who, disgusted by the manner in which Carrera had been treated, strongly advised against recognition. In a letter to Adams, Poinsett explained that "the present party in power" was composed of "corrupt and interested men." According to Poinsett, a change of government was imminent in Buenos Aires, so a delay in recognition was warranted. "Don Carlos Alvear is now in Montevideo and his partisans are numerous in Buenos Aires. . . . Carrera too is in Montevideo and breathes vengeance against the murderers of his brothers; he is active, daring and intelligent and has a powerful party in Chile."[22] Poinsett believed that recognizing Buenos Aires in the current circumstances would be a mistake, as it would strengthen the hand of Pueyrredon and San Martin.

As the year ended, Adams called Hyde de Neuville to discuss the status of the negotiations with Spain. The French ambassador, who acted as a mediator, said Onis had one condition: nonrecognition of Buenos Aires' independence. Hyde de Neuville asked Adams whether "the United States would give a pledge not to precipitate measures concerning South America" if Madrid agreed to sign a treaty. Getting more territory from Spain in exchange for delaying the recognition seemed like a good deal to Adams, who agreed. As to the rest of the colonies, "if Spain should come to terms with us, we would force nothing in South America by premature recognitions." However, Adams said that he could give no guarantees and "would never admit" to a connection between the two issues.

Meanwhile, although by mid-December the *National Intelligencer* reported that "Lallemand's military establishment in the Spanish province of Texas has been broken up." Onis was informed, incorrectly as it turns out, that Cochrane's squadron was near the island of Margarita.[23] The Spanish ambassador feared that Cochrane and MacGregor would jointly attack the Spanish possessions in Venezuela. He believed Cochrane planned to sail up the Orinoco River and cross over to Colombia while MacGregor attacked the fort of Portobello at the Isthmus of Panama and then marched across to the Pacific Ocean. If they succeeded, the Spanish empire in America would be split in two. Onis was convinced that the British government secretly supported Cochrane and MacGregor.[24] A report from New Orleans suggested that the Americans would try to use these British forces for their own purposes and attract Aury and Laffite, who would be "at the head of the enterprise." Once again, Pierre Laffite promised Onis to destroy in a single blow the plans of "all these adventurers" because "he loved his country."[25] We shall never know what kind of game Pierre was playing, but at the end of December he secretly met with David DeForest in Washington. There was a new plan under way and DeForest was convinced that the U.S. government would support him and his fellow conspirators.[26] The involvement of Graham, DeForest, and Laffite in this intrigue remains one of the murkiest episodes of the foreign policy of the Monroe administration. Whatever it was, it strengthened Adams's position in the negotiations with Onis.

Rumors about Lallemand's new plan to invade Mexico coincided with raids on the coast of Southern California by a Buenos Aires privateer sailing under the command of a Frenchman named Bouchard. The privateer had left Buenos Aires on an eastbound cruise in June in 1817 and had passed close to St. Helena. During the trip Bouchard told one of his officers that he was considering a plan to rescue Napoleon. He later abandoned the idea but his raids in California have always puzzled historians.[27] It is impossible to tell whether these raids were connected in any way with Lallemand, but the determined French general had not given up yet. At the end of the year, he obtained his American citizenship.[28] For someone as patriotically French as Lallemand this decision could serve only one purpose: to lead an invasion of Mexico under the U.S. flag. By late December the *New York Evening Post* reported that it was probable that Lallemand "will now direct his course into the interior of Mexico."[29]

A Bourbon King in Buenos Aires?

Buenos Aires, also, more than any other of the South American provinces, has been the theatre of foreign European intrigues.

—John Quincy Adams, 1823

By mid-1818 the Bonapartist émigrés in Buenos Aires were plotting a new offensive. Led by General Fressinet, they met regularly at the house of Aimé Bonpland, Malmaison's former botanist. So strident were the rantings of the émigrés that in July the government warned Bonpland about the "scandalous meetings taking place in his house" and expressed its "displeasure" at the conduct of his wife, Adeline, an ardent Bonapartist.[1] This warning, stricter police surveillance, and the arrest of a few opposition figures forced the conspirators to change tack. Major Bulewski left for Chile with messages for his comrades serving in the patriot army, while Jung, Mercher, Robert, and Lagresse traveled to Montevideo to coordinate their plans with Alvear and Carrera.

The time was ripe for a coup. Commodore Bowles, chief of the British naval station in Buenos Aires, believed that the fall of Supreme Director Pueyrredon, an ally of San Martin, was "almost certain" due to his growing unpopularity. "The party opposed to the existing authorities have lately recommenced their operations, and a plan for deposing the Director Pueyrredon, and securing his person was nearly matured when several of the principal conspirators . . . were seized and still remain in close confinement," Bowles reported in a dispatch to London. "I am also inclined to think that the ex-Director Alvear, who is now with many of his former associates residing at Montevideo under the protection of the Portuguese authorities, is more or less concerned in the present intrigues, although not likely to be restored to his former position or influence."[2]

Brayer arrived in Buenos Aires in the midst of this political turmoil still unsure about what role he would play next. After being expelled from the army by

San Martin, he had been confined in Mendoza for a few months. He was at least four months behind events in Europe and North America. And any influence Brayer could wield in this new phase of the campaign had been severely impaired: San Martin had made sure his reputation was ruined forever.[3] The fact that the charges against Brayer—incompetence and cowardice—were taken seriously in Buenos Aires is a testimony to San Martin's absolute hold on power. Nobody dared to question how a general who had risen through the ranks of the best army in the world, who had been present at many more battles than all the generals of the patriot army combined, and who had been wounded in action several times, could seriously be considered a coward and incompetent. But San Martin was a victorious native general and Brayer a foreigner with no connections. Very few people suspected San Martin's motivations at this time.

The news of Brayer's disgrace quickly reached Europe. In Paris the ultra-royalist *Journal des Débats* chose Napoleon's birthday to publish a special report on South America highlighting Brayer's cowardly conduct on the eve of the battle of Maipu. The newspaper quoted San Martin as saying that he had never really wanted Napoleon's veterans in his army and that he had been forced to accept them by orders from his superiors.[4] *La Minerve Française* was closer to the truth when it asserted months later that Brayer's disgrace was the result of a British intrigue to prevent a French general from emerging as the liberator of South America.[5]

A man of Brayer's character would not have let the accusations against him stand without demanding satisfaction, but by the time he arrived in Buenos Aires, San Martin had already left for Mendoza. Brayer was furious and tried at least to recover money owed to him by the government. During his two-month stay in Buenos Aires, Brayer also met Fressinet and Colonel Pierre Deschamps, one of the founders of the Vine and Olive colony who had just arrived from the United States.[6] It appears that the Bonapartist émigrés were considering two plans: One was to create a colony in Brazil similar to the one Lallemand planned to establish in Texas, the other to provoke a change of government in Buenos Aires and Chile that could open the door for an expedition to Peru. Bonpland thought Brazil "would be a better place to try our fortune."[7] But the Portuguese authorities had grown increasingly wary of the activities of foreigners, particularly the French.

Another former comrade of Brayer, Colonel Hilaire Le Moyne, had also arrived in Buenos Aires. The Duke of Richelieu had entrusted him with the mission of negotiating the establishment of a monarchy in the former Spanish viceroyalty as an antidote to Bonapartist designs. Le Moyne had also been instructed to neutralize the influence of Brayer and to discourage any support by the revolutionary government for the plans to rescue Napoleon from St. Helena. Soon after disembarking, Le Moyne arranged a secret meeting with Pueyrredon to discuss Richelieu's proposal. During the conversations, the French envoy raised the issue of the rescue plans and strongly advised against the employment of Lord Cochrane by the government of Chile.[8] The supreme director proposed the Duke of Orleans as the ideal candidate to be crowned in Buenos Aires. Le Moyne said it was a brilliant idea, so Pueyrredon sent an urgent message to Mendoza to get the approval of San Martin to this plan. Weeks later a secret emissary of the government traveled to Paris to continue the negotiations.[9]

San Martin was proceeding with a similar monarchical scheme for Chile. It was part of his grand scheme of establishing European monarchies in the Spanish colonies that he had communicated to Bowles. A French prince would rule in Buenos Aires, while in Chile, and probably Peru as well once it was liberated, the crown would be given to an English one. If a British royal was not available, a prince from the House of Orange or Braganza could be considered. Following orders from San Martin, O'Higgins had sent an envoy to Europe to pursue these negotiations.[10] Bowles informed London that a monarchical form of government was "actually decided upon" and that a foreign prince was "kept in view."[11]

Although the government tried to keep Le Moyne's presence secret, Bonpland reported his arrival to his friends in Montevideo. "Apparently he is a friend of our ambassador [Osmond]. Seems to have a lot of power and influence," he wrote to Captain Robert.[12] In fact, days after his meeting with Pueyrredon, Le Moyne contacted Brayer, who knew him from past campaigns.[13] During these meetings Le Moyne disclosed the negotiations he had started with Pueyrredon. Brayer in turn complained about San Martin and assured Le Moyne that he would return to the United States as soon as he settled his financial affairs with the government. But in truth Brayer decided to join Jose Miguel Carrera in Montevideo. Before leaving, he circulated among many influential people in Buenos Aires his own version of what had happened in Chile, which was very critical of San Martin.[14] News of Brayer's response soon reached San Martin, who accused the French general of being a "coward," a "wicked man," and a "rascal" and asked for his immediate arrest.[15] But by the time San Martin's orders arrived in Buenos Aires, Brayer had already left for Montevideo. At this time, another piece of the campaign planned in London by Wilson and Cochrane also fell apart. Admiral William Brown, who was to operate on the Pacific coast, was accused of insubordination as soon as he arrived in Buenos Aires and was conveniently imprisoned despite being the only naval hero of the revolution. He would regain his freedom a year later.[16]

In early September, Le Moyne reported to Osmond the success of his mission. Pueyrredon wholeheartedly supported the idea of crowning a foreign prince in Buenos Aires and proposed the Duke of Orleans as the ideal candidate. San Martin was inclined instead toward an agreement with England. Le Moyne reported that Joseph and Eugene of Beauharnais had also been considered as possible sovereigns. As for General Brayer, "He has been removed from the command of the troops he had under his orders. However, he still has some influence in Chile, where he established a good relationship with some of the chiefs of the government. Contrary to what is believed, he is not a supporter of the Bonapartes, although he appreciates them in their just measure. I have reason to believe that given his desire to reconcile himself to the King, he could be useful to us. Besides he no longer commands troops and cannot trouble us."[17]

Le Moyne was playing a double game or Brayer had lied to him. The French general would soon demonstrate that he could still cause plenty of trouble. As soon as he arrived in Montevideo, he joined Carrera, who was mad with rage at the brutal execution of his two brothers. A mutual hatred of San Martin cemented their friendship. Brayer also established a strong personal relationship with Alvear and even gave him a lock of Napoleon's hair in proof of his esteem.[18] In the coming weeks they met daily with Robert, Mercher, Jung, and Lagresse to plot the downfall of their enemies on both sides of the Andes.

As part of his campaign against San Martin, Brayer published a *Manifiesto* in which he accused San Martin of being a mediocre general who couldn't stand to have around him anybody with superior talent. He criticized the Argentine general for not pursuing the Spaniards after the victory of Chacabuco and blamed him for the disaster of Cancha Rayada. Brayer denied that he had refused to take part in the battle of Maipu and announced that he would return to the United States, "that great and generous nation in which hospitality is not exposed to the attack of men's passions."[19] But nothing was farther from Brayer's plans than returning to the United States. "I see him every day," Carrera wrote to Joel Roberts Poinsett weeks later. "He is healthy and wishes to return to Chile." Carrera also informed Poinsett that San Martin and O'Higgins planned to crown a Bourbon prince in South America.[20] As far as Brayer was concerned, his mission in South America was not over. Based on what he knew, Lallemand was advancing into Mexico and Cochrane was sailing to Chile to join the Peruvian campaign. And the monarchical intrigues crafted by Richelieu gave him an additional incentive to prolong his stay in South America.

Commodore Bowles reported to his government that Brayer had left for Montevideo and joined Alvear and "the remaining Carrera (who threatens signal vengeance against General San Martin for the execution of his two brothers in Mendoza)." Bowles noted that the three exiles were San Martin's mortal enemies and openly conspired to bring about his downfall.[21] Bowles expected a revolution to explode soon. Carrera agreed. He confidently assured his friends in the United States that "the time of reform that all good Americans have anxiously awaited will soon arrive."[22]

From Buenos Aires, Aimé Bonpland updated Wilson on the latest developments. The French botanist had kept up a regular correspondence with Wilson since they had met in Paris in the fall of 1816. In a letter couched in very cryptic language, Bonpland explained that Buenos Aires "was the center of a circle in which all the points of the circumference were agitated" and that Carrera and other "no less ambitious men" were at Montevideo rearming themselves and preparing to return to Chile, where the army refused to accept San Martin as its commander in chief. Bonpland offered to do "anything that would be useful to your projects."[23]

As part of their efforts to destabilize the government in Buenos Aires, Alvear, Brayer, and Carrera launched a media campaign, disclosing Pueyrredon's secret negotiations to establish a monarchy.[24] Bowles reported that their "inflammatory publications, which being printed there [in Montevideo] are sent up and distributed by their friends and agents in this city" were causing great impact.[25] This campaign was connected with Cochrane's imminent arrival from England, which would usher in a new phase in the campaign to liberate Peru.

In late October, as the mountain passes reopened, Major Bulewski, a veteran of Napoleon's legendary Polish Lancers, began a two-week journey to Santiago carrying secret messages for the French officers serving in the patriot army and Carrera's supporters. Bulewski was to be followed by Robert, Jung, and Mercher. All four had returned to Buenos Aires in early November after several months of planning in Montevideo with Alvear, Brayer, and Carrera. Lagresse would remain in Buenos Aires to coordinate with Alvear's supporters in Buenos Aires. Before departing for Chile, Robert wrote to Carrera: "The government of Pueyrredon is near its fall. . . . In Chile there is discontent with San Martin, if we get there we will have an easy task and achieve results. It will be easy to get rid of those two men. . . . There are many Frenchmen here to whom I have not said much, except to introduce them to you when you become Supreme Director of Chile."[26]

The government kept all Frenchmen under strict surveillance. Lagresse was aware of this, and to avoid having his communications with Brayer and Carrera intercepted, he relied on his compatriot Narcisse Parchappe, who was about to leave for Brazil on board a French merchant ship. The son of one of Napoleon's generals and a graduate of the Polytechnique, Parchappe had served as an artillery officer in the Grande Armée. Inside the package he carried was a letter from Bonpland to Le Breton, a fellow member of the Institut de France who lived in Rio de Janeiro and was also involved in the conspiracy. Bonpland acknowledged receipt of a letter to Fressinet and advised Le Breton that Parchappe would provide him all the details about "our project here." Bonpland's letter was filled with references to plants and trees that suggested a botanical endeavor. But on closer reading, its political overtones were evident. He not only discussed the plans for South America but also the restoration of the Bonaparte dynasty in France:

> The sending of plants to Bavaria that you told me about doesn't square at all with our hopes of seeing the small King of Rome on the throne of France. It seems to me that in such case, Prince Eugene should return to France and play a leading role. I say this because many people share this opinion. Besides, with his adoptive father at St. Helena I don't think Eugene can do anything great and useful for our country. It still pains me to remember his conduct after the first abdication of Napoleon. Nothing could have justified it or maybe he has been playing a role that was given to him perfectly well. Thanks for the news about our country and mainly for the great hopes you have; I haven't lost mine and I believe that there will be a change with the death of the King.

Bonpland suggested keeping a more regular correspondence. Evidently, the plans of the Bonapartists for Buenos Aires had encountered some serious problems. "I, and I believe many others, have been cruelly fooled in our hopes," he wrote to Le Breton. "I am guiltier than anybody else because I should have learned from the past, but because now we are in it, it will be necessary to leave with honor. . . . Our existence here would have been very nice and agreeable if it hadn't been for this unfortunate revolution and the party spirits that destroy the charms of society." But Bonpland had not lost all hope. "In two or three months hence, a great change is feared," he said.[27]

Somebody alerted the authorities and Parchappe was stopped before he could leave. A few days later, Lagresse was arrested. The turncoat was Jean Charles Durand, a French doctor who frequented the meetings at Bonpland's house and who for many years had been a student of Corvisart, Napoleon's personal doctor. Commodore Bowles reported that "several Frenchmen connected with General Brayer were arrested here on an accusation of having intended to assassinate General San Martin and the Director O'Higgins. It is said some of their associates have already left this city for Chile on this errand."[28] The government sent a detachment of troops to arrest Jung, Mercher, and Robert before they reached Chile. A week later, the three Frenchmen were captured. Although he didn't offer any resistance, Jung was shot and killed by one of the captors.

But the authorities had not yet found the letters carried by Parchappe, who had given them to his compatriot Augustin Dragumette. Again, somebody alerted the authorities who arrested Dragumette and seized the package he carried. A few days later, Robert and Mercher were brought back to Buenos Aires under heavy escort and thrown in jail with Lagresse, Parchappe, and Dragumette. The police searched Robert's luggage and found several letters that compromised not only Brayer and Carrera in their conspiracy but also Bonpland and Fressinet.[29]

Pueyrredon realized that he was facing a dangerous conspiracy. He warned San Martin that he had discovered a plan to kill him and advised him to "be careful with the Frenchmen that you have in your armies."[30] According to the intelligence gathered by the government, the plan of the conspirators was to promote a revolution in Buenos Aires and Santiago. Supposedly, Carrera and Alvear would return to Buenos Aires with a thousand men and depose Pueyrredon while their partisans in Chile killed San Martin and O'Higgins. British agents reported that the conspiracy to overthrow Pueyrredon and replace him with Alvear had originated in Montevideo "among the factious emigrants from Buenos Aires and the disappointed Frenchmen with General Brayer at their head."[31] And although "the intention of starting a revolution in Chile, an independent state from Buenos Aires, wasn't a motive strong enough for the Buenos Aires government to prosecute them," the six Frenchmen were accused of high treason.[32]

Pueyrredon took advantage of the alleged conspiracy to strengthen his grip on power and pursue the monarchical agenda he had agreed on with San Martin. The British consul in Buenos Aires informed the Foreign Office that the discovery of the conspiracy had coincided with the departure for England of Colonel Le Moyne "who came to this country with passports from the Marquis of Osmond in London. He either had or pretended to have instructions from the Duke of Richelieu to propose to this Government the placing here of the Duke of Orleans." The consul reported that the proposal had been well received by San Martin, who had long believed in "the necessity of establishing a monarchy in this country."[33]

Warned by Pueyrredon, San Martin took measures to protect his life, including posting sentries near his house. He also ordered the immediate arrest of Major Bulewski. Somebody had warned the Chilean authorities that he was a dangerous individual and should be put under surveillance.[34] The informer was none other than his compatriot and former comrade Colonel Skupieski, former equerry to Napoleon's mother, who had become a turncoat. The authorities in Santiago searched Bulewski's luggage for incriminating evidence but found only a manual of Freemasonry, a notebook with ciphers, and some letters of recommendation from Count Regnault. Under interrogation, Bulewski admitted that he knew Fressinet, that Jung was a personal friend, and that he was slightly acquainted with Mercher, Lagresse, and Robert. But he denied being involved in any conspiracy or knowing anything about Carrera.[35] Although there were no proofs to convict him, Bulewski remained under arrest and was later sent to Buenos Aires for trial.[36] It was another setback for Brayer.

33
Breakthrough at Jamestown

Is this indeed the tamer of the great,
Now slave of all could tease or irate
The paltry gaoler and the prying spy
The staring stranger with his note-book nigh?
                    —Lord Byron, *The Age of Bronze,* Canto 3

With O'Meara's departure, Lowe felt as if an "evil genius" had left the island. But if he hoped his relationship with Napoleon would improve, he was mistaken. Before leaving for Rio de Janeiro, Balmain told him that "it was a fixed idea in the minds of the French at Longwood that it was the intention of the British government to assassinate the Emperor, and that the Governor was the instrument to execute their design."[1] Napoleon didn't seem too disappointed that O'Meara had left. Apparently he had charged his doctor with a mission in England, as he would arrive just in time for the opening of the Congress of Aix-la-Chapelle and would be able to provide valuable information to the opposition in Parliament about what was really happening in St. Helena.[2] Since O'Meara's departure, Napoleon spent most of his time confined to his room, dictating his memoirs and reading. He was particularly interested in Wilson's recently published book about Russia and an earlier one about the Egyptian campaign.

In early September, Lowe received a dispatch from Bathurst confirming that "a clandestine correspondence to a considerable extent is carried on by the inhabitants of Longwood" and asking him to introduce "restraints on a liberty which it is evident has been so much abused."[3] A few days later Lowe made a discovery that "threw considerable light upon the conduct of persons both in England and St. Helena, and proved how little O'Meara and Balcombe were to be trusted."[4]

On September 19, a store-ship arrived from England carrying a letter addressed to Mr. Fowler, Balcombe's partner in St. Helena. When Fowler opened the box for O'Meara, he found that it contained nothing but an envelope addressed to a certain James Forbes. As he didn't know anybody with that name, he alerted Lowe, who opened the letter and found three letters for O'Meara. The first two letters were from William Holmes, O'Meara's agent in London. The first was dated June 26 and had enough obscure references, including one to Las Cases, to raise Lowe's suspicions.

> I have at length seen Mr. —— who I am sure will exert himself much for his friends at St. Helena. . . . He did think of going to the Continent for the benefit of his wife's health, but is fearful of improper motives being ascribed to the taking of the journey, and particularly as the tongue of slander has already been busy with his name. I told him that if business had anything to do with the object of his journey, I would be happy to go in his place, but he says he has only one commission to execute at Paris, which is so unimportant, that he would not trouble me; and that, indeed, his name being mentioned, he thought I could not effect it. If therefore you are aware of the nature of the commission, and that it is necessary still to execute it, you had better get me authorized to transact the business. I expect to hear from my friends at Rome and Munich, of which you shall have due information.

The unnamed person "lately come from St. Helena" with O'Meara's letter could be none other than Balcombe, who had left the island with Gourgaud under the pretext that his wife was ill. What sort of commission did Balcombe have to execute in Paris? Who were the friends in Rome and Munich? Lucien and Eugene? An even more suspicious postscript followed:

> All the parcels sent in July last by Mr. —— are safe; since which, two have been left by some unknown hand; one brought by B. and two by ——. This is the sum total of my receipts, except your letters of the 17th and 31st March and 2nd April. I intend starting for Paris next week to see Lafitte; and perhaps will see Las Cases, but I fear my journey will be useless from the insufficiency of the documents I hold. Seek every opportunity of writing me and sending what you can. S & P refused to pay Gourgaud's bill for £500 but they have since heard from Las Cases and it is settled. I understand the old general does not mean to publish, but should he, Perry of the *Chronicle* has promised his assistance. I under-

stand you are to draw for £1,800. You shall hear the issue of my visit to Lafitte, and if your remittances are paid, Trade of that kind can be carried on to any extent.

It appeared from this postscript that Holmes had gone to Paris to see the banker Jacques Lafitte, who unbeknownst to Lowe kept a substantial portion of Napoleon's personal fortune, and to Frankfurt to see Las Cases. Lowe may not have been familiar with Lafitte's name, but he considered Las Cases very dangerous. The reference to Gourgaud was puzzling. Before leaving St. Helena, Gourgaud had made a big deal about Napoleon not giving him £500. The letter suggested that Las Cases had paid him, obviously with Napoleon's approval. And what was Gourgaud going to publish with the aid of James Perry of the *Morning Chronicle?* The second letter, from Balcombe to O'Meara, had equally cryptic comments: "Holmes is indefatigable in his exertions in your cause and all my friends among the rest Sir George and Sir P . . . are of the same opinion with us. All communications whatever must be sent to Holmes. . . . Rest perfectly easy that no stone will be left unturned to serve our friends in the island." "Sir George" was Admiral Sir George Cockburn and "Sir P" was Admiral Sir Pulteney Malcolm, both of whom disapproved of the manner in which Lowe treated Napoleon. Cockburn had just been promoted to rear admiral and had joined the Lords of the Admiralty.

The third letter was from Holmes to doctor John Stokoe, a naval surgeon based in one of the warships anchored at Jamestown and a friend of O'Meara's: "If my friend and client O'Meara has left, oblige me by giving the enclosed to Count Bertrand in private, for although it is not of much importance, I nevertheless do not wish the governor to peruse it. Have the goodness also to give my address and desire any letters to be sent to my office. I have also sent you, a late publication of Las Cases, which when you have perused, give to those friends you think it will amuse."

The letter for Bertrand was dated in London on August 25 and was equally suspicious. It made reference to substantial investments that seemed beyond Bertrand's means and advised that "all other letters have been delivered."[5] Lowe thought Bathurst could make sense of all of this and sent him the intercepted correspondence aboard the HMS *Mosquito*, which departed Jamestown in late September.[6] He never imagined the storm the correspondence would cause in Europe.

Lowe was worried. In the past two months the sentries had not seen Napoleon. Was he still there? He threatened to enter Longwood by force to find out. "What does he want? Assassinate me?" said Napoleon when told by Montholon. "If they want to assassinate me, my position would make it easy."[7] Montholon assured Lowe that the "possibility of any plot or intrigue being carried on at St. Helena without being discovered" was zero. Besides, he added, "even if an attempt were made to get the Emperor off and he were told that a boat was ready for him to embark in he would refuse, for he would never go away like an adventurer, but would act as he did at Rochefort when he declined to try and escape."[8] Montholon was not telling the truth. Bertrand had just received a proposal to effect Napoleon's escape.[9] In fact, one of the best chances to liberate the illustrious prisoner was about to materialize.

In recent weeks an unidentified vessel had hovered around the island, and every time the British cruisers gave chase she disappeared.[10] The sightings and the unsuccessful cat-and-mouse game continued in early October.[11] The presence of this elusive ship near the island and the difficulty of ascertaining Napoleon's presence at Longwood troubled Lowe. The fast sailing ship that evaded the British cruisers was not the ghostly *Flying Dutchman** but the *Chacabuco,* a New York brig that had acquired fame as a privateer during the War of 1812 and now sailed under the flag of Buenos Aires. Thirty years later, the account of Lieutenant Thomas Sheffield, her second in command, was made public and threw some light on this episode. The owner of the *Chacabuco,* or whatever the ship's real name was,† was David DeForest, an American businessman who had become one of the biggest outfitters of privateers under the flag of Buenos Aires. DeForest was now linked to a new enterprise against Mexico with Laffite and Lallemand. He was also an associate of Captain Taylor of the *Morgiana,* a privateer who had participated in the Amelia Island occupation, and of David Jewett, captain of the *True Blooded Yankee* and a friend of Jose Miguel Carrera.

A "fancy craft that sailed like the wind," the *Chacabuco* had left Buenos Aires in August in search of two ships of the Royal Company of the Philippines bound for Spain with valuable cargoes. The Spanish prizes were expected to

---

* According to legend, the *Flying Dutchman* was a ship doomed to sail forever around the Cape of Good Hope.

† Given her description, the *Chacabuco* could have very well been the *True Blooded Yankee.* Both ships mounted sixteen guns.

stop at St. Helena for water. When the *Chacabuco* reached the island disguised as a Spanish merchantman, her captain sent a boat to shore to ascertain whether his targets had already passed. Since they had not, he positioned his vessel on the windward side of St. Helena to intercept them. As it turns out, the British cruiser patrolling that side of the island looked very similar to the *Chacabuco*, "so much in size and rig and general appearance, that the boatswain jocosely reported her a 'twin sister.'"

For several days the Buenos Aires privateer and the British cruiser played a game of cat and mouse. When the *Chacabuco* came close to shore, the cruiser would fire a gun and give chase, but only up to a certain point. In this way the captain of the *Chacabuco* was able to determine the British warship's cruising station and remain outside of it. As the days passed and his prey didn't appear, the corsair's crew grew increasingly anxious. One night a sudden and violent storm hit St. Helena and almost sank the *Chacabuco*. But daylight arrived and with it, clear skies and calm seas. The British cruiser was nowhere to be seen. Soon after, while the *Chacabuco* was lying a few leagues away from shore repairing the damage to her sails and rigging, Lieutenant Sheffield pulled out his telescope and saw Napoleon walking around his garden. The thought of rescuing him immediately crossed his mind and "thrilled his generous soul and aroused his ambition for the noble deed." Sheffield decided to hoist the English flag and impersonate the English cruiser. After obtaining approval from his captain he informed the crew, who fearing that the rich Spanish prizes would escape were not very enthusiastic. A moment of doubt and silence ensued. Sheffield let the moment pass and with it "departed forever the only and apparently a providential opportunity of rescuing a hero from an ignominious bondage!"[12]

Sheffield's account raises many questions. Everybody in the *Chacabuco* would have known that Joseph had offered a million dollars to anybody who rescued his brother. It is hard to imagine how the Spanish ships could be more valuable than Napoleon. The connection with DeForest also raises interesting questions that may never be answered. But this episode did actually take place. Months later the *Times* reported that "an American vessel, apparently dismasted, and otherwise injured, but purposely damaged to avoid suspicion, made her appearance off St. Helena." According to the London newspapers, pretending to be ill, "the wily Napoleon secretly quitted his bedroom about midnight. By means of the most artful he actually passed the guard, and eluding the vigilance of no less than seven sentinels succeeded in reaching the beach. . . . The means of escape which the ex-Emperor was led so confidently to expect, were, however, not yet perfected."[13]

Did Napoleon realize what was going on? One day, while walking around his garden, he suddenly asked Bertrand: "*Eh bien,* my dear Bertrand, will we ever leave this place? Shall we end our lives in this miserable island? I don't think so, but the question is complicated."[14]

34
The *Mosquito* Affair

If Napoleon, escaping from the clutches of his gaolers, were to retire to the United States, his gaze fixed on the Ocean would be enough to trouble the nations of the Old World.
—François René de Chateaubriand, *Le Conservateur,* November 1818

An article in the *Courier* confirmed that the British government was aware of the links between Cochrane, Wilson, MacGregor, Aury, and Lallemand. One of the government's spies was an English officer on half-pay who had enlisted in MacGregor's expedition. This officer had heard Maceroni, who was "the chief manager of MacGregor's affairs," say that the expedition was ready to depart for the Caribbean. Most of the troops had been recruited in Scotland and another contingent was to embark from Ireland. Maceroni had also said that MacGregor "had received several large sums from different merchants from London that [have] enabled him to carry on the expedition to a far greater extent then he first thought of . . . [and] that the British government was on their side and would lay no impediment in the way."[1] Reports from America indicated the conquest of Mexico was under way and that Joseph "had sent not less than 16,000 invitations individually to Frenchmen residing in France to join him in America."[2] The Admiralty had just been informed that Aury had occupied the islands of Providence and San Andres, from where he could easily attack the fortress of Portobello, the hinge of the Spanish empire in America.[3] And a recent dispatch from Commodore Bowles confirmed that the Chilean government had no funds to build a steamboat, as its financial situation was "very weak."[4]

These reports and others of Napoleon's seclusion at Longwood greatly troubled the Duke of Richelieu, who had just arrived at Aix-la-Chapelle, the small Prussian town where all the European sovereigns had gathered. Was Napoleon really at St. Helena? Napoleon's invisibility was "very disturbing because he could have escaped and Sir Hudson Lowe would find about it from London," Richelieu wrote to Osmond. He asked his ambassador in London to convince Bathurst to seek "other ways" of guarding the prisoner. The French minister still feared "a ministerial revolution in England," particularly if Lord Holland or Lord Grey led the new cabinet. "These gentlemen will not deal with the prisoner of St. Helena in a manner different from which they have expressed themselves in Parliament," Richelieu wrote.[5]

The main topic of discussion at Aix-la-Chapelle was the evacuation of the Allied troops from France. The fate of Napoleon at St. Helena was also unofficially part of the agenda. There was a link between the two issues. France was going through major political changes. Elections were looming and the army was being reorganized under the leadership of one of Napoleon's former generals. The *Courier* predicted that "great events will follow upon the heels of the retreating army of occupation." It was the ideal time for Napoleon's supporters "to make the utmost, the last exertions, to restore him to Europe." This explained why they had approached Marie Louise to intercede with her father, the emperor of Austria, to support proposals "to remove Napoleon to a climate more suited to his health and where he may follow his usual habits." Napoleon's enemies were particularly concerned about the tsar, who apparently intended "to require a change of air for him." The *Courier* predicted that as the time for withdrawing the Allied troops from France approached, "Buonaparte's sickness" would increase, as Paris was the only place that the former emperor would find suitable for his health. The efforts to relax the terms of his captivity were nothing but measures "for assisting his adherents to effect his escape."[6]

Relying on O'Meara's well-publicized reports, Las Cases had written letters to Alexander, Metternich, and Marie Louise arguing that the harsh climate at St. Helena would hasten Napoleon's death.[7] Eugene de Beauharnais joined these efforts and met secretly with the tsar to plead on behalf of his stepfather.[8] And Gourgaud, who had finally dropped the facade, also wrote to the tsar and to Marie Louise saying that Napoleon would die "the most cruel death" if he wasn't removed from St. Helena.[9] The publication of Gourgaud's letter to Marie Louise in the *Morning Chronicle* took many by surprise. Osmond was particularly upset, as he had been convinced of Gourgaud's "good faith" and had advocated his cause. He now wondered if he had "played a role or if it is necessary to attribute his conduct to the instability of his character."[10] Richelieu was less surprised; he had always been suspicious of Gourgaud, whose conduct only proved that "these men were far from wanting to retire quietly and that in their hearts they haven't lost hope."[11] He was right. According to the latest intelligence Gourgaud planned to join Lallemand. Aware of the efforts to soften the tsar, Richelieu decided to personally convince him of the importance of keeping Napoleon locked up at St. Helena.

The fate of the Spanish colonies was another unofficial topic of discussion at Aix-la-Chapelle. And it was also inextricably linked to Napoleon. According to the latest reports from the United States, which were at least five weeks old, the success of Lallemand's expedition was certain and Mexico seemed "destined at no distant day, to assume an imposing attitude and become a formidable Empire."[12] To obtain the military support of the Holy Alliance the envoy from Madrid argued that the insurrection in Spanish America threatened to upset Europe's political stability. "The discontented and criminals of Europe who have sought refuge in the United States in association with Bonaparte are trying to continue with their plans of ambition, usurpation and disorder in the New World," argued the Spanish minister. There was no longer any doubt that these plans had "an intimate relationship with the fate of Napoleon himself." Dangerous messages from St. Helena had inflamed the "imagination of his hotheaded supporters" and had led them to "new conspiracies." The cause of legitimacy had to be fought in America. The revolution in the Spanish colonies was the revolution of Europe, "only the Bonaparte family had been missing from the picture to make this a complete identity, and this had already happened."[13]

Spain's bid to enlist the Holy Alliance foundered thanks to Castlereagh's intervention. Castlereagh rejected force as a means to resolve the conflict in the colonies because it would damage British trade. Besides, Castlereagh had recently received a letter from San Martin proposing the establishment of several monarchies in the Spanish colonies with European princes.[14] Richelieu also disagreed with Spain's proposal, which he feared would trigger a dangerous conflict that would ultimately be to the Bonapartists' advantage. He insisted on his monarchical scheme, even though Russia considered it "chimerical."[15] Richelieu wanted a quick settlement between Spain and the United States. He instructed his ambassador in Madrid to emphasize to the Spanish government the need to sign a treaty with the United States at once and to avoid at all costs the recognition of the independence of Buenos Aires, even if it meant losing Florida.[16] Ferdinand VII agreed with this idea but rejected Richelieu's monarchical plans; he was still confident that a new expedition being prepared at Cadiz would put an end to the insurrection.[17] The anxiety of the French and Spanish courts about the situation in the New World subsided at the end of October, when the first reports of Lallemand's difficulties reached Europe. The *Courier* reported that "the French who have settled in the province of Texas have not yet made any incursion into Mexico nor is it expected that they will be in a condition to do so for some time."[18]

Wilson remained optimistic. He informed Lord Grey that he had met many French officers who had passed through England on their way to Texas. Wilson still hoped to see action in the upcoming campaign despite warnings from Lord Hutchinson that if the French émigrés "established themselves in any strength in the Champ d'Asile, the United States will interfere and soon put an end to their establishment. . . . Do you really think that they would ever suffer a French colony hoarded by French officers to interpose a wall between them and Mexico?"[19] The Champ d'Asile was just a "station on the road to Mexico," explained Wilson. And if any junior officer was put over his head in Chile, "I will go there [Texas] and get the command of a cohort so keep a candidate ready for Southwark."[20] Meanwhile, MacGregor's expedition was also making progress. Spanish spies again confirmed that the Scotsman would soon follow Cochrane at the head of a small fleet and a sizable army and would join Aury, who since July occupied the Island of New Providence. They would use this island as a base to launch an attack on Mexico or Panama.[21] This intelligence was consistent with the investigations carried out by Adams in Washington that proved that MacGregor, Aury, Cochrane, and Lallemand were all connected.[22] It also coincided with a report sent to Castlereagh by the Alien Office*:

> The arranged plan of the division of the Spanish insurgents now about to embark in the river under the command of MacGregor and clear out for Rio [de] Janeiro but instead proceeding thence to pass Trinidad island in Caracas to join the insurgents in Venezuela; they will then concentrate their force with that of New Granada where they have arranged to be joined also from the North by the French division under General Lallemand, stated to be four thousand from Mexico and the Champ d'Asile, when they expect to proceed without opposition and carry the whole of South America, particularly Peru. Maceroni, who conducts the French interests of this affair, will remain after MacGregor has sailed as commanding the recruiting depot in London. The French party of the insurgents intends establishing [Joseph] Buonaparte as emperor of Mexico.[23]

* Created in 1793, the Alien Office served as the domestic intelligence unit within the Home Office.

The British government decided it was time to derail these plans. Since Cochrane was gone and there was no evidence against Wilson, the government targeted O'Meara, MacGregor, and Gourgaud. On November 2, O'Meara was discharged from the Royal Navy and court-martialed for spreading "calumnious falsehoods." According to Wilson, these falsehoods consisted of accusing Lowe of charging him "with propositions & insinuations against Napoleon's life." Wilson assured Grey that O'Meara was "acting on the very best advice" and was preparing a strong reply to the charges.[24] Next on the list was Mac-Gregor, who in early November was accused of misappropriating funds belonging to Luis Lopez Mendez, Bolivar's recruiting agent in London.[25] Lopez Mendez publicly accused MacGregor of acting without the authorization of the government of Venezuela or any other independent republic of South America. Maceroni defended MacGregor and insisted that the rebel government of New Granada had authorized the expedition.[26] Somebody influential intervened and MacGregor was set free. Bathurst explained to the dismayed Spanish ambassador that it was impossible to keep him in prison as he had not violated any laws.[27]

On November 7, the HMS *Mosquito* arrived from St. Helena with evidence of the complicity of O'Meara and Balcombe in clandestine communications between Longwood and Europe. A secret cabinet meeting took place, as it was "conceived that it will be necessary to apprehend the party accused" and in "order that the arrival of any dispatches may be unknown in London as long as possible."[28] Wild rumors started to spread: Napoleon was dead, he had escaped or was about to escape. The *Times* claimed that Napoleon was still a prisoner but that "from the bustle at Lord Bathurst's office" some suspicious project had been discovered.[29] The *Courier* reported that Lowe had intercepted correspondence, "which proved the existence of a communication between that island and certain persons resident at Rome, Paris and Munich" for the purpose of liberating Napoleon. It was also rumored that "a miraculous sort of ship," hovered around St. Helena but was never caught by the British cruisers. The Tory newspaper linked these efforts to "a certain Lord who had tried to effect the escape of Napoleon" and who while in Paris had "boasted in a house which he was in the habit of frequenting, that he should like to have means enough to carry off the famous captive."[30] The unnamed person was Lord Cochrane, whose whereabouts at that time were unknown.

In Paris the rumors were even wilder: Bonaparte had escaped to New York and in England the lower classes celebrated.[31] Richelieu thought these rumors stirred the spirits in a way "that could be only harmful to public tranquility." Combined with other reports from the United States and the interception of clandestine correspondence at St. Helena, the reports confirmed that a Bonapartist plot would explode once the Allied troops evacuated French territory. "It is natural to think that the perfidious would seize such an occasion and we must thwart their intrigues by a more active surveillance and well concerted measures," Richelieu wrote to Osmond.[32]

The *Morning Chronicle* insisted that the British government had deliberately started the rumors to increase public anxiety about Napoleon.[33] According to the *Times,* the plot to rescue Napoleon involved "a banker's house in London . . . [and] two individuals in London, with others in the continent."[34] Goldsmith's *British Monitor* stressed that there was no doubt that plans "have been and still are forming to effect the escape of Napoleon." In fact, "the expeditions fitting out in our ports for the South American insurgents greatly assist the projects for Buonaparte's deliverance no one can doubt. All armed vessels which sail from the river with warlike stores, and even recruits on board, may go to St. Helena as well as to South America." How could anyone know their real destination? "I wish our ministers would look to this and they may be assured that Buonaparte's escape from St. Helena may be much easier effected by such means than by books or newspapers." Goldsmith also announced "that the Mexican insurgents have signed a pact of union with the refugees of the Champ d'Asile and that the crown of Mexico has been offered to Joseph Buonaparte."[35] As usual, he was well informed.

While Europe digested these rumors, a strange conspiracy was discovered in Brussels. From Aix-la-Chapelle, Castlereagh sent Bathurst details of a plot to kidnap Tsar Alexander and force him to sign a document stating that the Allied troops would leave France, that Napoleon would be brought back from St. Helena by the British government, and that the king of Rome would be proclaimed the new emperor of France. The leaders of the plot were two former officers of the Grande Armée.[36] Although Castlereagh requested that the "utmost secrecy may be observed," a week later the *Courier* reported the details of this alleged conspiracy.[37] The *Morning Chronicle* and the opposition accused Castlereagh and Richelieu of spreading false rumors to convince the tsar to take a harsher stance toward Napoleon.

The strategy worked well. On November 13 the tsar issued a statement deploring the accusations made by the "revolutionaries of all countries" regarding Napoleon's detention, which was "authorized by justice" and "demanded by necessity." The accusations of harsh treatment at St. Helena were "calumnies" de-signed to create "false compassion." Those who made these accusations did not want to improve Napoleon's condition but to facilitate his escape. Their campaign was designed to let "all enemies of public order know that their leader would return and infect France with a revolutionary virus." The revelations made by Gourgaud and the secret correspondence intercepted at St. Helena left no doubt about the existence of plans of escape, which Napoleon had deliberately postponed, said the tsar, who left Aix-la-Chapelle protected by a heavy escort.[38]

With the tsar's declaration, Napoleon's hopes of obtaining an improvement in his situation through political means were shattered. Richelieu and Castlereagh were ecstatic. For the British foreign secretary it was mission accomplished, as he informed Bathurst:

> I have not failed, from time to time, to communicate to the Conference such intelligence as Your Lordship has furnished me with relative to the proceedings at St. Helena and these communications have attracted the serious attention of the respective cabinets. Your Lordship is fully aware of the industry with which the disaffected press in different parts of Europe has systematically endeavored to represent the Emperor of Russia in particular, and also the Emperor of Austria, as highly incensed at the severities with which the confinement of Napoleon Bonaparte has been alleged to be attended, and that they had both interceded for his removal from St. Helena to a more wholesome and eligible abode.[39]

In London, Bathurst moved quickly to uncover all the ramifications of the plot discovered at St. Helena. William Balcombe was informed "that a correspondence of a very serious nature had been seized" in which he was implicated and summoned to testify in front of the cabinet. Balcombe declared his innocence and said that he did not remember having written any letters to O'Meara. He claimed to have avoided all French people at Longwood and denied having been asked to accept any commission to go to Paris before quitting St. Helena. Balcombe had clearly lied but maybe because he was the bastard son of the prince regent he was treated with leniency. As to Holmes, he admitted that he had sent the letter and books to O'Meara but insisted that he had done nothing improper. He explained that he had not been able to correspond openly with his client because Lowe had violated the privacy of their correspondence. The

British Monitor demanded a clearer explanation. "Mr. Holmes should also tell us who commissioned him to send books and papers to Longwood as he is not personally acquainted with any of those amiable exiles. . . . But Mr. Holmes at best is but the agent he should therefore make public the names of those Right Honorable Ladies in this country who have appointed him to be the agent of the worthy exiles of Longwood! I know who they are although Mr. Holmes keeps the secrets."[40] The writer was probably referring to Lady Holland, whose admiration for Napoleon was boundless.

Although Bathurst's investigation confirmed the existence of clandestine correspondence between Longwood and Europe, it did not find solid proof of a plan to rescue Napoleon that would allow the authorities "to adopt any legal measures against the parties concerned."[41] O'Meara was never brought to trial, probably because his accusations against Lowe would have a negative impact on public opinion. The Irish doctor counted on Balcombe as a witness to confirm that Lowe had once told him "that Bonaparte's life was of little consequence compared to the many that might fall was Napoleon to make his escape."[42] Realizing he had a very weak case, Bathurst instructed Lowe to send him any evidence "in the original" and by a reliable person "competent to swear to the place in which and to the circumstances under which they came into your possession."[43] He also said that even though Bonaparte's "friends" in London argued that escape was "quite out of his contemplation and that all alarm on that score is therefore inadequate" there were "good grounds for a very different opinion." Bathurst suspected that the American ship that put into St. Helena "on the plea of distress" and another unidentified ship that had hovered around the island without being intercepted "were connected with some attempt at escape."[44]

Among the evidence in Bathurst's hands was a suspicious letter from a certain Mr. Franklin dated at the Cape to an unnamed recipient in St. Helena. "Everything you wished has been finally settled upon, and a final decision is waited for and very probably you will soon see your friend. You may rely most implicitly upon every exertion being made for you. Three times your friend saw the person and the idea was much approved, as it will undoubtedly redound to your advantage and interest. PS: It is very sure that immediately one thing or other will speedily be done." Bathurst suspected it was connected "with the plans which there is every reason to believe are in agitation for the escape of General Bonaparte." He asked the authorities at the Cape to keep "a watchful eye on the correspondence and proceedings of Mr. Franklin" and to find out "whether the latter was in correspondence with any persons in Brazil, that being the quarter in which those of Buonaparte's adherents who were the most likely to embark on an enterprise to favor his evasion had established themselves."[45]

Following these investigations, the British government decided to arrest and deport Gourgaud.[46] Osmond and Bathurst had already concluded that the general had duped them. And Gourgaud's account of the battle of Waterloo, so unflattering to Wellington, had "inflicted a deep wound" in the heart of the Tories. Besides, Gourgaud had also "latterly associated entirely with Mr. O'Meara and other persons known to be in the confidence of General Buonaparte's friends," particularly Wilson, and planned to join Joseph in America.[47] In mid-November, Gourgaud was "torn from his bed by agents of the police" and arrested for "carrying on a correspondence with St. Helena and plotting the escape of Napoleon."[48] Colonel Paul Latapie, who had recently arrived in London and lodged at the same house, avoided arrest and secretly embarked for New York.[49]

Wilson informed Grey "that the ministers had no warranted charge against Gourgaud for communication with St. Helena or any other plot and that they have found no papers to justify their act. The approbation for his removal and fabrications came from the king of France. We have it from persons at Paris most entrusted in knowing the fact and who have evidence of it. This is indeed a degraded country when ministers dare commit such outrages without fear of responsibility." As to his being implicated in any way with Gourgaud, Wilson said there was no need to worry. "I do not believe he had any papers to implicate himself or anyone."[50]

The *Times* claimed that Gourgaud was "implicated in the plot or intrigue for the rescue of Buonaparte."[51] The *British Monitor* said there was no doubt that Gourgaud had faked a dispute with Montholon and had really been sent "on some errand" by Napoleon. Gourgaud had admitted that he "would shortly quit England to join Joseph Buonaparte in America." The ineffable Goldsmith, who had met Gourgaud several times, concluded: "This man, *in fine*, has been used too well, he should have been sent away from here long since."[52] An anonymous pamphlet, probably written by Wilson or Maceroni, defended Gourgaud: "If suspicion is a sufficient reason for subjecting him to so terrible a visitation who can remain exempt from fear?"[53] The *Morning Chronicle* accused the government of having deliberately invented a conspiracy to deport Gourgaud to Brussels. The *Mosquito* affair and the alleged plot to kidnap the tsar, were also "a machination of the English Ministry" to create "phantoms." Suffering a liver complaint, it was unlikely that Napoleon would attempt to escape, and "if death strikes him upon this rock, so miserable an end will only add to the *éclat* of his name and to the interests of his history," concluded the opposition newspaper.[54] The *Courier* accused the *Morning Chronicle* of taking "the whole tribe of the fugitive Buonapartists" under its protection and of trying "to persuade the public that the intelligence of any plan having been in contemplation for the escape of Buonaparte is altogether unfounded and ridiculous." The plan existed, as proved by the presence of "a fast-sailing privateer, supposed to be a South American" near St. Helena and the correspondence intercepted by Lowe.[55]

Fearing that he was next, MacGregor left for the Caribbean a few days after Gourgaud's arrest. The Alien Office reported that he had surmounted all obstacles preventing his departure by the offices of "good and powerful friends" at the Treasury and by the Duke of Sussex, "who came down with him in his vessel as far as Gravesend."[56] Maceroni remained in London recruiting more men with the help of Major Besant, a British officer on half-pay, and Count Sanchez de Lima, a Portuguese aristocrat who had served as aide-de-camp of Marshal Soult.[57] The *Globe* reported that "the second part of the expedition will clear out as soon as possible under the order of Colonel Maceroni, formerly aide-de-camp of Murat."[58] In fact, a few weeks later, the rest of MacGregor's expedition put to sea without Maceroni. It consisted of one brig of war and three transport vessels carrying more than thirty officers and four hundred men, "including several foreigners who formerly had served under Bonaparte in the French armies" and many British officers who "had served under Wellington in the late war." The objective was "to attempt the conquest of a kingdom in the New World," and the rendezvous with MacGregor had been fixed in Haiti.[59]

By now the British cabinet had no doubt that Cochrane, sailing across the South Atlantic, and other British subjects were involved in a conspiracy to rescue Napoleon and put him on the throne of South America. Castlereagh realized that the policy he had followed toward the Spanish colonies was no longer prudent. He started drafting a foreign enlistment act to prohibit British subjects from joining foreign armies and ordered the Admiralty to reinforce its naval presence in South America.

Richelieu must have been quite pleased with what had been accomplished at Aix-la-Chapelle. France was again accepted as a reliable European power; Allied troops would leave French territory; and the tsar had taken a strong stance against Napoleon. However, there was one important task pending: the creation of a Bourbon monarchy in South America. He thought that by consenting to the creation of a "kingdom composed of the states of Buenos Aires and

Chile" Spain would be able "to keep Peru and Mexico" and would "stop the influence of republican influences and doctrines." But a strange twist complicated his plans. Colonel Le Moyne, the envoy Richelieu had sent to Buenos Aires to negotiate a monarchical scheme, had written back with a counterproposal from Supreme Director Pueyrredon to crown the Duke of Orleans. Osmond recommended accepting it, as he thought it would offer many advantages to France and contribute to the consolidation of the Bourbon monarchy. And the Bonapartists would find a much less "benevolent audience" in South America for their projects.[60] Richelieu regarded this idea as crazy and told Osmond so: "The only thing we had charged Le Moyne with was to explore the attitude in Buenos Aires toward a monarchical government and suddenly he proposed the Duke of Orleans and nobody had charged him with that. The first and positive part of his mission was in accord with what I communicated with Spain, the second, which he took out of his own design, gives us an air of intrigue and falsity which if discovered will greatly embarrass us."[61]

Richelieu warned Osmond to "keep under the utmost secrecy all the details of this affair" and make sure Le Moyne did the same upon his return to London. But Richelieu had other problems to worry about. The liberal party had obtained a resounding victory in the recent legislative elections. As a result, at the end of December, the entire cabinet resigned. Richelieu went home with the satisfaction of knowing he had rendered valuable services to the king. With the help of Hyde de Neuville, Osmond, and Maler, he had derailed Napoleon's plans for the Spanish colonies. Even the British government now admitted that his worries had been well founded. But Napoleon had not yet been neutralized.

5
1819

35
Neutralizing Lallemand

Of the public history of Mr. Monroe's administration, all that will be worth telling to posterity hitherto has been transacted through the Department of State.

—John Quincy Adams, 1822

With Hyde de Neuville acting as mediator, Onis and Adams spent all of January 1819 trying to resolve the boundary disputes between their countries in Florida and Texas. The possibility of another military expedition led by Lallemand worried both European diplomats, most particularly Onis. Until the end of January, he remained convinced that an expedition involving Lallemand and Aury was afoot.[1] His informer was Pierre Laffite, who supposedly was also an active member of the expedition. Pierre and his brother again promised Onis that they would derail the expedition if given sufficient money.[2] Onis feared that if he didn't reach a quick agreement with the United States, Spain would lose not only Florida, but also Mexico and Peru. In his view this threat could only be neutralized with the help of the United States.

It is unclear what Lallemand was planning at this time. According to French agents in New Orleans, the intrigues surrounding Mexico were still very much alive and despite recent setbacks the redoubtable general was determined to charge again. In their view the American government, if not actively supporting Lallemand's plans, was at least aware of them.[3] Indeed, Lallemand had not abandoned his plan to conquer Mexico or another part of the Spanish empire. And encouraged by George Graham, Monroe's envoy to Galveston, he believed he could count on the support of the United States. This may explain why at the end of 1818 he became an American citizen.

The threat of a new expedition against Mexico was not simply in the imagination of French and Spanish diplomats. As late as mid-January, David DeForest, also reportedly linked with Lallemand's new enterprise, assured one of his associates that "the negotiations between this country and Spain appear to be pretty much at an end; and the United States cannot consider it any interference with her affairs if any enemy of Spain should take possession of Florida. The thing is practicable and I am confident the United States would not complain in the least."[4] It seems DeForest truly envisioned a new expedition against Florida. His connections with the privateers of Buenos Aires and a recent attempt to rescue Napoleon add an intriguing twist to his involvement in this affair.

The negotiations between Adams and Onis nearly failed several times. However, every time it seemed they would break down Hyde de Neuville managed to bring the parties back to the negotiating table. When a resolution with Spain seemed imminent, Adams sought a closer alliance with England and reiterated to the British ambassador his strong desire to act "in some concert with the British government with respect to the revolutionary movement in South America."[5] By mid-February, after arduous negotiations, Adams and Onis finally signed a treaty that settled all major outstanding border disputes between Spain and the United States.

The Adams-Onis treaty, as it became known, was a major coup for the secretary of state and a big step forward in America's expansionist policy. The United States not only moved its western border to the Sabine River, not far from Lallemand's Champ d'Asile, but also obtained Florida in exchange for surrendering any claims on Texas—only temporarily as it turned out—and obtaining Spain's recognition of American rights to Oregon.[6] The treaty was a sort of triumph for Onis too. A secret clause required the United States to strictly enforce its neutrality laws and to delay the recognition of the independence of the South American colonies for an indeterminate period of time. No more filibustering expeditions would sail from American ports to aid the insurgents in South America. As far as Onis was concerned, Florida was almost lost and Texas would be lost if Lallemand went ahead with his plans. It was strategically important for Spain to delay the recognition of Buenos Aires, particularly as a punitive expedition was preparing to sail from Cadiz to quash the rebels. Onis also feared that failure to reach an agreement with the United States would open a new war front for Spain and divert military resources needed to put down the insurgency in South America.

The secret clause in the Adams-Onis treaty was also a blow to Napoleon's American projects. Many influential politicians thought the long-term hemispheric interests of the United States had been sacrificed to satisfy England and

Spain. Clay accused Adams of being England's puppet: "If Lord Castlereagh says we may recognize, we do; if not, we do not. A single expression of the British minister to the present secretary of state, I am ashamed to say, has molded the policy of our government toward South America."[7] The court of Madrid very shrewdly delayed ratifying the Adams-Onis treaty until early 1821, thus tying the hands of the Monroe administration as far as the South American question was concerned.[8] By doing so it gained another two years to put down the rebellion in the colonies. Hyde de Neuville, who had played a critical role as mediator between Adams and Onis, also had reason to celebrate.[9] Richelieu had always feared that a war between Spain and the United States would benefit the Bonapartists. The Adams-Onis treaty eliminated this risk, neutralized Lallemand's designs on Mexico, and gave France more time to push for its own monarchical plans in South America.

It seemed as if the redoubtable Lallemand had finally been defeated. By the end of March, a month after the Adams-Onis treaty was signed, Spanish agents in New Orleans reported that Lallemand and his men roamed around the city without the means to survive.[10] But the French general still had considerable resources at his disposal, not only from the sale of the Tombigbee lands but from a public subscription organized in France to support the Champ d'Asile.[11] In fact, a few months later, the French consul in New Orleans reported rumors that Lallemand would join a new expedition against Mexico and that he still had important "pecuniary means."[12] The leader of this new expedition was James Long, a Natchez-based planter who believed that Adams had given away part of Louisiana to the Spaniards. In May 1819 Long assembled two hundred men. A month later he invaded Texas and declared its independence from Spain. Then he went to Galveston and asked Jean Laffite to help him. In no time Pierre Laffite alerted the Spanish consul in New Orleans and started playing the same game he and his brother had been playing since 1815.[13] This new expedition failed. Long was captured and shot.

It is unlikely that Lallemand actively participated in Long's expedition, but apparently General Humbert did.[14] At this point, it is hard to tell what Lallemand was planning. After the debacle of the Champ d'Asile his reputation had suffered enormously and he was involved in a grievous dispute with many of his men over the distribution of the funds raised in France. It must have been obvious to him that the American government had used him and no longer needed him.[15] Also, it is likely that Joseph, Napoleon, or both had decided to abandon the plans for Mexico. At this point, their attention was focused on Europe. By mid-1819 many die-hard Bonapartists who had followed Lallemand to Texas, such as Jean Schultz and Maurice Persat, returned to France, where important political changes were taking place.

36
England Sides with Spain

This is the commencement, if we are not much mistaken, of one of the most
important years that [we] have been seen for a long while.
—*Examiner*, London, January 3, 1819

News from South America took up to three months to reach London. At the
beginning of January 1819, letters from Buenos Aires suggested that "everything was tranquil" and that "the arrival of Lord Cochrane was anxiously expected."[1] At the same time, accounts from Spain confirmed that the greatest
"energy and activity prevail in every department of the Spanish government
to equip an expedition from Cadiz for South America."[2] Wilson was worried.
Even the fearless Cochrane would not be able to resist the massive armada fitting out at Cadiz. Maybe these developments convinced him that the liberation
of the Spanish colonies had to be accomplished in Europe. He left Maceroni in
charge of the expedition and turned his attention to Parliament, as he had been
recently elected to represent the borough of Southwark.

Wilson's maiden speech in the Commons focused on domestic politics. His
extreme views on reform not only offended the Tories but also many moderate
Whigs.[3] In another speech he criticized Gourgaud's deportation, pledging his
life that the French general "had not been guilty of any traitorous correspondence or of any attempt to disturb the peace of Europe." In his view Gourgaud's
treatment was irrefutable proof that "a police system was growing up in this
country, which, if not checked would become as odious as any of those under
which the continental nations groaned." Castlereagh rebutted these assertions
and advised Wilson "to be cautious how he pledged himself."[4]

Parliamentary oratory and backbenching could not hold Wilson's attention
for long. Events across the Channel again stirred his enthusiasm. The most radical change in French politics since Napoleon's abdication was about to take

place. "I am anxiously expecting further details from France but there can be no doubt of the fact that Decazes has triumphed," Wilson assured Grey in early January. His sister Fanny, who had returned to Paris after receiving a personal authorization from Decazes, kept him updated on the political situation.[5] Many believed the triumph of the liberals in the legislative elections was the first step to overthrowing the Bourbons. Wilson thought that France was "in high revolutionary progress."[6] The *Morning Chronicle* also hailed the triumph of the French liberals and predicted the appointment of Decazes as prime minister, which "could not fail to be productive of the utmost satisfaction to all who had the tranquility of France at heart."[7]

The changes in France were a consequence of the electoral laws approved in 1816 at the instigation of Decazes, which had allowed the liberal party to secure a majority in the Chamber of Deputies in the recent election. As a result, both Decazes and Richelieu tendered their resignations and the cabinet was disbanded. Richelieu expected to be reappointed but Decazes gained the upper hand and the king asked him to lead a new cabinet. Knowing his time had not arrived, Decazes proposed the Marquis Dessolles for that position. The fifty-two-year-old Dessolles was an old aristocrat and former general who had served Napoleon loyally until the first abdication. Although he was nominally prime minister, everybody knew that it was really Decazes who pulled the strings. Artois and the Ultras, who considered Decazes a closet Bonapartist, were not happy with this outcome. The meddling Russian ambassador in Paris, the Corsican Pozzo di Borgo, reported that "the democratic party which opposes the House of Bourbon and the independents who aspire to a change in the dynasty have supported the ambitions of Decazes, the favorite of the King and an extremely popular minister."[8] To the dismay of the Ultras, the new cabinet was composed mostly of men who at one point had served Napoleon. The only danger Wilson saw on the horizon was the possibility that England would intervene to support the Bourbons.[9]

The ascendance of Decazes in France raised hopes in the hearts of all Bonapartists that their political prospects would improve. Their optimism was not ill founded. (Before becoming a favorite of Louis XVIII, Decazes had served the Bonaparte family for years. He had long been rumored to be the lover of Hortense de Beauharnais and father of her son, the future Napoleon III.)[10] In fact, it was rumored that many ambassadors would be recalled. According to the *Morning Chronicle*, Hyde de Neuville was among them. It was also expected that the Royal Ordinance of 1815 "would be repealed and that many prominent émigrés would soon return to the country."[11] Among those pardoned were Marshal Grouchy, Generals Fressinet and Vandamme, and Count Regnault.[12]

Coincident with the political changes in France, rumors of Napoleon's escape intensified on both sides of the Atlantic. "Neither the governor nor any other Englishman knows anything more about him than that the orderly captain occasionally gets a glimpse of him through the window blinds," reported the *Morning Chronicle*.[13] A report from Barbados stated that St. Helena "had been attacked and Buonaparte rescued" and recent letters from New York indicated that "a number of sharp vessels" had left different ports of the United States "for the purpose of carrying off Bonaparte."[14] A liberal cabinet in power in France and the lack of accurate news from St. Helena worried the supporters of absolutism.

While France moved toward greater freedom, the rest of Europe and the Spanish colonies seemed destined to continue in the ways of despotism. Colonel Le Moyne arrived in London in February, just in time to learn that a change of government in France could derail the monarchical scheme he had negotiated with Supreme Director Pueyrredon in Buenos Aires. Le Moyne reported the results of his mission to Osmond, who had just resigned as France's ambassador. The colonel said that if France agreed to crown a prince in Buenos Aires, preferably the Duke of Orleans, Pueyrredon would not only relinquish sovereignty of the former Spanish viceroyalty but also assure its peaceful possession by the new monarch. Still convinced of the advantages of this scheme, Osmond prepared a long memorandum for Dessolles describing Le Moyne's secret negotiations and recommending their approbation. He explained that the objective of Le Moyne's mission had been "to remove the Bonapartists from the inner circle of Director Pueyrredon, to prevent any enterprise against St. Helena from Buenos Aires and to announce that all of Europe would watch with repugnance the establishment of a republic in South America." According to Osmond, "the success of the colonel has exceeded all our hopes."[15] Dessolles consulted Louis XVIII, who did not agree with the idea of crowning the Duke of Orleans in Buenos Aires and instead proposed the Duke of Lucca, the nineteen-year-old son of Maria Luisa de Borbon, queen of Etruria and sister of Ferdinand VII.*

---

*The Congress of Vienna had split the old grand duchy of Tuscany, which Napoleon had given to one of his sisters in 1807, into the duchies of Parma and Lucca. Parma had been left in the hands of the Archduchess Marie Louise, Napoleon's estranged wife, until her death, and Lucca had been returned to its former sovereign, Queen Maria Luisa, who in turn gave it as a duchy to her son who happened to be the nephew of Ferdinand VII, king of Spain.

To complete the scheme and convince Portugal to evacuate Montevideo, Dessolles proposed to marry Lucca to a Portuguese princess. At the end of April, he instructed his ambassador in Madrid to discuss this proposal with the Spanish cabinet.[16]

Meanwhile, Castlereagh pursued his solution for the Spanish colonies. In mid-February he called the American ambassador Richard Rush to discuss the situation. Castlereagh explained that he had opposed the use of force to resolve the issue, but Spain "seemed bent upon continuing the war with her own means and clung to the hope of bringing it to a close upon her own terms." England had "anxiously desired to see the controversy between Spain and her colonies at an end" and had always proposed to resolve it "upon the basis of a restoration of the supremacy of Spain" as the "materials of regular self-government among the colonies did not appear to exist." Although Buenos Aires had shown greater ability to exist as an independent entity than the other colonies and British trade there was important, Castlereagh had no intention of recognizing her independence, particularly as Spain prepared a massive expedition against the rebels. Unaware of the secret clause agreed on between Adams and Onis, Rush replied that the Monroe administration was in favor of recognizing independence. Castlereagh expressed regret that the United States "viewed the question of independence in the colonies differently from England."[17] Any regrets would soon disappear, as at this time, Adams assured Bagot that the United States wanted to act in unison with England on this subject.

Everything changed in late March, when news reached London that the United States had settled all boundary disputes with Spain and had obtained the much-coveted territory of Florida. The news shocked England's elite, which realized that the United States was embarking on an ambitious plan of territorial conquest.[18] The *Morning Chronicle* blamed Castlereagh's misguided foreign policy: "Few political changes have caused a deeper impression on the manufacturing and commercial classes of the British community than the recent transfer of the Floridas to the United States. . . . Everybody seems to ask what has our cabinet done in this important transaction? The French Revolution, the possession of Louisiana and the Floridas and the results of the late war with us have given to the United States the growth of a hundred years, and we say it plainly, if they forestall us in the affections of South America we shall have allowed them to acquire the growth of another century."[19]

Wilson prepared his own antidote for Castlereagh's mistakes but had not forgotten Napoleon. He had recently received reports that the emperor's health had deteriorated. "He has suffered an apoplectic attack" and his liver was "very much affected," he informed Lord Holland. "The constant attendance of a medical person at Longwood is increasingly necessary." Something "should be done on the subject," Wilson said.[20] What did he have in mind? The French ambassador in London reported that Lord Grey planned to introduce a motion regarding Napoleon in the House of Lords.[21] Did Wilson favor more forceful action? His underling Maceroni launched a campaign in favor of South American independence in the media. "The contest in South America has already lasted seven years with a variety of success but its general progress was for a time retarded by the prospect for reconciliation." It would be impossible for a foreign power to subdue Venezuela and New Granada, and although the situation in Mexico was still unclear, Buenos Aires, Chile, and possibly Peru were "already lost to Spain." Maceroni revealed that MacGregor would soon start his campaign at the head of at least one thousand veteran troops. "Five large ships full of veteran British soldiers, cavalry, infantry and artillery, have already sailed to join him, while several others are in progress of departure both from hence as well as from Ireland." Aury would join this expedition with "sixteen armed vessels and five hundred well-disciplined troops" in the Gulf of Darien. Once MacGregor took possession of the Isthmus of Panama, he "would immediately become the principal center of military strength and action in South America, whence from its geographical position it would be enabled to assist the cause of independence not only in Venezuela and in Peru, but at the same time, with the greatest ease achieve the liberation of Mexico."[22]

As time passed, criticism of Castlereagh's policy toward the Spanish colonies mounted. The *Morning Chronicle* reported the existence of secret articles in the Adams-Onis treaty and linked them to the demise of Lallemand's expedition and the reluctance of the United States to recognize the independence of Buenos Aires:

> The world has long been aware that the numbers of French discontented exiles assembled in the United States and under General Lallemand afterwards formed a colony in the province of Texas (New Spain) called the Champ d'Asile. It was always well understood that the Washington Government was not only privy to this new establishment but also under a secret understanding with its leaders and promoters. The reason of the Champ d'Asile, which had become extremely strong and flourishing, being suddenly broken up at the moment when a subscription in France had

been realized for its support and when nothing was to be apprehended from the Spaniards, has been a mystery to the public.

The *Morning Chronicle* revealed that the Monroe administration had ordered Lallemand "to withdraw from the province of Texas" as a result of "recent arrangements made between the United States and Spain."[23] Many powerful Whigs felt that Castlereagh's policy was contrary to British interests in South America. Free of the commercial monopoly imposed by Spain, the colonies offered great prospects to English manufacturers, who had endured years of stagnation. Since Waterloo, the recession in England had deepened and the government had been helpless to prevent it. It was no longer the specter of the French émigrés invading Mexico and setting up a Napoleonic empire that threatened England but the emergence of a territorially ambitious United States, argued the *Morning Chronicle*.[24]

Oblivious to criticism, Castlereagh sent new legislation to Parliament to ban British subjects from joining the armies of any nation not at war with England. The debate that followed gave Wilson an opportunity to criticize the government. "Spain could not force this bill on England," he said. In his view Castlereagh's policy favored the United States. After occupying Florida the United States would next demand Cuba, and "by intrigue and intimidation, she would ultimately extend her views of aggrandizement to Mexico, push her frontier from the Atlantic to the Pacific Ocean and in the end laugh at Great Britain as the dupe of her artifice." Wilson's prescient warning had no effect. To argue in favor of the legislation in the Upper Chamber, Bathurst used the example of MacGregor, who had "fitted out an expedition from the ports of this country, had embodied a force composed of British troops . . . his ships were British, the equipment British."[25] Across the Atlantic, Adams assured Congress that MacGregor was Bathurst's agent. The British Foreign Enlistment Act was approved at the end of June. England had finally taken sides in the contest in South America and placed her bets on despotic Spain.

Wilson was incensed. At a meeting to commemorate the first anniversary of his election to Parliament, attended by O'Meara and Maceroni, among others, he criticized the new legislation, which "was not only not neutral in its nature, but went, as far as the measure would go, to establish our vassalage to the most self debased government in the world." Amidst loud cheers, he continued his harangue. With this infamous act, England bound herself "to deliver over the South Americans into the hands of a master who never knew what it was to administer justice, much less to temper justice with mercy." Parliamentary reform was the only way to stop the Tories' despotism; without it, he said, "we might as well give up to the ministers a positive dictatorship." Wilson closed the proceedings with a toast to "our gallant and intrepid countryman Lord Cochrane and may his noble efforts to crush the chains of despotism be crowned with success." The meeting adjourned with the band playing "La Marseillaise."[26]

The Spanish government was quite relieved at the passing of the Foreign Enlistment Act. Ferdinand VII was convinced that without foreign help, the insurgency would collapse. So when the Spanish prime minister heard about the French proposal to crown the Duke of Lucca in Buenos Aires, he flatly rejected it. The colonies would soon be brought under control and the rebels would be severely punished he told the representative from Paris.[27] Despite Madrid's opposition, in early June, the French prime minister communicated his proposal to an envoy from Buenos Aires. The envoy, who thought the Duke of Orleans was the candidate, was taken aback and replied that a prince of the Spanish branch of the Bourbons would not be acceptable. Dessolles said that discussing any other alternative would be useless as it would never be accepted by Spain and therefore by none of the Allied powers.[28]

News of these negotiations gave rise to different interpretations. According to one, the French wanted to give the throne of Buenos Aires to the young Bourbon prince as part of a deal that would give the duchies of Parma, Piacenza, and Guastalla to Napoleon II, who had been disinherited. Louis XVIII reportedly supported the scheme because he feared that unless a throne was given to Napoleon's son, the Bonapartists would persist in their attempts to install him on the throne of France. The crown-swapping scheme was also supported by the emperor of Austria, who wasn't happy about the treatment of his grandson by the Holy Alliance. But not everybody thought Napoleon II was headed to northern Italy. Some suspected Decazes secretly planned to crown him king in Buenos Aires.[29]

37
Rendezvous at Portobello

So many valuable British lives were sacrificed by the imbecility and cowardice of the notorious MacGregor.

—Colonel Francis Maceroni, 1838

The news of Cochrane's arrival in Chile in late November 1818 quickly reached Lima. The Spanish viceroy lamented how it "must have much encouraged the audacity and confidence of the rebels." Even more worrying was that the former rebel MP from Westminster had arrived with his wife and son and had become a Chilean citizen, which meant he was planning to stay a long time. Besides, he had been welcomed in Santiago "with the most honorific demonstrations of consideration and been named commanding general of its naval forces."[1]

Cochrane arrived in Santiago just in time to witness the turmoil caused by the discovery in Buenos Aires of a conspiracy to depose San Martin and O'Higgins. If he had counted on Carrera or Brayer to execute his plans he would now have to improvise. Cochrane's reception was generally warm as neither his secret plans nor his political ideals were well known, but his military talents were much needed. Despite warnings from Buenos Aires, O'Higgins was delighted with his new admiral, who boasted that with his new steamship he would destroy the Spanish fleet. Despite being an enthusiastic Anglophile, San Martin did not like Cochrane, probably because of Commodore Bowles's warning. However, he made a special effort to woo Lieutenant Colonel James Charles, Wilson's loyal aide-de-camp, who had accompanied Cochrane to Chile. James would soon become Cochrane's right-hand man.

A clash between Cochrane and San Martin was inevitable. The Argentine general could not yet imagine that Cochrane planned to put Napoleon on the throne of South America, while Cochrane did not know that San Martin was trying to enlist Castlereagh's support to advance his monarchical schemes. It wouldn't take them long to figure out each other's plans. In the meantime there was a lot to do to preserve the cause of independence in South America. Despite San Martin's recent victory, Chile was vulnerable. The patriot army effectively occupied most of the Chilean territory but the Spaniards still held several coastal fortresses in the south and had control of the Pacific, a solid base for the massive armada that was being prepared at Cadiz.

After a few weeks in Santiago, Cochrane realized he had no time to lose. In mid-January he left Valparaiso at the head of his small squadron. His main objective was to neutralize the Spanish squadron anchored in Callao so he could sail freely along the Pacific. He also sent one of his ships to Panama to look out for MacGregor, as they had agreed to rendezvous at the Gulf of Panama sometime in early 1819. San Martin traveled to Mendoza, supposedly to recover his health. It was the beginning of one of the least understood chapters of his life. It is difficult to know whether his health problems were real or faked, although he claimed that his life was in danger.[2] Cochrane presented a serious obstacle to his plans and opened a rift between San Martin and O'Higgins. In a dispatch to London, Bowles reported that public opinion in Santiago had turned against the Argentine general as a result of the murders of the Carrera brothers and Manuel Rodriguez. He also noted that Cochrane's conduct in Santiago seemed calculated "to give us much trouble," and if he succeeded in his attempt at Callao "I have no doubt his insolence will be intolerable."[3]

San Martin had apparently lost hope that O'Higgins would support his expedition to Peru. "Since the fleet of this state [Chile] established its superiority in the Pacific they believed that the arms of the army of the Andes are no longer necessary," he complained to his allies in Buenos Aires. When Bowles learned that his friend and England's strongest ally in South America was thinking of resigning, he entreated him to reconsider the decision. "A general anarchy will be the outcome of such resolution," Bowles said. Obviously, it was not very convenient for England to lose its most valuable ally in South America at "such critical times." If San Martin resigned, foreign adventurers would take over and "plunge these countries into disasters hitherto unknown," Bowles said. He was referring to Cochrane and the exiles in Montevideo—Alvear, Brayer, and Carrera.[4] Bowles believed that the situation in Chile was so critical that O'Higgins would be ousted.[5] He warned the Admiralty that nothing "except a superior force, would protect our commerce and interests in this country."[6]

Meanwhile, in early February, Cochrane and his squadron arrived in the vicinity of Callao. It was the beginning of his distinguished naval career in

South America. Cochrane spent several days reconnoitering the heavily guarded harbor. His squadron was completely outgunned by the Spaniards, so surprise was essential for achieving victory. Cochrane planned to launch an attack on February 23, the last day of carnival, when he expected the crews of the Spanish ships anchored there and the troops manning the fort's artillery would be celebrating in Lima. To fool the Spaniards he disguised his ships as American men-of-war. Unfortunately, the dense fog that is so common in Callao at this time of the year delayed the attack for several days. When the fog finally cleared, Cochrane approached the harbor but the Spaniards didn't fall for the ruse and launched a fierce cannonade that forced Cochrane's ships to retreat behind the island of San Lorenzo. Cochrane remained in that position for a few more weeks, blockading the harbor and mulling his options. Realizing that a change in tactics was required, he resorted to a weapon he had used against the French in 1809: fire vessels.* But faulty powder and poor construction derailed his attack. Almost a month passed and Cochrane accomplished nothing. Impatient for results, at the end of March, he took his chances one more time. Once again, he met stiff resistance and failed. Cochrane's baptism by fire in South America was a complete disappointment. Without water and provisions, he withdrew and sailed north with his squadron to look out for MacGregor.

But MacGregor's expedition had also faced serious problems. During the voyage from England to the Bahamas there had been frequent riots and fights between the French and English troops, particularly among the lower ranks. One of the British officers in charge complained that the Frenchmen, all of them veterans of Napoleon's army, "could be kept in no kind of order."[7] When MacGregor arrived in the Bahamas in mid-January, he found that there was no cohesion or discipline among his troops. He took his expedition to Haiti to wait for the reinforcements that Captain Woodbine had promised to bring from Jamaica. But the British government had intervened and prevented Woodbine from recruiting a single man. Unaware of that, MacGregor sailed to Jamaica to find out what had happened and sent the rest of his expedition across the Caribbean to the island of San Andres, off the coast of Nicaragua. Together with the neighboring islands of Santa Catalina and Providence, San Andres was conveniently occupied by Louis Aury, MacGregor's erstwhile partner in the Amelia Island affair.[8] The archipelago was strategically located and could serve as a

---

*A fire vessel was a ship filled with powder, deliberately set on fire and steered (or, if possible, allowed to drift) into an enemy fleet, in order to destroy ships, or to create panic and make the enemy break formation.

base to attack the port of Veracruz or the fortress of Portobello at the Isthmus of Panama.

Aury's movements after leaving Amelia are unknown. According to one version he went to Buenos Aires, which is unlikely. Before leaving New York, Lallemand had instructed Aury to meet him at Galveston "with the greatest number of people possible" to support his invasion of Mexico, or if this plan failed, to help him in Venezuela.[9] Aury must have thought Venezuela was the objective, as in early 1818, before leaving Amelia, he sent Major Persat to the island of Margarita to confer with Simon Bolivar. Apparently, the leader of the Venezuelan patriots was not keen on combining his operations with Lallemand's, as at this point he was expecting his own reinforcements from England. Persat left Margarita quite disgusted with Bolivar.[10] Whether on his own initiative or following Lallemand's instructions, by mid-1818 Aury had taken possession of the islands of Providence and San Andres on behalf of the governments of Buenos Aires and Chile, although he had never received an official commission from either one.[11]

Meanwhile when MacGregor arrived in Jamaica he realized he would not be able "to effect the immediate embarkation of any force."[12] It seemed as if the story of Amelia Island was repeating itself. Hoping that with Aury's help he could take Portobello, after a few days he left Kingston. The chief of the British naval station in Jamaica reported that MacGregor's expedition would be "directed by the state of the winds and it will in all probability endeavor to fetch as far to the eastward on the Isthmus of Darien as possible."[13] Aury had also run into some difficulties and was repairing his fleet. MacGregor met the French corsair at Providence and explained the plan: take Portobello, cross the Isthmus of Panama, and join Cochrane in the Pacific. Aury agreed to help.[14]

Unknown to MacGregor his expedition was in grave danger. Since leaving Haiti his troops had been "considerably reduced by desertions" and after a few weeks at the island of San Andres, provisions were "nearly exhausted." At the end of March, his top lieutenants, having heard no news from MacGregor for two weeks, had called a council of war to decide whether to abandon the expedition. MacGregor's appearance in early April ended these deliberations and a few days later the entire expedition sailed toward Portobello.[15] MacGregor's unexpectedly long stay in Haiti and the trip to Jamaica had delayed his movements by about a month and made it difficult to meet the timetable agreed upon with Cochrane. While MacGregor prepared to attack Portobello, Cochrane was sailing up the coast of Ecuador. In mid-April, Cochrane subdued the small Spanish garrison of Paita. Cochrane loaded provisions and dispatched one of his ships to the Gulf of Panama to find MacGregor. At the beginning of May, not having heard from his compatriot, he sailed back to Callao.[16]

On the mainland, as late as the end of April, MacGregor's position and intentions were still a matter of speculation. Bolivar believed that MacGregor had at least four thousand veterans with him and was bound for Portobello "to take possession of the Isthmus."[17] Unbeknownst to Cochrane, on April 10, MacGregor surprised the Spanish garrison and succeeded in taking Portobello.[18] But his possession of the fortress was short lived. By late April the Spaniards had launched a counterattack and caught MacGregor by surprise. "Sir Gregor appeared for a moment confused and undecided," but some of his men attempted a spirited defense. One of them, a Frenchman named Gandon, a former captain of Napoleon's Grande Armée, died valiantly while defending the fortress's last redoubt. After intense combat, the Spanish forces regained control of Portobello. MacGregor ran toward the beach, threw his clothes off, and swam to his ship. The Spaniards followed him to the edge of the water and repeatedly fired at him but he escaped unhurt.[19] MacGregor blamed the fiasco on one of his officers.[20] There may be some truth in this assertion as the Spanish ambassador in London had infiltrated a spy in MacGregor's expedition. In any case, the rendezvous with Cochrane in the Pacific failed, putting the rest of the plan in jeopardy, as the Duke of San Carlos had predicted.

Having heard no news of MacGregor, Cochrane sailed back to Chile, where he arrived in mid-June. His naval campaign against the Spaniards had been disastrous and was beginning to damage his reputation. His enemies in Santiago, most of whom supported San Martin, were happy to see him defeated. Cochrane knew that unless he obtained a resounding victory, his career in South America would soon come to an inglorious end. Time was of the essence, as a massive punitive expedition was about to leave Spain to crush the rebels. Lieutenant Colonel James Charles kept Sir Robert Wilson abreast of what was happening in South America. "In speaking to the Director [O'Higgins] the other day respecting you, he mentioned his regret of you not having come out. I had already put him in possession [of] what had happened between you and Alvarez* on this subject, of this person's conduct whom he never approved." He also suggested that Wilson would receive a warm welcome in Santiago: "If your views are still directed towards S. America, do it by all means. This is a good op-

* Alvarez was San Martin's envoy in London.

portunity for you, on your deciding on it should it meet your approbation write to the Supreme Director he is much your friend and ally and eager to see you in any shape you choose to come and will give you that part to act which will be in perfect conformity to your wishes."

Charles also mentioned the tension between O'Higgins and San Martin. "It is not likely that general San Martin will continue the commander in Chief," he wrote. According to Charles, O'Higgins supported the expedition that Cochrane planned against Mexico and the Philippines. Cochrane expected MacGregor to attack Portobello, cross the Isthmus, and meet him somewhere along the Pacific coast. Despite all setbacks, Cochrane still planned to liberate Peru, which he believed he could accomplish with only three thousand men, "as the population was much opposed to the Spanish rule." He counted on Wilson to join him in this campaign. "Could you meet [us] with a force from England [at] both these places and do the same towards the middle of 1820?" Charles asked. "If you do not go to Portobello and Panama why can you not come to Buenos Aires? But to confess to you, I should like to see you attack Portobello." Charles also requested instructions from Wilson: "Write to me in duplicate letters, not to general San Martin, and keep Alvarez from the secret, for I am not altogether acquainted with the precise politics of the general or his aims, whether he is moderate or very ambitious. At all events, he is very sinister and I do not give him so much credit for the first or the last of these qualities. Alvarez is San Martin's friend and was placed in his present situation by him." In a postscript Charles said he would go to Panama if Wilson went to Portobello.[21]

Two weeks later, he wrote again and asked Wilson to give him "instructions with respect to your being ready to fit out a force to attack Portobello and cross to Panama." According to Charles, Cochrane was ready to launch his Peruvian campaign. Cochrane's plan was at odds with that of San Martin, who assured O'Higgins that at least six thousand men were necessary to liberate Peru. Cochrane's optimism was based on information he had gathered at Guayaquil, which was about to declare its independence. Unaware of MacGregor's fate, Charles tried to persuade Wilson to lead the attack of Portobello. From there, "the fleet would assist you in coming down and as there is no commander in chief with ability, you would be placed at the head of the army." And then he could share the laurels with Cochrane. "Let me repeat again, come to South America, it is a fine field for your talents."[22]

In Santiago, Cochrane pondered his next move. Things had not worked out as planned. He was beginning to appreciate the subtleties and intricacies of the politics of the revolution in South America. Although he got along relatively well with O'Higgins, his relationship with San Martin was openly hostile.

Meanwhile in Buenos Aires, by early April, Robert and Lagresse, the two Frenchmen who had conspired with Carrera to topple the governments on both sides of the Andes had been tried and executed. Their compatriots Mercher, Dragumette, and Parchappe were deported. Together with General Fressinet, who had also been implicated in the conspiracy, they sought refuge in Montevideo. Bonpland remained in Buenos Aires under strict police surveillance. Another conspirator, Major Jean Bulewski, was sent to Buenos Aires to stand trial. A member of an old aristocratic family from Poland, Bulewski was a diehard Bonapartist. Since 1812, he had worked under the Duke of Bassano at the Ministry of Foreign Affairs, and during the Hundred Days he had served in the Polish Lancers. The main witness for the prosecution was none other than Bulewski's compatriot and former comrade Colonel Antoine Skupieski. The infamous Baron Bellina, once suspected of being Joseph's spy, admitted having warned the Chilean authorities about Bulewski but, probably fearful of revenge, gave vague reasons for doing so. He claimed that Bulewski's conduct in Europe had made him fear for the security of "this country." When pressed to elaborate, the devious Pole said that while in Mendoza, Bulewski had tried to seduce a young girl from a distinguished local family.[23] Bulewski denied all charges and accused his compatriot of being an impostor. He insisted that Skupieski explain why he had written such alarming warnings about him. The trial eventually came to nothing; Bulewski was acquitted and Skupieski became a pariah among the Bonapartist émigrés in Buenos Aires. Even his beautiful Spanish wife, a fanatical Bonapartist who had just arrived from the United States, refused to see him.[24]

The execution of Robert and Lagresse dealt another blow to the plans of the Bonapartist émigrés in South America. England was the clear winner, as the American consul in Buenos Aires observed. British policy in South America "was similar to that they practiced in India, to set one chief against another, exhaust the strength of the country by fomenting parties and divisions and draining the country of all its plate and specie and inundating it with their manufactures." The American diplomat also noted that even though England's "great favorite" had always been San Martin, his prospects now seemed cloudy.[25] Doubts about San Martin's future were fueled by reports about his poor health. According to Commodore Bowles, San Martin had retired to Mendoza and had "very much injured his health (and perhaps his faculties) by the immoderate use of opium and spirits."[26] In truth, San Martin was pondering his next move. He had always favored an arrangement with England, which was now more remote than ever, as Castlereagh had decided to take sides with Spain. The independence of Buenos Aires was now in serious danger. The apprehension of the government was heightened "by the reports of a Spanish expedition and the certainty that Montevideo is to be surrendered on its arrival."[27] According to Bowles, the patriot army was in terrible shape and it would take time to reorganize it. "The present is the moment when a Spanish expedition would experience fewer difficulties than at any former period of the revolution."[28]

Aware that its survival was at stake, the faction ruling Buenos Aires placed all its bets on the monarchical scheme negotiated with the Duke of Richelieu. Unfortunately with the latter's resignation and the appointment of a new foreign minister in France, the prospects of this scheme were uncertain. Colonel Jean-Joseph Dauxion-Lavaysse, who had betrayed Carrera and now held the rank of general in the patriot army, wrote to Count Lally-Tollendal, a member of Louis XVIII's inner circle to lobby in favor of the proposal. In his letter Lavaysse described the recent political events in Buenos Aires and shed light on the role played by the Bonapartist émigrés. Lavaysse noted that in the last two years, three imperial tailors, a chaplain of the Imperial Guard, the chief wigmaker of Princess Hortense, and the shoemaker and *bonbonnier* of the king of Rome had arrived in Buenos Aires. Many other veterans of the Grande Armée had come to South America "with projects of gigantic military ambition . . . [and] had almost turned the country upside down." Robert and Lagresse had "imagined emulating Brissot and Genet and believed they had arrived at the country of the Iroquois and thought they would figure as great military men or ministers of state" even though they had not achieved the rank of captain in France. They had adopted Carrera as their leader, who had used them as emissaries. According to Lavaysse, the "worst of all these scoundrels and rascals" was General Fressinet, who had contributed more than anybody else "to excite the brains of these troublemakers." Fortunately, the execution of Robert and Lagresse "calmed them." Lavaysse also criticized Skupieski, who was the "appointed emissary of the imperial projects" designed by Grouchy and Clausel in Philadelphia and blamed Carrera for Brayer's troubles. By following the lead of this madman the general had "lost his head." Despite the negative image left by these Frenchmen in Buenos Aires, Lavaysse argued that France still had an opportunity to exert influence, as there was "great indignation in all classes of society against the narrow-minded and tortuous behavior of the government of the United States towards Spain and the independents of the South."[29]

Exiled in Montevideo, General Brayer was thirsty for revenge. Together with Alvear and Carrera he was planning another coup. Mercher, Parchappe, and Dragumette, who had just been expelled from Buenos Aires, joined them. General Fressinet returned to France. Courtesy of Decazes he had just obtained a royal pardon. With the liberal party in power, France opened up new possibilities to the Bonapartist cause.

38
Another Messenger Leaves St. Helena

Thy throne had still been thine, or never been;
For daring made thy rise as fall: thou seek'st
Even now to re-assume the imperial mien,
And shake again the world, the Thunderer of the scene!
—Lord Byron, *Childe Harold's Pilgrimage*, Canto 3

The year started with a bad omen at Longwood. Napoleon suffered an attack of vertigo and fainted. Bertrand urgently called Stokoe, surgeon of the HMS *Conqueror* and a friend of O'Meara, to come see him. By the time Stokoe arrived Napoleon had fully recovered. Despite his aversion to English doctors, Napoleon liked Stokoe and asked him to be his personal doctor with a very attractive pay package. The doctor had already been won over to his cause.

When days later Napoleon suffered a second attack, Bertrand again called Stokoe, who this time found the patient "in a very weak state, complaining of considerable pain in the right side, in the region of the liver, and with shooting pain in the right shoulder." Napoleon was convinced he had hepatitis. "How long might a man live with such a complaint?" he asked. Stokoe replied that he might live for a long time. Napoleon angrily clenched his fist and exclaimed: "I should have lived to the age of eighty if they had not brought me to this vile place."[1]

Stokoe prepared a report for Lowe and Plampin in which he stated that Napoleon was suffering from chronic hepatitis, the same diagnosis that O'Meara had made before leaving St. Helena and had so loudly publicized in Europe. Neither Lowe nor Plampin were willing to accept it. The admiral suspected Stokoe was playing a part in another of Napoleon's intrigues and asked him on what grounds he had based his diagnosis. The doctor responded that Napoleon had told him he was suffering from hepatitis and his symptoms confirmed that this was the case.[2] "You are a very dangerous character," Plampin replied.[3] Both he and Lowe believed Stokoe was "not entirely unaware of the use that was to be made of him as the clandestine medium of communication between the people of Longwood and their friends in Europe." As a result Plampin initiated court-martial proceedings against Stokoe for violating Lowe's regulations.[4] Unaware of that, in late January, the doctor requested permission to leave St. Helena, which was granted. He carried a letter from Napoleon to Joseph.

With Stokoe's departure Napoleon once again found himself without medical care. "Here is the second English doctor dismissed from Longwood, with the exception of Baxter, who the French say is a poisoner," wrote Balmain, who had just returned from a long vacation in Brazil.[5] Lowe's suspicions of the Russian commissioner had increased after he learned that while in Rio de Janeiro he had spent most of his time "in the society of the French party, who are known to be warmly attached to Buonaparte." Particularly troublesome had been his contacts with General Hogendorp, "who paraded his attachment to the ex-Emperor and increasingly expresses his regret at not having been fortunate enough to accompany him to St. Helena."[6] Balmain had also been in contact with the Archduchess Leopoldina, the younger sister of Marie Louise, who was married to the heir of the Portuguese throne and was suspected of Bonapartist sympathies. Lowe found out that Balmain had brought some messages from Hogendorp and a number of French émigrés.[7] He considered the Russian commissioner a "very intriguing and dangerous character, strongly imbued if not with French principles, at least with strong admiration of the principal French Revolutionary character."[8] Since Balmain's return from Brazil, Lowe had prevented him from visiting Longwood. "Bonaparte believes himself sustained and defended by the Russian Commissioner. That makes him capricious and intractable," he told the Russian. Balmain realized that he had "to break with the French" and for an entire month he saw no one from Longwood. He later discovered that "there had never been so much argument, intrigue, and gossip" as during the time he was in Brazil.[9]

Being left without a doctor was the least of Napoleon's troubles. His health was not as bad as he pretended. In fact, he told Bertrand that he was "the same [as] . . . when I left Austerlitz."[10] He followed the affairs of Europe and America through the London newspapers, particularly the *Morning Chronicle*. "It appears that England doesn't want the independence of the Spanish colonies," he told Bertrand. "England is the biggest enemy of freedom in Europe and the world." Napoleon still hoped for a change of cabinet in England. "We have friends there," he said, thinking of Grey, Holland, and Wilson. Sooner or later the government would have to bow to pressure from British merchants, whose interests were affected by Castlereagh's misguided policy toward the Spanish colonies. Besides, he said, "if the state of things in France continues, as it is probable, there will be motions in the Chambers in my favor, and public opinion will be so strong that even the Bourbons will have to take steps in my favor."[11]

If the *Courier* ever reached his hands, he must have learned that the British government suspected that Cochrane planned to rescue him from St. Helena. The idea of freedom was in Napoleon's mind. "If I were free, I would go to America and would gather all my family there," he told Bertrand in February.[12] Did this explain his change of behavior? Balmain reported the impact of the London papers of July and August. "Napoleon, convinced that the Allied Sovereigns, especially the Emperor of Austria, were beginning to take his side against the Governor of St. Helena, was awaiting them with extraordinary impatience, and had his suite translate word for word all the articles of the agreement of Aix-la-Chapelle. He was much dissatisfied, for the *Morning Chronicle,* his most zealous defender, hardly speaks of it. *The Courier* crushes him with reproaches and insults. And *The Observer* of August 12 is quite clear that it is our August Master who is handing him over to his destiny. He has again shut himself up in his workroom and sees nobody, so that it is impossible to know what he is doing, and whether he is well or ill."[13] Napoleon was in fact feeling quite well and spent most of the time reading and dictating his memoirs about the Egyptian campaign.

In early March, Napoleon learned that Gourgaud had been arrested for participating in a plot to rescue him.[14] The news almost coincided with the arrival of a ciphered dispatch for Montchenu from Richelieu. It was the last set of instructions that Montchenu would receive from the French government until mid-1820. The instructions had been written in November, shortly after the *Mosquito* affair. Richelieu expressly instructed Montchenu "to increase as much as possible his relations with Bertrand, Montholon, etc."[15] When Lowe learned about these instructions he was quite disturbed, as he considered any communication with Napoleon's entourage to be illegal and "contrary to the spirit of his regulations."[16]

Lowe was particularly sensitive as he had just been reprimanded by Bathurst for not reporting that in late 1818 an American vessel had put into St. Helena with a plea of distress and "that on examination it proved that she was only deficient in water, which deficiency was supposed to have been purposely created." The ship had sailed around St. Helena for several days and had been repeatedly chased by British cruisers but "all attempts to come up with her had failed, and that the same vessel had frequently, after being chased, reappeared in her original station and continued for a length of time to hover around the island." Bathurst was convinced that this mysterious ship was connected with some plan of escape. A chastised Lowe replied that "the only papers that have fallen into my possession, except what have been at different times forwarded to me from your Lordship's Department, have been communicated from America."[17] Bathurst's scolding hurt Lowe's pride, but learning that Gourgaud had fooled him was worse.[18] On the other hand, he was pleased to learn that O'Meara had been discharged from the Royal Navy and that "the famous ex general Brayer . . . [had] been disgraced by San Martin."[19]

By mid-April, Napoleon's mood had changed. Maybe he had heard the bad news about Brayer, as the news from France was very encouraging. The liberal party had finally triumphed. Dessolles, the new prime minister had been one of his generals and Decazes had been Hortense's secretary. An unexpected visitor to Longwood gave him an opportunity to vent his anger at Lowe. Charles Ricketts, an East India officer in Canton and a cousin of Lord Liverpool, had stopped at St. Helena on his way back to England. Napoleon agreed to meet him and pretended to be ill. From his bed and in a weak voice he complained about Lowe, who wanted to take from him the only thing he had left: his dignity. He also made a laundry list of requests that he wanted transmitted to the British government: to bring O'Meara back; to take him to another location, as St. Helena was bad for his hepatitis; to replace Hudson Lowe with "a man of honor"; and to have free correspondence with Liverpool, the royal princes, or Lord Holland without it being read by Bathurst.[20] For two weeks after Rickett's departure Napoleon did not show himself to the orderly officer. Lowe grew alarmed and did not know what to do.

Napoleon waited for news in his room. It was only in late May that the full impact of what had happened at Aix-la-Chapelle hit him. Napoleon realized that he could no longer expect anything either from the tsar or the Austrian emperor. The former seemed to be under the influence of the wily Pozzo di Borgo, who hated Napoleon, while the latter followed the advice of Metternich, who was equally unsympathetic. Napoleon was devastated by the news. To make matters worse, the role played by Balmain in establishing communications with the tsar had been discovered. In fact, the Russian foreign minister recalled him with "a rather dry letter." (Nonetheless, he remained in St. Helena for another year.) Balmain told Bertrand that the tsar had been shocked at the reports of escape plans and a conspiracy and as a result had agreed to sign a strong declaration against Napoleon. In Balmain's view, "the English had very skillfully managed the whole affair."[21]

This setback convinced Napoleon of the need to send another messenger to Europe. Just by reading the English newspapers, he must have known that Spain was preparing a massive expedition to quash the insurgents in the colonies, that Brayer had been expelled from Buenos Aires, that Lallemand had failed in Texas, and that the United States had just signed a treaty with Spain that complicated his plans for Mexico. Joseph had bungled it again, as he had done in Spain. It would be very difficult for Cochrane, and Wilson if he ever left England, to succeed in South America, particularly if the Spaniards sent a massive armada.

Reading Gourgaud's account of the battle of Waterloo forced Napoleon to reexamine his abdication. In his opinion, to properly evaluate this decision it was necessary to "represent him" in America, not at St. Helena. If he had gone to America he would have been closer to the throne of France than if he had remained in Paris and fought a bitter civil war.[22] But that was history. What could he do now? He wasn't prepared to die at St. Helena. Even though his American dream now seemed impracticable, he still wielded enormous power in Europe. In Italy his name remained popular; in France, Decazes was now pulling the strings and most of the cabinet had served under him for years. The new Chamber of Peers included many of his supporters. "If Louis XVIII died tomorrow, I would have a great chance for my son," Napoleon said to Montholon.[23] Maybe it was time to focus on placing his son on the throne of France. He had to send another message to his supporters.

The messenger was Albine de Montholon, who accepted the commission after negotiating an attractive life pension.[24] There had long been rumors that Albine shared the emperor's bed with the tacit approval of her husband. At the end of May, Montholon asked Lowe to allow his wife to return to Europe in consequence of an incurable liver ailment.[25] Having learned his lesson the hard way with Gourgaud, Lowe was reluctant to authorize her direct departure to England without the usual quarantine at the Cape. But on the advice of one of the British naval surgeons stationed at St. Helena, Lowe eventually relented. Balmain reported that her liver obstruction was incurable and strong doses of mercury had not dissolved it. "She is a woman of heart and head, very charming, and of great use to me at St. Helena," wrote the Russian.[26] Albine left the island in early July with her young daughter Josephine, who many believed was Napoleon's daughter. We don't know what messages she carried to Europe. However, we know she was instructed to contact Wilson, Las Cases, and Eugene de Beauharnais.

After Albine's departure, Napoleon resumed his game of hide-and-seek with the orderly officer, who made "a series of vain attempts to see him." Bertrand warned the poor fellow that the emperor would consider "any person who should enter his private apartments without his content" as an assassin and shoot him. The orderly officer took notice.[27] Lowe grew increasingly irritated and worried. Was Napoleon still there?

39
A Revolution in England?

Alas, the country! How shall tongue or pen
Bewail her now uncountry gentlemen?
The last to bid the cry of warfare cease,
The first to make a malady of peace.

—Lord Byron, *The Age of Bronze,* Canto 14

As the summer arrived, the changes in France were overshadowed by troubles in the German confederation that would have far-reaching consequences. A fanatical liberal student murdered August von Kotzebue, a German intellectual suspected of being an agent of the tsar. Kotzebue's murder raised fears that the revolutionary fever that had affected France would infect Austria. Metternich reacted quickly, convening a meeting at the city of Carlsbad to discuss measures to prevent a popular uprising. The resulting Carlsbad Decrees imposed restrictions on press freedom, a ban on dangerous books—anything written by Locke, Voltaire, or Paine—and strict surveillance of secret societies, thus reflecting "the reactionary views entertained by the Sovereigns of continental Europe."[1] The Austrian chancellor believed that Kotzebue's murder and recent student riots were part of a movement to establish liberal constitutions across the continent. With them Metternich accomplished what he had wanted to do since 1813, and which the tsar had always spoiled: to quash the democratic spirit and stop in its tracks the movement for constitutionalism in his area of influence.[2]

The Carlsbad Decrees, the Foreign Enlistment Act in England, and the imminent departure of the Spanish expedition to quash the South American rebels suggested an ominous future for the cause of freedom in Europe and America. As if this was not enough, in the early summer Wilson learned of the disastrous defeat suffered by MacGregor at Portobello.[3] Goldsmith's *British Monitor* claimed that MacGregor was a Spanish agent and that he had betrayed his men. "He is to be deprived of his command which has been offered to General Maceroni, the chief of his staff, who is still in England," Goldsmith said.[4]

The Parisian *Le Constitutionnel* also expressed doubts about "the sincerity of his [MacGregor's] projects and his demonstrations for the cause of the patriots" and wondered what "other motives have led him on his attempts at conquest."[5]

Wilson and Maceroni had no time to determine whether MacGregor was a traitor or merely incompetent. To salvage their plans they had no choice but to leave England. Maceroni left the day before the Foreign Enlistment Act was passed and continued his recruiting efforts in Brussels and France, which under a liberal administration proved hospitable to his efforts. By the end of the summer the Anglo-Italian intriguer had acquired two ships and recruited more than 150 French and Belgian officers to reinforce MacGregor. Colonel Sanchez de Lima, a Portuguese aristocrat who had served in the Grande Armée as aide-de-camp of Marshal Soult, was the leader of the new contingent, which was made up of "forty French and Italian officers of experience, almost all decorated with Legion of Honor, also sixty British veterans." This new expedition was expected to depart from Antwerp immediately to reinforce MacGregor.[6] Maceroni also sent an Irish adventurer resident in Baltimore named John Devereux to Dublin to recruit an additional 3,000 soldiers. Although Devereux claimed to be financing the expedition with his own means, the American ambassador Richard Rush was sure somebody else was providing the funds. "All this would appear to be an undertaking too much for private means" and too difficult "to reconcile all this with the strict enforcement of the Foreign Enlistment Bill," Rush reported.[7] Devereux and his Irish Legion embarked for South America at the end of July.

At the imminent departure of a Spanish armada from Cadiz, Castlereagh decided to reinforce its naval presence in South America to ensure British interests were well protected. Admiral Sir Thomas Hardy, one of the most senior officers in the Royal Navy, was named to replace Commodore Bowles as head of the South American Naval Station. The Court of Madrid was informed that "the actual state of Spanish America and the complicated warfare which may shortly ensue" had imposed upon England "the necessity of strengthening the British naval force in that quarter of the globe for the effective protection and property of British subjects."[8] But as reported by the *British Monitor*, Hardy's mission had another equally important objective: "to watch Lord Cochrane's motions."[9] The American ambassador confirmed that Hardy "was destined for this service in consequence of the operations of Lord Cochrane's ships in those seas" and to prevent him from having "sole command in the Pacific."[10] But this was not Hardy's sole mission. In recent months Castlereagh had received several reports about the French monarchical intrigues in Buenos Aires. He took them seriously enough to instruct Hardy to intercept any ship carrying "a French prince to Buenos Aires."[11] The Duke of Lucca was Italian. Who was Castlereagh thinking about?

Wilson watched all the preparations undertaken by Spain with great anxiety. No matter how many troops Maceroni managed to recruit, if the Spanish expedition went ahead, Cochrane was doomed, and with him the cause of independence for the Spanish colonies. The expedition had to be stopped before it left Cadiz. Many disaffected Spanish officers shared Wilson's idea. They belonged to the secret society of the Comuneros and their objective was to impose a liberal constitution in Spain and to allow her colonies to become independent.[12] In mid-1819 the Spanish government discovered the existence of a conspiracy among the troops bound for South America and took swift measures to derail it. But the seeds of mutiny were planted.

The Comuneros were not the only secret society determined to revive the revolutionary spirit in Europe. In Italy the Carbonari advocated the expulsion of the Austrians and the creation of an independent Italian republic.[13] A French version, the Charbonniers, was established in 1816 by disaffected army officers who had not abandoned the dream of placing Napoleon II on the throne of France.[14] The Carbonari, the Charbonniers, and the Comuneros communicated among themselves and with Wilson. The exact nature of Wilson's ties with these secret societies is unclear. While in Italy in 1814 he had met Eugene de Beauharnais and Murat. Some of Murat's top lieutenants were the leaders of the Carbonari. Wilson's network of freedom fighters included liberal army officers in Spain and Portugal, the Marquis de Lafayette in France, and General Savary, whom he helped to obtain passage to England.[15] As to Maceroni, as former aide-de-camp and agent of Murat, his ties to the Carbonari were probably even stronger.

But an unexpected obstacle appeared in Wilson's path. In early July, against everybody's advice, he returned to Paris. His friends warned him that it would be easier for him to enter France than to get out. The ostensible reason for the trip was the poor health of his sister Fanny, who had fallen ill. Fanny had never abandoned her enthusiasm for Napoleon's cause and continued to be involved in the intrigues to release him from St. Helena. She kept up an active correspondence with her brother, Aimé Bonpland, and other Bonapartists exiled in North and South America. She may even have been responsible for publishing Brayer's *Manifesto* in the liberal *Minerve Française*.[16] Wilson, never a welcome guest of the Bourbons, was allowed back into France with a special permission from Decazes. "This is an unavoidable journey and return must depend on circumstances beyond my control," he told Grey.[17]

Wilson's reappearance in France worried the Ultras, as it suggested that under Decazes "the instigators of trouble had nothing to fear."[18] The fact that he arrived in Paris in the company of Colonel Forbin-Janson, a former aide-de-camp of Napoleon exiled in London, naturally increased their suspicions. Coincidentally, many other English Bonapartists traveled to Paris that summer taking advantage of a more tolerant administration. Among them was Maceroni, who was trying to organize a new expedition to help MacGregor, supposedly with the secret support of the new French cabinet.[19] O'Meara also passed through Paris with an undisclosed objective.[20] The Irish doctor was trying to raise money for a new project. Or so said Edward Blaquiere, an enigmatic Irishman who had strong connections with Napoleon's family.* Blaquiere had lately been "on a mission to see what the Bonaparte family would do for O'Meara. Lafitte has large sums of Napoleon's, which he will not refund at all. Eugene Beauharnais has millions, and suffers himself to be a cat's-paw of the Emperor of Russia, with the hopes of being in the Regency when the Bourbon dynasty falls in France. . . . Hortense, living at Constance on £4,000 a year, is selling her diamonds."[21] But it wasn't simply about rewarding O'Meara. According to Maceroni, the Irish doctor wanted Cardinal Fesch and Eugene to finance the latest plan to rescue Napoleon.

Given Wilson's close relationship with O'Meara we can surmise that he was fully aware of these plans. Although Wilson was busy taking care of his sister, he had time for a Masonic ceremony organized in his honor. At the end of August, the Supreme Council of the Thirty-third Degree of the Ancient and Accepted Scottish Rite, which counted Decazes among its members, appointed Wilson as its representative in England.[22] The grand master reminded the French brothers attending the ceremony that "one life saved by him, gives him more title to our love than all the others he took while serving his country."[23] Wilson didn't have time to bask in his Masonic glory. Despite Fanny's deteriorating health, he was forced to return to England. It was the last time he saw his sister, as she died a few months later. Some of her friends suspected foul play.[24]

Wilson's sudden departure from Paris was prompted by news of political disturbances in England that presaged a revolution. In the middle of the summer the Radical leader Henry Hunt, an old acquaintance of Wilson and Cochrane,

* Edward Blaquiere (1779–1832) would later enlist Byron and others in the struggle for Greek independence.

convened a demonstration in Manchester in support of parliamentary reform. It had followed another demonstration Hunt had organized at Smithfield, on the outskirts of London. On that occasion Hunt had proposed a series of resolutions that were unanimously approved by the demonstrators. The last one stated that "this meeting unequivocally disclaim[s] any share or participation in the disgraceful and cowardly acts of the borough mongers in placing the brave Napoleon a prisoner, to perish upon a desert island, shut out from human society, and torn from his only son, whilst he is exposed to the brutal insolence of a hired keeper." The *Times* lambasted Hunt and judged "the commiseration of the Smithfield Orators despicable and wicked."[25]

Initially, Hunt chose August 16, coincidentally the day after Napoleon's birthday, as the date for the Manchester meeting, but he later changed it to the nineteenth. Almost sixty thousand people, carrying tricolor flags and bearing banners saying "Annual Parliaments," "Universal Suffrage," "Vote by Ballot," gathered to hear "Orator" Hunt. When Hunt appeared on the podium, he was greeted by a rapturous ovation. But as he prepared to deliver his speech, a regiment of the Manchester cavalry militia appeared. The troops, sent by the authorities to preserve the "public order," read Hunt the "Riot Act" and then put him under arrest. The demonstrators started booing and the situation quickly got out of control. The cavalrymen charged the crowd brandishing their swords and indiscriminately trampling over men, women, and children. Eleven people were killed and almost four hundred were wounded.[26] The Peterloo Massacre, as it was called, had a chilling effect throughout the country. Hobhouse thought "the end of it will be either a reform of parliament or a despotism."[27] An indignant Sir Francis Burdett demanded a parliamentary investigation. "What, kill men unarmed, unresisting and gracious God, women too!" he wrote to a friend, "Is this England? This is a Christian land? A land of Freedom? Can such things be and pass by us like a summer cloud, unheeded."[28] Unfazed by the critics, Lord Sidmouth, the home secretary, praised the Manchester magistrates in a highly publicized letter for their "prompt, decisive and efficient measures" to preserve "public tranquility."[29]

As soon as Wilson set foot in England, he joined the government critics and supported Burdett's motion for a parliamentary inquiry. In a speech he gave at the House of Commons he said that although he was "no radical" he believed that Radical reformers should not "be placed out of the pale of the constitution."[30] Wilson even shook hands with Hunt at a public meeting in London. Grey, who had long worried about Wilson's contacts with Hobhouse and Burdett, warned him that he was getting too close with "extremely radical company." Wilson replied that the real terrorists were not the Radicals but the government ministers. "I have very little [sympathy] for the former if the law be not outraged to check them and if reasonable concessions be granted to the spirit of reform." The government ministers were "tyrants in nature, education and habits" and Sidmouth's letter a "flagrant proof of their vicious designs against the constitution and humanity."[31]

In Wilson's view the only remedy for England's problems was parliamentary reform. He had put his plans to join Cochrane on hold due to the declining health of his sister and his wife.[32] But Wilson didn't forget Napoleon's cause. Albine de Montholon had just arrived in England and had been immediately deported to Belgium despite carrying a sick child. Wilson had not been able to meet or talk to Albine but proposed a parliamentary inquiry into her deportation. Not surprisingly, his motion was defeated. Shortly after Albine arrived in Brussels, her young daughter died.[33]

But Albine must have left a message for Wilson, for when Gourgaud learned of her travails he wrote to him from Hamburg asking for "news of all the persons whom she has just left." Although Gourgaud blamed the countess for his departure from St. Helena, he offered his services to her "to decrease the sufferings of the Emperor."[34] Gourgaud also wrote to Albine, reasserting his devotion to Napoleon.[35] He told Wilson he was determined to see the tsar to plead for the removal of the emperor from St. Helena.[36] But Tsar Alexander had no interest in helping Napoleon. Influenced by Metternich and spooked by a peasant rebellion at home, he saw the prisoner of St. Helena as the source of all the turbulence spreading throughout Europe.[37]

Despite the tragedy that had befallen her, Albine lost no time in contacting Eugene de Beauharnais and asking for his assistance in her efforts to obtain Napoleon's release. Unfortunately her letter has not survived, but Eugene's reply has. Eugene explained that he could not comply with her second request. "I would like to find among the ruins of my fortune the means of aiding in the recognition of those for whom I have proved to have these noble feelings. However I have a numerous family and I would compromise their interest and my security if I engage in enterprises that are above my forces. I hope you understand these observations."[38] Eugene's letters seems to suggest that he was trying to distance himself from any effort to ameliorate the situation of his stepfather. However this impression may be misleading. The problem with the very few letters of Napoleon's supporters that have survived is that we cannot be certain whether they express the writers' true opinions or whether the letters were deliberately misleading in the expectation that they would be intercepted. Eugene knew very well that he was under strict surveillance, and it is unlikely he would write anything that could compromise him. Wilson's experience in the Lavallette affair had shown that any sensitive information would have to be communicated in cipher or verbally. Therefore we cannot entirely dismiss the possibility that Eugene supported Albine's "enterprises," particularly since until the day he died, his name would continue to be linked with Bonapartist plots.

Back in London, Lord Liverpool called for extended parliamentary sessions. Many Whigs feared he took this step "for the purpose of infringing upon our liberties."[39] These fears were not unfounded, as in late November the ministers introduced legislation known as the "Six Acts," which severely limited the constitutional rights of every British subject and in fact declared that "every meeting for radical reform is an overt act of treasonable conspiracy against the King and his government." Wilson and other Whigs voted against the bill arguing that it "would encourage Radicals to become even more rebellious."[40] But the majority of the House approved the legislation. Wilson was convinced that England was veering toward despotism. The first victim of the Six Acts was John Cam Hobhouse, who was well known for his Bonapartism.[41] He was arrested for writing "a pamphlet likely to inflame people to violence."[42]

It was at this time that HMS *Owen Glendower* left for Buenos Aires under the command of Captain Robert Spencer, younger brother of John Spencer, Viscount Althorp, one of the most outspoken critics of the government in Parliament.[43] After the Peterloo incident Althorp criticized the government so strongly that the Tories accused him of sympathizing with "the Radical agitators." Althorp also voted with Wilson against the passing of the Six Acts.[44] Although only twenty-nine, Captain Spencer was an experienced seaman. Fluent in Spanish and French, he had served under Sir Alexander Cochrane in the campaign of New Orleans.[45] How much his political views were influenced by his brother is unclear, but what is certain is that his family's liberalism was as well known as their sympathy toward the prisoner of St. Helena. The Admiralty also made two other peculiar appointments. Frederick Maitland, the former captain of the *Bellerophon,* who still regretted having misled Napoleon into surrendering, was appointed to the Brazil naval station, and Frederick Marryat, who had served for many years with Cochrane and greatly admired him, was appointed to the St. Helena station.[46] With Spencer in Buenos Aires, Maitland in Rio de Janeiro, and Marryat at St. Helena, sending messages to Napoleon would be much easier.

40
Cochrane Alone

The fate of Chile in a great measure now depends on the circumstances, the exertions of the Government and those of Lord Cochrane.

— James Charles to Sir Robert Wilson, October 18, 1819

By mid-1819, if Brayer still entertained any hopes of liberating Napoleon from St. Helena, they depended on the success of the enterprise that Jose Miguel Carrera was about to launch. Determined to return to his native Chile, in recent months Carrera had forged an unlikely alliance with some provincial caudillos. They were united by their hatred of the faction that had ruled Buenos Aires since 1816 and now wanted to impose on them a foreign prince with the connivance of the Holy Alliance. If everything went well, Carrera expected to be in Santiago by the end of the year. According to the plan, Alvear would become supreme director in Buenos Aires and would provide all the "resources needed to invade Chile to oust O'Higgins and San Martin."[1] Alvear and Carrera counted on the support of most of Napoleon's veterans who had sought exile in Buenos Aires. On August 1, 1819, Carrera left Montevideo at the head of a band of partisans that included not only his loyal compatriots but also hard-core Bonapartists, including Brayer's son and a few officers who had served in Joseph's army in Spain. General Fressinet, who had been pardoned, had decided to return to France, where the prospects of Bonapartism seemed brighter.[2] He had no intention of keeping quiet.

In Santiago, Cochrane pushed O'Higgins to approve an expedition against Lima under his command. But O'Higgins dragged his feet. His lack of resolve was related to San Martin's attitude; he remained in Mendoza unsure what to do. On the one hand, he faced a serious threat to his power in Chile. On the other hand, the government of Buenos Aires had ordered him to come back to defend the city against the twin threats of a Spanish expedition and an attack by

Carrera, Alvear, and the provincial caudillos. San Martin was reluctant to obey.[3] He probably realized that his old allies were doomed.

Convinced that he could single-handedly liberate Peru, Cochrane asked the Chilean government to provide him with ten thousand experienced men, now under San Martin's command. He assured O'Higgins that with these troops "it would be possible to seize the forts of Callao and destroy all the Spanish vessels in the harbor." Alerted by one of his allies, San Martin made a counterproposal to O'Higgins.[4] Cochrane should immediately set sail and attempt to intercept the Spanish expedition in the South Atlantic before it arrived in Buenos Aires. In this way San Martin expected to kill two birds with one stone: to get rid of Cochrane and to avoid returning to the capital as he had been ordered. As soon as Cochrane learned about this proposal "he openly opposed it." In his view it was strategically unsound to move the squadron to the South Atlantic. To achieve victory he counted on a revolutionary weapon that had never been used before in America: the Congreve rocket. The rockets had been manufactured in Chile under the supervision of Wilson's aide-de-camp, Lieutenant Colonel James Charles, who had been trained in artillery at the Royal Academy at Woolwich. Weeks earlier Charles had personally tested the rockets and had been so satisfied with the results that he had asked Wilson to put "a paragraph in the *Morning Chronicle* respecting my improvements."[5] Cochrane was so confident that he told O'Higgins that he would respond "with his own head" if he was unable to destroy the Spanish squadron anchored at Callao.[6] San Martin remained skeptical and advised O'Higgins to dissuade the Scotsman by stimulating his "pecuniary" ambitions.[7] However, a new and desperate order from Buenos Aires, where he was needed with his troops "as soon as possible," forced San Martin's hand.[8]

In early September, after three months of negotiations with the Chilean government, Cochrane again put out to sea with his squadron. But he didn't get all the troops he had requested. Instead, the government had promised that he would be able to embark some regiments at Coquimbo, in northern Chile. His squadron included five warships and, aside from the Congreve rockets, it had the same firepower as his earlier expedition, since the Chilean government had not acquired any new vessels and, to Cochrane's frustration, the *Rising Star* was still docked on the Thames.* To make matters worse, his officers, mostly British or American veterans, had a hard time dealing with the inexperienced

*The *Rising Star* was allowed to sail to Chile at the end of 1821, when she was no longer needed.

local crews. San Martin and his allies in Santiago had laid a trap for Cochrane. When he arrived in Coquimbo, instead of finding the crack troops promised by O'Higgins, he found ninety men without training or uniforms. Indignant, he almost returned to Santiago to submit his resignation, but encouraged by the potential of the Congreve rockets, and the promise of additional reinforcements, he went ahead.

By the end of September, Cochrane's squadron was again at Callao, facing the formidable firepower of the Spanish batteries. In the next few days his men built rafts to launch his fearsome rockets. On October 19, Lieutenant Colonel Charles reconnoitered the bay by boat and tried to launch the Congreve rockets with no success. Days later he made a new attempt, which was equally unsuccessful. To prevent any damage to their ships, the Spaniards pulled down their rigs. Frustrated by the lack of results, Cochrane launched a new combined attack with rockets and mortars on November 2. But the hopes that he and Charles had placed on these weapons were again disappointed. The rockets were useless. Some exploded before being launched; others fired aimlessly; most of them simply didn't work. Apparently they had been built by Spanish prisoners who had deliberately mixed the powder with sand, sawdust, and even iron. Maybe there was another explanation. There were many powerful men in Santiago interested in Cochrane's failure. A subsequent attack with fire vessels also failed. It seemed Cochrane's career in South America had ended. Ignoring orders to return to Valparaiso, he took part of his squadron and sailed toward Guayaquil in search of a Spanish frigate carrying a valuable treasure. He also wanted to find MacGregor, whose whereabouts were unknown, and he sent another ship to explore the coast of Panama.[9]

Before leaving for Guayaquil, Cochrane ordered Lieutenant Colonel Charles to attack a Spanish fortress in Pisco with four hundred men, assuming it would be an easy victory. The night before the attack Charles wrote a long letter to Wilson describing what had happened in Chile since his arrival. Full of foreboding, he admitted that they had been too optimistic and that the results of the campaign so far had been disappointing. "The errors and horrors produced by a vacillating government must now be evident," lamented Charles. Instead of giving Cochrane "a military force with a discretionary power to dispose fit to the south of Lima, the most vulnerable and at this time the best point to have attacked Peru . . . his time was taken up in petty demonstrations, which had no other effect beyond not attacking the enemy." Cochrane had lost three valuable months and during this period of inactivity, "for which the Spaniards have to thank the legislative corps of Chile who control all plans, they [had] recovered from the shock [of] the blockade of their ports and the consequent stagnation of their commerce" and had sent reinforcements to Lima. "The fate of Chile in a great measure now depends on the circumstances, the exertions of the Government and those of Lord Cochrane." Charles once again asked Wilson to join the South American campaign:

> I am very much grieved you did not determine to leave England at the period you were negotiating with Alvarez.* You would certainly have been placed in the Command of the Army of Chile, for there are many jealousies and fear respecting the vices of the government of Buenos Aires that would make your presence, not only necessary but highly advantageous to this country. It would have also been more congenial to your pursuits and I am certain the fruits of your execution would pay you handsomely for the present sacrifice you might make, there your character as a military man would be enhanced for the whole world is interested in the liberty of South America. I am of the opinion with Lord Cochrane who often speaks kindly of you and regrets you not having come to this country. . . . Write to the Supreme Director don Bernardo O'Higgins to say you are on your way. A letter drawn up in your peculiar style would be such as to produce the feeling you ought to write. Chile has no good officers except one or two in subordinate situations, therefore the load is quite open to you.[10]

Unbeknownst to Charles, the plans of Wilson and Cochrane in London were about to suffer another blow. On the coast of Venezuela, MacGregor was adding another embarrassing fiasco to his career. Weeks after his humiliating escape from Portobello, he had returned to Haiti where he found the troops that Maceroni had recruited in Europe under the command of Colonel Sanchez de Lima, a Portuguese aristocrat who had served in the Grande Armée. Unsure about what to do, MacGregor accepted a proposal from Bolivar to launch a combined offensive against the Spaniards and prepared his men for an attack of the Spanish garrison at Rio Hacha, on the Venezuelan coast. He arrived there at the beginning of October, almost at the same time Cochrane reached Callao and, according to Maceroni, did everything "that imbecility and coward-

---

* Alvarez Condarco was San Martin's envoy in London.

ice" could do to derail the expedition. Instead of launching a surprise attack during the night, he announced his presence to the Spanish batteries and allowed them to organize their defense. The following day he put his men under the command of Sanchez de Lima, an Irish colonel named Eyre, and Lieutenant Colonel Borel, another veteran of the Grande Armée, and launched an attack against superior forces. After a bloody encounter, the Spaniards retreated. During this time MacGregor remained on his ship drinking, smoking, and singing patriotic hymns. Only after assuring himself that his men had succeeded did he disembark with a small escort. But the Spanish fortress was taken only due to the courage and intrepidity of Sanchez de Lima, Eyre, and Borel. And just like at Portobello, MacGregor took no precautions. Days later the Spaniards launched a surprise counterattack.[11] MacGregor quickly boarded his ship and left his three subordinates in charge of the defense. He later claimed that the British troops had deserted him on the eve of battle but his explanation was not very convincing.[12]

For whatever reason, MacGregor's expedition to Rio Hacha was even more disastrous than the one to Portobello. Colonel Eyre and most of the French officers died fighting. The few survivors, including Sanchez de Lima and more than a hundred British, Scottish, and Irish men, were taken prisoner and executed by the Spaniards.[13] The court of Madrid never heard a complaint from the Foreign Office about this cold-blooded massacre. MacGregor's attack was of great use to Bolivar, as it distracted the Spaniards and allowed him to march into Colombia without encountering any serious opposition. MacGregor's departure also allowed Bolivar to incorporate into his army the Irish Legion recruited by Devereux in Dublin, which was critical to his subsequent victories. The Venezuelan leader had never supported the Bonapartist plans for the Spanish colonies, and like San Martin, he believed that England was the natural ally of the independence movement. As for MacGregor, we shall never know whether he was a spy, an incompetent commander, or a coward. But he not only survived these disasters but years later was able to raise money for another ill-fated enterprise in South America.[14]

With Lallemand neutralized in New Orleans, Brayer exiled in Montevideo, and MacGregor defeated, the success of the South American campaign rested on Cochrane's shoulders and maybe Wilson's, if the health of his wife allowed him to leave England. But the project of liberating Napoleon to place him on the throne of a new American empire faced formidable obstacles.

In Buenos Aires the government had just received the proposal from Louis

XVIII to establish the Duke of Lucca as the country's new sovereign. It was the only hope of survival for the ruling faction. The supreme director urged the recently assembled Congress to accept the proposal. During a secret session, the deputies agreed to the plan if several conditions were met: (1) the Allied powers, particularly Spain and England, supported the plan; (2) France would facilitate the marriage of the young duke with a Portuguese princess and Portugal would relinquish her claims over Montevideo; (3) France would help the new sovereign to establish a monarchy in the old Spanish viceroyalty of the River Plate, including the province of Montevideo. Finally, if Spain rejected Dessolles's proposal and sent an expedition to Buenos Aires, France would send troops to defend the city.[15] Unknown to the approving deputies, another cabinet change had taken place in France. Baron Etienne Pasquier, who had served Napoleon for many years, was now at the head of the Ministry of Foreign Affairs and aborted the negotiations regarding the crowning of Lucca in Buenos Aires. Some suspected that Decazes had another candidate in mind: Napoleon's son.

With or without a foreign monarch, the ruling party in Buenos Aires faced serious threats: not only a Spanish expedition but also an attack by Carrera, Alvear, and the caudillos. The government once again ordered San Martin to return to the capital with his army. The Argentine general had awoken from his opium-induced lethargy. But as Bowles reported, he remained reluctant "to move from Mendoza." In fact, by this time San Martin had already left for Buenos Aires with a strong escort but halfway there he learned of the new offensive by Carrera. This news convinced him to return to Mendoza, disobeying his orders and abandoning his former allies to their fate, reportedly because he feared to do otherwise would derail his planned expedition to Peru, which he expected to launch at the end of the December.[16]

Meanwhile, in Peru, the results of Cochrane's expedition were almost as bad as MacGregor's. His rockets had failed miserably at Callao and the attack of Pisco ended tragically. The night before the attack, Charles learned that the Spanish garrison was much stronger than they had expected. It might have been prudent to reembark, especially as two-thirds of his men were new recruits, but the "remembrance of the disappointments before Callao produced an unanimous desire to attack." Instead of aborting the mission Charles launched an attack and was mortally wounded while leading it. "Cool and collected to the last moment, the manner in which he died would have done honor to any hero of ancient or modern times."[17] It was a great loss for Cochrane, who had come to rely heavily on Charles, and also for Wilson, who lost his loyal aide-de-camp.

The news of Cochrane's defeat reached Buenos Aires in mid-December just as Commodore Hardy was about to take command of the Buenos Aires naval station.[18] In contrast to Bowles, who had never got along with Cochrane, Hardy had known him for many years and although he didn't share his politics, he had great respect for his abilities as a naval officer. At Valparaiso, Cochrane licked his wounds. His first year as commander of the Chilean fleet had been a complete disaster. He was "greatly annoyed" at having failed at Callao and humiliated by the defeat at Pisco. His enemies in Santiago plotted his downfall. To frustrate their designs and assuage his "own wounded feelings" he decided to risk everything on a spectacular and daring coup.[19]

41
Toujours la France

Farewell to thee, France!—but when Liberty rallies
Once more in thy regions, remember me then,
The violet still grows in the depth of thy valleys;
Though wither'd, thy tear will unfold it again.

—Lord Byron, "Napoleon's Farewell"

By mid-1819 Napoleon had probably lost all hope that his American dream would ever become a reality. Lallemand had failed, and the United States would make any enterprise directed against Mexico very difficult, if not impossible. Brayer's disgrace in Chile suggested that South America was also out of reach. Maybe it had been a crazy idea after all. Maybe under the rule of the liberals France offered more hope for Napoleon II than the Spanish colonies. Louis XVIII was old and would probably die soon, and neither Artois nor any of his sons offered much hope for the survival of the Bourbon dynasty. The French cabinet was made up of men who had served him for years: Dessolles, Decazes, Pasquier, Molé, and Gouvion St. Cyr. Former marshals of the empire such as Davout, Monceau, and Jourdan had joined the Chamber of Peers and Grouchy, Exelmans, Fressinet, and other exiled Bonapartists had been pardoned. Despite the setback he had suffered at the Congress of Aix-la-Chapelle, Napoleon could see a ray of hope in France.

His fears of an assassination attempt resurfaced in August when Lowe violently put down a riot of Chinese laborers. He discontinued his walks and confined himself to his room. The orderly officer stationed at Longwood could only ascertain his presence because sometimes he heard him talking.[1] Unsure whether Napoleon was still there, Lowe fretted for a few weeks. To his great relief, in late August, the prisoner was sighted in the distance. Satisfied that Napoleon had not escaped, Lowe turned his attention to the physician Stokoe, who in early September returned to St. Helena to face a court-martial. After four sessions, the doctor was "unanimously declared guilty of the accusations brought against him and was condemned to be dismissed." Lowe had publicized the verdict and "almost persuaded people" that Stokoe would be hanged. Everybody wondered why O'Meara, who was supposedly much guiltier than his colleague, was not likewise tried "either before an ordinary jury on board the *Conqueror* or before an extraordinary tribunal at London."[2]

At the end of September a new set of companions for Napoleon arrived from England, including two priests, Buonavita and Vignali, a doctor named Francesco Antommarchi, and two chefs, all selected by Cardinal Fesch, Napoleon's uncle who lived in Rome under the watchful eye of the Vatican.[3] How much freedom Fesch had in selecting Napoleon's new companions is unclear. The Vatican states were under the control of Cardinal Consalvi, who was an implacable enemy of Bonapartism, constitutionalism, and liberalism in all their variations. Like Metternich, Consalvi feared the Carbonari, who advocated the creation of an independent republic in Italy.[4] It is hard to believe he would miss such a good opportunity to spy on Napoleon.

The new arrivals made up an odd group. Antommarchi, a Corsican by birth, was an anatomist and had never practiced medicine. He was a peculiar choice to take care of a patient who was supposedly suffering from a serious liver illness. Balmain thought Antommarchi was a "subtle and clever Corsican" but totally unsuited for his new position. Napoleon agreed. He found his new doctor presumptuous and uncouth. Why hadn't Fesch sent him a French doctor? Faced with the alternative of no medical treatment or having to see a British physician, Napoleon resigned himself. After a brief examination of his patient, Antommarchi diagnosed an obstruction of the liver.[5]

As to Father Buonavita, his presence at St. Helena was as inexplicable as Antommarchi's. Napoleon had never been religious. In addition, the sixty-seven-year-old priest was in very poor health and had recently suffered an attack of apoplexy. Montholon thought he was nearly moribund.[6] Surely there were many other candidates who could have taken his position. Why would Buonavita agree to go to an island whose climate would surely take him to his grave? Maybe he thought he was going to die anyway. Buonavita was completely devoted to Napoleon. In fact, he had once served as Napoleon's agent in Mexico promoting the insurrection against Spain.[7] Balmain thought that by detaching Napoleon "from the petty concerns of this world" Buonavita would "be the one of the five who will have been the most useful to him."[8] The last chapter on Buonavita remains to be written.

For the first time since arriving at St. Helena, Napoleon seemed resigned to his fate. His arguments with Lowe ceased. He sent a message to Balmain asking him to thank Tsar Alexander for the interest he had taken in his health. "I am a captive and so cannot prove my gratitude. Let him not abandon me forever." Napoleon also advised Balmain to try to get along with Lowe, whom he called "my assassin."[9] According to the Russian envoy, everything presaged "the end of intrigues" at Longwood, but maybe it was only the calm before a storm.[10] At this time Napoleon received a message of great interest. Bertrand did not provide any details about its contents but mentioned "a change of ministers."[11] Was he referring to France or England? Another piece of news that caught his attention was the passing of a Foreign Enlistment Act. Napoleon thought the filibustering expeditions organized in London would always serve England's interest. After all, France had been able to take possession of Haiti thanks to the filibusters.[12] And he had his own filibusters at work in South America.

Whatever the message was it improved Napoleon's mood and also his health. At the end of November, Balmain reported the latter as excellent, which was notable considering that with the advent of the spring, dysentery, liver diseases, and fevers wreaked havoc among the British troops stationed near Longwood. Even Balmain and Montchenu's secretary fell ill and complained of liver ailments. Napoleon instead was full of energy, "amusing himself with gardening" and putting "his whole suite hard at work—men, women, even old Father Buonavita."[13] Like Voltaire's Candide, Napoleon had decided to cultivate his own garden. Lowe reported that nothing could "exceed the bustle and activity which has been recently displayed by General Bonaparte, in giving directions about his flower garden and superintending the workmen employed at it. He is hemming it in all round with as bushy trees and shrubs as he can get transplanted."[14] Napoleon believed Lowe only wished for his death. "He calls for that moment; it comes too slowly to satisfy his impatience," he told Antommarchi. "But let him be comforted; this horrible climate is charged with the execution of the crime, and it will fulfill its trust sooner than he expects."[15]

The month of December passed uneventfully. Lowe was calmer. However, he grew suspicious about Antommarchi, who one night tried to leave Longwood without authorization.[16] Whom was the doctor trying to visit?

6
1820

Napoleon's Shadow Cast over Europe

Neglected or forgotten:—such was Spain;
But such she is not, nor shall be again.

—Lord Byron, *The Age of Bronze,* Canto 7

"The more however I think on the state of this miserable country the more I regret my inability to remove, but with a mind fully [bent] on so doing perhaps opportunity may be found," Wilson wrote to Grey in early 1820.[1] Wilson regretted not having been able to join Cochrane in South America and was quite disappointed at his parliamentary career. "Disgusted with public life," he had almost resolved to retire and move to France.[2] Wilson's spirits were raised a few weeks later when he learned that a military rebellion had occurred among the Spanish officers and soldiers "assembled at Cadiz for the purpose of being sent to South America."[3] The mutiny ended the hopes of Ferdinand VII of ever quashing the insurrection in the colonies and guaranteed the independence of Buenos Aires, and perhaps of the entire continent.[4] The leader of the rebellion was a young officer named Rafael del Riego, who had spent six years as a prisoner in France, where he had been indoctrinated with the ideas of the French Revolution and the principles of Freemasonry. Riego was a member of the Comuneros, a secret society linked to the Carbonari in France and Italy that sought to establish a liberal constitution in Spain.[5] It seemed Napoleon had been right: "Ferdinand, with all his rage, might try to hold on to his scepter; one of these mornings, it will slip out of his hands like an eel."[6] Wilson was ecstatic at the news. "Every man is at his post!" he exclaimed enthusiastically. He thought that the revolution in Spain would have "a very important influence in France."[7]

The European sovereigns and their ministers were dismayed. The French Bourbons, who felt the most threatened by Riego's rebellion, wanted to send troops across the Pyrenees to put it down. The tsar supported the military intervention of the Holy Alliance. But wary of Russia's growing power, Castlereagh and Metternich torpedoed this proposal. Their response was evidence of the fragility of the system crafted five years earlier at the Congress of Vienna. The massive social and political pressures that built up after Waterloo were about to explode. During 1820 the European monarchies faced their biggest challenge since Napoleon's return from Elba. Lord Liverpool's prediction that "at such a distance and in such a place [St. Helena], all intrigue would be impossible, and being withdrawn so far from the European world, he would very soon be forgotten" never seemed less fitting. Nobody had forgotten Napoleon; his presence was felt everywhere. His escape continued to be the subject of constant rumors. According to the latest, an English packet had brought to St. Helena a false order to move the illustrious prisoner to the Cape of Good Hope and "five privateers which had been equipped in a port of South America" planned to rescue him during the voyage.[8]

The difficult diplomatic negotiations between the Allied powers regarding Spain had barely started when all of Europe was shaken by the assassination of the Duke of Berri, nephew of Louis XVIII and heir to the throne. The murderer was a veteran of Napoleon's army named Louvel. Although he always claimed to have acted alone, there were strong suspicions of a broader conspiracy. The Prussian ambassador in Paris thought there was no doubt that Louvel had lied when "declaring that the crime was planned by himself alone" and that moral complicity in the crime was "shared by all the revolutionists and ultra liberals." Other foreign diplomats held similar views.[9] Interestingly, a few weeks before the assassination, the French police had been warned about a plot to kill the royal prince.[10]

Berri's murder was a clear attempt to end the Bourbon dynasty in France. Louis XVIII was a bachelor; Artois was old; and the Duchess of Angouleme was barren. All the hopes of the royalists had rested on the recently married young prince. With his death these hopes seemed dashed forever. The immediate consequence was a violent reaction against the liberal party. The Ultras blamed Decazes, whom they had long suspected of being a closet Bonapartist, for encouraging the extreme left and allowing the return to France of "all the outlaws, Jacobins, liberals who had armed the murderer and filled his head with crazy ideas." A member of the Ultra faction in the Chamber of Peers even proposed impeaching Decazes for being Louvel's accomplice.[11] Under enormous pressure, Decazes was forced to resign and Louis XVIII asked Richelieu to form a new cabinet. The Ultras were again in power. And to their relief, a few weeks later they found out that the Duchess of Berri was pregnant. Maybe the Bourbon dynasty would have an heir after all!

The prospects for the Spanish Bourbons were much bleaker. In March, under pressure from the revolutionaries, Ferdinand VII had accepted a liberal constitution. It was the first time since 1789 that an established European monarch had been forced to do so. Many exiled liberals returned to Spain to join the fight for freedom, including the famous *guerrillero* Francisco Espoz y Mina, whose nephew had led an ill-fated expedition to Mexico. Not surprisingly, he was in regular contact with Wilson.[12]

While Paris recovered from the shock of Berri's murder, London was stunned by the discovery of a plot to kill all cabinet ministers. The plot—known as the Cato Street conspiracy—was led by Arthur Thistlewood, who in 1816 had organized the Spa Field meetings that had indirectly led to Cochrane's arrest. Two months earlier Castlereagh had received a disturbing anonymous message warning him that on the last day of January a "horrid circumstance" would occur, to be followed "by a general rising of the disaffected."[13] Castlereagh told the American ambassador that by murdering all the ministers in a single night, the conspirators expected to overturn the government.[14] Countess Lieven, wife of the Russian ambassador, learned more details during a conversation with the Duke of Wellington whom Thistlewood had apparently chosen as his victim. "There had been a long fight over Castlereagh," she told Metternich. "They were to invite the populace and the army to join them, to announce the downfall of tyranny and to constitute themselves as the government of the people."[15]

The Tories were quick to find the real culprits. The *Courier* observed that some of the arrested plotters "ascribe their unfortunate situation to the influence of Hunt's speeches and Cobbett's writings" and that the conspiracy was "the legitimate offspring of Radical principles, which are themselves a compound of treason, infidelity and plunder."[16] In a very short period Thistlewood and his accomplices were tried, convicted, and executed. Hobhouse thought "they died like heroes" and that the Cato Street conspiracy was just "a trump card for the ministers just before the election." According to a modern historian, it was a "continuing conspiracy in which the government themselves were the conspirators."[17] Whether real or invented, the conspiracy was used by the government to crack down on the opposition. Burdett spent a few months in prison, and Hunt was convicted of being a person "of a wicked and turbulent disposition" and sentenced to two and a half years in prison. "The verdict against Hunt has intoxicated ministers with joy," Wilson complained. "They regard it as a complete justification but I hope the nation will think otherwise."[18]

The British government found comfort in reports suggesting that Cochrane's career in South America had ended in disgrace. The *Courier* gleefully announced: "The disasters attendant on the operations of Lord Cochrane follow in quick succession."[19] The *British Monitor* poked fun at the rebel admiral with the headline "Lord Cochrane's Bravado or Mock Congreve Rockets."[20] These reports were followed by accounts of MacGregor's disasters. Wilson was greatly affected by the news and particularly by the death of James Charles, his loyal aide-de-camp. It seemed as if the South American campaign would founder even without the threat of a Spanish expedition. These setbacks made him turn his attention to the struggle for freedom in Europe. He was in close contact with Lafayette, Mina, and other freedom fighters throughout the continent and was well aware of their plans.[21] It wouldn't be at all surprising if he had coordinated their efforts.

Meanwhile, the Austrian authorities discovered that Eugene de Beauharnais had transferred substantial funds to London. In Parma, Count Neipperg, the zealous and virile guardian of Marie Louise, had intercepted a letter from Joseph in which he said that he had "great hopes" for Napoleon's release and that Napoleon II would not be "an archbishop."[22] Metternich was furious. These damned Bonapartes never gave up! One of the few surviving letters from Joseph to Napoleon suggests that Metternich was right. Joseph said that he was alone, that only Pierre Real and the Lallemands had remained steadfast in their devotion, and that his house had burned. Joseph suspected the fire had been deliberately started to burn certain correspondence between Napoleon and the sovereigns of Austria and Russia during the Hundred Days that his brother had asked O'Meara to publish when he left St. Helena. Despite all these setbacks Joseph assured Napoleon that his cause was not lost and that the reaction against the policies of the Holy Alliance was strong all over Europe.[23]

In fact the boldest scheme to rescue Napoleon was under way. As Sir Walter Scott would reveal years later, a submarine "was to be the means of effecting this enterprise." Barry O'Meara, the man behind the project, had enlisted the aid of Thomas Johnstone, "a smuggler of an uncommonly resolute character."[24] At some point in his checkered career Johnstone had worked with Robert Fulton on the design and construction of a submarine, first for Napoleon and then for the Royal Navy.[25] His design, of wrought and cast iron, resembled "a porpoise" in shape. Twenty-seven feet long and five feet wide, it could sail on the surface of the water as an ordinary boat, but if necessary, her skipper could "immediately strike her yards and masts, plunge her to any depth he pleases under water and remain there 12 hours without any inconvenience or external communication" and it could navigate under water "at the rate of four knots an hour."[26] With the end of the war, the Admiralty shelved the project. Johnstone however, remained enthusiastic about submarines, perhaps because he saw their potential for smuggling. O'Meara had a different idea in mind and gave Johnstone money to start building a submarine in a shipyard at Blackwall Reach on the Thames. The shipyard workers were told that the vessel would be used for smuggling. The cost of building the submarine was estimated at £15,000, a considerable sum at the time. According to one version, Johnstone would skipper the vessel to St. Helena and then take Napoleon to Charleston.[27]

More likely, the plan was to approach St. Helena's windward side on a bigger vessel, sink the submarine during daylight to avoid being noticed and at night approach "the guarded rock without discovery."[28] Colonel Maceroni, who was involved in this project, claimed that "the mighty powers of steam were mustered to our assistance." Maybe the *Rising Star,* still docked on the Thames, was part of the plan. "Means of no insignificant character were insured" to rescue Napoleon, Maceroni said, including placing "friendly" British officers at St. Helena.[29] Unfortunately the third volume of Maceroni's memoirs—in which he promised to provide details of this plan—never saw the light as his publisher went bankrupt.[30] At this time Maceroni was organizing a new expedition to South America with the help of many Napoleonic veterans.[31] Were the two projects linked? Given the involvement of Maceroni and O'Meara in this new attempt to rescue Napoleon, we can safely assume that Wilson was at least aware of it. Maybe his sudden trip to Paris in the spring of 1820 had something to do with this project. Lady Holland had given him some "commissions to execute" in the French capital. Given her obsession with Napoleon, they may well have been connected with St. Helena. The French ambassador in London recommended keeping Wilson under strict surveillance.[32] By mid-April, Wilson reported from Paris that Lady Holland's "commands" were being carried out.[33] Having learned his lesson the hard way, he included no more details in his letter.

But an informer tipped off Castlereagh that a plan to rescue Napoleon was afoot. The foreign secretary was skeptical but immediately alerted Richelieu, who was as fearful as ever of Napoleon's escape. Castlereagh thought the plans were "the production of some very wild individual, if, in truth, they shall prove to have any existence whatsoever. I nevertheless think it right that they should be submitted to Your Excellency's inspection, however absurd in conception and design."[34] The warning revived Richelieu's worst nightmares. He immediately wrote back to Castlereagh asking if there was some way of obtaining "from the man who wrote to you more information about the means which he believes to be able to use to bring [about] the evasion of the prisoner of St. Helena without implicating your government." Richelieu was troubled that the alleged conspirators believed they would "be able to effect the escape of Buonaparte with only £20,000." Castlereagh replied that he had "not been able to obtain any satisfactory information regarding the individual in Poland Street to who[m] I am referred. . . . You will no doubt be enabled to ascertain whether the writer of the letters resides at Dunkirk and who he is. This may possibly suggest some expedient by which the means of the parties to undertake such a project may be estimated or put to the test, or by which their scheme, most probably framed for swindling purposes, may be detected." Castlereagh also promised any assistance necessary to dissipate "all anxiety which might result from the supposed ability of these parties to effectuate such an object."[35] But beyond putting Johnstone under surveillance, the government took no other measures to stop the submarine's construction.

Who had alerted Castlereagh? Who was the individual in Poland Street?* What about the Dunkirk connection? Coincidentally, a certain Daniel O'Meara, former colonel of Napoleon's Légion Irlandaise, lived there. Was he related to Napoleon's doctor? Unfortunately, O'Meara left no memoirs. However, two weeks after Castlereagh made his discovery, the Irish doctor paid a visit to John Cam Hobhouse and made an unusual request. Napoleon's mother, "who was willing to petition the English parliament" on behalf of her son, had asked O'Meara "to draw up the petition." O'Meara asked Hobhouse to write it. The objective was to show Napoleon that he had "nothing to expect from the English nation & must do what he can for himself." Maybe this would convince him to agree to escape in a submarine? Hobhouse thought O'Meara seemed "a clever, modest man."[36] He remains one of the least understood characters of the St. Helena saga.

With the arrival of spring, the survival of the ancien régime in Europe no longer seemed assured. Wilson believed that the fate of the Bourbons was sealed. "When and how may engage your speculations, but do not doubt the fact of

---

* Coincidentally, the poet Percy Bysshe Shelley once lived in Poland Street.

their expulsion from France," he wrote to Grey. Maybe he had learned something through his contacts in Paris with Lafayette and Savary.[37] How all of this turbulence would affect England was unclear Wilson said, but surely he had an idea, as while in Paris he had learned that Caroline of Brunswick was determined to reclaim her rights to the throne. Wilson had great hopes for Caroline and became one of her closest advisors.[38] In fact, he expected Caroline's arrival in England to provoke the resignation of the cabinet.[39] If she became queen she would agree to free Napoleon, so O'Meara suggested Joseph ask for her intercession.[40]

By late spring the specter of 1789 loomed ominously over Europe. Metternich was seriously troubled by the demands for a constitution made by the Spanish rebels. In his view a constitution limiting the powers of a sovereign undermined legitimacy.* It was all Napoleon's fault. Metternich believed that during the Hundred Days he had destroyed "the work of fourteen years during which he had exercised his authority" and had "set free the Revolution which he came to France to subdue."[41] Metternich worried about the "great conflict of parties" in France, the growing anarchy in Spain, and the volatile situation in England where "the relation between the King and the Ministry is very gloomy" because of Caroline.[42]

Any doubts about the political impact of Caroline's return disappeared in early June when she arrived in Dover after a five-year voluntary exile in Italy. Wilson was so excited that he went to greet her on the outskirts of London.[43] According to the *Times,* "neither at the landing of William the Conqueror nor at that of William III" had any arrival in England caused "such a sensation."[44] Lord Grey feared "a Jacobin revolution more bloody than that of France." Caroline became a symbol for the supporters of reform and the size of the demonstrations in her favor dwarfed those that had taken place at Peterloo. "I never saw more general agitation in the public," Wilson exclaimed.[45] Not surprisingly the *British Monitor* called her "the Queen of all the Radicals."[46]

The recently crowned George IV dreaded more than anybody the return of his wife and instructed his ministers to initiate divorce proceedings against her, which triggered a very negative public reaction. Lord Liverpool was never closer to resigning than during the summer and fall of 1820. His most likely successor was Lord Grey, a man known for his support of the French Revolution and his sympathy for Napoleon's plight. The political situation in England was watched

---

* In 1814 Louis XVIII accepted a soft constitution.

with increasing interest all over the continent, particularly at Paris and Vienna. "Fear of the consequences that could result from a change of Ministry and, consequently, of a new direction in the political agenda of the English cabinet," prompted Metternich to consider "if it would not be careful to adopt some precautions to insure Europe against the possibility of [setting] free the prisoner of St. Helena."[47] Precautions were certainly needed. Metternich warned his ambassador in London that the Bonapartists were spreading the rumor that "the English government, which for sometime past has allowed Bonaparte to enjoy far more liberty in his place of detention, would not in certain cases be opposed to his escape and might even connive at it."[48]

The turmoil caused by Caroline's divorce trial was momentarily eclipsed by the publication of the details of France's secret negotiations to crown a Bourbon prince in Buenos Aires. The newspapers published the correspondence between the rebel government and the French ministers, which included a memorandum "written in a manner particularly offensive to Britain."[49] In the House of Commons, Wilson demanded an explanation. Castlereagh objected to the motion and claimed ignorance of any negotiations between France and Buenos Aires.[50] In a private meeting with the American ambassador, Castlereagh insisted that the French monarchical scheme "was a total surprise [to] England, that the Cabinet had heard nothing of it until very recently, and were still willing to hope that it might not prove true to the extent stated, otherwise it showed a spirit of intrigue, which he had hoped had gone out of fashion among nations."[51] Wellington also appeared surprised by the news and hoped it would be proved false, because "if true, they would show an intrigue which England would not like, and not belonging to the age, which had excluded double-dealing from public affairs."[52] In truth, Castlereagh had long known of the French monarchical project. In fact, he not only did not oppose it he "approved it almost entirely."[53] He had himself proposed the idea in 1807 to neutralize Napoleon's designs on the Spanish colonies.[54]

Decazes, who had just arrived in London as the new French ambassador, also denied knowing anything and blamed the Marquis Dessolles for the negotiations with Buenos Aires. Pasquier, who was Dessolles's successor at the Foreign Ministry, believed the whole thing was "a big comedy" to distract public opinion from Caroline's divorce trial. Other European diplomats—possibly confusing Maria Luisa de Borbon for the Archduchess Marie Louise and the Prince of Parma for the Prince of Lucca—believed that Decazes had secretly intrigued to establish "a kingdom in South America for the Buonapartes."[55] Was this simply a confusion of names or had Decazes really tried to crown Napoleon's son in Buenos Aires? At this point, the Bonapartists would not settle for anything but France. Others believed Decazes had approved the negotiations on the "condition of an almost exclusive commercial liberty between France and South America."[56]

Richelieu also feigned complete ignorance of the negotiations with Buenos Aires even though he had personally authorized them at the end of 1818. Richelieu had other problems to worry about. The political situation in France had become increasingly volatile. By the beginning of summer, the Bourbons and their supporters were paranoid about the existence of an even more dangerous Bonapartist plot to bring about their downfall. Richelieu's worst fears were confirmed in early June when a massive student demonstration exploded in Paris and cries of "vive l'Empereur!" were heard in the streets.[57]

The demonstration was violently quashed by government troops and a young student was killed. Standing next to him was Major Persat. After the Amelia Island fiasco and the demise of Lallemand's Champ d'Asile, the hot-tempered Persat had returned to France. After the student demonstration the French capital was on the brink of a military insurrection. Madame Hamelin, who had returned to Paris and become an informer for Decazes, reported that the leader of the conspiracy was General Fressinet, "who had just arrived from Buenos Aires, from where he had been chased away for participating in a plot which had cost the lives of two talented young Frenchmen."[58] Fressinet was promptly arrested, while Persat escaped to Naples, where the Friends of Freedom planned their next strike.

The political upheaval caused by Caroline's divorce trial in England and the riots in Paris was soon overshadowed by a new revolution. This time it was Naples. Inspired by the revolution in Spain, a former officer of Murat named Guglielmo Pepe, a member of the Carbonari, led a military uprising and forced the king to accept a liberal constitution.[59] The Neapolitan revolution spread fear throughout Europe. From London, Countess Lieven wrote to Metternich, her lover, "Another revolution, *Mon Prince,* and a revolution which will have an immediate effect upon your movements. Here they are dumbfounded by the news. You will not be; you will act. You were a prophet."[60] Metternich had no doubts about the seriousness of the new upheaval. Naples, the largest Italian state, was tied to Austria by a treaty that prohibited a change to its institutions without consultation. Metternich believed the Neapolitan uprising threatened not only Austria but also all of Europe.[61]

The supporters of the ancien régime could see Napoleon's shadow behind the revolutionary menace. Pepe had fought under Napoleon's orders at Marengo, had served for many years under Joseph Bonaparte in Naples and Spain, and in the fall of 1815 had accompanied Murat on his last tragic adventure.[62] Not surprisingly, many die-hard Bonapartists such as Maurice Persat and Jean Schultz, veterans of Amelia Island and the Champ d'Asile, joined Pepe.[63] According to the French police, Eugene de Beauharnais provided money to the Neapolitan rebels through Prince Torlonia, the banker of the Bonaparte family in Rome.[64] When Napoleon learned about the Neapolitan revolution he was surprised. "Who would ever have guessed that a set of *Maccheronai* would ape the Spaniards, proclaim their principles and rival them in courage?"[65]

43
Cochrane the Liberator

Rashness, though often imputed to me, forms no part of my composition.
—Lord Cochrane, *The Autobiography of a Seaman*

Cochrane was deeply affected by the humiliating defeats he had suffered in Callao and Pisco and realized that his career in South America could end quickly and ignominiously, particularly if the massive Spanish punitive expedition sailed from Cadiz. He was also upset at his friend Edward Ellice for not sending him the *Rising Star,* which would have given him an enormous advantage at sea.[1] But Cochrane was determined to succeed and had decided to launch his most ambitious operation since arriving in South America: storming the fortress at Valdivia, the "Gibraltar" of the South Atlantic. With a defensive system that included seventeen strategically located forts and more than a 120 batteries pointing in every possible direction, Valdivia was considered to be completely impregnable to attacks by land or sea.[2] It was even more impregnable than St. Helena.

Cochrane knew that if he failed, his enemies in Chile would demand his head, so he carefully planned all the details of his new campaign. "Cool calculation would make it appear that the attempt to take Valdivia is madness," he told one of his men. "This is one reason why the Spaniards will hardly believe us in earnest, even when we commence, and you will see that a bold onset, and a little perseverance afterwards, will give a complete triumph; for operations unexpected by the enemy are when well executed almost certain to succeed, whatever may be the odds, and success will preserve the enterprise from the imputation of rashness."[3] But Cochrane faced enormous obstacles; under the influence of San Martin the Chilean government refused to give him any troops.

Cochrane went ahead with his plans. At the beginning of January he left Valparaiso at the head of his squadron. On January 18 he approached Valdivia and to fool the Spaniards he flew the Spanish colors. The ruse worked. A pilot and four officers sent to Cochrane's ship to help him navigate the channels were promptly taken prisoner. After a two-day reconnaissance, Cochrane decided on his plan of attack. He raised the necessary troops at Concepcion, whose governor was an enemy of San Martin and O'Higgins. Major George Beauchef, a Frenchman who had served under Brayer, was chosen to lead these troops.[4] Pleased to have a veteran of Napoleon's Imperial Guard under his orders, Cochrane treated Beauchef with distinction. During the voyage to Valdivia, Cochrane expressed his indignation at the way the British government had treated Napoleon, of whom, he confessed, he was an enthusiastic admirer. He also told Beauchef that he was thinking of taking his squadron to St. Helena to rescue the former emperor and bring him to South America to lead the fight against the Spaniards.[5]

But before embarking on this adventure, Cochrane needed a victory. Days later his squadron was in front of the fortress of Valdivia, ready to pounce on the Spaniards. On the morning of February 5 Cochrane ordered Beauchef to launch a surprise attack. Despite having superior numbers the Spaniards abandoned their positions and fled. The capture of Valdivia was perhaps "one of the most daring and successful on record."[6] It was also the turning point in Cochrane's campaign to liberate South America. Chile was no longer "in constant danger of losing the liberties."[7] Cochrane then turned his attention to the neighboring fortress of Chiloe, which was almost as impregnable as Valdivia and was defended by more than a thousand Spanish troops.[8] If it surrendered, Cochrane's dominance of the Pacific would be unchallenged. The attack took place at the end of February, but it failed. Cochrane was forced to withdraw; he returned to Santiago to claim the laurels for Valdivia.[9]

Although Cochrane had obtained a resounding victory for the patriot cause, some government officials suggested that he "deserved to lose his head for daring, unbidden, to attack such a place and for endangering the patriot soldiers, by exposing them to such hazard."[10] In fact, at the instigation of San Martin, the Chilean government initiated court-martial proceedings against him for insubordination.[11] But public sentiment was so strong in Cochrane's favor and his victory so decisive for the cause of independence that the proceedings were suspended.

By opening the doors to the invasion of Peru, Cochrane's victory made it imperative for Brayer, Alvear, and Carrera to succeed in Buenos Aires. Allied to the provincial caudillos, Carrera marched toward Buenos Aires at the head of a respectable army made up of Chilean patriots and French, Spanish, and Irish adventurers. Alvear and Brayer anxiously waited for his signal to enter the scene. In early February, Carrera and the caudillos defeated the army of Buenos Aires. From Montevideo, Brayer congratulated his friend:

> I don't want to be the last to congratulate you for your success. You have given a great proof of what can be done to liberate your country from the hands of the oppressors. . . . You are on the right path. . . . The happy successes of Buenos Aires must influence the plans that you are undoubtedly preparing for Chile and which cannot fail to have the same results. I regret that your desire to take advantage of the departure of [David] Jewett and A[lvear] doesn't leave me any time to talk to you about many interesting subjects. I will keep them for a future occasion and will wait until the departure of your sister. . . . You will undoubtedly be happy to learn that they have recalled General Fressinet and he is on his way back to France. I am hoping for the day in which I will receive the same justice.[12]

Although Carrera triumphed on the battlefield, Alvear's enemies were still powerful in Buenos Aires. To avoid an open confrontation, Alvear recommended that Carrera appoint one of his allies as the new governor. Once the situation stabilized, Alvear would return to take control of the army. At the end of February the new governor sent a secret message to Carrera assuring him "the door was open" for Alvear.[13] But rumors of the latter's return spread rapidly and stirred his enemies into action; they accused Alvear of planning to establish a military dictatorship. "No matter what his supporters say about his contrition, it cannot be anything but the same Napoleon had in the island of Elba."[14]

A new coup followed, and Alvear, who was biding his time on board Jewett's ship, decided to intervene. A revolution of sorts followed and Alvear barely escaped with his life. Realizing that Alvear would be strongly opposed, Carrera again placed his ally as governor. Alvear remained out of the city but Carrera's victory put an end to the French monarchical projects in Buenos Aires.[15] Its political impact would soon be felt in Europe. The new government gave Commodore Hardy copies of all the documentation regarding the secret negotiations held with France to crown a Bourbon prince. Hardy sent an urgent dispatch to London warning that the previous government had actually sent an emissary to Brazil "with the conditional acceptance by the Congress."[16] The presence of a French squadron in Rio de Janeiro raised Hardy's suspicions that the execution of this plan was under way. The full details of this monarchical intrigue soon reached Europe and the United States. Adams noted its "glaring" absurdity: "Being equally contrary to the true policy of this country, to the general feeling of all the native Americans, and to the liberal institutions congenial to the spirit of freedom, has produced its natural harvest of unappeasable dissensions, sanguinary civil wars, and loathsome executions, with their appropriate attendance of arbitrary imprisonments, a subdued [and] perverted press, and a total annihilation of all civil liberty." In Adams's view "the independence of an American nation can never be completely secured from European sway while it tampers for authority with the families of European sovereigns."[17] Recognizing the independence of Buenos Aires was definitely not worth risking a war with Spain.

At the end of March, news that Cochrane had taken Valdivia reached Buenos Aires. At this time, Alvear launched a second attempt to take power and again failed. "This country is in a sad troubled state having experienced three complete changes of government in as many months," Commodore Hardy wrote to his brother. "Those who are not satisfied with our government should come to this nice Republican country, where liberty is enjoyed only by the strongest and we live nearly by club law."[18]

Carrera was impatient. The time was right to return to Chile; in only three months the winter snows would close down the Andean passes. A French officer had arrived from Santiago to ask his assistance "to sustain a revolution."[19] Whoever liberated Peru would control the fate of South America. San Martin was well aware of this, so instead of heeding the calls for help from his partisans in Buenos Aires, he remained in Santiago preparing his army and fending off Cochrane's efforts to wrest away the supreme command of the campaign. San Martin's plan was to land a big force in Peru and lay siege to Lima, whereas Cochrane proposed to split the army in two and land at Lima and Guayaquil. Predictably O'Higgins leaned in favor of San Martin.[20] Disappointed at this decision, Cochrane tendered his resignation.

Carrera's dream of returning to Chile to lead the expedition to liberate Peru also ran into obstacles. San Martin's supporters were growing stronger in Buenos Aires. According to Captain Robert Spencer the natives were fed up with republicanism and instead wanted "to be led by any monarch, except the Spanish."[21] Carrera and Alvear had gathered a strong army and were considering storming the city. But as British troops had learned in 1806 and 1807, taking Buenos Aires by force would not be easy. A mutiny of several officers garrisoned in the city came to their aid. Ambrose Cramer and Jean Bulewski, two veterans of the Grande Armée who had been implicated in previous plots against San Martin, were among those who led the rebellion. Neither one had ever met Alvear or Carrera before. Clearly, they obeyed orders, probably from Brayer, who was on board a ship waiting for the right opportunity to disembark. But the authorities moved quickly to quash the mutiny and accused Brayer of being "constantly and closely allied with Carrera" and of trying to "disturb tranquility."[22] Napoleon's loyal general barely escaped arrest and was forced back to Montevideo. After three years of continued setbacks in South America, he was probably less sanguine about his prospects. And with the fall of Decazes, a royal pardon in France seemed less likely.

Disagreements between Alvear, Carrera, and their allies allowed the new governor, a partisan of San Martin, to strengthen the city's defenses.[23] But Carrera was confident of success, and by mid-June he predicted that he would be in Buenos Aires within two weeks "without firing a shot."[24] The prediction proved too optimistic. Instead he had to face his enemies on the battlefield. Alvear and Carrera were again victorious but the city refused to surrender. The partisans of San Martin and O'Higgins in Buenos Aires watched the unfolding situation with great concern. They suspected certain officers in Commodore Hardy's entourage—particularly Captain Spencer—supported Carrera and Alvear. All the Freemasons were on their side as well and were determined to take revenge on San Martin and O'Higgins for the death of their "brother" Luis Carrera.[25]

The turmoil in Buenos Aires was quickly felt in Santiago. As a precaution the authorities ordered the arrest of several *carreristas*.[26] San Martin was completely focused on the expedition to Peru before Carrera returned to Chile. However, the resignation of Cochrane and most of his officers had left him without a navy, and without a navy the Peruvian expedition was not viable. O'Higgins intervened and convinced Cochrane to withdraw his resignation.

After the death of his brother James, Lieutenant Claudius Charles had taken on the responsibility of keeping Wilson updated. At the end of June, Lieutenant Charles informed Wilson that "the expedition will sail from hence in about a month['s] time. . . . The object is to revolutionize Peru and arm the patriots against the Viceroy and the royalists."[27] His prediction proved too optimistic; in mid-July, Cochrane resigned for the second time after the government refused to pay his crew and give him absolute command of the naval operations in the Peruvian campaign. Most of his officers also tendered their resignations.[28] O'Higgins again pleaded with Cochrane, who relented after his conditions were met and San Martin's role was limited to commanding the land campaign.[29] Each expected to get rid of the other.

Cochrane had not forgotten what had brought him to South America. It was time to send a message to St. Helena. The problem was how to do it without raising suspicions. Maybe the answer was in Buenos Aires.

44
Blood Flows at Longwood

Conqueror and captive of the earth art thou!
She trembles at thee still, and thy wild name
Was ne'er more bruited in men's minds than now
That thou art nothing, save the jest of Fame.
          —Lord Byron, *Childe Harold's Pilgrimage,* Canto 3

The only thing Lowe deemed important enough to report at the beginning of 1820 was that Napoleon had shot a goat.[1] A few days later, some chickens and a cow were added to the list of victims. Their crime: eating the flowers of Napoleon's well-tended garden. It was a sign that Napoleon's health and spirits had fully recovered. "Blood is flowing at Longwood," Balmain reported. Montchenu, his French colleague, who often walked around Longwood to check that the prisoner was still there, was quite alarmed and asked Lowe "what would be done with General Bonaparte if he should happen to kill a man instead of a goat."[2] Lowe was unconcerned. For the first time in three years he was not worried about the possibility of Napoleon's escape. Napoleon led "a tranquil life," seemed to enjoy "the best of health," and was "extremely busy with his garden."[3] Lowe was in fact so unconcerned that he allowed Napoleon to roam freely around the island on horseback or on foot, unaccompanied by a British officer.[4] The only thing that upset the governor was Napoleon's refusal to see Sir Charles Somerset, governor of the Cape, who had applied to Montholon for an audience.

Lowe's worries resurfaced in mid-February when the news of political disturbances in England and the rest Europe reached St. Helena. Lowe feared that "the news of the disturbances at Manchester and the reference to his particular situation in the last of Mr. [Henry] Hunt's resolution at the Smithfield Meeting in July last, have probably inspired him with some hopes of a change and hence a great desire to see any fresh papers that might arrive here."[5] A letter from Admiral Pellew* suggested that public pressure could force the government's hand regarding Napoleon. "I hope you will soon have your Bird put into a stronger cage, as Gore† [tells] me the House [of Commons] gets forward fast. For my own part I should be very glad to hear he was put into a leaden case and sent across the line," wrote Pellew.[6] Coincidentally, Lowe found out that various pamphlets circulated widely around the island, "written obviously with the design to raise a spirit in favor of Bonaparte's liberation on the general ground of the injustice of his detention here."[7]

Lowe again tightened the security around Longwood and restricted the access of the foreign commissioners. Balmain, who had already announced his departure from St. Helena, complained that "it was so very necessary" that Napoleon should be seen by the commissioners, particularly Montchenu, France "being of all other nations, so deeply interested in knowing as much as possible about him." England was France's natural enemy, Balmain argued, and the British government "might have some political reason to conceal the real situation of Buonaparte from France and to keep her in ignorance about him so as to dispose of him as they pleased." He even suggested, and Montchenu agreed, that these regulations had been imposed so that Napoleon "might be removed from the island by the British government, unknown to the Foreign Commissioners for some political purpose."[8] Lowe in turn believed Montchenu was intriguing with Bertrand and Montholon. With France ruled by a cabinet made up of men who had served Napoleon for years, he suspected that the instructions of the French commissioner had changed and that Decazes wanted to release Napoleon or to enter into some negotiations with him. Although Montchenu had not received any instructions since late 1818, Lowe based his suspicions on a letter the marquis had just received from Baron Sturmer, who had been forced to leave St. Helena after the "Welle affair." Lowe knew that Sturmer "had gone to Paris to see his wife's relations and that the Baroness herself was mentioned."[9] The fact that Sturmer had been appointed Austrian ambassador to the Portuguese court also seemed suspicious. Lowe asked the British ambassador in Rio de Janeiro to keep him informed of any developments.

At the beginning of May, an East Indiaman brought the shocking news of the assassination of the Duke of Berri and of the Thistlewood conspiracy. Napoleon seemed in better health than at any time since 1816. According to Balmain he took "considerable exercise in his garden" but he still had trouble

---

* Admiral Sir Edward Pellew, Viscount Exmouth (1775–1833).
† Rear Admiral Sir John Gore (1772–1836).

with his "chronic disease, hepatitis, and often takes mercury." Napoleon's complexion was "fresh and healthy, his air pleasant; in other words, quite another man."[10] Napoleon started riding again, and Lowe, always wary of inconsistencies, again grew suspicious. Also at this time, Balmain and Montchenu received new instructions. The Russian commissioner was recalled and a few days later he embarked for London in the company of his brand new wife, who was Lowe's stepdaughter. Thus ended Balmain's four years at St. Helena. When he arrived in London he revealed that Napoleon was in love.[11] Was it Fanny Bertrand? The identity of Napoleon's lover is one of the many enigmas of St. Helena that Balmain chose not to disclose. Although there had been rumors about Balmain's recall since the Congress of Aix-la-Chapelle, his departure and the absence of a replacement raises the question: Did the tsar know or suspect that Napoleon was going to be murdered and refuse to be an accomplice, or was it simply coincidence?

With Balmain gone, Montchenu was the only foreign commissioner left on St. Helena. And the old marquis, who thought his government had forgotten him, was surprised to receive his first set of instructions since late 1818. Richelieu was back in power and as paranoid as ever about the escape of the prisoner on the rock. Shortly after receiving Richelieu's instructions, Montchenu started having private meetings with Montholon. What was he up to?

The first meeting took place in late June at Montchenu's house. It was a hot day and Montholon was quite talkative, particularly after drinking several glasses of the excellent port that his host kept for special occasions. After a discussion of O'Meara's recently published book, Montholon started talking about the murder of the Duke of Berri. He claimed that Napoleon had been much affected by the news. Montchenu was skeptical. Then they discussed the succession of Louis XVIII. Montholon said Napoleon believed that his son had "strong rights" to the throne. Before leaving, Montholon told Montchenu, "My obedience has only a very great devotion, this devotion is all the more generous as until now I have not [been] given proof that I made a success to please His Majesty. I leave myself to the magnanimity of the King." In a rambling dispatch to Richelieu filled with cryptic remarks, Montchenu said that Albine de Montholon, to whom he referred as a "viper," had been sent as Napoleon's "plenipotentiary minister to Europe." With her "fecundity of spirit" and "insinuating forms," the Bonapartists now viewed her as the "support" of the party.[12]

Two weeks later Lowe learned of another unauthorized meeting between

Montholon and Montchenu. He asked Bathurst for guidance, as it appeared that "a spirit of no ordinary intrigue" surrounded these meetings.[13] When questioned, Montchenu told Lowe that Montholon had only offered to send him some beans grown in Napoleon's garden and had asked whether he preferred them white or green. Montchenu asked for both. Lowe's suspicions were immediately stirred. He though that Montchenu "would have acted with more propriety if he had declined either or limited himself to a demand for the white alone."[14] Other developments increased his worries. He had just been informed about the "amusing" French monarchical plans in Buenos Aires.[15] Understanding South American politics was beyond Lowe's ability but his tortuous mind couldn't fail to see links between everything that happened around the world and Montchenu's recent visits to Longwood. What if they wanted to place Napoleon or his son in Buenos Aires?

Montholon prepared for his return to Europe, a decision he had already announced to both Napoleon and Lowe. He continued to visit Montchenu who, bored to no end, welcomed his visits, especially since Richelieu had told him that the king would "be grateful to you if you will keep him informed of all the projects and hopes of the inhabitants of Longwood."[16] Montchenu reported that Montholon had said that Napoleon's escape would be "very difficult not merely from its physical difficulties but owing to the morale of Bonaparte himself, whose mistrust was such that he would never confide his person to anyone but a member of his own family, or some individual amongst his former servants in whom he had equal confidence." Napoleon feared that if he were caught, his captors "would blow his brains out."[17]

With the passing months, Napoleon's health, which Balmain had reported as "excellent" in April, started to deteriorate. The first troubling signs appeared at the end of July, when Napoleon suffered a bilious attack followed by high fever. A few days later Lowe was surprised when scanning Longwood with his telescope to see Napoleon riding. He was even more surprised when he learned that the rider wasn't Napoleon but the Abbé Vignali, who had put on Napoleon's uniform and was mounted on one of his horses. Why would the Corsican priest impersonate Napoleon? Lowe wondered if there was a hidden meaning in all of this.[18]

45
The Revolutionary Virus Spreads

Have Carbonaro cooks not carbonadoed
Each course enough! Or doctors dire dissuaded
Repletion? Ah! In thy dejected looks
I read all France's treason in her cooks!
—Lord Byron, *The Age of Bronze,* Canto 12

By mid-1820 the supporters of the ancien régime were paranoid and saw Napoleon's hand behind the uprisings in Spain and Naples and the revolutionary movements spreading all over Italy. And even if Napoleon wasn't directly involved, his followers undoubtedly were, and as long as he lived they would continue to hope and to fight for his return. Even in Spain, which had steadfastly resisted Bonapartist rule, "a great change" had taken place in public opinion and Napoleon was becoming a popular figure.[1]

No member of the Bonaparte family was free of suspicion, even the octogenarian Madame Mere, who resided in Rome with her brother Cardinal Fesch. Having received reports that she had sent agents to Corsica to foment a Bonapartist insurrection and had offered Napoleon's fortune to finance it, the Duke of Richelieu asked the Vatican to increase its surveillance of her. Cardinal Consalvi bowed to this request and interviewed the old lady at her palace. When she heard the charges against her, Madame Mere replied, "I have no millions, but be good enough to tell the Pope, in order that my remarks may be repeated to King Louis XVIII, that were I fortunate enough to possess the fortune so charitably attributed to me, I should not employ it in fomenting troubles in Corsica, or to secure my son's partisans in France, for he has enough of them; but I should use it to equip a fleet with a special mission, that of proceeding to fetch the Emperor from St. Helena, where the most infamous and dishonorable conduct keeps him prisoner."[2] This reply added nothing to Richelieu's peace of mind.

Political turmoil was not limited to southern Europe. In England Caroline's divorce trial had divided the country. The Tories despised her. The Radicals, and many Whigs, as well as the majority of the English people, supported her. Wilson embraced Caroline's cause with his usual zeal. Not surprisingly, the Tories accused him of being "a renegade" and "a person so enamored of sedition that after making his first essay of service in foreign lands, he has returned to his native country to head the legions of tumult."[3] Even more worrisome to the Tories was the support that Caroline received from the Duke of Sussex, younger brother of the king, leader of the English Freemasons, and a renowned liberal. Sussex's popularity rose to such levels that many wondered whether he would replace his brother on the throne.[4] Countess Lieven warned Metternich that there would soon be "a serious crisis" in England. "The opposition believes there will be a revolution; the ministry perhaps fears it."[5]

The Tories were right to be worried, as Caroline held what were to them noxious political views. In a private conversation with John Cam Hobhouse she talked "in the strongest terms against Austria" and supported Italian independence. She also said she was in favor of parliamentary reform, that she would support "the little Napoleon coming to France with his mother," expressed great dislike for Wellington, whom she considered "her greatest enemy," and condemned "the confinement of Napoleon at St. Helena."[6] Caroline's accession to the throne of Europe's most powerful nation could have very serious consequences.

In France the situation was not much better. Wilson's warnings about an upcoming explosion were based on inside information. A military conspiracy to overthrow the Bourbons, put Napoleon II on the throne of France, and proclaim the constitution of the Hundred Days was about to explode. Thanks to a vast network of spies and informers, the French government learned about this conspiracy. Three groups were behind the plot, which became known as the conspiracy of the Bazar Française. The first and most important one was the Comité Rovigo, which was led by General Savary, Napoleon's former chief of police and one of his most loyal followers. Savary had recently returned to France after a brief stop in England, where he had been in touch with Wilson. This group also included generals Clausel, Vandamme, Foy, and Fressinet. The latter had been arrested after the June student demonstrations. The objective of the Comité Rovigo was to reestablish the Bonaparte dynasty in France. The plan was to send General Gourgaud to Vienna to get Napoleon's son and bring him back to Paris to succeed Louis XVIII. Lafayette, the chief of the liberal party, led the second group of conspirators. Although he disagreed with the Bonapartists about the form of government, he recognized that the only cause the army would support was crowning Napoleon II. The third group was the Comité de Grenoble led by Joseph Rey, a lawyer who had raised funds for Lallemand's Champ d'Asile and was a leader of the Charbonnerie.[7]

Some of the key plotters, alerted to their impending arrest by friends in the police, fled the country. Within days the conspiracy unraveled. The authorities managed to arrest and extract confessions from some of the lower-ranking conspirators. According to Pasquier, who was involved in the investigations, the conspiracy was "purely military and completely Bonapartist without dissimulation."[8] In a letter to Decazes he explained that the "unfortunate events in Spain and Naples have heated up the heads of some ambitious men who view the revolution as a means of advancement and fortune."[9] Pasquier was convinced not only that the Bonaparte family was involved but also that the plotters had received financial backing from the banker Jacques Lafitte, who held a large portion of Napoleon's vast fortune.[10] The discovery of this plot—the most serious against the Bourbons since March 1815—contributed to some serious discussion at the Pavillon Marsan* about how to neutralize Napoleon's insidious influence on the affairs of France and the rest of Europe.

A revolution in Portugal added a dangerous dimension to the turmoil spreading throughout Europe. This new revolution was no surprise to Wilson. He was now convinced that the cause of freedom would prevail and proudly informed Grey that the Lisbon uprising "was undertaken by old officers of my legion" who had avenged Gomes Freire, the ill-fated leader of the 1817 rebellion.[11] The English Radicals were ecstatic at the news. "This new revolution in Portugal comes earnestly in our aid," noted Major Cartwright, who advised Wilson "not [to] allow either unworthy jealousies or party maneuvers to divert us from a straightforward course in the cause of sacred freedom. The object we have in hand, if rightly conducted, may and must have great public effect. It is a cause that will sustain itself. . . . The events in Portugal will add much animation to the celebrations of Spanish and Neapolitan patriotism."[12] Portugal was followed by Piedmont. And this revolution threatened the core of the Austrian empire. Pasquier thought that no other event since Napoleon's return from Elba had caused as much of an impression in Europe as the revolution in Piedmont.[13] As in the case of Naples, the Bonapartist links were evident. The leader of the Piedmontese insurgents was Wilson's old friend General Vaudoncourt, who since 1816 had been involved in every intrigue to put Napoleon II on the throne of France.[14]

*This was the wing at the Tuileries Palace where the Comte d'Artois lived and the headquarters of the Ultras.

By the beginning of fall the political situation in Europe had become so un-
stable that those who in 1815 had favored Napoleon's execution instead of his
exile felt vindicated. The events in England, France, Spain, Portugal, and more
particularly Italy "rendered the safe custody of Napoleon a matter of even more
political importance than it had been at any time since his fall," as his escape
could have the "most formidable" consequences.[15] At the end of September,
Lord Bathurst sent Lowe his most serious warning since sending Napoleon to
St. Helena:

> The reports which you have recently made of the conduct of General
> Buonaparte and of his followers make me suspect that he is beginning to
> entertain serious thoughts of escaping from St. Helena and the accounts
> which he will have since received of what is passing in Europe will not
> fail to encourage this project. The overthrow of the Neapolitan Govern-
> ment, the revolutionary spirit which more or less prevails over all Italy, and
> the doubtful state of France itself, must excite his attention and clearly
> show that a crisis is fast approaching, if not already arrived, when his es-
> cape would be productive of important consequences. That his partisans
> are active cannot be doubted; and if he were ever willing to hazard the at-
> tempt, he will never allow such an opportunity to escape. You will there-
> fore exert all your attention in watching his proceedings, and call upon
> the Admiral to use his utmost vigilance, as upon the navy so much must
> ultimately depend. In what shape and in what manner this attempt will be
> made, I cannot judge, but I am satisfied this storm will not pass over un-
> noticed at Longwood. General Buonaparte has money at [his] command,
> he has partisans in abundance, he has means of communication which
> your regulations may occasionally intercept but cannot entirely prevent;
> the times are most favorable for the attempt; and, without thinking that
> he habitually courts a hazardous enterprise, I cannot persuade myself that
> he will shrink from one which, if successful, must now promise such im-
> portant results.

Bathurst ordered Lowe to review "all the different ways by which Buonaparte
may attempt his escape, and the best means therefore of preventing it."[16] The
British government started to take the plot to rescue Napoleon by submarine
more seriously. According to Maceroni, who was involved, "the object would
have been achieved, but money fell short." O'Meara had asked Eugene de Beau-

harnais, Madame Mere, and Cardinal Fesch for funds but returned to England "without having found any support from those who owed every penny they possessed to the illustrious prisoner."[17] Other evidence contradicts Maceroni's version. The Austrian police discovered that Eugene had transferred substantial funds to London in April, when the British government first learned about the submarine project. And according to Montholon more than six thousand *louis d'or** were spent on the construction of the submarine.[18]

In fact, at the end of 1820 the submarine was intercepted as it sailed down the Thames. According to an eyewitness account, on a dark November night, "she proceeded down the river (not being able to sink as the water was not deep enough). Anyhow, she managed to get below London Bridge" where it was stopped by government troops. Captain Johnstone, who was in command of the submarine, "threatened to shoot them. But they paid no attention to his threats, seized her and, taking her to Blackwall, destroyed her."[19] There are few other records of this extraordinary enterprise.

Rumors of Napoleon's escape were rife. At the end of November the *Times* reported that such rumors produced "a fall of half per cent in French stock."[20] And as the revolutionary fever spread throughout the continent, concerns about Napoleon's perfidious influence increased. Metternich realized that Austria's control over Italy was at stake and invited all the European sovereigns to the city of Troppau to discuss what measures should be taken. The meeting took place in October. Since France and England refused to participate, only Austria, Russia, and Prussia were represented. No decisions were taken with respect to Spain but at the suggestion of the tsar, Austria, Russia, and Prussia signed a treaty by which if any European monarchy was threatened by revolution, they would agree "by peaceful means, or if need be, by arms, to bring back the guilty state into the bosom of the Great Alliance." It was a big coup for Metternich, who got a free hand to send Austrian troops to quash the rebels in Piedmont and Naples. All parties agreed to meet again in early 1821 at Laybach to discuss a specific action plan for Spain. The message from Troppau was clear: Napoleon, "the representative of the Revolution," was to blame for Europe's troubles and any revolutionary attempt to disturb the status quo would be crushed with force by Austria and Russia.[21]

In London, Sir Robert Wilson organized his own conference to counteract the Congress of Troppau and "celebrate the triumph of liberty in Spain, Naples,

---

*This was roughly equivalent to 12,000 francs or approximately £9,000.

Sicily and Portugal." At a London tavern, Wilson chaired a great dinner attended by the leading figures of the opposition. Busts of Riego and Quiroga, the leaders of the Spanish insurrection, presided over the event. After dinner, a band played "La Marseillaise."[22] Wilson had not lost all hope of bringing freedom to England. He openly supported a petition by the borough of Southwark to dismiss Lord Liverpool's cabinet and became one of Caroline's most visible partisans. The popularity of the "unruly queen" grew every day, particularly after her divorce trial failed. At the end of November, Wilson escorted Caroline to a thanksgiving mass at St. Paul's with fellow radical John Cam Hobhouse. As they left the cathedral, a heckler shouted some insults at the uncrowned queen. According to Hobhouse it was the ineffable Lewis Goldsmith, "the *Anti-Gallican's* gourmet spy," who had been sent by the "ministers" to provoke "a disturbance." Wilson told Caroline to ignore the incident and the procession moved on.[23]

At the end of the year, Wellington advised Castlereagh "to watch very closely the Secret Societies" which had "certainly overturned the two governments in the Peninsula as well as that of Naples." The Iron Duke thought "the facility of communication is such in this country that their operations would be much easier and more effective."[24] He must have suspected that Wilson was involved. In fact, Wilson had just offered his sword to the Neapolitan rebels, who were preparing to resist the Austrian invasion. Metternich agreed that secret societies were one of the "most dangerous instruments used by the revolutionists of all countries" and a "plague" to be destroyed. But the real culprit was Napoleon. His return from Elba and the "false steps taken by the French government from 1815 to 1820, accumulated a mass of new dangers and great calamities for the whole civilized world." These influences threatened "with total ruin the work of restoration, the fruit of so many glorious efforts, and of a harmony between the greatest monarchs unparalleled in the records of history and they give rise to fears of indescribable calamities to society." But not everything was lost. Metternich noted that "for every disease there is a remedy."[25]

46
A Throne Awaits Napoleon

A most brilliant affair has taken place in the coast of Peru.
—Captain Searle, HMS *Hyperion*, November 1820

In mid-1820, after eighteen months of struggle as commander of the Chilean navy, Cochrane saw that the liberation of Peru was finally within his reach, and with it, his dream of putting Napoleon on the throne of South America. The rebellion in Cadiz had eliminated the risk of a punitive expedition from Spain and a temporary truce with San Martin had ensured his command of the patriot fleet. But peace between the two men would not last, as their agendas were incompatible. Given the political instability in Buenos Aires, San Martin now relied on his army and O'Higgins's support to achieve his goal of liberating Peru, which he considered a much more important political and economic objective than either Santiago or Buenos Aires. If San Martin occupied Lima he would be able to carry out his grandiose monarchical plans and maybe finally convince Castlereagh to send a British prince to the former Spanish viceroyalty.

The expedition left from Valparaiso at the end of August. Confident that the Spaniards would be defeated in only a few months, Cochrane decided the time was right to send a message to Napoleon. According to Lady Cochrane, his emissary was James Charles, "who personally knew the Emperor, to convey the sentiments of the New World."[1] But Charles had died at the end of 1819 while leading the attack of Pisco. Was Lady Cochrane trying to hide the true identity of the messenger? Maybe she confused James with his brother Claudius, who had arrived in Chile as a lieutenant in the Royal Navy and later joined the Chilean navy.[2] Or maybe she was referring to an earlier message.

Lady Cochrane played a role in conveying her husband's message to the exiled emperor. In his memoirs Cochrane revealed that soon after his departure for Peru, she "undertook a journey across the Cordillera to Mendoza" carrying "some dispatches of importance."[3] Cochrane's dispatches must have been really important for him to ask his own wife to undertake this journey. Crossing the Andes in the early spring was an enterprise fraught with danger. The mountain passes were still covered with snow and on her way back to Chile she barely escaped an assassination attempt! Why anybody would try to kill her is another mystery. From Mendoza, it would have taken no more than a week and half for a trusted courier to reach Buenos Aires. But then how would the message get to St. Helena? Maybe in one of the English warships anchored in Buenos Aires under Commodore Hardy's command.

At this time Hardy was trying to make sense of Buenos Aires' volatile politics. Following an initial victory, Alvear and Carrera had thought the city would quickly fall into their hands. They were betrayed once again by a caudillo, who negotiated a deal at their expense, and as a result their army was surprised and defeated. Alvear, who barely escaped alive, returned to Montevideo, where he rejoined a discouraged and frustrated Brayer. Carrera decided to emulate Napoleon after his escape from Elba and marched to Chile at the head of a band of determined followers. But even if he crossed the Andes it would be too late to stop San Martin.

An excellent opportunity to deliver Cochrane's message arose in late September when Hardy ordered Captain Robert Spencer of HMS *Owen Glendower* to transport a cargo of specie to St. Helena.[4] What prompted this decision is a mystery. Lowe occasionally needed currency but he usually obtained it directly from Brazil; there are no records of him ever making a request to Buenos Aires. And until late June, Spencer had expected to sail to the South Pacific instead of the South Atlantic.[5] Two weeks after ordering Spencer to go to St. Helena, Hardy informed the Admiralty of the situation and the movements of his squadron. With respect to the *Owen Glendower* he only mentioned that she had been taken to Montevideo to be caulked and refitted. Hardy omitted from his report the information that he had sent the ship to St. Helena, a detail that would have certainly been of interest to John Wilson Croker, secretary of the Lords of the Admiralty. Maybe the old admiral felt it was an irrelevant detail; on the other hand, some of the information he provided about other ships in his squadron is even less relevant.[6]

On October 2 Spencer departed for St. Helena carrying seven thousand dollars worth of gold, an insignificant amount given Lowe's needs. Almost at the same time, Captain David Jewett was approaching the Falkland Islands, located in the South Atlantic at the mouth of the Magellan strait, the main passage to the Pacific Ocean. In late October, as the *Owen Glendower* anchored at Jamestown, Jewett took possession of the Falklands in the name of the United Provinces of South America, a nonexistent political entity. Jewett had no orders to take the Falklands. In a proclamation he issued when taking possession of the islands he said that "one of the objects" was to preserve the resources needed to victual ships in transit. Jewett was linked to Burr, Poinsett, DeForest, Carrera, and Alvear. Like all of them he was a Freemason. He had also been the commander of the *True Blooded Yankee,* a privateer that had aroused the suspicions of British authorities at St. Helena. Was there any connection between his trip to the Falklands and Cochrane's plans? We can only speculate, as we have found no evidence linking them at that time. However, three years later when Cochrane took command of the Brazilian navy, Jewett became one of his top commanders. If Napoleon accepted Cochrane's proposal, the Falklands would be a necessary stop on the way to Lima. Better if they were in friendly hands.[7]

Meanwhile, the expedition to liberate Peru proceeded slowly. In early September, San Martin took possession of Pisco, and after some time "a thousand men were detached to the mountains in the rear of Lima." From Buenos Aires, Hardy reported that "the commanders of the Chilean expedition have not met with the success they were so sanguine in expecting."[8] Hardy was right. Instead of attacking Lima, San Martin remained inactive, signed an armistice with the Spanish viceroy, and started negotiations for the establishment of a constitutional monarchy in South America. As a result, the campaign to liberate Peru stalled.

Cochrane was furious. His relationship with San Martin had deteriorated beyond repair. The ineffable James Paroissien—former doctor, British spy, and one of San Martin's closest confidants—criticized Cochrane in the severest terms: "He is the most careless, unmethodical man I ever knew, promises everything and performs nothing. He appears only to be anxious about making money."[9] The antipathy was mutual. Cochrane thought Paroissien was "the basest" of San Martin's "vile agents."[10] He decided that the military resources of Chile "should not be wholly wasted without some attempt at accomplishing the object of the expedition."[11] In early November he attacked the Spanish fleet anchored in the port of Callao. It was his third attempt in almost two years, and this time it was a complete success. Cochrane personally led the capture of the powerful Spanish frigate *Esmeralda,* which "he carried together with a gun boat from under the batteries and out of their line of defense and in less than half an hour, had her under sail. This was done so quiet, and in so masterly a strike, that I had scarcely time to get [out] of the line of fire, and some of our merchant ships suffered considerably from not being able to move in time," wrote an admiring British captain.[12] With the *Esmeralda* in Cochrane's hands, the battle for the control of the Pacific effectively ended, making Lima's fall inevitable. San Martin, who had had no involvement whatsoever in this operation, issued a proclamation declaring that he had participated in its planning. Cochrane thought it beneath him to refute a "falsehood palpable to the whole expedition."[13]

When he learned of the capture of the *Esmeralda,* Hardy decided it was time to take his squadron to Chile. "We hear that Lord Cochrane has been very successful and has taken one of the Spanish frigates," he wrote to his brother. "Most likely I shall have the pleasure of seeing him and I have no doubt but we shall agree very well."[14]

Stuck in Montevideo, Brayer must have been quite disappointed at learning that the expedition to Lima had departed with San Martin at its head. His only consolation was that many Bonapartist officers, having avoided San Martin's purges, had embarked with the expedition. Among them were the loyal Beauchef; Alexis Bruix, the son of Admiral Bruix, and a former page to Napoleon; Frederic Brandsen, former aide-de-camp of Eugene de Beauharnais; and Pierre Raulet, Latapie's companion in the ill-fated adventure in Pernambuco.

From Buenos Aires to St. Helena

None stand by his low bed—though even the mind
Be wavering, which long awed and awes mankind:
Smile—for the fetter'd eagle breaks his chain,
And higher worlds than this are his again.
                                    —Lord Byron, *The Age of Bronze,* Canto 3

By August 1820 Napoleon had started riding again, taking full advantage of Lowe's relaxation of the regulations. His spirits were high, as if he knew that his situation would soon change. How much did he know about what was happening in France? If his supporters succeeded, his release from St. Helena would be only a matter of time. Lowe didn't sense any danger ahead until Montchenu shattered his tranquility at the end of August. The French commissioner informed him "of his intention to act upon" instructions originally issued by Richelieu at the end of 1818 and reiterated after his return to this ministry in March.[1] Montchenu explained that his mission was "to discover the schemes that were being hatched at Longwood" and carry "into effect the instructions he had received from the Duke de Richelieu which enjoin him to place himself in immediate and frequent communication with the French persons who are in attendance upon General Bonaparte." This meant that Montchenu not only intended "to assure himself simply of general Bonaparte's presence, but to see and converse with his followers." And to do so it would be necessary for him to enter Longwood. Greatly irritated at these demands, Lowe warned Montchenu that he could not enter Longwood's enclosure without his authorization. Unfazed by the threat, the marquis walked out determined to fulfill his instructions.[2]

Lowe immediately alerted Lord Bathurst. He found Montchenu's behavior rather strange and observed that the latest news from Europe, particularly the revolution in Spain, seemed to have again excited Napoleon's hopes of being released.[3] To add to Lowe's troubles, Count Bertrand had sent a letter to Lord Liverpool complaining about Napoleon's declining health.[4] With his uncanny ability to link totally unconnected events, Lowe suspected that there was a "degree of combination" between the inhabitants of Longwood and Montchenu. The insinuations of the French commissioner combined "very strangely" with Bertrand's letter. A detail that particularly caught Lowe's attention was hearing Montchenu refer to the prisoner as "Napoleon" when until now he had referred to him simply as Bonaparte. Lowe thought addressing the prisoner by his first name was "indecorous and insulting to the British government."[5]

The impasse was followed by an exchange of letters. Lowe again advised Montchenu to avoid unauthorized contact with the "French people" at Longwood.[6] Montchenu haughtily replied that he only answered for his "actions and intentions to the King of France." He reminded Lowe of certain troubling incidents that had taken place in France in recent months. The same day that an attempt was made on the life of the Duchess of Berri, pregnant with the heir of the Bourbon dynasty, popular demonstrations in Napoleon's support took place in the streets of Paris. The revolutionaries in France were daring to call back the man of St. Helena "in pamphlets plastered all over the city." It was evident to Montchenu that the troubles in France and the rest of Europe could be traced back to Longwood. "Do you want me to watch with guilty and cowardly indifference the flames spreading around me without trying to find out where they come from?" asked Montchenu. How could he be accused of violating Lowe's regulations when Napoleon could ride around the island without being escorted by a British officer? "It seems that the French Commissioner is the only dangerous person here," Montchenu said angrily. He reiterated his determination "to fulfill the instructions of my sovereign that you know well." On the "first beautiful day" he would visit Longwood, and if a sentinel tried to stop him, he would ignore his commands, as he didn't understand English.[7] This angry tirade did not allay Lowe's suspicions that Montchenu was conniving with Napoleon.

The standoff between Lowe and Montchenu continued for a few weeks. The French commissioner continued to exchange old newspapers with Montholon without permission. Lowe, who grew increasingly worried, complained to Bathurst about these provocations. In his view Montchenu had the means to ascertain Napoleon's presence at Longwood and had no need to enter the inner enclosure. His arguments "for desiring to communicate more freely with the followers of General Bonaparte might or might not have weight; at all events, they could form no ground of official discussion with me." Lowe was convinced that Montchenu's objective was to establish a secret channel of communication between Napoleon and Louis XVIII.[8] His suspicions increased when he learned that Montchenu had been heard saying that Napoleon would not live much longer due to his ill health.[9] Lowe was now sure that the marquis had either switched sides or had been duped into believing Napoleon's health was deteriorating and he needed to be transferred to a better climate. The possibility that Montchenu might have other reasons for being certain of Napoleon's demise apparently did not cross his mind. Montholon told Lowe at this time that he wanted to leave St. Helena.

Meanwhile, Napoleon's health continued to deteriorate. By the end of September, the pain in the liver that had started in July had returned. Antommarchi noted that his patient suffered from nausea, vomited quite regularly, and was getting weaker every day. In the first days of October, Napoleon took his last ride and came back to Longwood pale and completely exhausted.[10] At this time Lowe informed Bathurst that the communications between Montholon and Montchenu had become "exceedingly improper and indiscreet." Montchenu said they had simply exchanged some old French newspapers. They were generally sent with an open note from Montholon and returned also with an open note from the marquis.[11] During the rest of October, the deterioration of Napoleon's health was slow "but unceasing and visible." Antommarchi noticed that "it was particularly on the mind that its effect was marked."[12]

The unexpected arrival of the *Owen Glendower* from Buenos Aires at the end of October halted for a while the growing tensions between Lowe and Montchenu. Lowe would have generally welcomed the visit of someone with the pedigree of Captain Robert Spencer. But not on this occasion, as he knew Spencer belonged "to a family whose political opinions were in opposition to the Ministry." However, initially he didn't voice any concerns and simply explained to Bathurst that the *Owen Glendower* had just brought "a small amount of specie" from Buenos Aires.[13] Wondering why Commodore Hardy had sent Spencer to St. Helena, Lowe wrote him a polite note saying that he had been "much gratified and obliged by that consideration for our probable wants which has led you to allow of a small supply of dollars being sent here."[14]

Lowe feared Spencer would offer evidence to those voices in the opposition that criticized Napoleon's treatment and favored his release or at least his removal to a healthier climate.[15] His worries were well founded. Spencer's older brother John, Viscount Althorp, was not only a prominent Whig but had also been a friend and a disciple of the late Samuel Whitbread, one of Napoleon's most determined and fanatical supporters in England. Althorp had also been among the MPs who had supported Whitbread's quixotic efforts in the House of Commons to prevent the renewal of hostilities with France during the Hundred Days.[16] Althorp's opposition to the Tory ministry had steadily grown with the passage of time. The enactment of the Six Acts at the end of 1819 had convinced him that the Tories wanted "to establish a despotism" in England and he believed it was his duty "to take extraordinary steps in opposition to them."[17]

The day after disembarking, Spencer requested authorization from Admiral Lambert to see Napoleon as "a private individual." His request was not unusual, as most Englishmen of a certain standing who visited the island attempted to do the same, irrespective of their political views. Informed of the difficulties "that persons usually experienced in gaining admission" to the prisoner, Lambert referred him to Lowe, who authorized Spencer to visit as long as he avoided contact with Bertrand and made his application through Montholon. Since Napoleon would not let anyone be introduced except through Bertrand this guaranteed that the interview would never happen. Lowe explained to Bathurst that Spencer "had been already informed by the Admiral of the objections that prevailed against his applying through the channel of Count Bertrand. He did not even ask for permission to address himself to Count Bertrand but desired to know if I had any objection to his proceeding at once to Count Montholon and asking him to make known to general Bonaparte his desire of being presented to him. He said at the same time that being well acquainted with many of the Countess Bertrand's relations in England, he should desire on the same occasion to pay a visit to her. I told Captain Spencer I had not the most distant objection to his proposal on either head."[18]

Not surprisingly, Napoleon refused to see Spencer, even though he had a strong interest in seeing him, as at this precise time he was making a last-ditch effort to be removed from St. Helena.[19] In recent weeks Napoleon had ordered Bertrand to write letters to Lord Liverpool, Queen Caroline, and Lord Holland warning that if he wasn't moved to a better climate he would die.[20] Spencer, whose family was closely connected with both Holland and Grey, could easily take any of these letters back to England without Lowe ever finding out. The British captain could also give Napoleon news about what was happening in South America, a subject in which he was always interested. Did Napoleon refuse to see Spencer simply because of a question of etiquette or was it part of the ongoing psychological war he was waging against Lowe?

There was more going on than met the eye. Although Napoleon refused to see the young captain, he was keenly aware of his presence. Ever since Spencer's arrival, he had discarded the drab gardening outfit and straw hat he had been wearing in recent months. Instead he put on his black boots and the dark green uniform of the Chasseurs à Cheval of the Imperial Guard. And after weeks of seclusion, he was seen walking around his garden by a group of curious sailors from the *Owen Glendower.*

Two days after he disembarked, Spencer met Montholon at Longwood. He later paid a visit to Countess Bertrand and had "a long conversation with her."[21] When he returned to Plantation House, Spencer reported to Lowe details of his conversations with both. Lowe informed Bathurst that "the Countess Bertrand was particular in her enquiries as to the political connections of Captain Spencer's family; he did not disguise from her that they were in general not upon the side of the present administration when it appears she gave more full vent to her complaints. . . . Captain Spencer did not repeat to me all that Count Montholon said, but observed upon the disregard of truth evinced in their conversation generally."[22]

In a letter written to his father, Spencer explained that he had been unable to obtain an interview with Napoleon and had "to content myself with peeping at him through his garden rails and primping at Madame Bertrand's brain in my daily visits to her." The young captain admitted he could not help feeling "a curious emotion at being within a yard or two of Napoleon's room; he now and then visits her (although they live in separate houses) but hardly ever goes out." Although told that Napoleon was very ill, Spencer said that there were "very good reasons to doubt this in its full extent." However, he praised Countess Bertrand and Montholon "for their devoted and disinterested attachment to their master, whom they say, and with perfect truth with respect to her, they owe all their happy hours of life." Spencer also said that Lowe's conduct was as "liberal and conciliatory as the ticklish situation he holds admits of."[23] It is not clear whether Lowe read this letter but he started looking more favorably upon Spencer.

The next day Spencer returned to Longwood to pay another visit to Fanny Bertrand. He was told she had not risen and was indisposed, and while he waited outside, one of her sons invited him to come into the house. As he stepped in, Count Bertrand greeted him. The meeting seemed so accidental that the orderly officer reported that the captain "had been taken by surprise." Bertrand took advantage of the opportunity to complain bitterly about the conduct of the British government. On the way out, Spencer also almost ran into Napoleon, who was "walking at a short distance from him in the gardens." According to the orderly officer, Napoleon studiously avoided contact with the visitor and while walking impatiently outside the house had made "repeated inquiries whether Captain Spencer was gone, as he wished to see Madame Bertrand. And immediately on Captain Spencer leaving the house, General Bonaparte went to see her." He remained there for about an hour.[24]

Spencer's unauthorized contact with Bertrand and his near-encounter with Napoleon didn't raise Lowe's suspicions. In fact, his initial reservations about Spencer had been replaced by an unguarded enthusiasm. Viscount Althorp once observed that his younger brother possessed the extraordinary ability to influence his superiors "to a degree greater perhaps than ever belonged to a man."[25] Spencer had already exerted this extraordinary influence over Commodore Hardy. Now it was Lowe's turn, who reported to Bathurst that Spencer had one or two conversations with Montholon and Bertrand, who had spoken "freely to him, under the idea that he belonged to a party in England which espoused their views." Spencer had not been convinced by their arguments regarding Napoleon's situation, which he thought was "not as bad" as some people in England portrayed it.[26]

But as Lowe admitted, Spencer didn't tell him everything that went on during these meetings. At a minimum we know the captain violated Lowe's regulations and gave Napoleon a biography of the Duke of Marlborough sent by his uncle Robert Spencer and dedicated to the "Emperor Napoleon." Unfortunately, besides Spencer's letter to his father and two dispatches by Lowe, no other accounts of his visit to St. Helena have survived. Bertrand's diaries, which cover the entire period of Napoleon's captivity at St. Helena, have a gap during 1820. And Montholon in his memoirs never mentioned Spencer by name or his visit to Longwood, an omission that by itself is quite suggestive. Despite this oversight Montholon provided a clue about what happened.

On October 31 Napoleon had dinner with Montholon and the Bertrands. The orderly officer reported that the venetian shutters of the billiard room "were closed about the time the officers of the *Owen Glendower* arrived at Longwood and have not been opened since."[27] According to Montholon, in early November, "a naval captain" made a proposal of "great importance." Montholon did not provide the captain's name but said that "his vessel was returning from the Indies; he had arranged everything so as to be able to receive the emperor in a boat at a point of the coast previously designated and convey him to his vessel without his running the slightest risk of being stopped. He asked no reward for himself, but demanded a million of francs for the person whose concurrence was necessary, in order that the Emperor might safely pass from Longwood to the coast. This million was not to be payable until the Emperor had reached America and even landed; another condition was that the Emperor should only be accompanied by two persons."[28]

Was Spencer the captain Montholon referred to? It is unlikely that someone with his name and connections would participate in a scheme that could cost him not only his reputation but also his life. Besides, his ship was not returning from the Indies but had arrived from South America. As to whether he or somebody in the *Owen Glendower* brought a message from Cochrane it is impossible to tell. The logbooks of St. Helena show that only East Indiamen had arrived from the Cape in late October or early November.[29] But Cochrane's message could have arrived by other means. There was another ship anchored at Jamestown at this time, the *Perseverance,* a whaler that sailed between St. Helena, Rio de Janeiro, and the River Plate in the second half of 1820 and early 1821. In fact, the British ambassador in Brazil warned Lowe that her crew could be used "to get letters to and from the prisoner of St. Helena by a concert with M. Montholon or any other of his entourage."[30]

Napoleon's reaction to the new plan of escape was predictable. The news that the Duchess of Berri had given birth to a boy had not yet reached St. Helena and it is hard to believe Napoleon was not aware that his supporters were planning a coup d'état in France. Accepting Cochrane's offer of a throne in South America or any other plan of escape could jeopardize his son's dynastic chances. At this point Napoleon was more interested in restoring his son to the French throne than establishing himself in the New World. According to Montholon, Napoleon was determined "not to struggle against his destiny"; he refused the captain's offer and thanked him "for his devotedness."[31] According to Lady Cochrane, Napoleon was too sick and lacked the energy to undertake the ambitious project proposed by her husband.[32] We will probably never know the whole truth. Montholon said that around this time Napoleon also discarded another escape plan proposed by O'Meara "to be carried out by means of submarine vessels." If we are to believe his account, Napoleon had given up hope of ever leaving St. Helena. "We should always obey our destiny; everything is written in heaven; it is my martyrdom which will restore the crown of France to my dynasty," he said.[33]

Soon after, Lowe was informed that Montholon was sick. An English doctor went to see him and thought there was nothing wrong with him. Lowe "was sure there was something improper intended in all this."[34] In recent days he had grown increasingly worried about "the degree of communication which had been established between Montchenu and Montholon." He never imagined these communications would get "so direct" and so "exceedingly improper and indiscreet."[35] Later that day, Spencer returned to Longwood to visit Madame Bertrand "to take his leave." He later boasted to Lowe that he had been able "to combat the arguments which the Countess . . . still persevered in presenting." In the evening Lowe hosted a farewell dinner for Spencer. Montchenu showed no interest in meeting the guest of honor and complained about the apparent ease that he "enjoyed of communicating with the persons at Longwood."[36] Reportedly, the marquis suspected Spencer's visit entailed some danger.[37]

On November 2, in fine weather, the *Owen Glendower* sailed back to Buenos Aires. From Longwood's veranda, Napoleon would have seen the ship disappear over the horizon. We don't know whether the *Owen Glendower* or the *Perseverance* or one of the many whalers that sailed the South Atlantic brought Napoleon's response to South America, but Spencer arrived in Buenos Aires in early December and a few weeks later Brayer returned to Europe. Had Brayer been told that Napoleon had abandoned his American project? As for Spencer, his conduct in Buenos Aires raised many eyebrows. O'Higgins's agent singled him out as "an intimate friend of the anarchists."[38] To be a friend of Alvear and Carrera was an unusual position for a captain of the Royal Navy, as in the past they had all befriended San Martin. Spencer's political activities in South America remain as inexplicable as his trip to St. Helena.*

Lowe was quite pleased with Spencer's visit; he "came here with all those prepossessions that prejudiced or party views may have endeavored to excite in General Bonaparte's favor, and to lead to the opinion of his being harshly and severely treated here, and he has quitted the island as I have every reason to suppose, entirely the convert to a different opinion."[39] At Longwood, the excitement created by Spencer's visit and the recent offers of escape was replaced by a gloomy mood. Napoleon again fell ill and Fanny Bertrand cried "all the time."[40] By early December, Napoleon learned that the plot organized by his supporters in France had failed and that a new heir to the Bourbon dynasty had been born. It must have been a huge disappointment. Napoleon told Antommarchi that he no longer had "any strength, activity or energy left."[41]

Montchenu was also reported to be sick, and his secretary, Captain de Gors, met twice with Antommarchi. Lowe noted that the exchange of notes between

---

*A year later, Spencer interceded with San Martin to obtain the freedom of an Irishman who had followed Carrera in his last adventure.

Montchenu and Montholon continued and informed Bathurst that "if the meetings go on between Captain de Gors and the persons at Longwood, I must necessarily interfere, but hitherto they may have been from accident alone."[42] Lowe did not interfere. Antommarchi's conduct should also have raised his suspicions but didn't. The doctor was spotted visiting Montchenu after going to the pharmacy in Jamestown.[43] It is hard to believe that the ailing marquis would require treatment by someone as incompetent as Antommarchi when he had all the Royal Navy surgeons at his disposal.

On December 5, Montholon informed his wife that Napoleon's illness had "taken a turn for the worse."[44] It was around this time that Antommarchi started to give his patient a drink called orgeat to help "reduce gas."[45] Orgeat is a bittersweet syrup made with almonds, sugar, and rose water, which can also be used for other purposes.

Just as Lowe's fears had almost completely disappeared, he received a letter from Bathurst "respecting the probability of General Bonaparte" attempting an escape. Bathurst suggested showing it to Admiral Lambert. "Indeed I have written it in a great measure for that purpose; as it will enable you to take a review with him of all the different ways by which Bonaparte may attempt his escape and the best means therefore of preventing it. I am strongly impressed with the idea that very much depends upon the navy."[46] Montchenu also warned Lowe not to lower his guard, as the revolutionary ferment in Europe had not abated, as proved by the recent plot.[47] Lowe was convinced that with Lambert's cooperation there could be "no apprehension whatever of General Bonaparte's liberation."[48]

Epilogue
Prometheus Unbound

"Still alive and still bold," shouted Earth,
"I grow bolder and still more bold.
The dead fill me ten thousand fold
Fuller of speed, and splendour, and mirth."
—Percy Bysshe Shelley, "Lines Written on Hearing
the News of the Death of Napoleon"

For the supporters of legitimacy, the political situation in Europe at the beginning of 1821 presented a menacing aspect. The revolutionary virus had spread to Spain, Naples, Piedmont, and Portugal, nor did England and France seem immune to it. The mood was captured in a conversation in London between Wellington and Princess Lieven, wife of the Russian ambassador. The subject was Napoleon and the recent events in Naples. The Iron Duke was "not satisfied" with what was happening. "Things ought to be hurried up," he said. "What is to be done should be done at once; as it is, it will turn out ill."[1] At this precise time, Metternich was meeting with the emperors of Russia and Prussia at Laybach to decide what to do about all these revolutions, and also about Napoleon. At the end of March, the gathered sovereigns proclaimed their hostility to revolutionary regimes, agreed to abolish the Neapolitan constitution, and authorized the Austrian army to restore the monarchy in Naples. Almost at the same time, the Neapolitan rebels accepted an offer from Sir Robert Wilson to lead their armies "against the unjust aggression of Austria."[2] But before Wilson could enter the fray, Austrian troops marched into Naples and crushed the rebellion.

Three months after these events, at St. Helena, Sir Hudson Lowe visited Montchenu to congratulate him on the birth of the son of the Duke of Berri, which assured the continuation of the Bourbon bloodline. Lowe hoped to find Montchenu in a good mood and was surprised to find him extremely agitated. The police had just discovered a new conspiracy to murder the entire royal family and proclaim Napoleon II as the new sovereign of France. After calming down, Montchenu said that Montholon had congratulated him on behalf of "all the people at Longwood" and said that Napoleon "was the only man who could re-establish affairs in France" but that "he was very ill and did not want to meddle in affairs."[3]

A few days after this exchange, Montholon informed Lowe that Napoleon was seriously ill.[4] Still convinced that Napoleon's illness was a sham, Lowe noted in a dispatch to Bathurst that the date at which it had started "is also somewhat remarkable—that of Captain Spencer's arrival here." Lowe believed that the conversations that Montholon and Bertrand had had with Spencer had weakened "the expectation that there could be felt any particular interest regarding him upon grounds of complaint that were not real and from the mortification that must have sprung at finding the falsehood of so many of his complaints laid quite bare."[5] Bathurst was less skeptical about Napoleon's illness but suspected that it was "designedly" exaggerated. "His reluctance to admit an English physician is, of itself, suspicious," he wrote to Lowe. "The extreme desire which he expressed to go to Europe for his health, just at the time when the account of the commotions in Italy must have arrived in St Helena and the prescription of mineral waters by his own surgeon . . . make the accounts of his indisposition somewhat questionable." Bathurst was also wary of Montholon and Bertrand, who were "evidently weary of their duty and as his death would be their release, they may not take as lively an interest in persuading him to take medical advice." Despite his doubts, Bathurst advised Lowe to offer Napoleon proper medical attention and even bring an English doctor from the Cape.[6] Bathurst had not discarded the possibility of a rescue attempt but decided not to publish certain incriminating evidence after a fellow cabinet member advised him against it. "The cons seem much to preponderate, and yet it is impossible to be free from all anxiety till we have accounts of a subsequent date from St. Helena."[7]

Napoleon still dreamed about freedom. "If the choice were mine, I would go to America," he told Bertrand in early March. "First I would get my health back. Then I would spend six months touring the country. . . . I would see Louisiana." Days later he started reading a pamphlet by the Abbé de Pradt about the Spanish colonies.[8] But by the middle of the month he received disappointing news from Europe. Was it the resolution of the Congress of Troppau blaming him for the revolutions in Spain, Naples, and Piedmont? Whatever it was, Napoleon now placed all his hopes of being released on Caroline, who had returned to England to reclaim her title. Napoleon asked Montholon to write her a letter requesting her intercession.[9] But Caroline would have to defeat very powerful enemies before she could do anything. Even if she succeeded, it could be too late, as Napoleon's life was in serious danger.

Doctor Antommarchi's treatment—strong doses of tartar emetic—was wreaking havoc on the patient.* Napoleon's distrust of Antommarchi was so strong that he refused to drink anything he prescribed. But the Corsican doctor managed to enlist the unwitting support of Bertrand and Marchand, Napoleon's valet, who surreptitiously put the substance in his patient's drinks. Lowe informed Bathurst that "when pressed to take medicine, he [Napoleon] declined doing so, saying he had already taken too much, and ascribed his disease in a great degree to what he had taken. He had conceived a dislike therefore to Dr. Antommarchi." Napoleon's "apathy and indifference . . . were extreme . . . [and he] could not now bear the sight of him [Antommarchi] and it was only by stealth that he [Montholon] could get him into his room." Napoleon thought "it was owing to the medicine he had taken that he was so ill."[10]

On March 17 the Abbé Buonavita departed St. Helena after British doctors advised Lowe that he would die if he stayed on the island.† Lowe surprisingly agreed to let him go, not knowing that he carried a copy of Napoleon's will and letters for the Bonaparte family. The night of Buonavita's departure Lowe dined with Captain de Gors, Montchenu's secretary, who confidently said that Napoleon "could not live more than six months."[11] Lowe realized that Napoleon was not "shamming" his illness and that Captain Spencer's visit had had nothing to do with it. In fact, Lowe changed his opinion about Spencer when Napoleon donated a two-volume biography of the Duke of Marlborough to the officers of one of the British regiments garrisoned at St. Helena. The books had been given to Napoleon as a gift and were dedicated to "L'Empereur Napoléon" by Robert Spencer. Incensed, Lowe fired the orderly officer who had accepted the gift.[12]

The end was near. "If I finished my career now I would be happy," Napoleon told Bertrand in late March. "At times, I only wish to die. I am not afraid. It would make me happy to die in fifteen days. What else do I have to hope for? Maybe an even more unhappy ending."[13] Was Napoleon being poisoned? He certainly thought so. When given a drink that smelled strange he turned to

---

*Technically, antimony potassium tartrate. It is a highly toxic substance that is used in the textile industry to bind dyes to fabrics.

† Interestingly, Buonavita lived another twelve years, the last five in Mauritius, a French island in the middle of the Pacific. This was the island where the author Bernardin de St. Pierre had found the inspiration to write *Paul et Virginie,* one of Napoleon's favorite novels.

Montholon and said: "Here. Taste this. I do not know this smell." Only after receiving Montholon's assurances, did Napoleon agree to drink it. He then started talking about poisoning and observed that people "now rival in this respect the skill of Catherine de Médicis."[14] Shortly after this conversation, Bertrand asked Napoleon if he had drunk his tartar emetic. Napoleon furiously turned to Marchand: "Since when have you allowed yourself to poison me by putting emetic drinks on my table? Did I not tell you to offer me nothing I have not authorized? Did I not forbid that? Is this how you justify my confidence in you? You knew it. Get out!"[15]

With the passing weeks Antommarchi's behavior became more erratic. Montholon found his conduct "inexplicable."[16] Napoleon was fed up with his doctor and told Bertrand that he didn't want to see him ever again.[17] Lowe turned down Antommarchi's request to return to Europe. Even though the doctor "appeared much exhausted . . . and much agitated in his mind," Lowe believed he was "much embroiled with General Bonaparte."[18] Was Antommarchi the poisoner? Was he feeling remorse? Days earlier Antommarchi wrote to a friend: "I declare to you, to the Imperial family, to the whole world, that the malady from which the Emperor is suffering is due to the nature of the climate and that its symptoms are of the utmost gravity."[19]

By mid-April, Napoleon's health had deteriorated so much that Montholon and Bertrand agreed to call Archibald Arnott, an English doctor. Arnott initially thought the patient was fine but after a few days, he realized he was mistaken. Like Antommarchi, he recommended strong doses of calomel, a mercurial powder used as a purgative. The medicine immediately produced "a heavy evacuation of blackish matter, thick and partly hard, which resembled pitch or tar."[20] Napoleon grew suspicious. When Arnott suggested a dose of quinine, he asked if it had been prepared in Jamestown or at Longwood. Arnott replied that it had been prepared at Jamestown's pharmacy. "Had the pharmacist been stopped by Sir Thomas Reade?" Napoleon asked. The doctor didn't know. Then Napoleon asked for a drink. "Orgeat?" asked Bertrand, who was standing by his bed. "No," said Napoleon, "just water and wine."[21]

Despite his request to drink water and wine, in the last weeks of his life Napoleon was constantly given glasses of orgeat, which "suddenly appeared on his bedside table." The combination of orgeat and calomel can provoke arsenic poisoning "without recognition in the presence of physicians." Since the stomach naturally rejected this combination and provoked vomiting, the would-be poisoner first had to diminish the body's natural self-defense mechanism. The solution was to give the victim strong doses of tartar emetic, which in large quantities corrodes the lining of the stomach and prevents it from expelling poisons. Antommarchi had prescribed doses of tartar emetic to his patient for several weeks to induce vomiting. These doses were administered always "shortly prior to receiving his abnormally large dose of the purgative calomel."[22]

As he entered the last phase of his agony, an almost delirious Napoleon asked Bertrand, "Which is better, lemonade or orgeat?" "Orgeat is heavier, and less refreshing," responded Bertrand. "Which do the doctors advise?" asked Napoleon. "The one you fancy," the marshal said. "But lemonade's just as good?" Napoleon asked. "Yes, sire," was Bertrand's response. "Is orgeat made from barley?"* Napoleon asked. "No, Sire. From almonds," Bertrand replied. Napoleon then asked for a drink "made with cherries." None was available. During the night, he asked the same questions several times and requested a drink made with cherries—his favorite—to no avail.[23] Days later Napoleon turned to Arnott and said: "I am slowly assassinated with great precision, with premeditation, and the infamous Hudson Lowe is the executioner of your minister's high works."[24]

On the morning of May 2 Napoleon managed to stand up, but his sudden strength was undermined by another lethal combination of orgeat and calomel.[25] "What is this?" Napoleon asked before drinking it. "Orgeat," Bertrand said. "Ah, I understand! *Bonnet blanc et blanc bonnet,*" Napoleon said.† "The cause is lost," he muttered minutes later. For the next two days, he continued to receive intermittent doses of orgeat and calomel.[26] The deadly cocktail produced the desired effect and on May 5 Napoleon died.[27] His last thoughts were for his son, the king of Rome whom he hadn't seen in seven years. He hoped that one day he would rule France and left him detailed instructions on how to conduct himself. He also asked Joseph to do everything in his power to accomplish that goal.

In London, as late as the third week in May, the Tories denied that Napoleon was seriously ill. The *Courier,* which led the disinformation campaign, asserted that the rumors of his illness were just lies advanced by his inveterate English supporters such as Wilson and the *Morning Chronicle.* There was not "the slightest apprehension for his life."[28] Any speculation about Napoleon's health ended on the afternoon of July 4, when news of his death reached London.

* Barley was sometimes used as an antidote for arsenic poisoning.

† Colloquial French expression that is used to describe two situations that seem different but are actually the same.

"Buonaparte is no more!" reported the *Courier* and shamelessly added that he "was sensible until the end and died without pain." Then the newspaper made one of the most inaccurate predictions in the history of journalism: "The celebrity of this extraordinary man. . . is destined to decrease from age to age."[29]

The Tory ministers were quite relieved. At a minimum, Napoleon's death would save the British treasury "at least £300,000 a year."[30] When George IV was told that his "worst enemy" had died he celebrated, thinking he had gotten rid of Caroline. Caroline in turn thought Napoleon's death was "a black speck" on England's history.[31] The Duke of Sussex, her brother-in-law, agreed. In his view, Napoleon's death marked the end of "a most disgraceful transaction in which the Ministers have made this country to participate. To be the persecutor of fallen glory and the gaoler for the European sovereigns is not the situation in which England ought to have been placed. Peace to the remains of that great man, whom history will treat hereafter with greater justice than his contemporaries have hitherto done, while our disgrace will I fear be handled with all due severity."[32] Other English Bonapartists were devastated by the news. Wilson was "crushed," and according to the French ambassador he was one of the few English Bonapartists who openly mourned Napoleon's death.[33] Wilson believed the event would have a great impact all over Europe.[34] Henry Hunt, still serving a prison sentence for his participation in the Peterloo incidents, expressed sadness at the death of "the most wonderful man that ever existed!"[35] The news reached Paris a few days later and "produced a sort of excitement" in the general public and great relief, but probably no surprise, at the Bourbon court.[36] In Vienna the only person who cried at hearing the news was Napoleon II, who had been recently demoted in the royal hierarchy to a simple duke. Despite Metternich's brainwashing efforts, the ten-year-old boy never wavered in his affection and admiration for his father. No one in the Austrian court had expected him to "feel the loss of his father so deeply."[37]

Joseph learned of Napoleon's death in early August. The thought of his brother dying alone and away from his family on that wretched rock tortured him for a long time. Napoleon's mother refused to believe the news, convinced that Napoleon had already left St. Helena.[38] Maybe she knew something we don't know.

The news reached Lallemand in New Orleans. It was a big disappointment to him and many other exiled Bonapartists who, according to one version, at the end of 1820 had organized a scheme to rescue Napoleon from St. Helena. Together with Nicolas Girod, the mayor of New Orleans and other Frenchmen "equally devoted to the great man," they had raised money to commission the building of a fast ship named *La Seraphine.* Her commander was allegedly Dominique Youx, older brother of Jean Laffite. Girod even built a house for Napoleon in New Orleans, but before *La Seraphine* was able to put out to sea, the news of the emperor's death arrived.[39]

Together with other Bonapartists, Lallemand organized a memorial service. Hundreds of exiled French veterans donned their old uniforms to pay their last respects to the *petit caporal.* Lallemand, Humbert, and Lefebvre-Desnouettes led the funeral procession to the city's cathedral. It was a strange ceremony where Roman Catholic ritual mixed with Masonic symbols. The officiating priest was Father Antonio de Sedella, the head of Luis de Onis' spy network in New Orleans.[40] Napoleon's generals did not know that Sedella was partly responsible for derailing their plans. But Onis' plans were also overturned. Months later, Mexico became an independent kingdom with its own unlikely monarch, a former officer of the royalist army named Agustin de Iturbide.

Brayer heard of Napoleon's death while in Brussels, where he arrived in early 1821. A few weeks later he obtained a royal pardon and was allowed to return to Paris. The news caught up with Lord Cochrane in late August, two months after Lima fell to the patriot army. It must have been a bittersweet moment for him, having tried so hard to secure a throne for Napoleon in the Spanish colonies. "Poor Bonaparte!" he said. "I do regret the death of this man, the greatest that has ever lived in the pages of history and certainly the greatest man of our times."[41]

Doubts about the official cause of Napoleon's death—hereditary stomach cancer—surfaced almost immediately.[42] Hunt wondered whether Napoleon had died "by assassination or the quick or slow effect of the poisoned cup."[43] A fellow Bonapartist, Sir James Mackintosh, requested the opinion of O'Meara and another surgeon of the Royal Navy named Roberts. O'Meara insisted on his diagnosis of a liver obstruction, exacerbated by Lowe's vexations.[44] Roberts also rejected cancer as the cause of death. "Had he died of a protracted disease the body would have been extenuated, the adipose substance absorbed and universal derangement have ensued in the viscera." Stomach cancer was "wholly out of the question," as no person "ever died of that disorder *teres et rotundus** as he did." Roberts blamed poor medical care for hastening Napoleon's death and asserted that if Arnott had treated the patient earlier he would probably

---

*In such fine, well-shaped condition.

have survived. "It may not be irrelevant to notice what Desgenettes* told me at Paris in 1803 that Buonaparte had contracted while in Egypt the Leprosy (*Lepra Arabum*) for which he was then taking large doses [of] arsenic," Roberts added. "What effect this may have had upon his system I cannot determine."[45] The *Morning Chronicle* reported that "the idea of a hereditary cancer is treated irreverently by many of the faculty" and published a letter from O'Meara raising doubts about the supposed cause of Napoleon's death.[46]

Worried about the possibility that he might suffer from cancer, Joseph underwent a thorough medical examination but was found to be perfectly healthy. He lived another twenty-three years. "I can no longer doubt today that my brother died a victim to the cruelty of his enemies," Joseph wrote to a friend. "But for them, he would have lived in this country as healthy as I, who am older than he was and not so strong in constitution, and there would have been no discussion in order to find reasons for his death, which have nothing to do with the true one."[47]

Wilson asked Montholon and Bertrand when they returned to England and they both rejected "the idea of poison."[48] However, Montholon later admitted that Napoleon's liver "was much worse" than the autopsy report prepared by British doctors suggested.[49] Years later he was called as a witness for the defense in a slander trial that Lowe initiated against O'Meara and declared that Napoleon's life had been "shortened by the moral assassination of which he was the victim at St. Helena as much from the effect of the restrictions and administration of Sir Hudson Lowe as from the effect of the devouring climate of the said island."[50] Gourgaud also questioned the official explanation behind Napoleon's death. "It was not true that Napoleon died of [the] same illness as his father as asserted by the British government," he said decades later. "At St. Helena he never complained of stomach pains; two sisters have died and not of cancer, five brothers still live and never had symptoms of this hereditary illness." Gourgaud believed future historians would not give credit to this explanation and "grave suspicions would remain about the causes of Napoleon's death."[51]

But if there was a crime, a subject on which there is no consensus among historians, who was the assassin? Many accuse Montholon.[52] According to a popular theory, the wily count had a strong motive, as he stood to inherit most of Napoleon's fortune. Some historians claim he was Artois's secret agent, whereas

---

* René-Nicolas Desgenettes (1762–1837) served as a doctor in Napoleon's Egyptian campaign.

others suggest he sought revenge because Napoleon had seduced his wife. An even more far-fetched theory asserts that Napoleon ordered his own poisoning to get transferred out of St. Helena but that Montholon miscalculated the doses. Montholon's conduct certainly leaves many questions unanswered. The British government thought that there was "tolerably strong proof of the duplicity or ignorance of all [of] Buonaparte's attendants" and that Montholon "was either not speaking the truth in his letter to Princess Borghese or in his statement to Lowe as to the date when he first apprehended danger to Bonaparte's life."[53] When Montholon returned to Paris, there were rumors about his "not very honorable" conduct and resentment at his "grand airs."[54] However, these rumors never suggested he was Napoleon's murderer.

For those who believe that Napoleon was murdered the case against Montholon is far from conclusive. There are many other possible suspects. Napoleon himself suggested Colonel Reade, Lowe's right-hand man. And Lowe was not free from suspicion.[55] Another strong suspect is Antommarchi. Proponents of the poisoning theory exonerate him—too quickly perhaps—because he was Corsican and had been chosen by Cardinal Fesch. However, many of those who believed Napoleon had been murdered pointed their finger to "some Italians who were sent [to Saint Helena] some time ago from Rome."[56] Antommarchi's strange conduct during the last months of Napoleon's life raises serious questions. Napoleon blamed him for his illness and requested his replacement. Interestingly, Antommarchi "was himself conscious of his want of capacity" and knew that the effect of "what he prescribed frequently proved the very reverse of what he foretold and expected." Napoleon proposed several candidates to replace Antommarchi and "particularly desired that his family might be entirely excluded from all interference whatever in the choice of any of them." It was not so much "the fault of the family as of the position in which they were placed in an ecclesiastical state where they could not act with sufficient independence in making a selection," Napoleon had said. He wished therefore to leave it "entirely to the decision of the King of France and his ministers . . . nearly all of whom had served him in the same offices and who so well knew his habits and dispositions. For instance, there was Pasquier, who had been for ten years his minister. . . . There was Decazes himself, once his private secretary who knew him intimately for several years, and who was in possession of many secrets known to none but himself."[57]

But even if Antommarchi was the poisoner, he was clearly following orders. Who wanted to see Napoleon dead? The list was endless. The Count of Artois was probably at the top. Ever since 1815 the French Bourbons had asked themselves what would happen if "the English ministers had changed, and in their place [were] those who had declared against Buonaparte's detention?" What if he had escaped to America and then returned to France "to set all of Europe on fire and deluge it with blood?"[58] Metternich was also quite relieved at Napoleon's death, as he blamed him for all the troubles affecting Europe, particularly the uprisings in Italy, which threatened the stability of the Habsburg empire. Years later he revealed that Napoleon's only hope before his death "was the completion of a project which had been formed in America to get him off the island."[59]

The case against the British government is weak but cannot be dismissed out of hand. Bathurst admitted that as long as Napoleon lived "the large body of the discontented in France (and indeed elsewhere) had a rallying point to look to and there could be no doubt that his escape would at any time have been followed by a fearful result."[60] Napoleon certainly believed the English ministers would have no qualms about eliminating him. Interestingly, a month after the news of his death arrived in England, Queen Caroline also died. "It was a state murder, like Napoleon's," said one of her ladies-in-waiting. Hobhouse also noticed the coincidence and the *Examiner* argued that both Napoleon and Caroline had "by their treatment, been prepared for the catastrophe."[61]

A mob scene at Caroline's funeral proved to be Wilson's undoing. The gallant general led the funeral cortege and at one point prevented the Life Guards from charging the unruly mob that followed it. The incident gave the British ministers the perfect opportunity to get rid of an irritating thorn in their side. Wilson's conduct was found "unbecoming to an officer and a gentleman" and he was discharged from the army without a court-martial.[62] It was an act of "pure despotism," according to Cochrane.[63] Having heard of his friend's disgrace, he entreated him to "come to South America and leave behind the insuperable evils of the old, corrupt and still degenerating world." The mission of liberating South America had not been completed, Cochrane said. "We are every day expecting the reoccupation of Lima by the Spanish troops owing to the miscue of San Martin, who has proved himself to be a shallow, tough, cunning knave with the disposition of a vile satrap and a cruel tyrant."[64] San Martin gave himself the Cromwellian title of "protector" of Peru and lobbied England to send him a prince. Opposition to his despotic manner and monarchical schemes mounted and by late 1822 he was forced to resign, almost at the same time that Mexico's new monarch was ousted. After a brief interlude in Buenos Aires, he embarked on a lifelong exile to Europe. With the passing years, his victims, his attachment to England, and his monarchical intrigues were forgotten, and he became a symbol of nationalistic pride that continues to be used for political purposes.[65]

Although unsuccessful in their bid for power, Carrera and Alvear succeeded at least in derailing the monarchical schemes hatched by their enemies. After two years of struggle, in mid-1820 they parted ways and never saw each other again. Carrera attempted to reach Chile with a loyal band of followers but was captured and executed before reaching the Andes. Elated at the news, San Martin said, "Finally the damned Carrera has met the fate he deserved."[66] Alvear was luckier. In early 1822 his seven-year exile from Buenos Aires ended and a year later he was named ambassador to the United States. In the spring of 1824, while visiting Manhattan he was invited to dinner with a wealthy New York businessman, who asked him if he wanted to meet Joseph Bonaparte. Alvear politely declined. He knew his political career would never recover if rumors of such a meeting ever reached Buenos Aires.[67]

Wilson never set foot in South America.* Shortly after being discharged, he decided to "take my gallop into Spain."[68] With Italy subjugated by Austria, the fight for freedom had to be fought in the Peninsula. General Vaudoncourt, an old friend and fellow Bonapartist, who after leading the Piedmontese rebellion moved to Spain, encouraged Wilson.[69] But the French Bourbons decided that the revolutionary virus that had infected their neighbor was too dangerous and sent an army to restore Ferdinand VII. The affairs in the Peninsula provided Wilson and Lallemand an opportunity to join forces again. At the end of 1822 they met in London and organized the Legion Liberale to fight in Spain. Early the following year Wilson left England, ignoring the entreaties of his ailing wife. Lallemand followed him shortly after.

Was the revolution in Spain also part of Napoleon's grand plans? It was if we believe what Count Regnault revealed to MacGregor in March 1817. Whether part of a grand plan or not, the Bonapartist signs were evident everywhere. Although Brayer did not join this new campaign, Lallemand, Vaudoncourt, Latapie, Persat, Schultz, Fabvier, Maceroni, Pepe, and other well-known Bonapartists fought for the cause of freedom in Spain. One of the battalions fighting against the French and Spanish Bourbons was called Napoleon II and its officers were all veterans of the Grande Armée.[70] But Wilson never managed to get his campaign off the ground, and the liberal cause in Spain was eventually

* His son, however, became aide-de-camp to Bolivar.

crushed. The quixotic general was wounded and suffered a great indignity when the sovereigns of Russia, Austria, and Prussia stripped him of all his medals. A much more devastating blow was learning of the death of his wife. For five years her poor health had prevented him from going to South America. "I saw in an instant all my hopes destroyed, all my dreams vanished," Wilson wrote when he heard the news. "If I survive to days of tranquility I will at last do her memory justice and leave a record of utility as well as honor to her descendants."[71]

After the restoration of Ferdinand VII, Greece became the rallying cry of the Friends of Freedom. "Greece awaits a liberator. What a splendid wreath of glory is there! He can inscribe his name for eternity with those of Homer, of Plato, of Epaminondas! I myself was perhaps not far from doing it!" Napoleon had said at St. Helena.[72] Maybe the Friends of Freedom were inspired by his words. Byron died from a fever while fighting for the Greek cause. Not surprisingly, Cochrane and Lallemand as well as many other exiled Bonapartists also joined the Greek patriots after the fall of liberal Spain. But not Wilson. Overwhelmed with guilt over his wife's death and apparently in an effort to fulfill his promise to do justice to her memory, the knight-errant returned to England and sheathed his sword. And just when he had become an icon for freedom fighters around the world, he turned against the causes he had so passionately defended. As he grew older, he distanced himself from Grey, reconciled with Wellington, and supported the Tories. Wilson's strange ideological conversion explains why today he is relatively unknown. The Tories never forgot his youthful sins and the Whigs and the Radicals never forgave his betrayal. Had he died fighting for freedom in South America, Spain, or Greece, he would almost certainly have achieved the recognition he craved during his lifetime.

Cochrane outlived most of his fellow revolutionaries and eventually returned to England. Under the reign of Queen Victoria he was finally recognized as a national hero. His main preoccupation upon his return was to recover the title, the reputation, and the back pay he had lost during his trouble-making years, so he never disclosed what his true objectives had been when he left for South America. At the height of the Victorian empire, the fanatical attachment that he and other prominent Englishmen had felt for Napoleon seemed slightly ridiculous. They all managed to reinterpret their past. Not Brayer and Lallemand. Both remained devoted to Napoleon's memory until their death. Following the demise of the Spanish and Greek campaigns, Lallemand continued to fulfill important missions for Joseph. After the French revolution of 1830 he went to France to gather support for the return of Napoleon II. During the reign of Louis Philippe he was appointed governor of Corsica. He died in Paris at the end of 1839, a year before Napoleon's remains were brought back from St. Helena. As for Brayer, he settled in Strasbourg and remained close to the Bonaparte family. His daughter married Marchand, Napoleon's valet at St. Helena, who thus fulfilled his master's instructions "to marry the daughter of an officer of the old guard." Brayer died in November 1840, on the same day Napoleon's casket touched French soil.

Joseph lived in the United States for another ten years. Contrary to the myth of the "gentleman farmer," uninterested in politics and devoted to literature, women, and gardening, he never stopped intriguing to restore the Bonaparte dynasty to its former glory as Napoleon had instructed him on his deathbed. But he wasn't as capable or as determined as his brother had been.

Castlereagh, Richelieu, Tsar Alexander, and Metternich—the four individuals directly responsible for sending Napoleon to St. Helena and keeping him there—met very different fates. Castlereagh committed suicide almost a year after Napoleon's death. According to the official story he suffered a nervous breakdown. But many historians believe he was being blackmailed and killed himself by cutting his throat to avoid public humiliation.[73] Thistlewood's supporters couldn't have planned a sweeter revenge. Richelieu fell from power at the end of 1821 and died of a stroke six months later, almost at the same time as Castlereagh. Alexander died in 1825 at age forty-six of a mysterious illness.[74] Metternich lived until 1859 and had to witness the demise of the political system he had worked so hard to preserve when it was overwhelmed by the resurgence of liberal and nationalistic ideas. The return of Bonapartism to France must have been a bitter pill for the Austrian chancellor to swallow. Metternich's hopes that the death of Napoleon would end the revolutionary fever affecting Europe never came to pass. Instead, Napoleon's prediction came true. As Winston Churchill observed, the "ideals of liberty and nationalism, born in Paris" triumphed all over Europe.[75]

The Count of Artois, who many believe ordered Napoleon's murder, became king of France in 1824 as Charles X, but he was dethroned by a revolution six years later. His fall brought Joseph back into action. It was Joel Roberts Poinsett, the former American consul in Santiago, who after meeting Victor Hugo and other Bonapartists in Paris told Joseph that if he put himself at the head of the movement "the Duke of Reichstadt would be called to the French throne."[76]

Poinsett had evidently not abandoned his Bonapartist sympathies. It was the opportunity Joseph had been waiting for to fulfill Napoleon's instructions. After
receiving this message, he sent Lallemand to France to gather support for the
return of Napoleon II, who lived in Vienna under Metternich's strict surveillance.[77] In February 1832 Joseph wrote a letter to his nephew saying that it was
time to return to France.[78] The Duke of Orleans had reneged on the promises
made to the liberals and the country was again on the verge of revolution. But
despite Joseph's efforts, Napoleon's son was not to reign in France or anywhere
else. Soon after Joseph's letter reached Vienna, the young man died. The chess-
board of European interests "was too complicated to think seriously of taking him out of his obscurity, and his death, to which an intelligent poison was
doubtless not foreign, freed the two fearful monarchs from a constant menace."[79] As in the case of his father, his death was explained with detailed medical
reports. The cause was tuberculosis, from which he had been suffering for some
time. This explanation did not convince many Bonapartists, who believed that
Metternich had poisoned the young man.[80]

After the death of Napoleon II, the political weight of the Bonaparte family
waned for a few years. Joseph died in Florence in 1844, having tried for thirty
years to advance the dynastic interests of his family without success. Shortly
afterward the Bonapartes reemerged on the European political scene. Following the 1848 revolution, Joseph's nephew became emperor of France as Napoleon III. His plans to create an empire in Mexico ended disastrously and his
reign collapsed after the battle of Sedan.

The independence of the Spanish colonies was secured in 1824, when Bolivar's army defeated the royalists at the battle of Ayacucho. But the discord that
existed among the patriots in the early days of the revolution intensified. Once
the conflict between monarchism and republicanism was resolved, another pitting centralism against federalism followed. Because the former Spanish colonies lacked the institutional framework and political culture of the English
colonies, several decades passed before the republican form of government took
roots.

The Adams-Onis treaty didn't stop the United States' territorial expansion. Although the U.S. government agreed to relinquish any authority over
Texas, it encouraged occupation by American settlers, leading to the establishment of an independent republic in 1836. This was the first step on the road
to annexation. Mexico's refusal to recognize U.S. annexation in 1845 led to

the Mexican-American War (1846–48). In 1847 General Winfield Scott, who thirty years earlier had helped Xavier Mina organize an expedition to liberate Mexico, landed at Vera Cruz at the head of an army and secured a U.S. victory. As a result, the United States seized California and most of the Southwest. It was the beginning of an empire. Napoleon wouldn't have been surprised.

Notes

Abbreviations

Preface

1. Henry Chamberlain to Lord Castlereagh, Rio de Janeiro, November 15, 1817, NA FO 63/204, f.307.

2. Chamberlain to Captain Sharpe, Rio de Janeiro, November 18, 1817, NA FO 63/204, f.367.

3. Sir Charles Bagot to Castlereagh, October 21, 1817, NA FO 5/123.

4. Donald Thomas, *Cochrane: Britannia's Sea Wolf* (London: Cassell, 2002), 243–244.

5. Alexander von Humboldt, *Essai Politique sur le Royaume de la Nouvelle Espagne* (Paris: F. Schoell 1811), 1:5–7.

6. James Parton, "The Exploits of Edmond Genet in the United States," *Atlantic Monthly* 31, no. 186 (Apr. 1873): 385–405, and Harry Ammon, *The Genet Mission* (New York: Norton, 1973).

7. Carlos Villanueva, *Napoleón y la independencia de América* (Paris: Garnier Freres, 1911), 69.

8. William Hague, *William Pitt the Younger* (London: Harper Collins, 2004), 456.

9. Colonel Nemours, "Bonaparte et Saint-Domingue," *Revue des Etudes Napoléoniennes* 31 (July–Dec.1930): 156–158.

10. Jacques Sandeau, "La Révolution a Saint-Domingue et le désastre du corps expéditionnaire français, 1789–1803," *Revue de l'Institut Napoléon* 191 (2005–2), 7–44.

11. Conversation on March 10, 1821, Henri-Gratien Bertrand, *Cahiers de Sainte-Hélène: Manuscrit déchiffré et annoté par Paul Fleuriot de Langle* (Paris: Sulliver, 1949–1959), 3:96.

12. Mario Carneiro do Rego Melo, *A Maçonaria e a Revolução Republicana de 1817* (Recife: Imprensa Nery da Fonseca, 1912), 12.

13. Olivier Baulny, "Napoléon et les projets d'attaque du Brésil," *Revue de l'Institut Napoléon* 118 (1971): 25–33.

14. Robert Gardiner, *Memoir of Admiral Sir Graham Moore, G.C.B.* (London, 1844), 29–30.

15. Hague, *William Pitt,* 539.

16. Castlereagh, "Memorandum for the Cabinet, Relative to South America," dated 1807, Robert Stewart Viscount Castlereagh, 2nd Marquis of Londonderry, *Memoirs and Correspondence of Viscount Castlereagh Second Marquess of Londonderry* (London, 1848–1853), 7:320–323. Castlereagh's recommendations formed the basis of British policy toward Spanish America for most of the nineteenth century. H. S. Ferns, *Britain and Argentina in the Nineteenth Century* (Oxford: Clarendon Press, 1960), 47–48.

17. Miguel Artola, "Los afrancesados y América," *Revista de Indias* 10, no. 37–38 (1949): 541–78, and Jean-René Aymes, "Napoléon Ier et le Mexique," *Travaux de l'Institut d'Etudes Latino-Américaines de l'Université de Strasbourg* 11 (1971): 39.

18. Zea to Napoleón, July 1808, Alberto Miramón, *Política Secreta de Napoleón en Nueva Granada* (Bogotá: Ed. Kelly, 1978), 72–74, and Jose Ramón Mila de la Roca and Nicolas de Herrera to Joseph Bonaparte, Bayonne, June 28 and 29, 1808, Carraciolo Parra Pérez, *Bayona y la política de Napoleón en América* (Caracas: Tipografia Americana, 1939), 73–99.

19. Baulny, "Napoléon et les projets," 25–33.

20. Bernard de Sassenay, *Napoléon I et la fondation de la République Argentine, Jacques de Liniers Comte de Buenos-Ayres, Vice Roi de la Plata et le Marquis de Sassenay,*

1808–1810 (Paris: Plon, 1892), 5–8, 10, 131–134; Carlos Villanueva, *Napoleón y la independencia de América* (Paris: Garnier, 1911), 214–216; and Mario Belgrano, "Napoléon et l'Argentine: La mission de Sassenay (1808)," *Revue des Etudes Napoléoniennes* 24 (Jan.–June 1925): 219–238.

21. Manuel Palacio Fajardo, *Outline of the Revolution in Spanish America* (London: Longman, 1817), 79–87.

22. Aymes, "Napoléon Ier et le Mexique," 38–62. Regarding the activities of Napoleon's agents in the Spanish colonies, see Jacques Penot, *Meconnaissance, Connaissance, et Reconaisance de l'Independence du Mexique par la France* (Paris: Editions Hispaniques, 1975), 46–62; John Rydjord, *Foreign Interest in the Independence of New Spain* (Durham, N.C.: Duke University Press, 1935), 295–296; Analola Borges, "El Plan Bonaparte y sus Repercusiones en los Documentos Anglo-Españoles," in *Cuarto Congreso de Historia de América* (Buenos Aires: Academia Nacional de Historia, 1966), 7:205–237; Jacques Penot, *Les Relations entre la France et le Mexique de 1808 a 1840* (Paris: Champion, 1976); and William S. Robertson, *France and Latin American Independence* (Baltimore: Johns Hopkins Press, 1939), 73–74.

23. *Le Moniteur Universal,* Paris, December 14, 1809.

24. Aymes, "Napoléon Ier et le Mexique," 50.

25. Napoleon to Bassano, August 23, 1811, Napoleon, *Correspondance de Napoléon Ier* (Paris: Plon, 1858–1870), 22:506, and Bassano to Serurier, September 16, 1811, Villanueva, *Napoleón y la Independencia,* 278–280.

26. Russell to Monroe, Paris, September 2, 1811, William R. Manning, *Diplomatic Correspondence of the United States Concerning Independence of the Latin-American Nations* (New York: Oxford University Press, 1925), 2:1371.

27. Napoleon to Bassano, Paris, August 28, 1811, Napoleon, *Correspondance,* 22:525.

28. Napoleon to Decres, November 25, 1811, ibid., 23:41.

29. Before leaving Moscow, Napoleon invited Joel Barlow, the American ambassador in Paris, to meet him at Vilnius. Barlow arrived there in early December but after learning of the disastrous results of the campaign he concluded that Napoleon would be in no mood to negotiate, so he returned to Paris. He died of pneumonia during the trip. Jesse S. Reeves, *The Napoleonic Exiles in America: A Study in American Diplomatic History, 1815–1819* (Baltimore: Johns Hopkins Press, 1905), 114–134.

30. Armand A. L. de Caulaincourt, *With Napoleon in Russia* (New York: W. Morrow, 1935), 305–306.

31. Madison to Barlow, Washington, November 17, 1811, James Madison, *The Papers of James Madison: Presidential Series,* ed. Robert A. Rutland and Thomas A. Mason (Charlottesville: University Press of Virginia, 1984–2004), 4:22.

32. Gallatin to Madison, September 17, 1810, Madison, *Papers,* 2:545.

33. Serurier to Bassano, Washington, November 28, 1811, Villanueva, *Napoleón y la Independencia,* 282.

34. Barlow to Madison, Paris, December 30, 1811, Reeves, *The Napoleonic Exiles,* 126–131, and V. Vital-Hawell, "El Aspecto internacional de las usurpaciones americanas en las provincias españolas limítrofes con los Estados Unidos de 1810 a 1814," *Revista de Indias* 99–100 (Jan.–June 1965): 127.

35. John Quincy Adams, *Memoirs of John Quincy Adams Comprising Portions of His Diary from 1795 to 1848,* ed. Charles Francis Adams (Philadelphia: Lippincott, 1874–1877), 4:306.

36. Luis de Onis, *Memoir upon the Negotiations between Spain and the United States* (Baltimore: F. Lucas, 1821), 14–15.

37. Harris Gaylord Warren, *The Sword Was Their Passport: A History of American Filibustering in the Mexican Revolution* (Baton Rouge: Louisiana State University Press, 1943), 77–130.

38. Joseph Lockey, "The Florida Intrigues of Jose Alvarez de Toledo," *Florida Historical Quarterly* 12, no. 4 (Apr. 1934): 149–153.

39. Aymes, "Napoléon Ier et le Mexique," 55.

40. Onis to Captain General of Cuba, Philadelphia, August 20, 1813, Warren, *The Sword,* 77–78. According to Warren, Humbert was just a madman and an adventurer. In fact, he had the ideal profile of a filibuster, and French archives confirm that Napoleon sent Humbert on a mission to America. Jacques Baeyens, *Sabre au clair: Amable Humbert: General de la Republique: des Vosages a la Louisiane, 1789–1823* (Paris: Albatros, 1981), 128–129.

41. Some historians claim Humbert detested Napoleon but the evidence is contradictory. In fact, in 1813 Humbert refused the overtures of his old comrade and friend General Moreau to dethrone Napoleon. Henry Poulet, *Un soldat lorrain méconnu, le général Humbert, 1767–1823* (Nancy, 1928); Marie Louise Jacotey, *Le General Humbert: Un volontaire 1792 ou la Passion de la liberté* (Paris: Mirecourt, 1980); and Jean Sarrazin, *La descente des français en Irlande 1798* (Paris: La Vouivre, 1998).

42. Warren, *The Sword,* 93; Bennett Lay, *The Lives of Ellis P. Bean* (Austin: University of Texas Press, 1960), 88; and Penot, *Les Relations entre la France,* 1:155.

43. Buckner F. Melton Jr., *Aaron Burr: Conspiracy to Treason* (New York: Wiley, 2002), 154.

44. The documents presented by Burr to Napoleon's ministers are reproduced in Samuel Engle Burr, *Napoleon's Dossier on Aaron Burr* (San Antonio: Naylor, 1969); Aaron Burr, *Political Correspondence and Public Papers of Aaron Burr,* ed. Mary-Jo Kline (Princeton: Princeton University Press, 1983), 2:1099–1131; Ernesto de la Torre Villar, "Dos Proyectos para la Independencia de Hispanoamérica: James Workman y Aaron Burr," *Revista de Historia de América* 49 (1960): 55–67; and Walter F. McCaleb, *A New Light on Aaron Burr* (New York: Argosy, 1966), 139–143.

45. Palacio Fajardo, *Outline of the Revolution,* 352. Palacio Fajardo was the Venezuelan rebel who in 1813 went to Paris to request Napoleon's aid. Caracciolo Parra Pérez, *Una misión diplomática venezolana ante Napoleón en 1813* (Caracas: Publicaciones de la Secretaria General de la Décima Conferencia Interamericana, 1953); Robertson, *France and Latin American Independence,* 102–104; Francisco J. Urrutia, *Los Estados Unidos de América y las Repúblicas Hispano-Americanas* (Madrid: Editorial América, 1918), 49–50; and Miramón, *Política Secreta de Napoleón,* 87–90.

46. I. H. Vivian, *Minutes of a Conversation with Napoleon Bonaparte during His Residence at Elba, in January 1815* (London: Ridgway, 1839), 23.

47. Carlos Trelles y Govin, *Un precursor de la independencia de Cuba, Don Jose Alvarez de Toledo* (La Habana: Academia de la Historia, 1926), 33.

48. General Orders, General Jackson, New Orleans, January 21, 1815, Arsene Lacarrier Latour, *Historical Memoir of the War in West Florida and Louisiana in 1814–1815,* ed. Gene A. Smith (New Orleans: Historic New Orleans Collection; Gainesville: University Press of Florida, 1999), 339, and Jane Lucas de Grummond, *The Baratarians and the Battle of New Orleans* (Baton Rouge: Louisiana State University Press, 1961), 148–149.

Chapter 1

1. Winston S. Churchill, *A History of the English-Speaking Peoples* (London: Cassell, 1958), 2:309.

2. Anne-Jean-Marie-René Savary, *Memoirs of the Duke of Rovigo (M. Savary) Written by Himself* (London: H. Colburn, 1828), 2:113.

3. Antoine-Marie de Lavallette, *Memoirs of Count Lavallette* (London: Gibbins, 1894), 327.

4. Lazare H. Carnot, *Mémoires sur Lazare Carnot, 1753–1823* (Paris, 1907), 2: 527–528.

5. Savary, *Memoirs,* 2:117.

6. Hortense de Beauharnais, *The Memoirs of Queen Hortense,* ed. Prince Napoleon (London: Thornton Butterworth, 1928), 2:193.

7. Lucien to Pauline, June 26, 1815, Lucien Bonaparte, *Mémoires Secrètes* (Paris, 1818), 2:96.

8. Napoleon to N. Barber, Imperial Librarian, June 25, 1815, Napoleon, *Correspondance,* 28:300.

9. Henry Houssaye, *1815—La Seconde Abdication—Le Terreur Blanche* (Paris: Perrin, 1906), 215, and Henry Houssaye, *Le dernier jour de Napoléon a la Malmaison,* juin 29, 1815, Pièce en un acte (Paris: Perrin, 1914), 24.

10. Aimé Bonpland, *Londres Cuartel General Europeo de los Patriotas de la Emancipación Americana Archivo Bonpland IV* (Buenos Aires: Revista del Instituto de Botánica y Farmacología Julio A. Roca, 1940).

11. Frédéric Masson, *Napoleon at St. Helena* (New York: Medill McBride, 1950), 11.

12. Pierre Alexander Fleury de Chaboulon, *Memoirs of the Private Life of Napoleon* (London: J. Murray, 1820), 2:294–296.

13. Simon Bolivar to Camilo Torres, Kingston, August 22, 1815, Alberto Miramón, *Política Secreta de Napoleón,* 141–143.

14. In 1810, shortly after Caracas declared its independence, Bolivar visited London to seek the support of the British cabinet. See memorandum of Henry Wellesley, 1810, NA FO 72/106, f.20. Months later Venezuelan rebels reiterated their overtures to England. See Lopez Mendez to Wellesley, December 1811, NA FO 72/125, f.78, and Miranda to Vansittart, June 2, 1812, NA FO 72/171, f.27.

15. The messenger was General Becker, appointed by Fouché to watch over Na-

poleon at Malmaison. Savary, *Memoirs,* 2:123; Lavallette, *Memoirs,* 329; and Felix Martha-Beker, *Le Général Beker* (Paris, 1876), 74–75.

16. Charles Tristan de Montholon, *Récits de la captivité de l'Empereur Napoléon a Sainte-Helene, avec une introduction de M. Maillefer* (Paris, 1847), 2:203–205; François de Candé-Montholon, *Journal Secret d'Albine de Montholon, maitresse de Napoléon a Ste. Heléne* (Paris: Albin Michel, 2002), 171; and Joel T. Headley, *The Battles and Braveries of the Old Guard* (London, 1858), 60. According to Henri Lachouque the troops that arrived at Malmaison on June 29 were not part of Brayer's division but simply a regiment led by his nephew. Lachouque however doesn't provide any evidence to support this statement, which was probably based on Houssaye's account of Napoleon's last days at Malmaison. Henri Lachouque, *The Last Days of Napoleon's Empire* (New York: Orion Press, 1967), 144, and Houssaye, *1815—La Seconde Abdication,* 222. Montholon's version is also confirmed by Napoleon's valet and Brayer's son-in-law Louis Marchand, who asserted that the troops that appeared at Malmaison were a division from the army of the Vendée "commanded by their general," who was received by Napoleon. He couldn't have meant any other than Brayer. Louis Marchand, *Mémoires de Marchand,* ed. Jean Bourguignon (Paris: Tallandier, 1985), 244–245.

17. Regarding Brayer's military career see Georges Six, *Dictionnaire Biographique des Généraux et Amiraux de la Révolution e de L'Empire, 1792–1814* (Paris: G. Saffroy, 1934). For Brayer at Albuera see *Victoires, conquêtes, désastres, revers et guerres civiles des français, de 1792 a 1815* (Paris: Impr. C. L. F. Panckoucke, 1820), 20:242.

18. Alexis Belloc, *La telegraphie historique depuis les temps les plus reculés jusqu'à nos jours* (Paris: Firmin-Didot, 1894), 155.

19. Eugene de Vitrolles, *Mémoires et Relations Politiques du Baron de Vitrolles* (Paris: G. Charpentier, 1884), 2:285; Soult to Brayer, Paris, March 6, 1815, Belloc, *La télégraphie historique,* 156.

20. Antoine Henri de Jomini, *Precis Politique et Militaire de la Campagne de 1815* (Bruxelles: Meline, 1846), 39.

21. Lavallette, *Memoirs of Count Lavallette,* 269–280, 290; Benjamin Constant, *Mémoires sur les Cent-Jours* (Paris, 1961), 23–24. For an account of Napoleon's escape from Elba see Norman MacKenzie, *The Escape from Elba: The Fall and Flight of Napoleon, 1814–1815* (Oxford: Oxford University Press, 1982).

22. Fleury de Chaboulon, *Memoirs,* 1:193–194.

23. Napoleon, *Correspondance,* 31:70–71.

24. Montholon, *Récits,* 2:88.

25. Marchand, *Mémoires,* 179.

26. Jacques Etienne Macdonald, Duke of Tarento, *Souvenirs du Maréchal Macdonald, duc de Tarente* (Paris: Plon, 1892), 330–331.

27. Napoleon, *Correspondance,* 29:73, and Macdonald, *Souvenirs,* 337–338.

28. Marchand, *Mémoires,* 184, and Montholon, *Récits,* 2:88.

29. Gaspard de Gourgaud, *Journal de Sainte-Helene 1815–1818,* intro. and notes by Octave Aubry (Paris, 1944–47), 1:264–265, 336.

30. Louis E. St. Denis, *Napoleon: From the Tuileries to St. Helena* (New York and London: Harper and Bros., 1922), 117.

31. Marchand, *Mémoires,* 217, 223.

32. M. Theodore Muret, *Histoire des Guerres de l'Ouest* (Paris, 1848), 5:475–486, and *Victoires, conquêtes,* 24:252–255.

33. September 23, 1817, Montholon, *Récits,* 1:203–205.

34. Beauharnais, *The Memoirs of Queen Hortense,* 2:198, and Gilbert Martineau, *Napoleon Surrenders* (London: John Murray, 1973), 67.

35. Armand de Caulaincourt, *Souvenirs de Duc de Vicence, recueillis et publiés par Charlotte de Sor* (Paris, 1837), 2:256–257.

Chapter 2

1. Bennet to Creevey, Whitehall, July 1815, Thomas Creevey, *The Creevey Papers,* ed. John Gore (London: Folio Society, 1970), 154.

2. Robert T. Wilson, *Private Diary of Travels, Personal Services, and Public Events, during Mission and Employment with the European Armies in the Campaigns of 1812, 1813, 1814, from the Invasion of Russia to the Capture of Paris,* ed. H. Randolph (London: J. Murray, 1861), 2:339. Wilson faced Napoleon at Eylau, Friedland, Smolensk, Lutzen, Bautzen, Dresden, and Leipzig. Although he didn't command troops, he actively participated in military operations and his recommendations were often followed.

3. Henry Edward Fox, *The Journal of the Hon. Henry Edward Fox, 1818–1830,* ed. the Earl of Ilchester (London: Thornton Butterworth, 1923), 51.

4. Wellington to W. W. Pole, April 23, 1810, in Michael Glover, *A Very Slippery Fellow: The Life of Sir Robert Wilson, 1777–1849* (Oxford: Oxford University Press, 1978), 77. A more sympathetic biography can be found in Ian Samuel, *An Astonishing Fellow: The Life of General Sir Robert Wilson* (Bourne End: Kensal, 1985).

5. Erskine Neale, *Risen from the Ranks, or Conduct versus Caste* (London, 1853), 109.

6. Wilson accused Napoleon of poisoning his own wounded men at Jaffa and of massacring Turkish prisoners at Acre. Robert T. Wilson, *History of the Expedition to Egypt* (London, 1802).

7. Wilson, *Private Diary,* 2:365–366.

8. Glover, *A Very Slippery Fellow,* 147–149.

9. John Drinkwater, *Charles James Fox* (London: Ernest Benn, 1928), 352.

10. Regarding Napoleon's influence on English politics see Edward Tangye Lean, *The Napoleonists: A Study in Political Disaffection, 1760–1960* (London: Oxford University Press, 1970); Stuart Semmel, *Napoleon and the British* (London: Yale University Press, 2004); and Simon Bainbridge, *Napoleon and English Romanticism* (Cambridge: Cambridge University Press, 1995).

11. *Political Register,* London, July 8, 1815.

12. William Hazlitt, *Political Essays with Sketches of Public Characters* (London, 1819), 16.

13. Henry Hunt, *Memoirs of Henry Hunt, Esq. Written by Himself, in His Majesty's Jail at Ilchester* (London, 1822), 3:104–106, 189–194.

14. Hunt, *Memoirs,* 143.

15. Declaration of the Allied Powers, March 13, 1815, Foreign Office, *British and Foreign State Papers* (London: HMSO, 1841), 2:663.

16. John Belchem, *"Orator" Hunt: Henry Hunt and English Working-Class Radicalism* (Oxford: Clarendon, 1985), 46, and Daniel Green, *Great Cobbett: The Noblest Agitator* (London: Hodder and Stoughton, 1983), 376.

17. William Godwin, "Letters of Verax to the Editor of the *Morning Chronicle,* on the Question of a War to Be Commenced for the Purpose of Putting an End to the Possession of the Supreme Power in France by Napoleon Bonaparte," (London: Richard and Arthur Taylor, 1815), 32.

18. Lean, *The Napoleonists,* 93, 110, 113.

19. Marchand, *Mémoires,* 252–253.

20. Houssaye, *1815—La Seconde Abdication,* 359–360.

21. In 1812 at the head of a brigade of Chasseurs, Lallemand inflicted one of the most humiliating defeats on the British cavalry during the Peninsular War. David Gates, *The Spanish Ulcer: A History of the Peninsular War* (London: Pimlico, 2002), 361–362, and Charles A. Thoumas, *Les transformations de l'armée française: Essais d'histoire et de critique sur l'état militaire de la France* (Paris, 1887), 2:487–488.

22. Paul Charles F. A. H. D. Thiebault, *Mémoires du général baron Thiebault publiés sous les auspices de sa fille Mlle Claire Thiebault, d'après le manuscrit original, par Fernand Calmettes* (Paris: Plon, 1895–1897), 5:113–118.

23. Barry E. O'Meara, *Napoleon in Exile; or, A Voice from St. Helena* (London: Simpkin Marshall, 1822), 1:511–512. Regarding Lallemand's conspiracy see Etienne Denis Pasquier, *Histoire de mon temps: Mémoires du chancelier Pasquier* (Paris: Plon, 1893–1895), 3:136–138; Achille de Vaulabelle, *Histoire des Deux Restaurations* (Paris: Garnier, 1846), 2:185–186, 248–251; and Savary, *Memoirs,* 4:255.

24. Alexander Dumas, *My Memoirs* (London: Methuen, 1907), 1:384–386. Regarding the unraveling of Lallemand's plot see M. de Boutiaguine to Nesselrode, Paris, March 15, 1815, A. Polovtsoff, *Correspondance diplomatique des ambassadeurs et ministres de Russie en France et de France en Russie avec leurs gouvernements de 1814 a 1830* (St. Petersburg, 1902–), 1:165; Edouard Guillon, *Les Complots Militaires sous la Restauration* (Paris: Plon, 1895), 9–10; Antoine Augustin Pion des Loches, *Mes campagnes, 1792–1815: Notes et correspondence* (Paris: Firmin-Didot, 1889), 416–461; and *Victoires, conquêtes,* 24:21–23; Henry Houssaye, *1815 La Premiere Restauration-Le retour de l'ile d'Elbe-Les cent jours* (Paris: Perrin, 1899), 269–292.

25. Thirty years later, Dumas again met Lallemand at the house of Decazes and asked him if he remembered that day. Lallemand replied, "I remember it well! It is a date of great importance in my life." When Dumas asked if he remembered the boy who had offered him two pistols and fifty louis, Lallemand exclaimed, "*Sacrebleu!* Embrace me again!" Dumas, *My Memoirs,* 1:387–400.

26. Digby Smith, *Charge! Great Cavalry Charges of the Napoleonic Wars* (London: Greenhill, 2003), 239–240.

27. Frederic Guillaume de Vaudoncourt, *Histoire de Campagnes de 1814 et 1815* (Paris, 1826), 4:127. Christopher Kelly, *A Full and Circumstantial Account of the Memorable Battle of Waterloo, the Second Restoration of Louis XVIII, and the Deportation of Na-*

poleon Buonaparte to St. Helena (London, 1828), 189; and Vaulabelle, *Histoire,* 3:259–260, 269–270.

28. James Carret, "Recollections of 1815," in Charles Ingersoll, *History of the Second War between the United States of America and Great Britain* (Philadelphia: Lippincott, 1852), 1:368.

29. Houssaye, *1815—La Seconde Abdication,* 360; Claude Manceron, *Which Way to Turn? Napoleon's Last Choice* (London: Jonathan Cape, 1961), 101; Baudin to Bonnefoux, Maritime Prefect of Rochefort, July 5, 1815, Martineau, *Napoleon Surrenders,* 79; and Emmanuel de Las Cases, *Mémorial de Sainte-Helene, preface de Jean Tulard* (Paris: Editions du Seuil, 1999), 1:60.

30. Laure Junot, Duchesse d'Abrantés, *Mémoires sur la Restauration, ou souvenirs historiques sur cette époque, la Révolution de 1830, et les premières années du règne de Louis Philippe* (Bruxelles: Hauman, 1836), 4:24–26.

31. Charles Lacretelle, *Histoire de France Depuis la Restauration* (Paris: Dealaunay, 1829–1835), 1:342.

32. Georges Bertin, *Joseph Bonaparte en Amerique* (Paris: Librairie de La Nouvelle Revue, 1893), 44. Montholon, *Récits,* 1:75–81. Joseph Pelletreau, a Freemason in Bordeaux, made the arrangements to take Joseph to New York, Mailliard Family Papers, Yale University Library, Manuscripts and Archives, G341, B5, F1 (1804–1828).

33. Myron F. Brightfield, *John Wilson Croker* (Berkeley: University of California Press, 1940), 81.

34. Frederick Maitland, *The Surrender of Napoleon* (London: Blackwood, 1903), 225; Maitland to Keith, August 8, 1815, Martineau, *Napoleon Surrenders,* 216; and Las Cases, *Memorial,* 1:65.

35. Charles Antoine Lallemand, "Napoléon Refuse de Passer en Amérique," *French American Review* 2, no. 2 (Apr.–June 1949): 74–75.

36. Las Cases, *Mémorial,* July 15, 1815, 1:66.

37. William Lee, *A Yankee Jeffersonian: Selections from the Diary and Letters of William Lee of Massachusetts,* ed. Mary Lee Mann (Cambridge: Belknap Press of Harvard University Press, 1958), 158, and John Stokoe, *With Napoleon at St. Helena: Being the Memoirs of Dr. John Stokoe,* ed. Paul Frémeaux (London: John Lane, Bodley Head, 1902), 58.

38. John Whishaw to Sidney Smith, August 16, 1815, John Whishaw, *The "Pope" of Holland House: Selections from the Correspondence of John Whishaw and His Friends, 1813–1840,* ed. and annotated by Lady Seymour (London: Unwin, 1906), 113; George Home, *Memoirs of an Aristocrat and Reminiscences of the Emperor Napoleon* (London: Whittaker, 1838), 219; and Clement Shorter, *Napoleon and His Fellow Travelers* (London: Cassel, 1908), 305.

39. *Political Register,* July 29, 1815.

40. Maitland, *The Surrender of Napoleon,* 226.

41. William Warden, *Letters Written on Board HMS Northumberland and Saint Helena* (London, 1816), 2.

42. Mrs. Haviland to Benjamin R. Haydon, Plymouth, August 2, 1815, Benjamin R. Haydon, *Correspondence and Table Talk* (London: Chatto, 1876), 1:288.

43. Thomas, *Cochrane,* 216–223.

44. Conversation with Lord Ebrington at Elba, December 7, 1814, BL MSS Add 51526 HHP, f.32.

45. Thomas, *Cochrane,* 232.

46. Samuel Bamford, *Passages in the Life of a Radical* (London: Simpkin Marshall, 1844), 1:20.

47. Cochrane to James Guthrie, King's Bench Prison, June 1, 1815, NMM James Guthrie Papers.

48. Liverpool to Castlereagh, July 7, 1815, Castlereagh, *Memoirs,* 10:415.

49. Instructions to the Spanish envoy at the Congress of Vienna, 1815, Miramón, *Política Secreta de Napoleón,* 138–139.

50. Liverpool to Castlereagh, July 21, 1815, Castlereagh, *Memoirs,* 10:415.

51. Home, *Memoirs of an Aristocrat,* 252.

52. Napoleon's plans to attack St. Helena are detailed in Napoleon to Decres, Mayence, September 29, 1804, Napoleon Bonaparte, *Correspondance de Napoléon avec le Ministre de la Marine, depuis 1804 jusqu'en Avril 1815. Extraite d'un portefeuille de Sainte-Hélène* (Paris, 1837), 1:20; and Napoleon, *Correspondance,* 9:551–555.

53. Napoleon on board the *Bellerophon* at sea, August 4, 1815, Gaspard de Gourgaud, *The Campaign of 1815* (London, 1818), 233

54. George L. de St. M. Watson, *A Polish Exile with Napoleon: Embodying the Letters of Captain Piontkowski to General Sir Robert Wilson and Many Documents from the Lowe Papers . . .* (London: Harper and Bros., 1912), 142. Sir Francis Burdett planned to interpose a writ of habeas corpus to declare the illegality of Napoleon's detention but he desisted after Sir Samuel Romilly advised him that Napoleon would "not derive any benefit from such proceeding." Melville W. Patterson, *Sir Francis Burdett and His Times, 1770–1844* (London: Macmillan, 1931), 2:411, and Charles Milner Atkinson, *An Account of the Life and Principles of Sir Samuel Romilly* (Derby: Hobson, 1920), 185.

55. Martineau, *Napoleon Surrenders,* 180, and Croker to Keith, August 3, 1815, ADM 2/1382, f.197.

56. Croker to Peel, August 4, 1815, BL MSS Add 40183.

57. BL MSS Add 51525 HHP, f.6. Lyttelton was the brother-in-law of Captain Robert Spencer, who would later play a role in this story.

58. Lallemand, "Napoléon Refuse," 80.

Chapter 3

1. *Political Register,* London, August 12, 1815, and September 16, 1816.

2. Hunt, *Memoirs,* 3:266, and Belchem, *"Orator" Hunt,* 47.

3. Herbert M. A. Randolph, *Life of General Sir Robert Wilson from Autobiographical Memoirs* (London: J. Murray, 1862), 1:352–353.

4. Wilson to Grey, July 28, 1815, BL MSS Add 30120 SRWP, f.194.

5. Lean, *The Napoleonists,* 185. Lofft to Rev. George Summers, November 15, 1815, Watson, *A Polish Exile,* 291. For a review of the legal issues involved, see Rose

Melikan, "Caging the Emperor: The Legal Basis for Detaining Napoleon Bonaparte," *Tijdschrift voor Rechtsgeschiedenis* 67, no. 3–4 (1999): 349–362.

6. Holland to Carlyle, London, October 1821, BL MSS Add 51529 HHP, f.129.

7. Peter Virgin, *Sydney Smith* (London: Harper Collins, 1994), 117.

8. Lean, *The Napoleonists,* 169–170. Lady Holland's guest list is at BL MSS Add 51952 HHP.

9. *Political Register,* August 12, 1815.

10. Lord Hutchinson to Wilson, September 6, 1815, BL MSS Add 30125 SRWP, f.7.

11. Charles K. Webster, *The Foreign Policy of Castlereagh, 1812–1815: Britain and the Reconstruction of Europe* (London: G. Bell and Sons, 1950), 464–465.

12. Ernest Daudet, *La Police Politique: Chronique des Temps de la Restauration* (Paris: Plon, 1912), 100, 118–119. Antonello Pietromarchi, *Luciano Bonaparte* (Modena, 1981), 285.

13. Lacretelle, *Histoire de France,* 1:332.

14. *Victoires, conquêtes,* 20:376. Some historians incorrectly put Grouchy and Clausel on the second list. Marcel Doher, *Proscrits et Exilés après Waterloo* (Paris: Peyronnet, 1965).

15. Auguste Petiet, *Souvenirs militaires de l'histoire contemporaine* (Paris: SPM, 1844), 257, and Etienne Radet, *Mémoires du Général Radet d'après ses papiers personnels et les archives de l'état,* ed. Etienne A. Combier (Saint-Cloud: Belin Freres, 1892), 402–403.

16. Marshal Brune was killed by an angry mob at Avignon, and General Ramel was assassinated in Toulouse. Houssaye, *1815—La Seconde Abdication,* 430, 452, 478.

17. Louis Canler, *Mémoires de Canler* (Paris: Mercure de France, 1968), 72. Regarding la Congregation see Antoine Lestra, *Histoire secrete de la congregation de Lyon: De la Clandestinité a la fondation de la Propagation de la Foi* (Paris: Nouvelles Editions Latines, 1967), and Elizabeth Sparrow, *Secret Service: British Agents in France, 1792–1815* (Woodbridge, UK: Boydell Press, 1999), 391.

18. Decazes joined the Anacreon Lodge in 1808 and years later became the commander of the Supreme Council of the thirty-third degree of the Scottish Rite. Louis d'Estampes and Claudio Jannet, *La Franc-maçonnerie et la Revolution* (Avignon: Seguin Freres, 1884), 254.

19. Henri Lachouque, *The Anatomy of Glory: Napoleon and His Guard* (New York: Greenhill, 1995), 496.

20. Maurice Soulié, *Autour de l'Aigle Enchainé* (Paris: Marpon, 1938), 112; Doher, *Proscrits et Exilés,* 61. In April 1815, a London-based Societé Libre des Amies de la Patrie et la Liberté offered its leadership to Lazare Carnot, one of Napoleon's minister of interior during the Hundred Days. See Pierre F. Tissot, *Mémoires Historiques et Militaires sur Carnot* (Paris, 1824), 175, 345.

21. Michael Bruce to his father, July 16 and September 5, 1815, Ian Bruce, *Lavallette Bruce His Adventures and Intrigues before and after Waterloo* (London: H. Hamilton, 1953), 121–125 and 131–135.

22. Lavallette, *Memoirs,* 331–336.

23. Daudet, *La Police Politique,* 12–14; Canler, *Mémoires,* 72.

24. Wilson to Holland, Paris, October 5, 1815, BL MSS Add 51517 HHP, f.126.

25. Emmanuel de Grouchy, *Mémoires du Maréchal de Grouchy* (Paris: E. Dentu, 1873–74), 5:5–7; Gustave Le Doulcet de Pontecoulant, *Souvenirs historiques et parlementaires du comte de Pontécoulant, ancien pair de France: Extraits de ses papiers et de sa correspondance 1764–1848* (Paris: Levy, 1865), 4:17–18; and André Desfeuilles, "Réfugiés Politiques a New York," *Revue de l'Institut Napoléon* 7, (1959): 131–32.

26. Wilson to Grey, Paris, November 13, 1815, BL MSS Add 30120 SRWP, f.281.

27. Wilson to Grey, Paris, November 20, 1815, BL MSS Add 30120 SRWP, f.284.

28. Wilson to Holland, Paris, November 13, 1815, BL MSS Add 51517 HHP, f.133, and Holland to Kinnaird, December 5, 1815, BL MSS Add 51590 HHP, f.22.

29. Wilson to Grey, Paris, December 9, 1815, BL MSS Add 30120 SRWP, f.299.

30. Glover, *A Very Slippery Fellow,* 151–155.

31. Wilson to Grey, December 28, 1818, BL MSS Add 30108 SRWP, f.60.

32. Lavallette, *Mémoires,* 386–387; Lacretelle, *Histoire de France,* 2:30; and Auguste F. Marmont, *Mémoires du maréchal Marmont duc de Raguse* (Paris: Perrotin, 1857), 3:193–195.

33. J. Lucas-Dubreton, *L'evasion de Lavallette* (London: Harraps, 1928), 87.

34. M. Dupin, *Narrative of the Escape of the Count of Lavallette from France* (London, 1816), 11.

35. Rees H. Gronow, *The Reminiscences and Recollections of Captain Gronow* (London: J. C. Nemmo, 1889), 1:102–103.

Chapter 4

1. Madison to Monroe, September 12, 1815, Reeves, *The Napoleonic Exiles,* 19.

2. *Niles' Weekly Register,* September 15, 1815.

3. Edward H. Tatum, *The United States and Europe, 1815–1823: A Study in the Background of the Monroe Doctrine* (Berkeley: University of California Press, 1936), 63, and *Niles' Weekly Register,* September 30, 1815. Among those who deplored Napoleon's popularity was Albert Gallatin, secretary of the treasury under Madison. See Gallatin to Jefferson, November 27, 1815, in Albert Gallatin, *The Writings of Albert Gallatin,* ed. Henry Adams (Philadelphia: Lippincott, 1875), 1:666–667. For an analysis of American public opinion regarding Napoleon, see Ulane Bonnel, "Sainte-Hélène et l'Opinion Américaine," *Revue de l'Institut Napoléon* no. 120 (July 1971), and Kenneth Lee, "Le culte de Napoléon aux Etats-Unis jusque'a la Guerre de Sécession," *Revue de l'Institut Napoléon* no.125 (Dec. 1972): 146–147.

4. O'Meara, *Napoleon in Exile,* 1:185.

5. François Collaveri, *La Franc-Maçonnerie des Bonapartes* (Paris: Payot, 1982), 139; Robert Vallery-Radot, *Dictature de la Maçonnerie* (Paris: Grasset, 1934), 53–54; and François Collaveri, *Napoléon franc-maçon?* (Paris: Tallandier, 2003).

6. The Abbé Barruel, a French priest, was a forceful proponent of the theory of a secret conspiracy organized by the Freemasons to destroy the Church and the monarchy. See d'Estampes and Jannet, *La Franc-Maçonnerie,* 190, 222–235. For an opposite view

see Jean-Joseph Mounier, *De l'influence attribuée aux philosophes, aux francs-maçons et aux illuminés sur la Révolution de France* (Paris, 1801), 158–165.

7. Warren, *The Sword,* 120–130, and H. Yoakum, *History of Texas from Its First Settlement in 1685 to Its Annexation to the United States in 1846* (Redfield, 1856), 1:178.

8. Onis to Felix Maria Calleja, Viceroy of Mexico, Philadelphia, August 14, 1815, Louis-Jean Calvet, *Barataria L'etrange histoire de Jean Laffite, pirate* (Paris: Plon, 1998), 179.

9. Onis to Viceroy Calleja, Philadelphia, 16 September 1815, NA FO 72/189, f.355–356. This dispatch was intercepted by a Buenos Aires corsair and published in the *Gaceta de Buenos Aires* on September 5, 1816.

10. Yoakum, *History of Texas,* 1:196.

11. Jean Laffite, *The Journal of Jean Laffite: The Privateer-Patriot's Own Story* (New York: Vintage Press, 1958), 81. Many have questioned the authenticity of Laffite's memoirs. Warren believed they were the ramblings of an old man, full of inaccuracies but authentic. Harris Gaylord Warren, "Review of *The Journal of Jean Laffite: The Privateer-Patriot's Own Story,*" *Mississippi Valley Historical Review* 45, no. 4 (Mar. 1959): 665–666. For more on the Laffites see William C. Davis, *The Pirates Laffite: The Treacherous World of the Corsairs of the Gulf* (New York: Harcourt, 2005); Harris Gaylord Warren, "Documents Relating to the Establishment of Privateers at Galveston," *Louisiana Historical Quarterly* 21, no. 4 (Oct. 1938): 1088; Harris Gaylord Warren, ed., "Documents Relating to Pierre Laffite's Entrance into the Service of Spain," *Southwestern Historical Quarterly* 44, no. 1 (July 1940): 76–87; and Jose L. Franco, *La Batalla por el Dominio del Caribe y el Golfo de Mexico* (La Habana, 1964), 1:162.

12. Penot, *Les Relations,* 1:155.

13. Edouard de Montulé, *Voyage en Amérique, en Italie, en Sicile et en Egypte, pendant les années 1816, 1817, 1818 et 1819* (Paris, 1821), 27.

14. Cazeaux to Talleyrand, November 1815, Desfeuilles, "Réfugiés Politiques," 127–129.

15. Tatum, *The United States and Europe,* 190.

16. Onis, *Memoir,* 14–15.

17. Bowles to Croker, January 25, 1814, NA ADM 1/1565.

18. Miller to Monroe, July 26, 1813, NARA, Dispatches from U.S. Ministers to Buenos Aires, Dec. 1811–Nov. 1817, M70, Roll 1.

19. Bowles to Croker, January 25, 1814, NA ADM 1/1565.

20. Guillermo Gallardo, *Joel Roberts Poinsett: Agente Norteamericano, 1810–1814* (Buenos Aires: Emece, 1983), 279. In October 1804, Alvear's mother and his seven siblings were killed when the Royal Navy attacked a Spanish squadron that was bringing his family back to Spain. At the time of the attack, England and Spain were not at war. Robert Gardiner, *Memoir of Admiral Sir Graham Moore* (London, 1844), 33–34.

21. F. W. Seal-Coon, "Spanish American Revolutionary Masonry," *Ars Quatuor Coronatorum* 94 (1982): 97. There has been much debate among historians about whether the Caballeros Racionales were Masonic or not. There is not enough evidence to con-

firm it or deny it. Juan E. Hernández y Dávalos, *Colección de documentos para la historia de la guerra de independencia de México de 1808 a 1821* (México, 1877–82), 6:818–821; Jose Ferrer Benimeli, "Cadiz y las llamadas 'Logias' Lautaro o Caballeros Racionales," in *De la Ilustracion al Romanticismo* (Cadiz, 1998), 149–176; Juan Blazquez Miguel, *Introducción a la historia de la Masonería Española* (Madrid, 1989), 72; and Emilio Ocampo, "Inglaterra, la Masonería y la Independencia de América," *Todo es Historia* 473 (Feb. 2006).

22. It is unclear whether the letter reached its destination as the fugitive French officer was caught, but its timing was perfect. Napoleon had just declared his support for the rebels in the Spanish colonies. François Vigo-Rousillon, "La Guerre d'Espagne, Fragments des Mémoires du Colonel Vigo-Rousillon," *Revue des Deux Mondes* 116 (July 1891): 918–19.

23. Federico Zapiola, *Zapiola: Soldado de Chacabuco y Maipu* (Buenos Aires, 1956), 40.

24. Burr to Mariano Castilla, London, March 3, 1812, Burr, *Political Correspondence,* 2:1143–1144. The first of several meetings between Castilla and Burr occurred on December 12, 1811. Aaron Burr, *Private Journal of Aaron Burr* (New York, 1903), 2:261, 273, 288.

25. Castilla to Robert Staples, August 13, 1812, NA FO 72/157. Castlereagh sent a copy of this letter to the Spanish ambassador in London, the Count of Fernán Nuñez.

26. Staples to Wellesley, Buenos Aires, April 1, 1812, NA FO 72/171, f.38.

27. Heywood to Lord Melville, October 6, 1812, Edward Tagart, *A Memoir of Captain Peter Heywood* (London, 1832), 243; Heywood to Croker, October 13, 1812, Gerald S. Graham and Robert A. Humphreys, *The Navy and South America, 1807–1823* (London, 1962), 80. In his youth, Heywood was court-martialed for participating in the mutiny of the *Bounty.*

28. Heywood to Melville, Buenos Aires, December 4, 1812, and January 27, 1813, Tagart, *A Memoir,* 246–247, 262.

29. Heywood to Melville, Buenos Aires, February 13, 1813, ibid., 266.

30. Bowles to Croker, January 25, 1814, NA ADM 1/1565.

31. One of Alvear's allies, Nicolas Herrera, had many years earlier proposed to Joseph the creation of a Bonapartist empire in all of South America. Carraciolo Parra Pérez, *Bayona y la política de Napoleon,* 73–99.

32. Bowles to Croker, February 10, 1814, ADM 1/1557.

33. David Porter, *Journal of a Cruise Made to the Pacific Ocean by Captain David Porter, in the United States Frigate Essex, in the Years 1812, 1813, and 1814* (New York: Wiley and Halsted, 1822), 2:94–95, 98, 158–172.

34. Bowles's opinion of Carrera and Poinsett is in Bowles to Croker, November 18, 1813, Graham and Humphreys, *The Navy,* 116–117. Regarding Poinsett's role as U.S. agent see George B. Dyer and Charlotte L. Dyer, "The Beginnings of a United States Strategic Intelligence System in Latin America, 1809–1826," *Military Affairs* 14, no. 2 (Summer, 1950): 69–71.

35. Bowles to Supreme Director Posadas, February 19, 1814, ADM 1/1557.

36. Posadas to Madison, Buenos Aires, March 9, 1814, NARA, Dispatches from U.S. Ministers to Buenos Aires, Dec. 1811–Nov. 1817, M70, Roll 1.

37. Emilio Ocampo, *Alvear en la Guerra con el Imperio del Brasil* (Buenos Aires: Claridad, 2003), 92–102.

38. Strangford to Castlereagh, Rio de Janeiro, March 14, 1815, NA FO 63/169 Strangford, Brazil, January–April 1815, f.77. Percy to Dixon, HMS *Hotspur*, Buenos Aires, February 14, 1815, Graham and Humphreys, *The Navy*, 151; Thomas Halsey to Monroe, Buenos Aires, February 11, 1815, NARA M70 Dispatches from U.S. Ministers to Buenos Aires, Dec. 1811–Nov. 1817.

39. Manuel A. Pueyrredon, *Estudios Históricos* (Buenos Aires, 1929), 111, and William Yates, "A Brief Relation of Facts and Circumstances Connected with the Family of the Carreras in Chile," in Mary Graham, *Journal of a Residence in Chile during the Year 1822* (London, 1824), 468.

40. Graham, *Journal*, 20.

41. Henry Adams, *The War of 1812* (New York: Cooper Square Press, 1999), 239–240.

42. Bowles to Croker, Buenos Aires, September 22, 1816, NA ADM 1/1563.

43. Edgar S. Maclay, *A History of American Privateers* (New York: Appleton, 1924).

44. Lewis W. Bealer, "Los Corsarios de Buenos Aires," *Publicaciones del Instituto de Investigaciones Históricas, Universidad de Buenos Aires* 72 (1937): 15–18. Sonntag's original petition is in AGN S.10-C5-A1-N2. Regarding the *True Blooded Yankee* see Maclay, *History*, 275–276, 356.

45. Henry Hill, consul in Bahia, to Sumter, Bahia, December 9, 1814, NARA, Dispatches from U.S. Ministers to Brazil, May 1813–Feb. 1817.

46. Fred Lindeman, consul in Bahia, to Strangford, Bahia, December 8, 1814, NA FO 63/169, f.163.

Chapter 5

1. Candé-Montholon, *Journal Secret d'Albine de Montholon*, 100.

2. Joseph Lockwood, *A Guide to St. Helene Descriptive and Historical* (St. Helena, 1851), 9.

3. October 15, 1815, Gourgaud, *Journal*, 1:63.

4. Cockburn to Croker, October 22, 1815, BL MSS Add 20199 SHLP, f.43.

5. T. H. Brooke, *History of the Island of St. Helena* (London: Kingsbury, 1824), 71–72.

6. Wilks to Cockburn, n.d., BL MSS Add 20115 SHLP, f.44.

7. November 18, 1816, Gourgaud, *Journal*, 1:194.

8. Fréderic Masson, "Le comte de Montholon avant Sainte-Hélène," *Revue des Etudes Napoléoniennes* 1 (Jan.–Mar. 1912): 19–35; John T. Tussaud, *The Chosen Four* (London: Jonathan Cape, 1928), 98; and Candé-Montholon, *Journal Secret d'Albine de Montholon*, 49.

9. February 23, 1817, O'Meara, *Napoleon in Exile*, 1:456.

10. July 15, 1817, Gourgaud, *Journal,* 2:188.

11. Memorandum of Colonel Wilks, n.d., BL MSS Add 20115 SHLP, f.44.

12. Ken Denholm, "From Signal Gun to Satellite: A History of Communications on the Island of St. Helena" (Jamestown, 2001), 8–9.

13. Secret Orders for St. Helena, ADM 2/1382 f.296.

14. December 6, 1815, Gourgaud, *Journal,* 1:82.

15. December 29, 1815, Las Cases, *Memorial,* 1:324–325.

16. Fox, *Journal,* 83.

17. November 5, 1815, Gourgaud, *Journal,* 1:72.

18. Napoleon to Decres, September 29, 1804, *Correspondance de Napoléon avec le Ministre de la Marine,* 1:20. Also in Napoleon, *Correspondance,* 9:551–555. Donatello Grieco, *Napoleão e o Brasil* (Rio de Janeiro: Biblioteca do Exercito Editora, 1995), 50–51.

19. Raoul Brice, *Les espoirs de Napoleon a Sainte-Helene* (Paris: Payot, 1938), 176–179.

20. Wallace Hutcheon, *Robert Fulton: Pioneer of Undersea Warfare* (Annapolis: Naval Institute Press, 1981), 60.

21. Extracts from Admiral Cockburn's Diary, Edward Creasy, *Dramatic Incidents in the Life of Napoleon Bonaparte* (New York, 1892), 3:100.

22. December 1, 1815, Gourgaud, *Journal,* 1:80–81.

23. December 30, 1815, ibid., 1:91.

24. Watson, *A Polish Exile,* 176.

Chapter 6

1. Glover, *A Very Slippery Fellow,* 151–155.

2. Lavallette, *Memoirs,* 402.

3. Dupin, *Narrative,* 20–24.

4. Wilson to Grey, January 10, 1816, BL MSS Add 30120 SRWP, f.323. *A Full Report of the Trial of Major General Sir Robert Thomas Wilson* (London, 1816), 62–64.

5. N. Nicholson, *The Trial at Full Length of Major-General Sir Robert Thomas Wilson, Michael Bruce Esq., and Captain John Hely Hutchinson* (London, 1816), 23.

6. Sentence of the Cour Royale de Paris, Arrêt de la Cour d'Assises du département de la Seine, April 24, 1816, BL MSS Add 30127 SRWP, f.239.

7. Wilson to Holland, February 12, 1816, BL MSS Add 51517 HHP, f. 173.

8. Richelieu to Stuart, January 13, 1816, *A Full Report,* 6.

9. Richelieu to Osmond, January 30, 1816, Armand E. du Plessis Duke of Richelieu, *Lettres du Duc de Richelieu au Marquis d'Osmond 1816–1818 Publiées par Sébastien Charléty* (Paris: Gallimard, 1939), 3.

10. Pozzo di Borgo to Nesselrode, January 19, 1816, Carlo Andrea Pozzo di Borgo, conte de, *Correspondance Diplomatique du Comte Pozzo di Borgo et du Comte Nesselrode depuis la restauration des Bourbons jusqu'au Congres d'Aix-la-Chapelle, 1814–1818* (Paris: Calman-Levy, 1890–1907), 1:290.

11. Henry Brougham, *Historical Sketches of Statesmen Who Flourished in the Time of George III* (London: Knight, 1845), 1:152.

12. Hunt, *Memoirs*, 2:283.

13. Mary Berry, *Voyages de Miss Berry à Paris* (Paris: A. Robiot, 1905), 154.

14. William E. Frye, *After Waterloo: Reminiscences of European Travel, 1815–1819* (London: Heinemann, 1908), 147.

15. Frederic Guillaume de Vaudoncourt, *Quinze années d'un Proscrit* (Paris, 1835), 2:294–298.

16. Nicholson, *The Trial*, 26–27, 66.

17. Ibid., 19–23, and Kelly, *A Full and Circumstantial Account*, 246–259.

18. William H. Talbot to Lady Fielding, Paris, April 25, 1816, Correspondence of William Henry Fox Talbot, Document 00694, Collection LA16–015, University of Glasgow. Also Berry, *Voyages*, 169.

19. Wilson to Grey, April 25, 1816, BL MSS Add 30121 SRWP, f.91.

20. French ambassador to Richelieu, Madrid, April 22, 1816, AMAE CPEU, no. 73, f.20, and Richelieu to Osmond, July 5, 1816, Richelieu, *Lettres*, 46.

21. Daudet, *La Police Politique*, 224.

22. During the campaign of the Rhine in 1800, Brayer had fallen in love with Philippine and married her after divorcing his first wife. Octave Aubry, *St. Helena* (London: V. Gollancz, 1937), 364.

23. Alfred Marquiset, *Une Merveilleuse: Mme Hamelin, 1776–1851* (Paris: Champion, 1909), 170. Pozzo di Borgo to Tsar Alexander, October 5/7, 1815, Polovtsoff, *Correspondance diplomatique*, 1:319. Kinnaird had been under surveillance by the police. Eugene Fourgues, *Le Dossier Secret de Fouché Juillet-Septembre 1815* (Paris: Emile Paul, 1908), 76–77.

24. Baron de Cazes, chief of police at Lille, to Count Decazes, March 4, 1816, and 25 March 1816, Marquiset, *Une Merveilleuse*, 175–177.

25. Carlo Bronne, *Les Abeilles du Manteaux* (Brussels: La Renaissance du Livre, 1944), 148–156.

26. D'Abrantés, *Mémoires sur la Restauration*, 1:240; A. Lievyns, J.-M. Verdot, and Begat, *Fastes de le Légion d'Honneur* (Paris, 1845), 3:340. Regarding the Chevaliers de l'Epingle Noire see Pasquier, *Memoirs*, 4:104–105, and Vaudoncourt, *Quinze années*, 2:319–321.

27. *Morning Chronicle*, London, April 19, 1816.

28. Richelieu to Osmond, April 15, 1816, Richelieu, *Lettres*, 25.

29. Two emissaries were sent to Russia to ascertain what support could be expected from the tsar. The objective of this mission could have been to obtain Alexander's support for the young Napoleon. One of the men who participated in this mission was Nicolas Brice, a former major in the *chasseurs a cheval* who had participated in Charles Lallemand's plot in March 1815 and was a member of the Chevaliers de l'Epingle Noire. See Raoul Brice, *Le General Brice* (Nancy, 1923), 46–47.

30. Daudet, *La Police Politique*, 239.

31. *Anti-Gallican Monitor*, London, April 7, 1816.

32. Stuart to Castlereagh, Paris, May 27, 1816, FO 27/133.

33. Henry R. Fox, Lord Holland, *The Opinions of Lord Holland as Recorded in the Journals of the House of Lords from 1797 to 1841,* collected and ed. by D. C. Moylan (London, 1841), 84–85.

34. Whishaw to Smith, January 16, 1816, Whishaw, *The "Pope" of Holland House,* 141.

35. Gaspard de Gourgaud, *Lettre de Sir Walter Scott et Réponse du Général Gourgaud* (Paris, 1827), 40.

36. Act of British Parliament, April 11, 1816.

37. Great Britain, Parliament, *The Parliamentary Debates* (London: T. C. Hansard, 1816), 33:1020, hereinafter cited as *Hansard's Parliamentary Debates.*

38. Mollie Gillen, *Royal Duke: Augustus Frederick, Duke of Sussex (1773–1843)* (London: Sidgwick and Jackson, 1976), 186, and Henry R. Fox, Lord Holland, *Further Memoirs of the Whig Party, 1807–1821* (London, 1905), 220.

39. Hunt, *Memoirs,* 3:308–309.

40. Adams to Monroe, London, January 22, 1816, John Quincy Adams, *The Writings of John Quincy Adams,* ed. Worthington Ford (New York: Macmillan, 1917), 5: 487–90.

41. Servando T. de Mier, *The Memoirs of Fray Servando Teresa de Mier* (Oxford, 1998), 190–192.

42. Princess Lieven to Metternich, London, April 1820, Doroteya K. Lieven, *The Private Letters of Princess Lieven to Prince Metternich, 1820–1826,* ed. Peter Quennell (London: J. Murray, 1937), 28. Russell only briefly mentioned his meeting with Napoleon. See John Russell, *Recollections and Suggestions, 1813–1873* (London: Longmans, Green, 1875), 16. Later in life, Russell tried to distance himself from the Bonapartism of his youth. Lean, *The Napoleonists,* 148–149, 207, 281–282.

43. O'Meara, *Napoleon in Exile,* 1:211.

44. Conversation on February 9, 1816, Las Cases, *Memorial,* 1:412; Napoleon to Joseph, May 3, 1815, Albert du Casse, *Supplément à la correspondance de Napoléon Ier: lettres curieuses omises par le comité de publication: Rectifications* (Paris, 1886), 210–212; and Montholon, *Récits,* 2:436. Ortuño asserts that Mina did not receive any money from Napoleon during the Hundred Days. Other historians disagree. Manuel Ortuño Martinez in *Xavier Mina: Guerrillero Liberal Insurgente* (Navarra: Univ. Publica de Navarra, 2000), 196, and Martin L. Guzman, *Javier Mina: Héroe de España y de México* (Mexico: Cia. Gral. de Ediciones, 1955), 201.

45. Gordon to Castlereagh, May 28, 1816, Ortuño Martinez, *Xavier Mina,* 248, and Guadalupe Jimenez Codinach, *La Gran Bretaña y la Independencia de Mexico, 1808–1821* (Mexico, 1991), 293–295.

46. Known as the "Didier conspiracy," according to some historians it was an Orleanist plot. Vaulabelle, *Histoire,* 4:213–299; Guillon, *Les Complots Militaires,* 85–90. Also Joseph Rey, *Histoire de la Conspiration de Grenoble* (Grenoble, 1847), and Thomas Frost, *The Secret Societies of the European Revolution, 1776–1876* (London: Tinsley Brothers, 1876), 1:277.

47. Wilson to Grey, May 20, 1816, BL MSS Add 30121 SRWP, f.118.

48. *Anti-Gallican Monitor,* London, May 19, 1816.

49. Guillon, *Les Complots Militaires,* 83.

50. Richelieu to Osmond, May 8–9, 1816, Richelieu, *Lettres,* 32–33.

51. Wilson to Holland, La Force, June 10, 1816, BL MSS Add 51517 HHP, f.181.

Chapter 7

1. Las Cases, *Memorial,* 1:335

2. January 18, 1816, Montholon, *Récits,* 1:210.

3. January 18, 1816, Gourgaud, *Journal,* 1:102.

4. Extracts from Admiral Cockburn's Diary, Creasy, *Dramatic Incidents,* 70–71, 95.

5. Caulaincourt, *With Napoleon in Russia,* 305–306.

6. Burr, *Political Correspondence,* 2:1111.

7. Napoleon learned of Lefebvre-Desnouettes's arrival in New York in early January. O'Meara, *Napoleon in Exile,* 1:254.

8. Intercepted letters from Fanny Bertrand, January 1816, *British Monitor,* London, July 26, 1818.

9. January 3–5, 1816, Gourgaud, *Journal,* 1:93–95.

10. January 5, 1816, Las Cases, *Memorial,* 1:333–334.

11. January 6, 1816, Gourgaud, *Journal,* 1:95, and Lucia Elizabeth Balcombe Abell, *Recollections of the Emperor Napoleon during the First Three Years of His Captivity on the Island of St. Helena* (London, 1873), 76.

12. January 9, 1816, Gourgaud, *Journal,* 1:98.

13. January 15, 1816, Las Cases, *Memorial,* 1:346.

14. Extracts from Admiral Cockburn's Diary, Creasy, *Dramatic Incidents,* 70–71, 95.

15. Alexander Andrews, *The History of British Journalism* (London, 1859), 1:233. Goldsmith had a bad reputation and was on the payroll of the Spaniards. San Carlos to Casa Irujo, London, April 9, 1819, AGS Estado 8179.

16. Las Cases, *Memorial,* 1:163.

17. William Warden, *Letters Written on Board HMS Northumberland and Saint Helena* (London, 1816), 163–164.

18. March 6, 1816, Las Cases, *Memorial,* 1:444.

19. Cockburn to Roberts, St. Helena, March 14, 1816, NA ADM 1/67.

20. March 17, 1816, Las Cases, *Memorial,* 1:470.

21. April 10 and 13, 1816, ibid., 1:510–511, 520.

22. Bathurst to Lowe, London, September 12, 1815, NA CO 248/2, ff. 15–16.

23. Torrens to Lowe, Horse Guards, September 11, 1815, BL MSS Add 20114 SHLP, f.240.

24. April 19, 1816, O'Meara, *Napoleon in Exile,* 1:33.

25. Charles J. F. T. de Montholon, *History of the Captivity of Napoleon at St. Helena* (London: H. Colburn, 1846), 3:12.

26. May 6, 1816, Barry O'Meara, "Talks with Napoleon," *Century Magazine* 59 (Nov. 1899–Apr. 1900): 611.

27. May 5, 1816, O'Meara, *Napoleon in Exile,* 1:44–45.

28. May 16, 1816, Bertrand, *Cahiers,* 1:39.

29. May 18, 1816, Montholon, *Récits,* 1:278. It was probably the captain of the *Salcette* whose officers visited Longwood. Watson, *A Polish Exile,* 247, and Gourgaud, *Journal,* 1:136–137.

30. Paul-Philippe de Ségur, *Histoire et Mémoires, par le Général Comte de Ségur. Melanges, Souvenirs et Reveries d'un Octogenaire* (Paris: Firmin-Didot, 1873), 8:180.

31. A moon eclipse occurred on June 9, 1816. See NA ADM 50/123.

32. Watson, *A Polish Exile,* 248.

33. May 26, 1816, Las Cases, *Memorial,* 1:685–686.

34. May 25, 1816, Montholon, *Récits,* 1:286.

35. Ibid., 1:274.

36. Proclamation of Sir Hudson Lowe, St. Helena, June 12, 1816, BL MSS Loan 57/42 Bathurst Papers, f.54, and John Barnes, *A Tour through the Island of St. Helena* (London: J. M. Richardson, 1817), 206.

37. BL MSS Add 20204 SHLP, f.9.

38. Lowe to Cockburn, Plantation House, June 2, 1816, and enclosed letter, BL MSS Add 20115 SHLP, ff.183–185. Lord Rosebery thought these letters were "silly" and blamed Lowe for taking them seriously. Archibald Primrose, Lord Rosebery, *Napoleon: The Last Phase* (London: Harper, 1901), 133.

39. Wilson to Grey, November 30, 1816, BL MSS Add 30121 SRWP, f.219.

40. August 27, 1816, O'Meara, *Napoleon in Exile,* 1:103.

41. Princess Lieven to Alexander Benckendorff, London, January 9, 1816, Doroteya K. Lieven, Princess, *Letters of Dorothea, Princess Lieven, during her Residence in London, 1812–1834,* ed. Lionel G. Robinson (London: Longmans, 1902), 22.

42. Report no. 3, June 29, 1816, Aleksandr Antonovich de Balmain, *Napoleon in Captivity: The Reports of Count Balmain Russian Commissioner on the Island of St. Helena, 1816–1820,* ed. Julian Park (New York and London: Century, 1927), 15. Montchenu described the island in almost identical terms. Montchenu to Richelieu, June 21, 1816, Claude M. H. de Montchenu, *La Captivité de Sainte Helene d'apres les rapports inedits du marquis de Montchenu,* ed. Georges Firmin-Didot (Paris, 1894), 40–42, and Montchenu to Dineur, July 23, 1816, Charles Alexandre Geoffroy de Grandmaison, *Napoléon et ses recents historiens* (Paris, 1896), 326–32.

43. Norwood Young, *Napoleon in Exile at St. Helena* (London: Stanley Paul, 1915), 1:277.

44. June 18, 1816, Las Cases, *Memorial,* 1:853.

45. June 21, 1816, ibid., 1:857.

46. June 21, 1816, O'Meara, "Talks with Napoleon," 631.

47. June 7, 1816, Las Cases, *Memorial,* 1:782–783.

Chapter 8

1. Joseph to Julie Clary Bonaparte, New York, January 16, 1816, Gabriel Girod de l'Ain, *Désirée Clary* (Paris, 1959), 251–252.

2. Jean Thiry, *Les Cent-Jours* (Paris: Editions Berger-Levrault, 1943), 95–115, and Christopher Kelly, *A Full and Circumstantial Account,* 11–14.

3. Joseph had helped Girard recover one of his ships caught in the French blockade. Grouchy was introduced to Girard by Jacques Laffite, a prominent Parisian banker who held a big portion of Napoleon's fortune. John B. McMaster, *The Life and Times of Stephen Girard* (Philadelphia: Lippincott, 1918), 238–292, and Harry Emerson Wildes, *Lonely Midas: The Story of Stephen Girard* (New York: Farrar and Rinehart, 1943), 214.

4. Ann Spear to Elizabeth Patterson, Baltimore, May 30, 1816, Maryland Historical Society, MS 142, Elizabeth Patterson Bonaparte Papers, Section 1, Box 3.

5. Edward Biddle, "Joseph Bonaparte as Recorded in the Private Journal of Nicholas Biddle," *Pennsylvania Magazine of History and Biography* 55 (1931): 210.

6. *Niles' Weekly Register,* May 4, 1816.

7. Onis to Madison, Washington, January 2, 1816, AHN Estado 5641.

8. Onis to Cevallos, Washington, February 3, 1816, no. 25, AHN Estado 5641.

9. Onis to Cevallos, Washington, February 27, 1816, no. 26, AHN Estado 5641.

10. Onis to Cevallos, Washington, March 6, 1816, no. 39, AHN Estado 5641.

11. Martineau, *Napoleon's St. Helena,* 185.

12. O'Meara, *Napoleon in Exile,* 2:493.

13. See Horacio Zorraquin Becú, "De Aventurero Yanqui a Consul Porteño en los Estados Unidos: David C. de Forest, 1774–1825" *Anuario de Historia Argentina,* 1942; John W. de Forest, *The de Forests of Avesnes* (New Haven: Tuttle, Morehouse and Taylor, 1900), 124–125; and Benjamin Keen, *David Curtis de Forest and the Revolution of Buenos Aires* (New Haven: Greenwood Press, 1947).

14. Onis to Cevallos, May 27, 1816, Philadelphia, no. 72, AHN Estado 5641.

15. Once at sea, the *Orb* took the name *Congreso* and after a successful cruise she arrived in Buenos Aires in October. Bealer, "Los Corsarios de Buenos Aires," 19–20, 44, 54.

16. Consul Gilpin (Rhode Island) to Consul Baker (Washington), June 10, 1816, attached to Bagot's dispatch of July 4, 1816, NA FO 5/114.

17. See Urrutia, *Los Estados Unidos de América,* 49–50, and Miramón, *Política Secreta de Napoleon,* 87–90.

18. Maurice Persat, *Mémoires du commandant Persat, 1806 à 1844: Publiés avec une introduction et des notes par Gustave Schlumberger* (Paris: Plon, 1910), 33.

19. Lancaster Dabney, "Louis Aury: The First Governor of Texas under the Mexican Republic," *Southwestern Historical Quarterly* 42, no. 2 (1938–39): 109.

20. Rene Guillemin, *Corsaires de la République et de l'Empire* (Paris: France-Empire, 1982), 327–328. For a broad study of Napoleon's use of corsairs in the war against England see Ulane Bonnel, *La France et les Etats-Unis et la guerre de course, 1797–1815* (Paris: Nouvelles Editions Latines, 1961).

21. For a biography of Aury see Stanley Faye, "Commodore Aury," *Louisiana Historical Quarterly* 24 (July 1941): 611–97; Jaime Duarte French, *Los tres luises del Caribe: Corsarios o Libertadores* (Bogota: El Ancora Editora, 1988); and Carlos Ferro, *Vida de*

Luis Aury, corsario de Buenos Aires en las luchas por la independencia de Venezuela, Colombia y Centroamerica (Buenos Aires: Editorial Cuarto Poder, 1976).

22. In the *History of the Improved Order of Red Men* published in 1893, John S. Skinner is mentioned several times. He was a member of the Society of St. Tammany, or Columbian Order, an underground society formed by Revolutionary War soldiers. This order was organized out of the Sons of Liberty in Annapolis, Maryland, around 1771, and was absorbed by the Society of Red Men, formed in Philadelphia in 1813, during the War of 1812. Skinner delivered an address before the society on May 12, 1810, which was published in the May 19, 1810, issue of the *Maryland Republican.* Thanks to David Lintz, director of the Red Men Museum and Library, for this information.

23. Skinner to Adams, Baltimore, July 30, 1817, T. Frederick Davis, "Letters Relating to MacGregor's Attempted Conquest of East Florida, 1817," *Florida Historical Quarterly* 5, no. 1 (July 1926): 57–59.

24. Charles C. Griffin, "Privateering from Baltimore during the Spanish American Wars of Independence," *Maryland Historical Society* 35, no. 1 (Mar. 1940): 5–6.

25. Gilpin (Rhode Island) to Baker (Washington), June 10, 1816, attached to Bagot's dispatch of July 4, 1816. NA FO 5/114.

26. San Martin to Alvarez Thomas, Mendoza, November 20, 1815, Jose Miguel Carrera, *Archivo del General Jose Miguel Carrera,* ed. Armando Moreno Martín (Santiago: Sociedad Chilena de Historia y Geografía, 1992–2004), 15:288.

27. Griffin, "Privateering from Baltimore," 13.

28. In 1821 Poinsett was appointed deputy grand master of the Grand Lodge of South Carolina. See G. W. Baird, "Great Men Who Were Masons—Joel Roberts Poinsett," *New Age* 36, no. 12 (Dec. 1928): 716–730.

29. Charles J. Stillé, "The Life and Services of Joel R. Poinsett," *Pennsylvania Magazine of History and Biography* 12, no. 2 (1888).

30. J. Fred Rippy, *Joel R. Poinsett, Versatile American* (Durham N.C.: Duke University Press, 1935), 36.

31. William Miller Collier and Guillermo Feliú Cruz, *La primera misión de los Estados Unidos de América en Chile* (Santiago: Imprenta Cervantes, 1926), 33.

32. Ibid., 30–39. See also Dorothy Parton, *The Diplomatic Career of Joel Roberts Poinsett* (Washington, D.C.: Catholic University of America, 1934), 33, and William L. Neumann, "United States Aid to the Chilean Wars of Independence," *Hispanic American Historical Review* 27, no. 2 (May, 1947): 204–219.

33. Heywood to Melville, December 4, 1812, Tagart, *A Memoir,* 247, and Bowles to Croker, November 9, 1813. NA ADM 1/1556.

34. Travel Journal, February 19, 1816, Carrera, *Archivo,* 16:66.

35. Carrera to Luis Carrera, March 12, 1816, Carrera, *Archivo,* 16:123.

36. Baron de Montlezun, *Voyage Fait dans les années 1816 et 1817 de New York a la Nouvelle Orléans* (Paris: Gide Fils, 1818), 170–174.

37. Travel Diary, June 13, 1816, Carrera, *Archivo,* 16:282.

Chapter 9

1. July 16, 1816, Las Cases, *Memorial,* 1:946.

2. Conversation held on July 25, 1816, Clementina Malcolm, *A Diary of St. Helena (1816, 1817): The Journal of Lady Malcolm, Containing the Conversations of Napoleon with Sir Pulteney Malcolm,* ed. Sir Arthur Wilson, KCIE (London: A. D. Innes, 1899), 40.

3. Conversation between Madame Bertrand and O'Meara, July 17 and 19, 1816, O'Meara, "Talks with Napoleon," 783, 786.

4. July 27, 1816, Gourgaud, *Journal,* 1:169.

5. July 29, 1816, Bertrand, *Cahiers,* 1:93–94.

6. Bunbury [Bathurst's secretary] to Lowe, London, May 4, 1816, BL MSS Add 20115 SHLP f.109.

7. Carrera to Poinsett, Buenos Aires, July 2, 1815, Carrera, *Archivo,* 16:181.

8. Bunbury [Bathurst's secretary] to Lowe, London, May 4, 1816, BL MSS Add 20115 SHLP f.109.

9. Lowe to Chamberlain, August 6, 1816, BL MSS Add 20155 SHLP, f.381.

10. Lowe to Bathurst, July 9, 1816, BL MSS Add 20135 SHLP, ff.26–27.

11. Lowe to Bunbury [Bathurst's secretary], July 29, 1816, William Forsyth, *History of the Captivity from the Letters and Journals of the Late Lieut.-Gen. Sir H. Lowe, and Official Documents Not before Made Public* (London: J. Murray, 1853), 1:232–233.

12. Barnes, *A Tour through the Island of St. Helena,* 172.

13. August 4, 1816, Montholon, *Récits,* 1:348.

14. August 16, 1816, Las Cases, *Memorial,* 2:1105.

15. Report no. 5 and 6, Balmain, *Reports,* 21, 23, 31.

16. August 22, 1816, O'Meara, *Napoleon in Exile,* 1:99–100.

17. Barry O'Meara, *An Exposition of Some of the Transactions That Have Taken Place at St. Helena since the Appointment of Sir Hudson Lowe as Governor of That Island* (London: Ridgway, 1819), 15, 18.

18. Bathurst to Lowe, June 26, 1816, NA CO 248/2, f.36.

19. September 9, 1816, O'Meara, *Napoleon in Exile,* 1:116, 120.

Chapter 10

1. Berry, *Voyages,* 161.

2. Elizabeth B. White, *American Opinion of France: From Lafayette to Poincaré* (New York: A. Knopf, 1927), 42.

3. Jean Guillaume Hyde de Neuville, *Mémoires et Souvenirs du Baron Hyde de Neuville* (Paris: Plon, 1888), 2:261. Monroe to Gallatin, Washington, September 10, 1816, James Monroe, *The Writings of James Monroe, Including a Collection of His Public and Private Correspondence Now for the First Time Printed,* ed. S. M. Hamilton. (New York: G. P. Putnam's Sons, 1898–1903), 5:387.

4. Harry Ammon, *James Monroe: The Quest for National Identity* (Charlottesville: University Press of Virginia, 1990), 351.

5. Robert Christophe, *Napoleon on Elba* (London: Macdonald, 1964), 147. Regarding Skupieski see Danielle and Bernard Quintin, *Dictionnaire des Colonels de Napoleon* (Paris: SPM, 1996), and Andre Gavoty, "Deux Aventures Amoureuses de Napoléon," *Tout l'Histoire Napoleon* (Aug.–Oct. 1952): 256–257, 271. Joseph had last seen the Skupieskis at Malmaison, shortly after the abdication, when they attempted to follow Napoleon to the United States. St. Denis, *Napoleon,* 140; Gourgaud, *Journal,* 1:32–33; and Marchand, *Mémoires,* 249. Skupieski's arrival in the United States was reported in the *Boston Daily Advertiser,* December 15, 1815.·

6. Travel Journal, July 6, 1817, Carrera, *Archivo,* 17:1.

7. Manuel Ortuño Martinez, "El supuesto encuentro de Xavier Mina con el ex rey Jose Bonaparte en los Estados Unidos," *Huarte de San Juan Geografía e Historia* 9 (2002): 271–302, and Guadalupe Jimenez Codinach, "La Confederation Napoléonienne: El desempeño de los conspiradores militares y las sociedades secretas en la independencia de Mexico," *Historia Mexicana* 38, no. 1 (July–Sept. 1988): 43–68.

8. Harris Gaylord Warren, "The Origin of General Mina's Invasion of Mexico," *Southwestern Historical Quarterly* 42, no. 1 (July 1938): 8.

9. Hyde de Neuville to Richelieu, June 22, 1816, AMAE CPEU, no. 73, f.55.

10. Bagot to Castlereagh, July 4, 1816, NA FO 5/114.

11. Hyde de Neuville to Richelieu, July 12, 1816, AMAE CPEU, no. 73, f.62. Fournier had already been identified by Onis and French agents in Baltimore as one of the leaders of an expedition to rescue Napoleon.

12. Dispatch of June 24, 1816, AMAE Philadelphie, Consulat général, no. 11.

13. Travel Diary, May 19, 1816, Carrera, *Archivo,* 16:264. The recruiting agent was Martin Thompson, who would reappear later in the story. Enrique Gonzalez Louzieme, "La Misión Diplomática de Martin Jacobo Thompson en los Estados Unidos de Norte América en 1816," in *Cuarto Congreso de Historia de América* (Buenos Aires: Academia Nacional de Historia, 1966), 7:90–91.

14. Travel Journal, July 25, 1816, Carrera, *Archivo,* 17:1.

15. Travel Journal, August 1, 2 and 3, 1816, ibid., 17:37–38.

16. Travel Journal, August 4, 1816, ibid., 17:38.

17. Travel Journal, August 11 and 23, 1816, ibid., 17:39, 42.

18. Dauxion Lavaysse to Carrera, August 13, 1816, ibid., 17:59.

19. Charles W. Elliott, "Some Unpublished Letters of a Roving Soldier-Diplomat: General Winfield Scott's Reports to Secretary of State James Monroe, on Conditions in France and England in 1815–1816," *Journal of the American Military History Foundation* 1, no. 4. (Winter, 1937–38): 165–173; Edward Mansfield, *Life and Services of General Winfield Scott* (New York, 1852), 147–149. Scott's European tour is briefly discussed in John S. D. Eisenhower, *Agent of Destiny: The Life and Times of General Winfield Scott* (New York: Free Press, 1997), 103–107.

20. Inès Murat, *Napoleon and the American Dream* (Baton Rouge: Louisiana State

University Press, 1981), 177. Mina confirmed that Scott had been most helpful in a letter to Lord Holland, September 19, 1816, in BL MSS Add 51626 HHP, f.173.

21. Onis to Captain General of Cuba, August 21, 1816, Carrera, *Archivo*, 19: 330–332.

22. Onis to Cevallos, Philadelphia, August 10, 1816, AHN Estado 5641, vol.7. On Parish's links to Napoleon see Otto Wolff, *Ouvrard: Speculator of Genius, 1770–1846* (London: Barrie and Rockliff, 1962), 103–105. Regarding Parish, see Philip G. Walters; Raymond Walters Jr. "The American Career of David Parish," *Journal of Economic History* 4, no. 2 (Nov. 1944): 149–166.

23. Hyde de Neuville to Richelieu, New York, June 22, 1816, AMAE CPEU no. 74, f.55.

24. Grouchy to his wife, Philadelphia, June 27, 1816, Grouchy, *Mémoires*, 5:49–50.

25. Onis to Bardaxi, January 20, 1812, AHN Estado 5638.

26. Warren, *The Sword*, 157, and Harold A. Bierck Jr., *Vida Pública de Pedro Gual* (Caracas: Ediciones del Ministerio de Educación Nacional, 1947), 131–132.

27. Carrera to Grouchy, August 28, 1816, Carrera, *Archivo*, 17:82–83, 85.

28. Grouchy to Carrera, Bordentown, September 6, 1818, Carrera, *Archivo*, 16: 103–104.

29. Grouchy to Supreme Director of Buenos Aires, Philadelphia, September 1, 1816, Carrera, *Archivo*, 17:96–98.

30. Bierck, *Vida Publica de Pedro Gual*, 130.

31. Gual had first met Thornton in 1812 during his first visit to the United States. Bierck Jr., *Vida Publica de Pedro Gual*, 64–69; Harold A. Bierck Jr., "Pedro Gual and the Patriot Effort to Capture a Mexican Port, 1816," *Hispanic American Historical Review* (Aug. 1947): 463–464.

32. J. H. Powell, *Richard Rush, Republican Diplomat* (Philadelphia: University of Pennsylvania Press, 1942), 19, and Montlezun, *Voyage*, 117.

33. Travel Journal, August 30, 1816, Carrera, *Archivo*, 17:44.

34. Graham to Monroe, September 12, 1816, Lockey, "The Florida Intrigues of Jose Alvarez de Toledo," 163. Also Bierck, *Vida Publica de Pedro Gual*, 130.

35. For Burr's plans see, *Political Correspondence*, 2:1099–1131; Ernesto de la Torre Villar, "Dos Proyectos para la Independencia de Hispanoamérica: James Workman y Aaron Burr," *Revista de Historia de América*, no. 49 (1960): 55–67. Toledo's invitation is in Toledo to Burr, New York, September 30, 1816, Mathew L. Davis, ed., *Memoirs of Aaron Burr* (New York, 1836), 442–443.

36. Carrera to Poinsett, September 11, 1816, Carrera, *Archivo*, 17:136–138.

37. Warren, *The Sword*, 137–139, and Harris Gaylord Warren, "Jose Alvarez de Toledo's Reconciliation with Spain and Projects for Suppressing Rebellion in the Spanish Colonies," *Louisiana Historical Quarterly* 23, no. 3 (July 1940): 827–863.

38. Carrera to Luis Carrera, September 9, 1816, Carrera, *Archivo*, 17:98–99.

39. Carrera to Cortés de Madariaga, Montevideo, October 15, 1817, ibid., 18: 134–135.

40. Porter to Carrera, Washington, September 12, 1816, and Carrera to Didier, New York, September 29, 1816, ibid., 17:115–116, 148.

41. John McErlean, "Une Pretendue Conspiration au Canada en 1816," *Revue de l'Institut Napoléon* 136 (1980): 79–80. Maybe Story was repeating an old rumor. On the other hand, another Buenos Aires privateer was preparing to sail from New York to Cape Verde. It was the *Regent,* later renamed *Tupac Amaru.* See Keen, *David Curtis de Forest,* 118.

42. *Niles' Weekly Register,* September 21, 1816.

43. White, *American Opinion of France,* 48.

44. Onis to Cevallos, Philadelphia, September 17, 1816, AHN Estado 5641.

45. Travel Journal, September 19, 1816, Carrera, *Archivo,* 17:93.

46. Mina predicted he would obtain military results in three months. Mina to Lord Holland, September 19, 1816, BL MSS Add 51626 HHP, f.173.

47. Travel Journal, September 28, 1816, Carrera, *Archivo,* 17:95.

48. Onis' spy was Segundo Correa, the son of Diego Correa, a Spanish liberal exiled in London. Franco, *La Batalla por el Dominio,* 1:63.

49. Thompson to Supreme Director, September 2, 1816, AGN SX.C1.A5.N1 Misión Thompson 1816.

50. Burr, *Political Correspondence,* 2:1150. Regarding Hubbard see Marilyn Maple, "Ruggles Hubbard, Civil Governor of Fernandina," *Florida Historical Quarterly* 58, no. 3 (Jan. 1980): 315–319.

51. Burr had been for many years the leader of the society of Red Men and Hubbard was a sachem, or trustee. See Gustavus Myers, *The History of Tammany Hall* (New York, 1968), 61.

52. Before leaving, Skupieski had a violent dispute with another Polish veteran of the Grande Armée who accused him of being a fraud. The details of this incident and the negotiation between Thompson and Hubbard are in AGN SX.C1.A5.N1 Misión Thompson 1816.

53. Onis to Cevallos, no. 150, Philadelphia, September 27, 1816, AHN Estado 5641.

54. Travel Journal, October 7, and Carrera to Clausel, October 18, 1816, Carrera, *Archivo,* 17:183.

55. Carrera to Clausel, November 6, 1816, ibid., 17:231–232.

56. Onis to Cevallos, Philadelphia, October 31, 1816, AHN Estado 5641, f.177.

57. Lee to Madison, New York, November 8, 1816, Lee, *A Yankee Jeffersonian,* 180–184.

58. Alberic Cahuet, *Apres la mort de l'Empereur* (Paris: Emile-Paul, 1913), 78.

59. Brayer, who was a high-ranking Freemason, probably received protection from the "brothers" in Baltimore. Jean-Luc Quoy-Bodin, "La Franc Maçonnerie dans les Armes," *Revue de l'Institut Napoléon* 137 (1981): 70.

60. Carrera, *Archivo,* 18:45.

61. Onis to Cevallos, Philadelphia, November 16, 1816, AHN Estado 5641.

62. Carrera to Clausel, December 3, 1816, Carrera, *Archivo,* 17:288.

63. Skinner to Carrera, December 23, 1816, ibid., 17:323–324.

64. Proclamation of Jose Alvarez de Toledo, Philadelphia, December 1, 1816, Warren, "Jose Alvarez de Toledo's Reconciliation," 862.

65. Onis to Cevallos, Philadelphia, December 18, 1816, AHN Estado 5641.

Chapter 11

1. Wilson to Grey, June 26, 1816, BL MSS Add 30121 SRWP, f.132.

2. Frye, *After Waterloo,* 147, and General Orders, May 10, 1816, BL MSS Add 30108 SRWP, f.221.

3. Vaulabelle, *Histoire,* 3:125.

4. Richelieu to Osmond, 16 July 1816, Richelieu, *Lettres,* 46.

5. Gallatin to Monroe, Paris, July 12, 1816, Gallatin, *Writings,* 2:1–2.

6. Adams to John Adams, Ealing, August 1, 1816, Adams, *Writings,* 6:58–62.

7. Esterhazy to Metternich, London, August 31, 1816, Hans Schlitter, *Kaiser Franz I und die Napoleoniden, vom sturze Napoleons bis zu dessen Tode aus Schriftstücken des K. und K. Haus, Hof and Staatsarchivs* (Vienna: Tempsky, 1865), 347.

8. Croker to Peel, August 8, 1816, John Wilson Croker, *The Correspondence and Diaries of the Late Right Honourable John Wilson Croker, Secretary to the Admiralty from 1809 to 1830* (London: John Murray, 1885), 1:88.

9. Gordon to Croker, London, August 1816, ADM 1/4362.

10. Lord Sidmouth to Hiley Addington, July 24, 1816, Philip Ziegler, *Addington: A Life of Henry Addington, First Viscount Sidmouth* (London: Collins, 1965), 341.

11. Thomas B. Cochrane, *The Life of Thomas, Lord Cochrane, Tenth Earl of Dundonald* (London: R. Bentley, 1869), 84–85.

12. *Anti-Gallican Monitor,* London, August 4, 1816.

13. *Political Register,* London, August 24, 1816.

14. January 27, 1817, O'Meara, *Napoleon in Exile,* 1:354.

15. *Hampshire Chronicle and Courier,* Monday, August 26, 1816.

16. Wilson to Cochrane, London, March 14, 1823, Thomas Cochrane, *Observations on Naval Affairs* (London, 1857), 152–153.

17. Wilson to Grey, August 2, 1816, in BL MSS Add 30121 SRWP, f. 148.

18. BL MSS Add 30141 SRWP, f.2.

19. Fernan Nuñez to Cevallos, London, September 17, 1816, AGS Estado 8177.

20. Vaudoncourt, *Quinze années,* 2:294–295, and Frye, *After Waterloo,* 151.

21. Glover, *A Very Slippery Fellow,* 160.

22. *Anti-Gallican Monitor,* London, August 25, 1816.

23. The spy was Louis C. Hubert de Brivazac and he styled himself Comte de Beaumont. Born in 1780, he had been forced to immigrate to England with his father during the Revolution. He later returned to France and served as quartermaster in Napoleon's army in Spain. After the restoration of the Bourbons he was imprisoned for debt and then reappeared in London as a spy for the Bourbons. In 1822 he published a small tract titled *L'Europe et ses colonies* (Paris: Brissot Thivars et chez Delaunay, 1822). There is a

personal archive of Beaumont de Brivazac at the Archives Nationales that I have not been able to consult.

24. Richelieu to Osmond, September 12, 1816, Richelieu, *Lettres,* 62.

25. *Anti-Gallican Monitor,* London, September 29, 1816.

26. Charlton Whittall, memorandum of conversations with the Duc de Rovigo and General Lallemand, 1816, BL MSS Add 59654 Charlton Whittall Papers ff. 31–38. See also Savary, *Memoirs,* 4, 193.

27. Lascaris de Vintimille was a knight of Malta and a loyal Bonapartist. He had accompanied Napoleon to Egypt and had encouraged his dreams of a middle eastern empire. See Alphonse de Lamartine, ed., *Narrative of the Residence of Fatalla Sayeghir among the Wandering Arabs of the Great Desert* (Reading, UK: Garnet, 1996), 8–10, 199–200.

28. Frederique E. Planat de la Faye, *Vie de Planat de la Faye, aide-de-camp des Généraux Lariboisière et Drouot, officier d'ordonnance de Napoléon 1er: Souvenirs, lettres et dictées recueillis et annotés par sa Veuve* (Paris: Paul Ollendorff, 1895), 287.

29. Soulié, *Autour de l'Aigle enchaîné,* 36. See also Agustin Codazzi, *Memorias de Agustin Codazzi,* ed. Mario Longhena (Bogota: Talleres Gráficos del Banco de la República, 1973), 197–198, and Costante Ferrari, *Memorie Postume con introduzione e note di Mario Menghini* (Milano: Fasani, 1945), 430–432.

30. Savary, *Memoirs,* 4:191, and Planat de la Faye, *Vie de Planat de la Faye,* 286–287.

31. *Anti-Gallican Monitor,* London, October 20, 1816.

32. Soulié, *Autour de l'Aigle enchaîné,* 37–39.

33. Another Napoleonic veteran named Joseph Séve joined Mehmet Ali and became famous as Soliman Pasha. Jérôme Louis, "Soliman Pacha, 1788–1860," *Revue de l'Institut Napoléon* 186 (2003): 29–50.

34. Savary, *Memoirs,* 4:193.

35. *Anti-Gallican,* London, November 10, 1816.

36. *Times,* London, October 25, 1816.

37. *Anti-Gallican Monitor,* London, October 27, 1816.

38. Russell, *Recollections and Suggestions, 1813–1873,* 18.

39. Mitchell B. Garret and James L. Godfrey, *Europe since 1815* (New York, 1947), 99.

40. Wilson to Grey, November 8, 1816, BL MSS Add 30121 SRWP, f.201.

41. William Hone, *The Meetings in Spa Fields* (London, 1816).

42. Cochrane, *The Life,* 1:102.

43. Pietromarchi, *Luciano Bonaparte,* 286. The bankers of the Bonaparte family were Stephen Girard and David Parish in the United States and Giovanni Torlonia in Rome.

44. Vaudoncourt, *Quinze années,* 2:327–331, and Brice, *Le General Brice,* 49.

45. Schlitter, *Kaiser Franz I und die Napoleoniden,* 352.

46. BL MSS Add 20117 SHLP, f.42.

47. Vaudoncourt, *Quinze années,* 2:348–353.

48. Metternich to Vincent, Vienna, December 4, 1816, Schlitter, *Kaiser Franz I und die Napoleoniden,* 353.

49. According to the informer "certain committees were sitting in diverse parts of St. George Fields and that in that part there was on Thursday night between 12 and 1 o'clock two waggons from Birmingham loaded with sabres for the use of the mob that is to collect on Monday December 2nd. They are going to liberate Lord Cochrane and the prisoners in the bench prison and then proceed to enter Carlton House to see the Prince Regent," anonymous note, n.d., NA TS 11/199, loose folio.

50. David Johnson, *Regency Revolution: The Case of Arthur Thistlewood* (London: Compton Russell, 1974), 23–24.

51. Cochrane, *The Life*, 1:103.

52. Wilson to Grey, December 3, 1816, BL MSS Add 30121 SRWP, f.225.

53. *Political Register,* December 14, 1817.

54. Warren Tute, *Cochrane: A Life of Admiral the Earl of Dundonald* (London: Cassell, 1965), 164, and Belchem, "*Orator" Hunt*, 46.

55. Cochrane to Guthrie, Kings Bench, November 28, 1816, NMM Guthrie Papers.

56. Adams to Abigail Adams, December 11, 1816, Adams, *Writings*, 6:125–126.

57. Wilson to Grey, August 15 and November 25, 1816 in BL MSS Add 30121 SRWP, ff.166, 216.

58. Wilson, *Private Diary,* 2:343.

59. Francis Maceroni, *Memoirs of the Life and Adventures of Colonel Maceroni* (London, 1838), 2:174; Francis Maceroni, *Few Specimens of the Ars Logica Copleiana* (London, 1820), 11; Vaulabelle, *Histoire,* 3:316; and Fouché, *Mémoires,* 464.

60. Jonah Barrington, *Personal Sketches and Recollections of His Own Times* (Dublin: Ashfield Press, 1997), 353.

61. Wilson to Grey, London, December 12, 1816, BL MSS Add 30120 SRWP, f.236.

62. Wilson to Grey, London, December 9, 1816, BL MSS Add 30121 SRWP, f.234.

63. Grey to Wilson, December 19, 1816, Grey Papers, Durham University Library, GRE/B60/4/40.

64. Cochrane to Guthrie, London, December 25, 1816, NMM, James Guthrie Papers.

65. Wilson to Grey, December 26, 1817, BL MSS Add 30121 SRWP, f.249.

Chapter 12

1. Bathurst to Lowe, July 17, 1816, NA CO 248/2 f.54.

2. Extract from the logbook of the HMS *Hope,* Henry Elliot Commander, October 12, 1816, BL MSS Add 20116 SHLP, f. 160.

3. Onis to Cevallos, May 27, 1816, Philadelphia, no. 72, AHN Estado 5641. Also see Bealer, "Los Corsarios de Buenos Aires," 54.

4. Bathurst to Lowe, July 17, 1816, NA CO 248/2 f.54.

5. October, 3–4, 1816, O'Meara, *Napoleon in Exile,* 1:138–139.

6. O'Meara, *Napoleon in Exile,* 2:390, and Montholon, *Récits,* 1:406.

7. Bertrand, *Cahiers,* 1:137, and J. Chautard, *Noel Santini* (Paris: Ledoyen, 1854), 254.

8. Piontkowski to Wilson, n.d., Watson, *A Polish Exile,* 175.

9. Lowe to Bathurst, October 11, 1816, BL MSS Add 20116 SHLP, f.139.

10. O'Meara, *An Exposition,* 25–26.

11. Bathurst to Lowe, July 19, 1816, NA CO 248/2 ff.63, 70–72.

12. Bathurst to Lowe, August 21, 1816, NA CO 248/2 f.70; Forsyth, *History of the Captivity,* 1:309.

13. Candé-Montholon, *Journal Secret d'Albine de Montholon,* 165.

14. October 13 and 23, 1816, O'Meara, *Napoleon in Exile,* 1:151–152, 169–170.

15. October 29, 1816, Montholon, *Récits,* 1:427.

16. Report no. 6, September 10, 1816, Balmain, *Reports,* 41.

17. Las Cases to Lucien Bonaparte, November 1816, Forsyth, *History of the Captivity,* 1:476–485.

18. Lowe to Bathurst, December 3, 1816, BL MSS Add 20117 SHLP, f.97.

19. Forsyth, *History of the Captivity,* 1:368–370.

20. Lowe to Bathurst, 3 December 1816, BL MSS Add 20117 SHLP, f.97.

21. November 26, 1816, Gourgaud, *Journal,* 1:201.

22. December 14, 1816, ibid., 1:227.

23. December 5, 1816, O'Meara, *Napoleon in Exile,* 1:254.

24. December 9, 1816, Bertrand, *Cahiers,* 1:159.

25. November 29, 1816, O'Meara, *Napoleon in Exile,* 1:232.

26. December 29, 1816, ibid., 1:297.

27. Lowe to Bathurst, September 1, 1816, BL MSS Add 20135 SHLP, f.45.

28. O'Meara to Lowe, December 16, 1816, BL MSS Add 20117 SHLP, f.206.

29. December 9, 1816, O'Meara, *Napoleon in Exile,* 1:285.

30. Report no. 11, December 24, 1816, Balmain, *Reports,* 69.

Chapter 13

1. January 1, 1817, O'Meara, *Napoleon in Exile,* 1:302.

2. Marchand, *Mémoires,* 346.

3. Guy de l'Herault, *Histoire de Napoléon II, Roi de Rome suivie du testament politique de l'Empereur Napoléon 1er* (Paris, 1853), 145–146.

4. Report no. 2, January 28, 1817, Balmain, *Reports,* 78.

5. Montholon, *History,* 2:471–472.

6. March 1817, Montholon, *Récits,* 2:97.

7. January 30, 1817, ibid., 2:63.

8. January 30, 1817, Gourgaud, *Journal,* 1:305.

9. February 22, 1817, ibid., 1:336–337.

10. February 2, 1817, Bertrand, *Cahiers,* 1:193.

11. April 16, 1817, O'Meara, *Napoleon in Exile,* 1:511–512.

12. February 2, 1817, Bertrand, *Cahiers,* 1:193.

13. February 17, 1817, O'Meara, *Napoleon in Exile,* 1:389.

14. December 8, 1816, ibid., 1:260–262.

15. January 30, 1817, ibid., 1:360.

16. February 23, 1817, ibid., 1:422.

17. March 10, 1817, ibid., 1:423.

18. March 30, 1817, ibid., 1:474.

19. Goulbourn to Croker, September 18, 1817, NA ADM 1/4237.

20. May 3, 1817, Henry Meynell, *Conversations with Napoleon at St. Helena* (London: A. L. Humphreys, 1911), 60–61.

21. Third letter, May 1, 1817, *Letters from the Cape of Good Hope* (London, 1817), 59.

22. December 6, 1815, Las Cases, *Memorial,* 1:193.

23. March 4, 1817, Gourgaud, *Journal,* 2:21.

24. March 23, 1817, Montholon, *Récits,* 2:100–101.

25. Reade to Lowe, March 3, 1817, BL MSS Add 20118 SHLP, f.151.

26. April 13, 1817, Gourgaud, *Journal,* 2:71.

27. May 6, 1817, Gourgaud, *Journal,* 2:93.

28. April 11, 1817, ibid., 2:68.

Chapter 14

1. *Courier,* London, January 1, 1817.

2. *Courier,* London, January 7, 1817.

3. Metternich to Esterhazy, Vienna, January 23, 1817, Schlitter, *Kaiser Franz I und die Napoleoniden,* 356.

4. Richelieu to Osmond, January 9, 1817, Richelieu, *Lettres,* 90.

5. June 21, 1817, Gourgaud, *Journal,* 2:154.

6. Hunt, *Memoirs,* 3:427–428.

7. *Courier,* London, January 23, 1817.

8. Ziegler, *Addington,* 347.

9. Report of the Secret Committee to the House of Lords, February 18, 1817, NA TS 11/202, 1st pack.

10. Johnson, *Regency Revolution,* 22–23.

11. *Hansard's Parliamentary Debates,* 33:628.

12. Ziegler, *Addington,* 347–348, and Patterson, *Sir Francis Burdett,* 2:421–422.

13. Wilson to Grey, February 6, 1817, BL MSS Add 30121 SRWP, f. 279.

14. Chautard, *Noel Santini,* 277.

15. Maceroni, *Memoirs,* 2:425.

16. Piontkowski to Holland, London, Berwick St. no. 82, March 6, 1817, BL MSS Add 51528 HHP.

17. Watson, *A Polish Exile,* 157.

18. Francis Maceroni, *Interesting Facts Relating to the Fall and Death of Joachim Murat, the Capitulation of Paris in 1815, and the Second Restoration of the Bourbons* (London, 1817), 52.

19. Wilson to Grey, January 16 and 18, 1817, in BL MSS Add 30121 SRWP, ff.270, 276.

20. *Anti-Gallican Monitor,* London, January 27, 1817.

21. Schlitter, *Kaiser Franz I und die Napoleoniden,* 357.

22. Metternich to Esterhazy, Vienna, February 18, 1817, ibid.

23. Esterhazy to Metternich, London, February 19, 1817, ibid., 358.

24. Wilson to Grey, March 17, 1817, BL MSS Add 30121 SRWP, f. 288. Cockburn apparently had more favorable views of Napoleon than is generally supposed.

25. Piontkowski to Holland, London, March 17, 1817, BL MSS Add 51528 HHP 174.

26. Piontkowski to Gourgaud, March 20, 1817, Watson, *A Polish Exile,* 159–160.

27. Theodore E. Hook, *Facts Illustrative of the Treatment of Napoleon Buonaparte in St. Helena* (London, 1819), 21.

28. Wilson to Grey, March 14, 1817, BL MSS Add 30120 SRWP, f.286.

29. Primrose, *Napoleon: The Last Phase,* 157.

30. Maceroni, *Memoirs,* 2:425–429.

31. Wilson to Grey, March 19, 1817, BL MSS Add 30120 SRWP, f.292.

32. Report, London, March 20, 1817, Schlitter, *Kaiser Franz I und die Napoleoniden,* 418–419.

33. *Courier,* London, March 19, 1817.

34. *Anti-Gallican Monitor,* London, March 30 and April 6, 1817.

35. Wilson to Grey, March 26, 1817, BL MSS Add 30121 SRWP, f.301.

36. *Manuscript Transmitted from St. Helena by an Unknown Channel* (London, 1817), 146.

37. Mme. Regnault to her husband, 30 March 1817, *Revue Retrospective* 10 (1889): 134–136.

38. Richelieu to Osmond, 24 April 1817, Richelieu, *Lettres,* 107.

39. Conversation on September 7, 1817, O'Meara, *Napoleon in Exile,* 2:204, 207.

40. Princess de Tremoille to Hyde de Neuville, Paris, 10 May 1817, Hyde de Neuville, *Memoirs,* 2:287–288.

41. *Courier,* London, 28 March 1817.

42. Marquiset, *Une Merveilleuse,* 186.

43. Mme. Regnault to her husband, March 30, 1817, *Revue Retrospective* 10 (1889): 134–136.

44. Laure Junot, duchesse d'Abrantes, *Histoire des salons de Paris: Tableaux et portraits du grand monde, sous Louis XVI, le Directoire, le Consulat et l'Empire, la Restauration, et le règne de Louis-Philippe 1er* (Paris, 1837–1838), 6:369–370.

45. Hyde de Neuville to Richelieu, May 14, 1817, Carlos Villanueva, *La monarquía en América, San Martin y Bolívar* (Paris: Garnier, 1911), 62.

46. Charles K. Webster, *The Foreign Policy of Castlereagh, 1815–1822: Britain and the European Alliance* (London: G. Bell and Sons, 1934), 411–412.

47. Ibid., 423.

48. Ibid., 413–415.

49. Adams to Monroe, London, April 10, 1817, Adams, *Writings,* 6:174–176.

50. *Courier,* London, March 28, 1817.

51. Adams to John Adams, London, March 31, 1817, Adams, *Writings,* 6: 168–172.

52. Wilson to Grey, March 26, 1817, BL MSS Add 30121 SRWP, f.301.

53. Ian Grimble, *The Sea Wolf: The Life of Admiral Cochrane* (Edinburgh: Birlinn, 2000), 187.

Chapter 15

1. San Martin to Bowles, September 7, 1816, ADM 1/1563.

2. Bowles to Croker, Buenos Aires, September 22, 1816, NA ADM 1/1563.

3. Diego Barros Arana, *Recuerdos historicos: Un general polaco al servicio de Chile* (Santiago: Revista Chilena, 1875), 226.

4. In London, Bonpland had met Mina at Holland House. He had also met Servando de Mier, a defrocked priest who was a member of the Caballeros Racionales. Mier arrived in London in 1814 with Francisco Zea, a Colombian botanist with strong ties to the Bonapartes. In 1808, when Napoleon forced the abdication of the Spanish Bourbons, Zea had presented him a proposal for the establishment of a Bonapartist empire in Spanish America. Joseph appointed him head of Madrid's botanical gardens. After Joseph's downfall in 1813, Zea and Mier had followed him to France. It was Zea who introduced Mier to Bonpland. All three believed that with the return of absolutism to Europe, the New World offered the best hopes for freedom. Zea joined Bolivar in Venezuela; Bonpland went to Buenos Aires; and Mier joined Mina's expedition to Mexico. Miramón, *Política Secreta de Napoleón,* 72–74; Philippe Foucault, *Le pecheur d'orchidees Aimé Bonpland, 1773–1858* (Paris, 1990), 203–204, 209; Mier to Bonpland, August 20, 1815, Bonpland, *Londres Cuartel General Europeo,* n.p.

5. Bowles to Croker, April 9, 1817, NA ADM 1/23.

6. Bowles to Croker, January 10, 1817, and March 1, 1817, NA ADM 1/23.

7. Staples to Hamilton, Buenos Aires, April 11, 1817, NA FO 72/202 f.39

8. Pueyrredon to San Martin, February 25, 1817, Carrera, *Archivo,* 18:103–104.

9. Lavaysse to Skinner, April 16, 1817, ibid., 18:171–175.

10. Jean Joseph Dauxion Lavaysse, *Voyage aux îles de Trinidad, de Tobago, de la Margarite et dans diverses parties de Venezuela dans l'Amérique Méridionale* (Paris, 1813).

11. Beaubrun Ardouin, *Etudes sur l'histoire d'Haiti* (Paris: 1853–1860), 8:77–96, 129, and Miguel L. Amunategui, *La Dictadura de O'Higgins* (Madrid: Biblioteca Ayacucho, 1917), 155.

12. For a brief biography of Dauxion Lavaysse see Jacinto Yaben, *Biografías Argen-*

tinas y Sudamericanas (Buenos Aires, 1939), 3:375; Diego Barros Arana, "Don Claudio Gay y Su Obra," *Revista Chilena* 2 (1875): 125; and Johan Hoefer, *Nouvelle Biographie Generale* (Paris, 1852–66), 13:196. In 1817 Lavaysse was found guilty of bigamy and condemned to twenty years of forced labor.

13. Skinner to Carrera, July 31, 1817, Carrera, *Archivo,* 18:285.

14. Pueyrredon to San Martin, November 16, 1816, Carlos Pueyrredon, *La Campaña de los Andes* (Buenos Aires, 1942), Facsimile 67.

15. Pueyrredon to San Martin, November 25, 1816, ibid. f.72.

16. Pueyrredon to San Martin, December 17, 1816, Jose de San Martín, *Documentos del Archivo de San Martin* (Buenos Aires, 1910), 4:549, and Pueyrredon to San Martin, December 17, 1816, Pueyrredon, *La Campaña,* f. 76.

17. *Gazeta de Buenos Aires,* Buenos Aires, March 1, 1817.

18. Fernand Beaucour, "Plans to Deliver Napoleon from St. Helena," in Robert B. Holtman, ed., *Napoleon and America* (Pensacola: Perdido Bay Press, 1988), 226.

19. Bowles to Croker, April 8, 1817, NA ADM 1/23.

20. Staples to Hamilton, May 25, 1817, NA FO 72/202 f.48.

21. Bowles to Croker, June 31, 1817, NA ADM 1/23.

22. Augusto Rodríguez, "Ambrosio Cramer: Un soldado de la libertad," *Boletín de la Academia Nacional de Historia* 27 (Buenos Aires, 1956), 74.

23. San Martin to O'Higgins, April 8, 1817, Carrera, *Archivo,* 18:163.

24. Hector Viacava, "Andanzas, mentiras y desventuras de un coronel de Napoleón," *Todo es Historia* 157 (June 1980): 46.

25. San Martin to O'Higgins, April 8, 1817, ibid., 18:163. San Martin took the decision to expel Skupieski and had known him for less than two weeks.

26. Barros Arana, *Recuerdos Historicos,* 232.

27. Bowles to Croker, June 22, 1817, NA ADM 1/23.

28. Brayer to San Martin, Santiago, June 15, 1817, J. J. Biedma, ed., *Documentos referentes a la Guerra de la Independencia y Emancipación Política de la República Argentina y de otras secciones de América a que cooperó desde 1810 a 1828* (Buenos Aires, 1910–20), 2:147.

29. Jose Zapiola, *Recuerdos de Treinta Años* (Santiago, 1902), 196.

30. Feliú Cruz, *Memorias del coronel Beauchef,* 98.

31. Carrera to Grouchy, June 27, 1817, Carrera, *Archivo,* 18:252.

32. *Anti-Gallican Monitor,* London, June 23, 1816. French authorities were so afraid that this was the case that the ship was not allowed to carry any cannons. D. Hamy, "Les Voyages de Richard Grandsire de Calais dans l'Amérique du Sud," in *Journal de la Societé des Americanistes de Paris* 5 (1908), 3.

33. Jose Miguel Carrera to Luis Carrera, July 9, 1817, Carrera, *Archivo,* 18:270.

Chapter 16

1. Hyde de Neuville to Richelieu, January 10, 1817, AMAE CPEU, no. 73, f.202.

2. Engle Burr, *Napoleon's Dossier,* 37. .

3. Manuel Ortuño Martinez, *Xavier Mina: Fronteras de Libertad* (Mexico: Editorial Porrúa, 2003), 203–204.

4. Ibid., 205. See also William D. Robinson, *Memoirs of the Mexican Revolution* (London, 1821), 1:120–121 and 2:127.

5. Tulio Arends, *Sir Gregor MacGregor: Un escocés tras la aventura de América* (Caracas: Monte Avila Editores, 1991), 94.

6. Details of conversation with MacGregor, Bagot to Castlereagh, April 25, 1817, NA FO 5/122, f.57.

7. Montchenu to a friend in France, July 22, 1816, published in the *Evening Post,* New York, March 7, 1817.

8. *Niles' Weekly Register,* March 26, 1817.

9. MacGregor to Martin Tovar, March 18, 1817, Arends, *Sir Gregor MacGregor,* 100.

10. T. Frederick Davis, *MacGregor's Invasion of Florida, 1817* (Jacksonville: Florida Historical Society, 1928), 6–7, and Franco, *La Batalla por el Dominio,* 1:73.

11. Clemente to Jefe Supremo de Estado, Philadelphia, July 28, 1817, AGI Estado Caracas 12 (56).

12. The law was approved on March 3, 1817. See 14th Congress, 1817, Session 2, chap. 57–58, 370–371.

13. Joseph Rosengarten, *French Colonist and Exiles in the United States* (Philadelphia: Lippincott, 1907), 161–170.

14. Clay to Lakanal, Washington, March 20, 1817, Henry Clay, *The Papers of Henry Clay,* ed. James Hopkins (Lexington: University of Kentucky Press, 1961), 2:328–329.

15. Memorandum of Alvarez de Toledo, Madrid, April 8, 1817, Carlos M. Trelles y Govin, "Un Precursor de la Independencia de Cuba, Don Jose Alvarez de Toledo," *Academia de la Historia,* La Habana, Junio 1926, 114–119.

16. Onis to Pizarro, March 3, 1817, AHN Estado 5642, I.

17. White, *American Opinion of France,* 48.

18. *New York Evening Post,* New York, April 29, 1817.

19. MacGregor had already acted as a spy, agent, or informer of the British government. See MacGregor to Spencer Percival, Caracas, January 18, 1812, NA FO 72/171, f.1.

20. Davis, *MacGregor's Invasion of Florida,* 7. See also Frank Lawrence Owsley Jr. and Gene A. Smith, *Filibusters and Expansionists: Jeffersonian Manifest Destiny, 1800–1821* (Tuscaloosa: University of Alabama Press, 1997), 124.

21. Bagot to Castlereagh, April 25, 1817, NA FO 5/122, ff.57.

22. Onis to Pizarro, Washington, April 25, 1817, AHN Estado 5642, I, f.82.

23. Hyde de Neuville to Richelieu, March 20, 1817, Hyde de Neuville, *Mémoires et Souvenirs,* 2:269; Hyde de Neuville to Richelieu, May 14, 1817, AMAE CPEU, no. 74, f.11.

24. *United States Gazette,* May 10, 1817.

25. *Niles' Weekly Register,* May 24, 1817.

26. Hyde de Neuville to Richelieu, May 14, 1817, AMAE CPEU, no. 74, f.11.

27. *Niles' Weekly Register,* May 3, 1817.

28. Melo, *A Maçonaria e a Revoluçao Republicana,* 8–9; Francisco A. Pereira da

Costa, *La Ilha de Fernando de Noronha* (Pernambuco, 1887), 26–27, and Silvio de Mello Cahu, *A revoluçaõ nativista Pernambucana de 1817* (Rio de Janeiro, 1951), 15–18.

29. Hyde de Neuville to Richelieu, April 29, 1817, Hyde de Neuville, *Mémoires et Souvenirs,* 2:269–270.

30. Richelieu to Hyde de Neuville, April 18, 1817, AMAE CPEU, no. 73, f.292.

31. Da Cruz visited former president John Adams who expressed sympathy for the rebels. Da Cruz also met State Department officials. After this meeting, Joseph Ray was named consul in Pernambuco in 1816 but it seems that at a minimum the visit of Da Cruz hastened his departure. Adams to Jefferson, May 26, 1817, Agan, *The Diplomatic Relations of the United States and Brazil* (Paris: Jouve et cie, 1926), 88–97.

32. Chamberlain to Cockburn, Rio de Janeiro, April 17, 1816, BL MSS Add 20115 SHLP, f. 57.

33. Petry to Richelieu, Philadelphia, ciphered, May 21, 1817, AMAE CPEU, no. 74, f.49.

34. *Evening Post,* New York, June 17, 1817.

35. Hyde de Neuville to Richelieu, May 21, 1817, AMAE CPEU, no. 74, f.35.

36. Hyde de Neuville to Richelieu, June 17, 1817, AMAE CPEU no. 74, f.56.

37. *Niles' Weekly Register,* May 14, 1817.

38. Bagot to Castlereagh, October 8, 1817, BL MSS Add 20201 SHLP, ff.57.

39. Hyde de Neuville to Richelieu, May 21, 1817, AMAE CPEU, no. 74, f.35.

40. Hyde de Neuville to Richelieu, June 17, 1817, AMAE CPEU, no. 74, ff.82–83.

41. Jack Autrey Dabbs, trans., "Additional Notes on the Champ d'Asile," *Southwestern Historical Quarterly* 54, no. 3 (Jan. 1951): 347–358.

42. Davis, *MacGregor's Invasion of Florida,* 9–13, 18–19.

43. Thornton to Gual, Washington, July 8, 1817, Library of Congress, Thornton Papers, V01.5:ff.779–81, and Monroe to Madison, February 13, 1818, Monroe, *Writings,* 6:47. Monroe admitted that a conversation between Thornton and Rush took place regarding MacGregor's plans to sell Florida to the United States "for $1.5MM or 500,000 less than the United States had offered to Spain." Charles Carroll Griffin, *The United States and the Disruption of the Spanish Empire, 1810–1822* (New York: Columbia University Press, 1937), 111.

44. Onis to Adams, Philadelphia, July 9, 1817, Manning, *Diplomatic Correspondence,* 3:1942–1943.

45. Onis to Pizarro, no. 121, Washington, July 18, 1817, AHN Estado 5642, I.

46. Owen Connelly, *The Gentle Bonaparte: A Biography of Joseph, Napoleon's Elder Brother* (New York: Macmillan, 1968), 250–251, and T. Wood Clarke, *Emigrés in the Wilderness* (New York: Macmillan, 1941), 130–131.

Chapter 17

1. Hutchinson to Wilson, April 5, 1817, BL MSS Add 30125 SRWP, f.35.

2. Cochrane, *The Life,* 1:109.

3. Thomas Cochrane, *Narrative of Services in the Liberation of Chili, Peru, and Brazil from Spanish and Portuguese Domination* (London, 1859), 1:115.

4. *Courier,* London, May 28, 1817.

5. *Narrative of a Voyage to the Spanish Main in the Ship "Two Friends"* (London: J. Miller, 1819), 1–4, 28.

6. *Courier,* London, May 12, 1817.

7. Lucien to Lord Holland, Rome, April 2, 1817, BL MSS Add51527 HHP, f.10, and *Courier,* London, March 31, 1817.

8. T. Iung, *Lucien Bonaparte et ses Mémoires, 1775–1840* (Paris, 1882), 3:382.

9. Richelieu to Hyde de Neuville, April 18, 1817, AMAE CPEU, no. 73, f.292.

10. Schlitter, *Kaiser Franz I und die Napoleoniden,* 420; Warden to Lord Holland, London, April 24, 1817, BL MSS Add 51528 HHP (Napoleon), f.176; and Chautard, *Noel Santini,* 290–292.

11. Stuart to Castlereagh, May 15, 1817, NA FO 27/157 f.187.

12. *Times,* London, May 10, 1817.

13. *Courier,* London, May 26, 1817.

14. The details of the Pernambucan plot are in Alvear to Yrigoyen, April 25, 1817, attached to Chamberlain to Castlereagh, May 3, 1817, NA FO 63/203.

15. He had been elected to this position at the end of 1815. A. H. de Oliveira Marques, *Historia da Maçonaria em Portugal* (Lisbon, 1990), 110.

16. Teothonio Banha, *Apontamentos para a Historia da Legião Portugueza ao Serviço de Napoleão I* (Lisbon, 1863), 52.

17. Wilson to Grey, January 12, 1818, BL MSS Add 30122 SRWP, f.144.

18. Joao Brandao, *Vida e Morte de Gomes Freire,* Lisbon, 1990, 152–179.

19. Edward Blaquiere, *An Historical Review of the Spanish Revolution* (London, 1822), 251–256; Jose Luis Comellas, *Los Primeros Pronunciamientos en España 1814–1820* (Madrid, 1958), 229–243.

20. Vaulabelle, *Histoire,* 4:429–440; Comte de Fargues, *La verite Sur les évènemens de Lyon en mil huit cent dix-sept Reponse au Mémoire de M. le Colonel Fabvier* (Paris, 1818), 34, 81.

21. Cochrane, *Narrative,* 1:127.

22. Piontkowski to Holland, July 18, 1817, BL MSS Add 51528 HHP, f.186, and Esterhazy to Metternich, July 1817, NA FO 7/138.

23. Schlitter, *Kaiser Franz I und die Napoleoniden,* 421.

24. *Courier,* London, July 17, 28, and 22, 1817.

25. *Courier,* London, August 19, 1817.

26. Conversation with John Cam Hobhouse, March 28, 1818, BL MSS Add 47235 Broughton Papers, f.8.

27. Richelieu to Hyde de Neuville, August 11, 1817, AMAE CPEU no. 74, f.126, and Hyde de Neuville, *Memoirs,* 2:307–309.

28. *Anti-Gallican Monitor,* London, August 17, 1817.

Chapter 18

1. Bathurst to Lowe, February 23, 1817, BL MSS Add 20118 SHLP, f.112.

2. Bathurst to Lowe, March 5, 1817, BL MSS Add 20118 SHLP, f.162.

3. May 6, 1817, O'Meara, *Napoleon in Exile,* 2:20.

4. Piontkowski to Gourgaud, March 20, 1817, Watson, *A Polish Exile,* 159–160.

5. May 27, 1817, Gourgaud, *Journal,* 2:118.

6. May 28, 1817, ibid., 2:118.

7. O'Meara to Lowe, Longwood, June 5, 1817, Major Gorrequer Papers, NA J 76/4/4, f.38. Also in Forsyth, *History of the Captivity,* 2:388. Interestingly, O'Meara never publicized Napoleon's opinion about Maceroni.

8. May 30, 1817, Gourgaud, *Journal,* 2:121.

9. Observations dictated by Napoleon on Lord Bathurst's speech, Forsyth, *History of the Captivity,* 2:348, 350 and 364.

10. June 9, 1817, Gourgaud, *Journal,* 2:136.

11. June 11, 1817, ibid., 2:140.

12. June 21, 1817, ibid., 2:154.

13. May 31, 1817, O'Meara, *Napoleon in Exile,* 2:77–78.

14. June 12, 1817, Gourgaud, *Journal,* 2:141.

15. July 17, 1817, O'Meara, *Napoleon in Exile,* 2:132.

16. August 1817, ibid., 2:142.

17. June 29, 1817, Gourgaud, *Journal,* 2:165.

18. End of May 1817, Montholon, *Récits,* 2:130.

19. June 2, 1817, Gourgaud, *Journal,* 2:126.

20. 1 July 1817, ibid., 2:168.

21. Marchand, *Mémoires,* 417.

22. July 25, 1817, Bertrand, *Cahiers,* 1:249. Gourgaud mentions this episode a month later. Gourgaud, *Journal,* 2:217–218.

23. Marchand, *Mémoires,* 406.

24. Bathurst to Lowe, July 1817, BL MSS Add 20119 SHLP, f.55.

25. July 14, 1817, Montholon, *Récits,* 2:151.

26. July 14, 1817, Gourgaud, *Journal,* 2:184–186.

27. Donald M. Liddell, *Chessmen* (London: Harrap and Co., 1938), 59.

28. Solomon's role became evident to Lowe only after Napoleon's death when some half-burnt papers were found at Longwood. BL MSS Add 20128 SHLP, f.3.

29. August 15, 1817, Montholon, *Récits,* 2:164.

30. June 11, 1817, Gourgaud, *Journal,* 2:138.

Chapter 19

1. *National Intelligencer,* Washington, July 14, 1817.

2. MacGregor to Skinner, Fernandina, July 17, 1817, and Skinner to Adams, July 30, 1817, are reproduced in T. Frederick Davis, "Letters Relating to MacGregor's Attempted Conquest of East Florida, 1817," 55–60.

3. Ammon, *James Monroe,* 361.

4. Adams to Abigail Adams, London, 16 May 1817, Adams, *Writings,* 6:179–182.

5. Ammon, *James Monroe,* 361.

6. Adams to Alexander Everett Hill, Washington, September 29, 1817, Adams, *Writings,* 6:200–204.

7. Adams to Abigail Adams, Paris, March 19, 1815, Adams, *Writings,* 5:290–294. See also Adams, *Memoirs,* 3:171, 176.

8. Robert Remini, *Henry Clay, Statesman for the Union* (New York: Norton, 1991), 154. For Clay's description of Napoleon see his speech to Congress on March 30–31, 1824, Clay, *Papers,* 3:720.

9. Clay to William H. Crawford, London, March 23, 1815, Clay, *Papers,* 2:11.

10. Adams to James Monroe, London, 22 January 1816, Adams, *Writings,* 5: 487–490.

11. Adams to Alexander Everett Hill, Washington, December 29, 1817, Adams, *Writings,* 6:280–283.

12. Griffin, *The United States and the Disruption,* 133–135. Clay was also a brilliant lawyer and high-ranking Freemason who in 1806 had defended Burr in his first grand jury trial for conspiracy and high treason. Buckley, *Aaron Burr,* 113–117.

13. Adams, *Memoirs,* 4:515.

14. Hyde de Neuville to Richelieu, July 3 and 20, 1817, AMAE CPEU, no. 74, ff.82–83, 93.

15. Hyde de Neuville to Richelieu, July 20, 1817, AMAE CPEU, no. 74, f.93.

16. Hyde de Neuville to Bagot, July 19, 1817, NA FO 5/122, f. 229.

17. Bagot to Castlereagh, July 26, 1817, NA FO 5/122, f. 225.

18. Hyde de Neuville to Richelieu, July 26, 1817, AMAE CPEU, no. 74, f.99.

19. Hyde de Neuville to Richelieu, New Brunswick, August 4, 1817, AMAE CPEU, no. 74, ff.132–138.

20. Usurping identities was not uncommon in those days and Raoul's name had been many times spelled without the "a." See Dossier Jacques Roul, Archive de l'Armée de Terre, Chateau de Vincennes, and Quintin's *Dictionnaire des Colonels de Napoléon.* At this time Nicholas Raoul was in Rome serving as tutor to the future Napoleon III. The similarity between the names of Roul and Raoul has led many historians to confuse their identities. Raoul was the son of a French general and a graduate of the prestigious Ecole Polytechnique. When Napoleon left for Elba after his first abdication he brought along a battalion of the Imperial Guard and Raoul was one of the officers chosen to accompany him. At Elba, Napoleon appointed him aide-de-camp and commander of his escort. Raoul "had no fortune but his sword" and was wholly devoted to his master. His only fault was to fall in love with one of Pauline Bonaparte's ladies-in-waiting who apparently had also caught the emperor's attention. In 1818 Raoul went to the United States to join Lallemand. When the Champ d'Asile collapsed, Raoul joined the Alabama settlement with other French émigrés such as Clausel and Lefebvre-Desnouettes. Years later Raoul left for Central America and became the liberator and national hero of Guatemala. Fleury de Chaboulon, *Memoirs,* 1:192; *A Year of the Life of the Emperor Napoleon* (New York, 1815), 13; and St. Denis, *Napoleon,* 77–78, 109. For a biography of Raoul see Adan Szaszdi, *Nicolás Raoul y la República Federal de Centro América* (Madrid, 1958), 38–39.

21. Beaucour, "Plans to Deliver Napoleon from St. Helena," 219–239.

22. Hyde de Neuville to Richelieu, New Brunswick, August 4, 1817, AMAE CPEU, no. 74, ff.115–126.

23. Doher, *Proscrits,* 138–139.

24. Hyde de Neuville to Richelieu, August 11, 1817, AMAE CPEU, no. 74, f.127.

25. Onis to Pizarro, no. 124, Washington, August 16, 1817, AHN Estado 5642.

26. Wilder to Robertson, July 3, 1817, BL MSS Add 20119 SHLP, f.90.

27. Robertson to Bagot, July 28, 1817, BL MSS Add 20119 SHLP, f193.

28. Bagot to Castlereagh, September 1, 1817, NA FO 5/125 f.366, and BL MSS Add 20201 SHLP, f.309. Robert Oden to Castlereagh, August 23, 1817, NA FO 5/125 f.371.

29. Max Dorian, *Un Bordelais: Stephen Girard, premier millionaire americaine* (Paris: Albatross, 1977), 137.

30. Robertson to Bagot, August 7, 1817, BL MSS Add 20119 SHLP, f.219 and f.221.

31. *Niles' Weekly Register,* August 16, 1817. The Spanish consul in New York warned the district attorney general that the vessels being prepared in New York were bound for Amelia Island in violation of the neutrality laws of the United States. See American State Papers, 15th Congress, 1st Session, Foreign Relations, 4:199–201.

32. *Niles' Weekly Register,* August 9, 1817.

33. Burr, Hubbard, and Skinner belonged to the Order of the Red Men. See Myers, *The History of Tammany Hall,* 61, and George W. Lindsay, Charles C. Conley, and Charles H. Litchman, *Official History of the Improved Order of Red Men,* ed. Carl R. Lemke (Waco, Tex.: Davis Bros., 1964), 185, 249.

34. Alderson to Burr, November 5, 1817, Burr, *Political Correspondence,* 2:1174.

35. Luis Peru de Lacroix, *Diario de Bucaramanga* (Caracas: Ministerio de Educación Nacional, Dirección de Cultura, 1949), 257.

36. Montulé, *Voyage en Amerique,* 316.

37. Gravier to Pizarro, January 30, 1818, AHN Estado 5643, I.

38. Onis to Pizarro, Washington, 31 August 1817, 134, AHN Estado 5642.

39. Anonymous to Hyde de Neuville, August 25, 1817, AMAE CPEU no. 74, f.155. The Lakanal Papers start on f.158. For a biography of Douarche see Quintin and Quintin, *Dictionnaire des Colonels,* 288.

40. Hyde de Neuville to Richelieu, August 31, 1817, AMAE CPEU no. 74, f.158.

41. Onis to Pizarro, Philadelphia, September 16, 1817, AHN Estado 5642.

42. Jose Cienfuegos to Juan Ruiz de Apodaca, Habana, October 30, 1817, Jose R. Guzman, "Los Hermanos Lallemand en Texas," *Boletín del Archivo General de la Nación* 11, no. 1–2 (1970): 167.

43. Hyde de Neuville to Bagot, September 22, 1817, NA FO 5/123, f.57.

44. Meeting on September 23, 1817, Adams, *Memoirs,* 4:9.

45. Adams to Hyde de Neuville, Washington, September 24, 1817, Adams, *Writings,* 6:190–191.

46. September 26, 1817, Adams, *Memoirs,* 4:11.

47. Lee to Adams, September 27, 1817, MHS JQA Papers, Reel 439.

48. September 29, 1817, Adams, *Memoirs,* 4:11.

49. Clay to Robert Walsh, September 6, 1817, Clay, *Papers,* 376–378.

50. Monroe to Adams, Washington, September 25, 1817, Adams, *Writings,* 6: 191–192.

51. Adams to Monroe, September 27, 1817, Library of Congress, *Papers of and Relating to James Monroe,* microfilm (Washington, 1960), Roll 7, Series 2.

52. Letter from the French consul in Boston, M. de Valnais, August 16, 1816, AMAE CPEU Philadelphie, Consulat général, no. 12.

53. Anonymous letter, Philadelphia, September 15, 1817, attached to De Grand to Adams, September 20, 1817, MHS JQA Papers, Reel 439. Unfortunately the records seem to be incomplete.

54. Aury arrived at Amelia Island two weeks after Hubbard. Davis, *MacGregor's Invasion of Florida,* 24–34. Richard Wavell, *Campañas y Cruceros Durante la Guerra de Emancipacion Hispano Americana* (Caracas: Academia Nacional de Historia, 1973), 6. The group that left from New York included Maurice Persat, a former officer of dragoons; the Italians Codazzi and Ferrari, former officers of Eugene de Beauharnais who had met with Lallemand at Constantinople; and Colonel Gravier del Valle. Persat, *Mémoires,* 18–25; Charles H. Bowman Jr., *Vicente Pazos Kanki* (La Paz: Editorial Los Amigos del Libro, 1975), 136; Charles H. Bowman, "Vicente Pazos and the Amelia Island Affair, 1817," *Florida Historical Quarterly* 53, no. 3 (Jan. 1975): 280–282; Ferrari, *Memorie Postume,* 462, and Codazzi, *Memorias,* 251.

55. Adams to Peter Paul Francis de Grand, September 29, 1817, Adams, *Writings,* 6:205n.

56. Adams to Monroe, Washington, September 29, 1817, ibid., 6:204–206.

57. Bagot to Castlereagh, October 6, 1817, BL MSS Add 20120 SHLP, ff.25–29.

58. Bagot to Castlereagh, October 8, 1817, NA FO 5/123 and BL MSS Add 20201 SHLP, ff.8–59.

59. Bagot to Castlereagh, October 21, 1817, NA FO 5/123.

Chapter 20

1. Mole to Richelieu, September 22, 1817, Montchenu, *La captivité,* 284–286.

2. Richelieu to Osmond, September 8, 1817, Richelieu, *Lettres,* 133.

3. Stuart to Castlereagh, September 1, 1817, BL MSS Add 20119 SHLP, f.332

4. Goulbourn to Lowe, September 15, 1817, and Goulbourn to Croker, September 15, 1817, NA CO 248/2, f.73 and f.180.

5. Wilson to Grey, September 12, 1817, BL MSS Add 30122 SRWP, f.31.

6. Robert T. Wilson, *A Sketch of the Military and Political Power of Russia in the Year 1817* (London, 1817), 7, 95.

7. *Quarterly Review,* September 1817, and *Courier,* London, September 12, 1817.

8. Wilson to Grey, September 13, 1817, BL MSS Add 30122 SRWP, f.33.

9. Osmond to Castlereagh, September 11, 1817, BL MSS Add 20119 SHLP, f.353.

10. Osmond to Maler, September 11, 1817, Montchenu, *La captivité,* 282–283.

11. Extract of an anonymous letter written from Philadelphia, July 24, 1827, BL MSS, Add 20119 SHLP, ff.114. Translated version reproduced in Watson, *A Polish Exile,* 287–89.

12. Stuart to Castlereagh, September 8, 1817, NA FO 27/162.

13. After being taken to Milan, Santini was imprisoned at the fortress of Mantua. Three months later he would be sent to Vienna for further interrogation. Chautard, *Noel Santini,* 290–292 and 300–301.

14. Richelieu to Osmond, September 8, 1817, Richelieu, *Lettres,* 133.

15. Hyde de Neuville to Richelieu, July 26 and 29, August 4, 1817, AMAE CPEU no. 74, ff.99, 103 and 115–126. An extract in French is in BL MSS Add, 20119 SHLP, ff.114, and a translated version in English is reproduced in Watson, *A Polish Exile,* 287–89.

16. In his memoirs Bernard Poli doesn't directly admit being part of this scheme to kidnap Napoleon II. However, he admits that he was obsessed with rescuing Napoleon from St. Helena. "Mémoires du Commandant Bernard Poli: Officier de Napoléon Ier," *Etudes Corses* 74, no. 2 (July 1954): 10, and no. 7–8 (Dec.1955): 63–64.

17. Richelieu to Osmond, September 11, 1817, Richelieu, *Lettres,* 135.

18. Unsigned letter to Sir Robert Wilson, Genoa, November 25, 1817, BL MSS Add 30108 SRWP, f.355, and Schlitter, *Kaiser Franz I und die Napoleoniden,* 424.

19. Piontkowski was imprisoned at the fortress of Mantua and for a long time his whereabouts were unknown. Lofft to Holland, December 27, 1817, BL MSS Add 51528 HHP, f.224. See also Watson, *A Polish Exile,* 165; Schlitter, *Kaiser Franz I und die Napoleoniden,* 426.

20. Wilson to Grey, October 13, 1817, BL MSS Add 30122 SRWP, f.64.

21. Wilson to Grey, October 27, 1817, BL MSS Add 30122 SRWP, f.74.

22. Wilson to Grey, October 31, 1817, BL MSS Add 30122 SRWP, ff.80–84.

23. Wellesley to Castlereagh, Madrid, October 5, 1817, NA FO 72/200.

24. Wellesley to Castlereagh, Madrid, December 23, 1817, NA FO 72/200.

25. Wilson to Grey, October 13, 1817, BL MSS Add 30122 SRWP, f.64.

26. Wilson to Grey, October 31, 1817, BL MSS Add 30122 SRWP, ff.80–84.

27. Wilson to Grey, November 4, 1817, BL MSS Add 30122 SRWP, f.88.

28. Grey to Wilson, November 30, 1817, Grey Papers, Durham University Library, GRE/B60/4/63.

29. Hutchinson to Wilson, postmarked November 11, 1817, BL MSS Add 30125 SRWP, f.50.

30. San Carlos to Court, London, November 11, 1817, AGS Estado 8289, f.162. Jimenez Codinach, *La Gran Bretaña,* 332.

31. Among the troops sent to reinforce Clausel's Army of the Pyrenees was a Spanish regiment made up of *josefinos* and others disaffected with the regime of Ferdinand VII. See Davout to Napoleon, May 13, 1815, Charles de Mazade, ed., *Correspondance du*

marechal Davout, prince d'Eckmuhl: Ses commandements, son ministere, 1801–1815 (Paris, 1885), 4:528. Regarding Renovales, see Franco, *La Batalla por el Dominio,* 1:262–266.

32. February 3, 1818, O'Meara, *Napoleon in Exile,* 2:367.

33. *Courier,* London, October 6, 1817.

34. Robert Fulton had adopted a similar solution for the *Demologos* (later renamed the *Fulton*), the steam-powered warship he had built in 1814. See Hutcheon, *Robert Fulton,* 134.

35. Grey to Wilson, December 10, 1817, Grey Papers, Durham University Library, GRE/B60/4/64.

36. Wilson to Grey, December 14 and 15, 1817, BL MSS Add 30122 SRWP, f.122 and f.125.

Chapter 21

1. Thomas de Souza Safra to Luiz de Rego Barreto, Paraiba, 25 August 1817, *Documentos do Arquivo do Pernambuco,* 1:323–324.

2. F. J. Fetis, *Biographie Universelle des Musiciens* (Paris, 1883), 7:94–95.

3. John Miller, *Memoirs of General Miller* (London, 1829), 2:343.

4. Joseph Ray to Richard Rush, Pernambuco, 21 July 1817, NARA, Consular Correspondence Pernambuco (1817–1819).

5. José Inácio Borges, Governor of Rio Grande do Norte to Luiz de Rego Barreto, Natal, 2 September 1817, *Documentos do Arquivo do Pernambuco,* 1:195–197.

6. Thomas de Souza Safra to Luiz de Rego Barreto, Paraiba, September 11, 1817, *Documentos do Arquivo do Pernambuco,* 1:323–324.

7. Ray to Sumter, October 3, 1817, NARA Correspondence of U.S. Consuls in Pernambuco, Mic. T344.

8. Manuel de Oliveira Lima, *Dom João no Brasil* (Rio de Janeiro, 1945), 2:807–808.

9. Diego Barros Arana, *Historia Jeneral de Chile* (Santiago, 1890), 11:223–230; Domingo Pérez to O'Higgins, Santiago, August 30, 1817, Carrera, *Archivo,* 18:334–335.

10. Sharpe to Croker, Secret, *Hyacinth,* off Buenos Aires, October 8, 1817, NA FO 72/218, f.122.

11. Cramer was accused of allowing a duel between two officers of his regiment and for not keeping discipline among his troops. He never had a court-martial. Zapiola, *Recuerdos de Treinta Años,* 195. Drouet had promoted an insurrection among O'Higgins's troops. See O'Higgins to San Martin, Concepcion, July 14, 1817, San Martin, *Documentos del Archivo,* 5:368.

12. To Intendente de Cuyo, September 9, 1817, AGN S.X-C5-A5-N9.

13. Brayer was also under the watchful eye of James Paroissien, chief surgeon of the army and San Martin's spy. Paroissien was an Englishman of French Huguenot ancestry who had been sent to Buenos Aires in 1808 by Admiral Sir Sidney Smith, England's master spy during the Napoleonic Wars. His mission was to prepare a third invasion of Buenos Aires by organizing a coup to oust the local government. But the hapless doctor was discovered, found guilty of spying, and imprisoned. After spending almost

eighteen months in jail, Paroissien was freed and remained in Buenos Aires as an active member of the British intelligence network. R. A. Humphreys, *Liberation in South America, 1806–1827: The Career of James Paroissien* (London: University of London, 1952), 19–21, Carlos Roberts, *Las invasiones inglesas del Rio de la Plata* (Buenos Aires: Peuser, 1938), 340–352.

14. Luzuriaga to Secretario de Estado de Gobierno, Mendoza, November 24, 1817, AGN S.X-C5-A5-N9, f.223.

15. Carrera to Skinner, September 17 1817, Carrera, *Archivo,* 19:108.

16. Skinner to Carrera, November 27, 1817, ibid., 19:187–191.

17. Carrera to Alvear, October 3, 1817, ibid., 19:129.

18. Alvear to Carrera, November 22, 1817, ibid., 19:173–174.

19. Casa Florez to Fernan Nuñez, Rio de Janeiro, November 15, 1817, AHN Estado 5845/1. Governor Rego Barreto later claimed that Latapie had confessed to him after being released that while in Philadelphia he and his fellow passengers had learned about the revolution in Pernambuco. Joseph Bonaparte, with whom they had connections, had asked them to come to Brazil to learn more about the nature of the revolution. His objective was to find the right occasion to prepare a small flotilla to facilitate Napoleon's escape from St. Helena. Rego Barreto quickly reported his findings to Rio de Janeiro. Dispatch of Luiz Rego Barreto, March 2, 1818, Augusto Ferreira da Costa, "Napoléon Ier au Brésil," *Revue du Monde Latin* 8 (May 1886): 213.

20. Chamberlain to Castlereagh, Rio de Janeiro, November 15, 1817, NA FO 63/204.

21. Paul Latapie, *Mémoire du Général Latapie, Prévenu de s'être servi, en 1815, au mois d'octobre, d'un faux ordre de route, pour se soustraire a la surveillance de l'autorité militaire et a l'action des cours prévôtales* (Paris, 1836), 11.

22. Chamberlain to Castlereagh, December 3, 1817, NA FO 63/204.

23. Chamberlain to Sharpe, Rio de Janeiro, November 18, 1817, NA FO 63/204.

24. Sharpe to Chamberlain, Buenos Aires, December 4, 1817, NA FO 63/211, f.7.

25. Bowles to Chamberlain, November 2, 1817, NA FO 63/211, f.1.

26. San Martin to the Earl of Fife, December 9, 1817, NA FO 72/215, f.184.

27. Carrera to Porter, December 12, 1817, Library of Congress, *Papers of and Relating to James Monroe,* Roll 7, Series 2.

28. O'Higgins to San Martin, Concepcion, October 1, 1817, Bernardo O'Higgins, *Archivo de don Bernardo O'Higgins* (Santiago, 1946–), 18:46.

29. O'Higgins, battle report on the action at Talcahuano, December 10, 1817, Guillermo Feliú Cruz, *Memorias del Coronel Beauchef* (Santiago: Editorial Andrés Bello, 1964), 301–302.

Chapter 22

1. James Lewis, *John Quincy Adams Policymaker for the Union* (Wilmington: SR Books, 2001), 44.

2. Adams to Monroe, Washington, October 6, 1817, Adams, *Writings,* 6:213.

3. De Grand to Adams, Boston, October 6, 1817, MHS, JQA Papers, Reel 440.

4. Charles and Henri Lallemand to William Lee, October 3, 1817, MHS JQA Papers, Reel 440.

5. Apparently MacGregor met Aury before leaving Amelia Island. See *Narrative of a Voyage to the Spanish Main*, 96.

6. *Charleston Courier*, November 14, 1817.

7. Carlos Ferro, *Vida de Luis Aury* (Buenos Aires, 1976), 51, and Persat, *Mémoires*, 29–30.

8. Adams to Monroe, Washington, October 8, 1817, Adams, *Writings*, 6:213–214.

9. Hyde de Neuville to Duc de Richelieu, New Brunswick, October 11, 1817, AMAE CPEU no. 74, ff.241–244.

10. Years later Latour joined Laffite and at the Battle of New Orleans he served as General Jackson's chief engineer. Latour was probably a double agent. In 1834 he went to Corsica to visit Lallemand, who had been appointed commander of the island's military garrison. Latour, *Historical Memoir of the War in West Florida and Louisiana*.

11. Franco, *La Batalla por el Dominio*, 1:85.

12. Galabert to Joseph, June 18, 1808, Parra-Pérez, *Bayona y la política de Napoleón*, 49.

13. Skinner to Carrera, November 27, 1817, Carrera, *Archivo*, 19:187–191. Skinner may have been exaggerating as, at least officially, the value never exceeded $5.23 per acre. Rafe Blaufarb, *Bonapartists in the Borderlands* (Tuscaloosa: University of Alabama Press, 2005), 134–135.

14. Onis to Pizarro, no. 175, Philadelphia, October 9, 1817, AHN Estado 5642/1.

15. Memorandum to Cabinet, October 1817, Monroe, *Writings*, 6:31.

16. Charles Bowman Jr., "Vicente Pazos and the Amelia Island Affair, 1817," 292.

17. Hyde de Neuville to Duc de Richelieu, New York, November 6, 1817, AMAE CPEU no. 74, ff.264–270.

18. Onis to Pizarro, no. 180, Washington, October 26, 1817, AHN Estado 5642/1.

19. Hyde de Neuville to Duc de Richelieu, New Brunswick, October 17, 1817, AMAE CPEU no. 74, ff.251–256.

20. Lakanal to Joseph, November 24, 1817, John C. Dawson, *Lakanal the Regicide* (University: University of Alabama Press, 1948), 117.

21. Alderson to Burr, November 5, 1817, Burr, *Political Correspondence*, 2:1168–1169.

22. November 9, 1817, Adams, *Memoirs*, 4:18–20.

23. Adams to De Grand, November 13, 1817, Adams, *Writings*, 6:205.

24. Monroe to Madison, November 24, 1817, Monroe, *Writings*, 4:33.

25. Adams to Rodney, Bland and Graham, Washington, November 21, 1817, Manning, *Diplomatic Correspondence*, 1:47–48.

26. Message of James Monroe to Congress, December 2, 1817, Monroe, *Writings*, 6:33–44.

27. Adams to Hyde de Neuville, December 5, 1817, Reeves, *The Napoleonic Exiles*, 76.

28. Onis to Adams, December 6, 1817, *British Foreign and State Papers* (London, 1841), 5:477.

29. Onis to Pizarro, no. 180, Washington, December 2–10, 1817, AHN Estado 5642/1.

30. Biddle to Monroe, Philadelphia, December 11, 1817, Library of Congress, *The Papers of and Relating to James Monroe*, Roll 7, Series 2.

31. Blaufarb, *Bonapartists,* 135.

32. Etienne Laborde, *Napoleon et sa Garde* (Paris, 1840), 89–93.

33. Dabbs, "Additional Notes," 351.

34. Petry to Richelieu, Philadelphia, December 31, 1817, AMAE CPEU no. 74, ff.327–332.

35. Robertson to Bagot, December 16, 1817, BL MSS Add 20120 SHLP, ff.346.

36. Onis to Pizarro, no. 209, Washington, December 18, 1817, AHN Estado 5642/1.

37. Onis to Pizarro, no. 215, Washington, December 24, 1817, AHN Estado 5642/1.

38. Petry to Richelieu, Philadelphia, December 18, 1817, AMAE CPEU no. 74, ff.297–300.

39. Petry to Richelieu, Philadelphia, December 31, 1817, AMAE CPEU no. 74, ff.327–332.

40. Aury to Monroe, December 23, 1817, Foreign Office, *British and Foreign State Papers,* vol. 5, 773. Aury's emissary was Vicente Pazos. See Bowman, "Vicente Pazos, Agent for the Amelia Island Filibusters," 428–442.

41. December 24, 1817, Adams, *Memoirs,* 4:30.

42. December 26, 1817, ibid., 4:31.

43. Adams to Charles Collins, Washington, December 31, 1817, Adams, *Writings,* 6:283–286.

Chapter 23

1. July 18, 1817, O'Meara, *Napoleon in Exile,* 2:151.

2. Basil Hall, *Narrative of a Voyage to Java, China, and the Great Loo-Choo Island* (London: E. Moxon, 1840), 76–81.

3. August 26, 1817, Montholon, *Récits,* 2:172, and August 29, 1817, Gourgaud, *Journal,* 2:227.

4. Montholon, *Récits,* 2:203.

5. Ibid., 2:205.

6. This episode was recorded by Montholon and Gourgaud on September 14, 1817. However, Montholon suggests that Napoleon was referring to Australia. Montholon, *Récits,* 2:197, and Gourgaud, *Journal,* 2:250.

7. August 22, 1817, O'Meara, *Napoleon in Exile,* 2:154–155.

8. September 16, 1817, Gourgaud, *Journal,* 2:251.

9. September 27, 1817, ibid., 2:264.

10. O'Meara to Lowe, September 13, 1817, NA J 76/4/4.

11. September 26, 1817, O'Meara, *Napoleon in Exile,* 2:240–241.

12. October 19, 1817, Montholon, *Récits,* 2:218–220.

13. October 26, 1817, Gourgaud, *Journal,* 2:264.

14. October 4, 1817, ibid., 2:271–274.

15. Bathurst to Lowe, August 19, 1817, BL MSS Add 20200 SHLP f.32.

16. October 19, 1817, Montholon, *Récits,* 2:218, and October 19, 1817, Gourgaud, *Journal,* 2:289.

17. Report of a conversation with Mr. Robinson, July 7, 1817, BL MSS Add 20204 SHLP, f.35.

18. Robinson to Lowe, October 31 1817, BL MSS Add 20120 SHLP, ff. 184.

19. Lowe to Bathurst, October 31, 1817, BL MSS Add 20120 SHLP, f.185.

20. October 4, 1817, Gourgaud, *Journal,* 2:278.

21. October 18, 1817, O'Meara, *Napoleon in Exile,* 2:280.

22. November 4 1817, ibid., 2:291–292.

23. Goulbourn to Lowe, September 15, 1817, CO 248/2 f.173 also BL MSS Add 20200 SHLP, f.78.

24. J. B. Urmston to Reade, December 1817, BL MSS Add 20120 SHLP, ff.308–314.

25. Memorandum by Joshua Wilder, Philadelphia, n.d., BL MSS Add 20119 SHLP, f.190.

26. Report no. 23, November 2, 1817, Balmain, *Reports,* 143.

27. November 18, 1817, Gourgaud, *Journal,* 2:302.

28. December 18, 1817, Montholon, *Récits,* 2:237–239.

29. November 23, 1817, Gourgaud, *Journal,* 2:305.

30. Report no. 27, December 13, 1817, Balmain, *Reports,* 146.

Chapter 24

1. Adams, *Memoirs,* 4:35.

2. Onis to Pizarro, Washington, January 6, 1818, AHN, 5643/1 1818.

3. *New York Evening Post,* January 6 and 7, 1818.

4. *National Intelligencer,* Washington, January 7, 1818; Beatrice Starr Jenkins, *William Thornton: Small Star of the American Enlightenment* (San Luis Obispo, Calif.: Merritt Starr, 1982), 126.

5. *National Intelligencer,* Washington, January 8, 1818.

6. Robert Kagan, *Dangerous Nation* (New York: Knopf, 2006), 186–87.

7. January 8, 1817, Adams, *Memoirs,* 4:36.

8. January 10, 1817, ibid., 4:37–38.

9. January 12, 1818, ibid., 4:39–40.

10. Message of Monroe to Congress, January 13, 1818, *American State Papers* (Washington, 1834), 4:139.

11. January 13, 1818, Adams, *Memoirs,* 4:40.

12. January 21, 1818, ibid., 4:44–47.

13. Extract of a letter to Adams, January 19, 1818, *British and Foreign State Papers,* 5:771.

14. Davis, *MacGregor's Invasion of Florida,* 67.

15. Anonymous letter published in 1822 in *Journal des Voyages, decouvertes et Navigations modernes,* reproduced and translated in Dabbs, "Additional Notes," 353.

16. John B. Novion to Louis Aury, New York, January 2, 1818, Guzman, "Los Hermanos Lallemand en Texas," 168–169. Months earlier Novion had been accused of privateering activities in violation of U.S. neutrality laws. He had obtained a privateering patent from the Republic of Cartagena through Pedro Gual, and Louis Aury was the captain of the ship. It was Aaron Burr who got Novion out of jail. Milton Lomask, *Aaron Burr* (New York: Farrar, Straus and Giroux, 1982), 368–369.

17. Henri Lallemand to Stephen Girard, February 7, 1818, APS Girard Papers, Reel 65, f.152.

18. Henri Lallemand to Stephen Girard, February 14, 1818, APS Girard Papers, Reel 65, f.175.

19. Pierre Laffite to Jean, New Orleans, February 17, 1818, Stanley Faye, "The Great Stroke of Pierre Laffite," *Louisiana Historical Quarterly* 23 (1940), 785–786.

20. January 22, 1818, Adams, *Memoirs,* 4:48.

21. Lee to Adams, January 20, 1818, Reeves, *The Napoleonic Exiles,* 67–68.

22. De Grand to Adams, January 15, 1818, MHS JQA Papers, Reel 442.

23. Adams to De Grand, Washington, January 21, 1818, Adams, *Writings,* 6: 289–291.

24. De Grand to Adams, Boston, January 28, 1818, MHS JQA Papers, Reel 442.

25. Skinner to John Mason, February 19, 1818, MHS JQA Papers, Reel 442.

26. Bagot to Castlereagh, Washington, February 8, 1818, Castlereagh, *Memoirs,* 11:404.

27. February 8, 1818, Adams, *Memoirs,* 4:53.

28. February 13, 1818, ibid., 4:54.

29. February 23, 1818, ibid., 4:61.

30. Biddle to Monroe, February 25, 1818, Reeves, *The Napoleonic Exiles,* 78. Biddle saw Joseph frequently in Philadelphia and considered him "the most interesting stranger that I have ever known in this country," Biddle, "Joseph Bonaparte as Recorded in the Private Journal of Nicholas Biddle," 209.

31. Onis to Pizarro, Washington, February 20, 1818, and Gravier to Pizarro, January 30, 1818, AHN, 5643/1.

32. Lallemand to Gravier, July 5 1817, and Gravier to Lallemand, New York, July 10, 1817, AHN, 5643/1.

33. Bowman, "Vicente Pazos, Agent for the Amelia Island Filibusters," 432.

34. *Evening Post,* New York, February 24, 1818.

35. Adams to Peter Paul Francis de Grand, Washington, March 1, 1818, Adams, *Writings,* 6:299–300.

36. Biddle to Monroe, March 5, 1818, Reeves, *The Napoleonic Exiles,* 78. In fact,

during the last months of 1817 and the first of 1818, total sales of Tombigbee lands amounted to more than thirty thousand dollars, and most of this money was used to finance the Champ d'Asile. Blaufarb, *Bonapartists,* 135.

37. Guillemin to Artois, March 4, 1818, AMAE Etats-Unis, no. 75, f.80.

38. Adams, *Memoirs,* March 18, 1818, 4:61.

39. Onis to Pizarro, Washington, March 13, 1818, AHN, 5643/1.

40. H. R. 27, March 19, 1818, Bills and Resolutions of Congress.

41. Henry Clay, speech to Congress, March, 1818, John Latané, *The Diplomatic Relations of the United States and Spanish America* (Baltimore: Johns Hopkins Press, 1900), 59. Clay also supported the presentation in the House of Representatives of a memorial of Vicente Pazos, Aury's representative, and requested all relevant documentation from the State Department.

42. Adams, *Memoirs,* 4:90. Among the documents in the dossier were extracts from a letter sent to Adams by John Stuart Skinner, without the section in which Skinner denied a connection between MacGregor and the British government. *American State Papers,* 4:602–605.

43. House Journal, Session of March 26, 1818, *Journal of the House of Representatives of the United States, 1817–1818,* 338.

44. Pizarro to Onis, Madrid, February 20, 1818, AHN Estado 5660/1 1818.

45. *National Intelligencer,* Washington, March 28, 1818.

46. Henri Lallemand to Girard, February 20, 1818, APS Girard Papers, Reel 66, f.198.

47. Henri Lallemand to Girard, March 30, 1818, APS Girard Papers, Reel 66, f.339.

48. Lorenzo de Zavala, *Ensayo Historico de las Revoluciones de Mexico desde 1808 hasta 1830* (Mexico, 1845), 1:79

49. Guillemin to Richelieu, New Orleans, February 16, 1818, AMAE CPEU no. 75, f.59.

50. L. Hartmann and M. Maillard, *Le Texas ou Notice Historique sur le Champ d'Asile comprenant tout ce qui s'est passé depuis la formation jusqu'a la dissolution de cette colonie* (Paris: Beguin, 1819), 12.

51. Just Girard, *Les Aventures d'un Capitaine Français a Texas* (Tours, 1860), 65.

Chapter 25

1. Hutchinson to Wilson, February 26, 1818, BL MSS Add 30125 SRWP, f.63 and Wilson to Grey, January 12, 1818, BL MSS Add 30122 SRWP, f.144.

2. Wilson to Grey, February 21, 1818, BL MSS Add 30122 SRWP, f.169.

3. Las Cases to Wilson, Hamburg, February 11, 1818, BL MSS Add 30108 SRWP, f.385.

4. In 1817, while cruising the Caribbean the Royal Navy confiscated one of Brown's prizes. As a result, Brown went to London to obtain an indemnification. Guillermo Brown, *Memorias del Almirante Brown* (Buenos Aires, 1957), 187.

5. San Carlos to Castlereagh, January 23, 1818, AGS Estado 8289. (A copy also NA FO 72/216 Duke of San Carlos, f.6.) See also San Carlos to Pezuela, Virrey del Peru, London, February 7, 1818, San Martin, *Documentos del Archivo,* 5:173–174.

6. Renovales to Castlereagh, London, January 9, 1818, NA FO 72/218.

7. Hamilton (Foreign Office) to Harrison (Customs House), January 31, 1818, NA FO 72/218, f.82 and f.84.

8. Osmond to Richelieu, no. 173, January 6, 1818, AMAE CPA, no. 611, 1818.

9. Richelieu to Osmond, January 22, 1818, Richelieu, *Lettres,* 148.

10. Richelieu to Noailles, Paris, January 20, 1818, Polovtsoff, *Correspondance diplomatique.* 2:556.

11. Richelieu to Osmond, January 29, 1818, Richelieu, *Lettres,* 151–152.

12. Richelieu to Osmond, February 5, 1818, ibid., 152–153.

13. Castlereagh to San Carlos, February 11, 1818, AGS Estado 8289.

14. San Carlos to Court, London, no. 70, March 4, 1818, AGS Estado 8289.

15. Confidential Note no. 4, London, February 6, 1818, AGS Estado 8312, and San Carlos to Castlereagh, February 6, 1818, NA FO 72/216, f.44.

16. Osmond to Richelieu, no. 178 February 3, 1818, AMAE CPA, 1818.

17. Harrison to Hamilton, February 10, 1818, NA FO 72/218, f. 173.

18. Osmond to Richelieu, no. 179, February 6, 1818, AMAE CPA, 1818.

19. Osmond to Richelieu, no. 181, February 13, 1818, AMAE CPA, 1818.

20. Richelieu to Osmond, February 9, 1818, Richelieu, *Lettres,* 153–154.

21. Richelieu to Osmond, February 16, 1818, ibid., 154.

22. Richelieu to Osmond, February 23 and March 29, 1818, ibid., 159, 170.

23. *Courier,* London, March 28, 1818, and *British Monitor,* London, March 29, 1818.

24. A. G. Claveau, *De la Police de Paris, de ses abus, et des réformes dont elle est susceptible, avec documents anecdotiques et politiques, pour servir a l'histoire judiciaire de la Restauration* (Paris, 1831), 442–443. Cantillon was later acquitted for lack of evidence and Napoleon rewarded him in his will.

25. Richelieu to Osmond, February 23, and March 29, 1818, Richelieu, *Lettres,* 159, 170.

26. *La Minerve Française,* Paris, March 15, 1818.

27. Richelieu to Osmond, March 19, 1818, Richelieu, *Lettres,* 169.

28. *Courier,* London, March 28, 1818.

29. *British Monitor,* London, March 1, 1818.

30. *British Monitor,* London, March 29, 1818.

31. Wilson to Grey, March 9, 1818, BL MSS Add 30122 SRWP, f.184.

32. *Examiner,* London, April 12, 1818, and *Courier,* London, April 6, 1818.

33. Wilson to Grey, March 19, BL MSS Add 30122 SRWP, f.190.

34. Samuel, *An Astonishing Fellow,* 188, and Bruce, *Lavallette Bruce,* 315.

35. March 26–28, 1818, in BL MSS Add 47235 Broughton Papers, f.8.

36. Wilson to Grey, March 10, 1818, BL MSS Add 30122 SRWP, f.186.

37. Hutchinson to Wilson, April 2, 1818, BL MSS Add 30125 SRWP, f.65.

38. *Courier,* London, March 28, 1819.

39. San Carlos to Castlereagh, Confidential, April 13, 1818, NA FO 72/216, f.137.

40. *British Monitor,* London, May 10, 1818.

41. San Carlos to Court, no. 191, June 2, 1818, AGS Estado 8289.

42. Franco, *La Batalla por el Dominio,* 1:273–274.

43. Le Moyne to Osmond, March 23, 1818 in Mario Belgrano, *La Francia y la Monarquía en el Plata* (Buenos Aires: Librería de A. Garcia Santos, 1933), 20. Also in Joaquín Pérez, *Artigas y San Martín y los proyectos monárquicos en el Río de la Plata y Chile 1818–1820* (Montevideo, 1960), 28.

44. Osmond to Richelieu, March 31, 1818, Belgrano, *La Francia y la Monarquía,* 21–24.

45. Richelieu to Osmond, March 30, 1818, Richelieu, *Lettres,* 172. Some Argentine historians have mistakenly asserted that Le Moyne first proposed the mission to Osmond and then traveled to Paris to convince Richelieu. It is another example of careless research. Ernesto J. Fitte, "Los Franceses en 1819: Del Periodismo a la Conspiracion," *Separata de la Revista Historia* 46 (1966).

46. Serurier to Richelieu, Paris, April 20, 1818, Villanueva, *La monarquía en América,* 72.

Chapter 26

1. Chamberlain to Sharpe, Rio de Janeiro, November 18, 1817, NA FO 72/218, f.246.

2. Ray to Adams, Pernambuco, February 18, 1818, NARA, Consular Correspondence Pernambuco (1817–1819), Roll 1.

3. Ferreira da Costa, Napoleon Ier au Brésil, 215–216.

4. Fréderic Masson, *Napoleon et sa famille,* Paris, 1918, 12:249.

5. Decatur to Daniel Smith, April 1818, Irvin Anthony, *Decatur* (New York: C. Scribner, 1931), 270.

6. Ferreira da Costa, "Napoleon Ier au Brésil," 340–341.

7. Bowles to Croker, February 14, 1818, NA ADM 1/23.

8. Chamberlain to Castlereagh, April 6, 1818, NA FO 63/211, ff.257–260.

9. Emilio Ocampo, "Brayer, Un general de Napoleón que desafió a San Martin," *Todo es Historia* 455 (June 2005): 60–77.

10. Leopoldo Ornstein, *De Chacabuco a Maipo Continuación de "La campaña de los Andes a la luz de las doctrinas de guerra modernas"* (Buenos Aires: Circulo Militar, 1933), 117.

11. Alejandro Chelen Rojas, *El Guerrillero Manuel Rodríguez y su hermano Carlos. Precursores de la democracia y la libertad* (Santiago: Ed. Pla., 1964), 97.

12. Ricardo A. Latcham, *Vide de Manuel Rodríguez: El guerrillero* (Santiago: Edit. Nascimento, 1932), 242–243.

13. Samuel Haigh, *Sketches of Buenos Ayres and Chile* (London, 1831), 197.

14. Francisco Encina, *Historia de Chile desde la prehistoria hasta 1891* (Santiago:

Edit. Nascimento, 1947), 7:502; Latcham, *Manuel Rodríguez,* 235–243; and Ocampo, "Brayer, Un general de Napoleón," 60–77.

15. O'Higgins to San Martin, September 9, 1817, San Martin, *Documentos del Archivo,* 5:399.

Chapter 27

1. Las Cases to Joseph, Frankfurt, February 21, 1818, and Bertrand to Joseph, March 15, 1818, in Joseph Bonaparte, *Mémoires et Correspondance Politique et Militaire du Roi Joseph,* ed. A. du Casse (Paris: Perrotin, 1853–1854), 10:248, 250.

2. Dorian, *Un Bordelais: Stephen Girard,* 140.

3. Ivo Rens, *Introduction au Socialisme Rationnel de Colins* (Neuchatel: La Baconniere, 1968), 34–65. Colins's aerostat project is also discussed in Beaucour, "Plans to Deliver Napoleon from St. Helena," 232.

4. *National Intelligencer,* Washington, April 23, 1818.

5. Adams to Peter Paul Francis de Grand, Washington, April 20, 1818, Adams, *Writings,* 6:310–311.

6. *National Intelligencer,* Washington, April 29, 1818.

7. Henri Lallemand to Stephen Girard, April 30, 1818, APS Girard Papers, Reel 66, f.389.

8. Onis to Pizarro, Washington, April 6, 1818, AHN Estado 5642/1.

9. Jacques Galabert, "Las Americas, Los Ingleses, Los Estados Unidos y la España," Philadelphia, April 25, 1818, AGI Estado Leg. 90, 1226.

10. Joseph to Girard, April 24, 1818, APS Girard Papers, Reel 66, f.446.

11. Jose L. Franco, *Documentos para la Historia de Mexico* (La Habana: Archivo Nacional de Cuba, 1961), 214–215.

12. *L'Abeille Americaine,* Philadelphia, April 23, 1818.

13. Hyde de Neuville to Richelieu, April 28, 1818, AMAE CPEU no. 75, ff.154–158.

14. Onis to Pizarro, Washington, April 22, 1818, 72, AHN Estado 5643/2.

15. Onis to Pizarro, Washington, April 28, 1818, AHN Estado 5643/2.

16. April 30, 1818, Adams, *Memoirs,* 4:83–84.

17. Bagot to Castlereagh, May 6, 1818, NA FO 5/132, f.38.

18. Onis to Hyde de Neuville, May 1, 1818, AMAE CPEU no. 75, f.159.

19. Onis to Pizarro, Washington, May 8, 1818, AHN EUA Estado 5643/2.

20. Hyde de Neuville to Onis, May 8, 1818, AMAE CPEU no. 75, f.169.

21. Hyde de Neuville to Richelieu, May 8, 1818, AMAE CPEU no. 75, f.169.

22. Onis to Adams, May 7, 1818, Manning, *Diplomatic Correspondence,* 3:1966.

23. May 25, 1818, Adams, *Memoirs,* 4:100.

24. Adams to Rush, May 19 and 20, 1818, Adams, *Writings,* 6:312–327.

25. Robertson to Bagot, Philadelphia, May 28, 1818, Castlereagh, *Memoirs,* 11: 441–443.

26. Henri Lallemand to Girard, Philadelphia, May 28, 1818, APS Girard Papers,

Reel 66, f.560. Parts also reproduced in McMaster, *The Life and Times of Stephen Girard,* 2:342–343

27. Petry to Hyde de Neuville, May 19, 1818, AMAE CPEU no. 75, ff.178–180.

28. Report by Guillemin, New Orleans, May 25, 1818, AMAE CPEU no. 75, ff.283–293.

29. Hyde de Neuville to Richelieu, June 4, 1818, Hyde de Neuville, *Mémoires,* 367–371.

30. Adams to Graham, June 2, 1818, Walter Pritchard, "George Graham's Mission to Galveston in 1818," *Louisiana Historical Quarterly* 20, no. 3 (July 1937), 640–642.

31. Adams to Louisa Catherine Adams, Washington, 7 October, [1821], Adams, *Writings,* 7:33.

32. Monroe to Jackson, December 28, 1817, Philip Coolidge Brooks, *Diplomacy and the Borderlands: The Adams-Onis Treaty of 1819* (Berkeley: University of California Press, 1939), 140.

33. Robert Remini, *The Life of Andrew Jackson* (New York: Penguin, 1990), 122.

34. Remini, *Henry Clay,* 154.

35. Adams, *Memoirs,* June 15, 1818, 4:105–108.

36. *National Intelligencer,* Washington, July 11, 1818.

37. Bagot to Castlereagh, June 29, 1818, Castlereagh, *Memoirs,* 10:458. Also Adams, *Memoirs,* 4:104–105.

38. Hyde de Neuville to Richelieu, July 15, 1818, Hyde de Neuville, *Mémoires,* 374.

39. John Quincy Adams to George Erving, Ambassador in Madrid, November 28, 1818, Hubert Bruce Fuller, *The Purchase of Florida: Its History and Diplomacy* (Cleveland: Burrows Brothers, 1906), 340, 350, and 352.

40. See Kent Gardien, "Take Pity on Our Glory: Men of Champ d'Asile," *Southwestern Historical Quarterly* 87, no. 3 (Jan. 1984): 241–268.

41. Anonymous letter, Reeves, *The Napoleonic Exiles,* 89–90.

42. Fatio to Cienfuegos, New Orleans, June 27, 1818, Guzman, "Los Hermanos Lallemand en Texas," 172.

Chapter 28

1. Baron Sturmer to Prince Metternich, January 8, 1818, Barthelemi von Sturmer, *Napoléon a Sainte-Hélène, Rapports Officiels du Baron Sturmer commissaire du gouvernement autrichien,* ed. Hans Schlitter (Paris: Librairie illustrée, 1885), 148.

2. January 5, 1818, Gourgaud, *Journal,* 2:329.

3. Bertrand, *Cahiers,* 2:53.

4. January 1, 1818, Gourgaud, *Journal,* 2:326–327.

5. Report no. 1, January 1, 1818, Balmain, *Reports,* 153.

6. Plampin to Melville, St. Helena, 25 January 1818, M. Dechaux, "Un projet d'evasion de Sainte-Hélène," *Revue des Etudes Napoléoniennes* 34 (Jan.–June 1932): 302, and Sharpe to Chamberlain, December 4, 1817, NA FO 63/211, f.7.

7. Sturmer's report dated March 14, 1818, Sturmer, *Napoleon a Sainte-Hélène,* 169.

8. Unnumbered report, February 15, 1818, Balmain, *Reports,* 162.

9. January 28, 1818, Montholon, *Récits,* 2:249.

10. January 28 and 30, 1818, Gourgaud, *Journal,* 2:343, 346, and January 30, 1818, Bertrand, *Cahiers,* 2:19.

11. Report no. 3, January 15, 1818, Balmain, *Reports,* 161.

12. February 1, 1818, Gourgaud, *Journal,* 2:348.

13. January 30, 1818, Bertrand, *Cahiers,* 2:42, 138–139.

14. February 3, 1818, O'Meara, *Napoleon in Exile,* 2:369–370.

15. Bertrand, *Cahiers,* 2:59.

16. Montholon to the Chevalier de Beauterne, 1841, in Primrose, *Napoleon: The Last Phase,* 48.

17. February 2, 1818, Gourgaud, *Journal,* 2:349–351.

18. January 11, 1818, Montholon, *Récits,* 2:247.

19. January 30, 1818, Bertrand, *Cahiers,* 2:52–53.

20. February 11, 1818, Sturmer's report, Sturmer, *Napoléon a Sainte-Helene,* 150.

21. February 4, 1818, Montchenu, *La Captivité,* 138–139.

22. Sturmer to Metternich, May 14, 1818, in Sturmer, *Napoléon a Sainte-Helene,* 150, and Young, *Napoleon in Exile,* 2:88–89. Gourgaud later refuted many of the assertions made by Sturmer. Gourgaud, *Lettre de Sir Walter Scott,* 16–19.

23. Bertrand, *Cahiers,* 2:101.

24. February 10, 1818, Montholon, *Récits,* 2:251.

25. Forsyth, *History of the Captivity,* 2:247.

26. Montholon to Gourgaud, n.d., Fréderic Masson, *Autour de Sainte-Hélène, cinquieme edition* (Paris: P. Ollendorff, 1909), 1:90–91.

27. Marchand, *Mémoires,* 429–430.

28. Goulbourn to Lowe, January 6, 1818, NA CO 248/2.

29. Forsyth, *History of the Captivity,* 3:43–44.

30. Marchand, *Mémoires,* 432.

31. Bertrand to Joseph, March 15, 1818, Joseph Bonaparte, *Mémoires et Correspondance Politique,* 10:250.

32. Report of March 14, 1818, Balmain, *Reports,* 164.

33. April, 1818, Bertrand, *Cahiers,* 2:52–53.

34. Balmain's report no. 13, April 15, 1818, Balmain, *Reports,* 170.

35. Balmain no. 17, May 11, 1818, ibid., 177.

36. April 10, May 9 and May 16, 1818, O'Meara, *Napoleon in Exile,* 2:399–401.

37. Bertrand, *Cahiers,* 2:133–134.

38. Bathurst to Lowe, April 23, 1818, Forsyth, *History of the Captivity,* 3:43–44.

39. Balmain to Lieven, July 28, 1818, BL MSS Add 47272 Balmain's Correspondence with Lieven, f.24.

40. July 25, 1818, O'Meara, *Napoleon in Exile,* 2:416.

41. Bertrand, *Cahiers,* 2:124–125, 209.

42. Report no. 23, July 23, 1818, Balmain, *Reports,* 184.

Chapter 29

1. D. Hamy, "Les Voyages de Richard Grandsire de Calais dans l'Amérique du Sud," *Journal de la Societé des Americanistes de Paris* 5 (1908): 1–20.

2. The Bonapartists criticized Maler for his conduct in this affair. *La Minerve Française,* Paris, August 1818 and April 1819.

3. Villanova to Casa Florez, May 30, 1818, attached to Casa Florez to Fernan Nuñez, Rio de Janeiro, August 8, 1818, AHN EUA 5846.

4. Chamberlain to Castlereagh, Rio de Janeiro, May 30, 1818, NA FO 63/212.

5. Guillon, *Les Complots Militaires,* 7.

6. Philibert Fressinet], *Appel Aux Generations Presente et Futures* (Geneve, 1817), 42–43, and Eugene Vitrolles, *Mémoires et relations politiques du baron de Vitrolles, publiés, selon le vœu de l'auteur, par Eugene Forgues* (Paris: Charpentier, 1884) 3:87.

7. Interrogation of Bulewski, AGN SX.C.29.A10.N2 Exp. 139–161

8. Jung's name is sometimes spelled Yung or Young. He led the Corps francs de la Moselle, which under General Meriage slowed the advance of the Prussian army after Waterloo. Vaulabelle, *Histoire,* 3:410, and Guillaume de Vaudoncourt, *Quinze années,* 2:137–138. Another officer who accompanied Jung was Colonel Fabvier, who will play a role later in the story. Antonin Debidour, *Le Général Fabvier: Sa vie militaire et politique* (Paris: Plon, 1904), 105.

9. Declarations of Mercher, Bulewski, and Lagresse, 1818 and 1819 in AGNA SX.C.29.A10.N5, 227–272 and SX.C.29.A10.N2, 139–161.

10. Henri Papillaud, *Le journalisme français a Buenos Aires de 1818 jusqu'a nos jours* (Buenos Aires: Lasserre, 1947).

11. Amunategui, *La Dictadura de O'Higgins,* 105.

12. O'Higgins to San Martin, September 9, 1817, San Martin, *Documentos del Archivo,* 5:399.

13. Haigh, *Sketches,* 246.

14. Ibid., 243.

15. Worthington to Adams, Buenos Aires, March 7, 1819, Manning, *Diplomatic Correspondence,* 1:434–435.

16. Ibid., 243–244, and W. B. Stevenson, *A Historical Narrative of Twenty Years' Residence in South America* (London: Hurst, Robinson, 1825), 3:189–190.

17. Bowles to Croker, December 6, 1818, NA ADM 1/24. Many historians however insist that San Martin had nothing to do with the execution of the Carrera brothers. It is absurd to argue that a decision with such massive political implications would be taken without the approval of San Martin and Pueyrredon. Joaquín Pérez, *San Martín y José Miguel Carrera* (Buenos Aires: Univ. Nac. Eva Peron, 1954), 78–89, for a defense of San Martin.

18. Zapiola, *Recuerdos de Treinta Años,* 197–198.

19. Haigh, *Sketches,* 215. See also Ocampo, "Brayer, Un general de Napoleón," 60–77.

20. Chamberlain to Castlereagh, May 20, 1818, NA FO 63/212.

21. San Martin to Castlereagh, Santiago, April 11, 1818, NA FO 72/215, f.204.

22. Bowles to Croker, June 10, 1818, Buenos Aires, British mediation, NA ADM 1/23.

23. Skinner to Carrera, Baltimore, March 28, 1818, Carrera, *Archivo*, 21:72.

Chapter 30

1. *Courier*, London, May 7, 1818.

2. Bathurst to Lowe, May 5, 1818, BL MSS Add 20201 SHLP, ff.114 also NA CO 248/2, ff.226–227.

3. Goulbourn to Bathurst, May 10, 1818, BL MSS Add 20201 SHLP. Gourgaud later asserted that the report prepared by Goulbourn distorted their conversation. See Gourgaud, *Lettre de Sir Walter Scott*, 20.

4. Goulbourn to Croker, May 14, 1818, NA ADM 1/4237.

5. Jacques Macé, "Journal Inedit du General Gourgaud, 1818–1821," *Revue de l'Institut Napoléon* 187, 2:(2003), 76.

6. Richelieu to Osmond, May 11, 1818, Richelieu, *Lettres*, 183.

7. Richelieu to Osmond, May 17, 1818, ibid., 185.

8. Richelieu to Osmond, May 18, 1818, ibid., 186.

9. *British Monitor*, London, May 17, 1818.

10. Osmond to Richelieu, May 15 1818, Masson, *Autour de St. Helene*, 1:239.

11. San Carlos to Castlereagh, May 11, 1818, NA FO 72/216.

12. Duke of San Carlos to Pizarro, London, May 3, 1818, Belgrano, *La Francia y la Monarquía*, 20–24.

13. *Narrative of a Voyage*, 1–4 and 28.

14. Richelieu to Osmond, May 25, 1818, Richelieu, *Lettres*, 188–189.

15. Richelieu to Osmond, May 27, 1818, ibid., 189–190.

16. Richelieu to Osmond, May 28, 1818, ibid., 193.

17. *Examiner*, London, June 19, 1818.

18. The meeting took place on May 16, 1818. Macé, "Journal Inedit du General Gourgaud," 78.

19. Lieven to Nesselrode, May 23, 1818, Masson, *Autour*, 1:242.

20. Osmond to Richelieu, May 26, 1818, ibid., 1:241.

21. Macé, "Journal Inedit du General Gourgaud,"81.

22. Gallatin to Monroe, Paris, June 18, 1818, Manning, *Diplomatic Correspondence* 2:1379.

23. Richelieu to Osmond, June 25 and 29, 1818, Richelieu, *Lettres*, 200–201.

24. Wilson to Grey, July 17, 1818, BL MSS Add 30122 SRWP, f. 218.

25. *Hansard's Parliamentary Debates*, 32:1150; *Courier*, London, June 5, 1818.

26. Tute, *Cochrane*, 169.

27. Loose note, AGS Estado 8312.

28. *Naval Chronicler,* 39:280.

29. Richelieu to Osmond, July 27, 1818, Richelieu, *Lettres,* 210.

30. *British Monitor,* London, June 14, 1818.

31. Osmond to Richelieu, no. 198, London, July 17, 1818, in AMAE CPA, no. 611, 1818.

32. San Carlos to Pizarro, London, July 10, 1818, AGS Estado 8277. See also Edmundo A. Heredia, "Un plan Europeo para la Independencia Americana (Londres, 1818)," *Anuario de Estudios Americanos* 35, no. 1 (1978): 179–196.

33. Richelieu to Osmond, August 6, 1818, Richelieu, *Lettres,* 212.

34. Osmond to Richelieu, no. 200, August 14, 1818, AMAE CPA, 1818.

35. Goulbourn to Lowe, August 1818, BL MSS Add 20201 SHLP f.162.

36. Testimony by captain Wauchope, commander of HMS Eurydice, BL MSS Add 20155 SHLP, f.52.

37. Wilson to Grey, September 1818, BL MSS Add 30122 SRWP, ff.244–245.

38. Esterhazy to Metternich, London August 7, 1818, Schlitter, *Kaiser Franz I und die Napoleoniden,* 431.

39. Wilson to Grey, September 1818, BL MSS Add 30122 SRWP, ff.244–245. Gourgaud's meetings with Wilson are reported in his own diary. Macé, "Journal Inedit du General Gourgaud," 85. Latapie also confirmed his meetings with Gourgaud. Latapie, *Mémoire du Général Latapie,* 11.

40. *Courier,* London, October 1, 1818.

41. *Journal des Debats Politiques et Literaires,* Paris, August 15, 1818.

42. San Carlos to Pizarro, London, August 31, 1818, no. 313, AGS Estado 8289, and Faye, "Commodore Aury," 647.

43. Richelieu to Osmond, August 6, 1818, Richelieu, *Lettres,* 212.

44. National Archives of Scotland, Papers of Lord Cochrane, GD233 Box 44 23 Alexander Galloway correspondence on *Rising Star.*

45. Bertrand to Las Cases, St. Helena, March 15, 1818, Joseph Bonaparte, *Mémoires et Correspondance Politique,* 10:250.

46. Las Cases to Joseph, Frankfurt, August 16, 1818, ibid., 10:250–251.

47. Richelieu to Montmorency-Laval, August 6, 1818, Mario Belgrano, *La Francia y la Monarquía,* 77.

48. *Courier,* London, September 7, 1818.

49. *Courier,* London, September 18, 1818.

50. *Globe,* London, September 18, 1818, and *Examiner,* London, September 23, 1818.

Chapter 31

1. *Niles' Weekly Register,* August 8, 1818.

2. Petry to Richelieu, Philadelphia, August 29, 1818, AMAE CPEU no. 75, f.39.

3. Adams to De Grand, Washington, August 17, 1818, MHS JQA Papers, Reel 147.

4. Petry to Richelieu, Philadelphia, August 31, 1818, AMAE CPEU no. 75, f.43.

5. Lallemand to Girard, Champ d'Asile, July 10, 1818, APS Girard Papers, Reel 66, f.704 ss.

6. Hartmann and Millard, *Le Texas,* 58.

7. Graham to Adams, n.d., Pritchard, "George Graham's Mission to Galveston," 645–647.

8. Faye, "The Great Stroke of Pierre Laffite," 798; Harris G. Warren, "Documents Relating to George Graham's Proposal to Jean Laffite," *Louisiana Historical Quarterly* 21 (1938), 213–219; and Jimenez Codinach, "La Confederation napoléonienne," 59.

9. Guillemin to Cabinet, New Orleans, September 16, 1818, AMAE CPEU no. 75, ff. 65–67.

10. Guillemin to Hyde de Neuville, New Orleans, September 25, 1818, AMAE CPEU no. 75, f.74.

11. San Carlos to Pizarro, London, July 10, 1818, AGS Estado 8277.

12. Renovales to Fatio, New Orleans, September 12, 1818, Franco, *La Batalla por el Dominio,* 1:284.

13. Renovales to Intendente Ramirez, New Orleans, September 30, 1818, ibid., 1:285.

14. Hartmann and Maillard, *Le Texas,* 63.

15. Ibid., 67.

16. Guillemin to Hyde de Neuville, New Orleans, October 3, 1818, AMAE CPEU no. 75, f.76.

17. Guillemin to Hyde de Neuville, New Orleans, October 8, 1818, AMAE CPEU no. 75, f.76.

18. Agreement between Felipe Fatio and Mariano Renovales, New Orleans, December 5, 1818, AGS Estado 8312.

19. Onis to Pizarro, October 31, 1818, no. 163, AHN Estado 5644.

20. Emmanuel de Grouchy, *Observations sur la Relation de la Campagne de 1815 publiee par le General Gourgaud* (Philadelphia, 1818). Apparently, Napoleon was disappointed by Gourgaud's account of the battle of Waterloo. Lowe to Bathurst, May 14, 1821, BL MSS Add 20133 SHLP, f.205.

21. Onis to Pizarro, November 20, 1818, and Onis to Pizarro, November 25, 1818, AHN Estado 5644. Also Keen, *David Curtis de Forest,* 146–149.

22. Poinsett to Adams, November 4, 1818, Manning, *Diplomatic Correspondence,* 1:441.

23. *National Intelligencer,* Washington, December 12, 1818.

24. Onis to Casa Irujo, December 23, 1818, no. 221, AHN Estado 5644.

25. Onis to Casa Irujo, December 29, 1818, no. 242, AHN Estado 5644.

26. Keen, *David Curtis de Forest,* 150–152.

27. Miguel Angel de Marco, *Los Corsarios Argentinos* (Buenos Aires: Planeta, 2002), 182–183.

28. Gardien, "Take Pity on Our Glory" 258.

29. *New York Evening Post,* New York, December 17, 1818.

Chapter 32

1. Daniel Hamerly Dupuy, "El Naturalista Bonpland y la Conspiracion de Jose Carrera contra O'Higgins y San Martin," *Revista Historia* 13 (1958): 84.

2. Bowles to Croker, Secret, Buenos Aires, August 20, 1818, NA FO 72/221, f.282.

3. Manuel A. Pueyrredon, *Memorias Inéditas* (Buenos Aires, 1947), 258–262, Bernardo O'Higgins, "Indicación de O'Higgins a la cita del teniente general don Miguel Brayer," in Carrera, *Archivo*, 22:59–77, and Juan R. Balcarce and others, *Contestación de los Jefes del Ejercito Unido de los Andes y Chile al manifiesto del ex mayor general D. Miguel Brayer, sobre su conducta en el tiempo que permaneció en Sud-América* (Santiago, 1818).

4. *Journal des Debates Politiques et Literaires,* Paris, August 15, 1815.

5. *La Minerve Française,* Paris, August 1818, and April 1819.

6. Bonpland to Robert, Buenos Aires, September 7, 1818, AGN SX.C.29.A10. N5 Sumarios Militares Letra C Expedientes 227–272. Regarding Colonel Deschamps see Danielle and Bernard Quintin, *Dictionnaire des Colonels de Napoleon* (Paris: SPM, 1996).

7. Bonpland to Robert, Buenos Aires, August 28, 1818, AGN SX.C.29.A10.N5, 227–272.

8. Le Moyne to Osmond, London, February, 19 1819, Miguel Cané, *La diplomacia de la revolución: El Director Pueyrredón y el enviado Le Moyne* (Buenos Aires: Ed. Devenir, 1960), 46–48.

9. Patricia Pasquali, *San Martín Confidencial* (Buenos Aires: Planeta, 2000), 116.

10. Pérez, *Artigas y San Martín,* 39–40.

11. Bowles to Croker, Buenos Aires, August 8, 1818, ADM 1/24.

12. Bonpland to Robert, Buenos Aires, September 7, 1818, AGN S.X-C29-A10-N5, 227–272.

13. Quintin, *Dictionnaire des Colonels,* 529.

14. Brayer to Robert, Buenos Aires, August 27, 1818, AGN S.X-C29-A10-N5, 227–272.

15. San Martin to Guido, October 7, 1818, Pasquali, *San Martín Confidencial,* 115.

16. Brown, *Memorias,* 188.

17. Le Moyne to Osmond, September 2, 1818, Cané, *La diplomacia de la revolución,* 33.

18. Hugo Chumbita and Diego Herrera Vegas, *El Manuscrito de Joaquina: San Martín y el Secreto de la familia Alvear* (Buenos Aires: Ed. Catálogos, 2007), 60.

19. Miguel Brayer, *Manifiesto de la conducta del Teniente General Brayer, en el tiempo que ha permanecido en la América del Sud,* Montevideo, 1818, Carrera, *Archivo,* 21:77–85. Many contemporaries thought Cramer's intervention was crucial for the victory. See Miguel L. Amunategui, *Don Bernardo O'Higgins juzgado por algunos de sus contemporáneos, según documentos inéditos* (Santiago: Imprenta Universitaria, 1917), 34. See also Patrick Puigmal, "Diálogo de Sordos entre San Martin y Brayer; Cartas, Artículos y Manifiestos Argentinos, Chilenos y Franceses durante la Independencia Chilena (1817–1819)," *V Congreso Argentino Chileno de Integración Cultural* (San Juan, 2003).

20. Carrera to Poinsett, October 9, 1818, Carrera, *Archivo,* 21:72.

21. Bowles to Croker, Buenos Aires, November 19, 1818, NA ADM 1/24.

22. Carrera to Porter, Montevideo, October 10, 1818, Library of Congress, *Papers of and relating to James Monroe,* Roll 7, Series 2.

23. Bonpland to Wilson, Buenos Aires, October 20, 1818, BL MSS Add 30108 SRWP, f.424.

24. Pérez, *Artigas y San Martín,* 59.

25. Bowles to Croker, Buenos Aires, November 19, 1818, NA ADM 1/24.

26. Robert to Carrera, November 12, 1818, Carrera, *Archivo,* 22:132–133.

27. Bonpland to Le Breton, Buenos Aires, November 1818, AGN S.X-C29-A10-N5 Sumarios Militares Letra C Expedientes, 227–272, no. 78.

28. Bowles to Croker, November 22, 1818, NA FO 72/229 Spain Domestic, f.154.

29. Maria Rosa Labastie, "El Complot de los Franceses y sus vinculaciones con la Emancipación Americana," *IV Congreso Internacional de Historia de América,* Buenos Aires, 1966, 2:345–363. Other articles on the subject are: Hector Viacava, "La Conspiración de los franceses," *Revista Todo es Historia* 150 (Nov. 1979): 52–69; Jorge C. Bohdziewicz, "Resumen Documentado de la Causa Criminal Seguida y Sentenciada contra los Reos Carlos Robert, Juan Lagresse, Agustin Dragumette, Narciso Parchappe y Marcos Mercher por el Delito de Conspiración" (Buenos Aires: Biblioteca F.V., 1976); Ernesto Fitte, *Los Franceses en 1818: Del Periodismo a la Conspiración* (Buenos Aires: Talleres Gráficos Dorrego, 1966). With respect to Bonpland's role in the conspiracy see Dupuy, "El Naturalista Bonpland y la Conspiración de Jose Carrera contra O'Higgins y San Martin," 83–94.

30. Pueyrredon to San Martin, November 24, 1818, Carrera, *Archivo,* 22:132. Hipolito Villegas to Bernardo O'Higgins, Santiago, November 27, 1818, Archivo Historico de la Provincia de Buenos Aires, *Documentos del Congreso de Tucumán* (La Plata, 1947), 245.

31. Chamberlain to Castlereagh, Rio de Janeiro, January 23, 1819, NA FO 63/220, f.63.

32. Tomás de Iriarte, *Memorias* (Buenos Aires: Ediciones Argentinas SIA, 1944–1951), 1:191–193.

33. Staples to Hamilton, Buenos Aires, December 3, 1818, NA FO 72/215.

34. Hilarion de la Quintana to San Martin, Santiago, December 29, 1818, AGN S.X-C29-A10-N2, 139–161, and Tagle to San Martin, Confidential, November 24, 1818, AGN SX.C.29.A10.N2.

35. AGN SX.C.29.A10.N2

36. San Martin to Pueyrredon, December 29, 1818, AGN SX.C.29.A10.N2.

Chapter 33

1. Forsyth, *History of the Captivity,* 3:52.

2. Bertrand, *Cahiers,* 2:157.

3. Bathurst to Lowe, May 5, 1818, BL MSS Add 20201 SHLP, ff.114.

4. Forsyth, *History of the Captivity,* 3:57.

5. BL MSS Loan 57/43 Bathurst Papers, ff.251–253 and NA ADM 1/67 Cape of Good Hope 1816–1817.

6. Lowe to Bathurst, September 29, 1818, and Lowe to Bathurst, 26 December 1818, f.58 in BL MSS Add 20137 SHLP, f.9, 58. O'Meara refuted the accusations made by Croker in a separate pamphlet. Barry O'Meara, "A Letter to Lord Holland on the Review of Napoleon in Exile," *Quarterly Review* 55 (1823). The text of the letters in Croker's is different from the one in Lowe's archives.

7. Bertrand, *Cahiers,* 2:158–159.

8. Forsyth, *History of the Captivity,* 3:68.

9. Bertrand, *Cahiers,* 2:177.

10. *Courier,* London, November 16, 1818.

11. Admiral Plampin logbook, October 2 and 14, 1818, NA ADM 50/138.

12. "Napoleon at St. Helena: The Rumor of an Attempted Rescue in 1818," *American Whig Review* 6, no. 1 (1847): 88. Apparently, the author of this article was Joseph E. Sheffield, whose brother Thomas had been on board the *Chacabuco* as second lieutenant. Fifty years later, De Forest's nephew disclosed the name of the officer. Perhaps this is the vessel alluded to in one of De Forest's letters, where he orders "a fast sailing brig for privateering purposes." See de Forest, *The de Forests of Avesnes,* 131.

13. *Times,* London, January 5 and 23, 1819.

14. Bertrand, *Cahiers,* 2:218.

Chapter 34

1. The informant was on the payroll of the Duke of San Carlos. See Beckett to Hamilton, September 2, 1818, NA FO 72/221, f.11.

2. *Courier,* London, October 1, 1818.

3. Croker to Hamilton, September 29, 1818, NA FO 72/221.

4. Bowles to Croker, July 14, 1818, Buenos Aires, NA ADM 1/23. According to a Chilean historian, Cochrane's brother was ruined because Chile never paid him back the amounts he contributed for the completion of the ship. Alamiro de Avila Martel, *Cochrane y la Independencia del Pacífico* (Santiago: Ed. Universitaria, 1976), 76.

5. Richelieu to Osmond, September 7, 1818, Richelieu, *Lettres,* 223.

6. *Courier,* London, September 16, October 2, and October 16, 1818.

7. William Holmes to Lord Holland, September 8, 1818, BL MSS Add 51529 HHP, f.25. Las Cases to the Congress of Aix-la-Chapelle, Mannheim, November 13, 1818, Schlitter, *Kaiser Franz I und die Napoleoniden,* 571.

8. Adalberto de Baviera, *Eugenio Beauharnais* (Madrid, 1942), 387.

9. Gourgaud to Marie Louise, London, August 25, 1818, Gourgaud to Alexander, October 2, 1818, and Gourgaud to Francis II, October 25, 1818, Gaspard de Gourgaud, *The St. Helena Journal of General Baron Gourgaud* (London: J. Lane, Boadley Head, 1932), 348–352.

10. Osmond to Bathurst, October 1818, Masson, *Autour,* 1:242.

11. Richelieu to Osmond, October 20, 1818, Richelieu, *Lettres,* 230.

12. *Courier,* London, October 21, 1818.

13. Jose Garcia de León y Pizarro, *Memorias* (Madrid, 1953), 2:280–285.

14. Lieven to Nesselrode, September 4, 1818, Webster, *The Foreign Policy of Castlereagh 1815–1822,* 423, 563.

15. Gallatin to Monroe, Paris, August 10, 1818. Manning, *Diplomatic Correspondence,* 2:1383.

16. Richelieu to Montmorency-Laval, Aix-La-Chapelle, 5 October 1818, Villanueva, *La monarquía en América,* 85.

17. Montmorency- Laval to Richelieu, Madrid, November 12, 1818, ibid., 85.

18. *Courier,* London, October 28, 1818.

19. Hutchinson to Wilson, October 10, 1818, in BL MSS Add 30125 SRWP, f.81.

20. Wilson to Grey, October 4 and 30, 1818, BL MSS Add 30122 SRWP, ff.248, 258 and 274.

21. San Carlos to Pizarro, London, no. 365, October 17, 1818, AGS Estado 8289.

22. San Carlos to Pizarro, London, October 30, and November 2, 1818, AGS Estado 8289.

23. Secret Report from Alien Office, no. 9, November 2 and 3, 1818, NA FO 72/221, f.207, 209.

24. Wilson to Grey, London, November 4, 1818, BL MSS Add 30122 SRWP, f. 280.

25. Secret Report from Alien Office. no. 9, November 2 and 3, 1818, NA FO 72/221, f.207, 209.

26. Francis Maceroni, *An Appeal to the British Nation on the Affairs of South America* (London, 1819), 27, 34–37, and letter from Francis Maceroni, *Morning Chronicle,* London, November 5, 1818.

27. Bathurst to San Carlos, November 2, 1818, NA FO 72/217 Duke of San Carlos 1818, f.151.

28. Viscount Melville to Bathurst, November 8, 1818, Historical Manuscripts Commission (HMC), *Report on the Manuscripts of Earl Bathurst, Preserved at Cirencester Park* (London: HMSO, 1923), 459.

29. *Times,* London, 9–10 November 1818.

30. *Courier,* London, November 8, 1818.

31. *Le Conservateur,* Paris, November 17, 1818, and J. Lucas-Dubreton, *Le Culte de Napoléon* (Paris: Albin Michel, 1959), 102.

32. Richelieu to Osmond, November 30, 1818, Richelieu, *Lettres,* 232.

33. *Morning Chronicle,* London, November 16, 1818.

34. *Times,* London, November 16, 1818.

35. *British Monitor,* London, November 15, 1818.

36. Castlereagh to Bathurst, Aix-la-Chapelle, Most Secret and Confidential, November 12, 1818, NA FO 92/38 ff.224, 227.

37. *Courier,* London, November 20, 1818.

38. Protocole, Aix-la-Chapelle, November 13, 1818, Schlitter, *Kaiser Franz I und die Napoleoniden,* 571–579.

39. Castlereagh to Bathurst, Aix-la-Chapelle, November 19, 1818, NA FO 92/38. Many suspected that the Ultras had been behind the scheme to kidnap the tsar with the objective of influencing his view vis-à-vis Napoleon. *Le Censeur,* Paris, vol. 12 (Apr. 1819): 281–82.

40. *British Monitor,* London, December 6, 1818.

41. Bathurst to Lowe, several dispatches, November 1818, BL MSS Add 20201 SHLP, ff.193–201.

42. Balcombe to O'Meara, Plymouth, December 31, 1818, BL MSS ADD 51529 HHP, f.28.

43. Goulbourn to Lowe, November 16, 1818, BL MSS Add 20201 SHLP, f.181.

44. Goulbourn to Lowe, November 18, 1818, BL MSS Add 20201 SHLP, f.187.

45. Bathurst to Somerset, December 30, 1818, Forsyth, *History of the Captivity,* 3:98.

46. M. Froment, *La Police Devoilée depuis La Restauration, et notamment sous Messieurs Franchet et Delavau* (Paris: Lemonnier, 1829), 1:286.

47. Goulbourn to Lowe, November 18, 1818, BL MSS Add 20201 SHLP, f.187.

48. *A Letter to the Right Hon. Earl Grey on the Subject of the Late Arrest and Removal of General Gourgaud* (London, 1819), 2.

49. Latapie, *Mémoire,* 11.

50. Wilson to Grey, November and December 4, 1818, BL MSS Add 30122 SRWP, ff.262 and 295.

51. *Times,* London, November 17, 1818.

52. *British Monitor,* London, November 22, 1818.

53. *A Letter to the Right Hon. Earl Grey,* 2.

54. *Morning Chronicle,* London, February 24, 1819.

55. *Courier,* London, November 16 and 17, 1818.

56. Report from Alien Office, no. 14, November 12, 1818, NA 72/221, f.245.

57. W. Davidson Weatherhead, *An Account of the Late Expedition against the Isthmus of Darien under the Command of Sir Gregor MacGregor* (London, 1821), 3.

58. *Globe,* London, November 12, 1818.

59. John Besant, *Narrative of the Expedition under General MacGregor against Portobello, including an account of the voyage* (London, 1820), 8–10.

60. Osmond to Richelieu, London, November 24, 1818, Villanueva, *La monarquía en América,* 102.

61. Richelieu to Osmond, November 30, 1818, Richelieu, *Lettres,* 232.

Chapter 35

1. Onis to Casa Irujo, January 20, 1819, AHN Estado 5645 Estados Unidos 1819.

2. Onis to Casa Irujo, January 30, 1819, AHN Estado 5645 Estados Unidos 1819.

3. Guillemin to Ministere des Affaires Etrangeres, New Orleans, January 12, 1819, AMAE CPEUNew Orleans, 2mi1961 vol 2, 58.

4. De Forest to Henry Didier, Georgetown, January 13, 1819, Keen, *David Curtis de Forest,* 152.

5. Bagot to Castlereagh, January 4, 1819, Castlereagh, *Memoirs,* 12:99.

6. For more details about the negotiations that led to the Adams-Onis treaty and Hyde de Neuville's role as mediator see Brooks, *Diplomacy and the Borderlands,* 143–151, and Bradford Perkins, *Castlereagh and Adams: England and the United States, 1812–1823* (Berkeley: University of California Press, 1964), 299–302.

7. Henry Clay, speech to Congress, March 20, 1820, Latané, *The Diplomatic Relations,* 59.

8. Ibid., 61.

9. Adams to De Grand, May 21, 1819, Adams, *Writings,* 6:545–550.

10. Onis to Casa Irujo, March 24, 1819, AHN Estado 5645.

11. *La Minerve Française,* Paris, May 1819, 291.

12. Report de Cónsul Guillemin, New Orleans, July 10, 1819, AMAE CPEU, vol. 2, 70.

13. Davis, *The Pirates Laffite,* 393–399.

14. Penot, *Les Relations entre la France et le Mexique,* 1:218, and Lillian E. Fisher, "American Influence upon the Movement for Mexican Independence," *Mississippi Valley Historical Review* 18, no. 4 (Mar. 1932): 473–474.

15. Report of Consul Guillemin, New Orleans, July 15, 1819, AMAE CPEU Nouvelle Orleans, 2mi1961, vol. 2, 70.

Chapter 36

1. *Morning Chronicle,* London, January 7 and 8, 1819.

2. *Morning Chronicle,* London, January 9, 1819.

3. John Cam Hobhouse's diary, February 22 and 27, 1819, BL MSS Add 56540 Broughton Papers vol. 14, ff.48, 50.

4. *Hansard's Parliamentary Debates,* 39:1355, 1369, and 1373.

5. Decazes to Fanny Wallis, March 28, 1817, BL MSS Add 30108 SRWP, f.324. Soon after arriving in Paris, Hamelin became a spy for Decazes under the pseudonym of Madame Deschamps. See Daudet, *La Police Politique,* 246.

6. Wilson to Grey, January 1819, BL MSS Add 30123 SRWP, f.1 and 25.

7. *Morning Chronicle,* London, January 1, 1819.

8. Pozzo di Borgo to Nesselrode, Paris, January 24, 1819, Polovtsoff, *Correspondance diplomatique,* 3:14–15.

9. Wilson to Grey, January 1819, BL MSS Add 30123 SRWP, f.28.

10. Jasper Ridley, *Napoleon III and Eugenie* (New York: Viking Press, 1979), 14.

11. *Morning Chronicle,* London, January 15, 1819.

12. *Morning Chronicle,* London, March 16, 1819. Regnault de St. Jean d'Angely died two months after returning to Paris.

13. *Morning Chronicle,* London, January 11, 1819.

14. *Times,* London, January 5 and 23, 1819, and *Morning Chronicle,* London, March 18, 1819.

15. Osmond to Dessolles, London, February 15, 1819, and Le Moyne to Osmond, London, February 19, 1819, Cané, *La diplomacia de la revolución,* 46.

16. Dessolles to Montmorency-Laval, Paris, April 25, 1819, Villanueva, *La monarquía en América,* 154.

17. Memorandum on conversation with Castlereagh, February 12, 1819, Richard Rush, *The Court of London from 1819 to 1825* (London: R. Bentley, 1873), 3–7.

18. Caraman to Dessolles, London, March 26, 1819, AMAE CPA no. 612, f.214.

19. *Morning Chronicle,* London, April 5, 1819.

20. Wilson to Lord Holland, April 9, 1819, BL MSS Add 51617 HHP, f. 189.

21. Caraman to Dessolles, April 6, 1819, AMAE CPA no. 612.

22. Francis Maceroni, *An Appeal to the British Nation,* 19–22 and 30–32.

23. *Morning Chronicle,* London, April 21, 1819.

24. *Morning Chronicle,* London, April 28, 1819.

25. *Hansard's Parliamentary Debates,* 40:867, 1377, and 1381.

26. Robert T. Wilson, *A Full Report of the Speeches Delivered at the Anniversary Dinner Given by the Free Electors of Southwark* (London, 1819).

27. Montmorency-Laval to Dessolles, Madrid, May 11, 1819, Villanueva, *La Monarquía en América,* 142.

28. Belgrano, *La Francia y la monarquía,* 156, and Cané, *La diplomacia de la revolución,* 143.

29. Irisarri to O'Higgins, London, July 21, 1819, Pérez, *Artigas y San Martín,* 156.

Chapter 37

1. Pezuela to de la Serna, Lima, January 12, 1819, Jose de San Martin, *Documentos para la Historia del libertador general San Martín* (Buenos Aires: Instituto Nacional Sanmartiniano, 1953), 10:167.

2. San Martin to Supreme Director, January 12–14, 1819, San Martin, *Documentos para la Historia,* 10:176–179.

3. Bowles to Croker, February 27, 1819, Buenos Aires, NA ADM 1/24.

4. Bowles to San Martin, Buenos Aires, February 27, 1819, ibid., 10:154.

5. Bowles to Croker, February 27, 1819, Buenos Aires, NA ADM 1/24.

6. Bowles to Croker, March 15, 1819, Buenos Aires, NA ADM 1/24.

7. Besant, *Narrative of the Expedition,* 8–10.

8. Weatherhead, *An Account of the Late Expedition,* 4, and Jaime Duarte French, *América de Norte a Sur* (Bogota, 1975), 253.

9. J. B. Novion to Aury, New York, January 2, 1818, Guzman, "Los Hermanos Lallemand en Texas," 168–169.

10. Persat, *Mémoires,* 34–35, 40.

11. Aury had obtained an authorization to occupy these islands from Jose Cortes de Madariaga on behalf of the independent republics of Buenos Aires and Chile. But Madariaga was not empowered to do so. It was a situation reminiscent of Amelia Island.

Nicolas Perazzo, *José Cortés de Madariaga* (Caracas: Comisión Nacional del Cuatricentenario de Caracas, 1966), 123–125.

12. Besant, *A Narrative of the Expedition,* 29–30.

13. Popham to Croker, Jamaica, March 18, 1819, NA ADM 1/270.

14. Codazzi, *Memorias,* 339–340, and Weatherhead, *An Account of the Late Expedition,* 19.

15. Besant, *Narrative of the Expedition,* 29–30, and Duarte French, *América de Norte a Sur,* 254.

16. Miller, *Memoirs,* 1:218.

17. Bolivar to Zea, Angostura, April 20, 1819, Duarte French, *América de Norte a Sur,* 265.

18. Maceroni, *Memoirs,* 2:439.

19. Weatherhead, *An Account of the Late Expedition,* 49–50, and Codazzi, *Memorias,* 341.

20. MacGregor to Editor of the *Edinburgh Star,* September 28, 1821, Gustavus Hippisley, *Acts of Oppression Committed under the Administration of M. de Villéle* (London, 1831), 112.

21. Charles to Wilson, on board HMS *Andromache,* Valparaiso, June 19, 1819, in BL MSS Add 30109 SRWP, f.19.

22. Charles to Wilson, Santiago, July 7, 1819, in BL MSS Add 30109 SRWP, f.31.

23. Declaration of Skupieski, April 6 and June 9, 1819, AGN SX.C.29.A10.N2 Sum. Mil. Letra B Exp. 139–161.

24. Second Declaration by Bulewski, June 9, 1819, AGN SX.C.29.A10.N2 Sum. Mil. Letra B Exp. 139–161.

25. Worthington to Adams, Buenos Aires, March 7, 1819, Manning, *Diplomatic Correspondence,* 1:434–435.

26. Bowles to Croker, Buenos Aires, May 28, 1819, NA ADM 1/24.

27. Bowles to Croker, February 27, 1819, NA ADM 1/24.

28. Bowles to Croker, April 1, 1819, NA ADM 1/24.

29. Lavaysse to Lally Tollendal, July 3, 1819, Archivo del General Bartolomé Mitre, Buenos Aires.

Chapter 38

1. Stokoe, *Memoirs,* 91–92.

2. Reports of conversation between Plampin and Stokoe, January 19, 1819, NA ADM 1/67.

3. Stokoe, *Memoirs,* 110.

4. Plampin to Croker, January 30, 1819, NA ADM 1/67.

5. Balmain Report no. 3, January 30, 1819, Balmain, *Reports,* 203.

6. Chamberlain to Lowe, October 8, 1818, NA FO 63/123, f.127.

7. Lowe to Bathurst, December 15, 1818, and January 1, 1819, BL MSS Add 20137 SHLP, f.45, 59.

8. Lowe to Bathurst, May 15, 1819, BL MSS Loan 57/44 Bathurst Papers, f.128.

9. Report no. 1, January 19, 1819, Balmain, *Reports,* 201.

10. January 21, 1819, Bertrand, *Cahiers,* 2:249.

11. February 8, 1819, ibid., 2:292–295.

12. February 20, 1819, ibid., 2:308.

13. Report no. 4, March 1, 1819, Balmain, *Reports,* 209.

14. March 5, 1819, Bertrand, *Cahiers,* 2:312.

15. Report no. 5, March 18, 1819, Balmain, *Reports,* 211.

16. Report no. 9, April 22, 1819, ibid., 215.

17. Lowe to Bathurst, April 12, 1819, BL MSS Add 20137 SHLP, f.135.

18. Goulbourn to Lowe, November 1818, Forsyth, *History of the Captivity,* 3:151.

19. Chamberlain to Lowe, Rio de Janeiro, January 17, 1819, BL MSS Add 20233 SHLP, f.81.

20. April 1819, Bertrand, *Cahiers,* 2:324–325, 330.

21. May 1819, Bertrand, *Cahiers,* 2:357.

22. May 1819, ibid., 2:364.

23. Montholon, *Récits,* 2:409.

24. Albine H. de Montholon, *Souvenirs de Sainte-Helene par la Comtesse de Montholon 1815–1816* (Paris: Emile-Paul, 1901), 225.

25. Forsyth, *History of the Captivity,* 3:161.

26. Report no. 15, July 1, 1819, Balmain, *Reports,* 218.

27. Forsyth, *History of the Captivity,* 3:171–173.

Chapter 39

1. John Hall, *The Bourbon Restoration* (London: Alston Rivers, 1909), 239.

2. Henry Kissinger, *A World Restored: Metternich, Castlereagh, and the Problems of Peace, 1812–1822* (London: Weidenfeld and Nicholson, 1999), 244.

3. It was an old acquaintance, Sir Home Popham, British governor in Jamaica, who gave Wilson the bad news. "What a vagabond your friend MacGregor has turned out to be!" Popham to Wilson, Jamaica, June 21, 1819, BL MSS Add 30109 SRWP, f.24.

4. *British Monitor,* London, July 4 and 11, 1818.

5. *Le Constitutionnel,* Paris, August 31, 1819.

6. Maceroni, *Memoirs,* 2:442.

7. Rush to Adams, October 5, 1819, Rush, *The Court of London,* 164–166.

8. Wellesley to Gonzalez Salmon, Madrid, August 4, 1819, NA ADM 1/3543 Secret Service.

9. *British Monitor,* London, July 25, 1819.

10. Memo, September 3, 1819, Rush, *The Court of London,* 3–7.

11. Villanueva, *La monarquía en América,* 1:134–135.

12. Iris M. Zavala, *Masones, Comuneros y Carbonarios* (Madrid: Siglo XXI, 1971), 68–70, and Jose Luis Comellas, *Los Primeros Pronunciamientos en España: 1814–1820* (Madrid: Consejo Superior de Investigaciones Científicas, 1958).

13. Guillaume Pepe, *Memoirs of General Pepe Comprising the Principal Military and Political Events of Modern Italy* (London: R. Bentley, 1846), 1:15–16. Frost, *The Secret Societies,* 209–210, and Hall, *The Bourbon Restoration,* 297.

14. Lucien de la Hodde, *Histoire de las Sociétés Secrètes et du Parti Républicain de 1830 a 1848. Louis-Philippe et la révolution de Février, portraits, scènes de conspirations, faits inconnus* (Paris, 1853), 19–20; Pierre-Arnaud Lambert, *La Charbonnerie Française, 1821–1823* (Lyon: Presses Universitaires de Lyon, 1995), 96–97.

15. Savary to Wilson, June 6, 1819, BL MSS Add 30109 SRWP, f.15.

16. *La Minerve Française,* Paris, August 1819, 38–46.

17. Wilson to Grey, London, July 12, 1819, BL MSS Add 30109 SRWP, f.63.

18. Pozzo di Borgo to Nesselrode, July 20, 1819, Polovtsoff, *Correspondance diplomatique,* 3:151–152.

19. Synopsis of unpublished volumes 3 and 4, Maceroni, *Memoirs,* 2:i.

20. Maurice d'Herisson, *The Black Cabinet* (London: Longmans, Green, 1887), 157.

21. John Cam Hobhouse, 20 July 1819, BL MSS Add 56540 Broughton Papers.

22. BL MSS Add 30138 SRWP.

23. *Le Constitutionnel,* Paris, August 31, 1819.

24. Vaudoncourt, *Quinze années,* 2:303.

25. *Times,* London, July 22, 1819.

26. Joyce Marlowe, *The Peterloo Massacre* (London: Rapp and Whiting, 1971).

27. BL MSS Add 56540 Broughton Papers.

28. Burdett to Lord Langdale, August 22, 1819, Patterson, *Sir Francis Burdett,* 2:490.

29. Ziegler, *Addington,* 371–374.

30. *Hansard's Parliamentary Debates,* 41:360–362, and Robert Walmsley, *Peterloo: The Case Reopened* (Manchester: Manchester University Press, 1969), 386–387.

31. Samuel, *An Astonishing Fellow,* 193–194.

32. Wilson to Grey, London, September 20, 1819, BL MSS Add 30109 SRWP, f.73.

33. Albine to Charles Montholon, Brussels, October 4, 1819, Philippe Gonnard, *Lettres du Comte et de la Comtesse de Montholon 1819–1821* (Paris, 1906), 37.

34. Gourgaud to Wilson, Hamburg, September 19, 1819, BL MSS Add 30109 SRWP, f.43.

35. Gourgaud to Madame Montholon, October 19, 1819, BL MSS Add 30109 SRWP, f.68.

36. Gourgaud to Wilson, December 1, 1819, BL MSS Add 30109 SRWP, f.67.

37. Henri Troyat, *Alexander of Russia: Napoleon's Conqueror* (New York: Dutton, 1982), 249–250.

38. Eugene to Albine de Montholon, Munich, October 13, 1819, Candé-Montholon, *Journal Secret d'Albine de Montholon,* 200–201.

39. Althorp to Second Earl Spencer, October 24, 1819, BL MSS Add 76377 Althorp Papers.

40. *Hansard's Parliamentary Debates,* 41:764.

41. John Cam Hobhouse, 20 July 1819, BL MSS Add 56540 Broughton Papers.

42. Bruce, *Lavallette Bruce,* 315.

43. Althorp to 2nd Earl Spencer, December 21, 1819, BL MSS Add 76377 Althorp Papers.

44. Denis Le Marchant, *Memoir of John Charles, Viscount Althorp, Third Earl Spencer* (London: R. Bentley, 1876), 198.

45. *Royal Naval Biography* (London, 1829), 256–260.

46. Florence Marryat, *Life and Letters of Captain Marryat* (London: R. Bentley, 1872), 1:28.

Chapter 40

1. Lucio Mansilla, "Memorias Inéditas," in Santiago Moritán, *Mansilla Ramírez Urquiza* (Buenos Aires, 1945), 33.

2. Maler to Dessolles, Rio de Janeiro, August 20, 1819, Cané, *La diplomacia de la revolución,* 87–88.

3. Bowles to Croker, Buenos Aires, August 31, 1819, NA ADM 1/24.

4. Las Heras to San Martin, Santiago, June 30, 1819, San Martin, *Documentos para la Historia,* 13:279.

5. Charles to Wilson, Santiago, July 7, 1819, BL MSS Add 30109 SRWP, f.31.

6. Guido to San Martin and O'Higgins to San Martin, August 7, 1819, San Martin, *Documentos para la Historia,* 14:3, 6–7.

7. San Martin to O'Higgins, August 12, 1819, San Martin, *Documentos para la Historia,* 14:19.

8. Rondeau to San Martin, August 11, 1819, ibid., 14:16.

9. Popham to Croker, December 22, 1819, NA ADM 1/270.

10. Charles to Wilson, Callao, October 18, 1819, BL MSS Add 30109 SRWP, f. 50.

11. Maceroni, *Memoirs,* 2:445.

12. MacGregor to editor of *Courant,* Edinburgh, October 17, 1821, Hippisley, *Acts of Oppression,* 108.

13. Juan Friede, "La Expedición de MacGregor a Rio Hacha-Año 1819," *Boletín Cultural y Bibliográfico* 10, no. 9 (1967): 69–85.

14. David Sinclair, *Sir Gregor MacGregor and the Land That Never Was* (London: Headline Book, 2003). See also Matthew Brown, "Gregor MacGregor: Clansman, Colonizer, and Conquistador," in *Colonial Lives across the British Empire: Imperial Careering in the Nineteenth Century,* ed David Lambert and Alan Lester (Cambridge: Cambridge University Press, 2006).

15. Villanueva, *La monarquía en América,* 150.

16. Bowles to Croker, *Creole,* Buenos Aires, November 15, 1819, NA ADM 1/25 f. 12. San Martin to O'Higgins, November 11, 1819, Miguel A. Cárcano, *La Política Internacional en la Historia Argentina* (Buenos Aires: Editorial Universitaria de Buenos Aires, 1973), book 3, 2:751–752.

17. Miller, *Memoirs,* 1:235–236.

18. Bowles to Hardy, *Creole,* Buenos Aires, December 25, 1819, NA ADM 1/25 f. 32.

19. Cochrane, *Narrative,* 1:34.

Chapter 41

1. Report no. 21, August 25, 1819, Balmain, *Reports,* 220.

2. Report no. 22, September 22, 1819, Balmain, *Reports,* 223.

3. September 1819, Bertrand, *Cahiers,* 2:396.

4. Consalvi to Metternich, January 4, 1818, d'Estampes and Jannet, *La Franc-maçonnerie,* 248–249, 256.

5. Report no. 25, October 1, 1819, Balmain, *Reports,* 223.

6. Montholon to Albine, October 31, 1819, Montholon, *Lettres du Comte et de la Comtesse de Montholon 1819–1821* (Paris, 1906), 40.

7. Aymes, "Napoléon Ier et le Mexique," 46.

8. Report no. 24, September 22, 1819, Balmain, *Reports,* 223.

9. Report no. 25, October 1, 1819, ibid., 225.

10. Report no. 26, October 25, 1819, ibid., 226.

11. October 5, 1819, Bertrand, *Cahiers,* 2:401.

12. October 6, 1819, ibid., 2:402.

13. Report no. 29, December 1, 1819, Balmain, *Reports,* 228.

14. Lowe to Bathurst, December 1, 1819, Forsyth, *History of the Captivity,* 3:198.

15. Francesco C. Antommarchi, *The Last Days of the Emperor Napoleon* (London: H. Colburn, 1825), 1:114.

16. Forsyth, *History of the Captivity,* 3:203.

Chapter 42

1. Wilson to Grey, January 20, 1820, BL MSS Add 30123 SRWP, f.107.

2. The Diary of John Cam Hobhouse, January 19, 1820, BL MSS Add 56540 and 56541 Broughton Papers.

3. *Courier,* London, January 25, 1820.

4. Timothy Anna, *Spain and the Loss of America* (Lincoln: University of Nebraska Press, 1983), 218.

5. Pasquier, *Mémoires,* 5:295.

6. Conversation on February 9, 1816, Las Cases, *Memorial,* 1:412.

7. Wilson to Grey, February 9 and 15, 1820, BL MSS Add 30123 SRWP, f.123–130.

8. Liverpool to Castlereagh, July 21, 1815, Castlereagh, *Memoirs,* 10:415; *Courier,* London, January 12, 1820.

9. Count Goltz to the King of Prussia, Paris, February 19, 1820, d'Herisson, *The Black Cabinet,* 58.

10. The informer was Joseph Antinori, self-styled Duke of Brindisi, a Neapolitan intriguer. D'Herisson, *The Black Cabinet*, 76. For more on Antinori see Alessandro Cutolo, *Il Duca di Brindisi* (Milan, 1960); Adams, *Memoirs*, 4:68–69; and Castlereagh, *Memoirs*, 12:39.

11. Lacretelle, *Histoire de France*, 2:370.

12. Wilson to Grey, February 12, 1820, BL MSS Add 30123 SRWP, f.126.

13. Anonymous to Castlereagh, Paris, December 28, 1819, NA FO 95/4/5, f.416.

14. Memorandum on conversation with Castlereagh, February 24, 1820, Rush, *The Court of London*, 217.

15. Lieven to Metternich, London, February 25, 1820, Lieven, *Private Letters*, 17–20.

16. *Courier*, London, February 29 and March 3, 1820.

17. John Stanhope, *The Cato Street Conspiracy* (London: J. Cape, 1962), 150–151.

18. Wilson to Grey, March 29, 1820, BL MSS Add 30123 SRWP, f.145.

19. *Courier*, London, March 31, 1820, and April 12, 1820.

20. *British Monitor*, London, May 14, 1820.

21. Wilson to Grey, March 10, 1820, BL MSS Add 30123 SRWP, f.140.

22. Schlitter, *Kaiser Franz I und die Napoleoniden*, 478–480.

23. Joseph to Napoleon, May 9, 1820, Candé-Montholon, *Journal Secret d'Albine de Montholon*, 202–204, and Joseph to O'Meara, May 1, 1820, Albert Du Casse, *Les Rois Freres de Napoléon 1er* (Paris: Bailliere, 1883), 74–75.

24. Walter Scott, *The Life of Napoleon Buonaparte, Emperor of the French* (London, 1828), 9:284. Some authors give Johnstone's name as Johnson or Johnston. See Henry Shore, *Smuggling Days and Smuggling Ways* (London: E. P. Publishing, 1972); Henry N. Shore and Charles G. Harper, *The Smugglers* (London, 1923), 1:195–198; and David Whittet Thomson, "They Wanted to Rescue Napoleon," *U.S. Naval Institute Proceedings* 69 (Sept.–Dec. 1943): 794–800.

25. Tom Pocock, *The Terror before Trafalgar: Nelson, Napoleon, and the Secret War* (London: J. Murray, 2002), 150, and Holden Furber, "Fulton and Napoleon in 1800: New Light on the Submarine Nautilus," *American Historical Review* 39, no. 3 (Apr. 1934): 489–494.

26. *Naval Chronicle* (London, 1814), 31:287.

27. James Cleugh, *Captain Thomas Johnstone, 1772–1839: Smuggler's Reach* (London: A. Melrose, 1955), 305. Cleugh unfortunately does not disclose his sources. Thomson, "They Wanted to Rescue Napoleon," 797, and Pocock, *The Terror*, 25–26, 40–41.

28. Scott, *Life of Napoleon*, 9:285.

29. Maceroni, *Memoirs*, 2:423–426.

30. Maceroni's publisher enlisted a then-unknown writer named William Thackeray to edit his memoirs. Thackeray found Maceroni's adventures "so interesting" that he proposed to rewrite them and make a best seller. "The book must be rewritten, and will cause a world of trouble," Thackeray wrote to the publisher. "The Colonel must give you *carte-blanche* about alterations, and not disown the book when published. We may make a hero of him by these means; if after the work's publication he blusters or denies it, the sale will be seriously injured." Thackeray to John Macrone, London, July 26,

1837. Grateful thanks to Peter Shillingsburg, professor of English at the University of North Texas, for sending me an excerpt from this letter. Maceroni died in 1846 completely destitute. See NA HO 44/31, f.548, and Maceroni's letters in Brougham's Archives at University College, London.

31. Duque de Frias to D. Evaristo Perez de Castro, London, 23 August 1820, AGI Estado 146, Cajon 1, Legajo 15 (87).

32. Caraman to Pasquier, April 4, 1820, AMAE CPA, no. 613, 1820, f.41.

33. Wilson to Lord Holland, April 16, 1820, BL MSS Add 51617 HHP, f.192.

34. Castlereagh to Richelieu, April 10, 1820, Castlereagh, *Memoirs,* 12:239.

35. Castlereagh to Richelieu, April 28, 1820, ibid., 12:251.

36. May 6, 1820, BL MSS Add 56541 Broughton Papers, f.33

37. Wilson to Grey, May 1, 1820, BL MSS Add 30123 SRWP, f.147.

38. The Diary of John Cam Hobhouse, February 13, 1820, BL MSS Add 56541 Broughton Papers, f.4.

39. Wilson to Grey, May 5, 1820, BL MSS Add 30123 SRWP, f.151.

40. Joseph to O'Meara, May 1, 1820, Du Casse, *Les Rois Freres,* 74–75.

41. Metternich to Tsar Alexander, February 15, 1820, Clement von Metternich, *Memoirs of Prince Metternich* (London: R. Bentley, 1880–82), 3:462.

42. Metternich to Emperor Francis, Vienna, May 18, 1820, ibid., 3:432.

43. Flora Fraser, *The Unruly Queen: The Life of Queen Caroline* (London: Macmillan, 1996), 367.

44. *Times,* June 7, 1820.

45. Wilson to Grey, June 6, 1820, BL MSS Add 30123 SRWP, f.169.

46. *British Monitor,* London, August 20, 1820.

47. Report of Count Caraman, Rome, June 1820, Edmond Bonnal, *Les Royalistes contre l'Armée, D'apres les archives du Ministere de la guerre* (Paris, 1906), 2:348.

48. Metternich to Esterhazy, Prague, June 3, 1820, Pierre Paul Ebeyer, *Revelations Concerning Napoleon's Escape from St. Helena* (New Orleans: Windmill, 1947), 366.

49. *Times,* London, July 1, 3, and 5, 1820, and Webster, *The Foreign Policy of Castlereagh, 1815–1822,* 424.

50. Caraman to Pasquier, July 7, 1820 in AMAE CPA, no. 613, 1820, f.67. *Hansard's Parliamentary Debates,* London, n.s. vol. 2, 1820 (June 27–Sept. 7), 382.

51. Memorandum of a meeting with Castlereagh, July 13, 1820, Rush, *The Court of London,* 278–279.

52. Memorandum of a meeting with Castlereagh, July 22, 1820, ibid., 288–290

53. Irisarri to O'Higgins, London, July 12, 1820, Benjamin Vicuña Mackenna, *El Ostracismo del general Bernardo O'Higgins* (Valparaiso, 1860), 376. In fact, in 1807 Castlereagh had argued for precisely this solution. Castlereagh, *Memoirs,* 12:322.

54. Memorandum for the Cabinet, South America, 1807, Castlereagh, *Memoirs,* 7:322.

55. Count Munster to Count de Grote, London, July 11, 1820, d'Herisson, *the Black Cabinet,* 69–70.

56. Count Goltz to the King of Prussia, Paris, July 15, 1820, ibid., 69.

57. Louis Blanc, *Histoire de diz ans: 1830–1840* (Paris, 1842), 1:89–90, and Pasquier, *Mémoires,* 4:424–426.

58. Hamelin to Decazes, June 1820, Marquiset, *Une Merveilleuse,* 209–210.

59. Frost, *The Secret Societies,* 240, and R. M. Johnston, *The Napoleonic Empire in Southern Italy and the Rise of Secret Societies* (London: Macmillan, 1904), 2:78–87.

60. Lieven to Metternich, July 20, 1820, Lieven, *Private Letters,* 53.

61. Metternich to Rechberg, Vienna, December 31, 1820, Metternich, *Memoirs,* 2:448. Kissinger, *A World Restored,* 251.

62. Pepe, *Memoirs,* 1:126.

63. Persat, *Mémoires,* 64–66.

64. The author of this report was the Duke of Brindisi, the perennial intriguer. Cutolo, *Il Duca di Brindisi,* 147. The Austrians suspected Eugene was involved in the plot. Baviera, *Eugenio Beauharnais,* 399–400.

65. January 21, 1821, Antommarchi, *The Last Days,* 1:395.

Chapter 43

1. BL MSS Add 56541 Broughton Papers, f.55.

2. Cochrane, *Narrative,* 1:34–35, and Avila Martel, *Cochrane y la Independencia,* 198.

3. Miller, *Memoirs,* 1:243.

4. Cochrane, *Narrative,* 1:36.

5. Barros Arana to Vargas, Santiago, 4 July 1902, Jose Miguel Barros, "Lord Cochrane y Napoleón Bonaparte," *El Mercurio,* Santiago de Chile, August 5, 2001.

6. Graham, *Journal of a residence in Chile,* 58.

7. Cochrane, *Narrative,* 1:55.

8. Miller, *Memoirs,* 1:253–254.

9. Cochrane, *Narrative,* 1:52.

10. Graham, *Journal,* 59.

11. Tute, *Cochrane,* 188.

12. Brayer to Carrera, Montevideo, March 1, 1820, Carrera, *Archivo,* 23:171–172.

13. Sarratea to Carrera, February 26, 1820, Carrera, *Archivo,* 23:145.

14. Anonymous letter to the Gaceta of Buenos Aires, February 26, 1820, Carrera, *Archivo,* 23:166.

15. Zañartu to O'Higgins, Buenos Aires, March 21, 1820, O'Higgins, *Archivo,* 6:204.

16. Hardy to Croker, *Owen Glendower,* off Buenos Aires, April 12, 1820, NA ADM 1/25 f.173.

17. Adams to Rodney, Washington, May 17, 1823, Adams, *Writings,* 7:424–441.

18. Hardy to Joseph Hardy, March 24, 1820, A. M. Broadley and R. G. Bartelot, *Nelson's Hardy: His Life, Letters, and Friends* (London: J. Murray, 1909), 181–182.

19. Yates, "A Brief Relation," 400.

20. Ignacio Zenteno, *Documentos Justificativos sobre la Expedición Libertadora del Peru Refutación de las Memorias de Lord Cochrane* (Santiago, 1861), 48–49.

21. Spencer to Earl Spencer, May 19, 1820, BL MSS Add 76662 Althorp Papers.

22. Quintana to Soler, May 23, 1820 in Carrera, *Archivo,* 24:68–69.

23. Hardy to Croker, *Owen Glendower,* off Buenos Aires, June 13, 1820, NA ADM 1/25 f.249.

24. Carrera to del Corro, June 14, 1820, Carrera, *Archivo,* 24:84–85.

25. Zañartu to O'Higgins, Montevideo, July 23, 1820, Carrera, *Archivo,* 24: 122–123.

26. Hardy to Croker, *Owen Glendower,* off Buenos Aires, July 11, 1820, NA ADM 1/25 f.249.

27. Claudius Charles to Wilson, June 27, 1820, BL MSS Add 30109 SRWP, f.115.

28. Cochrane, *Narrative,* 1:65.

29. Cochrane, *Narrative,* 1:70.

Chapter 44

1. Lowe to Bathurst, January 21, 1820, Bathurst Papers, BL Loan 57/45 f.23.

2. Lowe to Bathurst, February 16, 1820, Bathurst Papers, BL Loan 57/45 ff.35–38.

3. Report no. 1 and 2, January 10 and 28, 1820, Balmain, *Reports,* 231–232.

4. Forsyth, *History of the Captivity,* 3:204.

5. Lowe to Bathurst, February 16, 1820, BL Loan 57/45 Bathurst Papers, ff.35–38.

6. Admiral Edward Pellew, Baron Exmouth, to Lowe, September 26, 1819, BL MSS Add 36297 Misc. Autographs, f.20.

7. Lowe to Plampin, February 27, 1820, BL MSS Add 20129 SHLP Papers, ff.208–210.

8. Memorandum of conversation between Balmain and Gorrequer, March 10, 1820, BL MSS Add 20129 SHLP, f.244.

9. Lowe to Bathurst, March 10, 1820, BL Loan 57/45 Bathurst Papers, f.45.

10. Report no. 8, April 18, 1820, Balmain, *Reports,* 235–236.

11. Philipp von Neumann, *The Diary of Philipp von Neumann, 1819–1850,* trans. and ed. E. Beresford Chancellor (London: Allan, 1928), 1:27.

12. Montchenu to Richelieu, St. Helena, June 23, 1820, BL Loan 57/22 Bathurst Papers, 3:f.253.

13. Lowe to Bathurst, July 20, 1820, BL Loan 57/45 Bathurst Papers, f.117.

14. Forsyth, *History of the Captivity,* 3:223.

15. Lowe to Bathurst, June 22, 1820, BL Loan 57/45 Bathurst Papers, f.111.

16. Ralph Korngold, *The Last Years of Napoleon: His Captivity on St. Helena* (New York: Harcourt, Brace, 1959), 137.

17. Forsyth, *History of the Captivity,* 3:232.

18. Ibid., 3:233–234.

Chapter 45

1. Edward Blaquiere, *An Historical Review of the Spanish Revolution* (London, 1822), 120. Regarding the resurgence of Bonapartism in Spain see Irene Castells Olivan and Jordi Roca Vernet, "Napoleón y el mito del Héroe Romántico. Su proyección en España (1815–1831)," *Hispania Nova Revista de Historia Contemporánea* 4 (2004), http://hispanianova.rediris.es/4/articulos/04_001.htm.

2. Lascelles Wraxall and Robert Wehrhan, eds., *Memoirs of Queen Hortense, Mother of Napoleon III* (London, 1862), 2:148–150.

3. Samuel, *An Astonishing Fellow*, 176.

4. Lean, *The Napoleonists*, 120.

5. Lieven to Metternich, London, August 12, 1820, Lieven, *Private Letters*, 59.

6. The Diary of John Cam Hobhouse, October 2, 1820, in BL MSS Add 56541 Broughton Papers, f.78.

7. This account is based mainly on Pasquier, *Mémoires*, 4:441–462. Others denied that the Bonaparte family had any involvement in the conspiracy. Marmont, *Mémoires*, 7:268–280. See also Vaulabelle, *Histoire*, 5:183–193. The classic study of the military plots during the Bourbon restoration including the plot of August 1820 is Guillon, *Les Complots Militaires*, 110–139. See also Alan B. Spitzer, *Old Hatreds and Young Hopes: The French Carbonari against the Bourbon Restoration* (Cambridge: Harvard University Press, 1971), 235–240. On Fabvier's role see Marmont, *Mémoires*, 7:270–272. Regarding Brice's participation in this plot see Brice, *Le General Brice*, 53.

8. Minister of French Police to Decazes, August 20, 1820, NA FO 27/240 France 1820.

9. Pasquier to Decazes, August 20, 1820, NA FO 27/240 France 1820.

10. Pasquier, *Mémoires*, 4:445–446.

11. Wilson to Grey, September 11 and 14, 1820, BL MSS Add 30123 SRWP, ff.195, 198.

12. Cartwright to Wilson, September 12, 1820, BL MSS Add 30109 SRWP, f.124.

13. Pasquier, *Mémoires*, 5:170.

14. Guillon, *Les Complots Militaires*, 336, and Hall, *The Bourbon Restoration*, 297.

15. Scott, *Life of Napoleon*, 9:287.

16. Bathurst to Lowe, 30 September 1820, Forsyth, *History of the Captivity*, 3:250–251.

17. Maceroni, *Memoirs*, 1:428–429.

18. Montholon, *Récits*, 2:434.

19. Pocock, *The Terror*, 226–227. Another reference to Johnsone's failed attempt to launch a submarine is in G. W. Hovgaard, *Submarine Boats* (London, 1887), 16.

20. *Times*, London, November 20, 1820.

21. Dominique Georges Frédéric de Riom de Prolhiac de Fourt de Pradt, *Europe and America in 1821* (London, 1822), 1:214.

22. Cartwright to Florez Estrada, October 1820, John Cartwright, *The Life and Cor-*

respondence of Major Cartwright, ed. Francis D. Cartwright (New York: A. M. Kelley, 1969), 2:201–3, and *Niles' Weekly Register,* November 11, 1820.

23. The Diary of John Cam Hobhouse, November 29, 1820, in BL MSS Add 56541 Broughton Papers, f.115.

24. Wellington to Castlereagh, London, November 26, 1820, Webster, *The Foreign Policy of Castlereagh 1815–1822,* 575.

25. Secret memo from Metternich to Alexander, December 15, 1820, Metternich, *Memoirs,* 3:462.

Chapter 46

1. Lady Cochrane, n.d., Tute, *Cochrane,* 176.

2. Claudius Charles to Wilson, off Valparaiso, June 27, 1820, BL MSS Add 30109 SRWP, f.115.

3. Cochrane, *Narrative,* 1:94.

4. Hardy ordered Spencer to go to St. Helena on September 1, 1820. See Hardy to Spencer, September 1, 1820, NA ADM 50/145 Commodore Sir Thomas Hardy, August 1819-May 1822. Spencer spent almost a month refitting his ship on the Uruguayan coast and left for St. Helena on October 2, 1820.

5. Spencer to Earl and Lady Spencer, Buenos Aires, June 24, 1820, BL MSS Add 76662.

6. Hardy to Croker, *Augusta,* off Buenos Aires, September 17, 1820, NA ADM 1/25, f.330.

7. Most Argentine historians argue that Jewett took possession of the Falklands following orders from the government of Buenos Aires although no documentary evidence supports this assertion. Jose Antonio da Fonseca Figueira, *David Jewett: Una biografía para la historia de las Malvinas* (Buenos Aires: Sudamericana/Planeta, 1985), 84–115.

8. Hardy to Croker, *Creole,* December 9, 1820, NA ADM 1/26, f.42.

9. Grimble, *The Sea Wolf,* 220.

10. Cochrane to Place, Valparaiso, October 16, 1822, BL MSS Add 37949, f.119.

11. Cochrane, *Narrative,* 1:83.

12. Searle to Hardy, *Hyperion* off Callao, November 8, 1820, NA ADM 1/26, f.96.

13. Cochrane, *Narrative,* 1:97–98.

14. Hardy to Joseph Hardy, Buenos Aires, January 14, 1821, Broadley and Bartelot, *Nelson's Hardy,* 184–185.

Chapter 47

1. Lowe to Bathurst, August 22, 1820, BL Loan 57/45 Bathurst Papers, f.141.

2. Lowe to Bathurst, August 31, 1820, BL MSS Add 20138 SHLP f.147.

3. Lowe to Bathurst, September 1, 1820, BL MSS Add 20131 SHLP, f.1.

4. Bertrand to Liverpool, September 2, 1820, BL MSS Add 20131 SHLP, f.8.

5. Lowe to Bathurst, September 3, 1820, BL Loan 57/45 Bathurst Papers, f.147.

6. Lowe to Montchenu, September 8, 1820, BL MSS Add 20131 SHLP, f.27.

7. Montchenu to Lowe, September 9, 1820, BL MSS Add 20131 SHLP, f.28.

8. Lowe to Bathurst, September 12, 1820, BL MSS Add 20131 SHLP, f.39.

9. Lowe to Bathurst, September 21, 1820, BL MSS Add 20131 SHLP, f.66.

10. October 29, 1820, Antommarchi, *The Last Days,* 1:362.

11. Lowe to Bathurst, October 11, 1820, BL MSS Add 20138 SHLP f.332.

12. Antommarchi, *The Last Days of the Emperor Napoleon,* 1:333–335.

13. Lowe to Bathurst, October 28, 1820, BL MSS Add 20131 SHLP, f.141.

14. Lowe to Hardy, November 1, 1820, BL MSS Add 20131 SHLP, f.164.

15. Forsyth, *History of the Captivity,* 3:246.

16. Le Marchant, *Memoir,* 153, 162.

17. Althorp to 2nd Earl Spencer, October 31, December 21, 1819, and January 17, 1820, BL MSS Add 76377 Althorp Papers.

18. Lowe to Bathurst, November 7, 1820, BL MSS Add 20131 SHLP, f.183.

19. Lowe to Bathurst, October 28, 1820, BL MSS Add 20131 SHLP, f.141.

20. Bertrand to Lord Holland, September 2, 1820, Henry R. Fox, *Foreign Reminiscences by Henry Richard Lord Holland,* ed. Henry E. Fox (London, 1851), 335.

21. Lowe to Bathurst, October 28, 1820, BL MSS Add 20131 SHLP, f.141.

22. Lowe to Bathurst, November 7, 1820, BL MSS Add 20131 SHLP, f.183.

23. Spencer to Earl Spencer, October 28, 1820, BL MSS Add 75946 Althorp Papers, loose folio.

24. Lutyens to Gorrequer, Longwood, October 30, 1820, and Lowe to Bathurst, November 7, 1820, BL MSS Add 20131 SHLP, ff.145, 183.

25. Le Marchant, *Memoir,* 221.

26. Lowe to Bathurst, November 7, 1820, Add 20131 SHLP, f.183, and Forsyth, *History of the Captivity,* 3:246–247.

27. Lutyens to Gorrequer, October 31, 1820, BL MSS Add 20131 SHLP, f.146

28. Montholon, *History,* 3:140–141, and Montholon, *Récits,* 2:433–434.

29. Lists of ships and vessels arriving at Jamestown, BL MSS Add 20161 SHLP.

30. Edward Thornton to Lowe, Rio de Janeiro, February 3, 1821, BL MSS Add 45517 SHLP, f.69.

31. Montholon, *History,* 3:140–141, and Montholon, *Récits,* 2:433–434.

32. Tute, *Cochrane,* 175–176.

33. Montholon, *History of the Captivity,* 3:140–141, and *Récits,* 2:433–434.

34. Lowe to Bathurst, November 1, 1820, BL Loan 57/45 Bathurst Papers, f.149 and f.167.

35. Lowe to Bathurst, November 6, 1820, BL MSS Add 20138 SHLP, f.342.

36. Lowe to Bathurst, November 6, 1820, BL MSS Add 20131 SHLP, f.175.

37. Reade to Lowe, November 2, 1820, BL MSS Add 20131 SHLP, f.167.

38. Zañartu to O'Higgins, January 10 and 27, 1821, Carrera, *Archivo,* 25:40, 60.

39. Lowe to Bathurst, November 7, 1820, BL MSS Add 20131 SHLP, f.183. An extract of this letter is in Forsyth, *History of the Captivity,* 3:246–247.

40. Charles to Albine de Montholon, November 6, 1820, Gonnard, *Lettres,* 60–61.

41. Antommarchi, *The Last Days,* December 26, 1820, 1:362.

42. Lowe to Bathurst, November 16, 1820, BL Loan 57/45 Bathurst Papers, ff.188–189.

43. Report of Lieutenant Crand, November 22, 1820, BL MSS Add 20131 SHLP, f.234.

44. Charles Montholon to Albine, December 5, 1820, Gonnard, *Lettres,* 63.

45. Antommarchi, *The Last Days,* October 29, 1820, 1:381.

46. Bathurst to Lowe, September 22, 1820, BL MSS Add 20131 SHLP, f.66.

47. Montchenu to Lowe, December 28, 1820, BL MSS Add 20131 SHLP, f.357.

48. Lowe to Bathurst, December 27, 1820, BL MSS Add 20131 SHLP, f.355.

Epilogue

1. Lieven to Metternich, January 6, 1821, Lieven, *Private Letters,* 60–62.

2. Prince de Limitile to Wilson, London, March 31, 1821, BL MSS Add 30109 SRWP, f.180, and C. P. Brand, *Italy and the English Romantics: The Italianate Fashion in Early Nineteenth-Century England* (Cambridge: Cambridge University Press, 1957), 27–28.

3. Lowe to Bathurst, January 3, 1821, BL MSS Add 20132 SHLP, ff.6–11.

4. Report of a conversation with Montholon, January 1821, BL MSS Add 20132 SHLP, f.76.

5. Lowe to Bathurst, February 15, 1821, BL MSS Add 20132 SHLP, f.148.

6. Bathurst to Lowe, February 16, 1821, NA CO 248/2.

7. The Earl of Harrowby to Bathurst, March 1, 1821, HMC, *Report on the Manuscripts of Earl Bathurst,* 494.

8. March 10, 1821, Bertrand, *Cahiers,* 3:96.

9. Montholon to Queen Caroline, Longwood, March 17, 1821, BL MSS Add 30, 109 SRWP f.168.

10. Lowe to Bathurst, March 20, 1821, and Gorrequer's Report, BL MSS Add 20132 SHLP, f.283–284, f.289.

11. Lowe to Bathurst, March 17, 1821, and Gorrequer's Report, BL MSS Add 20132 SHLP, f.268.

12. The books had been sent to Napoleon by Lord Robert Spencer, Captain Spencer's uncle. Engelbert Lutyens, *Letters of Captain Engelbert Lutyens,* ed. Lees Knowles (London: John Lane, 1915), 109, 139, 184, and Forsyth, *History of the Captivity,* 3:277. Lutyens was the orderly officer stationed at Longwood who received the books from Napoleon.

13. March 27, 1821. Bertrand, *Cahiers,* 3:105.

14. Montholon, *Récits,* 2:499.

15. March 27, 1821, Marchand, *Mémoires,* 528.

16. Charles to Albine de Montholon, April 9, 1821, Gonnard, *Lettres,* 78.

17. April 9, 1821. Bertrand, *Cahiers,* 3:110.

18. Lowe to Bathurst, April 10, 1821, BL MSS Add 20133 SHLP, f.33.

19. Ben Weider and David Hapgood, *The Murder of Napoleon* (New York: Congdon and Lattes, Distributed by St. Martin's Press, 1982), 218.

20. St. Denis, *Napoleon,* 271.

21. April 18, 1821, Bertrand, *Cahiers,* 3:128.

22. Ben Weider and Sten Forshufvud, *Assassination at St. Helena Revisited* (New York: Wiley, 1995), 430–434. Ben Weider and John Harry Fournier, "Activation Analyses of Authenticated Hairs of Napoleon Bonaparte Confirm Arsenic Poisoning," *American Journal of Forensic Medicine and Pathology* 20, no. 4 (Dec. 1999): 378–382.

23. April 29, 1821, Bertrand, *Cahiers,* 3:177.

24. Marchand, *Mémoires,* 543–544.

25. May 3, 1821, Antommarchi, *The Last Days,* 2:150.

26. April 18, 1821. Bertrand, *Cahiers,* 3:187.

27. For theories that Napoleon didn't die at St. Helena see Ebeyer, *Revelations concerning Napoleon's Escape,* and Thomas G. Wheeler, *Who Lies Here? A New Inquiry into Napoleon's Last Years* (New York: Putnam, 1974).

28. *Courier,* London, May 19, 1821.

29. *Courier,* London, July 4, 1821.

30. E. Beresford Chancellor, *The Diary of Philipp von Neumann* (London, 1928), 64.

31. The diary of John Cam Hobhouse, July 4, 1821, BL MSS Add 56542 Broughton Papers, f.44.

32. Gillen, *Royal Duke,* 186.

33. Caraman to Pasquier, 6 July 1821, AMAE CPA, no. 614.

34. Wilson to Grey, n.d., 1821 in Grey Papers, Durham University Library, GRE /B60/4/121.

35. Hunt, *Memoirs,* 2:29.

36. D'Herisson, *The Black Cabinet,* 266, and *Morning Chronicle,* London, July 18, 1821.

37. Alan Palmer, *Napoleon and Marie Louise: The Emperor's Second Wife* (New York: St. Martin's Press, 2001), 214.

38. Nicolas Planat de la Faye, *Rome et Sainte-Hélène de 1815 a 1821* (Paris, 1862), 17.

39. Joseph to Mr. Hopkinson, Point Breeze, December 24, 1821, F. Marion Crawford, "Joseph Bonaparte in Bordentown," *Century Magazine* 46, no. 1 (May 1893): 87–88.

40. Fréderic Masson, *Napoléon et sa famille* (Paris, 1918), 12:250–252.

41. Simone de la Souchère Deléry, *Napoleon's Soldiers in America* (Gretna, La. Pelican, 1950), 92.

42. Cochrane to Monteagudo, August 29, 1821, Carrera, *Archivo,* 26:59.

43. Schubart to Murray, Paris, July 26, 1821, d'Herisson, *The Black Cabinet,* 266, and Georges Lote, "La Mort de Napoléon et l'opinion Bonapartiste en 1821," *Revue des Etudes Napoléoniennes* 31 (July–Dec.1930): 43–46.

44. Hunt, *Memoirs,* 2:29.

45. O'Meara to Mackintosh, August 26, 1821, BL MSS Add 52453 Mackintosh Papers, f.70.

46. Roberts to Mackintosh, London, August 26, 1821, BL MSS Add 52453 Mackintosh Papers, f.68.

47. *Morning Chronicle,* London, July 6 and 10, 1821.

48. Wilson to Grey, August 1821, BL MSS Add 30123 SRWP, f.243.

49. Montholon to Joseph, London, October 5, 1821, Joseph Bonaparte, *Mémoires et Correspondance Politique,* 10:259. At the end of this letter Montholon wrote three lines in cipher but the key has never been found.

50. Montholon's testimony, April 11, 1823, BL MSS Add 20230 SHLP, f.134.

51. Gourgaud, *Lettre de Sir Walter Scott,* 30–32.

52. For the case against Montholon see Sten Forshufvud, *Assassination at St. Helena: The Poisoning of Napoleon Bonaparte* (Vancouver: Mitchell Press, 1978); Weider and Hapgood, *The Murder of Napoleon,* and Francois de Candé-Montholon and Rene Maury, *L'énigme Napoléon résolue. l'extraordinaire découverte des documents Montholon* (Paris: Albin-Michel, 2000). For a defense of Montholon see Jacques Macé, *L'honneur retrouvé du général de Montholon, de Napoléon 1er à Napoléon III* (Paris: Ed. Christian, 2000).

53. Goulbourn to Bathurst, August 3, 1821, BL Loan 57/13 Bathurst Papers. Goulbourn was referring to a letter from Napoleon's sister asking permission to go to St. Helena.

54. Planat to Eugene Leblon, Paris, November 10, 1821, Planat de la Faye, *Vie de Planat de la Faye,* 406.

55. Maximilien Lamarque, *Mémoires et Souvenirs* (Paris, 1835), 2:213.

56. Fazakerly to W. Ord, Paris, July 12, 1821, d'Herisson, *The Black Cabinet,* 262. See also Lamarque, *Mémoires,* 1:21, and Planat to Eugene Leblon, Paris, July 11, 1821, Planat de la Faye, *Vie de Planat de la Faye,* 393.

57. Report of a conversation with Montholon by Gorrequer, January 1821, BL MSS Add 20132 SHLP, f.76.

58. M. Stafford to the Earl of Carlisle, Paris, July 9, 1821, d'Herisson, *The Black Cabinet,* 258–260. The quote belongs to the Marquis of Castel-Cicala, the representative of Bourbon Naples in Paris and a fanatical royalist.

59. Gentz to Lowe, Vienna, December 9, 1825, and unsigned memorandum, Vienna, December 1825, BL MSS Add 20233 SHLP, f.256 and f.260.

60. Bathurst to Sir Walter Scott, July 2, 1827, Sir Walter Scott's Papers, National Library of Scotland.

61. Hobhouse to Byron, London, August 12, 1821, Peter Graham, *Byron's Bulldog: The Letters of John Cam Hobhouse to Lord Byron* (Columbus: Ohio State University Press, 1984), 315, and *Examiner,* London, 1821.

62. Wilson to the Duke of York, London, October 8, 1821, BL MSS Add 30109 SRWP, f.252

63. Thomas Cochrane, Tenth Earl of Dundonald, *The Autobiography of a Seaman,* (London: R. Bentley and Son, 1890), 1:426, 430.

64. Cochrane to Wilson, August 14, 1822, BL MSS Add 30110 SRWP, f.56.

65. Building San Martin into a myth had strong political overtones. See Jose Ignacio

García Hamilton, *Por qué crecen los paises* (Buenos Aires: Editorial Sudamericana, 2006), 167–215.

66. San Martin to O'Higgins, Lima, September 29, 1821, O'Higgins, *Archivo,* 18:199.

67. Iriarte, *Memorias,* 3:143–144.

68. Wilson to Grey, n.d., 1821 in Grey Papers, Durham University Library, GRE /B60/4/121

69. Frederic Guillaume de Vaudoncourt, *Letters on the Internal Political State of Spain* (London, 1824), 12.

70. Walter Bruyer-Ostells, "Les Officiers de la Grande Armée de l'Espagne liberale de 1823," *Revue de l'Insitut Napoléon* 186, 2:2003, 55–78; Sylvia Neely, *Lafayette and the Liberal Ideal, 1814–1824: Politics and Conspiracy in an Age of Reaction* (Carbondale: Southern Illinois University Press, 1991), 97–117, 206–209.

71. Samuel, *An Astonishing Fellow,* 232–233.

72. March 10–12, 1816, Las Cases, *Memorial,* 1:456.

73. John W. Derry, *Castlereagh* (London: A. Lane, 1976), 227, and H. Montgomery Hyde, *The Strange Death of Lord Castlereagh* (London: Heinemann, 1959), 189.

74. Troyat, *Alexander of Russia,* 301–305. For an interesting account of Alexander's strange vanishing act, see Alexander Troubetzkoy, *Imperial Legend: The Mysterious Disappearance of Tsar Alexander I* (New York: Arcade, 2002).

75. Churchill, *A History of the English-Speaking People,* 3:312

76. Victor Hugo to Joseph, September 6, 1831 in Victor Hugo, *Correspondence* (Paris, 1947), 1:502–503; Ingersoll, *History,* 2:398.

77. Joseph to Lafayette, September 7, 1830, Joseph Bonaparte, *Mémoires et Correspondance Politique,* 10:335.

78. Joseph to Napoleon II, February 15, 1832, ibid., 10:378.

79. D'Herisson, *The Black Cabinet,* 337.

80. L'Herault, *Histoire de Napoléon II,* 185–245.

Bibliographic Essay

The Emperor's Last Campaign is based mostly on documentary sources, both published and unpublished, from several public and private archives on both sides of the Atlantic, particularly in Great Britain. Most of these archives are listed in the acknowledgments. Other important primary sources include published memoirs and diaries of all the main characters of the St. Helena saga and of other leading figures of the Napoleonic period, as well as contemporary newspapers from England, France, and the United States. The archives of Jose Miguel Carrera, meticulously compiled by Armando Moreno Martin in more than thirty volumes, were of particular value to my research efforts, as they provided strong evidence of the links between Joseph Bonaparte and the South American insurgents. Noted Brazilian historian Augusto Ferreira da Costa described the Pernambucan plot based on Portuguese sources in an article published in 1898 in the *Revue de Deux Mondes,* and Austrian historian Hans Schlitter compiled several valuable documentary pieces from Vienna's diplomatic archives.

Among the many secondary sources that cover these events, the following were particularly helpful: *Napoléon et sa famille* by Frederic Masson, *Les espoirs de Napoléon a Sainte-Hélène* by Raoul Brice, *Autour de l'Aigle Enchaîné* by Maurice Soulié, *The Napoleonic Exiles in America* by Jesse S. Reeves, *The Sword Was Their Passport* by Harris G. Warren, *Napoléon a Sainte-Hélène* by Gilbert Martineau, *Sainte-Hélène, terre d'exil* by Ulane Bonnel, *Proscrits et Exilés après Waterloo* by Marcel Doher, and *Napoléon et le rêve Américain* by Inès Murat. Also worth mentioning are works by Napoleonic scholar Fernand Beaucour and

Mexican American historian Guadalupe Jimenez Codinach, which focus on certain aspects of the emperor's last campaign. The activities of the Bonapartist émigrés in North America have been covered in detail by Rafe Blaufarb in *Bonapartists in the Borderlands*. French historian Patrick Puigmal has published several articles on Napoleonic influence in the wars for South American independence, and Chilean historians Fernando Berguño and José Miguel Barros published articles on Cochrane's plans to rescue Napoleon.

An expanded version of this book with a detailed bibliography was published in Spanish in 2007.

Index